Understanding
Human Communication

Understanding Human Communication

● ● ● ● ● Second Canadian Edition ● ● ●

Ronald B. Adler | George Rodman | Alexandre Sévigny

OXFORD
UNIVERSITY PRESS

OXFORD
UNIVERSITY PRESS

8 Sampson Mews, Suite 204, Don Mills, Ontario M3C 0H5
www.oupcanada.com

Oxford University Press is a department of the University of Oxford.
It furthers the University's objective of excellence in research, scholarship,
and education by publishing worldwide in

Oxford   New York

Auckland   Cape Town   Dar es Salaam   Hong Kong   Karachi
Kuala Lumpur   Madrid   Melbourne   Mexico City   Nairobi
New Delhi   Shanghai   Taipei   Toronto

With offices in

Argentina   Austria   Brazil   Chile   Czech Republic   France   Greece
Guatemala   Hungary   Italy   Japan   Poland   Portugal   Singapore
South Korea   Switzerland   Thailand   Turkey   Ukraine   Vietnam

Oxford is a trade mark of Oxford University Press
in the UK and in certain other countries

Published in Canada by Oxford University Press

Copyright © Oxford University Press Canada 2011

The moral rights of the author have been asserted

Database right Oxford University Press (maker)

First Published 2011

Original edition published by Oxford University Press, Inc.,
198 Madison Avenue, New York, NY 10016-4314, USA.
Copyright © 2003 Oxford University Press, Inc.

Previous edition copyright © 2008 Oxford University Press Canada

Library and Archives Canada Cataloguing in Publication

Adler, Ronald B. (Ronald Brian), 1946–
Understanding human communication / Ronald B. Adler,
George Rodman, Alexandre Sévigny.—2nd Canadian ed.

Includes bibliographical references and index.
ISBN 978-019-543127-8

1. Communication—Textbooks.   2. Communication—Canada—Textbooks.
I. Rodman, George R., 1948–   II. Sévigny, Alexandre   III. Title.

P90.A318 2011   302.2   C2010-907270-7

Cover image: Fancy Photography/Veer

This book is printed on permanent (acid-free) paper ∞
which contains a minimum of 10% post-consumer waste.
Printed and bound in United States of America.

4 5 6 7 8 – 17 16 15 14 13

BRIEF CONTENTS

PART I

Elements of Communication

CONTENTS

Chapter 3
Language 83

Chapter 4
Listening 129

PART II

Interpersonal Communication

PART III

Communication in Groups

PART IV
Persuasion and Public Communication

Chapter 13
Public Speaking 491

PREFACE

Before putting the first Canadian edition of *Understanding Human Communication* together in 2006, I asked the students in my Introduction to Communication course at McMaster University what their ideal introductory human communication text-book would contain. While preparing this second Canadian edition, I became even more convinced that our pedagogy should reflect our students' needs, desires, and dreams. I have, therefore, again spent a lot of time asking students what improvements could be included to ensure that their first contact with the field of communication would be a memorable and positive one.

My students made it clear that a good textbook should spell out how theory and research relate to everyday life. The ideal text should be full of bright colours and be visually inviting, with interesting boxed features, images, and examples that help to clarify the subject matter. Its tone should be student-friendly, conversing with readers rather than talking down to them or over their heads. It should have a strong Canadian perspective, especially in its examples. For it to 'feel comfortable', the content should also reflect Canadian social and cultural life in its visual elements. Some students also stated that they wanted to see more profiles of successful recent graduates. Others requested profiles of senior communicators, in which seasoned practitioners would share a few words of wisdom. Above all, they indicated that a good text should give students the tools to master the material and to earn a grade of which they can be proud.

The concerns of students are vitally important, but so too are the needs of instructors. Therefore, I asked my colleagues what they think distinguishes a good textbook. They told me that a good text must present an accurate and comprehensive picture of the academic work it addresses. It should also be manageable within the length of an academic term. An ideal text would make life easier for instructors by giving students plenty of learning support.

Basic Approach

A lot of effort has gone into this second Canadian edition to help it meet the needs of both students and their instructors in the ways described above. If I have succeeded, students will find this book clear, interesting, and useful, with tools that will help them succeed in their first serious exploration of human communication. Instructors, meanwhile, will find that the book does justice to the discipline and helps render their teaching more efficient, engaging, and effective.

This edition builds on the approach that has served more than half a million students and their professors well in the past. Rather than take sides in debates on theory versus skill, *Understanding Human Communication* treats scholarship and skill development as mutually reinforcing. Its reader-friendly approach strives to present material clearly without being overly simplistic. A wealth of examples helps make concepts clear and interesting. A dynamic and inviting new design and colour scheme make the material inviting, as do a collection of stimulating photos, interesting readings, amusing and instructive cartoons, and well-chosen quotations. Key theoretical terms are defined in a running glossary, and definitions of cultural idioms help students whose first language is not English make sense of colloquial expressions.

Every chapter of this book emphasizes the influence of both culture and technology on human communication. Along with discussion in the text itself, boxed features highlight key topics in this area, many of which include thought-provoking and sometimes controversial questions that encourage students to think and talk about the role of communication in the lives of Canadians. 'Understanding Diversity' boxes address subjects of interest to an increasingly diverse student audience in Canada: how French and English Canadians have different levels of self-definition and how minority languages, such as those of Canada's Aboriginal peoples, are increasingly endangered, to name just two. 'Understanding Communication Technology' boxes focus on topics ranging from how people's relationships in their virtual lives, lived out on sites such as Second Life, differ from their real-world relationships to how Facebook is changing people's lives. The 'Communication Onscreen' boxes showcase examples of communication skills and processes from film and television.

Various strategies and techniques also highlight the cultural similarities and differences between Canada's founding peoples: Aboriginal peoples, French Canadians, and English Canadians. For instance, numerous boxes draw attention to their contributions to Canada's identity, in addition to presenting insightful academic research that compares and contrasts these groups. This material, in particular, stems from a firm, personal belief that Canadians must get to know one another better for our country to continue to flourish as a beacon of hope and possibility for our own citizens, as well as for foreigners who seek peace, order, and good government. Critical thinking probes boxes pose intriguing ethical scenarios.

Second Edition: A Major Revamp

This second edition features a new structure to better suit a contemporary student audience. So much has changed in the last five years—e-mail has become a 'dated technology', and social media has swept through the world of mediated communication, changing the cultural landscape for everyone, especially students. There is a generation of people who are growing up digital, and digital communication is becoming a core literacy. As educators, we must account for these changes in our textbooks. It is crucial that we provide critical instruction on what's out there as well as the benefits and dangers. For this reason, this edition includes a new chapter on social media and communication theory (Chapter 8), a refurbished chapter on persuasion, audiences, and persuasive writing (Chapter 11), and a 'condensed' discussion of public speaking (Chapters 12 and 13).

The new chapter on social media was considered a must for a book on human communication, given the overwhelming majority of students who use social media on a daily basis. Social media are becoming a huge part of the workplace as well, as organizations integrate them into normal business practices and use them to do background checks on potential employees. Understanding the opportunities and perils of this new communication landscape is of the utmost importance for students entering the workforce and wanting to make sense of the world around them. To meet this need, this chapter examines the strengths and weaknesses of various social networking media that were current at the time of this text. As part of the effort to be comprehensive and critical, the text also includes various tips and processes on how to build a personal brand, how to encourage collaboration using social media, and how to avoid the dangers of social media.

The chapter on persuasion reflects my belief that we are entering a new era of rhetoric and constant media influence through the omnipresent stream of highly tailored persuasive information which we receive through our smartphones, our tablet devices, and our computers. We are just at the beginning of this age of personally tailored persuasion—we haven't seen anything yet! Giving students the tools to identify, use, and criticize the techniques of persuasion that they will certainly face in both their private and professional lives was a serious priority in composing this chapter.

This Age of Social Media that is upon us is also an Age of Writing—especially persuasive writing. To bring in an expert voice on the topic of persuasive professional writing, I enlisted Dr Philip Savage, a colleague in the Department of Communication Studies and Multimedia, to write a section of the chapter. Philip brings a wealth of academic and industry experience to the task, having served as the director of research for CBC Radio for many years before pursuing a career in academic research. Philip and I co-direct the COMM-Lab: McMaster Communication Metrics Laboratory, which is devoted to bringing Canadian students to the cutting edge of communication and media research.

The final two chapters of the text present a more succinct exploration of public speaking than was offered in the previous edition, without losing any important information. While the chapter on speech writing introduces the necessary skills, planning, and strategies students need to compose a speech, the chapter on public speaking covers the strategic and tactical knowledge necessary to overcome stage fright, use visual aids effectively, and connect with the audience, among many other essential skills. These two chapters retain the popular sample speeches from great Canadian communicators such as Jean Chrétien and Pierre Elliott Trudeau that were featured in the previous edition. However, they also offer the latest information on using the Internet and social media to communicate effectively in a Canadian context.

Another key feature of this edition is profiles of successful communicators. Each chapter contains a profile of a communications graduate who has gone on to do some neat things with his or her degree. These profiles are inspiring, hip, and fun; they show what amazing futures await those who invest their time, energy, and enthusiasm in communication studies. They are aspirational in aim—I want students using this book to see that others have put these ideas to work and have achieved success. Four profiles of senior Canadian communications leaders are also included. These leaders have contributed short notes to students, sharing a little wisdom and explaining what skills and attitudes students should focus on to become successful communicators.

Acknowledgements

Anyone involved with creating a textbook knows that the authors wouldn't succeed without the contributions of many people.

For help in addressing the aims of this textbook, I worked with two editorial assistants from McMaster, Tom Aylward-Nally and Morgan Harper. Tom and Morgan found modern Canadian content and made significant suggestions regarding the text's art program. They also helped a lot in brainstorming the new edition's reorganization. Tom and Morgan were both exemplary assistants and became my friends through the process of putting this second edition together. I have since worked on communications consulting projects with Tom; and Morgan assisted me as I founded a new journal, the *Journal of Professional Communication*.

I would also like to thank the following reviewers and the four anonymous reviewers for their constructive and invaluable suggestions that assisted in the development of both editions of this text: Paula Dworatzek, Brescia University College; Anne Price, Red Deer College; Jennifer Sipos-Smith, Glendon College, York University; and Ruth Stewart, Grant MacEwan College.

Working with the professionals at Oxford University Press Canada has been an absolute delight. In particular, I am grateful to Stephen Kotowych, acquisitions editor, who nudged me into accelerating work on this textbook and meeting deadlines. I would also like to thank Rebecca Ryoji, developmental editor, and Janna Green, copyeditor, who were both a great pleasure to work with.

Several of my colleagues at McMaster provided valuable feedback and encouragement: Laurence Mussio, David Ogborn, Philip Savage, and Stephen Svenson from the Department of Communication Studies and Multimedia, as well as Michael Kliffer and Stephanie Posthumus from the Department of French. A special thanks to Terry Flynn, from the DeGroote School of Business and former president of the Canadian Public Relations Society, who has opened the world of communications management to my students and me. I would also like to thank Suzanne Crosta, our generous and visionary dean of the Faculty of Humanities, who has always mentored me on how to successfully blend research and teaching and provided a professional environment wonderfully conducive to scholarly writing. I owe particular thanks to Lars Wessman, blogger (piratasum.com) and president of the Wessman Group in Porto, Portugal, who is a true philosopher and friend; our 19-year running conversation has inspired, shaped, and coloured many of the examples and anecdotes that have found their way into this book. Joey Coleman, higher education blogger with *The Globe and Mail* and journalist with *The Hamilton Spectator* has been a friend throughout the process of editing this book—his advice, commentary, and critique have been invaluable in keeping the examples I used relevant.

I would also like to thank some friends from the realm of industry who have given me their views on what would be practical for students to know for successful communication careers: Andrew Laing, president, Cormex Research; Megan Coppolino, communications rockstar, kitestring.ca; David Estok, vice-president of communications, Sick Kids Foundation; Natalie Ott, compassion mobilizer, The Meeting House and former director of communications, Briercrest College; Bianca Freedman, communications coordinator, The Credit Valley Hospital Foundation; Rebecca Edgar, communications consultant and my student in the Master of Communications Management Program; and Elena Yunusov, communications specialist, Office of the Ontario Ombusdman.

These acknowledgements would not be complete without a nod to my furry feline companion, the glamorous and Rubenesque Gigi, whose unconditional love is a comfort in lonely moments.

Finally, I would like to thank my parents, brother, and grandmother for their good-natured tolerance and support throughout this project.

Alex Sévigny

21 January 2011

Important Features of This Edition

The second Canadian edition of *Understanding Human Communication* builds on the success of the previous edition to give first-time students a compelling and accurate introduction to the academic study of human communication. This edition retains many valuable features that will be familiar to long-time users, including a seamless integration of Canadian themes and issues, an outstanding breadth of coverage, and engaging real-life examples. Alexandre Sévigny has thoroughly revised the text and assembled vital new materials for this updated edition.

Highlights Include

- a *new* chapter on social media with thorough, up-to-date coverage of the history, characteristics, uses, benefits, and dangers of social media;
- *new* 'Communication Onscreen' boxes that highlight classic and recent films and TV shows and connect character and story to communication theories;
- a *new* section on persuasive professional writing, written by Dr Philip Savage, which provides tips on writing news releases, op-eds, blogs, and briefing notes;
- updated 'Young Communicator Profile' boxes featuring successful Canadian communicators in various high-profile positions;
- discussions of technology, gender, cultural diversity, as well as communication styles and methods, that are based on the most up-to-date information available; and
- a comprehensive ancillary package that includes a companion website for students and additional resources for instructors (an instructor's manual, test generator, and PowerPoint slides).

Elements of Communication

Part I

Professional Profile:

Rikia Saddy

Though I directed my friends in pretend television commercials as a child and paid more attention to the ads than the programs when watching TV, I wasn't aware of the industry as a career until I landed at a graduate school with a strong advertising program.

After graduation, I joined the New York advertising world, and worked day and night to become the best in my business. The qualities it took to succeed then are the same as today: intense curiosity, a genuine interest in why people behave as they do, the ability to hold competing thoughts at the same time, lateral thinking, hard work, and an obsession with never missing a detail. None of this is taught in school, but you can learn it there.

The communications industry is the most creative field in business, and you will become part of an exciting, influential tribe. There are more media channels today, and less bureaucracy to reach them. Get to know the needs of every medium. Know which likes to launch the newest thing, which will repeat what you provide verbatim, who is overworked and will thank you for doing their job, and who needs total control. Most importantly, know your strengths and what you have to offer. Build your own brand while you build your clients'.

Do not shy away from technology. It is easy to stay current now, but in 20 years will there be a group of kids that knows more than you? The key to a successful career is to become the best at something. Choose a path that will make that journey fun.

In recent years, I've turned my attention to the world around me and grown my company to include political strategy. Like marketing strategy, it involves educating and informing the public. There is a tendency for politicians to govern by poll results, but the true path lies in finding a way to communicate the strengths and position of a leader without resorting to gimmicks.

All good marketing and communication is authentic. Your job, regardless of the field you choose, is to connect.

Rikia Saddy is a principal at Rikia Saddy Strategy, a marketing and political strategy firm in Vancouver. She has worked in Canada, the United States, and Europe.

After studying the material in this chapter . . .

You should understand:

- the working definition and characteristics of communication;
- the types of communication covered in this book;
- the needs satisfied by communication;
- the characteristics of linear and transactional communication models;
- the characteristics of competent communication; and
- common misconceptions about communication.

You should be able to:

- define communication and give specific examples of the various types of communication introduced in this chapter;
- describe the needs you attempt to satisfy by communicating;
- judge the competence of communication (yours or others') in a specific situation and suggest ways of increasing the competence level; and
- identify how misconceptions about communication can create problems and suggest how a more accurate analysis of the situations you describe can lead to better outcomes.

Human Communication: What and Why

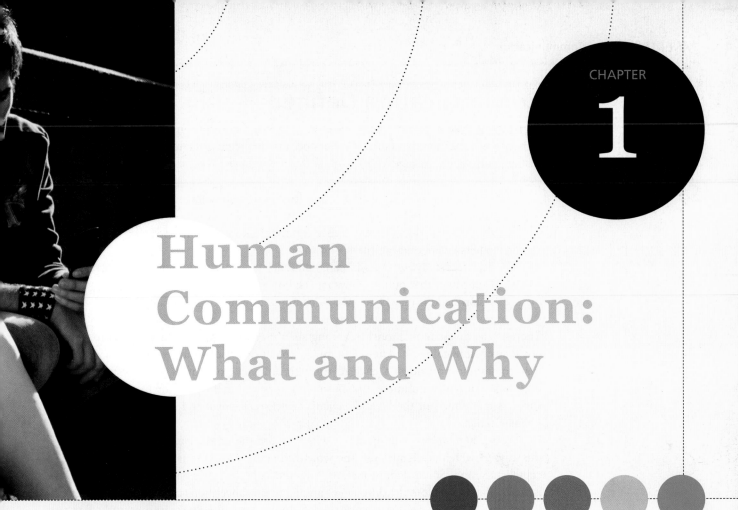

Chapter Highlights

Communication, as examined in this book, possesses three important characteristics:

- It occurs between humans.
- It is a process.
- It is symbolic.

This chapter introduces several types of communication:

- intrapersonal,
- dyadic/interpersonal,
- small-group,
- public, and
- mass.

Communication helps satisfy a number of needs in our lives:

- physical needs,
- identity needs,
- social needs, and
- practical needs.

Two models of communication help us understand what is involved in this process:

- the linear model; and
- the transactional model

Communication competence indicates a person's knowledge of how to be a good communicator. This chapter explores competence by

- defining the nature of competence and how it is acquired, and
- outlining the characteristics of competent communicators.

The field of communications contains several misconceptions. We will consider the following clarifications.

- Communication doesn't always require complete understanding.
- Communication isn't always a good thing.
- No single person or event causes another's reaction.
- Communication won't solve all problems.
- Meanings rest in people, not in words.
- Communication isn't as simple as it often seems.
- More communication isn't always better.

Communication Defined

Because this book is about communication, it makes sense to begin by defining that term. This task is not as simple as it might seem because people use the term in a variety of ways that are only vaguely related:

- Family members, co-workers, and friends describe their relationships in terms of communication ('We just can't communicate'; 'We communicate perfectly').
- Business people talk about 'office communications systems', which consist of computers, telephones, printers, and so on.
- Scientists study and describe communication among ants, dolphins, and other animals.
- Companies that publish newspapers, books, and magazines or own radio and television stations may be known as 'communications conglomerates'.

There is clearly some relationship among such uses of the term, but we need to narrow our focus before going on. After all, a quick look at this book's table of contents will show that communication doesn't have to do with animals, computers, or newspapers. Nor is it about Holy Communion, the 'bestowing of a material thing', or many of the other subjects mentioned in the *Oxford Canadian English Dictionary's* 1,200-word definition of *communication*.

What, then, *are* we talking about when we use the term *communication*? A survey of the ways in which academics use the word will show that there is no one universally accepted meaning. Some definitions are long and complex, others brief and simple. This isn't the place to explore the differences among these conceptions or to defend one against the others. What we need is a working definition that will help us in our study. For our purposes we will say that **communication** is a continuous, irreversible, transactive process involving communicators who occupy different but overlapping environments and are simultaneously senders and receivers of messages, many of which are distorted by physical and psychological noise.

A point-by-point examination of this definition reveals some important characteristics of communication as we will be studying it.

communication
A continuous, irreversible, transactive process involving communicators who occupy different but overlapping environments and are simultaneously senders and receivers of messages, many of which are distorted by physical and psychological noise.

Communication Is Human

In this book we'll be discussing communication between human beings. Animals clearly do communicate. Bees, for instance, instruct their hive-mates about the location of food by means

The Many Meanings of Communication

Few words have as many meanings as communication. The term can refer to everything from messages on T-shirts to presidential speeches, from computer code to chimpanzee behaviour. Communication has been the professional concern of philosophers, scientists (social, biological, and physical), poets, politicians, and entertainers, to name just a few. Responding to this diversity, Brent Ruben asked, 'How does being interested in communication differ from being interested in life?'

There are several reasons why the term *communication* has so many different meanings. Understanding them will help explain how and why this word refers to a broad range of subjects.

Interdisciplinary Heritage

Unlike most subjects, communication has captured the interest of scholars from a wide range of fields. Ever since classical times, philosophers have studied the meaning and significance of messages. In the twentieth century, social scientists joined the field. Psychologists examine the causes and effects of communication as it relates to individuals. Sociologists and anthropologists examine how communication operates within and between societies and cultures. Political scientists explore the ways communication influences government affairs. Engineers use their skill to devise methods of conveying messages electronically. Zoologists focus on communication between animals. With this kind of diversity, it's no surprise that *communication* is a broad and sometimes confusing term.

Field and Activity

Sometimes the word *communication* refers to a field of study (of non-verbal messages or effects of televised violence on children, for example). In other cases it denotes an activity that people do. This confusion doesn't exist in most disciplines. People may study history or sociology, but they don't 'historicate' or 'sociologize'. Having only one word that refers to both the field of study and the activity that it examines leads to confusion.

Humanities and Social Science

Unlike most disciplines, communication straddles two very different academic domains. It has one foot firmly planted in the humanities, where it shares concerns with disciplines like English and philosophy. At the same time, other scholars in the field take an approach like their colleagues in the social sciences, such as psychology, sociology, and anthropology. And to confuse matters even further, communication is sometimes associated with the performing arts, especially in the area of oral interpretation of literature.

Natural and Professional Communication

This is a natural activity that we all engage in unconsciously. At the same time, there are professional communication experts whose specialized duties require training and skill. Careers such as marketing, public relations, broadcasting, speech making, counselling, journalism, and management all call for talent that goes far beyond what is required for everyday speaking and listening.

Communication and Communications

Even the name of the field is confusing. Traditionally, *communications* (with an 's') has been used when referring to activities involving technology and the mass media. *Communication* is typically used to describe face-to-face and written messages, as well as the field as a whole. With the growth of communication technology, the two terms are being used interchangeably more often.

—Brent Ruben, Communication and Human Behavior

Question: The author asserts that communication is a multidisciplinary field. Why do you think a professional communicator must be aware of several fields of knowledge to be effective?

of a special dance. Chimpanzees have been taught to express themselves with the same sign language used by deaf humans, and a few have developed impressive vocabularies. And on a more commonplace level, pet owners can testify to the variety of messages their animals can express. Although the subject of animal communication is fascinating and important, it goes beyond the scope of this book.[1]

Communication Is a Process

We often talk about communication as if it consisted of individual units, such as one person's utterance or a conversation between two people. In fact, communication is a continuous process. Consider, for example, a friend's compliment about your appearance. Your interpretation of those words will depend on a long series of experiences stretching far back in time: How have others judged your appearance? How do you feel about your looks? How honest has your friend been in the past? How have you been feeling about one another recently? All this history will help shape your response to the friend's remark. In turn, the words you speak and the way you say them will shape the way your friend behaves toward you and others—both in this situation and in the future.

This simple example shows that it's inaccurate to talk about 'acts' of communication as if they occurred in isolation. To put it differently, communication isn't like a series of photos posted on Facebook but rather like a Twitter feed, in which the meaning comes from the unfolding of a series of interrelated microblogging messages. The fact that communication is a process is reflected in the transactional model introduced later in this chapter.

Communication Is Symbolic

Symbols are used to represent processes, ideas, or events in ways that make communication possible. Chapter 3 explores the nature of symbols in more detail, but this idea is so important that it needs an introduction now. The most significant feature of symbols is their *arbitrary* nature. For example, consider words as symbols. There's no logical reason why the letters in the word *book* should stand for the object you're reading now. French speakers call it *un livre*, and Germans call it a *Buch*. Even in English, another set of letters would work just as well as long as everyone agreed to use it in the same way. We overcome the arbitrary nature of symbols by following linguistic rules and customs. Effective communication depends on agreement among people about these rules. This is easiest to see when we observe people who don't follow or aren't aware of linguistic conventions. For example, think of how unusual the speech of children sounds before they have managed to learn all the conventions.

Words are one type of symbol, but non-verbal behaviour can also have symbolic meaning. Like words, some non-verbal behaviours, though arbitrary, have clearly agreed-upon meanings. For example, to most Canadians a nod of the head means 'yes'. But

A word after a word after a word is power.

Margaret Atwood,
'Spelling'

symbol
An arbitrary sign used to represent a thing, person, idea, event, or relationship in ways that make communication possible.

CRITICAL THINKING PROBE

MUST COMMUNICATION BE INTENTIONAL?

Some theorists believe that any behaviour that has meaning to others should be considered communication, whether it is intentional or not. To them, an involuntary grimace or overheard remark is worthy of study. Other scholars believe that only messages that are intentionally sent and received should be considered communication. They argue that the broader definition means that the study of communication has no boundaries. Which position do you take? Be prepared to support your answer in a discussion with others who hold the opposing viewpoint.

non-verbal behaviours, even more than words, are ambiguous. Does a frown signify anger or unhappiness? Does a hug stand for a friendly greeting or a sign of romantic interest? You can't always be sure. We'll have more to say about non-verbal communication in Chapter 5.

Types of Communication

Within the domain of human interaction there are several types of communication. Each occurs in a different context, and, despite the features that they all share, each has its own characteristics. In the following section we'll examine the features of five different types of communication.

Intrapersonal Communication

By definition, **intrapersonal communication** means 'communicating with oneself'.[2] You can tune in to one way that each of us communicates internally by listening to the little voice that lives in your mind. Take a moment now and listen to what it is saying. Did you hear it? It may have been saying something like, 'What little voice? I don't have any little voice!' This voice is the 'sound' of your thinking.

We don't always think in verbal terms, but whether the process is apparent or not, the way we mentally process information influences our interactions with others. Thus, even though intrapersonal communication doesn't fit the 'face-to-face' element of our definition of *communication,* it does affect those forms of interaction. You can understand the role of intrapersonal communication by imagining your thoughts in each of the following situations:

- You are about to introduce yourself to a classmate you've never spoken to.
- You scrutinize an audience of 30 strangers before beginning a 10-minute speech.
- The CEO yawns in the middle of your project proposal.
- You wonder if you're the cause of a friend's recent irritability.

The way you handle each of these situations would depend on the intrapersonal communication that precedes or accompanies your overt behaviour. Much of Chapter 2 deals with the perception process in everyday situations.

Dyadic/Interpersonal Communication

Social scientists call two people interacting a **dyad,** and they describe this type of communication as **dyadic communication.** A dyad is the most common setting for communication. One study revealed that university students spend almost half of their total communication time interacting with one other person.[3] Observation

Cultural Idiom

tune in to
focus on

dyad
A two-person unit.

dyadic communication
Two-person communication.

intrapersonal communication
Communication that occurs within a single person.

A man is but the product of his thoughts.
What he thinks, he becomes.

Mohandas Gandhi

interpersonal communication
Communication in which the parties consider one another as unique individuals rather than as objects. It is characterized by minimal use of stereotyped labels; unique, idiosyncratic social rules; and a high degree of information exchange.

public communication
Communication that occurs when a group becomes too large for all members to contribute. It is characterized by an unequal amount of speaking and by limited verbal feedback.

small-group communication
Communication that occurs in a group whose size allows each member to participate actively with the other members.

Cultural Idiom

operate in a vacuum
function as if there was no one around

in a variety of settings—playgrounds, shopping malls, railway stations—shows that most communication is dyadic in nature.[4] Even communication within larger groups (think, for instance, of classrooms, parties, and family gatherings) consists of multiple, often shifting dyadic encounters.

Dyadic interaction is sometimes considered identical to **interpersonal communication**, but as we will see in Chapter 6, not all two-person interaction can be considered interpersonal in the fullest sense of the word. At the same time, the qualities that characterize interpersonal communication aren't limited to pairs but may also be present in three-person interactions or even in small groups.

Small-Group Communication

In **small-group communication** every person can participate actively with the other members. Small groups are common in everyday life. Your family is one. So is a collection of students or co-workers collaborating on a project. Even the players on a recreational hockey team can be considered a small group.

Whatever their makeup, small groups possess characteristics that are not present in a dyad. For instance, two or more members of a group can form a coalition to defend their position against other members, whereas in a dyad the members face each other as individuals, without support from others. In a group, the majority of members can, either consciously or unconsciously, put pressure on those in the minority to conform; in a dyad no such pressures exist. Conformity pressures can also be comforting, giving group members the confidence to take risks they would not dare to take if they were alone or in a dyad. With their greater size, groups also have the ability to be more creative than dyads. Finally, communication in groups is affected strongly by the type of leader. Groups are such an important communication setting that chapters 9 and 10 focus exclusively on them.

Public Communication

Public communication takes place when a group becomes too large for all members to contribute. One characteristic of public communication is an unequal amount of speaking. A small number of people—sometimes even just one—will do almost all the talking, while the rest of the group becomes an audience. This leads to a second characteristic of public communication: limited verbal feedback. Audience members aren't able to respond in a two-way conversation the way they might in a dyadic or small-group setting. However, this doesn't mean that speakers operate in a vacuum when delivering their remarks. Audiences often have a chance to ask questions and make brief comments, and their non-verbal reactions offer a wide range of clues about their reception of the speaker's remarks. This type of communication is commonly seen in talk shows, such as CBC's *The Hour*, hosted by George Stroumboulopoulos.

Public speakers usually have a greater chance to plan and structure their remarks than do communicators in smaller settings. For this reason, the final two chapters of this book describe the steps you can take to prepare and deliver an effective speech.

Mass Communication

Mass communication consists of messages that are transmitted to large, widespread audiences via electronic and print media: the Internet, television, radio, newspapers and magazines, and so on. Mass communication differs from interpersonal, small-group, and public communication in several ways. First, mass messages are aimed at large audiences without any personal contact between senders and receivers. Second, most of the messages sent via mass communication channels are developed, or at least financed, by large organizations. In this sense, mass communication is far less personal and more of a finished product than the other types we have examined so far.

Of course, the Internet has made it possible for individuals without the backing of large organizations to broadcast their ideas on blogs and on sites like YouTube and, in this sense, has changed traditional mass communication. However, even most Internet users consult sites that are produced and maintained by large organizations such as the CBC, Canada.com, *The Globe and Mail,* and the Government of Canada. As Donald Smith, director of operations, Public Affairs Branch, Canada Revenue Agency (CRA), wrote, the CRA depends on the Internet to reach key audiences and stakeholders.[5] Finally, mass communication is almost always controlled by many gatekeepers who determine what messages will be delivered to consumers, how they will be constructed, and when they will be delivered. Sponsors (whether corporate or governmental), editors, producers, reporters, and executives all have the power to influence mass messages in ways that don't affect most other types of communication. Because of these and other unique characteristics, the study of mass communication raises special issues and deserves special treatment. Sometimes, mass communication can serve a very powerful democratic purpose, as Kim Morris discusses in a case study she wrote about crisis communications in rural communities in northeastern Ontario.[6]

mass communication
The transmission of messages to large, usually widespread audiences via broadcast means (such as radio and television), print (such as newspapers, magazines, and books), multimedia (such as CD-ROM, DVD, and the Internet), and other forms of media such as recordings and movies.

Functions of Communication

Now that we have a working understanding of the term *communication,* it is important to discuss why we spend so much time exploring this subject. Perhaps the strongest argument for studying communication is its central role in our lives. Most of us are surrounded by others with whom we try to build understandings: family, friends, co-workers, teachers, and strangers. The amount of time we spend communicating is staggering. And many of us are replacing 'face time' with social media time. One study measured the amount of time a sample group of Canadians spent communicating using social media such as Facebook, Twitter, and MySpace.[7] The researchers found that 49 per cent of the subjects used social media to communicate with other people or with organizations, such as companies, stores, not-for-profit agencies, or governments, at least once per day.

Whatever medium we choose to communicate through, there's a good reason why we speak, listen, read, and write so much: communication satisfies most of our needs.

Physical Needs

Communication is so important that it is necessary for physical health. In fact, evidence suggests that an absence of satisfying communication can even jeopardize life itself. Medical

Young Communicator
PROFILE

Caroline Gdyczynski, News
Writer, Canadian Broadcasting
Corporation

The communications and media industry has always been intriguing to me, and at a very young age I began wondering how I could become part of its world.

Academic work was where I placed most of my efforts. I started out by taking communication technology courses in high school, followed through with a BA Honours in communication studies and multimedia, and finally finished with a post-graduate diploma in journalism. In all of my post-graduate experiences, both academically and professionally, I have been able to draw on the knowledge and experience I gained while studying communication and mass media.

The classes, group projects, oral presentations, and lectures allowed me to become completely immersed in the study and practice of the communications industry. Through it all, I gained practical and valuable experience that I put to use as a communications assistant for an NGO with consultative status at the United Nations. In addition to what I learned in the classroom, volunteering and working for the student newspaper prepared me for the deadline driven atmosphere at the CBC, where I interned and now work with News Network. I believe that I will continue to draw from what I learned while studying communications in all the future years of my professional life.

researchers have identified a wide range of hazards that result from a lack of close relationships.[8] For instance,

- People who lack strong relationships have two to three times the risk of early death, regardless of whether they smoke, drink, or exercise regularly.
- Terminal cancer strikes socially isolated people more often than it does those who have close personal relationships.

- Divorced, separated, and widowed people are 5 to 10 times more likely to need hospitalization for mental problems than are their married counterparts.
- Pregnant women under stress and without supportive relationships have three times more complications than pregnant women who suffer from the same stress but have strong social support.
- Socially isolated people are four times more susceptible to the common cold than those who have active social networks.[9]

Other studies have shown that social isolation is a major risk factor contributing to coronary disease,[10] and three recent articles in *The Globe and Mail* have discussed how loneliness has been linked to increased risk of heart attack, high blood pressure, and cancer. Not surprisingly, the quality of personal relationships has an even more significant bearing on health. This has to do with the difference between *structural support*—a person's basic network of social relationships, including friends, family, and romantic partners—and *functional support,* which refers to the quality of those relationships and whether or not a person believes, for example, that his or her friends will be there in a time of need.[11] A Quebec study found that psychiatric patients, in comparison with people from the general population, consistently reported less satisfaction with their social support, suggesting that functional support—that is, actual or perceived strength of social ties—is a predictor of mental health outcomes.[12]

People who have higher levels of social support are more likely to eat healthy foods, drink alcohol in moderation, and refrain from smoking. A University of Alberta study even found that adults who reported higher levels of social support expressed a greater intention to exercise.[13] A Statistics Canada study published in 2002 showed that rates of depression and alcohol dependence were lower among immigrants than among Canadian-born comparison groups, owing mainly to the strength and frequency of communication patterns within the cultural groups.[14] Another unusual fact uncovered by this study was that the 'Immigrant Health Effect' was greater among more recent immigrants. Also, a study by Siavash Jafari, Souzan Baharlou, and Richard Mathias demonstrated that one of the key determinants of the mental health of Iranian immigrants to Canada was communication.[15]

Other studies suggest that high levels of humour are associated with a stronger immune system.[16] A study from the University of Waterloo found that women with high levels of coping humour had lower systolic blood pressure than women with low levels of coping humour. The findings differed for male subjects, however, leading the authors to surmise that female humour, which is often self-directed and better promotes social cohesion, is possibly healthier than male humour, which tends to be hostile and at the expense of others.[17] Presumably, men would derive more health benefits if their humour was more pro-social in its focus.

This research demonstrates the importance of having satisfying personal relationships. Remember, though, that not everyone needs the same amount of contact, and the quality of communication is almost certainly as important as the quantity. The main point here is that personal communication is essential for our well-being. To paraphrase an old song, 'people who need people' aren't 'the luckiest people in the world'—they're the *only* people!

Identity Needs

Communication does more than enable us to survive. Indeed, it is the only way we have to learn who we are. As you'll read in Chapter 2, our sense of identity comes from the way

Whether the consequence of a mental attitude or a living condition, loneliness affects millions, usually for the worse. Death certificates read heart attack, cancer, or suicide; but coroners are missing the point. With no one to love or to love us, we tend to smoke, drink, brood, or simply cry ourselves into earlier graves.

Don E. Hamachek, *Encounters with Others*

Feeding the Need for Native News: Duncan McCue

Duncan McCue, educated as a lawyer, is a national reporter for CBC-TV *News in Vancouver, and his current affairs documentaries are featured on the* CBC's The National. *Nominated for Gemini and Webster awards, he has received an* RTNDA *Award for investigative reporting and multiple honours from the Native American Journalists Association for investigative, news, and feature reporting. McCue is Anishinaabe and a member of the Chippewas of Georgina Island First Nations in southern Ontario. Throughout his career, he has worked diligently to bring Native stories into the mainstream media. He was recently appointed the first visiting professor in Media and Indigenous Peoples at the* UBC *School of Journalism.*

. . .

As an Aboriginal journalist, did you face obstacles moving into the mainstream media?

The most obvious obstacle was that when I started I didn't know what I was doing. I worked for a show called *Road Movies* and for YTV News, but that was an unusual experience in that they were asking for me to do commentaries. I could write whatever I wanted, and they encouraged me to express my point of view. Journalism is a very different beast. The learning curve was huge for me, and the CBC, bless their hearts, took me on and I learned on the job. I was also the only Native reporter at CBC Vancouver for a long time. And still, there aren't many of us. Also, I had some strong views about the ways that Aboriginal communities had been covered in the mainstream media and I wanted to change that. I found that it wasn't as easy as I thought it was going to be. It's

not that there was resistance to my ideas, but the definition of what makes news and what the lead story is—that definition has been around for a long time, and my idea of what is newsworthy wasn't always what my producers thought was newsworthy.

In the first couple of years, I was racing off to blockades and things like that, which was exciting and fun. But then after a while I thought, 'There's more to life in Native communities than blockades.' That's when I started to pitch different ideas, and that's when it became tougher for me.

You have covered some very difficult stories addressing social and political issues. How do you balance reporting on hard issues and reporting on the positive?

I think that is partly why I have been at the CBC so long. I don't mind tackling tough issues in the Native community, whereas a lot of young Native people who come into the system want to tell positive stories. There's an old line about the 'Four Ds' of news coverage for Native people. They were either 'drunk, dead or drumming or dancing'. And if you are not doing one of those things then you're not going to make it on the news that night.

So there have been a lot of people who have said they want to promote more positive role models. I think there are all kinds of problems in Native communities that need to be addressed. Whether we are poaching eagles, or our kids are working the streets and being abused, or we're dealing with financial accountability—those are all tough issues that

we interact with other people. Are we smart or stupid, attractive or ugly, talented or inept? The answers to these questions don't come from looking in the mirror. We decide who we are based on how others react to us. Deprived of communication with others, we would have no sense of identity. In his book *Bridges, Not Walls*, John Stewart dramatically illustrates this fact by citing the case of the famous 'Wild Boy of Aveyron', who spent his early childhood without any apparent human contact. The boy was discovered in January 1800 while digging for vegetables in a French village garden.[18] He showed none of the behaviours that one would expect in a social human. The boy could not speak but uttered only weird cries. More significant than this absence of social skills was his lack of any identity as a human being. As author Roger Shattuck put it, 'The boy had no human sense of being in the world.

communities are grappling with. I think Native reporters have a responsibility to try to report on those, and I can put things in context in a way that non-Native reporters might not be able to.

. . .

Do you feel you are becoming a role model?

Yeah, I guess I am. But someone described me as the 'first' professor of Indigenous Media the other day, and I think that's an awful thing. I think of Judge Scow coming to UBC and all throughout his career being described as the 'first Indian lawyer' and the 'first Aboriginal judge', and I think 'poor Judge Scow'. First of all, being on your own for that length of time, but also that it's not a thing to celebrate [being the first]. There should be a bunch of Aboriginal journalists. There are more today, but there are still not enough, which is part of the reason I have started teaching. There are no Aboriginal students at the journalism school right now . . . and there need to be. If my going there helps some Native kid or even some middle-aged Native person think they can do it, then great.

Tell me more about what inspired you to become an educator.

CBC is a really great place to be. It is maybe not like it was 30 years ago, but it is still one of the premier training grounds for young journalists and technicians in Canada. Training has always been part of the CBC, to ensure we produce the kind of quality we expect of ourselves and that Canadians expect from us. Two or three years ago, I realized that if I am at all good at my craft, it's in part due to the training I had, and that I wanted to pass that on—particularly because I despair about the small number of Native people who are going into journalism. There's a strong network of Native newspapers and radio stations, and now we have APTN, so there's lots of people interested in working within Indigenous media. But there are very few who want to make that crossover into the mainstream, and there needs to be Native voices in the mainstream, otherwise our voices are not being heard in the full complexity that they should be.

What is the next career step for you?

I don't know, but I am looking forward to finding out! I've always said if I get a gold watch from the CBC then I'll be disappointed with myself because at some point I'd really like to help build the Indigenous media capacity in the country, and help shape it. And I haven't done that yet, and I do feel a really strong responsibility. At some point, I would like to take some of the skills I have learned and try to blend it with my experience in the Native community and create something that would really knock the socks off of Native communities, and the rest of Canada.

—*UBC Alumni Profiles, law.ubc.ca/alumni/profiles/alumni/ Mccue.html*

Question: Professor McCue's research and writing discuss a specific demographic group: Native Canadians. How does his success story demonstrate the importance of communication to business, cultural, and political causes?

He had no sense of himself as a person related to other persons.'[19] Only with the care and attention of a loving 'mother' did the boy begin to behave—and, we can imagine, think of himself—as a human.

Contemporary stories support the essential role that communication plays in shaping identity. In 1970, authorities discovered a 12-year-old girl (they called her 'Genie') who had spent virtually all her life in an otherwise empty, darkened bedroom with almost no human contact. The child could not speak and had no sense of herself as a person until she was removed from her family and 'nourished' by a team of caregivers.[20] A more recent case involved a Toronto boy, Jeffrey Baldwin, who for most of his short life was confined to his room by his grandparents, unable to communicate with other children. We can only imagine how this experience affected his sense of identity and self before his tragic death at the age of six.[21]

No one is born with a ready-made sense of identity. We become aware of who we are from the ways others define us. As Chapter 2 will discuss, the messages we receive in early childhood are the strongest, but the influence of others continues throughout life. Chapter 2 also explains how we use communication to manage the way others view us.

Some scholars have argued that we are most attracted to people who confirm our identity.[22] This confirmation can come in different forms, depending on the self-image of the communicator. People with relatively high self-esteem seek out others who verify their value and, as much as possible, avoid those who treat them poorly. Conversely, people who regard themselves as unworthy may look for relationships in which others treat them badly. This principle offers one explanation for why some people stay in unsuccessful or abusive relationships. If you view yourself as worthless, you may associate with others who will confirm that self-perception. Of course, relationships can change a communicator's identity as well as validate it. Supportive relationships can transform feelings of inadequacy into self-respect, and damaging ones can lower self-esteem.

The role of communication in shaping identity works in a second way. Even as others' messages are working to shape who we think we are, we are sending messages (sometimes consciously, sometimes not) intended to shape the way others see us. For example, the choices we make about how to dress and otherwise shape our appearance are almost always attempts to manage our identity.

Social Needs

Besides helping to define who we are, communication provides a vital link with others. Researchers and theorists have identified a range of social needs that we satisfy by communicating: the need for *pleasure* (e.g., we communicate 'because it's fun' or 'to have a good time'); the need for *affection* (e.g., 'to help others' or 'to let others know I care'); the need for *inclusion* (e.g., 'because I need someone to talk to or be with', 'because it makes me less lonely'); the need for *escape* (e.g., 'to put off doing something I should be doing'); the need for *relaxation* (e.g., 'because it allows me to unwind'); and the need for *control* (e.g., 'because I want someone to do something for me', 'to get something I don't have').[23]

Just how vital is the need for pleasure in communication? Several Canadian researchers have investigated the benefits of humour in communication, including Rod Martin, who, with his research group at the University of Western Ontario, outlined four models that describe how humour and laughter can have a positive impact on health.[24] First, a physiological model focuses on the possibility that physiological changes associated with laughter contribute to improved health. Second, an emotion model is based on the idea that humour produces positive emotions that, in turn, contribute positively to health. Third, a stress-moderation model posits that humour, together with other processes that contribute to a positive outlook on the world, acts as a buffer to mitigate stress, thereby improving health. Finally, a social support model suggests that the benefits of humour are mediated by the increased social support that comes from being a fun-loving and outgoing individual.

As you look at the rest of the items on the list of social needs satisfied by communication, imagine how empty your life would be if these needs weren't met. Then notice that it would be impossible to fulfill these needs without communicating with others. Because relationships with others are so vital, some theorists have gone as far as to argue that communication is the primary goal of human existence. Anthropologist Walter Goldschmidt has called the drive for meeting social needs the 'human career'.[25]

Practical Needs

We shouldn't overlook the important everyday functions that communication serves. Communication is the tool that lets us tell the hair stylist to take just a little off the sides, explain to the police officer why we were driving 60 kilometres per hour in a 40-kilometre zone, and inform the contractor that the leaking roof needs attention right now!

Beyond these obvious needs, a wealth of research demonstrates that communication is an important key to effectiveness in a variety of everyday settings. For example, a survey of over 400 American employers identified 'communication skills' as the top characteristic that employers seek in job candidates.[26] It was rated as more important than technical competence, work experience, or academic background. A study by the Conference Board of Canada found that an employee's ability to communicate effectively is also implicitly favoured because communication skills underpin other desired skills such as teamwork.[27]

Communication is just as important outside of work. University roommates who are both willing and able to communicate effectively report higher satisfaction with one another than do those who lack these characteristics,[28] and students who demonstrate communication competence have higher grade point averages than those who do not have this skill.[29] Married couples who were identified as effective communicators reported happier relationships than did spouses with poorer communication skills.[30] In 'getting acquainted' situations, communication competence played a major role in whether a person was judged physically attractive, socially desirable, and good at the task of getting acquainted.[31]

COMMUNICATION ON-SCREEN

Cast Away (2000)
Directed by Robert Zemeckis.

Chuck Noland (Tom Hanks) is a hard-driving executive who is the only survivor of a plane crash. Stranded for what may be the rest of his life on an otherwise uninhabited Pacific island, he creates a 'companion' by drawing a face on a volleyball and naming it Wilson (the name of the sporting goods company that made the volleyball). Even though Chuck is hungry, thirsty, sun-baked, and in physical pain, he retains his will to go on because he keeps talking and 'interacting' with Wilson to meet his communication needs. This story illustrates how our physical, identity, and social needs are met through communication. For Chuck, communicating with something was better than communicating with no one—it also may have saved his life.

Modelling Communication

So far we have introduced a basic definition of *communication* and looked at the functions it performs. This information is useful, but it only begins to describe the process we will be examining throughout this book. One way to understand more about what it means to communicate is to look at some models that describe what happens when two or more people

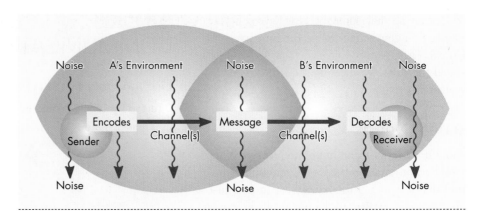

Figure 1.1

Linear Communication Model

interact. As you will see, over the last half-century scholars have developed an increasingly accurate and sophisticated view of this process.

A Linear Model

Until about 50 years ago, researchers viewed communication as something that one person 'does' to another.[32] In this **linear communication model**, communication is like giving an injection: a **sender encodes** ideas and feelings into some sort of **message** and then conveys them to a **receiver**, who **decodes** them (see Figure 1.1).

One important element of the linear model is the communication **channel**—the method by which the message is conveyed. For most people, face-to-face contact is the most familiar and obvious channel. Writing is another channel. In addition to these long-used forms, **mediated communication** channels include telephone, e-mail, instant messaging, faxes, voice mail, and even video conferencing. (The word *mediated* reflects the fact that these messages are conveyed through some sort of communication medium.)

---

channel
Medium through which a message passes from sender to receiver.

decode
The process in which a receiver attaches meaning to a message.

encode
The process of putting thoughts into symbols, most commonly words.

linear communication model
A characterization of communication as a one-way event in which a message flows from sender to receiver.

mediated communication
Communication sent via a medium other than face-to-face interaction, e.g., telephone, e-mail, instant messaging. Can be both mass and personal.

message
A sender's planned and unplanned words and non-verbal behaviours.

receiver
One who notices and attends to a message.

sender
The originator of a message.

Marshall McLuhan

A foundational communication theorist, Marshall McLuhan was one of the most successful and prominent Canadian intellectuals throughout the 1960s. His theory that communication media are actually extensions of the body revolutionized the way marketers, psychologists, and public relations professionals thought of the telephone, the automobile, and many other everyday technologies. McLuhan's radical ideas such as 'the wheel extends the leg' and 'clothing extends the skin' made social scientists and philosophers, as well as communications professionals, rethink how to model communication. He argued that the technologies we use to communicate are just as important as the messages we send. McLuhan was an example of how Canadian communication theorists have had a huge impact on communications theory and the communications professions since World War II.

TABLE 1.1 Factors to Consider When Choosing a Communication Channel

	Time Required for Feedback	Amount of Information Conveyed	Sender's Control Over How Message Is Composed	Control Over Receiver's Attention	Effectiveness for Detailed Messages
Face-to-face	Immediate (after contact established)	Highest	Moderate	Highest	Weak
Telephone	Immediate (after contact established)	Vocal, but not visual	Moderate	Less than in face-to-face setting	Weakest
Voice mail	Delayed	Vocal, but not visual	Higher (since receiver can't interrupt)	Low	Weak
E-mail	Delayed	Lowest (text only, no formatting)	High	Low	Better
Instant messaging	Immediate	Lowest (text only, no formatting)	High	Modest	Weak
Hard copy (e.g., handwritten or typed message)	Delayed	Words, numbers, and images, but no non-verbal cues	Highest	Low	Good

Source: Adapted from R.B. Adler and J.M. Elmhorst, *Communicating at Work: Principles and Practices for Business and the Professions,* 8th edn (New York: McGraw-Hill, 2005), 32–3.

The channel you choose can make a big difference in the effect of your message. For example, a typewritten love letter probably wouldn't have the same effect as a handwritten note or card. Likewise, ending a relationship by leaving a voice-mail message would make a very different statement than delivering the bad news in person. As Table 1.1 suggests, we can improve the quality of our relationships by choosing the communication channel with the best chance of success in any particular situation. As Canadian communication theorist Marshall McLuhan famously claimed, 'The medium is the message.'[33]

The linear model also introduces the concept of **noise**—a term used by social scientists to describe any forces that interfere with effective communication. There are three types of noise—external, physiological, and psychological—and they can disrupt communication at every stage of the process. *External noise* (also called *physical noise*) includes those factors outside the receiver that make it difficult to hear or concentrate on the message being delivered. A television switched on in a restaurant might make it hard for you to pay attention to the person sitting across the table from you, and a back-row seat in a crowded auditorium might make a speaker's remarks unclear. External noise can disrupt communication almost anywhere in our model—in the sender, in the channel, in the message, or in the receiver.

Physiological noise occurs when biological factors in the receiver or sender—illness, fatigue, and so on—interfere with accurate reception. *Psychological noise* refers to forces within a communicator that interfere with the ability to express or understand a message accurately. For instance, an angler might exaggerate the size of a catch in order to convince others of his or her talents. In the same way, a student might become so upset upon receiving a 'D' on an essay that he or she would be unable (or perhaps unwilling) to understand clearly what went wrong.

A linear model shows that communicators often occupy different **environments**—fields of experience that help them understand others' behaviour. In communication terminology, *environment* refers not just to a physical location but also to the personal experiences and

environment

Both the physical setting in which communication occurs and the personal perspectives of the parties involved.

noise

External, physiological, and psychological distractions that interfere with the accurate transmission and reception of a message.

cultural backgrounds that participants bring to a conversation. Consider some of the factors that might contribute to different environments:

- *A* might belong to one ethnic group and *B* to another.
- *A* might be rich and *B* poor.
- *A* might be rushed and *B* have nowhere to go.
- *A* might have lived a long, eventful life, and *B* might be young and inexperienced.
- *A* might be passionately concerned with the subject and *B* indifferent to it.

Environments aren't always so obvious. Consider, for instance, the findings of an American study that showed that college students who have been enrolled in debate classes become more argumentative and verbally aggressive than those who have not been exposed to this environment.[34]

When you look at the linear model in Figure 1.1 you will see that the environments of *A* and *B* overlap. This area represents the background that the communicators must have in common. As the shared environment becomes smaller, communication becomes more difficult. Consider a few examples in which different perspectives can make understanding difficult:

- Employers who have trouble understanding the perspective of their employees will be less effective managers, and workers who do not appreciate the challenges of being in charge are more likely to be uncooperative.
- Parents who have trouble recalling their youth are likely to clash with their children, who do not yet know and may not appreciate the responsibility that comes with parenting.
- Members of a dominant culture who have never experienced being 'different' may not appreciate the concerns of people from other cultures, whose own perspectives make it hard to understand the apparent cultural blindness of the majority.

transactional communication model

A characterization of communication as the simultaneous sending and receiving of messages in an ongoing, irreversible process.

Differing environments make understanding one another challenging but certainly not impossible. Hard work and many of the skills described in this book provide ways to bridge the gaps that separate all of us. For now, recognizing the challenge that comes from dissimilar environments is a good start. You can't solve a problem until you recognize that it exists.

A Transactional Model

Despite its simplicity, the linear model doesn't do a very good job of representing the way most communication operates. The **transactional communication model** in Figure 1.2 presents a more accurate picture in several respects.

Simultaneous Sending and Receiving

Although some types of mass communication flow in a one-way, linear manner, most types of personal communication are two-way exchanges.[35] The transactional model reflects the fact that we usually send and receive messages simultaneously. The roles of sender and receiver that seemed separate in the linear model are now superimposed and redefined as those of 'communicators'. This new term reflects the fact that at a given moment we are capable of receiving, decoding, and responding to another person's behaviour, while at the same time that other person is receiving and responding to ours.

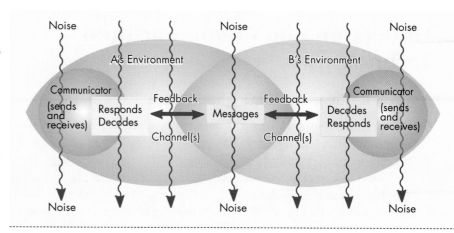

Figure 1.2

Transactional Communication Model

Consider, for instance, the significance of a friend's yawn as you describe your romantic problems. Or imagine the blush you may see as you tell one of your raunchier jokes to a new acquaintance. Non-verbal behaviours like these show that most face-to-face communication is a two-way affair. The discernible response of a receiver to a sender's message is called **feedback.** Not all feedback is non-verbal, of course. Sometimes it is oral, as when you ask for clarification from an instructor who has just announced a test or when you reply to a friend who has asked what you think of her new haircut. In other cases it is written, as when you answer the questions on a mid-term exam or respond to a letter from a friend. Figure 1.2 makes the importance of feedback clear. It shows that most communication is, indeed, a two-way affair.

Another weakness of the traditional linear model is the questionable assumption that all communication involves encoding. We certainly do choose symbols to convey most verbal messages. But what about the many non-verbal cues that occur whether or not people speak: facial expressions, gestures, postures, vocal tones, and so on? Cues like these clearly do offer information about others, although they are often unconscious and thus don't involve encoding. For this reason, the transactional model replaces the term *encodes* with the broader term *responds,* because it describes both intentional and unintentional actions that can be observed and interpreted.[36]

feedback

The discernible response of a receiver to a sender's message.

A new idea is delicate. It can be killed by a sneer or a yawn; it can be stabbed to death by a joke or worried to death by a frown on the right person's brow.

Charles Brower

Communication Is Fluid, Not Static

Besides illustrating the simultaneous nature of face-to-face interaction, the examples we just considered show that it's difficult to isolate a single discrete 'act' of communication from the events that precede and follow it. The way a friend or family member reacts to a sarcastic remark you make will probably depend on the way you have related to one another in the past. Likewise, the way you'll act toward each other in the future depends on the outcome of this conversation. Research conducted on partners in romantic relationships confirms the importance of context. As communication researcher Steve Duck put it, 'Relationships are best conceived . . . as unfinished business.'[37]

Communication Is Relational, Not Individual

The transactional model shows that communication isn't something we do *to* others; rather, it is something we do *with* them. In this sense, communication is rather like dancing—at least the kind of dancing we do with partners. Like dancing, communication depends on the involvement of a partner. And like good dancing, successful communication isn't something

Understanding Communication Technology

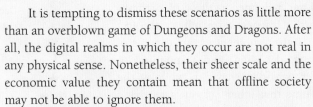

Are You Ready for Avatar Rights?

The world has seen its share of rights movements in recent years. That may not prepare it for the claims of the latest group seeking recognition—digital people.

As online computer games soar in popularity, the distinction between animated characters and their real life creators is eroding. This has given rise to perplexing new questions about the extent to which we have rights in our digital identities.

The popularity of avatars has much to do with the emergence of the online self. Avatars are the custom-designed figures created by computer users to play video games or to participate in a variety of online worlds. Recently, some nasty events have befallen these avatars, bringing moral or financial injury to their creators.

Consider one famous example.

In 2006, digital representatives of real-world news outlets arranged an interview inside the online world known as Second Life with an avatar named Anshe Chung. Chung had arrived to discuss how she had become the largest real estate magnate inside the game and, by doing so, a millionaire outside of it. Instead, the interview was derailed when Chung was bombarded by a montage of giant phalluses introduced to the online studio by a hacker. The incident remains a hit item on YouTube.

The Chung story is only one such episode. Avatars have also been victims of fraud, murder (by so-called 'character killers') and even sexual assault. At the same time, the provenance of certain avatars is becoming the subject of ethical scrutiny amid reports of Asian gaming sweatshops that produce characters for export.

It is tempting to dismiss these scenarios as little more than an overblown game of Dungeons and Dragons. After all, the digital realms in which they occur are not real in any physical sense. Nonetheless, their sheer scale and the economic value they contain mean that offline society may not be able to ignore them.

With more than four million inhabitants, Second Life has a larger population than New Zealand. The game uses a currency (called Linden dollars) that can be exchanged for real-world greenbacks and it contains a diverse collection of merchants hawking a variety of products and services. Moreover, major companies like American Apparel and Toyota and even national governments are staking out a presence in Second Life and other games.

As these online worlds grow in scale so, too, are the conflicts that are emerging within them. Some disputes are already spilling into real-world courts.

Sarah Dale-Harris has an opportunity to be the first Canadian lawyer to have a digital client. She and other associates at her firm, Davis LLP, have created avatar versions of themselves to staff an office they opened in Second Life.

While acknowledging that the notion of avatar rights may seem far-fetched, Dale-Harris notes that courts in other countries have begun to transpose computer game events into real-world judgments. She cites a divorce case in China where the divided assets included virtual property from a video game.

'Countries like Korea and Taiwan are taking it very seriously because of their population's engagement in MMORGs (Massively multiplayer online role-playing games). It's forced them to step up.'

that depends just on the skill of one person. A great dancer who doesn't consider and adapt to the skill level of his or her partner can make both people look bad. In communication and dancing, having two talented partners does not guarantee success. When two talented dancers perform without coordinating their movements, the results feel bad to the dancers and look foolish to an audience. Finally, relational communication—like dancing—is a unique creation that arises out of the way in which the partners interact. The way a person dances varies depending on the partner because of its co-operative, transactional nature. Likewise, the way you communicate almost certainly varies with different partners.

Dale-Harris admits that so far her firm's digital office has been largely a marketing and recruitment tool but that she would be willing to represent an avatar-based claim in Canadian court. She notes that legal action will likely emerge in response to criminal actions within online games or as a consequence of game companies closing the accounts of players without providing compensation for their assets.

'Canada may have to react in the future. It doesn't really have a choice.'

While it is becoming apparent that people have rights within digital realms, it remains uncertain how those rights should be defined.

In the case of Chung (victim of the flying penis attack), her real-world husband attempted to use copyright law to force media outlets to remove images related to the incident. He retracted the threats after a number of groups complained that the demands amounted to news censorship.

Copyright and other forms of property rights have so far formed the basis of the handful of lawsuits from online realms that are trickling into the world's courts. These cases typically involve plaintiffs who have lost virtual assets through the termination of their accounts or who have had their merchandise in a game illegally copied by digital counterfeiters.

The notion of using forms of property law to protect online characters does not seem far-fetched. Indeed, Dale-Harris, the Canadian lawyer, suggests that individuals should consider registering their avatars as a means of protecting them.

A harder question is whether these digital creatures should also enjoy personal rights. For instance, it seems somehow perverse to rely on a notion like property damage to address a cyber-rape (the first instance of which was reported in 1993).

To avoid relying on property concepts, one scholar has written that avatars should enjoy the protection of defamation law. Her argument is that online characters rely on reputation when interacting in the virtual world and that slights to their reputation carry over to their real-world counterparts.

Despite the popularity of online computer games, the extent to which digital people should be endowed with actual rights remains an open question.

In this country, it appears the distinction between avatars and individuals will remain intact for the foreseeable future.

'The whole of online gaming space is becoming bigger and bigger and the legal implications are growing in importance,' says Michael Geist, an authority on copyright and Internet law at the University of Ottawa.

He adds, however, that there is no immediate need for the courts or legislature to get involved.

'I think we can take a hands-off approach until there's an identifiable problem.'

At the same time, the millions of people whose everyday lives leave them with little time to create a digital self might have a further piece of advice for those fretting about their avatar's latest peccadillo: Turn off the computer.

—Jeff Roberts, Special to *The Star*, 5 July 2008. Jeff Roberts is a lawyer and recent graduate of McGill University where he studied law and economics.

Question: The author discusses how someday soon, avatars on Second Life could have rights and pursue lawsuits against people who infringe upon those rights. What effects do you imagine the possibility of being sued would have on how people communicate on Second Life?

Psychologist Kenneth Gergen captures the relational nature of communication well when he points out how our success depends on interaction with others. As he says, 'one cannot be "attractive" without others who are attracted, a "leader" without others willing to follow, or a "loving person" without others to affirm with appreciation.'[38]

Because communication is transactional, it's often a mistake to suggest that just one person is responsible for a relationship. Consider the cartoon on page 22. Both of the characters had good intentions, and both probably could have handled the situation better. It would have been far better to ask, 'How did we handle this situation poorly, and what can we do to make it better?'

The transactional nature of communication shows up in school, where teachers and students influence one another's behaviour. For example, a teacher who regards some students negatively may treat them with subtle or overt disfavour. As a result, these students are likely to react negatively, which reinforces the teacher's original attitudes and expectations.[39] It isn't necessary to resolve the 'who started it' issue here to recognize that the behaviours of teachers and students are part of a transactional relationship.

The transactional character of communication also figures dramatically in relationships between parents and their children. We normally think of 'good parenting' as a skill that some people possess and others lack. We judge the ability of a mother and father in terms of how well their children turn out. In truth, the question of good parenting isn't quite so clear. Research suggests that the quality of interaction between parents and children is a two-way affair, that children influence parents just as much as the other way around.[40] For example, children who engage in what social scientists call 'problematic behaviour' evoke more high-control responses from their parents than do co-operative children. By contrast, children with mild temperaments are less likely to provoke coercive reactions by their parents than are more aggressive children. Parents with low self-esteem tend to send more messages that weaken the self-esteem of their children, who in turn are likely to act in ways that make the parents feel even worse about themselves. Thus, a mutually reinforcing cycle arises in which parents and children shape one another's feelings and behaviour. In cases like this it is at least difficult and probably impossible to identify who is the 'sender' and who is the 'receiver' of messages. It's more accurate to acknowledge that parents and children—just like husbands and wives, managers and staff, teachers and students, and any other people who communicate with one another—act in ways that mutually influence one another. The transactional nature of relationships is worth re-emphasizing: we don't communicate *to* others, we communicate *with* them.

By now you can see that a transactional model of communication should be more like a video clip than a slide show of still images. Although Figure 1.2 does a fair job of illustrating the phenomenon we call communication, an animated version in which the environments, communicators, and messages constantly change would be an even better way of capturing the process.

Communication Competence: What Makes an Effective Communicator?

It's easy to recognize good communicators, and even easier to spot poor ones. But what are the characteristics that distinguish effective communicators from those who are less successful? Answering this question has been one of the leading challenges for communication scholars.[41] Although not all of the answers are in, research has identified a great deal of important and useful information about communication competence.

Communication Competence Defined

Defining **communication competence** isn't as easy as it might seem. Although scholars are still struggling to agree on a precise definition, most would concur that effective communication involves achieving one's goals in a manner that, ideally, maintains or enhances the relationship in which it occurs.[42] This definition may seem both vague and verbose, but a closer look shows that it suggests several important characteristics of communication competence.

There Is No 'Ideal' Way to Communicate

Your own experience will show you that a variety of communication styles are effective. Some very successful communicators are serious, while others use humour; some are gregarious, while others are quiet; and some are straightforward, while others hint diplomatically. Just as there are many kinds of beautiful music and art, there are many kinds of competent communication.

You will also find that the type of communication that succeeds in one situation might be a colossal blunder in another. The joking insults you routinely trade with a friend might be insensitive and discouraging if he or she has just suffered a personal setback. The language you use with your peers might offend a family member, and last Saturday night's romantic approach would probably be out of place at work on Monday morning. For this reason, being a competent communicator requires flexibility in understanding what approach is likely to work best in a given situation.[43]

Cultural differences also call for different approaches to communication. What qualifies as competent behaviour in one culture might be completely inept, or even offensive, in another.[44] Habits like belching after a meal or appearing nude in public, to note two obvious examples, might be appropriate in some parts of the world but would of course be considered outrageous in others. But there are more subtle differences in competent communication. For example, such qualities as being self-disclosing and speaking clearly, which are valued among Americans and English Canadians, are likely to be considered overly aggressive and insensitive in many Asian cultures, where subtlety and indirectness are considered important.[45]

Even within a single society, people from different cultural backgrounds may have different notions of appropriate behaviour. One American study, for instance, revealed that ideas of how good friends should communicate varied from one ethnic group to another:[46] Latinos, as a group, valued relational support most highly, whereas African Americans valued respect and acceptance. Asian Americans emphasized a caring, positive exchange of ideas, and Anglo-Americans prized friends who recognized their needs as individuals.

Now, consider for a moment the cultural diversity of Canada. People of African ancestry make up a tiny fraction of the Canadian population, but they come from a very wide variety of geographic origins in Africa and the Caribbean. People of Asian descent, who make up 60 per cent of Canadian visible minorities, come from all parts of Asia, including mainland China, Hong Kong, Taiwan, Macao, Korea, India, and Sri Lanka. And the fact that Canadians of European origin are much more likely than their American counterparts to be fluent in a language other than English makes it much more difficult to categorize them as a single group. At the same time, a recent study showed that Canadians generally feel a much stronger

e-mail: CLOSETOHOME@COMPUSERVE.COM 10-27

'I SAID, "I have trouble developing close relationships with people!" For cryin' out loud, clean out your ears, fathead!'

communication competence
Ability to maintain a relationship on terms acceptable to all parties.

Cultural Idiom

visible minorities
people whose physical appearance identifies them as members of a particular ethnic group

Cultural Idiom

sure-fire
certain to succeed

attachment to regional cultures, such as those of the Maritimes, the North, or Quebec, than Americans do.[47] This cultural complexity makes it difficult to generalize about cultural and communication competence in English Canada. By contrast, the identity of French Canada is relatively homogeneous, and therefore easier for most immigrants to assimilate to. Some argue that this is the reason that French-Canadian television, current affairs programs, and celebrities have relatively much higher profiles than their English-Canadian counterparts.

Findings like these mean that there can be no sure-fire list of rules or tips that will guarantee your success as a communicator. They also suggest that competent communicators are able to adapt their style to suit the individual and cultural preferences of others.[48] Throughout this book, you will be introduced to a variety of communication skills. Although all of them are likely to be effective at one time or another, they aren't meant to replace other approaches that you already use. The skills you learn from this book will broaden your repertoire of choices about how to communicate. When you combine them with other approaches, you'll be likely to recognize a change for the better in your interactions with others.

Competence Is Situational

Because competent behaviour varies so much from one situation and person to another, it's a mistake to think that communication competence is a trait that a person either possesses or lacks. It's more accurate to talk about degrees or areas of competence.[49] You and the people you know are probably quite competent in some areas and less so in others. You might deal quite skilfully with peers, for example, but feel clumsy interacting with people much older or younger, wealthier or poorer, or more or less attractive than yourself. In fact, your competence with one person may vary from one situation to another. This means that it's an overgeneralization to say, in a moment of distress, 'I'm a terrible communicator!' It would be more accurate to say, 'I didn't handle this situation very well, even though I'm better in others.' In a place as diverse as Canada it's especially important to remember that people who seem to be having difficulty communicating in one particular context may do much better in a different setting.

Competence Is Relational

Because communication is transactional, behaviour that is competent in one relationship isn't necessarily competent in others.

A fascinating study on relational satisfaction illustrates that what constitutes satisfying communication varies from one relationship to another.[50] Researchers Brant Burleson and Wendy Samter hypothesized that people with sophisticated communication skills (such as managing conflict well, giving ego-support to others, and providing comfort to relational partners) would be better than less-skilled communicators at maintaining friendships. To their surprise, the results did not support this hypothesis. In fact, friendships were most satisfying when partners possessed matching skill levels. Apparently, relational satisfaction arises in part when our styles match those of the people with whom we interact. This idea of 'communication compatibility' is at the heart of eHarmony.ca, the highly successful Canadian dating website. Users of this service answer a battery of questions about themselves, the purpose of which is to determine their compatibility with other singles on the website.

The same principle holds true in the case of jealousy. Researchers have uncovered a variety of ways by which people deal with jealousy in their relationships.[51] These include keeping closer tabs on the partner, acting indifferent, decreasing affection, talking the matter over, and acting angry. The researchers found that no type of behaviour was effective or ineffective in

Cultural Idiom

keeping closer tabs on
paying closer attention to

every relationship, leading them to conclude that approaches that work with some people would be harmful to others. Findings like these demonstrate that competence comes from developing ways of interacting that work for you and for the other people involved.[52]

Competence Can Be Learned

To some degree, biology is destiny when it comes to communication style.[53] Studies of identical and fraternal twins suggest that traits including sociability, anger, and relaxation are partly a function of our genetic makeup. Fortunately, biology isn't the only factor that shapes how we communicate: communication is a set of skills that anyone can learn. As children grow, their ability to communicate effectively develops. For example, older children learn to use more sophisticated techniques of persuasion.[54] Along with maturity, systematic education (including classes such as the one in which you are now enrolled) can boost communicative competence. Even a modest amount of specialized training can produce dramatic results. After just 30 minutes of instruction, one group of observers became significantly more effective at detecting deception in interviews.[55] Even without systematic training, it's possible to develop communication skills through the processes of trial-and-error and observation. One study revealed that university students' communication competence increases over their undergraduate studies, regardless of whether or not they're enrolled in human communication courses.[56] Finally, we learn from our own successes and failures, as well as from observing other models—both positive and negative.

> **Cultural Idiom**
>
> **common denominators**
> features that all share
>
> **counting on**
> depending on
>
> **soften the blow of**
> ease the effect of

Characteristics of Competent Communicators

Although competent communication varies from one situation to another, scholars have identified several common denominators that characterize effective communication in most contexts.

A Wide Range of Behaviours

Effective communicators are able to choose their actions from a wide range of behaviours. To understand the importance of having a large communication repertoire, imagine that one of your friends repeatedly tells jokes that you find offensive. You could respond to these jokes in a number of ways. You could:

- say nothing, figuring that the negative consequences of raising the subject would be greater than the benefits;
- ask a third party to say something to your friend about the offensiveness of the jokes;
- hint at your discomfort, hoping that your friend would get the point;
- joke about your friend's insensitivity, counting on humour to soften the blow of your criticism;
- express your discomfort in a straightforward way, asking your friend to stop telling the offensive jokes, at least around you; or
- simply demand that your friend stop.

With these possible responses at your disposal (and you can probably think of others as well), you could pick the one that had the best chance of success. But if you were able to use only one or two of these responses when raising a delicate issue—always keeping quiet or always hinting, for example—your chances of success would be much smaller. Indeed,

I witnessed recently a striking and barely believable
example of such [inappropri-
ate] behaviour at a wedding
ceremony. One of the guests
said loud enough for those of
us on my side of the chapel
to hear, 'Think it through,
Jerry' just at the point where
the rabbi had asked Jerry if
he took this woman to be his
lawful wedded wife, according to (no less) the laws of
Moses and Israel. So far as I
could tell, the wedding guest
was not drunk or embittered.
He merely mistook the synagogue for Shea Stadium . . .

Neil Postman,
Crazy Talk, Stupid Talk

many poor communicators are easy to spot by their limited range of responses. Some are chronic jokers; others are always belligerent; and still others are quiet in almost every situation. Like a pianist who knows only one tune or a chef who can prepare only a few dishes, these people are forced to rely on a small range of responses again and again, whether or not they are successful.

Ability to Choose the Most Appropriate Behaviour

Simply possessing a large array of communication skills isn't a guarantee of effectiveness. It's also necessary to know which of these skills will work best in any particular situation. Choosing the best way to send a message is like choosing a gift: what is appropriate for one person won't be appropriate for another one at all. This ability to choose the best approach is essential because a response that works well in one setting might flop miserably in another one. Although it's impossible to say precisely how to act in every situation, there are at least three factors to consider when you are deciding which response to choose: the context, your goal, and the other person.

Skill at Performing Behaviours

After you have chosen the most appropriate way to communicate, it's still necessary to use the required skills effectively. There is a big difference between simply being aware of alternatives and skilfully putting them to work. Similarly, just reading about communication skills in the following chapters won't guarantee that you can start using them flawlessly. As with any other skills—those required to play an instrument or learn a sport, for example—the road to competence in communication is not a short one. You can expect that your first efforts at communicating differently will be awkward. After some practice you will become more skilful, although you will still have to think about the new way of speaking or listening. Finally, after practising the new skill again and again, you will find you can use it without conscious thought.

Empathy/Perspective-Taking

People have the best chance of developing an effective message when they understand the other person's point of view. And because others aren't always good at expressing their thoughts and feelings clearly, the ability to imagine how an issue might look from the other's point of view is an important skill. The value of taking the other's perspective is one reason why listening is so important. Not only does it help us understand others, but it also gives us information to develop strategies about how to best influence them. Because empathy is such an important element of communicative competence, much of Chapter 4 is devoted to this topic.

cognitive complexity

The ability to construct a variety of frameworks for viewing an issue.

Cognitive Complexity

Cognitive complexity is the ability to construct a variety of frameworks for viewing an issue. It is an ingredient of communication competence because it allows us to make sense of people by using a variety of perspectives. For instance, imagine that a long-time friend seems to be angry with you. One possible explanation is that your friend is offended by something you've done. Another possibility is that something upsetting has happened in another part of your friend's life. Or perhaps nothing at all is wrong, and you're just being overly sensitive. Researchers have found that the ability to analyze the behaviour of others in a variety of ways leads to greater 'conversational sensitivity', increasing the chances of acting in ways that will produce satisfying results.[57]

Self-Monitoring

Psychologists use the term **self-monitoring** to describe the process of paying close attention to one's behaviour and using these observations to shape the way one behaves. Self-monitors are able to separate a part of their consciousness and observe their behaviour from a detached viewpoint, making observations such as

- 'I'm making a fool out of myself.'
- 'I'd better speak up now.'
- 'This approach is working well. I'll keep it up.'

Chapter 2 explains how too much self-monitoring can be problematic. Still, people who are aware of their behaviour and the impression it makes are more skilful communicators than people who are low self-monitors.[58] For example, they are more accurate in judging others' emotional states, better at remembering information about others, less shy, and more assertive. By contrast, low self-monitors aren't even able to recognize their incompetence. (Calvin, in the cartoon below, does a nice job of illustrating this problem.) One study revealed that poor communicators were blissfully ignorant of their shortcomings and more likely to overestimate their skill than were better communicators.[59] For example, experimental subjects who scored in the lowest quartile on joke-telling skill were more likely than funnier people to grossly overestimate their sense of humour.

Commitment to the Relationship

One feature that distinguishes effective communication in almost any context is commitment. People who seem to care about the relationship communicate better than those who don't.[60] This concern shows up in commitment to the other person and to the message being expressed.

Calvin and Hobbes   by Bill Watterson

self-monitoring

The process of paying close attention to one's behaviour and using these observations to shape the way one behaves.

*Ha! whaur ye gaun, ye
        crowlin ferlie?
Your impudence protects you
        sairly;
I canna say but ye strunt
        rarely,
Owre gauze and lace;
Tho', faith! I fear ye dine but
        sparely
On sic a place.*

*Ye ugly, creepin, blastit
        wonner,
Detested, shunn'd by saunt
        an' sinner,
How daur ye set your fit
        upon her-
Sae fine a lady?
Gae somewhere else and seek
        your dinner
On some poor body.*

*Swith! in some beggar's
        haffet squattle;
There ye may creep, and
        sprawl, and sprattle,
Wi' ither kindred, jumping
        cattle,
In shoals and nations;
Whaur horn nor bane ne'er
        daur unsettle
Your thick plantations.*

*Now haud you there, ye're
        out o' sight,
Below the fatt'rels, snug and
        tight;
Na, faith ye yet! ye'll no be
        right,
Till ye've got on it-
The verra tapmost, tow'rin
        height
O' Miss' bonnet.*

Clarifying Misconceptions about Communication

Having spent time talking about what communication *is*, we also ought to identify some things it is *not*.[61] Recognizing some misconceptions is important, not only because they should be avoided by anyone knowledgeable about the subject but also because following them can get you into trouble.

Communication Does Not Always Require Complete Understanding

Most people operate on the implicit but flawed assumption that the goal of all communication is to maximize understanding between communicators. Although some understanding is necessary for us to comprehend one another's thoughts and feelings, there are some types of communication in which understanding as we usually conceive it is not the primary goal.[62] Consider the following examples:

- *Social rituals.* 'How's it going?' you ask. 'Great,' the other person replies. The primary goal in exchanges like this one is mutual acknowledgement; there's obviously no serious attempt to exchange information.
- *Attempts to influence others.* A quick analysis of most TV commercials shows that they are aimed at persuading viewers to buy products, not to understand the content of the ad. In the same way, many of our attempts at persuading someone to act as we wish have little to do with getting the other person to understand what we want; they're designed to get that person to comply with our wishes.
- *Deliberate ambiguity and deception.* When you decline an unwanted invitation by saying 'I can't make it,' you probably want to create the impression that the decision is really beyond your control. If your goal was to be perfectly clear, you might say: 'I don't want to get together. In fact, I'd rather do almost anything than accept your invitation.' As Chapters 3 and 6 explain in detail, we often equivocate precisely because we want to obscure our true thoughts and feelings.
- *Coordinate action.* This term is used to describe situations in which participants interact smoothly with a high degree of satisfaction but without necessarily understanding one another perfectly.[63] **Coordination** without understanding can be satisfying in many important situations. Consider the many meanings of the phrase 'I love you': 'I admire you'; 'I feel great affection for you'; 'I want you'; 'I am grateful to you'; 'I feel guilty'; 'I want you to be faithful to me'; or even 'I hope you love me'.[64] It's not hard to picture a situation in which partners gain great satisfaction—even over

coordination
Interaction in which participants interact smoothly, with a high degree of satisfaction but without necessarily understanding one another well.

a lifetime—without completely understanding that the mutual love they profess is actually quite different for each of them.

At the conversational level, some scholars have compared coordinated communication to what musicians call 'jamming'.[65] In this sort of musical interaction, musicians play off one another, improvising melodies and riffs based on what others have contributed. There's no plan, and no attempt at understanding. Some conversations resemble this sort of jamming in several respects:

- *Coordination is more important than understanding.* Musicians in a jam session focus on and gain satisfaction from making music together, not on understanding one another. In coordinated conversations, satisfaction comes principally from being together—laughing, joking, exchanging confidences, and telling stories. The act of conversation is more important than its content.
- *Participants follow rules.* In a jam session, musicians agree on fundamentals such as the key in which they will play, the tempo, and the overall structure of the music. In coordinated communication, participants tacitly agree on things like the level of seriousness, the amount of time they will spend, and what topics are off limits. They may not understand the content of one another's messages, but they do understand how to behave with one another.
- *Everyone gets a solo.* Each musician in a jam session gets a time to take the lead, with others following. Conversations work only when the participants take turns, giving each other time to talk.
- *Sessions go to new places.* When musicians improvise, every session is unique. Likewise, no two conversations are identical in words or tone. One person's decision about what to say and how to say it triggers the other's response, which in turn results in a unique reaction. The communication is truly transactional, as described earlier.
- *Jamming builds rapport.* Musicians who jam with one another build unspoken bonds. In the same way, communicators who converse smoothly with one another feel a connection—even if the topic isn't very important or the participants don't completely understand one another.[66]

Communication Is Not Always a Good Thing

For most people, belief in the value of communication rates somewhere close to loyalty, charity, or parenthood in their hierarchy of important values. In truth, communication is neither good nor bad in itself. Rather, its value comes from the way it is used. In this sense, communication is similar to fire: flames in the fireplace on a cold night keep you warm and create a cozy atmosphere, but the same flames can do serious damage if they spread into your living room. Communication can be a tool for expressing warm feelings and useful facts, but under different circumstances the same words and actions can cause both physical and emotional pain. An excellent example was recently related to one of the authors:

Professor Sévigny, I recently met someone with whom I shared so many things in common. We loved the same cultural activities, found each other attractive, and enjoyed each others' company on the couple of dates that we went on. We had exchanged over 50 e-mails, almost daily. But one night, I had had the worst day of my life—bad at work, bad

My sooth! right bauld ye set your nose out,
As plump an' grey as ony groset:
O for some rank, mercurial rozet,
Or fell, red smeddum,
I'd gie you sic a hearty dose o't,
Wad dress your droddum.

I wad na been surpris'd to spy
You on an auld wife's flainen toy;
Or aiblins some bit dubbie boy,
On's wyliecoat;
But Miss' fine Lunardi! fye!
How daur ye do't?

O Jeany, dinna toss your head,
An' set your beauties a' abread!
Ye little ken what cursed speed
The blastie's makin:
Thae winks an' finger-ends, I dread,
Are notice takin.

O wad some Power the giftie gie us
To see oursels as ithers see us!
It wad frae mony a blunder free us,
An' foolish notion:
What airs in dress an' gait wad lea'e us,
An' ev'n devotion!

Robert Burns,
'To a Louse'

COMMUNICATION ON-SCREEN

Pontypool (2008)
Directed by Bruce McDonald.

The idea that communication isn't always desirable is taken to a rather exaggerated but entertaining end in this Canadian independent film, released under the apt tagline 'Shut Up or Die.' *Pontypool* re-imagines the basic zombie setup with an innovative twist: unlike other recent portrayals (*28 Days Later, Dawn of the Dead*) where the 'affliction' is treated as if it were a physical disease, the crazed hordes that overrun the town of Pontypool, Ontario, spread their infection to others through speech. Literalizing the colloquial metaphor that ideas 'go viral' in our communication-rich world, the film's cast is presented with a truly unique puzzle. After all, nobody's written a survival handbook for dealing with a linguistic epidemic.

at school, bad at the charity I volunteer with—and I asked her some prying, judgmental questions over text message. She was insulted and told me to go to sleep because I had a lot of work to do in the morning. I felt heartsick about having insulted her and then sent her an 'e-mail in text messages'. I guess there were about 30 messages in total. My last one said: 'I should really have sent this as an e-mail—all these text messages are awkward.' Well, I woke up the next day to find a text message from her saying 'I woke up to over 30 text messages from you! That is more than creepy to me. I would appreciate it if you didn't contact me anymore.' Professor Sévigny, you don't know how much I regret sending those text messages instead of an e-mail!

No Single Person or Event Causes Another's Reaction

Although communicative skill can often make the difference between pleasant and unpleasant outcomes, it's a mistake to suggest that any single thing we say or do causes an outcome. Many factors play a role in how others will react to your communication in a given situation. Suppose, for example, that you lose your temper and say something to a friend that you regret as soon as the words escape your lips. Your friend's reaction will depend on a whole host of events besides your unjustified remark: her frame of mind at the moment (uptight or mellow), elements of her personality (judgmental or forgiving), your relational history (supportive or hostile), and her knowledge of any factors in your life that might have contributed to your unfair remark. Because communication is a transactional, ongoing, collaborative process, it's usually a mistake to think that any event occurs in a vacuum.

Communication Will Not Solve All Problems

'If I could just communicate better . . .' is the sad refrain of many unhappy people who believe that if they could just express themselves better, their relationships would improve. Though this is sometimes true, it's an exaggeration to say that communicating—even communicating clearly—is a guaranteed remedy for relationship woes.

Meanings Rest in People, Not in Words

We hinted that meanings rest in people, not in words, when we said earlier that the symbols we use to communicate are arbitrary. It's a mistake to think that, just because you use a word in one way, others will do so, too.[67] Sometimes differing interpretations of symbols are easily caught, as when we might first take the statement 'He's loaded' to mean that the subject has had too much to drink, only to find out that he is quite wealthy (and sober). In other cases, however, the ambiguity of words and non-verbal behaviours isn't so apparent, and thus can have more far-reaching consequences. Remember, for instance, a time when someone said to you, 'I'll be honest and tell you the truth,' and only later did you learn that those words hid precisely the opposite fact. In Chapter 3 we'll look more closely at the problems that come from mistakenly assuming that meanings rest in words.

Communication Is Not Simple

Most people assume that communication is an aptitude that people develop without the need for training—rather like breathing. After all, we've been swapping ideas with one another since early childhood, and there are lots of people who communicate pretty well without ever taking a class on the subject. Though this picture of communication as a natural ability seems accurate, it's actually a gross oversimplification.[68]

Throughout history there have been cases of infants raised without human contact. In all these cases, the children were initially unable to communicate with others when brought into society. Only after extensive teaching (and not even then, in some cases) were they able to speak and understand language in ways we take for granted. But what about the more common cases of effective communicators who have had no formal training and yet are skilful at creating and understanding messages? The answer to this question lies in the fact that not all education occurs in a classroom. Many people learn to communicate skilfully because they have been exposed to models of such behaviour by those around them. This principle of modelling explains why children who grow up in homes with stable relationships between family members have a greater chance of developing such relationships themselves. They know how to do so because they've seen effective communication in action.

Does the existence of these good communicators mean that certain people don't need courses like the one you're taking? Hardly. Even the best communicators aren't perfect: they often suffer the frustration of being unable to get a message across effectively, and they frequently misunderstand others. Furthermore, even the most successful people you know can probably identify ways in which their relationships could profit by better communication. These facts show that communication skills are rather like athletic ability: even the most inept of us can learn to be more effective with training and practice, and those who are talented can always become better.

More Communication Is Not Always Better

Although it's certainly true that not communicating enough is a mistake, there are also situations when too much communication is wrong. Sometimes excessive communication is simply unproductive, as when we 'talk a problem to death', going over the same ground again and again without making any headway. And there are times when communicating too much can actually aggravate a problem. We've all had the experience of 'talking ourselves into a hole'—making a bad situation worse by pursuing it too far. As McCroskey and Wheeless put it, 'More and more negative communication merely leads to more and more negative results.'[69]

There are even times when no communication is the best course. Any good salesperson will tell you that there comes a time when it's best to stop talking and let the customer think about the product. And when two people are angry and hurt, they may say things they don't mean and will later regret. At times like these it's probably best to spend a little time cooling off, thinking about what to say and how to say it.

One key to successful communication, then, is to share an adequate amount of information in a skilful manner. Teaching you how to decide what information is adequate and what constitutes skilful behaviour is one major goal of this book.

After several minutes of utterly dull conversation I began to think of her not as a woman but as a human, then not as a human but as an animal, then not as an animal but as a source of high-grade protein.

Mark Gooley

Summary

This chapter began by defining communication as it will be examined in this text: a process involving communicators occupying different but overlapping environments and simultaneously sending and receiving messages, many of which are distorted by physical and psychological noise.

It introduced four communication contexts that will be covered in the rest of the book: intrapersonal, dyadic, small-group, and public. The chapter also identified several types of needs that communication satisfies: physical, identity, social, and practical.

A linear and a transactional communication model were developed, demonstrating the superiority of the transactional model in representing the process-oriented nature of human interaction.

The chapter went on to explore the difference between effective and ineffective exchanges by discussing communication competence, showing that there is no single correct way to behave and that competence is situational, that it is relational in nature, and that it can be learned. Competent communicators were described as those who are able to choose and perform appropriately from a wide range of behaviours; they are cognitively complex self-monitors, who can take the perspective of others and who have committed to important relationships.

After spending most of the chapter talking about what communication is, we concluded by discussing what it is not by refuting several common misconceptions. We demonstrated that communication doesn't always require complete understanding and that it is not always a good thing that will solve every problem. We showed that more communication is not always better; that meanings are in people, not in words; that no single person or event causes another's reactions; and that communication is neither simple nor easy.

Key Terms

channel 16

cognitive complexity 26

communication 4

communication
   competence 23

coordination 28

decode 16

dyad 7

dyadic communication 7

encode 16

environment 17

feedback 19

interpersonal
   communication 8

intrapersonal
   communication 7

linear communication
   model 16

mass communication 9

mediated
   communication 16

message 16

noise 17

public communication 8

receiver 16

self-monitoring 27

sender 16

small-group
   communication 8

symbol 6

transactional communication
   model 18

Activities

A. Analyzing Your Communication Behaviour

Prove to yourself that communication is both frequent and important by observing your interactions during a single day. Record every occasion on which you are involved in some sort of communication as it is defined on pages 7–8. Based on your findings, answer the following questions:

1. What percentage of your waking day is involved in communication?
2. What percentage of time do you spend communicating in the following contexts?
    a. intrapersonal
    b. dyadic
    c. small-group
    d. public
3. What percentage of your communication is devoted to satisfying each of the following types of needs?
    a. physical
    b. identity
    c. social
    d. practical
    (Note that you might try to satisfy more than one type at a time.)

Based on your analysis, describe 5 to 10 ways you would like to communicate more effectively. For each item on your list of goals, describe who is involved (e.g., 'my parents', 'people I meet when I'm out') and how you would like to communicate differently (e.g., 'act less defensively when criticized', 'speak up instead of waiting to be approached'). Use this list to focus your studies as you read the remainder of this book.

B. Choosing the Most Effective Communication Channel

Decide which communication channel would be most effective in each of the following situations. Be prepared to explain your answer.

1. In class, an instructor criticizes you for copying work from other sources when the work was your own. You are furious, and you don't intend to accept the charge without responding. Which approach(es) would be best for you to use?
    a. Send your instructor an e-mail or write a letter explaining your objections.
    b. Telephone your instructor and explain your position.
    c. Schedule a personal meeting with your instructor.
2. You want to see whether the members of your extended family are able to view the photos you've posted on your own website. How can you ensure that they can access the site?
    a. Demonstrate the website at an upcoming family get-together.
    b. E-mail them a link to the site.
    c. Phone them individually to inquire about their ability to access websites.

3.   You want to be sure the members of your office team are able to use the new voice-mail system. What should you do?
     a. Send each employee an instruction manual for the system.
     b. Ask employees to e-mail any questions about the system.
     c. Conduct one or more training sessions where employees can try out the system and you can clear up any questions.
4.   You've just been given two free tickets to tomorrow night's concert. What is the best way to find out whether your friend can go with you?
     a. Send her an e-mail and ask for a quick reply.
     b. Leave her a voice mail asking her to phone you back.
     c. Send her a text message.

C. Increasing Your Communicative Competence

Prove to yourself that communication competence can be increased by following these steps.

1.   Identify a situation in which you are dissatisfied with your present communication skill.
2.   Identify at least three separate approaches you could take in this situation that might be more successful than the one you have taken in the past. If you are at a loss for alternatives, consider how other people you have observed (both real and fictional characters) have handled similar situations.
3.   From these three alternatives, choose the one you think would work best for you.
4.   Consider how you could become more skilful at performing your chosen approach. For example, you might rehearse it alone or with friends, or you might gain pointers from watching others.
5.   Consider how to get feedback on how well you perform your new approach. For instance, you might ask friends to watch you. In some cases, you might even be able to ask the people involved how you did.

     This systematic approach to increasing your communicative competence isn't the only way to change, but it is one way to take the initiative in communicating more effectively.

Further Reading

Coupland, Nikolas, Howard Giles, and John M. Wiemann, eds. *Miscommunication and Problematic Talk*. Newbury Park, CA: Sage, 1991.
This collection of readings explores the many ways in which communication can be unsuccessful. Chapters focus on communication problems involving gender, age, physical disabilities, and culture. Other selections look at communication problems in different settings, such as medical, legal, and organizational.

Heath, Robert L., and Jennings Bryant. *Human Communication Theory and Research*, 2nd edn. Mahwah , NJ: Erlbaum, 2000.
Separate chapters describe the body of research and theorizing on communication competence and new communication technologies.

Stiebel, David. *When Talking Makes Things Worse! Resolving Problems When Communication Fails*. Kansas City, MO: Andrews and McMeel, 1997.
The author offers many examples from his experience as an adviser to Fortune 500 companies, showing how even clear communication can create problems instead of solving them. The author also offers guidelines for deciding when talking will only make matters worse.

Study Questions

1. Describe an incident that illustrates how communication is a symbolic process.
2. Using your own experience, describe two or three examples from everyday life of each type of communication: intrapersonal, dyadic/interpersonal, small-group, public, and mass.
3. Discuss one or more typical communication transactions intended to satisfy each type of need: physical, identity, social, and practical.
4. Use an incident from everyday life to illustrate the transactional process of communication (pages 18–22).
5. Use the characteristics of competent communication (pages 25–7) to evaluate one transaction you have observed or experienced.
6. Show how avoiding common misconceptions about communication (pages 28–31) can make relationships more satisfying.

After studying the material in this chapter . . .

You should
understand:

- how common perceptual tendencies and situational factors influence perception;
- the influence of culture on perception and the self-concept;
- the importance of empathy in communication;
- the communicative influences that shape the self-concept;
- how self-fulfilling prophecies influence behaviour;
- how the process of identity management can result in presentation of multiple selves; and
- the reasons for and the ethical dimensions of identity management.

You should be
able to:

- explain how the tendencies outlined in this chapter have led you to develop distorted perceptions of yourself and others;
- use perception-checking and empathy to be more accurate in your perceptions of others' behaviour;
- identify the ways you influence the self-concepts of others and the ways significant others influence your self-concept;
- identify the communication-related self-fulfilling prophecies that you have imposed on yourself, that others have imposed on you, and that you have imposed on others; and
- describe the various identities you attempt to create and the ethical merit of your identity management strategies.

Perception, the Self, and Communication

Chapter Highlights

Our perceptions of others shape the way we communicate with them. Several factors influence these perceptions:

- our success at constructing shared narratives through communication;
- our tendency to make several perceptual errors;
- factors arising from our own experience and from our prior relationship with that person;
- our cultural background; and
- our ability to empathize.

The skill of perception-checking can help us clarify mistaken perceptions, leading to a shared narrative and smoother communication.

Communication depends on the way we perceive ourselves, as well as others. You will appreciate the importance of the self as you read about

- how communication shapes the self-concept;

- the way culture shapes our self-perceptions;
- the role of personality in shaping our perceptions; and
- how self-fulfilling prophecies can lead either to more satisfying or to less productive communication.

As Chapter 1 explained, one reason we communicate is to persuade others to view ourselves as we want to be seen. To understand how this principle of identity management operates, Chapter 2 explains

- the difference between perceived and presenting selves;
- how we communicate to manage our identities, via both face-to-face and mediated channels; and
- reasons why we communicate to manage our identities.

- Two students, one Métis and the other English Canadian, are discussing their latest reading assignment for their Canadian history class. 'Louis Riel was quite a guy,' the English-Canadian student says sincerely to his classmate. 'You must be very proud of him.' The Métis student is offended at what sounds like a condescending remark.
- A student is practising his first speech for a public speaking class in front of several friends. 'This is a stupid topic,' he laments. The others assure him that the topic is interesting and that the speech sounds good. Later in class he becomes flustered because he believes that his speech is awful. As a result of his unenthusiastic delivery, he receives a low grade on the assignment.
- In biology class, a shy but earnest student mistakenly uses the term *orgasm* instead of *organism* when answering the professor's question. The entire class breaks into raucous laughter. The student remains quiet for the remainder of the semester.
- Despite her nervousness, a graduating student does her best to look and sound confident in a job interview. Although she leaves the session convinced she botched a big chance, a few days later she is surprised to receive a job offer.
- A young woman allows a friend to take silly photos of her on a 'girls' night out' at the pub and to post them on Facebook. During an interview for a teaching position in a religious school, one of her interviewers mentions the photos and questions her personal judgment. She is deeply embarrassed and messes up the interview.
- A man gets into a heated conversation with an ex-girlfriend via Twitter, in which he says some very personal and demeaning things. Feeling remorseful a few hours later, he deletes all his offensive tweets and begs her forgiveness. However, she has already posted his tweets to Facebook and to her blog. His reputation is ruined, as many of his business contacts have seen his abusive comments. He contacts her and says that he thought the tweets were 'just between them'. She feels bad for having posted them, but the damage is done.

You're probably familiar with stories like these, but would you believe that each of them illustrates principles that affect our communication more than almost any others we'll discuss in this book? For example,

- Two or more people often perceive the world in radically different ways, which presents major challenges for successful communication.
- The set of beliefs each of us holds about ourselves—our self-concept—has a powerful effect on our own communication behaviour.
- The messages we send can shape others' self-concepts and thus influence their communication.
- The image we present to the world varies from one situation to another.

These simple truths play a role in nearly all the important messages we send and receive. The goal of this chapter is to demonstrate the significance of these truths by describing the nature of perception and showing how it influences the way we view ourselves and how we relate to others.

Perceiving Others

Suppose you woke up tomorrow in another person's body. Imagine how different the world would seem if you were 15 years older or younger, a member of the opposite sex or a different ethnic group, far more or less intelligent, vastly more attractive or ugly, more wealthy

---

Cultural Idiom

botched
destroyed, ruined

or poverty-stricken. It doesn't take much imagination to understand that the world feels like a different place to each of us, depending on our physical condition as well as our social and personal backgrounds.

Narratives and Perception

Each of us has our own story of the world, and often our stories are quite different from those of others. A family member or roommate might think your sense of humour is inappropriate, whereas you think you're quite clever. You might blame an unsatisfying class on the instructor, whom you think is an arrogant bore who likes nothing more than the sound of his own voice. On the other hand, the instructor might characterize

"I know what you're thinking, but let me offer a competing narrative."

the students as superficial and lazy and blame the class environment on them. (Chapter 3 will examine the sort of name-calling embedded in the previous sentences.)

Social scientists call the personal stories that we and others create to make sense of our personal world **narratives**.[1] In a few pages we will look at how a tool called 'perception-checking' can help bridge the gap between different narratives. For now, though, the important point is that differing narratives can lead to problematic communication.

After they take hold, narratives offer a framework for explaining behaviour and shaping future communication. One study of sense-making in organizations illustrates how the process operates on the job.[2] Researchers tracked down employees who had participated in office discussions about cases where a fellow worker had received 'differential treatment' from management in matters such as time off, pay, or work assignments. The researchers then analyzed the conversations that employees held with their colleagues about the differential treatment. The analysis revealed that, during these conversations, employees created and reinforced the meaning of the co-worker's behaviour and management's response. For example, consider Jane, who has a habit of taking long lunches. As Jane's co-workers discuss her behaviours, they might decide that her long lunches aren't fair, or they might agree that they aren't a big deal. Either way, the co-workers' narrative of office events defines those events. Once their perceptions have been defined in this way, co-workers tend to seek reinforcement for their perceptions by keeping a mental scorecard rating their fellow employees and management. ('Did you notice that Luis came in late again today?' 'Did you hear that Nadia was picked to go on that trip to Nunavut?')

Although most of us like to think we form judgments about others on our own, the research on sense-making in organizations suggests that sense-making is an *interactive* process. And, as University of Western Ontario psychologist Anne Wilson suggests, any errors of judgment we may be guilty of in the course of our sense-making do not always reflect cognitive shortcomings but the common goals and strategies we all rely on to understand our world and generate meaningful conversation.[3] In other words, reality in the workplace and elsewhere isn't 'out there'; rather, we create it with others through communication.

Research on long-term happy marriages demonstrates that shared narratives don't have to be accurate to be powerful.[4] Couples who report being happily married after 50 or more years seem to collude in a relational narrative that doesn't always jibe with the facts. They

narrative
The stories people create and use to make sense of their personal worlds.

Cultural Idiom

jibe
agree

yardsticks
standards of comparison

COMMUNICATION ON-SCREEN

Rashōmon (1950)

Directed by Akira Kurosawa.

Foreign film buffs can talk giddily about *Rashōmon* for hours. A truly trail-blazing film, *Rashōmon* arrived on Western shores from Japan a mere five years after World War II and proceeded to not only launch the then-unknown director Akira Kurosawa as a titan of global cinema (he would go on to make the classics *The Seven Samurai, Ikiru, Throne of Blood,* and *Yojimbo*) but also rewrite the book on cinematography, prompt the creation of the Best Foreign Film category at the Academy Awards, and almost single-handedly familiarize the Western public with Japan's samurai era.

Of course, lost in its historical success is *Rashōmon's* abiding status as the quintessential film about the nature of contradictory narratives. The story unfolds in flashback as the four main characters—a bandit, a samurai, the samurai's wife, and a nameless woodcutter—recount how on one afternoon in a wooded grove a series of events unfolded that resulted in the woman's rape and the apparent murder of her husband. Each account of those events, though entirely plausible, is completely incompatible with the others. The audience is left questioning not only who is telling the truth but also the very nature of truth itself.

self-serving bias
The tendency to interpret and explain information in a way that casts the perceiver in the most favourable light.

might agree that they rarely have conflict even though objective analysis reveals that they do have their share of disagreements and challenges. Without overtly agreeing to do so, they choose to blame outside forces or unusual circumstances for problems instead of attributing responsibility to one another. They offer the most charitable interpretations of one another's behaviour, each believing that his or her spouse acts with good intentions when things don't go well. They seem willing to forgive, or even forget, transgressions. Examining this research, one scholar wonders:

> Should we conclude that happy couples have a poor grip on reality? Perhaps they do, but is the reality of one's marriage better known by outside onlookers than by the players themselves? The conclusion is evident. One key to a long happy marriage is to tell yourself and others that you have one and then to behave as though you do![5]

Common Perceptual Tendencies

Shared narratives may be desirable, but they can be hard to achieve. Some of the greatest obstacles to understanding and agreement arise from errors in what psychologists call *attribution*—the process of attaching meaning to behaviour. We attribute meaning to both our own actions and the actions of others, but we often use different yardsticks. Research has uncovered several perceptual errors that can lead to inaccurate attributions—and to troublesome communication.[6] By becoming aware of these errors, we can guard against them and avoid unnecessary conflicts.

We Often Judge Ourselves More Charitably than We Judge Others

In an attempt to convince ourselves and others that the positive face we show to the world is true, we tend to judge ourselves in the most generous terms possible. Social scientists have labelled this tendency the **self-serving bias**.[7] When others suffer, we often blame the problem on their personal qualities. On the other hand, when we suffer, we find explanations outside ourselves. This 'cognitive conceit' occurs when we overestimate the accuracy of our beliefs and judgments, and reconstruct the memory of our past in self-serving ways. The more favourably we perceive some dimension of ourselves—our intelligence or our athletic ability, for example—the more we will tend to use that dimension as a basis for judging others.[8] Consider a few examples:

- When others botch a job, we might think they weren't listening well or trying hard enough; when we botch a job, it's because the directions weren't clear or we weren't given enough time.

- When someone lashes out angrily, we say he or she is being moody or too sensitive; when we lash out, it's because we're under a lot of stress at the moment.
- When she gets caught speeding, we say she should have been more careful; when we get caught, we deny or downplay the speeding infraction, or rhyme off a list of factors we think should have mitigated the offence under the circumstances.

Cultural Idiom

lashes out
attacks with words

rhyme off
recite a series of items rapidly and spontaneously

The egocentric tendency to rate ourselves more favourably than others would has been demonstrated experimentally.[9] In one study, members of a random sample of men were asked to rank themselves on their ability to get along with others.[10] Defying mathematical laws, all subjects—every last one—put themselves in the top half of the population. Sixty per cent of the subjects rated themselves in the top 10 per cent of the population, and an amazing 25 per cent believed they were in the top 1 per cent. In the same study, 70 per cent of the men ranked their leadership skills in the top 25 per cent of the population, whereas only 2 per cent thought they were below average. Sixty per cent said they were in the top 25 per cent in athletic abilities, whereas only 6 per cent viewed themselves as below average. How could this be? In another study, researchers discovered that people tend to process and recall information about themselves more efficiently than they do information about others. As a result, they perceive themselves more favourably.[11]

These data suggest we often give ourselves more credit than we deserve. A famous example of this self-serving bias surrounds Frederick Banting and John Macleod, who shared the 1923 Nobel Prize for their role in the discovery of insulin. Each man thought the discovery was primarily his own. Banting claimed that Macleod—who headed the lab, provided one of his research assistants (Charles Best), and actively supported the research—was more of a hindrance than a help. And Macleod did not mention Banting's name, let alone his contribution to the research, when speaking in public about the discovery.

Evidence such as this suggests how uncharitable attitudes toward others can affect communication. Your harsh opinions of others can lead to judgmental messages, and self-serving defences of your own actions can result in a defensive response when others question your behaviour.[12]

Egotist, n.
A person of low taste, more interested in himself than in me.

Ambrose Bierce,
The Devil's Dictionary

We Are Influenced by What Is Most Obvious

Every time we encounter another person, we are bombarded with more information than we can possibly take in. You can appreciate this by spending two or three minutes just reporting on what you can observe about another person through your five senses. ('Now I see you blinking your eyes . . . Now I notice you smiling . . . Now I hear you laugh and then sigh . . . Now I notice you're wearing a red shirt . . .') You will find that the list seems almost endless and that every time you seem to be nearing the end, a new observation presents itself.

Faced with this tidal wave of sense data, we need to whittle down the amount of information we will use to make sense of others. There are three factors that cause us to notice some messages and ignore others: we pay attention to stimuli that are *intense* (loud music, people dressed in bright clothing), *repetitious* (dripping faucets, persistent people), or *contrastive* (a normally happy person who acts grumpy or vice versa). *Motives* help determine what information we select from our environment. If you're anxious about being late for a date, you'll notice whatever clocks may be around you; if you're hungry, you'll become aware of any restaurants, markets, and billboards advertising food in your path. Motives also determine how we perceive people. For example, during the 2008 Canadian federal election, the

Conservative Party focused on Liberal leader Stéphane Dion's lack of English fluency and linked it to the idea that Dion was not competent to govern. A few days before the election, Dion had to do several takes during an English interview. Senator Mike Duffy, then the host of *Mike Duffy Live*, replayed Dion's stumbling outtakes announcing that the show would discuss 'Stephane Dion's struggle with the English language [which] is going to be one you will be talking about for days.' The outtakes were replayed many times by national newscasts. The Conservatives' branding of Dion stuck—he was perceived as not only a poor communicator but also a poor leader. Despite his many accomplishments as a former leader of the Liberal Party and cabinet minister, a leader in the passing of the Kyoto Accord, and a university professor, Dion is still remembered by many for his awkwardness as an English-language communicator.

If intense, repetitious, or contrastive information were the most important thing to know about others, there would be no problem. But the most noticeable behaviour of others isn't always the most important. For example,

- When two children (or adults, for that matter) fight, it might be a mistake to blame the one who lashes out first. Perhaps the other one was at least equally responsible, by teasing or refusing to co-operate.
- You might complain about an acquaintance whose malicious gossiping or arguing has become annoying, forgetting that, by previously tolerating that kind of behaviour, you have been at least partly responsible.
- You might blame an unhappy working situation on your manager, overlooking factors beyond her control, such as a change in the economy, policies imposed by upper management, or the demands of customers or other workers.
- When you are working with someone who is obviously of a different ethnic or religious background from your own, you may pay more attention to superficial things, such as his or her physical appearance or manner of dress, than you do to his or her work or contribution to your common project.

We Cling to First Impressions, Even If Wrong

Labelling people according to our first impressions is an inevitable part of the perception process. These labels are a way of making interpretations. 'She seems cheerful.' 'He seems sincere.' 'They sound awfully conceited.'

If they're accurate, impressions like these can be useful ways of deciding how best to respond to people in the future. Problems arise, however, when the labels we attach are inaccurate, because after we form an opinion of someone, we tend to hang on to it and make any conflicting information fit our image.

Suppose, for instance, you mention the name of your new neighbour to a friend. 'Oh, I know him,' your friend replies. 'He seems nice at first, but it's all an act.' Perhaps this appraisal is off-base. The neighbour may have changed since your friend knew him, or perhaps your friend's judgment is simply unfair. Whether the judgment is accurate or not, once you have accepted your friend's evaluation, it will probably influence the way you respond to the neighbour. You'll look for examples of the insincerity you've heard about—and you'll probably find them. Even if the neighbour were a saint, you would be likely to interpret his behaviour in ways that fit your expectations. 'Sure he seems nice,' you might think, 'but it's probably just a front.' Of course, this sort of suspicion can become a self-fulfilling prophecy, transforming a genuinely nice person into someone who truly becomes an undesirable neighbour as he reacts to your suspicious behaviour.

Given the almost unavoidable tendency to form first impressions, the best advice we can offer is to keep an open mind and be willing to change your opinion as events prove that the first impressions were mistaken.

We Tend to Assume That Others Are Similar to Us

People commonly imagine that others have the same attitudes and motives that they do. For example, research shows that people with low self-esteem imagine that others view them un-favourably, whereas people who like themselves imagine that others like them, too.[13] Another study points to our tendency to arrive at a 'false consensus' by believing that certain of our opinions and behaviours—in particular those that are undesirable—are much more common than they are.[14] The frequently mistaken assumption that others' views are similar to our own applies in a wide range of situations. For example,

- You've heard an off-colour joke that you found funny. You might assume that it won't offend a somewhat conservative friend. It does.
- You've been bothered by an instructor's tendency to stray off topic during lectures. If you were a professor, you'd want to know if anything you were doing was creating problems for your students, so you decide that your instructor will probably be grateful for some constructive criticism. Unfortunately, you're wrong.
- You lost your temper with a friend a week ago and said some things you regret. In fact, if someone said those things to you, you would consider the relationship finished. Imagining that your friend feels the same way, you avoid making contact. However, your friend actually feels that he was partly responsible and has avoided you because he thinks you're the one who wants to end things.

Examples like these show that others don't always think or feel the way we do, and assuming that similarities exist can lead to problems. For instance, one study revealed that men consider women who initiate first dates to be more interested in sex than do the women themselves.[15]

How can you find out the other person's real position? Sometimes by asking directly, sometimes by checking with others, and sometimes by making an educated guess after you've thought the matter out. All these alternatives are better than simply assuming that everyone feels the same way you do.

Cultural Idiom
a front
a pretense

I have heard students say things like, 'It was John's fault, his speech was so confusing nobody could have understood it.' Then, two minutes later, the same student remarked, 'It wasn't my fault, what I said could not have been clearer. John must be stupid.' Poor John! He was blamed when he was the sender and when he was the receiver. John's problem was that he was the other person, and that's who is always at fault.

Stephen W. King

Understanding Diversity

PM'S IRON-WILLED DECISION TO EXPOSE JAFFER–GUERGIS SCANDAL INTENDED TO PROTECT HIS CONSERVATIVE BASE

RAHIM

A top Conservative commentator says Prime Minister Stephen Harper's iron-willed decision to 'cut the cancer out' by exposing Rahim Jaffer's undeclared lobbying over the past year and throwing Helena Guergis overboard is intended to end the brewing scandal before it spreads.

But political observers and opposition MPs believe Prime Minister Harper (Calgary Southwest, AB) is also trying to ensure the unusually lurid details of the furor involving the husband and wife team does not erode crucial financial and electoral backing for the federal Conservative Party from perhaps its single most important base—the conservative Christian right.

And, even though Conservatives believe Mr Harper's decision to draw attention of the media, MPs, and the federal lobbying commissioner with a trail of e-mails showing Mr Jaffer's lobbying efforts after his 2008 election defeat will put the government in a transparent light, the e-mails themselves suggest the strategy could backfire and lead to new questions about backroom government pressure on public servants.

'There's no question these documents will come back to haunt the conservatives,' said NDP MP Pat Martin (Winnipeg Centre, MB).

A bundle of e-mails and letters the government distributed to selected journalists after sending it off to Lobbying Commissioner Karen Shepherd last week included more than 40 e-mails involving odd schemes Mr Jaffer and his Green Power partner Patrick Glémaud were promoting through Conservative MP Brian Jean (Fort McMurray–Athabasca, AB), a friend of Mr Jaffer's who had been designated as the government gatekeeper for the $1-billion Green Infrastructure Fund, and Sébastien Togneri, then director of parliamentary affairs, to Public Works Minister Christian Paradis (Mégantic–L'Érable, QC).

One of the e-mail chains involved a biofuel proposal that would process trees destroyed by the pine beetles. Sites for the proposed plants included locations in British Columbia and Calgary, but also Guelph, ON, Waterloo, ON, and Simcoe County, inside Ms Guergis's riding. 'Not really Pine Beetle territory,' a public servant or aide to Mr Jean noted in the margin. 'How do I advise Mr Glémaud?'

But a series of other e-mails could be even more hazardous to Mr Harper and his government. They centre on a proposal Mr Jaffer and Mr Glémaud were pushing at Public Works and Government Services Canada that would have installed solar panels on the roofs of federal office buildings in Ontario. Edward Morofsky, a buildings control specialist in the department, rejected the scheme in an internal response.

'I'll skip over the competitive issue as I'm sure it will be treated by others,' he wrote before pointing out glaring technical problems, including the fact that new roofs would be required 'or we will be left with a seriously compromised roof service' and the proposal implied the department would have to repair and maintain the units. 'This is just another reason for competitive bidding . . .' Mr Morosky wrote.

As the department sat on the request, Mr Togneri e-mailed an adviser to the deputy minister saying: 'The sector has had this for weeks, what's the holdup?' Mr Togneri then instructed the bureaucrat to 'set the meetings' to discuss the proposal from Mr Jaffer and Mr Glémaud on 30 September 2009 and 'please invite me.'

Opposition MPs point out that the offices of at least eight cabinet ministers should have been aware of the lobbying, particularly since many of the e-mails were exchanged around the time last September when the Ontario Provincial Police created a flurry of media attention by disclosing Mr Jaffer had been charged with cocaine possession and drunk driving. The opposition says cabinet ministers involved, including Transport Minister John Baird (Ottawa West–Nepean, ON), Environment Minister Jim Prentice (Calgary Centre North, AB), and Mr Paradis, now the minister of Natural Resources, should have intervened or reported Mr Jaffer to Ms Shepherd.

Despite questions that arise over the time it took for Mr Harper to discover the lobbying, likely a contravention of his own Public Accountability Act because Mr Jaffer and Mr Glémaud did not register as lobbyists or report their meetings, Conservative Party commentator Tim Powers said the government's decision to release details as the Commons Government Operations Committee probes the affair was designed to cut short the controversy.

'I think the reason is if you have material to share, share it all at once so you're not subject to an ongoing saga of drippings and droppings that comes when you don't put all the information out at once,' Mr Powers told *The Hill Times*. 'The best way to deal with that problem is to do what he [Mr Harper] has done, you put the cancer out, which is what he's done, in terms of remedies, in terms of people not currently in the caucus, and give them all the information they want.'

Mr Powers rejected the view that Mr Harper's attempt to nip the scandal in the bud by disclosing the information, combined with his abrupt expulsion of Ms Guergis from Cabinet and the Conservative caucus two weeks ago, along with what seemed a precipitous decision to call in the Mounties, was also intended to buff up the government's image for its core base.

There is little question seamy allegations that are part of the affair—cocaine use, partying with escorts and 'busty hookers', links to organized crime and the Hell's Angels—would not be attractive to tens of thousands of supporters represented by organizations such as Focus on the Family and the Canadian Family Action Coalition, both of which have close links to the Conservative Party and its members.

'I think the Prime Minister has reasonably well-inoculated himself from any wounding from the base, because of his swift action as it relates to Guergis,' said Mr Powers. 'He won't lose sleep at night by being criticized, as some are now doing to him, for acting precipitously.'

Others, however, say a perfect storm of government actions that have taken place over the past few weeks, including a sudden announcement Canada would not fund abortions through its support for an international maternal health program Mr Harper is proposing, attacks against the Liberals over the federal gun registry, and the figurative lynching of Mr Jaffer and Ms Guergis indicate that is exactly what the government is doing.

Considering Mr Harper has also indicated he is ready to fight a snap election over secret government documents about possible prisoner torture in Afghanistan, it makes sense the Prime Minister may be trying to batten down hatches on the right wing, critics say.

'It would make eminently good sense that they're trying to change the channel on this as quickly as possible,' said Mr Martin. 'The image, the optics, offend their traditional base and they need that base desperately if we're inching, if we're on the precipice of an election.'

A political scientist and University of Ottawa law professor agrees Mr Harper is attempting to keep secure the party's substantial base among Christian conservatives, and his forceful measures in the controversy sparked by Mr Jaffer and Ms Guergis are part of the effort.

'For financing, it's huge,' Professor Errol Mendes told *The Hill Times*. 'It's constant, it's not just this, it's the gun registry. They can't hold on to power if they lose their fundraising base or the support. It accounts for 30 per cent of their support.'

The executive director of one of the largest Christian organizations that pins its political goals with the Conservatives admitted the Jaffer/Guergis affair may be damaging the party's image.

'That's the one thing that I've probably heard more than anything,' said Brian Rushfeldt, executive director of the Canadian Family Action Coalition.

'Even in private discussions, certainly I know it's always coming up,' he told *The Hill Times*. 'I hear it whenever I'm out and around in various circles I hear it coming up and then talking about it, but as far as knowing whether from a partisan standpoint it's made any impact I wouldn't even venture a guess.'

—*Tim Naumetz, The Hill Times, 3 May 2010, hilltimes.com/page/printpage/scandal-05-03-2010.*

Questions: This article focuses on reputation. It takes the behaviour of a small number of MPs and extends it to entire political parties. In your opinion, is this article's discussion of the reputation of the Conservative Party credible? Why or why not? How are Prime Minister Harper's actions explained by the perceptual tendencies described in this chapter?

We Tend to Favour Negative Impressions Over Positive Ones

What do you think about Hector? He's handsome, hardworking, intelligent, and honest. He's also very conceited.

Did the last quality mentioned make a difference in your evaluation? If it did, you're not alone. Research shows that when people are aware of both the positive and the negative traits of another person, they tend to be more influenced by the negative. In one study, for example, researchers found that job interviewers were likely to reject candidates who revealed negative information even when the total amount of information was highly positive.[16]

Sometimes this attitude makes sense. If the negative quality clearly outweighs any positive ones, you'd be foolish to ignore it. A surgeon with shaky hands and a teacher who hates children, for example, would be unsuitable for their jobs whatever their other virtues. But much of the time it's a bad idea to pay excessive attention to negative qualities and overlook positive ones. This is the mistake some people make when screening potential friends or dates. They find some who are too outgoing or too reserved, others who aren't intelligent enough, and still others who have the wrong sense of humour. Of course, it's important to find people you truly enjoy spending time with, but expecting perfection can lead to unnecessary loneliness.

Don't misunderstand: we don't always commit the kind of perceptual errors described in this section. Sometimes, for instance, people are responsible for their misfortunes, and sometimes our problems are not our fault. Likewise, the most obvious interpretation of a situation may be the correct one. Nonetheless, a large amount of research has proven again and again that our perceptions of others are often distorted in the ways listed here. The moral, then, is clear: don't assume that your first judgment of a person is accurate.

Situational Factors Influencing Perception

Along with the attribution errors described in the preceding pages, we consider a whole range of additional factors when trying to make sense of others' behaviour.

CRITICAL THINKING PROBE

PERCEIVING OTHERS AND YOURSELF

1. You can gain appreciation for the way perceptual errors operate by proposing two different explanations for each of the situations that follow. First, explain the behaviour as you would if you were the person involved. Second, explain it as you would if the person involved were someone you dislike.
   - dozing off in class
   - getting angry at a customer on the job
   - dressing sloppily in public
   - being insensitive to a friend's distress
   - laughing at an inappropriate or offensive joke
2. If your explanations for these behaviours differ, ask yourself why. Are the differing attributions justifiable, or do they support the tendency to make the perceptual errors listed on pages 40–43, 46?
3. How do these perceptual errors operate in making judgments about others' behaviour, especially when those others come from different social groups?

Relational Satisfaction

The behaviour that seems positive when you are in a satisfying relationship might seem completely different when the relationship isn't going well. For example, you might regard the quirks of a housemate with amusement when things are going smoothly but find them very annoying when you are unhappy with his or her other behaviours. In this sense, our willingness to tolerate the potentially bothersome behaviour of people we like is rather like the amusement we feel when the beloved family pet takes food while nobody is looking.

Degree of Involvement with the Other Person

We sometimes view people with whom we have (or seek to have) a close relationship more favourably than those whom we observe from a detached perspective.[17] One study revealed how this principle operates in everyday life. A group of male subjects was asked to critique presentations by women who allegedly owned restaurants. Half of these presentations were designed to be competent and half were incompetent. The men who were told they would be having a casual date with the female speakers judged their presentations—whether competent or not—more highly than did those who didn't expect any involvement with the speakers.[18]

Past Experience

What meaning do similar events hold? If, for example, you've been gouged by landlords in the past, you might be skeptical about an apartment manager's assurances that your careful housekeeping and diligence about repairs will guarantee the refund of your security deposit.

> **Cultural Idiom**
> **been gouged by**
> been charged an excessive amount

Expectations

Anticipation shapes interpretations. If you imagine that your boss is unhappy with your work, you'll probably feel threatened by a request to 'see me in my office first thing Monday morning.' On the other hand, if you imagine that your work will be rewarded, your weekend will probably be pleasant. As Natalia Villegas, a communications consultant based in Oakville, Ontario, describes in a recently published case study, effective internal communications can lead to more harmony in an organization by helping to manage expectations around authenticity, cultural diversity, and employee needs.[19]

Social Roles

Social relationships can influence the way we perceive others. For example, a study of communication in the workplace revealed that observers—both men and women—interpret facial expressions differently depending on their status relative to the other person.[20] Subjects were shown photos of people and asked to judge how each person was feeling. When the person pictured was described as a manager, subjects tended to see less fear than when they were told that the person pictured was an employee. Gender also makes a difference in how we perceive others: presented with two photos, one of a woman and one of a man, both showing anger of the same intensity, subjects saw more anger and less fear in a man's expression than in a woman's, probably because gender stereotypes of emotion guided their interpretations.

Knowledge

If you know that a friend has just been jilted by a lover or been fired from a job, you'll interpret his aloof behaviour differently than you would if you were unaware of what had happened.

If you work in an environment where socializing is common and colleagues have friendly relationships, you may be less likely to perceive a fellow worker's remark as sexual harassment than you would if you were in an unfamiliar environment.[21]

Self-Concept

When you're feeling insecure, the world is a very different place from the world you experience when you're full of confidence. For example, self-concept has proven to be the single greatest factor in determining whether people who are on the receiving end of teasing interpret the teaser's motives as being friendly or hostile and whether they respond with comfort or defensiveness.[22] And a McGill University study found that people with low self-esteem experienced significantly more difficulty processing rejection words than acceptance words, whereas people with high self-esteem showed no such difference.[23] These results are consistent with those of another Canadian study, which demonstrated that self-esteem is affected by and influences our interpersonal relationships so completely that we are often completely unaware of it.[24] Clearly, the way we feel about ourselves strongly influences how we interpret others' behaviour.

When I meet someone from another culture, I behave in the way that is natural to me, while the other behaves in the way that is natural to him or her. The only problem is that our 'natural' ways do not coincide.

Raymonde Carroll

Perception and Culture

Perceptual differences make communication challenging enough between members of the same culture. But when communicators come from different cultures, the potential for misunderstanding is even greater. Culture serves as a perceptual filter that influences the way we interpret even the simplest events. A study carried out at Northwestern University and the University of Calgary, for example, found that adults of Chinese cultural background were just as likely to categorize concepts on the basis of relationship as they were on the basis of similarity; that is, given pictures of three items—a car, a bus, and a tire—they were as likely to group 'car' with 'tire' (a relational grouping) as they were 'car' with 'bus' (similarity). By contrast, English-Canadian and American adults were more likely to categorize concepts based on similarity.[25]

The same principle causes people from different cultures to interpret similar events in different ways. Blinking while another person talks may be hardly noticeable to English Canadians, but the same behaviour is considered impolite in Taiwan. A 'V' sign made with two fingers means 'victory' in most of the Western world—as long as the palm is facing out. But in some European countries the same sign with the back of the hand facing out means roughly 'shove it'. The beckoning 'come-hither' finger motion that is familiar to North Americans is an insulting gesture in most Middle and Far Eastern countries.

Even beliefs about the very value of talk differ from one culture to another.[26] English-Canadian culture views talk as desirable and uses it to achieve social purposes as well as to perform tasks. Silence in conversational situations has a negative value in English- or French-Canadian culture. It is likely to be seen as evidence of a lack of interest, an unwillingness to communicate, hostility, anxiety, shyness, or interpersonal incompatibility. English and French Canadians are uncomfortable with silence, which they find embarrassing and awkward. Furthermore, the kind of talk that English Canadians admire is characterized by straightforwardness and honesty. Being indirect or vague—'beating around the bush', it might be labelled—has a negative connotation. French Canadians, on the other hand, have a significantly higher tolerance for allusion, metaphor, and indirect speech. That's why English Canadians can find French Canadians a little 'flowery' in the way that they sometimes speak about relationships, using what seem to be over-the-top expressions of affection when they greet one another: 'What a pleasure to find myself in the company of an old and cherished friend!' This greeting would seem a little awkward to a typical English Canadian, unless the two people truly had been best friends and hadn't seen each other for a long time.

On the other hand, most Asian cultures discourage the expression of thoughts and feelings. Silence is valued, as Taoist sayings indicate: 'In much talk there is great weariness' or 'One who speaks does not know; one who knows does not speak.' Unlike westerners, who are uncomfortable with silence, Japanese and Chinese people believe that remaining quiet is appropriate when there is nothing to be said. To easterners, a talkative person is a show-off or is insincere. And when an Asian person does speak up on social matters, he or she is likely to phrase the message indirectly to 'save face' for the recipient.

It is easy to see how these different views of speech and silence can lead to communication problems when people from different cultures meet. Both the talkative westerner and the silent easterner are behaving in ways they believe are proper, yet each views the other with disapproval and mistrust. Only when they recognize the different standards of behaviour can they adapt to one another, or at least understand and respect their differences.

Perceptual differences are just as important right at home when members of different co-cultures interact. Failure to recognize co-cultural differences can lead to unfortunate and unnecessary misunderstandings. For example, a Canadian man on a date with an Indonesian woman may interpret her silence as shyness and keep talking in an effort to put her at ease, when in fact she is behaving politely by allowing him to speak, even though she thinks he's rude for dominating the conversation.

Eye contact differs significantly between people from different cultural backgrounds. Whereas the European tradition is to look away from a partner while speaking and make eye contact when listening, the African tradition is just the reverse: looking at a partner more when talking and less when listening.[27] A speaker from Ireland, therefore, might interpret a Kenyan listener's lack of eye contact as a sign of inattention or rudeness, when exactly the opposite is true.

Our perceptions of people from different cultures can lead to preferring one group over another. A cross-cultural communication study by social psychologist Wallace Lambert showed that English-Canadian women preferred English-Canadian to French-Canadian men, rating them as taller, kinder, more dependable, and more entertaining. The French-Canadian men were perceived as lacking integrity and being less socially attractive. English-Canadian men held less negative views about French-Canadian men. In the same study, French-Canadian women showed a preference for French-Canadian men and expressed admiration for English-Canadian women's assertive qualities.[28]

Along with ethnicity and nationality, geography also can influence perception. A fascinating series of studies revealed that climate and geographic latitude were remarkably accurate predictors of communication predispositions.[29] People living in southern latitudes of the United States were found to be more socially isolated, less tolerant of ambiguity, higher

> **Cultural Idiom**
>
> **save face**
> protect one's dignity

●●●●●

COMMUNICATION ON-SCREEN

Bon Cop, Bad Cop (2006)
Directed by Erik Canuel.

An unlikely pairing is created as a French-Canadian police officer from the *Sûreté de Québec*, David Bouchard (Patrick Huard), joins forces with an anglophone member of the Ontario Provincial Police, Martin Ward (Colm Feore), to investigate a crime committed on the provincial border. The two must find a way to resolve their different approaches to police work and communication if they are to have any success in solving the case.

empathy
The ability to project oneself into another person's point of view, so as to experience the other's thoughts and feelings.

sympathy
Compassion for another's situation.

We have a marvellous gift, and you see it develop in children, this ability to become aware that other people have minds just like your own and feelings that are just as important as your own, and this gift of empathy seems to me to be the building block of our moral system.

Ian McEwan

in self-esteem, more likely to touch others, and more likely to verbalize their thoughts and feelings. This sort of finding helps explain why communicators who travel from one part of a country to another find that their old patterns of communicating don't work as well in their new location. A southerner whose relatively talkative, high-touch style seemed completely normal at home might be viewed as pushy and aggressive to a northerner.

Empathy and Perception

By now it is clear that differing perceptions present a major challenge to communicators. One solution is to increase the ability to empathize. **Empathy** is the ability to re-create another person's perspective, to experience the world from the other's point of view.

Dimensions of Empathy

As we'll use the term here, *empathy* has three dimensions.[30] On one level, empathy involves *perspective-taking*—the ability to take on the viewpoint of another person. This understanding requires a suspension of judgment, so that for the moment you set aside your own opinions and take on those of the other person. Besides cognitive understanding, empathy has a second, emotional dimension that allows us to experience the feelings that others have. We know their fear, joy, sadness, and so on. When we combine the perspective-taking and emotional dimensions, we see that empathizing allows us to experience the other's perception—in effect, to become that person temporarily. A third dimension of empathy is genuine concern for the welfare of the other person. When we empathize we go beyond just thinking and feeling as others do; we genuinely care about their well-being.

It is easy to confuse empathy with **sympathy**, but the concepts are different in two important ways. First, sympathy means you feel compassion *for* another person's predicament, whereas empathy means you have a personal sense of what that predicament is like. Consider the difference between sympathizing with an unwed mother or a homeless person and empathizing with them—imagining what it would be like to be in their position. Despite your concern, sympathy lacks the degree of identification that empathy entails. When you sympathize, it is the other's confusion, joy, or pain; when you empathize, the experience becomes your own, at least for the moment. Both perspectives are important ones, but empathy is clearly the more complete of the two.

Empathy is different from sympathy in a second way. We sympathize only when we accept the reasons for another's pain as valid, whereas it is possible to empathize without feeling sympathy. You can empathize with a difficult relative, a rude stranger, or even a criminal without feeling much sympathy for the person. Empathizing allows you to understand another person's motives without requiring you to agree with them. After empathizing, you will almost certainly understand a person better, but sympathy won't always follow.

The ability to empathize seems to exist in a rudimentary form in even the youngest children.[31] Virtually from birth, infants become visibly upset when they hear another infant crying, and children who are just a few months old cry when they observe another child crying.

Young children have trouble distinguishing others' distress from their own. If, for example, one child hurts his finger, another child might put her own finger in her mouth as if she were feeling pain. Researchers report cases in which children who see their parents crying wipe their own eyes, even though they are not crying.

While infants and toddlers may have a basic capacity to empathize, studies with twins suggest that the degree to which we are born with the ability to sense how others are feeling varies according to genetic factors. But although some people may be born with a greater potential for empathy, environmental experiences are the key to developing this skill. Specifically, the way in which parents communicate with their children seems to affect children's ability to understand others' emotional states. When parents point out to their children the distress that others feel from their misbehaviour ('Look how sad Samika is because you took her toy. Wouldn't you be sad if someone took away your toys?'), they gain a greater appreciation that their acts have emotional consequences than they do when parents simply label behaviour as inappropriate ('That was a mean thing to do!').

Total empathy is impossible to achieve. Completely understanding another person's point of view is simply too difficult a task for humans with different backgrounds and limited communication skills. Nonetheless, it is possible to get a strong sense of what the world looks like through another person's eyes.

"Hey, YOU have got great empathy!"

The value of empathy is demonstrated by the results of a simple experiment in which university students were asked to list their impressions of people either shown in a videotaped discussion or described in a short story.[32] Half of the students were instructed to empathize with the person shown as much as possible, and the other half were not given any instructions about empathizing. The results were impressive: the students who did not practise empathy were prone to explain the person's behaviour in terms of personality characteristics. For example, they might have explained a cruel statement by saying that the speaker was mean, or they might have attributed a divorce to the partners' lack of understanding. The empathetic students, on the other hand, were more aware of possible elements in the situation that might have contributed to the reaction. For instance, they might have explained a person's unkind behaviour in terms of job pressures or personal difficulties. In other words, practising empathy seems to make people more tolerant.

An ability to empathize can make a difference in everyday disputes. For instance, in a study conducted at the Catholic University of the Sacred Heart in Milan, researchers found that empathy and forgiveness were reliable predictors of a marriage's strength: partners in stronger marriages were more likely to give each the benefit of the doubt in disagreements and were more likely to forgive. It's worth noting that the correlation between empathy and forgiveness was stronger among husbands; among wives, the severity of the

Understanding Diversity

ABORIGINAL CARTOON MIXES SATIRE WITH POP CULTURE, SMALL-TOWN LAUGHS

It's being billed as Canada's first Aboriginal cartoon series.

But with its blend of pop-culture references, quirky small-town humour and the odd political jab, *By the Rapids* should speak to anyone—Aboriginal or not—who has struggled to find a place in the world, says Joseph Lazare, the show's creator, writer, and director.

The cartoon, which debuts Thursday on APTN, has been a five-year undertaking for the 24-year-old filmmaker, who drew inspiration from his own background in crafting a satirical look at an urban teenager who's forced to live in his parents' small Aboriginal hometown.

'I wanted to have a show that was special to our community but wasn't neglecting people from the outside,' says Lazare, who grew up in Kahnawake, a Mohawk reserve just outside Montreal, and moved to Toronto a few years ago.

'There's some stuff we do that I think is just an Aboriginal-people joke and (non-Aboriginals are) like, "That's funny! I don't know why, but I think it's really funny," and they can't stop laughing. So then they ask me a question: "Why is that funny? What does that mean?" And so I'm really excited about how we can do certain things on the show that'll get people asking questions and kind of doing their own research.'

The show revolves around pampered teen Cory Littlehorn, a gadget-crazed kid who has spent his whole life in the big city until his parents drop him off with relatives in the fictional Mohawk community of By the Rapids.

Cut off from his friends, the Internet, and city lifestyle, Cory must find a way to get along with his no-nonsense grandma Hazel, his macho uncle Regis, his older cousin Karen, and Karen's scatterbrained boyfriend Derek.

Cory soon realizes he knows next to nothing about Aboriginal culture, and slowly warms up to life on the rez as he's introduced to powwows, Indian tacos, the Mohawk language, and local slang. His rural relatives get schooled in urban oddities, too, such as when Cory impulsively picks up fresh dog poop from the sidewalk and looks for a trash bin to deposit it. In another episode, Cory is embarrassed by a flustered cashier when he tries to take advantage of Aboriginal tax exemptions at a local big-box store.

Lazare said he was eager to offer a show that incorporates a mix of realism, fantasy, and pop culture, and profile a light-hearted side to Aboriginal life that's little seen in mainstream media.

'A lot of Aboriginal media, if it is not hard-hitting, it's kind of soft, so what we like to do is be humorous but a little bit edgy in some ways,' he says.

More fantastical elements come from a storyline following Cory's parents. The stuffy pair head off on vacation to mend their marital troubles, but when their chartered plane crash-lands on a remote island they're thrown into a series of outlandish adventures. The duo must learn to rely on each other for survival as they fend off wild animals, freakish monsters, and a murderous colony of plane crash survivors reminiscent of the cast of the TV hit series *Lost*.

Lazare, who figured out his way around a camera by fiddling with his dad's video equipment as a teen, cut his teeth at a drop-in youth centre that offered film gear and a place to work out ideas. From there, his work made it to the Sundance Film Institute's gen-Y program in 2001, and three years later Lazare premiered an animated/live action short at the Sundance Film Festival.

blame they attributed to their husbands was a more reliable predictor of how likely they were to forgive (in other words, the milder their accusations, the more likely they were to forgive).[33]

You might argue here, 'Why should I be more tolerant? Maybe the other person's position or behaviour isn't justified.' Perhaps so, but research clearly shows that, as mentioned earlier, we are much more charitable when we find explanations for our own behaviour.[34] When explaining our own actions, we are often quick to suggest situational causes: 'I was

This led to a paid internship at Big Soul Productions, a Toronto-based Aboriginal production company, at age 18. It wasn't long before Lazare was pitching ideas for an Aboriginal cartoon, in between making photocopies and fetching coffee.

Lazare says getting the production company's support was easy, but it was another story courting television networks like APTN.

'The hardest part is convincing people how cool your idea is,' he says. 'And that's what comes with the territory of creating something that's cutting-edge and groundbreaking stuff. I think the first feeling from a lot of people was: "Well, what do you mean it's funny?" You know, and that's so foreign to people, because it's Aboriginal.'

Confidence is so high on the series, APTN has already ordered a second season to follow the initial six episodes.

Lazare says he hopes the show can be inspiring to viewers, both Aboriginal and non-Aboriginal, who have seen little diversity in how his community has been portrayed.

'It's very humorous and positive,' he says. 'So that's basically what I want people to get out of it—just have a good time, and see these wacky characters just being really funny people.'

—*Cassandra Szklarski, The Canadian Press, 12 November 2008.*

Questions: Why do you think it's important to increase the visibility of Aboriginal people in the mass media? Is having a cartoon show effective for promoting positive messages about Aboriginal culture? Why or why not?

tired', 'She started it.' In other words, we often excuse ourselves by saying, 'It wasn't my fault!' Perhaps becoming more empathetic can help even the score a bit, enabling us to treat others at least as kindly as we treat ourselves. The most important point to remember here is that all communication happens in a context. Just as in the examples given at the beginning of this chapter, words and pictures that seem appropriate in one context can be damning in another. While it is important to be generous in your judgment of others, it is also crucial to be aware of the context of your own communication lest you be judged yourself.

Perception-Checking

Having good intentions and making a strong effort to empathize are good ways to begin understanding others. Along with a positive attitude, however, there is a simple tool that can help you interpret the behaviour of others more accurately. To see how this tool operates, consider how often others jump to mistaken conclusions about your thoughts, feelings, and motives. We've all been addressed with questions or statements like these:

1. 'Why are you mad at me?' (Who said you were?)
2. 'What's the matter with you?' (Who said anything was the matter?)
3. 'Come on now. Tell the truth.' (Who said you were lying?)

As we'll see in Chapter 7, even if the interpretation is correct, dogmatic, mind-reading interrogations like the ones above are likely to generate defensiveness. The skill of **perception-checking** provides a better way to handle your interpretations. A complete perception check has three parts:

- a description of the behaviour you noticed;
- at least two possible interpretations of the behaviour; and
- a request for clarification about how to interpret the behaviour.

Perception checks for the preceding three examples would look like this:

1. 'When you stomped out of the room and slammed the door [*behaviour*], I wasn't sure whether you were mad at me [*first interpretation*] or just in a hurry [*second interpretation*]. How did you feel [*request for clarification*]?'
2. 'You haven't laughed much in the last couple of days [*behaviour*]. I wonder whether something's bothering you [*first interpretation*] or whether you're just feeling quiet [*second interpretation*]. What's up [*request for clarification*]?'
3. 'You said you really liked the job I did [*behaviour*], but there was something about your voice that made me think you might not like it [*first interpretation*]. Maybe it's just my imagination, though [*second interpretation*]. How do you really feel [*request for clarification*]?'

Perception-checking is a tool for helping us understand others accurately instead of assuming that our first interpretation is correct. Because its goal is mutual understanding, perception-checking is a co-operative approach to communication. Besides leading to more accurate perceptions, it cuts down on defensiveness by allowing the other person to save face. Instead of saying, in effect, 'I know what you're thinking,' a perception check takes a more respectful approach that states or implies, 'I know I'm not qualified to judge you without some help.'

Sometimes a perception check won't need all three parts to be effective:

'You haven't dropped by lately. Is anything the matter [single interpretation combined with request for clarification]?'

'I can't tell whether you're kidding me about being cheap or if you're serious [*behaviour combined with interpretations*]. Are you mad at me?'

'Are you sure you don't mind driving? I can use a ride if it's no trouble, but I don't want to take you out of your way [*no need to describe behaviour*].'

perception-checking
A three-part method for verifying the accuracy of interpretations, including a description of the sense data, two possible interpretations, and a request for confirmation of the interpretations.

Retrospectively, one can ask 'Who am I?' But in practice, the answer has come before the question.

J.M. Yinger

Of course, a perception check can succeed only if your non-verbal behaviour reflects the open-mindedness of your words. An accusing tone of voice or a hostile glare will contradict the sincerely worded request for clarification, suggesting that you have already made up your mind about the other person's intentions.

Perception-checking is helpful to see what others are really thinking or feeling, but a perception check can also be usefully directed inward to see if we're presenting the thoughts and feelings we mean to. Two University of Manitoba studies showed that many people have a faulty perception of emotional transparency. The first suggested that we tend to overestimate the degree to which others can perceive our emotional states.[35] The second[36] reinforces this idea, indicating that we are least likely to be aware of how others perceive us when we are most immersed in what we know about ourselves. In other words, the clearer our self-understanding, the more likely we are to assume that others understand us just as well, when in fact this may not be the case at all. This type of self-directed bias, where we assume that everyone sees in us what we know about ourselves, makes perception-checking a must for successful communication. You might know, for example, that you are a very joyful person but be so comfortable in your self-knowledge that you fail to be joyful with others. A quick perception check will tell you that others are not seeing your joyful self and that you should make it more manifest. We'll have more to say about self-perception in the next section.

Perceiving the Self

It should be clear by now that our perceptions of others are subjective and that it takes a real effort to bridge the gap between our ideas about others and the way they view themselves. But as we've just seen, the way we perceive ourselves—and the way we think others perceive us—plays a vital role in communication. In this section we will turn our examination inward, exploring how our self-perceptions affect our communication.

---

self-concept

The relatively stable set of perceptions each individual holds of him- or herself.

Self-Concept Defined

The **self-concept** is a set of relatively stable perceptions that each of us holds about ourselves. The self-concept includes our conception about what makes us unique and what makes us similar to and different from others. To put it differently, the self-concept is like a mental mirror that reflects how we view ourselves: not only our physical features but also our emotional states, talents, likes and dislikes, values, and roles.

We will have more to say about the nature of the self-concept shortly, but first you will find it valuable to gain a personal understanding of how this theoretical construct applies to you. You can do so by answering the following questions: Who are you? How do you define yourself? As a student? A man, a woman, or transgendered? By your age? Your religion? Your occupation?

There are many ways of identifying yourself. Take a few minutes and list as many ways as you

can to identify who you are. You'll need this list later in this chapter, so be sure to complete it now. Try to include all the characteristics that describe you:

- your moods or feelings;
- your appearance and physical condition;
- your social traits;
- your talents and limitations;
- your intellectual capacity;
- your strong beliefs; and
- your social roles.

A list of 20 or even 30 terms would be only a partial description. To make this written self-portrait complete, your list would have to be hundreds—even thousands—of words long.

Of course, not all items on such a list would be equally important. For example, the most significant part of one person's self-concept might have to do with social roles, whereas for another it might relate to physical appearance, health, friendships, accomplishments, or skills. And for some people, their self-concept might have much to do with negative qualities and skills that they lack, though many of us have difficulty identifying our less favourable traits. Two studies conducted at Concordia University showed that ego-involved people (that is, people who have high self-awareness) tended to recall a greater number of positive words about themselves, suggesting that we have a general positivity bias when we process information.[37]

Nationality or citizenship can be an important part of a person's self-concept. In Canada, most people outside Quebec identify themselves as Canadian, despite the country's emphasis on multiculturalism and the ethno-cultural mosaic. (Quebecers are more likely to identify themselves as Québécois than Canadian.) For many people, 'being Canadian' means not only tolerance and respect for difference but also having the right to opt out of any cultural identity, whether mainstream French or English or one's own defined ethnic or cultural heritage.

Another factor that can determine the self-concept is race. A study conducted by Monica Das of the University of Alberta examined how four individuals of mixed race in western Canada negotiated their identities. The participants shared their life stories with Das, who uncovered five key factors that played a role in the identity development of mixed-race people: family, childhood experiences, adult experiences, physical appearance, and racism.[38]

An important element of the self-concept is **self-esteem**: our evaluations of self-worth. One person's self-concept might include being religious, tall, or athletic. That person's self-esteem would be shaped by how he or she felt about these qualities: 'I'm glad that I am athletic' or 'I am embarrassed about being so tall', for example.

Self-esteem has a powerful effect on the way we communicate.[39] People with high self-esteem are more willing to communicate than people with low self-esteem. They are more likely to think highly of others and expect to be accepted by others. They aren't afraid of other people's reactions and perform well when others are watching them. They work harder for people who demand high standards of performance, and they are comfortable with those they view as superior in some way. When confronted with critical comments, they are comfortable defending themselves.

By contrast, people with low self-esteem are likely to be critical of others and expect rejection from them. They are also critical of their own performances. They are sensitive to possible disapproval of others and perform poorly when being watched. They work harder for undemanding, less critical people. They feel threatened by people they view as superior in some way and have difficulty defending themselves against others' negative comments.

self-esteem
The part of the self-concept that involves evaluations of self-worth.

Communication and Development of the Self

So far we've talked about what the self-concept is; but at this point you may be asking what it has to do with the study of human communication. We can begin to answer this question by looking at how you came to possess your own self-concept.

Our identity comes almost exclusively from communication with others. As psychologists Arthur Combs and Donald Snygg put it,

> The self is essentially a social product arising out of experience with people. . . . We learn the most significant and fundamental facts about ourselves from . . . 'reflected appraisals', inferences about ourselves made as a consequence of the ways we perceive others behaving toward us.[40]

The term **reflected appraisal**, coined by Harry Stack Sullivan,[41] is a good one because it captures, metaphorically, the idea that we develop an image of ourselves from the way we think others view us. This notion of the 'looking-glass self' was introduced in 1902 by Charles H. Cooley, who suggested that we put ourselves in the position of other people and then, in our mind's eye, view ourselves as we imagine they see us.[42]

As we learn to speak and understand language, verbal messages—both positive and negative—also contribute to the developing self-concept. These messages continue later in life, especially when they come from what social scientists term **significant others**—people whose opinions we especially value. Although this term has entered colloquial usage in the past two decades with the more narrow meaning of 'romantic partners', in the original academic sense significant others could be a teacher from long ago, a close friend or respected relative, or perhaps a barely known acquaintance you hold in high regard: all can leave an imprint on how you view yourself. To see the importance of significant others, ask yourself how you arrived at your opinion of yourself as a student, as a romantic partner, as an employee, and so on, and you will see that these self-evaluations were probably influenced by the way others regarded you. Jennifer Bartz and John Lydon, psychologists at McGill University, conducted two studies to examine the interaction between working self-concept and personal relationships. The studies looked at how the social interactions of participants varied depending on the nature of the relationship on which they had been 'primed', in other words, whether the relationship was secure, avoidant, anxious–ambivalent, avoidant–dismissive, and so on. Their findings showed that those primed with a secure relationship increased their sense of being together, whereas those primed with less secure relationships—say, anxious–ambivalent or avoidant–fearful—increased the sense of having to act as an individual within the relationship.[43]

As we grow older, the evaluations of others still influence beliefs about the self in some areas, such as physical attractiveness and popularity. A study out of Wilfrid Laurier and Simon Fraser universities suggests that our responses to social comparisons (for instance, when we are compared with someone more or less

reflected appraisal
The theory that a person's self-concept matches the way that person believes others regard him or her.

significant other
A person whose opinion is important enough to affect one's self-concept strongly.

Understanding Diversity

CULTURE AND NATIONAL IDENTITY

Shared Values

A few years ago, a *Globe and Mail* editorial sought to give voice to 'the Canadian idea', what 'we stand for as a nation':

> Most of us already know in our hearts. We are against the idea that people should be treated differently because of their skin colour, language, religion, or background. We are for the idea that all Canadians should be treated as full citizens. We are against the idea that any person is more purely Canadian than another, no matter how far back his or her Canadian ancestry goes. We are for the idea that everyone should have an equal chance to succeed on his or her merit. We are against ethnic nationalism, in which people of common ethnicity rule themselves—masters in their own house. We are for civic nationalism, in which people of different backgrounds come together under the umbrella of common citizenship to form a community of equals. Ours is a modern nationalism: liberal, decent, tolerant, and colour-blind. That is what Canada represents to the millions of people who come here from other countries. That is the idea of Canada. (*The Globe and Mail*, 4 November 1995, p. D6)

This brief discussion is useful because it spells out the values and behaviours that Canada's 'national newspaper' says makes us what we are as a nation. But it is important to note that there is no mention of cultural nationalism or the need for a pervasive and intrusive broadcasting policy to ensure adequate Canadian content on radio or television stations. Further, as Globerman . . . points out, 'acknowledging that Canadians may possess certain shared values and convictions [the Massey Commission concept of social identity] is not tantamount to specifying the nature of Canada's 'identity.'

So why does the federal government intervene in cultural activities and, in particular, establish elaborate Canadian content regulations in broadcasting? Is the policy attributable to a weak sense of national identity?

Weak National Identity: English Canada versus French Canada

Professor Edward Grabb . . . notes that Canadians

> are notorious for wondering about who and what we are, and inevitably seem to define our own identity by comparing ourselves with Americans. More than a few observers have suggested that, in fact, Canadian identity is very difficult to describe or explain, except as a negative. In other words, whatever Canadians are, the one certainty is that they are not Americans. . . .

> Grabb . . . notes that several analysts have suggested that 'our relatively weak national identity [as compared to that of Americans], especially among English Canadians, . . . is one reason why Canada is able to accommodate such diversity in its cultural composition.' He notes that Canada's foreign-born population (16 per cent of the total)

successful) are strongest when they come from someone with whom we share an extremely close relationship and whom we consider an important part of our identity, such as a parent or a spouse.[44] On the whole, however, the influence of significant others is less powerful as we age.[45] The looking glass of the self-concept becomes distorted, so that it shapes the input from others to make it conform with our existing beliefs. For example, if your self-concept includes the element 'poor student', you might respond to a high grade by thinking 'I was just lucky' or 'The professor must be an easy grader.'

You might argue that not every part of one's self-concept is shaped by others, insisting there are certain objective facts that are recognizable by self-observation. After all, nobody needs to tell you that you are taller than others, speak with an accent, can run quickly, and so on. These facts are obvious.

is more than twice that of the US and ranks as one of the highest in the world. . . .

One interpretation of this situation is that Ottawa has sought to make a virtue out of a notable weakness. Having little sense of who we are, it is easy to trumpet diversity as Canada's 'unique identity'. This diversity includes regional and linguistic diversity (but only to a limit of two official languages) and multiculturalism which is reinforced by a host of federal government policies. The result is a 'mosaic', rather than a 'melting pot'. In summary, it is argued that Canada's identity is its diversity or multiplicity of different identities. But we know that individuals do not thrive on multiple identities or internal diversity. Those who have this characteristic may be diagnosed as schizophrenics. Can a nation thrive with multiple identities?

In contrast to most English Canadians, 'French Canadians are believed to have a very clear understanding of who they are as a people and, in this way, are much more like Americans in their nationalism and patriotic fervour' for Quebec, not Canada . . . . As a result, support for Canadian content in Quebec, i.e., French-language programming, has always been strong.

When television began in Canada in 1952, Montreal quickly became the world's second-largest centre of French-language TV production. Ever since, Quebec television and radio have been dominated by indigenous production. For example, TVA, the province's largest TV broadcaster, includes only one US drama series in its weekday prime-time schedule. To the envy of producers in English Canada, the unprompted allegiance of Quebecers to home-grown shows has been enough to make TV production a largely profitable business within the province. . . .

The data indicate that francophones watch much more Canadian content than do anglophones (about 69 per cent versus 32 . . .). The difference is very likely due to language. In Quebec, the use of French is like a small island in a large sea of English spoken elsewhere in North America. In Quebec, Canadian content is largely locally produced French-language programming. Recently, however, some Quebecers have become concerned that US cultural products (notably TV programs) have become more popular and that Quebec's culture is being threatened. . . .

While the federal government uses a host of policies to differentiate Canada from the United States, Quebec employs at least as many policies differentiating itself from the rest of Canada. The motto must be *Vive la différence!* Indeed, much of the political (and cultural) elite in Quebec is determined to create a new nation-state so as to [be] better able to express their concept of a unique identity. . . . Canada's tolerance for diversity goes so far as to subsidize the federal party which is openly and energetically devoted to the creation of a sovereign Quebec. . . .

Clearly, both the existence of a national identity and the nature of that identity for Canadians is contested. It is also hard to agree on the key values shared by most Canadians. The national identity of francophones seems to be better defined than that of anglophones. No wonder there is so much debate about the role of Canadian content regulations in shaping national identity. . . .

—*The Fraser Institute, Fraser Forum Online August 1998*

Questions: Why do you think French Canadians are perceived to have a better sense of their identity? Do you think English Canadians should celebrate what defines them more? Why or why not?

Though it's true that some features of the self are immediately apparent, the *significance* we attach to them—the rank we assign them in the hierarchy of our list and the interpretation we give them—depends greatly on our social environment. The interpretation of characteristics such as weight depends on the way people important to us regard them. Being anything less than trim and muscular is generally regarded as undesirable because others tell us that slenderness is an ideal. In one study, young women's perceptions of their bodies changed for the worse after watching just 30 minutes of televised images of the 'ideal' female form.[46] Furthermore, these distorted self-images can lead to serious behavioural disorders such as depression and eating disorders. However, in cultures and societies where greater weight is considered beautiful, a Western supermodel would be considered unattractive. In the same way, the fact that one is single or married, solitary or sociable, aggressive or passive takes on meaning depending on the interpretation that society attaches to those traits. Thus, the importance of a given characteristic in your self-concept has as much to do with the significance that you and others attach to it as with the existence of the characteristic.

Culture and the Self-Concept

Canadians have long been alert to the challenges and opportunities that come from cultural diversity. But the influence of culture is far more basic and powerful than most people realize. Although we seldom recognize the fact, our whole notion of the self is shaped by the culture in which we have been reared.[47]

The most obvious expression of a culture is the language its members use. If you live in an environment where everyone speaks the same tongue, then language will have little noticeable impact. But when your primary language is not the one spoken or written by the majority, or when it is not prestigious, your sense of being a member of what social scientists call the 'out-group' is likely to be strong. As a speaker of a non-dominant language, you can react in one of two ways: either you may feel pressured to assimilate by speaking the 'better' language, or you may refuse to accede to the majority language and maintain loyalty to the non-dominant language.[48] In either case, the impact of language on your self-concept is powerful. On one hand, you might feel you're not as 'good' as speakers of the native language; on the other, you might believe there's something unique and worth preserving in the language you use.

Cultures affect the self-concept in more subtle ways, too. Most Western cultures are highly individualistic, whereas other cultures—most Asian ones, for example—are traditionally much more collective.[49] When asked to identify themselves, Canadians, Americans, Australians, and Europeans would probably respond by giving their first name, surname, street, town, and country. Many Asians would do it the other way around.[50] Steven Heine, a psychologist at the University of British Columbia, studied differences between Asian and Anglo-North American selves and found that East Asians are more likely than Anglo-North Americans to incorporate people with whom they have very close relations into the self and emphasize the distance of 'outgroup' members. East Asians were also more likely to view self-criticism as an important way to motivate an individual.[51] Meanwhile, if you ask Hindus for their identity, they will give you their caste and village as well as their name. The Sanskrit formula for identifying one's self begins with lineage, goes on to family and house, and ends with one's personal name.[52]

These conventions for naming aren't just cultural idiosyncrasies: they reflect very different ways of viewing one's self.[53] In collective cultures a person gains identity by belonging to a group. This means that the degree of interdependence among members of the society and its subgroups is much higher. Feelings of pride and self-worth are likely to be shaped not only by what the individual does but also by the behaviour of other members of the community. This linkage to others explains the traditional Asian denial of self-importance—a strong contrast to the self-promotion that is common in individualistic Western cultures. In Chinese written language, for example, the pronoun 'I' looks very similar to the word for 'selfish'.[54] Table 2.1 summarizes some differences between individualistic Western cultures and more collective Asian ones.

This sort of cultural difference isn't just a matter of anthropological interest. It shows up in the level of comfort or anxiety that people feel when communicating. In societies where the need to conform is great, there is a higher degree of communication apprehension. For example, as a group, residents of China, Korea, and Japan exhibit significantly more anxiety about speaking out than do members of individualistic cultures such as those of Canada and the United States.[55] It's important to realize that different levels of communication apprehension don't mean that shyness is a 'problem' in some cultures. In fact, just the opposite is true:

In Japan, in fact, everything had been made level and uniform—even humanity. By one official count, 90 percent of the population regarded themselves as middle-class; in schools, it was not the outcasts who beat up the conformists, but vice versa. Every Japanese individual seemed to have the same goal as every other—to become like every other Japanese individual. The word for 'different,' I was told, was the same as the word for 'wrong.' And again and again in Japan, in contexts varying from the baseball stadium to the watercolor canvas, I heard the same unswerving, even maxim: 'The nail that sticks out must be hammered down.'

Pico Iyer,
Video Night in Katmandu

TABLE 2.1 The Self in Individualistic and Collectivistic Cultures

Individualist Cultures	Collectivistic Cultures
Self is separate, unique individual; should be independent, self-sufficient	People belong to extended families or in-groups; 'we' or group orientation
Individual should take care of self and immediate family	Person should take care of extended family before self
Many flexible group memberships; friends based on shared interests and activities	Emphasis on belonging to a very few permanent in-groups, which have a strong influence over the person
Reward for individual achievement and initiative; individual decisions encouraged; individual credit and blame assigned	Reward for contribution to group goals and well-being; co-operation with in-group members; group decisions valued; credit and blame shared
High value on autonomy, change, youth, individual security, equality	High value on duty, order, tradition, age, group security, status, hierarchy

Source: Adapted by S. Sudweeks from H.C. Triandis, 'Cross-cultural Studies of Individualism and Collectivism', in J. Berman, ed., Nebraska Symposium on Motivation 37 (Lincoln, NE: University of Nebraska Press, 1990), 41–133, and E.T. Hall, *Beyond Culture* (Garden City, NY: Doubleday, 1976).

reticence is valued in these cultures. When the goal is to avoid being the nail that sticks out, it's logical to feel nervous when you make yourself appear different by calling attention to yourself. A self-concept that includes 'assertive' might make a westerner feel proud, but in much of Asia it would more likely be cause for shame.

The Self-Concept, Personality, and Communication

Whereas the self-concept is an internal image we hold of ourselves, the personality is the view others hold of us. The term **personality** describes a relatively consistent set of traits people exhibit across a variety of situations.[56] We use the notion of personality to characterize others as friendly or aloof, energetic or lazy, smart or stupid, and in literally thousands of other ways. In fact, one survey revealed almost 18,000 trait words in the English language that can be used to describe a personality.[57] People do seem to possess some innate personality traits. Psychologist Jerome Kagan reports that 10 per cent of all children seem to be born with a biological disposition toward shyness.[58] Babies who stop playing when a stranger enters the room, for example, are more likely than others to be reticent and introverted as adolescents. Likewise, Kagan found that another 10 per cent of children seem to be born with especially sociable dispositions. Research with twins also suggests that personality may be at least partly a matter of genetic destiny.[59] For example, identical twins are much more similar in terms of sociability than are fraternal twins. These similarities are apparent not only in infancy but also in adulthood, and they are noticeable even when the twins have had different experiences growing up.

Canadian researchers Kelly Schwartz and Gregory Fouts asked 164 Canadian adolescents to fill out a survey to measure personality characteristics of three groups of music listeners: those preferring light qualities of music, those preferring heavy qualities of music, and those who had eclectic preferences. They found that each of the three groups demonstrated a specific personality profile.[60]

Despite its common use, the term *personality* is often an oversimplification. Much of our behaviour isn't consistent. Rather, it varies from one situation to another. You may be quiet around strangers but gregarious around friends and family. You may be optimistic about

personality
A relatively consistent set of traits a person exhibits across a variety of situations.

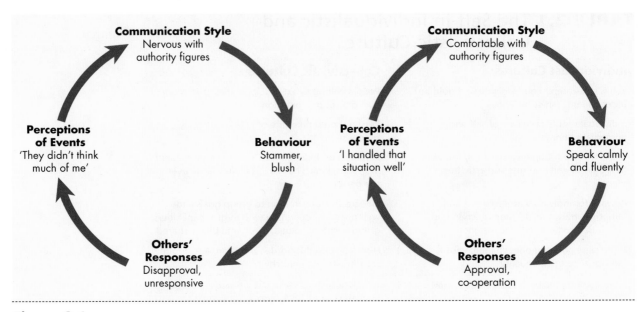

Figure 2.1
The Relationship between the Self-Concept and Behaviour

your schoolwork or career but pessimistic about your love life. The term *easygoing* might describe your behaviour at home, whereas you might be a fanatic at work. Inconsistencies of this kind are not only common but are also often desirable. The argumentative style you use with friends wouldn't be well received by the judge in traffic court when you appeal a citation. Likewise, the affectionate behaviour you enjoy with a boyfriend or girlfriend in private wouldn't be welcomed by a stranger in public. As you read in Chapter 1, a wide range of behaviours is an important ingredient of communication competence. In this sense, a consistent personality can be more of a liability than an asset—unless that personality is 'flexible'.

Figure 2.1 illustrates the relationship between the self-concept and behaviour. It shows how the self-concept both shapes and is shaped by much of our communication behaviour. We can begin to examine the process by considering the self-concept you bring to an event. Suppose, for example, that one element of your self-concept is 'nervous with authority figures'. That image probably comes from evaluations you have received in the past from significant others—teachers, perhaps, or former employers. If you view yourself as nervous with authority figures such as these, you will probably feel nervous when you encounter them in the future, such as in a teacher–student conference or a job interview. That nervous behaviour is likely to influence how others view your personality, which in turn will shape how they respond to you—probably in ways that reinforce the self-concept you brought to the event. Finally, the responses of others will affect the way you interpret future events: other job interviews, meetings with professors, and so on. This cycle illustrates how the chicken-and-egg nature of the self-concept, which is shaped by significant others in the past, helps to govern your present behaviour and influences the way others view you.

The Self-Fulfilling Prophecy

The self-concept is such a powerful force on the personality that it not only determines how we communicate in the present but can also actually influence our behaviour, and that of others, in the future. Such occurrences come about through a phenomenon called the self-fulfilling prophecy.

A **self-fulfilling prophecy** occurs when a person's expectation of an outcome makes the outcome more likely to occur than would otherwise have been true. Self-fulfilling prophecies occur all the time, although they might never have been labelled as such. For example, do any of the following situations sound familiar?

- You expected to become nervous and botch a job interview and ultimately did so.
- You anticipated having a good (or terrible) time at a social affair and found your expectations being met.
- A teacher or boss explained a new task to you, saying that you probably wouldn't do well at first. You did not do well.
- A friend described someone you were about to meet, saying that you wouldn't like the person. The prediction turned out to be correct.

In each of these cases, there is a good chance that the outcome happened because it had been predicted. You needn't have botched the interview; the party might have been boring only because you helped make it so; you might have done better on the new task if your boss hadn't spoken up; and you might have liked the new acquaintance if your friend hadn't planted preconceptions. In other words, what helped make each outcome occur was the expectation that it would.

There are two types of self-fulfilling prophecies. The first type occurs when your own expectations influence your behaviour. Like the job interview and the party described earlier, there are many times when an unnecessary outcome occurs because you expect it to. If you play sports you have probably psyched yourself into playing better than usual on at least one occasion, so that the only explanation for your performance was your attitude—your expectation that you would behave differently. The same principle operates for anxious public speakers: communicators who feel nervous about facing an audience often create self-fulfilling prophecies about doing poorly.[61] (Chapter 13 offers advice on overcoming this kind of stage fright.)

Research has demonstrated the power of self-fulfilling prophecies. A study of Ontarians suffering from social phobia disorder (which causes people to fear doing certain things in public, such as eating) demonstrated the debilitating effects that anticipation can have on a person, causing marked reduction in the quality of life.[62] In another study, communicators who believed they were incompetent proved less likely than others to pursue rewarding relationships and more likely to sabotage their existing relationships than did people who were less critical of themselves.[63] On the other hand, students who perceived themselves as capable achieved more academically.[64] Research conducted at the University of Waterloo demonstrated the effect of overachieving fourth-year students on the self-perception in first-year students: when first-year students read a profile of a star fourth-year student, they tended to evaluate themselves more positively because the star fourth-year student represented what they could become.[65]

Cultural Idiom

chicken-and-egg
a reference to the philosophical question, 'Which came first, the chicken or the egg?'

Cultural Idiom

psyched yourself
affected your behaviour by changing your thinking

"My objective is to have each student become more insightful, compassionate, introspective, and empathetic. In your case I will settle for quiet."

In another study, subjects who were sensitive to social rejection tended to expect it, perceive it where it might not have existed, and overreact to their exaggerated perceptions in ways that jeopardized the quality of their relationships.[66]

The self-fulfilling prophecy also operates on the job. For example, salespeople who perceive themselves as effective communicators were found to be more successful than those who perceive themselves as less effective, despite the fact that there was no difference in the approach that members of each group used with customers. In other words, the apparent reason that some salespeople do well is that they expect to succeed. Self-fulfilling prophecies can be physiologically induced: putting a smile on your face, even if you're not in a good mood, can lead to a more positive disposition.[67]

A second type of self-fulfilling prophecy occurs when the expectations of one person govern another's actions. The classic example was demonstrated by Robert Rosenthal and Lenore Jacobson:

> Twenty per cent of the children in a certain elementary school were reported to their teachers as showing unusual potential for intellectual growth. The names of these 20 per cent were drawn by means of a table of random numbers, which is to say that the names were drawn out of a hat. Eight months later these unusual or 'magic' children showed significantly greater gains in IQ than did the remaining children who had not been singled out for the teachers' attention. The change in the teachers' expectations regarding the intellectual performance of these allegedly 'special' children had led to an actual change in the intellectual performance of these randomly selected children.[68]

In other words, some children may do better in school not because they are any more intelligent than their classmates but because they learn that their teacher, a significant other, believes they can achieve.

To put this phenomenon in context with the self-concept, we can say that when a teacher communicates to students the message 'I think you're bright,' they accept that evaluation and change their self-concepts to include that evaluation. Unfortunately, we can assume that the same principle holds for those students whose teachers send the message 'I think you're stupid.'

This type of self-fulfilling prophecy has been shown to be a powerful force for shaping the self-concept, and thus the behaviour, of people in a wide range of settings beyond schools. In medicine, patients who unknowingly receive placebos—substances such as sugar pills that have no curative value—often respond just as favourably to this treatment as do people who receive the actual drug. The patients believe they have taken a substance that will help them feel better, and this belief brings about a 'cure'. Rosenthal and Jacobson describe several studies suggesting that psychotherapy patients who believe they will benefit from treatment do so, regardless of the type of treatment they receive. In the same vein, when a doctor expresses to a patient a belief that he or she will improve, the patient may do so precisely because of this expectation, whereas another person for whom the doctor gives little hope often fails to recover. Apparently the patient's self-concept as sick or well—as shaped by the doctor—plays an important role in determining the true state of health.

The self-fulfilling prophecy operates in families as well. If parents tell their children often enough that they never do anything right, the children's self-concepts will soon incorporate this idea, and they will fail at many or most of the tasks they attempt. On the other hand, if children are told they are capable, lovable, or kind, there is a much greater chance of their behaving accordingly.[69]

There is an old joke about a man who was asked if he could play a violin and answered, 'I don't know. I've never tried.' This is psychologically a very wise reply. Those who have never tried to play a violin really do not know whether they can or not. Those who say too early in life and too firmly, 'No, I'm not at all musical,' shut themselves off prematurely from whole areas of life that might have proved rewarding. In each of us there are unknown possibilities, undiscovered potentialities—and one big advantage of having an open self-concept rather than a rigid one is that we shall continue to discover more and more about ourselves as we grow older.

S.I. Hayakawa

SELF-FULFILLING PROPHECIES

Explore how self-fulfilling prophecies affect your communication by answering the following questions:

1. Identify three communication-related predictions you make about others. What are the effects of these predictions? How would others behave differently if you did not impose these predictions?
2. Identify three self-fulfilling prophecies you impose on yourself. What are the effects of these prophecies? How would you communicate differently if you did not subscribe to them?

The self-fulfilling prophecy is an important force in communication, but it doesn't explain all behaviour. There are certainly times when the expectation of an outcome won't bring it about. Your hope of drawing an ace in a card game won't in any way affect the chance of that card's turning up in a shuffled deck, and your belief that good weather is coming won't stop the rain from falling. In the same way, believing you'll do well in a job interview when you're clearly not qualified for the position is unrealistic. And there will probably be people you don't like and occasions you won't enjoy, no matter what your attitude. To connect the self-fulfilling prophecy with the 'power of positive thinking' is an oversimplification.

In other cases, your expectations will be borne out because you are a good predictor and not because of the self-fulfilling prophecy. For example, children are not equally equipped to do well in school, and in such cases it would be wrong to say that a child's performance was shaped by a parent or teacher even though the behaviour did match what was expected. In the same way, some workers excel and others fail, some patients recover and others don't—all according to our predictions but not because of them.

As we keep these qualifications in mind, it's important to recognize the tremendous influence that self-fulfilling prophecies play in our lives. To a great extent we are what we believe we are. In this sense we and those around us constantly create our self-concepts and thus ourselves.

> **Cultural Idiom**
>
> **in the same vein**
> similarly
>
> **turn the tables**
> reverse the point of view

Identity Management: Communication as Impression Management

So far we have described how communication shapes the way communicators view themselves and others. In the remainder of this chapter we turn the tables and focus on **impression management**—the communication strategies people use to influence how others view them. In the following pages you will see that many of our messages aim at creating desired impressions.

> **impression management**
> Strategies used by communicators to influence the way others view them.

Public and Private Selves

To understand why impression management exists, we have to discuss the notion of self in more detail. So far we have referred to the 'self' as if each of us had only one identity. In truth, each of us possesses several selves, some private and others public. Often these selves are quite different.

face
The socially approved identity that a communicator tries to present.

facework
Verbal and non-verbal behaviour designed to create and maintain a communicator's face and the face of others.

perceived self
The person we believe ourselves to be in moments of candour. It may be identical with or different from the presenting and ideal selves.

presenting self
The image a person presents to others. It may be identical to or different from the perceived and ideal selves.

People often say that this or that person has not yet found himself. But the self is not something one finds, it is something one creates.

Thomas Szasz,
The Second Sin

The **perceived self** is a reflection of the self-concept, the person you believe yourself to be in moments of honest self-examination. We can call the perceived self 'private' because you are unlikely to reveal all of it to another person. You can verify the private nature of the perceived self by reviewing the self-concept list you developed while reading page 56. You'll probably find some elements of yourself there that you would not disclose to many people, and some that you would not share with anyone. You might, for example, be reluctant to share some feelings about your appearance ('I think I'm rather unattractive'), your intelligence ('I'm not as smart as I wish I was'), your goals ('the most important thing to me is becoming rich'), or your motives ('I care more about myself than about others'). In contrast to the perceived self, the **presenting self** is a public image—the way we want to appear to others. In most cases the presenting self we seek to create is a socially approved image: diligent student, loving partner, conscientious worker, loyal friend, and so on. Social norms often create a gap between the perceived and presenting selves. Table 2.2 summarizes the results of a study of the difference between the perceived and presenting selves of male and female university students. As you will see, the self-concepts of the male and female students were quite similar, but their public selves were different in several respects both from their private selves and from the public selves of the opposite sex.[70]

Sociologist Erving Goffman used the word **face** to describe the presenting self, and he coined the term **facework** to describe the verbal and non-verbal ways we act to maintain our own presenting image and the images of others.[71] He argued that each of us can be viewed as a kind of playwright/performer who creates and then acts out roles that we want others to believe.

Facework involves two tasks: managing our own identity and communicating in ways that reinforce the identities that others are trying to present.[72] You can see how these two goals operate by recalling a time when you've used self-deprecating humour to defuse a potentially unpleasant situation. Suppose, for example, that you were late getting to a party

TABLE 2.2 Self-Selected Adjectives Describing Perceived and Presenting Selves of College Students

Perceived Self		Presenting Self	
Men	**Women**	**Men**	**Women**
1. Friendly	1. Friendly	1. Wild	1. Active
2. Active	2. Responsible	2. Able	2. Responsible
3. Responsible	3. Independent	3. Active	3. Able
4. Independent	4. Capable	4. Strong	4. Bright
5. Capable	5. Sensible	5. Proud	5. Warm
6. Polite	6. Active	6. Smart	6. Funny
7. Attractive	7. Happy	7. Brave	7. Independent
8. Smart	8. Curious	8. Capable	8. Proud
9. Happy	9. Faithful	9. Responsible	9. Sensible
10. Funny	10. Attractive	10. Rough	10. Smart

Source: Adapted from C.M. Shaw and R. Edwards, 'Self-Concepts and Self-Presentations of Males and Females: Similarities and Differences', *Communication Reports* 10 (1997): 55–62.

because a friend gave you confusing directions. 'Sorry I got lost,' you might have said. 'I'm a terrible navigator.' This sort of mild, self-directed putdown accomplishes two things at once. It preserves the other person's face by implicitly saying, 'It's not your fault.' At the same time, your mild self-debasement shows that you're a nice person who doesn't find faults in others or make a big issue out of small problems.[73]

Characteristics of Identity Management

Now that you have a sense of what identity management is, we can look at some characteristics of this process.

We Strive to Construct Multiple Identities

In the course of even a single day, most people play a variety of roles: the respectful student, the joking friend, the friendly neighbour, and the helpful worker, to suggest just a few. We even play a variety of roles with the same person. As you grew up you almost certainly changed characters as you interacted with your parents. In one context you acted as the responsible adult ('You can trust me with the car!'), and in another context you were the helpless child ('I can't find my socks!'). At some times—perhaps on birthdays or holidays—you were a dedicated family member, and at other times you may have played the role of rebel. Likewise, in romantic relationships we switch among many behaviours, depending on the context: friend, lover, business partner, scolding critic, apologetic child, and so on.

The ability to construct multiple identities is one element of communication competence. For example, the style of speaking or even the language spoken can reflect a choice about how to construct one's identity. We recall a neuroscience professor who was always very strict and reserved with his students but who changed demeanour entirely when participating in his Catholic parish activities in Montreal. On campus or in the lab, he was quiet and demanding, whereas at church he was open, smiling, and full of jokes. In a similar vein, a University of Waterloo study looked at how bicultural Chinese Canadians who experience unfavourable circumstances in one culture (either Chinese or English Canadian) maintain their sense of well-being by shifting to their other cultural identity.[74]

Identity Management Is Collaborative

As we perform like actors trying to create a front, our 'audience' is made up of other actors who are trying to create their own characters. Identity-related communication is a kind of process theatre in which we collaborate with other actors to improvise scenes in which our characters mesh.

You can appreciate the collaborative nature of identity management by thinking about how you might handle a grievance against a roommate or family member who has failed to pass along a phone message that arrived while you were out. Suppose you decide to raise the issue tactfully in an effort to avoid seeming like a nag (desired role for yourself: 'nice person') and also to save the other person from the embarrassment of being confronted (hoping to avoid casting the other person in the role of 'screw-up'). If your tactful bid is accepted, the dialogue might sound like this:

You: By the way, Jenny told me she called yesterday. If you wrote a note, I guess I missed seeing it.

Other: Oh . . . sorry. I meant to write a note, but as soon as I hung up, the doorbell rang, and then I had to run off to class.

You (*in friendly tone of voice*): That's okay. Try to leave me a note next time, though.

Other: No problem.

In this upbeat conversation, you and the other person have accepted one another's bids for identity as basically thoughtful people. As a result, the conversation ran smoothly. Imagine, though, how different the outcome would be if the other person didn't accept your role as 'nice person':

You: By the way, Jenny told me she called yesterday. If you wrote a note, I guess I missed seeing it.

Other (*defensively*): Okay, so I forgot. It's not that big a deal. You're not perfect yourself, you know!

Your first bid as 'nice, face-saving person' was rejected. At this point you have the choice of persisting in your original role ('Hey, I'm not mad at you, and I know I'm not perfect!') or switching to the new role of 'unjustly accused person' and giving your roommate the gears ('I never said I was perfect. But we're not talking about me here . . .').

As this example illustrates, *collaboration* doesn't mean the same thing as *agreement*.[75] The small issue of the phone message might mushroom into a fight in which you and the other

person both adopt the role of combatant. The point here is that virtually all conversations provide an arena in which communicators construct their identities in response to the behaviour of others. As we discussed in Chapter 1, communication isn't made up of discrete events that can be separated from one another. Instead, what happens at one moment is influenced by what each party brings to the interaction and by what has happened in their relationship up to that point.

Identity Management Can Be Conscious or Unconscious

At this point you might object to the notion of strategic identity management, claiming that most of your communication is spontaneous and not a deliberate attempt to present yourself in a certain way. However, you might acknowledge that some of your communication involves a conscious attempt to manage impressions.

There's no doubt that sometimes we are highly aware of managing impressions. Most job interviews and first dates are clear examples of conscious identity management. But in other cases we unconsciously act in ways that are really small public performances.[76]

For example, experimental subjects expressed facial disgust in reaction to eating sandwiches laced with a supersaturated saltwater solution only when there was another person present; when they were alone, they made no faces when eating the same sandwiches.[77] Another study showed that communicators engage in facial mimicry (such as smiling or looking sympathetic in response to another's message) in face-to-face settings only when their expressions can be seen by the other person. When they are speaking over the phone and their reactions cannot be seen, they do not make the same expressions.[78] Studies such as these suggest that most of our behaviour is aimed at sending messages to others, even though reactions like the ones described are often instantaneous and unconscious. In other words, we engage in identity management even when we're not aware that we're doing it.

In the same way, many of our choices about how to act in the array of daily interactions aren't deliberate, strategic decisions. Rather, they rely on 'scripts' that we have developed over time. You probably have a variety of roles for managing your identity from which to choose in familiar situations such as dealing with strangers, treating customers at work, interacting with family members, and so on. When you find yourself in such situations you probably slip into these roles quite often. Only when those roles don't seem quite right do you deliberately construct an approach that reflects how you want the scene to play out.

Despite the claims of some theorists, it seems like an exaggeration to suggest that all behaviour is aimed at making impressions. Young children certainly aren't strategic communicators. A baby spontaneously laughs when pleased and cries when sad or uncomfortable, without any notion of creating an impression in others. Likewise, there are almost certainly times when we, as adults, act spontaneously. But when a significant other questions the presenting self we try to put forward, the likelihood of taking actions to prop it up increases. This process isn't always conscious: at a non-conscious level, we monitor others' reactions and swing into action when our face is threatened—especially by significant others.[79]

People Differ in Their Degree of Identity Management

Some people are much more aware of their impression management behaviour than others. High self-monitors have the ability to pay attention to their own behaviour and others' reactions, adjusting their communication as necessary to create the desired impression. By contrast, low self-monitors express what they are thinking and feeling without much attention to the impression their behaviour creates.[80]

There are certainly advantages to being a high self-monitor.[81] People who pay attention to themselves are generally good actors who can create the impression they want, acting interested when bored or friendly when they really feel quite the opposite. This allows them to handle social situations smoothly, often putting others at ease. They are also good 'people-readers' who can adjust their behaviour to get the desired reaction from others. But along with these advantages are some potential drawbacks. Their analytical nature may prevent high self-monitors from experiencing events completely, because a portion of their attention will always be devoted to viewing the situation from a detached position. Their ability to perform means that it is difficult to tell how they are really feeling. In fact, because high self-monitors change roles often, they may have a hard time knowing how they really feel.

People who score low on the self-monitoring scale live life quite differently from their more self-conscious counterparts. They have a simpler, more focused idea of who they are and who they want to be. Low self-monitors are likely to have a narrower repertoire of behaviours, so that they can be expected to act in more or less the same way regardless of the situation. This means that low self-monitors are easy to read. 'What you see is what you get'

Cultural Idiom

'scripts'
practised responses

to play out
to proceed to a conclusion

Prepare a face to meet the faces that you meet.

T.S. Eliot,
'The Love Song of J. Alfred Prufrock'

might be their motto. Although this lack of flexibility may make their social interaction more awkward in many situations, low self-monitors can be counted on to be straightforward communicators.

By now it should be clear that neither extremely high nor extremely low self-monitoring is the ideal. There are some situations when paying attention to yourself and adapting your behaviour can be useful, but there are other situations when reacting without considering the effect on others is a better approach. This need for a range of behaviours demonstrates again the notion of communicative competence outlined in Chapter 1: flexibility is the key to successful relationships.

Why Manage Impressions?

Why bother trying to shape others' opinions? Sometimes we create and maintain a front to follow social rules. As children we learn to act polite, even when bored. Likewise, part of growing up consists of developing a set of manners for various occasions: meeting strangers, attending school, going to religious services, and so on. Young children who haven't learned all the do's and don'ts of polite society often embarrass their parents by behaving inappropriately ('Mummy, why is that man so fat?'), but by the time they enter school, behaviour that might have been excusable or even amusing just isn't acceptable. Good manners are often aimed at making others more comfortable. For example, able-bodied people often mask their discomfort upon encountering someone with a disability by acting nonchalant or stressing similarities between themselves and the disabled person.[82]

Social rules govern our behaviour in a variety of settings. It would be impossible to keep a job, for example, without meeting certain expectations. People in sales are obliged to treat customers with courtesy. Employees need to appear reasonably respectful when talking to their managers. Some forms of clothing would be considered outrageous in the workplace. By agreeing to take on a job, you are signing an unwritten contract that you will present a certain face at work, whether or not that face reflects the way you might be feeling at a particular moment.

Even when social roles don't dictate the proper way to behave, we often manage impressions for a second reason: to accomplish personal goals. You might, for example, dress up for a visit to traffic court in the hope that your front ('responsible citizen') will persuade the judge to treat you sympathetically. You behave affably toward your neighbours so they will respect your request that they keep their dog off your lawn. We also try to create a desired impression to achieve one or more of the social needs described in Chapter 1: affection, inclusion, control, and so on. For instance, you might act friendlier and more lively than you feel upon meeting a new person so that you will appear likeable. You could sigh and roll your eyes when arguing politics with a classmate to gain an advantage in a debate. You might smile to show the attractive stranger at a party that you would like to get better acquainted. In situations like these you aren't being deceptive as much as putting your best foot forward.

All these examples show that it is difficult—even impossible—*not* to create impressions. After all, you have to send *some* sort of message. If you don't act friendly when meeting a stranger, you have to act aloof, indifferent, hostile, or in some other manner. If you don't act businesslike, you have to behave in an alternative way: casual, goofy, or whatever. Often the question isn't whether or not to present a face to others; the question is only which face to present.

Not all messages are about identity, but identity is part of all messages.

Michael L. Hecht

While studying communications at McMaster University, I learned about platforms from the printing press to the Internet. Today, I find myself applying old-school theories to social media, making sense of how new tools revolutionize the way we communicate. My academic background has inspired my passion for communication innovation and its crucial impact on Canadian business.

I never thought that within two years of graduating, I'd be consulting for a national magazine brand or developing a strategic communication plan for a $45 million fundraising campaign. But the truth is, I am . . . and you can too. Organizations are seeking educated, enthusiastic professionals to help them to adapt and capitalize on new communications opportunities.

Working for The Credit Valley Hospital Foundation, I get to apply my skills in social media and corporate communications to a cause I believe in. Healthcare is a challenging and fulfilling environment, with real and compelling stories to share. My favourite part of my job is meeting patients and sharing their experiences with the world online.

I believe that my degree in communications combined with a college certificate in public relations has prepared me for an exciting career ahead. Research, writing, analysis, and presentation skills combined with a zest for constant learning are in demand. I leave you with Marshall MacLuhan's words, 'We become what we behold. We shape our tools and then our tools shape us' (*Understanding Media*, 1964).

Young Communicator
PROFILE

Bianca Freedman, Communications Coordinator, The Credit Valley Hospital Foundation

How Do We Manage Impressions?

How do we create a public face? In an age when technology provides many options for communicating, the answer depends in part on the medium of communication chosen.

Face-to-Face Impression Management

In face-to-face interaction, communicators can manage their impression in three ways: through manner, appearance, and setting.[83] *Manner* consists of a communicator's words and non-verbal actions. Physicians, for example, display a wide variety of manners as they conduct physical examinations. Some are friendly and conversational, whereas others adopt a brusque and impersonal approach. Still others are polite but businesslike. Much of a communicator's manner comes from what he or she says. A doctor who remembers details about your interests and hobbies is quite different from one who sticks to clinical questions. But along with the content of speech, non-verbal behaviours play a big role in creating impressions. A doctor who greets you with a friendly smile and a handshake comes across quite

Cultural Idiom

lust after
strongly desire to own

sticks to
focuses solely on

Cultural Idiom

'richness'
completeness

straightened up
cleaned and/or organized

differently from one who gives nothing more than a curt nod. The same principle holds in personal relationships: your manner plays a major role in shaping how others view you. Chapters 3 and 5 will describe in detail how your words and non-verbal behaviours create impressions. Because you have to speak and act, the question isn't whether or not your manner sends messages but whether or not these messages will be intentional.

Along with manner, a second dimension of impression management is *appearance*—the personal items people use to shape an image. Sometimes appearance is part of creating a professional image. A physician's lab coat and a police officer's uniform both set the wearer apart as someone special. A tailored suit and a rumpled outfit create very different impressions in the business world. Off the job, clothing is just as important. We choose clothing that sends a message about ourselves, sometimes trendy and sometimes traditional. Some people dress in ways that accent their sexuality, whereas others hide it. Clothing can say 'I'm an athlete,' 'I'm wealthy,' or 'I'm an environmentalist.' Along with dress, other aspects of appearance play a strong role in impression management. Do you have any tattoos or piercings? What is your hair style?

A third way to manage impressions is through the choice of *setting*—physical items we use to influence how others view us. Consider the items that people use to decorate the space where they live. Think, for example, of how the posters and other objects a student uses to decorate her dorm room function as a kind of 'who I am' statement.[84] In modern Western society the automobile is a major part of impression management. This explains why many people lust after cars that are far more expensive and far less fuel-efficient than they really need. Whether it's a sporty red convertible or an imposing black SUV, a vehicle doesn't just get people from one place to another: it also makes a statement about the kind of person driving it.

The physical setting we choose and the way we arrange it are other important ways to manage impressions. What colours do you choose for the place you live? What artwork? What music do you play? Of course, we choose a setting that we enjoy; but in many cases we create an environment that will present the desired front to others. If you doubt this fact, just recall the last time you straightened up your home before important guests arrived. You might be comfortable with a messy place when you're 'backstage', but the front you put on in public—at least to some people—is quite different.

Impression Management in Mediated Communication

At first glance, computer-mediated communication (CMC) seems to have limited potential for identity management. E-mail messages, for example, appear to lack the 'richness' of other channels. They don't convey the postures, gestures, or facial expressions that are an important part of face-to-face communication. They even lack the vocal information available in telephone messages. These limitations might seem to make it harder to create and manage an identity when communicating via computer.

Recently, though, communication scholars have begun to recognize that what is missing in computer-mediated communication can actually be an advantage for communicators who want to manage the impressions they make.[85] E-mail users can edit their messages until they create just the desired impression.[86] They can choose the desired level of clarity or ambiguity, seriousness or humour, logic or emotion. Unlike face-to-face communication, electronic correspondence allows a sender to say difficult things without forcing the receiver to respond immediately, and it permits the receiver to ignore a message rather than give an unpleasant response. Options like these show that CMC can serve as a tool for impression management at least as well as face-to-face communication.

In CMC, communicators have much greater control over what kinds of information to reveal or hide. A web designer who doesn't want to be judged by his appearance (his age, his gender, his looks, etc.) can hide or manipulate these characteristics in ways that aren't possible in face-to-face settings. A telecommuter working at home can close a big deal via computer while cursing about the client, chomping on an apple, or feeding the dog—none of which is recommended in face-to-face business dealings.

In addition to providing greater control over *what* messages say, mediated channels enhance communicators' control over *how* the message is shaped, whether to enhance their own identity or to preserve the face of others. On the Internet, it's possible to shape a message until it creates just the desired impression. You can edit remarks to get the right tone of sincerity, humour, irony, or concern—or not send any message at all, if that is the best way to maintain face. This kind of identity management is important in personal communication as well as in business communication. The CBC television program *Streetcents*, in an episode devoted to on-line dating, reported that more than 25 per cent of the people who have looked for dates online admit to having misrepresented themselves. The most common misrepresentations involved age, appearance, and marital status.[87]

Some statistics from a survey by the Pew Internet and American Life Project reveal how much people—especially younger ones—manage their identities on the Web. Fifty-six per cent of online teens had more than one screen name or e-mail address, and many reported that they used some of these names to hide their real identities from strangers, and even

COMMUNICATION ON-SCREEN

Alias (2001–06)
Created by J.J. Abrams.

A highly stylized spy drama, *Alias* follows secret agent Sydney Bristow (Jennifer Garner) as she kicks, punches, and shoots her way through a Byzantine series of international conspiracies while maintaining two, three, or sometimes four parallel identities. As the series' title less-than-subtly suggests, Bristow's blur of assumed identities are at the heart of its premise, and elaborate impression management exercises crop up in virtually every episode. Watching the show, it's easy—often too easy—to notice how Bristow's impression management toolbox tends to involve plenty of off-camera visits to an unusual CIA wardrobe facility stocked with all manner of lace and rubber items. But equally fascinating, if somewhat less titillating, are the adjustments to verbal and non-verbal behaviours we see in Bristow's assumed identities. Those aspects of impression management helped earn Garner a Golden Globe Award and a raft of Emmy nominations for her acting, a feat virtually unheard of in the action genre.

Cultural Idiom

preserve the face of others
protect the dignity of others

"I loved your E-mail, but I thought you'd be older."

Understanding Communication Technology

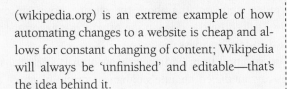

Web 3.0

Have you heard of Web 3.0? You may not have yet, but it's been planned for the last 10 years and you are now seeing it directly affect your life in Facebook's Open Graph initiative (opengraphprotocol.org/). Web 3.0 is a marketing term for something that is technically called the 'semantic web', which is a variation of the term 'Web 2.0' which Tim O'Reilly (radar.oreilly.com/tim/), the owner of O'Reilly Media Inc., popularized. 'Semantic Web' describes the move from an Internet dominated by static web pages to an Internet made mostly of web pages filled with 'dynamic content'.

Discussing Web 3.0 is easier if you understand what Web 2.0 is. Let's define Web 2.0.

A static web page is one where the user doesn't interact with the web page. Students who are old enough will remember a web filled with pages they read and only interacted with when they filled in forms. Web 2.0 is defined by web pages that have dynamic content. This can mean two things:

1. Web pages are no longer just collections of text, pictures, and video. Rather, Web 2.0 web pages are actually software applications that you can use to do things with information. Think of Google Docs or Hotmail as examples.
2. In Web 2.0, web pages are constantly 'under construction' in a way that they weren't before. Web page content has never been fixed. Web pages are constantly added to, edited, adapted, or even deleted, as any user of the Internet has experienced, when trying to consult a trusty web page about a personal interest, such as fishing or camping or gaming, only to find that it has been moved or changed. During the Web 2.0 period, this process was largely automated so that the cost of changing content is greatly reduced. Wikipedia

(wikipedia.org) is an extreme example of how automating changes to a website is cheap and allows for constant changing of content; Wikipedia will always be 'unfinished' and editable—that's the idea behind it.

There's a social dimension to Web 2.0 as well. Web 2.0 sites are set up to take advantage of user-created content. Rather than going through the expensive and time consuming process of creating content for a website, Web 2.0 sites concentrate on building a community on and around the website. Once the community is built, it is the members of that community who create the content for the site. In fact, one could say that the community IS the content of the Web 2.0 site. This model can make large websites relatively cheap to start up because most of the work is done by the users of the site. For example, Wikipedia is at the time of this writing, the fifth most popular site on the Internet and has 34 full-time employees. Wikipedia employees work to support a community of about 100,000 regular content editors who volunteer their time and effort, and hundreds of millions of users every month (upload. wikimedia.org/wikimedia/pt/2/2d/2010-Wikipedia_ Academy_Portugal_April_2010_Global_Collab.small.pdf presentation slides in English).

Tim Berners-Lee (w3.org/People/Berners-Lee/) created the HTTP protocol, URL addresses, and the HTML markup language, all of which are part of the technical foundation of the Internet, and he is currently the head of the W3 Consortium, which is the international organization that sets Internet Standards. Berners-Lee calls static websites and Web 2.0 websites the 'Internet of documents'. Documents are things that humans can trade, look at, and understand, so the Internet of documents is where information is created, traded, and given meaning by humans.

Tim Berners-Lee talks about there being another Internet, the 'Internet of data'. In the Internet of data, it is the computers themselves which trade information amongst themselves, create it, and give it meaning. It is the Internet of data that we are referring to when we say 'Web 3.0'.

How does Web 3.0 work? Humans trade information among themselves in human languages, such as French, English, or Japanese. Computers don't understand human language very well, despite our best efforts to train them, so computer programmers need to encode information in a format that is easy for computers to deal with. To this end, programmers created various formats to do this, most of which have arcane-sounding names like RDF, OWL, or XML. These formats boil down to a simple relationship: any two objects must have a link between them and each object has a unique description that can be accessed on the Internet using an URL. These descriptions of the data, if one looks at all of the descriptions linked to in a document, can often contain more information than the data being commented on by the descriptions. All this complexity is there to allow each person to describe the world the way they see it, and still have a computer be able to understand the description and have it make sense with other descriptions of the same thing, much like we can understand different descriptions of the same flower by different people.

Databases filled with information like this can be located all over the Internet. A computer only needs to know where the information is located to make use of it. For example, a website that provides information about houses to prospective homebuyers might get information from databases on crime in the area where the house is located, information about the neighbors found on social networking sites, and information about building inspections from the city hall. The website could then give the buyer information about the desirability of a particular house, whether the asking price is reasonable as well as information about homes with similar profiles. The website could even provide unexpected sorts of information, such as similar homes with neighbors who have demonstrated an interest in environmental issues. If the prospective homebuyer is concerned for the environment, he or she might want to be around neighbors for whom the environment is also top of mind.

By collecting information from different sources and systematically searching and organizing the information in a process called 'data-mining', computers can create new information. There are ways of analyzing relationships found in data that actually create new information about the data and about the world. Consider the website flightcaster.com. Flightcaster.com has collected information about the conditions under which flights get delayed. The website applies a proprietary method for finding patterns in that data and, on the basis of that analysis, promises to be able to predict when a plane will be delayed at least six hours before the delay will actually be announced by the airline. This sort of 'intelligence' will transform our lives in the near future.

The possibilities for services built on collecting data from different sites and creating new data on-the-fly are endless. Web 3.0 is about increasing our power to know about the world around us. When Web 3.0 is coupled with mobile computing, it becomes a second nervous system and brain for each of us, connecting us together and showing us more of the world than we would be able to see without it.

—piratasum.com (aka Lars Wessman)

Questions: The Web 3.0 revolution will make the World Wide Web much more interactive and customizable through the use of artificial intelligence. These virtual machines will do our bidding and make decisions for us about what to read and look at. What is it that makes the idea of artificial intelligence so appealing? How will impression management in the world of intelligent machines differ from the real-world kind, especially when the machines are capable of finding out all sorts of information about us?

friends. Roughly a quarter of the online teens said they had given false information about themselves in e-mails or instant messages.[88]

Recent research has revealed that communicators who are concerned with impression management don't always prefer computer-mediated channels. People are generally comfortable with face-to-face interaction when they feel confident that others support the image they want to present. On the other hand, people are more likely to prefer mediated channels when their own self-presentation is threatened.[89]

Impression Management and Honesty

After reading this far, you might think that impression management sounds like an academic label for manipulation or phoniness. If the perceived self is the 'real' you, it might seem that any behaviour that contradicts it would be dishonest.

There certainly are situations where impression management is dishonest. A manipulative date who pretends to be interested in a long-term relationship but is really just after a one-night stand is clearly unethical and deceitful. So are job applicants who lie about academic records or salespeople who pretend to be dedicated to customer service when their real goal is to increase their commissions. But managing impressions doesn't necessarily make you a liar. In fact, it is almost impossible to imagine how we could communicate effectively without making decisions about which front to present in one situation or another. It would be ludicrous for you to act the same way with strangers as you do with close friends, and nobody would show the same face to a two-year-old as to an adult.

Each of us has a repertoire of faces—a cast of characters—and part of being a competent communicator is choosing the best role for the situation. Consider a few examples:

- You offer to teach a friend a new skill—playing the guitar, operating a computer program, or sharpening a tennis backhand. Your friend is making slow progress with the skill, and you find yourself growing impatient.
- At a party with a companion, you meet someone you find very attractive, and you are pretty sure that the feeling is mutual. You feel an obligation to spend most of your time with the person you came with, but the opportunity here is very appealing.
- At work you face a belligerent customer. You don't believe that anyone has the right to treat you this way.
- A friend or family member makes a joke about your appearance that hurts your feelings. You aren't sure whether to make an issue of the remark or pretend that it doesn't bother you.

In each of these situations—and in countless others every day—you have a choice about how to act. It is an oversimplification to say that there is only one honest way to behave in each circumstance and that every other response would be insincere and dishonest. Instead, impression management involves deciding which face—which part of yourself—to reveal. For example, when teaching a new skill you can choose to display the patient instead of the impatient side of yourself. In the same way, at work you have the option of acting hostile or nondefensive in difficult situations. With strangers, friends, or family you can choose whether or not to disclose your feelings. Which face to show to others is an important decision, but in any case you are sharing a real part of yourself. You may not be revealing everything—but, as you will learn in Chapter 6, complete self-disclosure is rarely appropriate.

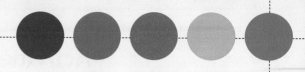

Summary

Perceptions of others are always selective and are often distorted. The chapter began by describing how personal narratives shape our perceptions. It then outlined several perceptual errors that can affect the way we view and communicate with others. Along with universal psychological influences, cultural factors affect perceptions. Increased empathy is a valuable tool for increasing understanding of others and hence communicating more effectively with them. Perception-checking is one tool for increasing the accuracy of perceptions and for increasing empathy.

Perceptions of one's self are just as subjective as perceptions of others, and they influence communication at least as much. Although individuals are born with some innate personality characteristics, the self-concept is shaped dramatically by communication with others, as well as by cultural factors. Once established, the self-concept can lead us to create self-fulfilling prophecies that determine how we behave and how others respond to us.

Impression management consists of strategic communication designed to influence others' perceptions. Impression management operates when we seek, consciously or unconsciously, to present one or more public faces to others. These faces may be different from the private, spontaneous behaviour that occurs outside of others' presence. Identity management is usually collaborative: communication goes most smoothly when we communicate in ways that support others' faces, and they support ours. Some communicators are high self-monitors who are highly conscious of their own behaviour, whereas others are low self-monitors who are less aware of how their words and actions affect others.

Impression management occurs for two reasons. In many cases it is designed for following social rules and conventions. In other cases it is meant to achieve a variety of content and relational goals. In either case, communicators engage in creating impressions by managing their manner, appearance, and the settings in which they interact with others. Although impression management might seem manipulative, it can be an authentic form of communication. Because each person has a variety of faces that he or she can present, choosing which one to put forth doesn't have to be dishonest.

Key Terms

empathy 50

face 66

facework 66

impression
   management 65

narratives 39

perceived self 66

perception-checking 54

personality 61

presenting self 66

reflected appraisal 57

self-concept 55

self-esteem 56

self-fulfilling
   prophecy 62

self-serving bias 40

significant others 57

sympathy 50

Activities

A. Exploring Narratives

Think about a situation where relational harmony is created because you and others involved in the situation share the same narrative. Then think of another situation where you both use different narratives to describe the same situation. What are the consequences of having different narratives in this situation?

B. Experiencing Another Cyber-Culture

Spend at least an hour in an online forum that reflects a culture that is unfamiliar to you and where you are a minority. For example, visit a website such as Second Life or World of Warcraft and explore alternative identities where a cultural group other than your own is the majority; spend time on a discussion site with people whose political views are radically different from your own; visit an online community where people of a different age group make up the majority; or attend an online meeting of an organization or a religious group of which you are not a member. Observe how communication practices differ from those of your own culture. Based on your experience, discuss what you can do to facilitate communication with people from other cultural backgrounds whom you may encounter in your everyday life. (As you develop a list of ideas, keep in mind that what you might consider helpful behaviour could make online communicators from different cultures even more uncomfortable.)

C. Understanding Empathy

Choose a disagreement you've been having or have had with another person or group. The disagreement might be a personal one—an argument about how to settle a financial problem, for instance—or it might be a dispute over a contemporary public issue, such as what the provincial or federal government should be doing to stop climate change.

1. In 300 words or so, describe your side of the issue. State your position and explain why you believe as you do, just as if you were presenting your position to a panel of judges.

2. Now write another 300 words, in the first-person singular, to describe the position of the other person or group. For a short while get in touch with how the other person feels and thinks.

3. Show the description you wrote to your 'opponent', the person whose beliefs are different from yours. Have that person read your account and correct any statements that don't reflect his or her position accurately. Remember: you're doing this so that you can more clearly understand how the issue looks to the other person.

4. Make any necessary corrections in the account you wrote and again show it to your partner. When your partner agrees that you understand his or her position, have your partner sign your paper to indicate this.

5. Now record your conclusions to this experiment. Has this perceptual shift made any difference in how you view the issue or how you feel about your partner?

D. Perception-Checking Practice

Practise your perception-checking ability by developing three-part verifications for the following situations:

1. You made what you thought was an excellent suggestion to an instructor. The instructor looked uninterested but said she would check on the matter right away. Three weeks have passed, and nothing has changed.
2. A neighbour and good friend, who is normally quite friendly, has not responded to your 'Good morning' greeting for three days in a row.
3. You haven't received the usual weekly phone call from the folks back home in over a month. The last time you spoke, you had an argument about where to spend the holidays.
4. A friend with whom you have shared the problems of your love life for years has recently changed around you: the formerly casual hugs and kisses have become longer and stronger, and the occasions where you 'accidentally' brush up against one another have become more frequent.

E. Identifying Your Identities

Keep a one-day log of the identities you create in different situations: at school, at work, with strangers, with various family members, and with different friends. For each identity,

1. describe the persona you are trying to project (e.g., 'responsible son or daughter', 'laid-back friend', 'attentive student'), and
2. explain how you communicate to promote this identity. What kinds of things do you say (or not say)? How do you act?

F. Honesty and Multiple Identities

This text argues that presenting different identities to the world isn't inherently dishonest. Nonetheless, there are certainly cases when it is deceitful to construct an identity that doesn't match your private self.

Explore the ethics of multiple identities by identifying a time in your life when

1. you presented a public identity that didn't match your private self in a manner that wasn't unethical, and
2. a situation (real or hypothetical) in which you have presented or could present a dishonest identity.

Based on the situations you and your classmates present, develop a code of ethics that identifies the boundary between ethical and unethical identity management.

Further Reading

Bauby, Jean-Dominique. *The Diving Bell and the Butterfly*. London: HarperCollins, 2007.
Bauby was the publisher of *Elle* magazine in Paris until a stroke left him almost completely paralyzed; the only part of his body he could control was his left eyelid. Even though his mind remained active, his ability to communicate was restricted to blinking. Bauby's case illustrates how the 'self' or mind can soar even when the body is paralyzed.

Bolter, David J. 'Identity', in Thomas Swiss, ed., *Unspun: Key Concepts for Understanding the World Wide Web*. New York: NYU Press, 2000.
This essay points out ways in which we can create desired identities on the Internet that differ fundamentally from identity management in face-to-face relationships.

Cupach, William R., and Sandra Metts. *Facework*. Thousand Oaks, CA: Sage, 1994.
The authors summarize research on how communicators manage their own identity and maintain the face of others, especially in problematic situations.

Gergen, Kenneth. *The Saturated Self: Dilemmas of Identity in Contemporary Life*.
New York: Basic Books, 1992.
Gergen's thesis is that, in today's fast-paced society, traditional notions of the self are being crowded out by a variety of alternatives. Chapter 6, 'From Self to Relationship', describes how creating (and communicating) any self-image one desires is becoming increasingly possible in emerging postmodern society.

Ickes, William E., ed. *Empathic Accuracy*. New York: Guilford, 1997.
This edited volume offers an array of scholarly articles describing the nature and importance of empathic accuracy. Chapters deal with topics including the evolutionary and social factors that contribute to empathy, the psychological characteristics and influences that affect empathic ability, and the relationship between empathy and gender.

Luntz, Frank. *What Americans Really Want . . . Really: The Truth About Our Hopes, Dreams, and Fears*. New York: Hyperion, 2009.
Luntz takes us on a guided tour of what Americans really think about many things. His findings are based on more than 25,000 interviews and surveys that he conducted over the last 20 years. Luntz attacks several of American culture's sacred cows and presents a set of counter-intuitive, but highly insightful and timely, observations about what motivates Americans to communicate and behave the way they do.

Macrae, C. Neil, Charles Stangor, and Miles Hewstone, eds. *Stereotypes and Stereotyping*.
New York: Guilford, 1996.
This collection of scholarly works provides a comprehensive look at stereotyping. Chapters deal with the formation and development of stereotypes, how stereotyping operates in everyday interaction, and how to minimize the harmful effects of stereotyping.

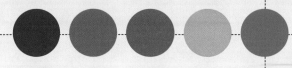

O'Brien, Jodi, and Peter Kollock, eds. *The Production of Reality: Essays and Readings on Social Interaction*, 3rd edn. Thousand Oaks, CA: Pine Forge Press, 2001.
Part III of this fascinating collection includes six selections describing how the self is a product of social interaction. Part IV offers five readings illustrating how the self-fulfilling prophecy operates in a variety of contexts ranging from first impressions in social situations to mental institutions.

Rapaille, Clothaire. *The Culture Code: An Ingenious Way to Understand Why People Around the World Live and Buy As They Do.* New York: Broadway, 2007.
Rapaille left a successful practice as a psychologist helping autistic children and as a psychoanalyst to troubled people to apply his knowledge and skills to the problem of 'decoding' American culture. In this book he offers insightful and convincing analyses of why people around the world relate to one another differently and why certain things make us feel comfortable and secure while others repel us. He examines the large areas of concern for most people: dating, sexuality, prestige, food, intergenerational communication, and safety, among many others.

Walther, Joseph B., and Malcolm R. Parks. 'Cues Filtered Out, Cues Filtered In: Computer-Mediated Communication and Relationships', in Mark L. Knapp and John A. Daly, eds, *Handbook of Interpersonal Communication*, 3rd edn. Thousand Oaks, CA: Sage, 2002.
The authors point out some ways in which computer-mediated communication differs from face-to-face interaction. A section of this reading focuses on how identity management operates in online relationships.

📓 Study Questions

1. Describe a situation in which a Canadian and someone visiting from another country might have incompatible narratives.
2. Discuss how common perceptual tendencies (pages 40–6), situational factors (pages 46–8), and cultural differences (pages 48–50) can lead to friction. How can greater empathy help people communicate more smoothly?
3. Explain some of the factors (personal and cultural) that have helped shape your self-concept.
4. Using yourself or someone you know as an example, describe how the process of identity management operates during an average day. Discuss the ethics of presenting multiple identities.

After studying the material in this chapter . . .

You should understand:

- the symbolic, person-centred nature of language;
- the phonological, syntactic, semantic, and pragmatic rules that govern language;
- the ways in which language shapes and reflects attitudes;
- the different types of troublesome language and the skills required to deal with each;
- the gender and non-gender factors that characterize the speech of men and women; and
- the verbal styles that distinguish various cultures, and the effect that language can have on worldview.

You should be able to:

- discuss how you and others use phonological, syntactic, semantic, and pragmatic rules and how these rules affect the way a message is understood;
- identify at least two ways in which language has shaped your attitudes;
- identify at least two ways in which language reflects your attitudes;
- recognize and suggest alternatives for equivocal language, slang and jargon, relative terms, and overly abstract language;
- identify and suggest alternatives for fact–inference and fact–opinion confusion and for emotive statements;
- suggest appropriate alternatives for unnecessary or misleading euphemisms and equivocal statements; and
- identify the degree to which your speech reflects gender stereotypes and then reflect on the effect your cultural speech patterns have on others.

Language

Chapter Highlights

Language has several important characteristics:

- It is symbolic.
- Its meanings reside in the minds of people, not in words themselves.
- It is governed by several types of rules, and understanding those rules helps us understand one another.

Beyond simply expressing ideas, language can be very powerful.

- It can shape our attitudes toward things and toward one another.
- It can reflect the way we feel about things and people.

Some kinds of language can create problems by unnecessarily

- disrupting relationships,
- confusing others, or
- avoiding important information.

Gender plays an important role in the way language operates.

- The content of male and female speech varies somewhat.
- Men and women often have different reasons for communicating.
- Male and female conversational styles vary in some interesting ways.
- Gender isn't always the most important factor shaping language use.

Cultural factors can shape the way we see and understand language.

- Different cultures have different notions of what language styles are and aren't appropriate.
- The language we speak can shape the way we view the world.

At one time or another, every one of us has suffered the limits and traps of language. Even when the words we are using are familiar, it's clear that we often don't use them in ways that allow us to communicate smoothly with one another.

In the following pages we will explore the nature of linguistic communication. By the time you have finished reading this chapter, you will better appreciate the complexity of language, its power to shape our perception of people and events, and its potential for incomplete and inaccurate communication. Perhaps more important, you will be better equipped to use the tool of language more skilfully to improve your everyday interaction.

. . . words strain,
Crack and sometimes break,
under the burden
Under the tension, slip, slide,
perish,
Decay with imprecision, will
not stay in one place,
Will not stay still.

T.S. Eliot,
'Burnt Norton', from *Four Quartets*

language
A collection of symbols, governed by rules and used to convey messages between individuals.

The Nature of Language

Humans speak about 10,000 language varieties.[1] Although most of these sound different from one another, all possess the same characteristics of **language**: a collection of symbols governed by rules and used to convey messages between individuals. A closer look at this definition can both explain how language operates and suggest how we can use it more effectively.

Language Is Symbolic

There's nothing natural about calling your loyal four-pawed companion a 'dog' or the object you're reading right now a 'book'. These two words, like virtually all language, are symbols—arbitrary constructions that represent a communicator's thoughts. Not all linguistic symbols are spoken or written words. Furthermore, speech and writing aren't the only forms of language. Sign language, as 'spoken' by most deaf people, is symbolic in nature and not the pantomime it might seem. There are literally hundreds of different sign languages spoken around the world that represent the same ideas in different ways.[2] These distinct languages include Canadian Sign Language, Langue des signes québécois, British Sign Language, French Sign Language, Danish Sign Language, Chinese Sign Language—even Australian Aboriginal and Mayan sign languages.

'What part of oil lamp next to double squiggle over ox don't you understand?'

Symbols are more than just labels: they are a way of experiencing the world. You can prove this fact by trying a simple experiment.[3] Work up some saliva in your mouth, and then spit it into a glass. Take a good look, and then drink it up. Most people find this process mildly disgusting. But ask yourself why this is so. After all, we swallow our own saliva all the time. The answer arises out of the symbolic labels we use. After the saliva is in the glass, we call it *spit* and think of it in a different way. In other words, our reaction is to the name and the concept, not the thing.

The naming process operates in virtually every situation. How you react to a stranger will depend on the symbols you use to categorize him or her: gay (or straight), religious (or not), attractive (or unattractive), and so on.

Meanings Are in People, Not in Words

Ask a dozen people what the same symbol means, and you are likely to get 12 different answers. Does a Canadian flag bring up associations of peacekeeping missions around the world? Rowdy hockey fans streaming out of bars into the streets after an international victory? Inukshuks, totem poles, and other items associated with the country's Aboriginal populations? Saint-Jean-Baptiste Day parades in Montreal? How about a cross, a crescent, or a menorah: what do they represent? Sunday school? Religious imperialism? The necklace your sister always wears?

As with physical symbols, so with language, the place to look for meaning is not in words themselves but rather in the way people understand them. An unfortunate episode illustrating that truth occurred in Washington, DC, when the city ombudsman described an approach to budget-making as 'niggardly' and some African-American critics accused him of uttering an unforgivable racial slur.[4] Although his defenders pointed out that the word, which means 'miserly', is Scandinavian in origin and has no connection at all with the word it resembles, the incident was a reminder that, correct or not, the meanings that people associate with a word have far more significance than any dictionary definition.

Linguistic theorists C.K. Ogden and I.A. Richards illustrated the fact that meanings are social constructions in their well-known 'triangle of meaning' (Figure 3.1).[5] This model shows that there is only an indirect relationship—indicated by the broken line—between a word and the thing it claims to represent. Some of these 'things', or referents, do not exist in the physical world. For instance, some referents are mythical (such as unicorns), some are no longer tangible (such as Elvis, if he really is dead), and others are abstract ideas (such as love).

Problems arise when we mistakenly assume that others use words in the same way we do. It's possible to have an argument about *environmentalism* without ever realizing that you and the other person are using that term to represent entirely different things. The same goes for *conservative*, *distinct society*, *national health care*, *rock music*, and thousands upon thousands of other words and phrases. Words don't mean; people do—and often in widely different ways.

Despite the potential for linguistic problems, the situation isn't hopeless. We do, after all, communicate with one another reasonably well most of the time. And with enough effort, we can clear up most of the misunderstandings that do occur. The key to more accurate use of language is to avoid assuming that others interpret words the same way we do. In

Man's achievements rest upon the use of symbols . . . we must consider ourselves as a symbolic, semantic class of life, and those who rule the symbols, rule us.

Alfred Korzbyski,
Science and Sanity

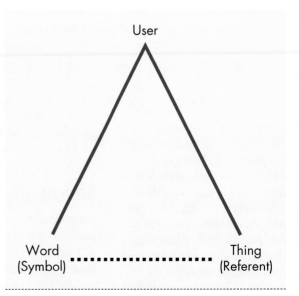

Figure 3.1
Ogden and Richards's Triangle of Meaning

Understanding Communication Technology

First Museum in the World to Introduce an Innovative Mobile Application for BlackBerry Users

. . . The Canadian Museum of Civilization today became the first museum in the world to introduce a BlackBerry application for access to its audioguides and other museum information. This follows on a similar first for an application accessible to iPhone and iPod Touch in December 2009.

Owners of these popular handheld devices now can obtain one-stop access to museum information from anywhere in the world. They can plan a visit to the museum by accessing interactive floor maps, a calendar of events and information about hours of operation, admission fees, and public services.

'The museum is constantly looking for innovative ways to broaden its audience and reach people in Canada and around the world,' said Dr Victor Rabinovitch, president and CEO of the Canadian Museum of Civilization Corporation. 'We are delighted to be the first museum in the world to provide this progressive and convenient technology to the public. The Canadian Museum of Civilization strives to preserve Canadian heritage and to share our country's fabulous story with Canadians and the world.'

The Museum of Civilization's Mobile Application for BlackBerry Bold 9700, developed in partnership with Tristan Interactive of Ottawa, is now available for free on BlackBerry App World in both official languages. 'Tristan's support for the BlackBerry—the North American smartphone market leader—now allows millions of BlackBerry users the best access to museum multimedia. Tristan is proud to be the first in the world to build this technology,' said Chris McLaren, CEO of Tristan Interactive Inc.

In addition to automatic updates about new museum programs and exhibitions, two audioguides, which were previously accessible only on museum-supplied headsets, are now available on these personal handheld devices. Visitors can use their mobile devices to visit two of the museum's largest and most popular exhibition galleries. At the touch of a button, BlackBerry owners have access to Canada Hall, which relays the history of Canada from year 1000 to the present and the First Peoples Hall, which shares with listeners how Canada's First Peoples shaped our country as we now know it. In essence, the history of the foundation of Canada is brought to Canadians and the world through this new application.

. . .

—Canadian Museum of Civilization Press Release, 29 March 2010. Available at civilization.ca/cmc/media/press-releases/2010/first-museum-in-the-world-to-introduce-an-innovative-mobile-application-for-blackberry-users.

> *The problem with defending the purity of the English language is that English is about as pure as a cribhouse whore. We don't just borrow words; on occasion, English has pursued other languages down alleyways to beat them unconscious and rifle their pockets for new vocabulary.*
>
> James Nicoll

truth, successful communication occurs when we negotiate the meaning of a statement.[6] As one French proverb puts it, the spoken word belongs half to the one who speaks it and half to the one who hears.

Language Is Rule-Governed

Languages contain several types of rules. **Phonological rules** govern how words sound when pronounced. For instance, the words *champagne*, *double*, and *occasion* are spelled identically in French and English but are pronounced differently in each language. English is notable for having particularly inconsistent phonological rules, as a few examples illustrate:

He could lead if he would get the lead out.
A farm can produce produce.

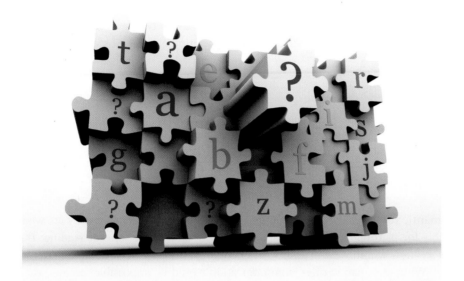

phonological rules
Linguistic rules governing how sounds are combined to form words.

syntactic rules
Linguistic rules that govern the ways in which symbols can be arranged as opposed to the meanings of those symbols.

The dump was so full it had to refuse refuse.
The present is a good time to present the present.
I did not object to the object.
The bandage was wound around the wound.
I shed a tear when I saw the tear in my clothes.

Non-native English speakers are plagued by the apparent anarchy of the language's phonological rules, especially in contrast to languages with highly regularized phonology such as Spanish and German. While those languages rigorously re-spell words as they borrow them from other tongues to ensure a word's pronounced and written form are consistent, English has compiled its vast collection of borrowed words without much concern for consistency.

Phonological rules aren't the only ones that govern the way we use language to communicate. **Syntactic rules** govern the structure of language—the way symbols can be arranged. For example, the rules of English syntax require that most English sentences have a subject, a verb, and an object, in that order. It also prohibits sentences such as 'Have you the cookies brought?', which is a perfectly acceptable word order in German. Although most of us aren't able to describe the syntactic rules that govern our language, it's easy to recognize their existence by noting how odd a statement that violates them appears.

Syntactic rules and pronunciation can vary even within a language. In Canada, for instance, the English language is fairly uniform except in the Atlantic provinces (Newfoundland and Labrador, Nova Scotia, New Brunswick, Prince Edward Island), where Irish, Scottish, Gaelic, and French have heavily influenced spoken English. Quebec French also shows massive regional variation in phonology and syntax. There are as many accents and dialects in the province of Quebec as there are regions. As well, the French spoken in different provinces varies enormously: Franco-Ontarians, Franco-Albertans, Acadians, and many others have significantly different ways of pronouncing words and organizing sentences.

Leet: A derivative of the 80s software piracy scene. Originally 'elite' was used to show status on a BBS [Bulletin Board System]. Commonly the people who cracked the software, or had sysop access on a board would be referred to as Elite. Later it became common to just use 'leet'. With the Internet explosion it was later used to describe hackers as well as crackers. Due to it being great to be known as leet, newbies started adopting the term and using [it] to describe themselves, often with numerical variations. Anyone who considers themselves 'leet' should be able to tell you who/what Razor1911 is, anyone failing to answer this question should be laughed at.

'Wow, those guys that run this new board are leet, they had win 3.1 a week before it came out!'

The Urban Dictionary

Technology has spawned sub-versions of English, each with its own syntactic rules.[7] For example, users of instant messaging on the Internet have devised a streamlined version of English, sometimes called *leet* or *geekspeak*,[8] that speeds up typing in real-time communication (although it probably makes teachers of composition grind their teeth in anguish):[9]

A: Hey

B: r u at home?

A: yup yup

B: ok I'm getting offline now

A: no! why?

B: i need t study for finals u can call me tho bye

A: kbye

Semantic rules deal with the meanings of specific words. Semantic rules are what make it possible for us to agree that 'bikes' are for riding and 'books' are for reading; they also help us to know whom we will and won't encounter when we open doors marked 'men' or 'women'. Without semantic rules, communication would be impossible, because each of us would use symbols in unique ways, unintelligible to one another.

Semantic misunderstandings occur when words can be interpreted in more than one way, as the following humorous headlines prove:

Police Begin Campaign to Run Down Jaywalkers
British Left Waffles on Falkland Islands
Prostitutes Appeal to Pope
Panda Mating Fails; Veterinarian Takes Over
Astronaut Takes Blame for Gas in Spacecraft
New Study of Obesity Looks for Larger Test Group

Pragmatic rules govern how people use language in everyday interaction.[10] Consider the example of an employer telling a First Nations employee to 'Hold the fort while I am away.' It's easy to imagine how the subordinate might be offended by a cultural idiom that the boss didn't think twice about. Scholars of language have pointed out several levels at which the rules each person uses can differ. You can understand these levels by imagining how they would operate in our example:

Each person's self-concept
Employer: Views himself as a nice guy.
Employee: Self-conscious because of historical stereotypes of First Nations people.

The episode in which the comment occurs
Employer: A casual remark upon stepping out of the office.
Employee: A hurtful reminder of the era when the fort was a colonial outpost that had to be held secure against Indigenous 'enemies'.

Perceived relationship
Employer: Views employees like members of the family.
Employee: Depends on boss's goodwill for advancement.

. . . a clever Toronto lawyer was deep into a technical argument before the Supreme Court. His position was dependent upon a close reading of the legal text and turned on the letter of the law. Suddenly the chief justice, Beverley McLachlin, leaned forward and asked the counsel if his argument also worked in French. After all, the law is the law in both languages and a loophole in one tends to evaporate in the other. Only an argument of substance stands up. The lawyer had no idea what to reply.

John Ralston Saul,
A Fair Country

Understanding Diversity
● ● ● ● ● **ENDANGERED LANGUAGES**

Of the six or seven thousand languages spoken in the world today, 90 per cent are in danger of extinction within the next two or three generations.

The situation in which the Mi'kmaq people of Atlantic Canada find themselves is typical of the situation facing many Aboriginal communities everywhere. The Mi'kmaq occupy a reasonably well-defined territory, exercise increasing political autonomy with respect to both the federal and provincial governments, and have a language with a number of mutually understandable dialects. Today, however, that language is perilously close to becoming extinct. Among the greatest obstacles to preserving the Mi'kmaq language is disunity: disunity among those responsible for passing it on through education, and disunity among its speakers. This is in part a systemic problem, stemming from inadequate teaching resources. But it is also a result of the way the colonial period affected Mi'kmaq perceptions, identity, and self-definition.

For centuries it was the policy first of the colonial government, then of the federal and provincial governments, to divide the First Nations by confining them to reserves, banning the celebration of their cultural traditions, and attempting to assimilate their children by placing them in residential schools. This policy served to devalue the Mi'kmaq language and culture while reinforcing the majority English or French worldview, which in many respects conflicted with the Mi'kmaq worldview. In time,

the Mi'kmaq language was largely forgotten, replaced by a language that was not historically linked to Mi'kmaq social life. This new language, which the Mi'kmaq had to use to organize their thoughts and perceptions of the world, was a translated worldview, a hybrid created through the imposition of English or French culture. Without a common language and culture, the people drifted apart—both linguistically and politically.

Today the situation is slowly improving. Academics, politicians, and lobbyists have all agreed that the strategies for preserving endangered Indigenous languages should come from Indigenous communities, not from non-Native 'experts'. There is a push towards openness and economic development, as well as better governance, education, and natural resource stewardship, in Mi'kmaq communities. Young and old alike are working to revive the old ways and adapt them to the modern realities of diverse, multicultural, information-age Canada. The Mi'kmaq are beginning to make peace with their past pains while asserting their rights and moving boldly forward as players in the Canada of tomorrow. The only question that remains is whether they will be doing it in English, French, Mi'kmaq, or a combination of all three.

Question: How do you think communication technologies could help or hinder the preservation of an endangered language such as Mi'kmaq?

Cultural background

Employer: Member of generation in which hurtful comments about First Nations were commonplace.

Employee: Member of generation sensitive to reminders of past wrongs against First Nations.

As this example shows, pragmatic rules don't involve semantic issues, since the meanings of the words themselves are usually understood well by almost everybody. Instead, they involve connotations—the extended meanings of those words.

The Power of Language

On the most obvious level, language allows us to satisfy basic functions such as describing ideas, making requests, and solving problems. But beyond these functions, the way we use language also influences others and reflects our attitudes in more subtle ways, which we will examine now.

Language Shapes Attitudes

The most powerful stimulus for changing minds is not a chemical. Or a baseball bat. It is a word.

George A. Miller

The power of language to shape ideas has been recognized throughout history. The first chapters of the Bible report that Adam's dominion over animals was demonstrated by his being given the power to give them names.[11] As we will now see, our speech—sometimes consciously and sometimes not—shapes others' values, attitudes, and beliefs in a variety of ways.

Naming

'What's in a name?' Juliet asked rhetorically. If Romeo had been a social scientist, he would have answered, 'A great deal.' Research has demonstrated that naming is more than just a simple means of identification: names shape the way others think of us, the way we view ourselves, and the way we act.

At the most fundamental level, some research suggests that even the phonetic sound of a person's name affects the way we regard him or her, at least when we don't have other information available. For example, in Canadian politics, having a name that could be either French or English, such as that of former prime minister Paul Martin, is beneficial because it allows both francophone and anglophone voters to feel comfortable with the candidate. In American politics, names that are simple, appealing, easily pronounced, and rhythmic are judged more favourably than those that are not.[12] Consider the names of the winning candidates in one series of US elections: Sanders beat Pekelis, Rielly defeated Dellwo, Grady outpolled Schumacher, Combs trounced Bernsdorf, and Golden prevailed over Nuffer. Names don't guarantee victory, but in 78 elections studied, 48 outcomes supported the value of having an appealing name.

An excellent contemporary example of the importance of names in politics is First Lady of the United States Michelle Obama's telling of how she was surprised that this man with 'a funny name' asked her out, but that she accepted him as her boyfriend anyhow.

She repeated this story countless times during the Democratic nomination race and the presidential campaign in an effort to neutralize the idea that the name Barack Hussein Obama made her husband alien or threatening, especially to a public dealing with the Iraq War and terrorism. In Canada, which is a more multicultural nation than the United States, there are many politicians whose names indicate origins that are neither British nor French Canadian. Only one has made it to the prime minister's chair thus far—John Diefenbaker, whose name is of German origin.

The Bible's book of Proverbs (22:1) proclaims 'a good name is rather to be chosen than great riches.' Social science research confirms this position.[13] In one study, psychologists asked university students to rate over a thousand names according to their likeability, their masculinity or femininity, and how active or passive they seemed. The names Michael, John, and Wendy were viewed as likable and active and were rated as possessing the masculine or feminine traits of their sex. The names Percival, Isadore, and Alfreda were judged less likable, and their sexual identity was less clear.

Credibility

Scholarly speech is a good example of how speaking style influences perception. We refer to what has been called the Dr Fox hypothesis:[14] 'An apparently legitimate speaker who utters an unintelligible message will be judged competent by an audience in the speaker's area of apparent expertise.' The Dr Fox hypothesis got its name from one Dr Myron L. Fox, who delivered a talk followed by a half-hour discussion on 'Mathematical Game Theory as Applied to Physical Education'. The audience included psychiatrists, psychologists, social workers, and educators. Questionnaires collected after the session revealed that these educated listeners found the lecture clear and stimulating.

Despite his warm reception by this learned audience, Fox was a complete fraud. He was a professional actor whom researchers had coached to deliver a lecture of double-talk—a patchwork of information from a *Scientific American* article mixed with jokes, non sequiturs, contradictory statements, and meaningless references to unrelated topics. When wrapped in a linguistic package of high-level professional jargon, however, the meaningless gobbledy-gook was judged as important information. In other words, the reaction of Fox's audience was based more on the credibility that arose from his use of impressive-sounding language than from the ideas he expressed.

The same principle seems to hold for academic writing.[15] A group of 32 management professors rated material according to its complexity rather than its content. When a message about consumer behaviour was loaded with unnecessary words and long, complex sentences, the professors rated it highly. When the same message was translated into more readable English, with shorter words and clearer sentences, the professors judged the same research as less competent. Steven Pinker, a Canadian cognitive scientist teaching at Harvard, indicated that far more ungrammatical sentences can be found in speeches delivered at academic conferences than in the everyday speech of average people.[16]

Status

In the classic musical *My Fair Lady*, Professor Henry Higgins transforms Eliza Doolittle from a lowly flower seller into a high-society woman by replacing her cockney accent with an upper-crust speaking style. Decades of research have demonstrated that the power of speech to influence status is a fact.[17] Several factors combine to create positive or negative impressions: accent, choice of words, speech rate, and even the apparent age of a speaker. In most cases, speakers of standard language varieties are rated higher than non-standard speakers in a variety of ways: they are viewed as more competent and more self-confident, and the content of their messages is rated more favourably. The unwillingness or inability of a communicator to use the standard dialect fluently can have serious consequences. For instance, studies have shown that speakers of African-American Vernacular English (also known as 'Black English')—a distinctive

> *The name of a man is a numbing blow from which he never recovers.*
>
> Marshall McLuhan,
> *Understanding Media*

"No, this is not Mel's secretary. This is Mel."

Idiom-Proof

After a screening of the rough cut of *Shrek* a few years ago, it was decided there was a problem with the film's title character, a lonely ogre played by Mike Myers. The problem wasn't the dialogue or the animation; it was the accent. Myers, a native of Toronto, had delivered his lines in his regular voice, making the creature a southern Ontario ogre. That just wasn't funny.

Myers decided to re-dub the part in a Scottish brogue that reminded him of the voices his own mother, who was English, used when she read fairy tales to her children. Crowds roared at the Scottish Shrek and were forgiving of instances where the actor, according to at least one critic, lapsed into Canadian.

There are those who might take umbrage at being told their accent isn't worthy of an animated green monster. Canadians are more likely to be grateful that Mike Myers's linguistic passport was read at all. The Canadian dialect is so subtle it is routinely mistaken as non-existent, or at least as indistinguishable from generic American.

Dialects, of course, are comprised equally of accent and idioms. There isn't a uniform Canadian accent, just as there isn't a uniform British, or American, or Indian accent. But there are definite characteristics to Canadian speech, and they show very little variation from the Ottawa River to the Pacific. Generally, Mainland Canadian speech is most similar to the speech of the American West. Our speech is clipped and evenly cadenced. Linguists also write about the phenomenon of 'Canadian raising', whereby the initial vowel element

in certain vowel clusters is spoken higher in the mouth than in American versions, with a shorter glide to the second element. We say 'couch' with an 'ouch' and our 'house' sounds like 'lout', rather than 'loud'. We are rumoured to say 'ahboot' for 'about', though that may simply be how others hear these high and fast diphthongs.

According to Henry Rogers, a linguist at the University of Toronto, the Canadian accent is actually moving further away from the American. 'Something called the Northern Cities Vowel Shift is taking place in the US,' he says. 'Vowels are sort of shifting in one direction, whereas in Canada they're shifting in the other direction.' And there are linguists, at the McGill Dialectology and Sociolinguistics Lab, for instance, who study regional variation in pronunciation within Canadian speech.

Still, not all experts are convinced that Canadian English is faring well. There are academic papers charting its disappearance. A few hard-headed linguists even declare the very notion of a Canadian dialect a myth, fabricated to bolster a wobbly national identity.

As for the other component of dialect, there is evidence of distinctly Canadian expressions. The most recent *Collins English Dictionary* includes some 150 new 'Canadian' terms. 'Status Indian' and 'equalization payment' probably won't excite linguistic pride. But a 'saw-off', for a compromise, and 'idiot strings', for the ties that keep children's mittens attached to their coats, are lively enough. Then there are our drinking words: a 'two-four' and a 'twenty-

dialect with its own accent, grammar, syntax, and semantic rules—are rated as less intelligent, professional, capable, socially acceptable, and employable by speakers of standard English.[18] Another study found that some First Nations women in British Columbia felt 'invalidated' by their verbal interactions with the health care system.[19]

Studies have also shown that people learning English as a second language struggle to overcome the perception that the content of their messages is less credible because they are not fluent. Suzanne Romaine, a sociolinguist, reports that when kindergarten students in Toronto were asked who was most likely to succeed and who was most likely to fail, those who had English as a second language were regarded as twice as likely to fail as native English speakers.[20] She explains that this leads to a vicious cycle where the children are less frequently encouraged to participate and thus have fewer chances to practise speaking English.

sixer' and a 'mickey' of rye, the latter often sipped out of a brown paper bag.

That said, Canadian English, at least from Ottawa westward, can't come close to Irish or Australian for wit and inventiveness. It can't even rival the other major Canadian dialect, the one belonging to Newfoundland. Some of this, according to Charles Boberg, the director of the McGill dialectology lab, has to do with dialect variation. 'Old, densely populated areas like England or the eastern US have a lot of dialect variation,' he says. 'More recently and sparsely settled regions, like western Canada and the western US, exhibit more homogeneity over large areas.'

We drift toward the pronunciation that surrounds us, and cities, where most Canadians now live, aren't necessarily the best places to preserve existing accents, or acquire new ones.

On Canada's East Coast, on the other hand, geographical isolation, along with deep Scottish and Irish roots, ensured that the pronunciation would remain distinct from that of the more heterogeneous middle of the country. There are entire dictionaries that catalogue the vocabularies of Prince Edward Island and Nova Scotia's Cape Breton and South Shore. And out on the Rock, the speech remains musical and loose and nicely barbed.

An off-the-cuff remark by the Newfoundland comedian Mary Walsh, who declared someone to be 'still having the mark of the bucket on her arse', started the television critic John Doyle wondering how she gets away with it. Doyle, who recalled the insult from his own Irish childhood, concluded that the line would have been unacceptable on Canadian TV

'if it had been delivered in less colourful language, and without the accent'.

The question is, do most Canadians want to leave such a strong impression? The linguistic impulses of most of the English-speaking nation have tended toward moderation and, sometimes, disguise. Generations of Canadian actors and newsreaders have counted on both to launch careers in the States.

There could also be a class dimension to how the majority of us talk. Middle-class, urban societies tend to avoid strong or idiosyncratic speech, finding such verbal energy unruly. For all their appeal, regional idioms, especially those from the historically poorer 'Celtic' regions of Canada, with their culturally ingrained admiration of wordplay and irreverence, have made scant impact on the wider nation. Most of the country hasn't taken into its collective mouth 'having a scoff' for eating a meal, or being 'stogged' for being stuffed up; it doesn't declare, about blackflies, 'If you kill one, 50 more come to its funeral.' Few Manitobans, say, delight in explaining that 'scluttery' means fatty, or that a guy who has 'chowdered it' has messed something up.

If we did, perhaps Mike Myers would have stayed with his Canadian accent. Shrek, after all, would have made a fine Newfoundland ogre.

—*Charles Foran,* The Walrus, *April/May 2004*

Questions: Do you feel that you have an accent? How does your accent reflect your identity? Do you feel more or less Canadian because of your accent? Or does your accent make you identify more with your specific town, province or country of origin?

Sexism and Racism

By now it should be clear that the power of language to shape attitudes goes beyond individual cases and influences how we perceive entire groups of people. For example, Casey Miller and Kate Swift argue that some aspects of language suggest women are of lower status than men. They contend that, except for words referring by definition to females, such as *mother* and *girl*, English defines many non-sexual concepts as male. Most dictionaries, in fact, define *effeminate* as the opposite of *masculine*, although the opposite of *feminine* is closer to *unfeminine*. They also argue that incorrect use of the pronoun *he* to refer to both men and women can have damaging results:

On the television screen, a teacher of first-graders who has just won a national award is describing her way of teaching. 'You take each child where you find him,' she says. 'You watch to see what he's interested in, and then you build on his interests.'

Bilingualism or Multilingualism for Canada?

When the federal government passed the new Official Languages Act in 1988, the legislation had three purposes. First, it was designed to ensure respect for English and French as the official languages of Canada and to guarantee equality of status, rights, and privileges in all federal institutions. Second, it set out the powers, duties, and functions of federal institutions with respect to those languages. Third, it mandated that the federal government support the development of English- and French-speaking minority communities and generally advance the equality of status and use of the English and French languages within Canadian society (ocol-clo.gc.ca/legislation/ola_llo.asp?Lang=English).

This was a big step for Canada, enshrining language rights from sea to sea and laying the groundwork for the preservation of French as a living language of work and social life across the country. The Act was quite controversial in western Canada, where tiny francophone minorities were granted the right to receive all communication in French. It was also controversial in Quebec, where the provincial government saw it as an attempt to impose English as one of the official languages of that province. However, beyond the occasional flare-up of anti-bilingualism sentiment in isolated parts of the country since 1988, the Act is generally considered to have been successful in promoting the use of both official languages throughout Canada. It has also enabled francophone Canadians to feel at home anywhere in Canada, encouraging a sense of belonging confidence that was not possible in more oppressive times.

The Official Languages Act has also had an interesting effect among citizens for whom neither English nor French is a first language. Children of immigrant families who speak a language other than French or English at home are now exposed to both French and English at school. The result is not bilingualism but multilingualism.

Many supporters of Aboriginal culture and language, however, object to the Official Languages Act on the grounds that it excludes the languages of Canada's other founding peoples. They argue that Indigenous languages should be privileged as official languages like French and English. This has raised the hackles of large language minorities such as the Chinese-Canadian community, whose lobbyists sometimes argue for a regional bilingualism model: since people of Chinese origin make up a large part of the population of British Columbia, for example, Cantonese or Mandarin should be given official language status in that province.

Most of the problems arising from the multiplicity of linguistic and ethnic identities in Canada will probably resolve themselves over time. As immigrant populations become more settled in Canada, they will likely blend and fade into the majority culture, just as the Italian community became integrated into the fabric of life in Canada's great cities.

The issue of Indigenous language rights is much thornier, however. It is tangled with a history of oppression, discrimination, and pain that cannot be ignored.

Questions: How do you think Canada's linguistic identity will evolve over the next 50 years? Will a policy of official bilingualism still make sense? Will Canada move to a more pragmatic model of 'regional bilingualism'? What will become of Native languages? Would official recognition preserve them?

A five-year-old looking at the program asks her mother, 'Do only boys go to that school?'

'No,' her mother begins, 'she's talking about girls too, but—'

But what? The teacher being interviewed on television is speaking correct English. What can the mother tell her daughter about why a child, in any generalization, is always *he* rather than *she*? How does a five-year-old comprehend the generic personal pronoun?[21]

Although French has a separate, neutral pronoun, *on*, to refer to an individual whose sex is not known, it still offers many examples of sexist usage. Fabienne Baider, a sociolinguist, argues that in French, adjectives that would have a positive connotation when used to modify a masculine noun have a very negative connotation when used to modify a feminine noun. For example, to call a man 'galant' means that he is chivalrous and kind, whereas a 'galant' woman is one who is morally loose.[22]

It's usually easy to find alternatives for sexist language. For example, the term *mankind* may be replaced by *humanity*, *human beings*, *human race*, or *people*; the adjective *man-made* may be replaced by *artificial*, *manufactured*, or *synthetic*; and *manpower* may be replaced by *human power*, *workers*, or *workforce*. Likewise,

- *Firemen* may be called *firefighters*.
- *Actresses* may be called *actors*.
- *Foremen* may be called *supervisors*.
- *Policemen* and *policewomen* may be called *police officers*.
- *Waitresses* may be called *servers*.
- *Stewardesses* may be called *flight attendants*.

The use of labels for racist purposes has a long and ugly history. Names have been used to stigmatize groups that other groups have disapproved of.[23] By using derogatory terms to label some people, the out-group is set apart and pictured in an unfavourable light. In a report about racial profiling for the Ontario Human Rights Commission,[24] a young Native man, injured during an arrest, is quoted as saying:

After that [the arrest], I grew up with a lot of hatred towards the cops, especially white cops. And I forgot to mention also that they used racial slurs against us as they were beating us against the fence.

Another young man, also injured during an arrest, said:

It is really hard when I teach my kids to have respect and to do what is right, and then to get treated like that from the court system and put down, you know, they are not being given a fair chance.

The power of racist language to shape attitudes is difficult to avoid, even when it is obviously offensive. In one study, experimental subjects who heard a derogatory label used against a member of a minority group expressed annoyance at this sort of slur; despite their disapproval, the negative emotional terms did have an impact.[25] Not only did the subjects rate the minority individual's competence lower when that person performed poorly, but they also found fault with others who associated socially with the minority person—even members of the subject's own ethnic group. An excellent example of racist usage is the common practice of using expressions that are offensive to Indigenous people without even knowing it. Calling someone 'Chief' is very derogatory to an Indigenous person because it can be interpreted as a mocking reference to an Indigenous leader.

COMMUNICATION ON-SCREEN

My Fair Lady (1964)
Directed by George Cukor.

In this Academy Award-winning musical, linguistics professor Henry Higgins (Rex Harrison) takes on the professional challenge of his life: teaching cockney flower seller Eliza Doolittle (Audrey Hepburn) to masquerade as royalty by learning proper elocution.

The story of Higgins and Doolittle originated as George Bernard Shaw's 1912 stage comedy *Pygmalion*—itself loosely based on an ancient Greek myth by the same name—and had previously been adapted into an acclaimed non-musical film in 1938. Shaw's play has since inspired countless other remakes, ranging from the 1990 film *Pretty Woman* to a 2001 episode of *Family Guy*. *My Fair Lady* is among the best at illustrating—albeit in a romanticized manner—Shaw's original message about the importance of language as a marker of social status.

The only jobs for which no man is qualified are human incubators and wet nurse. Likewise, the only job for which no woman is or can be qualified is sperm donor.

Wilma Scott Heide

TABLE 3.1 Powerless Language

Type of Usage	Example
Hedges	'I'm kinda disappointed . . .' 'I think we should . . .' 'I guess I'd like to . . .'
Hesitations	'Uh, can I have a minute of your time?' 'Well, we could try this idea . . .' 'I wish you would—er—try to be on time.'
Intensifiers	'So that's how I feel . . .' 'I'm not very hungry.'
Polite forms	'Excuse me, sir . . .'
Tag questions	'It's about time we got started, isn't it?' 'Don't you think we should give it another try?'
Disclaimers	'I probably shouldn't say this, but . . .' 'I'm not really sure, but . . .'

Language Reflects Attitudes

Besides shaping the way we view ourselves and others, language reflects our attitudes. Feelings of control, attraction, commitment, responsibility—all these and more are reflected in the way we use language.

Power

Communication researchers have identified a number of language patterns that add to, or detract from, a speaker's ability to influence others and that reflect how a speaker feels about his or her degree of control over a situation.[26] Table 3.1 summarizes some of these findings by listing several types of 'powerless' language.

You can see the difference between powerful and powerless language by comparing the following statements:

1. Excuse me, sir, I hate to say this, but I . . . uh . . . I guess I won't be able to turn in the assignment on time. I had a personal emergency and . . . well . . . it was just impossible to finish it by today. I'll have it in your mailbox on Monday, okay?
2. I won't be able to turn in the assignment on time. I had a personal emergency, and it was impossible to finish it by today. I'll have it in your mailbox on Monday.

Although the powerless speech described in Table 3.1 can often lead to unsatisfying results, it would be a mistake to assume that it's always best to sound as powerful as you can. Along with gaining compliance, another common conversational goal is to build a supportive, friendly relationship, and sharing power with the other person can help you in this regard. For this reason, many everyday statements will contain a mixture of powerful speech and powerless speech. Our student–teacher example illustrates how combining the two can help the student get what he wants while staying on good terms with the instructor:

> Excuse me, Professor Sévigny. I want you to know that I won't be able to turn in the assignment on time. I had a personal emergency, and it was impossible to finish it by today. I'll definitely have it in your mailbox on Monday.

The Language of Oppression

Whether or not the instructor finds the excuse acceptable, it's clear that this last statement combines the best features of powerful speech and powerless speech, namely self-assurance and goodwill.

Simply counting the number of powerful or powerless statements won't always reveal who has the most control in a relationship. Social rules often mask the real distribution of power. Sociolinguist Deborah Tannen describes how politeness can be a face-saving way of delivering an order:

> I hear myself giving instructions to my assistants without actually issuing orders: 'Maybe it would be a good idea to . . .'; 'It would be great if you could . . .'; all the while

The power which comes from names and naming is related directly to the power to define others—individuals, races, sexes, ethnic groups. Our identities, who and what we are, how others see us, are greatly affected by the names we are called and by the words with which we are labelled. The names, labels, and phrases employed to 'identify' a people may in the end determine their survival.

Haig A. Bosmajian

knowing that I expect them to do what I've asked right away [. . .] . This rarely creates problems, though, because the people who work for me know that there is only one reason I mention tasks—because I want them done. I like giving instructions in this way; it appeals to my sense of what it means to be a good person [. . .] taking others' feelings into account.[27]

As this quote suggests, high-status speakers often realize that politeness is an effective way to get their needs met while protecting the face of the less powerful person. The importance of achieving both content goals and relational goals helps explain why a mixture of powerful speech and polite speech is usually most effective.[28] Of course, if the other person misinterprets politeness for weakness, it may be necessary to shift to a more powerful speaking style.

Powerful speech that gets the desired results in mainstream North American and European culture doesn't succeed everywhere with everyone.[29] In Japan, saving face for others is an important goal, so communicators from that country tend to speak in ambiguous terms and use hedge words and qualifiers. In most Japanese sentences the verb comes at the end of the sentence so the 'action' part of the statement can be postponed. The traditional culture of the Mi'kmaq First Nation, with its strong emphasis on the other, makes a priority of using language to create harmony in interpersonal relationships rather than taking a firm or oppositional stance in order to make others feel more at ease. This focus on the other is so ingrained in Mi'kmaq that, as Canadian researchers Danielle Cyr and Alexandre Sévigny point out, the conventional ordering of grammatical persons in English (where the 'first person' is *I*, the 'second person' *you*) does not apply in Mi'kmaq grammar.[30] Koreans are another cultural group who prefer 'indirect' to 'direct' speech.

Affiliation

Power isn't the only way language reflects the status of relationships. Language can also be a way of building and showing solidarity with others. An impressive body of research has demonstrated that communicators who want to show affiliation with one another adapt their speech in a variety of ways, including their choice of vocabulary, rate of talking, number and placement of pauses, and level of politeness.[31] On an individual level, close friends and lovers often develop special terms that serve as a way of signifying their relationship.[32] Using a shared vocabulary sets these people apart from others, reminding themselves and the rest of the world of their relationship. The same process works among members of larger groups, ranging from street gangs to military personnel. Communication researchers call this linguistic accommodation **convergence**.

When two or more people feel equally positive about one another, their linguistic convergence will be mutual. But when communicators want or need the approval of others they often adapt their speech to suit the others' style, trying to say the 'right thing' or speak in a

convergence
Accomodating one's speaking style to another person, who usually is desirable or has higher status.

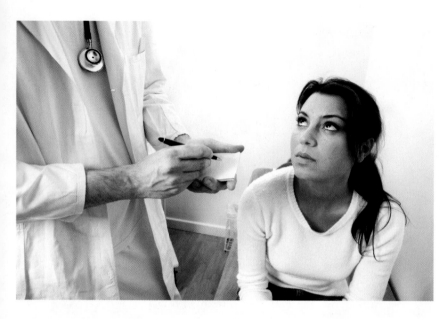

divergence

A linguistic strategy in which speakers emphasize differences between their communicative style and others' in order to create distance.

way that will help them fit in. We see this process when immigrants who want to gain the rewards of material success in a new culture strive to master the prevalent language. Likewise, employees who seek advancement tend to speak more like their superiors: supervisors adopt the speech style of managers, and managers converge toward their bosses.

The principle of speech accommodation works in reverse, too. Communicators who want to set themselves apart from others adopt the strategy of **divergence**, speaking in a way that emphasizes their difference from others. For example, members of an ethnic group, even though fluent in the dominant language, might use their own language variety as a way of showing solidarity with one another—a sort of 'us against them' strategy. British-born black people of Caribbean descent, for instance, have adopted a vernacular that celebrates their ancestry and separates them from the white majority.[33] Divergence also operates in other settings. A physician or an attorney who wants to establish credibility with her client might speak formally and use professional jargon to create a sense of distance. The implicit message here is 'I'm different from (and more knowledgeable than) you.'

Attraction and Interest

Social customs discourage us from expressing like or dislike in many situations. Only an idiot would respond to the question 'What do you think of the cake I baked for you?' by saying, 'It's terrible.' Bashful or cautious suitors might not admit their attraction to a potential partner. Yet even when people are reluctant to speak candidly, the language they use can suggest their degree of interest in or attraction toward a person, object, or idea. Morton Wiener and Albert Mehrabian outline a number of linguistic clues that reveal these attitudes:[34]

- **Demonstrative pronoun choice:** saying _These_ people want our help (positive) versus _Those_ people want our help (less positive)
- **Negation:** saying It's _good_ (positive) versus It's _not bad_ (less positive)
- **Sequential placement:** saying _Dick_ and Jane (where Dick is more important) versus _Jane_ and Dick (where Jane is more important)

It's worth noting that sequential placement isn't always significant. You may put 'toilet bowl cleaner' at the top of your shopping list simply because it's in aisle 1 of the grocery store, while 'ice cream', further down on your list, is in aisle 9.

Responsibility

In addition to suggesting the extent of a speaker's liking or appreciation for a person or thing, language can reveal the speaker's willingness to accept responsibility for a message. Consider the following ways of accepting—or passing off—responsibility:

- **'It' versus 'I' statements:** saying *It's not finished* (less responsible) versus *I haven't finished it* (more responsible)
- **'You' versus 'I' statements:** saying *Sometimes you make me angry* (less responsible) versus *Sometimes I get angry when you do that* (more responsible); 'I' statements are more likely to generate positive reactions from others[35]
- **'But' statements:** saying *It's a good idea, but it won't work* or *You're really terrific, but I think we ought to spend less time together* (*but* cancels everything that went before the word)
- **Questions versus statements:** saying *Do you think we ought to do that?* (less responsible) versus *I don't think we ought to do that* (more responsible)

Troublesome Language

Besides being a blessing that enables us to live together, language can be something of a curse. We have all known the frustration of being misunderstood, and most of us have been baffled by another person's overreaction to an innocent comment. In the following pages we will look at several kinds of troublesome language, with the goal of helping you communicate in a way that makes matters better instead of worse.

The Language of Misunderstandings

The most obvious language problems are semantic: they occur when we simply don't understand others completely or accurately. Most misunderstandings arise from some common problems that are easily remedied—after you recognize them.

Equivocal Language

Equivocal words have more than one dictionary definition. Some equivocal misunderstandings are simple, at least after they are exposed. A nurse once told her patient that he 'wouldn't be needing' the materials he requested from home. He interpreted the statement to mean he was near death; the nurse merely meant that he would be going home soon. A colleague once sent some confidential materials to the wrong person after his boss had instructed him to 'send them to Richard'—without specifying which Richard. Some equivocal misunderstandings can be particularly embarrassing, as one woman recalls:

> In the fourth grade the teacher asked the class what a period was. I raised my hand and shared everything I had learned about girls' getting their period. But he was talking about the dot at the end of a sentence. Oops![36]

Equivocal misunderstandings can have serious consequences. Communication researchers Michael Motley and Heidi Reeder suggest that equivocation at least partly explains why men sometimes persist in attempts to become physically intimate when women have expressed unwillingness to do so.[37] Interviews and focus groups with university students revealed that women often used ambiguous phrases to say 'no' to a man's sexual advances, especially when they hoped to see the man again; these phrases include 'I'm

equivocal words
Words that have more than one dictionary definition.

confused about this,' 'I'm not sure that we're ready for this yet,' 'Are you sure you want to do this?', 'Let's be friends,' and even 'That tickles.' (The researchers found that women were more likely to give a direct response when they wanted to end the relationship.) Whereas women viewed indirect statements as equivalent to saying 'no', men were more likely to interpret them as less clear-cut requests to stop. The researchers concluded that 'male/female misunderstandings are not so much a matter of males hearing resistance messages as "go", but rather their not hearing them as "stop".' Under the law, *any instruction to stop, even an ambiguous instruction, means stop*, and anyone who argues otherwise can be in for serious legal problems.

Relative Words

Relative words gain their meaning by comparison. For example, is the school you attend large or small? This depends on what you compare it to: alongside a campus like that of the University of Toronto, with its enrollment of over 68,000 students, it probably looks small; on the other hand, compared to a smaller institution, it might seem quite large. In the same way, relative words like *fast* and *slow*, *smart* and *stupid*, *short* and *long* depend for their meaning on what they're compared to. (In some movie theatres, a 'large' bag of popcorn is the smallest you can buy; the other sizes are 'extra large' and 'jumbo'.)

Some relative words are so common that we mistakenly assume that they have a clear meaning. In one study, graduate students were asked to assign numerical values to terms such as *doubtful*, *toss-up*, *likely*, *probable*, *good chance*, and *unlikely*.[38] There was a tremendous variation in the meaning of most of these terms. For example, the responses for *possible* ranged from 0 to 99 per cent. A *good chance* meant between 35 and 90 per cent, whereas *unlikely* fell between 0 and 40 per cent.

Using relative words without explaining them can lead to communication problems. Have you ever responded to someone's question about the weather by saying it was warm, only to find out that what was warm to you was cold to the other person? Or have you followed a friend's advice and gone to a 'cheap' restaurant, only to find that it was twice as expensive as you expected? Have you been disappointed to learn that classes you've heard were 'easy' turned out to be hard, that journeys you were told would be 'short' were long, that 'unusual' ideas were really quite ordinary? The problem in each case came from failing to anchor the relative word used to a more precise or measurable word.

Slang and Jargon

Slang is language used by a group of people whose members belong to a similar subculture or other group. Some slang is related to specialized interests and activities. For instance, cyclists who talk about 'bonking' are referring to running out of energy. Fans of hip-hop and rap know that 'bling' refers to jewellery and a 'whip' is a nice-looking car.

Other slang consists of regionalisms—terms that are understood by people who live in one geographic area but that are incomprehensible to outsiders. This sort of use illustrates how slang defines insiders and outsiders, creating a sense of identity and solidarity.[39] For instance, many southern Ontarians spend their weekends or summers in 'cottage country', but if you live in northern Ontario or Manitoba, you might call your summer retreat a 'camp'. Western Canadians call their cottages 'cabins', while English-speaking Quebecers prefer the term 'chalet'. In Newfoundland and Labrador and in parts of the Maritimes, a summer residence—even a luxurious one—may be called a 'shack', while the same dwelling in Cape Breton may be referred to as a 'bungalow'.[40]

relative words
Words that gain their meaning by comparison.

slang
Language used by a group of people whose members belong to a similar co-culture or other group.

In the East End of London, England, cockney dialect uses rhyming words as substitutes for everyday expressions: 'bacon and eggs' for 'legs', and 'Barney Rubble' for 'trouble'. If you've ever referred to the derisive spitting noise made with the tongue and lips as a 'raspberry', you've used rhyming slang, though you might not have known it: 'raspberry' is short for 'raspberry tart', rhyming slang for 'fart'. This sort of use also illustrates how slang can be used to identify insiders and outsiders: with enough shared rhyming, slang users can talk about outsiders without the clueless outsiders knowing that they are the subject of conversation ('Lovely set of bacons, eh?', or 'Stay away from him—he's Barney.').

Slang can also be age-related. Most university students know that 'sick' is used to signal approval or appreciation (as in 'He pulled off a 720 Mctwist that was just sick'), not illness or disgust, as their parents are more likely to assume. Canadian students know that a 'bird course' is one that shouldn't be too difficult to pass.

Almost everyone uses some sort of **jargon**: the specialized vocabulary that functions as a kind of shorthand among people with common backgrounds and experiences. Snowboarders have their own language to describe manoeuvres: 'ollie', 'fakie', and 'mute', to name just a few. Some jargon consists of acronyms—initials of terms that are combined to form a word. Canada's intelligence service is known as CSIS (pronounced 'see-siss'); Canadian communications academics are forever pursuing grants from a government body called SSHRC (pronounced 'sherk'); and English-language learners will be familiar with LINC (pronounced like 'link') programs offering Language Instruction for Newcomers to Canada.

The digital age has spawned its own vocabulary of jargon. For instance, computer users know that a 'Wi-Fi' hotspot will give them wireless Internet access. Some jargon goes beyond being descriptive and conveys attitudes. For example, cynics in the high-tech world sometimes refer to being fired from a job as being 'uninstalled'. They talk dismissively about the non-virtual world as the 'carbon community', to books and newspapers as 'treeware', and to the brain as 'wetware'. Some technical support staffers talk of 'banana problems', meaning those that could be figured out by monkeys, as in 'This is a two-banana problem at worst.'[41]

Jargon can be a valuable kind of shorthand for people who understand its use. The trauma team in a hospital emergency ward can save time, and possibly lives, by speaking in shorthand, referring to 'emerg' (the emergency room), 'GSWs' (gunshot wounds), 'chem 7' lab tests, and so on, but the same specialized vocabulary that works so well among insiders can mystify family members of the patient, who don't understand the jargon. The same confusion may be experienced by bank customers, who, on any trip to their local branch, are likely to encounter a dizzying array of acronyms, including 'CSB' (Canada Savings

Slang is a language that rolls up its sleeves, spits on its hands, and goes to work.

Carl Sandburg

jargon

The specialized vocabulary that is used as a kind of shorthand by people with common backgrounds and experiences.

COMMUNICATION ON-SCREEN

Firefly (2002–03)
Created by Joss Whedon.

In his first two television series, *Buffy the Vampire Slayer* and *Angel*, Joss Whedon developed a reputation for turning out scripts stuffed with his own distinctive brand of quirky dialogue. His third pushed into more peculiar territory still. *Firefly*—which ran just 13 episodes and prompted the follow-up feature film *Serenity*—was, put simply, a western set in outer space in the distant future. And not just any old distant future but one where China is co-dominant with America in shaping humanity's cultural melting pot. Accordingly, *Firefly's* dialogue is at times barely written in English at all but is a sort of pidgin blending hillbilly yokelisms, smatterings of Mandarin, and completely fabricated terms that are evidently period slang.

What's fascinating is how eminently comprehensible it all is. Context alone makes it quite clear what functions slang terms like 'gorram', 'backbirth', and 'shiny' serve in this future. Whedon consciously chose not to subtitle the Mandarin so as to make its incorporation into English speech all the more seamless, and the spurts of Mandarin that do crop up—often rather colourful expletives that would make for some dicey subtitling anyway—hardly impact the overall lucidity of the onscreen communication. In making its manner of communication so exotic, *Firefly* achieves that sense of 'otherworldliness' so central to science fiction far more immersively than any number of rubber-foreheaded extras could achieve.

Bond), 'GIC' (Guaranteed Investment Certificate), 'RRSP' (Registered Retirement Savings Plan), 'RESP' (Registered Educational Savings Plan), 'CPP' (Canada Pension Plan), and many more.

Misunderstandings can arise when insiders in a particular industry use their own language with people who don't share the same vocabulary. Jeffrey Katzman of the William Morris Agency's Hollywood office experienced this sort of problem when he met with members of a Silicon Valley computer firm to discuss a joint project:

> When he used the phrase 'in development', he meant a project that was as yet merely an idea. When the techies used it, on the other hand, they meant designing a specific game or program. Ultimately, says Katzman, he had to bring in a blackboard and literally define his terms. 'It was like when the Japanese first came to Hollywood,' he recalls. 'They had to use interpreters, and we did too.'[42]

Overly Abstract Language

Most objects, events, and ideas can be described with varying degrees of specificity. Consider the material you are reading right now. You could call it:

- a book,
- a textbook,
- a communication textbook,
- *Understanding Human Communication*,
- Chapter 3 of *Understanding Human Communication*,
- page 102 of Chapter 3 of *Understanding Human Communication*, and so on.

abstraction ladder
A range of more to less abstract terms describing an event or object.

abstract language
Language that lacks specificity or does not refer to observable behaviour or other sensory data.

In each case your description would be more and more specific. Semanticist S.I. Hayakawa created an **abstraction ladder** to describe this process.[43] This ladder consists of a number of descriptions of the same thing. Lower items focus specifically on the person, object, or event, whereas higher terms are generalizations that include the subject as a member of a larger class. To talk about 'university', for example, is more abstract than to talk about a particular school.

Higher-level abstractions are helpful because without them language would be too cumbersome to be useful. It's faster, easier, and more useful to talk about 'Europe' than to list all of the countries on that continent. In the same way, using relatively abstract terms like *friendly* or *smart* can make it easier to describe people than listing their specific actions.

Abstract language—speech that refers to observable events or objects—serves a second, less obvious function. At times it allows us to avoid confrontations by deliberately

Understanding Communication Technology

E-mail, IM, and Texting Abbreviations

E-mail users have coined numerous abbreviations that enable them to insert common phrases into their correspondence quickly and easily. Many of these have been adopted with enthusiasm by cellphone users, who depend on the brevity of this kind of shorthand to make text messaging as quick and efficient as possible. Anyone who is accomplished at instant messaging (IM) will be familiar with most, if not all, of the abbreviations below. Notice that several of them (such as <G>, LOL, ROTFL) are specifically designed to clarify the sender's intentions, which aren't always clear in the sterile format of e-mail or IM text.

AFAIK	As far as I know	IRL	In real life
ASAP	As soon as possible	JK	Just Kidding
BAK	Back at keyboard	LOL	Laughing out loud
BBL	Be back later	LTNC	Long time no chat
BC	Because	NM	Nothing much/Never mind
BF/GF	Boyfriend/Girlfriend	NP	No problem
B4N	Bye for now	NRN	No reply necessary
BRB	Be right back	OMG	Oh my god
BTW	By the way	PLS	Please
F2F	Face to face	POS	Parents over shoulder
FWIW	For what it's worth	POV	Point of view
FYVM	'Frack' you very much	PPL	People
FYI	For your information	ROTFL	Rolling on the floor laughing
<G>	Grinning	RSN	Real slow now
G2G	Got to go	TIA	Thanks in advance
GTGB	Got to go bye	TMI	Too much info
IDK	I don't know	TTFN	Ta ta for now
IIRC	If I remember correctly	TX	Thanks
IM	Instant message	TY	Thank you
IMHO	In my humble opinion	U	You
IMO	In my opinion	U2	You too
INALB	I'm not a lawyer but	<Y>	Yawning
IOW	In other words		

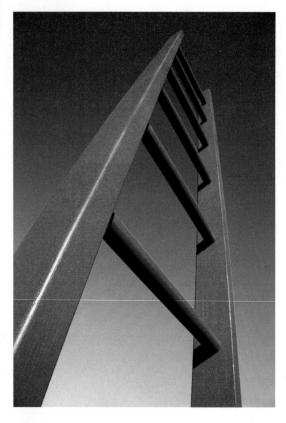

being unclear.[44] Suppose, for example, your boss is enthusiastic about a new approach that you think is a terrible idea. Telling her the truth might seem too risky, but lying—saying 'I think it's a great idea'—wouldn't feel right either. In situations like this, an abstract answer can hint at your true belief without a direct confrontation: 'I don't know. . . . It's sure unusual. . . . It might work.' The same sort of abstract language can help you avoid embarrassing friends who ask for your opinion with questions like 'What do you think of my new haircut?' An abstract response like 'It's really different!' may be easier for you to deliver—and for your friend to receive—than the clear, brutal truth: 'It's really ugly!' We will have more to say about this strategy of equivocation later in this chapter.

Although vagueness does have its uses, highly abstract language can cause several types of problems. The first is *stereotyping.* Consider claims like 'All whites are bigots,' 'Men don't care about relationships,' 'The police are a bunch of goons,' or 'Professors around here care more about their research than they do about students.' Each of these claims ignores the very important fact that abstract descriptions are almost always too general, that they say more than we really mean.

Besides fostering stereotypes, abstract language can lead to the problem of confusing others. Imagine the lack of understanding that results from imprecise language in situations like this:

> A: We never do anything that's fun anymore.
> B: What do you mean?

A: We used to do lots of unusual things, but now it's the same old stuff, over and over.
B: But last week we went on that camping trip, and tomorrow we're going to that party where we'll meet all sorts of new people. Those are new things.

A: That's not what I mean. I'm talking about really unusual stuff.
B: (*becoming confused and a little impatient*): Like what? Taking hard drugs or going over Niagara Falls in a barrel?

A: Don't be stupid. All I'm saying is that we're in a rut. We should be living more exciting lives.
B: Well, I don't know what you want.

behavioural description
An account that refers only to
observable phenomena.

The best way to avoid this sort of overly abstract language is to use **behavioural descriptions** instead (see Table 3.2). Behavioural descriptions move down the abstraction ladder to identify the specific, observable phenomenon being discussed. A thorough description should answer three questions:

1. **Who is involved?** Are you speaking for just yourself or for others as well? Are you talking about a group of people ('the neighbours', 'classmates') or specific individuals ('the people next door with the barking dog', 'Tamsin and Jenny')?
2. **In what circumstances does the behaviour occur?** Where does it occur: everywhere or in specific places (at parties, at work, in public)? When does it occur: when

TABLE 3.2 Abstract and Behavioural Descriptions

	Abstract Description	Behavioural Description			Remarks
		Who Is Involved	In What Circumstances	Specific Behaviours	
Problem	I talk too much.	People I find intimidating	When I want them to like me	I talk (mostly about myself) instead of giving them a chance to speak or asking about their lives.	Behavioural description more clearly identifies behaviours to change.
Goal	I want to be more constructive.	My roommate	When we talk about household duties	Instead of finding fault with her ideas, suggest alternatives that might work.	Behavioural description clearly outlines how to act; abstract description doesn't.
Appreciation	'You've really been helpful lately.'	(Deliver to fellow worker)	'When I've had to take time off work because of personal problems . . .'	'You took my shifts without complaining.'	Give both abstract and behavioural descriptions for best results.
Request	'Clean up your act!'	(Deliver to target person)	'When we're around my family . . .'	'Please don't tell jokes that involve sex.'	Behavioural description specifies desired behaviour.

you're tired or when a certain subject comes up? The behaviour you are describing probably doesn't occur all the time. In order to be understood, you need to pin down what circumstances set this situation apart from other ones.

3. **What behaviours are involved?** Though terms such as *more co-operative* and *helpful* might sound like concrete descriptions of behaviour, they are usually too vague to do a clear job of explaining what's on your mind. Behaviours must be observable, ideally both to you and to others. For instance, moving down the abstraction ladder from the relatively vague term *helpful*, you might come to behaviours such as *does the dishes every other day*, *volunteers to help me with my studies*, or *fixes dinner once or twice a week without being asked*. It's easy to see that terms like these, as opposed to fuzzier abstractions, are easier for both you and others to understand.

Behavioural descriptions can improve communication in a wide range of situations, as Table 3.2 illustrates. Research also supports the value of specific language. One study found that well-adjusted couples had just as many conflicts as poorly adjusted couples, but the way the well-adjusted couples handled their problems was significantly different. Instead of blaming one another, the well-adjusted couples expressed their complaints in behavioural terms.[45]

You can dismiss an abstraction . . . You can mistreat an object . . . But as soon as you come upon a human being, you will be moved to share yourself with him, to care for him. It will be far more difficult to hurt his feelings or ignore him or simply analyze him. It will be almost impossible to kill him or cheer his death, which is why this sort of orientation can put armies out of business.

Alfie Kohn

Disruptive Language

Not all linguistic problems come from misunderstandings. Sometimes people understand one another perfectly and still end up in conflict. Of course, not all disagreements can, or

should be, avoided. But eliminating three bad linguistic habits from your communication repertoire can minimize the kind of clashes that don't need to happen, allowing you to save your energy for the unavoidable and important struggles.

Confusing Facts and Opinions

Factual statements are claims that can be verified as true or false. By contrast, **opinion statements** are based on the speaker's beliefs. Unlike matters of fact, they can never be proved or disproved. Consider a few examples of the difference between factual statements and opinion statements:

factual statement
A statement that can be verified as being true or false.

inferential statement
A conclusion arrived at from an interpretation of evidence.

opinion statement
A statement based on the speaker's beliefs.

Fact	Opinion
Vancouver receives a greater accumulation of rain per year than does Winnipeg.	The climate in Winnipeg is better than in Vancouver.
Wayne Gretzky is the all-time leading goal scorer in the National Hockey League.	Gretzky is the greatest hockey player in the history of the game.
Per capita income in Canada is lower than in several other countries.	Canada is not the best model of economic success in the world.

When factual statements and opinion statements are set side by side like this, the difference between them is clear. In everyday conversation, we often present our opinions as if they were facts, and in doing so we invite an unnecessary argument. For example:

- 'That was a dumb thing to say!'
- 'Spending that much on _____ is a waste of money!'
- 'You can't get a fair shake in this country unless you're a white male.'

Notice how much less antagonistic each statement would be if it was prefaced by a qualifier like 'In my opinion . . .' or 'It seems to me . . .'.

Everyone is entitled to their own opinions, but they are not entitled to their own facts.

Daniel Patrick Moynihan

Confusing Facts and Inferences

Labelling your opinions can go a long way toward relational harmony, but developing this habit won't solve all linguistic problems. Difficulties also arise when we confuse factual statements with **inferential statements**—conclusions arrived at from an interpretation of evidence. Consider a few examples:

Cultural Idiom

a fair shake
honest treatment

to weasel out of
to get out of doing something

Fact	Inference
He hit a lamppost while driving down the street.	He was daydreaming when he hit the lamppost.
You interrupted me before I finished what I was saying.	You don't care about what I have to say.
You haven't paid your share of the rent on time for the past three months.	You're trying to weasel out of your responsibilities.
I haven't gotten a raise in almost a year.	My employer is exploiting me.

There's nothing wrong with making inferences as long as you identify them as such: 'She stomped out and slammed the door. *It looked to me* as if she were furious.' The danger comes when we confuse inferences with facts and make them sound like the absolute truth.

One way to avoid fact–inference confusion is to use the perception-checking skill described in Chapter 2 to test the accuracy of your inferences. Recall that a perception check has three parts: a description of the behaviour being discussed, your interpretation of that behaviour, and a request for verification. For instance, instead of saying,

Why are you laughing at me? you could say,
When you laugh like that [description of behaviour], *I get the idea you think something I did was stupid* [interpretation]. *Are you laughing at me* [question]?

Emotive Language

Emotive language contains words that sound as if they're describing something when they are really announcing the speaker's attitude toward something. Do you like that old picture frame? If so, you would probably call it 'an antique', but if you think it's ugly, you would likely describe it as 'a piece of junk'. Emotive words may sound like statements of fact but are always opinions.

American singer, actor, and director Barbra Streisand once pointed out how some people use emotive language to stigmatize behaviour in women that they admire in men:

A man is commanding—a woman is demanding.
A man is forceful—a woman is pushy.
A man is uncompromising—a woman is a ball-breaker.
A man is a perfectionist—a woman's a pain in the ass.
He's assertive—she's aggressive.
He strategizes—she manipulates.
He shows leadership—she's controlling.
He's committed—she's obsessed.
He's persevering—she's relentless.
He sticks to his guns—she's stubborn.
If a man wants to get it right, he's looked up to and respected.
If a woman wants to get it right, she's difficult and impossible.[46]

Problems occur when people use emotive words without labelling them as such. You might, for instance, have a long and bitter argument with a friend about whether a third

emotive language
Language that conveys the sender's attitude rather than simply offering an objective description.

I use emotion for the many and reserve reason for the few.

Adolf Hitler

CRITICAL THINKING PROBE

EMOTIVE LANGUAGE

Test your ability to identify emotive language by playing the following word game.

1. Take an action, object, or characteristic and show how it can be viewed either favourably or unfavourably, depending on the label it is given. For example,
   a. I'm casual.
      You're careless.
      He's a slob.
   b. I read adult love stories.
      You read erotic literature.
      She reads pornography.
2. Now create three-part descriptions of your own, using the following statements as a start:
   a. I'm tactful.
   b. She's a liar.
   c. I'm conservative.
   d. You have a high opinion of yourself.
   e. I'm quiet.
   f. You're pessimistic.
3. Now recall two situations in which you used emotive language as if it were a description of fact. How might the results have differed if you had used more objective language?

person was 'assertive' or 'obnoxious', when a more accurate and peaceable way to handle the issue would be to acknowledge that one of you approves of the behaviour and the other doesn't.

euphemism
A pleasant-sounding term used in place of a more direct but less pleasant one.

Evasive Language

None of the troublesome language habits we have described so far is a deliberate strategy to mislead or antagonize others. Now, however, we'll consider euphemisms and equivocations, two types of language that speakers use by design to avoid communicating clearly. Although both of these have some very legitimate uses, they also can lead to frustration and confusion.

Euphemisms

A **euphemism** (from a Greek word meaning 'to use words of good omen') is a pleasant term substituted for a more direct but potentially less pleasant one. We use euphemisms when we say that someone has 'passed away' (as opposed to 'died') or when we describe someone as being 'plump' or 'heavy-set' instead of 'fat' or 'overweight'. In Canada, common euphemisms for 'toilet' range from bathroom, restroom, washroom, and little boys'/girls' room to john, throne, loo, and head. Then there are the euphemisms we substitute for swear words in polite company or in front of the children. 'Fuddle-duddle', famously attributed to former prime minister Pierre Trudeau, is an example of

'Be honest with me Roger. By "mid-course correction" you mean divorce, don't you.'

this. There certainly are cases where the euphemistic pulling of linguistic punches can be face-saving. It's probably more constructive to question a possible 'statistical misrepresentation' than to call someone a liar, for example. Likewise, it may be less disquieting to some to refer to people as 'senior citizens' than as 'old people'.

Like many businesses, the airline industry uses euphemisms to avoid upsetting already nervous flyers.[47] For example, rather than saying 'turbulence', pilots and flight attendants use the less frightening term 'bumpy air'. Likewise, they refer to thunderstorms as 'rain showers' and fog as 'mist' or 'haze'. And savvy flight personnel never use the words 'your final destination'.

Despite their occasional advantages, many euphemisms are not worth the effort it takes to create them. Some are pretentious and confusing, such as the renaming of one university's Home Economics Department as the Department of Human Ecology, or a junior high school's labelling of hallways as 'behaviour transition corridors'. Other euphemisms are downright deceptive, such as the military usage 'friendly fire', which leaves one to wonder what can possibly be friendly about it if it kills people, or the term 'peacemaking mission', which really means a military campaign against another country to change its political regime. Steven Pinker, in his 2001 address to incoming undergraduates at the Massachusetts Institute of Technology, warned students of the 'euphemism treadmill', in which euphemisms eventually become taboo words as unpalatable as the ones they were designed to replace by taking on the negative connotations of the concepts they designate.[48] In fact, 'toilet' itself is a classic example, originally used as a euphemism for earlier terms such as 'lavatory' or 'privy'.

Equivocation

It's 8:15 p.m., and you are already a half-hour late for your dinner reservation at the fanciest restaurant in town. Your partner has finally finished dressing and confronts you with the question 'How do I look?' To tell the truth, you hate your partner's outfit. You don't want to lie, but on the other hand you don't want to be hurtful. Just as important, you don't want to lose your table by waiting around for your date to choose something else to wear. You think for a moment and then reply, 'You look amazing. I've never seen an outfit like that before. Where did you get it?'

Your response in this situation is an **equivocation**—a deliberately vague statement that can be interpreted in more than one way. Earlier in this chapter we talked about how unintentional equivocation can lead to misunderstandings. But our discussion here focuses on intentionally ambiguous speech that is used to avoid lying on one hand and telling a painful truth on the other. Equivocations have several advantages. They spare the receiver the embarrassment that might come from a completely truthful answer, and they spare the sender the discomfort of being honest.

Despite these benefits, there are times when equivocation is used by communicators as a way to weasel out of delivering important but unpleasant messages. Suppose, for example, that you are unsure about your standing in one of your courses. You approach the professor and ask how you're doing. 'Not bad,' the professor answers. This answer isn't too satisfying. 'What grade am I earning?' you inquire. 'Oh, lots of people would be happy with it' is the answer you receive. 'But will I receive an A or B this semester?' you persist. 'You could' is the reply. It's easy to see how this sort of evasiveness can be frustrating.

As with euphemisms, high-level abstractions, and many other types of communication, it's impossible to say that equivocation is always helpful or harmful. As we explained in

Euphemisms are not, as many young people think, useless verbiage for that which can and should be said bluntly; they are like secret agents on a delicate mission, they must airily pass by a stinking mess with barely so much as a nod of the head, make their point of constructive criticism and continue on in calm forbearance. Euphemisms are unpleasant truths wearing diplomatic cologne.

Quentin Crisp

'Euphemism' is a euphemism for lying.

Bobby Gentry

equivocation
A vague statement that can be interpreted in more than one way.

My name is Melonie Fullick, and I am a graduate student currently working on my PhD in education. Previously I completed my BA in communication studies and my MA in linguistics. As my background shows, the study of human communication can be wide-ranging and interdisciplinary. One of the things I enjoyed most about my degree in communication studies was that the subject brought together so many different yet interrelated phenomena around a relevant theme. I was encouraged to make my own meaningful connections, using theory from multiple 'fields' such as linguistics, media theory, and social psychol-

ogy. Adopting this flexible approach has allowed me to create and pursue a unique research path that incorporates a variety of academic interests. I have also found that studying communication has given me insight into the workings of the social world around me, from the interpersonal level to the study of institutions such as the mass media and the education system. My current research examines the ways in which the governance of universities is affected by broader changes in Canadian political and economic life. I hope to pursue a career as an academic or in the civil service once I have completed my PhD.

Chapter 1, competent communication behaviour is situational. Your success in relating to others will depend on your ability to analyze yourself, the other person, and the situation when deciding whether to be equivocal or direct.

Gender and Language

So far we have discussed language use as if it were identical for both sexes. Some theorists and researchers, though, have argued that there are significant differences between the way men and women speak, whereas others have argued that any differences are not significant.[49] What are the similarities and differences between male and female language use?

Content

Although there is a great deal of variation within each gender, on the average, men and women discuss a surprisingly different range of topics. The first research on conversational topics was conducted over 60 years ago. Despite the changes in men's and women's roles since then, the results of more recent studies are remarkably similar.[50] In these studies, women and men ranging in age from 17 to 80 described the range of topics each discussed with friends of the same sex. Certain topics were common to both sexes: work, movies, and television proved to be frequent subjects for both groups. And men and women alike reserved discussions of sex and sexuality for members of the same gender. The differences between men and women were more striking than the similarities, however. Female friends spent much more time discussing personal and domestic subjects, relationship problems, family, health and reproductive matters, weight, food and clothing, men, and other women. Men, on the other hand, were more likely to discuss music, current events,

sports, business, and other men. Men and women were equally likely to discuss personal appearance, sex, and dating in same-sex conversations. True to one common stereotype, women were more likely to gossip about close friends and family. By contrast, men spent more time gossiping about sports figures and media personalities. Women's gossip was no more derogatory than men's.

These differences can lead to frustration when men and women try to converse with one another. Researchers report that *trivial* is the word often used by both sexes to describe topics discussed by the opposite sex. 'I want to talk about important things,' a woman might say, 'like how we're getting along. All he wants to do is talk about the news or what we'll do this weekend.'

Reasons for Communicating

Research shows that the notion that men and women communicate in dramatically different ways is exaggerated. Both men and women, at least in the dominant cultures of Canada and the United States, use language to build and maintain social relationships. Regardless of the sex of the communicators, the goals of almost all ordinary conversations include making the conversation enjoyable by being friendly, showing interest in what the other person says, and talking about topics that interest the other person.[51] *How* men and women accomplish these goals is often different, though. Although most communicators try to make their interaction enjoyable, men are more likely than women to emphasize making conversation fun. Their discussions involve a greater amount of joking and good-natured teasing. By contrast, women's conversations focus more frequently on feelings, relationships, and personal problems. In fact, communication researcher Julia Wood flatly states that 'for women, talk is the essence of relationships.'[52] When a group of women was surveyed to find out what kinds of satisfaction they gained from talking with their friends, the most common response was a feeling of empathy—'To know you're not alone,' as some put it.[53] Whereas men commonly

COMMUNICATION ON-SCREEN

I Love You, Man (2009)
Directed by John Hamburg.

Peter Klaven (Paul Rudd) is pretty happy about where things stand: he has a stable—if perhaps a bit boring—job selling real estate by day and goes home to spend loving—if perhaps a bit tame—evenings with his fiancée, Zooey (Rashida Jones). A moment of unguarded frankness from Zooey, however, leads Peter to the harsh realization that he lacks any kind of strong male friendships. With his nuptials looming, Peter sets out to find himself a male best friend and, he hopes, a best man.

Although the nuances of friendship between women have been frequently explored onscreen, *I Love You,* Man is one of comparatively few films to tackle the nature of bond-building between males, or at least do so outside the frame of a mud-spattered warzone. As Peter strikes up a friendship with Sydney (Jason Segal), the film explores the sorts of everyday behaviour that males indulge in to meet their social needs. The nature of male-to-male communication (and miscommunication—this is a comedy, after all) features prominently.

Cultural Idiom

to one-up
to do better than

If two men agree on everything, you may be sure that one of them is doing the thinking.

Lyndon B. Johnson

described conversations with other males as something they *liked*, women characterized their woman-to-woman talks as a kind of contact they *needed*. The greater frequency of female conversations reflects their importance. Nearly 50 per cent of the women surveyed said they called friends at least once a week just to talk, whereas less than half as many men did so. In fact, 40 per cent of the men surveyed reported that they never called another man just to talk.

Because women use conversation to pursue social needs, their speech typically contains statements designed to show support for the other person, demonstrate equality, and keep the conversation going. With these goals, it's not surprising that female speech typically contains statements of sympathy and empathy: 'I've felt just like that myself,' 'The same thing happened to me!' Women are also inclined to ask lots of questions that invite the other person to share information: 'How did you feel about that?' 'What did you do next?' The importance of nurturing a relationship also explains why female speech is often somewhat powerless and tentative. Saying, 'This is just my opinion . . .' is less likely to put off a conversational partner than a more definite 'Here's what I think . . .'.

Men's speech tends to be driven by quite different goals. For instance, men are more likely to use language to accomplish the job at hand than to nourish relationships. This explains why men are less likely than women to disclose their vulnerabilities, which would be a sign of weakness. When someone else is sharing a problem, instead of empathizing, men are prone to offer advice: 'That's nothing to worry about . . .' or 'Here's what you need to do . . .'. Besides taking care of business, men are more likely than women to use conversations to exert control, preserve their independence, and enhance their status. This explains why men are more likely to dominate conversations and one-up their partners. Men frequently interrupt their conversational partners to assert their own experiences or points of view. (Women interrupt, too, but they usually do so to offer support: quite a different goal.) But just because male talk is competitive doesn't mean it's not enjoyable. Men often regard talk as a kind of game: when researchers asked men what they liked best about their all-male talk, the most frequent answer was its ease.[54] Another common theme was appreciation of the practical value of conversation: new ways to solve problems. Men also mentioned enjoying the humour and rapid pace that characterized their all-male conversations.

Conversational Style

Women and men behave differently in conversations.[55] For example, women ask more questions in mixed-sex conversations—nearly three times as many as men do, according to one study. Other research has revealed that in mixed-sex conversations, men interrupt women far more often than the other way around. Some theorists have argued that differences like these result in women's speech being less powerful and more emotional than men's. Research has supported these theories—at least in some cases. Even when clues about the speakers' sex were edited out, raters found clear differences between transcripts of male speech and female speech.

In one study, women's talk was judged more aesthetic, whereas men's talk was seen as more dynamic, aggressive, and strong. In another, male job applicants were rated more fluent, active, confident, and effective than female applicants.

Other studies have revealed that men and women behave differently in certain conversational settings. For example, in mixed-sex dyads, women talk less than men do, whereas in situations with other women, they speak for a longer time. In larger groups, men talk more, whereas in smaller groups, women talk more. There are subtler differences, too, between men's and women's conversation: women talking with other women use more questions, justifiers, intensive adverbs, personal pronouns, and adverbials. Men talking to men use more directives, interruptions, and filler words to begin sentences.[56]

Given all these differences, it's easy to wonder how men and women manage to communicate with one another at all. One reason why cross-sex conversations do run smoothly is that women accommodate to the topics men raise. Both men and women regard topics introduced by women as tentative, whereas topics that men introduce are more likely to be pursued. In effect, women seem to grease the wheels by doing more work than men to maintain conversations. A complementary difference between men and women also promotes cross-sex conversations: men are more likely to talk about themselves with women than with other men; and because women are willing to adapt to this topic, conversations are likely to run smoothly, if one-sidedly.

An accommodating style isn't always a disadvantage for women. One study revealed that women who spoke tentatively were actually more influential with men than those who used more powerful speech.[57] On the other hand, this tentative style was less effective in persuading women. (Language use had no effect on men's persuasiveness.) This research suggests that women who are flexible in their approach can persuade both other women and men—as long as they are not dealing with a mixed-sex audience.

Gender differences are apparent not only in speech but also in writing. A study by Sarah Marinelli, a recent honours communications graduate of McMaster University, investigated the identity of op-ed writers across Canada. She found that only 20 per cent of op-eds published in major Canadian newspapers were written by women. She also found that 10 per cent of women wrote outside of their field of expertise, whereas 50 per cent of men did so. This research suggests that Canadian op-ed writing is still strongly gendered.[58]

> **Cultural Idiom**
>
> **to grease the wheels**
> to facilitate

Non-Gender Variables

Despite the differences in the ways men and women speak, the link between gender and language use isn't as clear-cut as it might seem. In fact, several research reviews have found many more similarities than differences in the ways that women and men communicate. For example, one analysis of over 1,200 research studies found that only 1 per cent of variance in communication behaviour resulted from sex difference.[59] There is no significant difference between male speech and female speech in areas such as use of profanity, use of qualifiers such as 'I guess' or 'This is just my opinion', tag questions, and vocal fluency.[60] Some on-the-job research shows that male and female supervisors in similar positions behave the same way and are equally effective. In light of the considerable similarities between the sexes and the relatively minor differences, some communication scholars suggest that the 'men are from Mars, women are from Venus' idea overstates the case.[61] It might be more accurate to say that men are from Vancouver and women from Victoria.

You Just Don't Understand: Women and Men in Conversation

A growing body of research has revealed other factors that influence language use as much as, or even more than, gender does. For example, social philosophy plays a role: women who are feminists talk longer than their partners do, whereas non-feminist wives speak less than their husbands. Orientation toward problem-solving also plays a role in conversational style: the orientations of speakers—co-operative or competitive—have more influence than gender on how speakers interact.

The speaker's occupation and social role also influence speaking style. For example, the speech used by male early childhood educators to the children they're teaching resembles the language of women childcare workers more closely than it resembles the language of fathers at home. Overall, doctors interrupt their patients more often than the reverse, although male patients do interrupt female physicians more often than they do male physicians. At work, task differences exert more powerful effects on whether speakers use gender-inclusive language (such as 'he or she' instead of just 'he') than does biological sex.[62] A close study of trial transcripts showed that the speaker's experience on the witness stand and occupation had more to do with language use than did gender. If women generally use 'powerless' language, this may reflect their social role in society at large. As the balance of power grows more equal between men and women, we can expect many linguistic differences to shrink.

Why is the research on gender differences so confusing? In some studies, male speech and female speech seem identical, whereas other studies reveal important differences. As we have already said, one reason for the confusion is that factors besides gender influence the way people speak: the setting in which conversation takes place, the expertise of the speakers, their social roles (husband/wife, boss/employee, and so on). Also, women's roles are changing so rapidly that many women simply don't use the conversational styles that characterized their older sisters and mothers. But in addition to these factors, another powerful force that influences the way individual men and women speak is their **sex role**—the social orientation that governs behaviour—rather than their biological gender. Researchers have identified three sex roles: masculine, feminine, and androgynous. These sex roles don't always line up neatly with gender. There are 'masculine' females, 'feminine' males, and androgynous communicators who combine traditionally masculine and feminine characteristics.

Research shows that linguistic differences are often a function of these sex roles more than the speaker's biological sex. Masculine sex-role communicators—whether male or female—use more dominant language than either feminine or androgynous speakers. Feminine speakers have the most submissive speaking style, whereas androgynous speakers fall between these extremes. When two masculine communicators are in a conversation, they often engage in a one-up battle for dominance, responding to the other's bid for control with

> *If women speak and hear a language of connection and intimacy, while men speak and hear a language of status and independence, then communication between men and women can be like cross-cultural communication, prey to a clash of conversational styles. Instead of different dialects, it has been said they speak different genderlects.*
>
> Deborah Tannen

sex role
The social orientation that governs behaviour, in contrast to a person's biological gender.

a counter-attempt to dominate the interaction. Feminine sex-role speakers are less predictable. They use dominance, submission, and equivalent behaviour in an almost random fashion. Androgynous individuals are more predictable: they most frequently meet another's bid for dominance with a symmetrical attempt at control, but then move quickly toward an equivalent relationship.

All this information suggests that when it comes to communicating, 'masculinity' and 'femininity' are culturally recognized sex roles, not biological traits. Research suggests that neither a stereotypically male style nor female style is the best choice. For example, one study showed that a 'mixed gender strategy' that balanced the stereotypically male, task-oriented approach with the stereotypically female, relationship-oriented approach received the highest marks from both male and female respondents.[63] As opportunities for men and women become more equal, we can expect that the differences between male and female use of language will become smaller.

Culture and Language

Anyone who has tried to translate ideas from one language to another knows that communication across cultures can be a challenge.[64] Sometimes the results of a bungled translation can be amusing. The American manufacturers of Pet condensed milk, for instance, unknowingly introduced their product in French-speaking markets without realizing that in French the word *pet* means 'fart'.[65] Likewise, the naive English-speaking representative of a US soft drink manufacturer drew laughs from Mexican customers when she offered free samples of Fresca soda pop: in Mexican slang, *fresca* means 'lesbian'. English-Canadian food growers and canners who have to use bilingual packaging will often use the phrase 'sans préservatifs' to indicate that a can of organic tomatoes (for example) contains no preservatives; in French, however, a *préservatif* is a condom.

Even knowing the right words is no guarantee that non-native speakers will use an unfamiliar language correctly. For example, Japanese insurance companies warn their policyholders who are visiting the United States to avoid their cultural tendency to say 'excuse me' or 'I'm sorry' if they are involved in a traffic accident.[66] In Japan, apologizing is a traditional way to express goodwill and maintain social harmony, even if the person offering the apology is not at fault. In the United States, however, an apology can be taken as an admission of guilt and could result in Japanese tourists being held accountable for accidents for which they are not responsible. Canadians, whose obliging and conciliatory culture often leads them to apologize for things they aren't directly responsible for, face the same danger when travelling in the United States.

Difficult as it may be, translation is only a small part of the communication challenges facing members of different cultures. Differences in the way language is used and the very worldview that a language creates make communicating across cultures a challenging task.

> **Cultural Idiom**
> **bungled**
> done something imperfectly

> *The whole object of travel is not to set foot on foreign land; it is at last to set foot on one's own country as a foreign land.*
>
> Gilbert K. Chesterton

Verbal Communication Styles

Using language is more than just choosing a particular group of words to convey an idea. Each language has its own unique style that distinguishes it from others. And when a communicator tries to use the verbal style from one culture in a different one, problems are likely to arise.[67]

Direct–Indirect

One way in which verbal styles vary is in their directness. Anthropologist Edward Hall identified two distinct cultural ways of using language.[68] **Low-context cultures** use language primarily to express thoughts, feelings, and ideas as clearly and logically as possible. To low-context communicators, the meaning of a statement is in the words spoken. By contrast, **high-context cultures** value language as a way to maintain social harmony. Rather than upset others by speaking clearly, communicators in these cultures learn to discover meaning from the context in which a message is delivered: the non-verbal behaviours of the speaker, the history of the relationship, and the general social rules that govern interaction between people. Table 3.3 summarizes some key differences between the ways low- and high-context cultures use language.

Anglo-North American culture falls toward the direct, low-context end of the scale. English-speaking residents of Canada and the United States value straight talk and grow impatient with 'beating around the bush'. By contrast, most Asian and Middle Eastern cultures fit the high-context pattern. In many Asian cultures, for example, maintaining harmony is important, and so communicators will avoid speaking plainly if doing so would threaten another person's face. For this reason, Japanese or Korean people are less likely than English Canadians or Americans to offer a clear 'no' to an undesirable request. Instead, they would probably use roundabout expressions like 'I agree with you in principle, but . . .' or 'I sympathize with you . . .'.

Low-context Anglo-North Americans may miss the subtleties of high-context messages, but people raised to recognize indirect communication have little trouble decoding them. A look at Japanese child-rearing practices helps explain why. Research shows that Japanese mothers rarely deny the requests of their young children by saying 'no'. Instead, they use other strategies: ignoring a child's requests, raising distractions, promising to take care of the matter later, or explaining why they cannot or will not say 'yes'.[69] Sociolinguist Deborah

high-context culture

A culture that avoids direct use of language to express information, especially about relational matters. Instead, members of the culture rely on the context of a message to convey meaning.

low-context culture

A culture that relies heavily on language to make messages, especially of a relational nature, explicit.

Cultural Idiom

beating around the bush
approaching something in an indirect way

TABLE 3.3 Low- and High-Context Communication Styles

Low Context	High Context
Majority of information carried in explicit verbal messages, with less focus on the situational context.	Important information carried in contextual clues (time, place, relationship, situation). Less reliance on explicit verbal messages.
Self-expression valued. Communicators state opinions and desires directly and strive to persuade others.	Relational harmony valued and maintained by indirect expression of opinions. Communicators refrain from saying 'no' directly.
Clear, eloquent speech considered praiseworthy. Verbal fluency admired.	Communicators talk 'around' the point, allowing others to fill in the missing pieces. Ambiguity and use of silence admired.

Tannen explains how this indirect approach illustrates profound differences between high- and low-context communications:

> . . . saying no is something associated with children who have not yet learned the norm. If a Japanese mother spoke that way, she would feel she was lowering herself to her child's level precisely because that way of speaking is associated with Japanese children.[70]

Tannen goes on to contrast the Japanese notion of appropriateness with the very different one held by dominant Anglo-North American society:

> Because American norms for talk are different, it is common, and therefore expected, for American parents to 'just say no'. That's why an American mother feels authoritative when she talks that way: because it fits her image of how an authoritative adult talks to a child.[71]

The clash between cultural norms of directness and indirectness can aggravate problems in cross-cultural situations. Consider, for example, encounters between straight-talking, low-context English Canadians—who value speaking clearly—and French Canadians, whose high-context culture stresses smooth interaction. It's easy to imagine how the clash of cultural styles could lead to misunderstandings and conflicts between English Canadians and their French-Canadian neighbours. English Canadians could see their French-speaking counterparts as evasive, whereas the latter could perceive the anglophones as being insensitive and blunt.

As with the differences between English and French Canadians, subcultures within a single country can have varying notions about the value of direct speech. For example, the communication style of many Aboriginals is closer to that of high-context Japan or Korea than to low-context English Canada.[72] As a group, Aboriginal people value social harmony and avoid confrontation, which leads them to systematically speak in an indirect way to avoid giving offence. Researchers Laura Leets and Howard Giles suggest that the traditional Asian tendency to favour high-context messages sheds light on the difference: adept at recognizing hints and non-verbal cues, high-context communicators are more sensitive to messages that are overlooked by people from cultural groups that rely more heavily on unambiguous, explicit low-context messages.[73]

It's worth noting that even generally straight-talking residents of Canada raised in the low-context English-Canadian tradition often rely on context to make their point. When you decline an unwanted invitation by saying 'I can't make it,' it's likely that both you and the other person know that the choice of attending isn't really beyond your control. If your goal was to be perfectly clear, you might say, 'I don't want to get together.'

Elaborate—Succinct

Another way language styles can vary across cultures is in terms of whether they are *elaborate* or *succinct*. Speakers of Arabic, for instance, commonly use language that is much more rich and expressive than the language

preferred by most communicators who use English. Strong assertions and exaggerations that would sound ridiculous in English are a common feature of Arabic. This contrast in linguistic style can lead to misunderstandings between people from different backgrounds. As one observer put it,

> . . . [A]n Arab feels compelled to over-assert in almost all types of communication because others expect him [or her] to. If an Arab says exactly what he [or she] means without the expected assertion, other Arabs may still think that he [or she] means the opposite. For example, a simple 'no' to a host's requests to eat more or drink more will not suffice. To convey the meaning that he [or she] is actually full, the guest must keep repeating 'no' several times, coupling it with an oath such as 'By God' or 'I swear to God.'[74]

Succinctness is most extreme in cultures where silence is valued. In many Aboriginal cultures, for example, the favoured way to handle ambiguous social situations is to remain quiet.[75] When you contrast this silent style to the talkativeness common in French- and English-Canadian cultures when people first meet, it's easy to imagine how the first encounter between an Inuit, Haida, or Mohawk and a European person might feel uncomfortable to both.

Formal–Informal

A third way languages differ from one culture to another involves *formality* and *informality*. The informal approach that characterizes relationships in countries like Canada, the United States, Australia, and New Zealand is quite different from the great concern for using proper speech in many parts of Asia and Africa. Formality isn't so much a matter of using correct grammar as of defining social position. In Korea, for example, the language reflects the Confucian system of relational hierarchies.[76] Korean has special vocabularies for both sexes, for different levels of social status, for different degrees of intimacy, and for different types of social occasions. There are different degrees of formality for speaking with old friends, non-acquaintances whose background one knows, and complete strangers. One sign of being a learned person in Korea is the ability to use language that recognizes these relational distinctions. When you contrast these sorts of distinctions with the casual friendliness many Anglo-North Americans use even when talking with complete strangers, it's easy to see how a Korean might view communicators in Canada as boorish and how a Canadian might view Koreans as stiff and unfriendly.

Language and Worldview

Different linguistic styles are important, but there may be even more fundamental differences that separate speakers of various languages. For almost 150 years, some theorists have put forth the notion of **linguistic determinism**: the theory that the worldview of a culture is shaped and reflected by the language its members speak. For instance, bilingual speakers seem to think differently when they change languages.[77] In one study, French-speaking North Americans were asked to interpret a series of pictures. When they spoke in French, their descriptions were far more romantic and emotional than when they used English. Likewise, when students in Hong Kong were asked to complete a values test, they expressed more traditional Chinese values when they answered in Cantonese than when they answered in English. In Israel, both Arab and Jewish students saw greater distinctions between their group

---

Tact is the ability to describe others as they see themselves.

Abraham Lincoln

The basic tool for the manipulation of reality is the manipulation of words. If you can control the meaning of words, you can control the people who must use the words.

Philip K. Dick

linguistic determinism

The theory that a culture's worldview is unavoidably shaped and reflected by the language its members speak.

Understanding Diversity

● ● ● ● ● **LOYALISTS TO LOONIES: A VERY SHORT HISTORY OF CANADIAN ENGLISH**

Many Canadians have but one, fearful, question about their language: is it becoming more American? In light of Canadian history, this is quite ironic, since the roots of Canadian English (other than Newfoundland English, which derives from the dialects of southwest England and of Ireland) are in the speech of the United Empire Loyalists who fled the United States during and after the Revolution. At its origins, then, Canadian English *was* American English, so it is hard to know how it could become *more* American. This common origin explains why Canadians share so many words with Americans and sound more like Americans from the northern states than they sound like the British. Much of the vocabulary that distinguishes North American English from British English is an inheritance of older words that have survived over here but been superseded by other words in the UK (*fall* for *autumn*, *diaper* for *nappie*, etc.). Likewise, we retain some older pronunciations (*herb* with a silent *h*, for instance, which can be traced back to the Middle Ages). But Canadian English is different from American English, and our history accounts for that.

Ever since our arrival in Canada, English speakers have co-existed with French speakers and Aboriginal peoples. We have happily borrowed many words from both, a process that continues to this day. From early fur-trade borrowings such as *voyageur*, to nineteenth-century borrowings like *tuque* to our most recent acquisitions like *poutine*, Canadian English includes a lot of French! Words like *saskatoon* reveal our indebtedness to native languages.

In the nineteenth century, vast numbers of people from the British Isles were encouraged to settle in British North America to ward off any lurking nefarious American influence. Although their children inevitably ended up sounding like their playmates rather than their parents, some British linguistic traits managed to impose themselves. It is to this time that we owe our 'British spellings', our use of 'zed' rather than 'zee', and the pronunciations that some (but not all) of us use (*leftenant*, *shedule*, *herb* with an *h*). Scots in particular left their mark on Canadian English. In the Maritimes, southwestern Ontario, and the Prairies, people use Scottish words like *storm-stayed* and *a skiff of snow*, but other Scottish words have made it into English across the country: *bursary* for a particular type of scholarship, *bannock* for a kind of quick bread (this usage probably thanks to the high numbers of 'Orkneymen' in the employ of the Hudson's Bay Company).

Another phenomenon of the nineteenth century was the hybrid language used on the west coast known as 'Chinook Jargon'. This mixture of several Aboriginal languages, particularly Nuu-chah-nulth and Chinook, with English and French, facilitated communication between the various groups. It was widely used but has now died out, though remnants of it survive in such words as *chum* (*salmon*), *Siwash sweater*, and *saltchuck*.

The twentieth century brought waves of immigrants from non-English speaking countries, as we saw with our look at Ukrainian and Italian words in Canadian English. As we borrow from other languages, we continue to invent new words (*stagette*) from and apply new senses (*download*) to the existing English vocabulary.

Canadians may be consumed by the fear of being swallowed up entirely by US English, but we have already managed to maintain our linguistic distinctiveness despite living right next door to this behemoth for almost 250 years, with citizens travelling back and forth freely between both countries, and Canadians bombarded constantly by a barrage of American publishing and media, the like of which other English-speaking countries never experience. I believe that Canadian English will continue to survive and thrive. Just so long, of course, as we don't run out of loonies.

—*Katherine Barber, Six Words You Never Knew Had Something To Do With Pigs. Copyright © 2006 Oxford University Press Canada. Reprinted by permission of the publisher.*

Questions: The author describes how Canadian English has evolved differently from both American and British English. How do you think Canadian English will evolve over the next 50 years? The next hundred? What factors will influence this evolution?

Cultural Idiom

tongue
language

Sapir–Whorf hypothesis
The theory that the structure of a language shapes the worldview of its users.

and 'outsiders' when using their native language than when they used English, a neutral tongue. Examples like these show the power of language to shape cultural identity—sometimes for better and sometimes for worse.

Exponents of linguistic determinism believe that linguistic influences start early in life. For instance, they cite the fact that English-speaking parents often label the mischievous pranks of their children as 'bad', implying that there is something immoral about acting wild. On the other hand, French parents are more likely to say *Sois sage!*—'Be wise!'; the linguistic implication is that misbehaving is an act of foolishness. Swedes would correct the same action with the words *Var snall!*—'Be friendly, be kind.' By contrast, German adults would use the command *Sei artig!*—literally, 'Be of your own kind'—in other words, get back in step, conform to your role as a child.[78] Cognitive psychologists such as Judith Rich Harris have persuasively challenged the 'nurture hypothesis' (which states that parents have a large influence on the development of their children's cognitive abilities and personality). Harris has demonstrated that it is a combination of *genes and environment* that shape children's identities, and that parents—and their words—have only a very small part to play in the process.[79] This puts her and most of cognitive neuroscience squarely at odds with those who believe in linguistic determinism.

The best-known declaration of linguistic determinism is the **Sapir–Whorf hypothesis**, formulated in the 1930s by anthropologist Edward Sapir and Benjamin Whorf, an amateur linguist.[80] Following Sapir's theoretical work, Whorf suggested that the language spoken by the Hopi, a Native American people living mainly in Arizona, represents a view of reality dramatically different from more familiar tongues. For example, he claimed that the Hopi language makes no distinction between nouns and verbs, and therefore the people who speak it see the entire world as though it were constantly in process. The difference between the Hopi and English worldviews, according to this theory, would be similar to that between a video clip and a still photo. More recently, however, linguist and social activist Noam Chomsky and cognitive scientist Steven Pinker have argued that Whorf's methods were shoddy and his knowledge of the Hopi language non-existent.

Similarly, poor research and wishful thinking on the part of proponents of linguistic determinism are believed to be responsible for the popular myth that the Inuit have—depending on who is telling the tale—anywhere from 9 to 200 words for snow. Common Inuktitut, in fact, has only two words for snow: *aput*, meaning snow as a substance, and *qanik*, which is used most often like the verb 'to snow'. Like German, Inuktitut words can be extended by attaching anywhere from one to dozens of suffixes to convey more meaning, but linguists note that this practice is not substantively different from how English uses modifiers to produce compound terms like 'blowing snow', 'snowdrifts', or 'wet snow'. Inuktitut, however, is noteworthy by lacking a word for 'guilt', which has contributed to some particular complexities in Nunavut's justice system.[81]

Current research in the cognitive science of language has largely discredited the Sapir–Whorf hypothesis and linguistic determinism as bad science. In fact, the links between language and thinking appear to become weaker with each passing year. But although there is little support for the extreme linguistic deterministic viewpoint that it is impossible for speakers of different languages to view the world identically, the more moderate notion of **linguistic relativism**—the idea that language exerts a strong influence on perceptions—does seem valid. As one scholar put it, 'the differences between languages are not so much in what can be said, but in what it is relatively easy to say.'[82] Some languages contain terms that have no exact English equivalents.[83] Consider the following, for example:

- *nemawashi* (Japanese) the process of informally feeling out all the people involved with an issue before making a decision;
- *lagniappe* (Louisiana Creole) an extra gift given in a transaction that wasn't expected by the terms of a contract;
- *lao* (Mandarin) a respectful term used for older people, showing their importance in the family and in society;
- *dharma* (Sanskrit) each person's unique, ideal path in life and the knowledge of how to find it;
- *schadenfreude* (German) a feeling of malicious enjoyment derived from observing someone else's misfortune; and
- *koyaanisquatsi* (Hopi) nature out of balance; a way of life so crazy it calls for a new way of living.

Once words like these exist and become a part of everyday life, the ideas they represent are easier to recognize. But even without such words, each of the concepts mentioned is still possible to imagine. Thus, speakers of a language that includes the notion of *lao* would probably treat older members respectfully, and those who are familiar with *lagniappe* might be more generous, but the words aren't essential to follow these principles. Although language may shape thoughts and behaviour, it doesn't dominate them absolutely.

Language Use in Anglo–North American Culture

The importance of language as a reflection of worldview isn't just a matter of interest for anthropologists and linguists. The labels we use in everyday conversation both reflect and shape the way we view others and ourselves. This explains why businesses often give employees impressive titles and why a woman's choice of the label 'Ms' or 'Mrs' can be a statement about her identity. Women in Western society make a conscious choice about how to identify themselves when they marry. They may follow the tradition of taking their husband's last name, hyphenate their birth name with their husband's, or keep their birth name. A fascinating study found that a woman's choice is likely to reveal a great deal about herself and her relationship with her husband.[84] Surveys suggested that women who have taken their husbands' names place the most importance on relationships, with social expectations of how they should behave placing second, and issues of self coming last. By contrast, women who have kept their birth names put their personal concerns ahead of relationships and social expectations. Women with hyphenated names fall somewhere between the other groups, valuing self and relationships equally.

In the same way, the labels that members of an ethnic group choose to define themselves say a great deal about their sense of identity. Over the years, labels of racial identification have

linguistic relativism
A moderate form of linguistic determinism that argues that language exerts a strong influence on the perceptions of the people who speak it.

Cultural Idiom

feeling out
finding out others' opinions without directly asking them

gone through cycles of popularity.[85] In Anglo-North America, the first freed slaves preferred to be called *Africans*. In the late nineteenth and early twentieth centuries, *coloured* was the term of choice; later *Negro* became the respectable word. Then, in the 1960s, the term *black* grew increasingly popular—first as a label for militants and later as a term preferred by more moderate citizens of all colours. More recently, *African American* and *Afro-Canadian* have gained popularity.[86] In Canada, the situation is a little more complicated, particularly because of the diverse origins of Canadians of African descent.[87] A recent study showed that although *black* was the most preferred label, it was but one of four identified terms (the others being *Africentric*, *Caribbean*, and *Canadian*). Decisions about which name to use reflect a person's attitude. For example, one survey revealed that individuals who prefer the label *black* choose it because they consider it to be 'acceptable' and 'based on consensus' of the larger culture.[88] They describe themselves as patriotic, accepting of the status quo, and attempting to assimilate into the larger culture. By contrast, people who choose the term *Afro-American* derive their identity from their ethnicity and do not want to assimilate into the larger culture, only to succeed in it. The label others choose can also be revealing. In the United States, political liberals are more likely to use the term *African American* than are conservatives.[89]

Canadian sociolinguists Ruth King and Sandra Clarke have identified a similar complexity surrounding the word *newfie*.[90] Members of mainstream Canadian culture often use *newfie* as a derogatory and marginalizing term, but the network of its meanings is actually very complex. Originally, *newfie* denoted a happy-go-lucky fisher who didn't shoulder the cares of the world. The Newfoundland rock band Great Big Sea has attempted to re-appropriate the term and represent a positive and enlightened view of Newfoundland to the rest of Canada. King and Clarke cite Bob Benson, a staff reporter of *The Telegram*, a Newfoundland newspaper, who explicitly links *newfie* with the extremely derogatory term *nigger*. Interestingly, when speaking amongst themselves or in their own media, Newfoundlanders are completely unselfconscious about using *newfie*, even going so far as to characterize objections to the word as examples of political correctness.

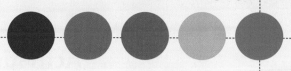

Summary

Language is both one of humanity's greatest assets and the source of many problems. This chapter highlighted the characteristics that distinguish language and suggested methods of using it more effectively.

Any language is a collection of symbols governed by a variety of rules and used to convey messages between people. Because of its symbolic nature, language is not a precise tool: meanings rest in people, not in words themselves. In order for effective communication to occur, it is necessary to negotiate meanings for ambiguous statements.

Language not only describes people, ideas, processes, and events, but it also shapes our perceptions of them in areas including status, credibility, and attitudes about gender and ethnicity. Along with influencing our attitudes, language reflects them. The words we use and our manner of speech reflect power, responsibility, affiliation, attraction, and interest.

Many types of language have the potential to create misunderstandings. Other types of language can result in unnecessary conflicts. In other cases, speech and writing can be evasive, avoiding expression of unwelcome messages.

The relationship between gender and language is a confusing one. There are many differences in the ways men and women speak: the content of their conversations varies, as do their reasons for communicating and their conversational styles. Not all differences in language use can be accounted for by the speaker's gender, however. Occupation, social philosophy, and orientation toward problem-solving also influence the use of language, and psychological sex role can be more of an influence than biological sex.

Language operates on a broad level to shape the consciousness and communication of an entire society. Different languages often shape and reflect the views of a culture. Low-context cultures like that of English Canada use language primarily to express feelings and ideas as clearly and unambiguously as possible, whereas high-context cultures avoid specificity to promote social harmony. Some cultures value brevity and the succinct use of language, whereas others value elaborate forms of speech. In some societies formality is important, whereas in others informality is important. Beyond these differences, there is the controversial concept of linguistic relativism—the notion that language exerts a strong influence on the worldview of the people who speak it.

Key Terms

abstraction ladder 102
abstract language 102
behavioural
   description 104
convergence 97
divergence 98
emotive language 107
equivocal words 99
equivocation 109
euphemism 108

factual statement 106
high-context culture 116
inferential statement 106
jargon 101
language 84
linguistic determinism 118
linguistic relativism 121
low-context culture 116
opinion statement 106
phonological rules 86

pragmatic rules 88
relative words 100
Sapir–Whorf
   hypothesis 120
semantic rules 88
sex role 114
slang 100
syntactic rules 87

Activities

A. Powerful Speech and Polite Speech

Increase your ability to achieve an optimal balance between powerful speech and polite speech by rehearsing one of the following scenarios:

1. Describing your qualifications to a potential employer for a job that interests you.
2. Requesting an extension on a deadline from one of your instructors.
3. Explaining to a merchant why you want a cash refund on an unsatisfactory piece of merchandise when the store's policy is to issue credit.
4. Asking your boss for three days off so you can attend a friend's out-of-town wedding.
5. Approaching your neighbours about their dog, which barks while they are away from home.

Your statement should gain its power by avoiding the types of powerless language listed in Table 3.1. You should not become abusive or threatening, and your statement should be completely honest.

B. Slang and Jargon

Find a classmate, neighbour, co-worker, or other person whose background differs significantly from yours. In an interview, ask this person to identify the slang and jargon terms that he or she finds confusing. Explore the following types of potentially baffling terms:

1. regionalisms
2. age-related terms
3. technical jargon
4. acronyms

C. Low-Level Abstractions

You can develop your ability to use low-level abstractions by following these steps:

1. Use your own experience to write each of the following:
   a. a complaint or gripe
   b. one way you would like someone with whom you interact to change
   c. one reason why you appreciate a person with whom you interact
2. Now translate each of the statements you have written into a low-level abstraction by including:
   a. the person or people involved
   b. the circumstances in which the behaviour occurs
   c. the specific behaviours to which you are referring
3. Compare the statements you have written in steps 1 and 2. How might the lower-level abstractions in Step 2 improve the chances of having your message understood and accepted?

D. Gender and Language

1. Note differences in the language use of three men and three women you know. (Include yourself in the analysis.) Your analysis will be most accurate if you record the speech of each person you analyze. Consider the following categories:
   a. conversational content
   b. conversational style
   c. reasons for communicating
   d. use of powerful/powerless speech
2. Based on your observations, answer the following questions:
   a. How much does gender influence speech?
   b. What role do other variables play? Consider occupational or social status, cultural background, social philosophy, competitive–co-operative orientation, and other factors in your analysis.

E. Sexist and Racist Language

One of the most treasured civil liberties is freedom of speech. At the same time, most people would agree that some forms of racist and sexist speech are hateful and demeaning to their targets. As you have read in these pages, language shapes the attitudes of those who hear it.

How do you reconcile the principle of free speech and the need to minimize hateful and discriminatory messages? Do you think laws and policies can and should be made to limit certain types of communication? If so, how should those limits be drafted to protect civil liberties? If not, can you justify the necessary protection of even sexist and racist language?

F. Euphemisms and Equivocations

For most people, 'telling it like it is' is usually considered a virtue, and 'beating around the bush' is a minor sin. You can test the function of indirect speech by following these directions:
1. Identify five examples of euphemisms and equivocations in everyday interaction.
2. Imagine how matters would have been different if the speakers or writers had used direct language in each situation.
3. Based on your observations, discuss whether equivocations and euphemisms have any place in face-to-face communication.

Further Reading

Ellis, Donald G. *From Language to Communication*, 2nd edn. Hillsdale, NJ: Lawrence Erlbaum, 1999.
This book covers a wide range of topics, including the origins of language, a review of the field of linguistics, a look at the mental processes that govern language use, and how language operates in everyday conversations.

Jacot de Boinod, Adam. *The Meaning of Tingo and Other Extraordinary Words from Around the World*. New York: Penguin Press, 2005.
One day BBC researcher Adam Jacot de Boinod noticed that an Albanian dictionary contained nearly 30 different words each for eyebrows and mustache. This observation began the author's research through hundreds of foreign dictionaries and the collective wisdom of over 154 languages, in order to compile a genuinely informative guide to the world's strangest— and most useful—words. This intriguing book is arranged by theme, allowing the reader to compare international attitudes about common and everyday items and activities.

Pinker, Steven. *The Blank Slate*. New York: Viking, 2004.
In this highly controversial and fascinating book, Steven Pinker explores the idea of human nature and its moral, emotional, and political colourings. He shows how many intellectuals have denied the existence of human nature by embracing three linked dogmas: The Blank Slate (the mind has no innate traits), The Noble Savage (people are born good and corrupted by society), and The Ghost in the Machine (each of us has a soul that makes choices free from biology). Each dogma carries a moral burden, so their defenders have engaged in desperate tactics to discredit the scientists who are now challenging them.

Rheingold, Howard. *They Have a Word For It*. Los Angeles: Tarcher, 1988.
Rheingold has collected a lexicon of words and phrases from languages around the world that lend support to the Sapir–Whorf hypothesis. This entertaining 200-page compendium of 'untranslatable phrases' illustrates that speaking a new language can, indeed, prompt a different worldview.

Rich Harris, J. *The Nurture Assumption: Why Children Turn Out the Way They Do*. New York: Free Press, 1999.
This lucidly written and wide-ranging work of cognitive psychology puts to rest the notion that parents are largely to blame for their children's development. The author also challenges the idea that language shapes our perception of reality.

Smith, Neil. *Language, Bananas and Bonobos: Linguistic Problems, Puzzles and Polemics*. Oxford: Blackwell, 2002.
Smith highlights many interesting and amusing quirks of language, cognition, and the brain. This very funny and accessible book will bring you up to date on the latest linguistic and cognitive scientific theorizing.

Tannen, Deborah. *Gender and Discourse*. New York: Oxford University Press, 1995;
You Just Don't Understand: Women and Men in Conversation. New York: Morrow, 1990;
Talking from 9 to 5. New York: Morrow, 1994.
Gender and Discourse provides a more scholarly look at the connection between gender and communication than Tannen's trade books. One chapter describes how social class interacts with gender to affect the interaction between men and women.

Wood, Julia. *Gendered Lives*, 6th edn. Belmont, CA: Wadsworth, 2005.
Chapter 5, 'Gendered Verbal Communication', offers a good survey of the relationship between language and the way we think about men and women in society.

Study Questions

1. Describe an incident illustrating how meanings reside in people, not words.
2. Recall incidents when (a) language shaped your attitudes, and (b) your own choice of words reflected your attitudes.
3. Explain how the types of troublesome language described on pages 99–105 have caused problems in a situation you experienced or observed.
4. Based on your experience of English-Canadian culture, describe how the gender and non-gender variables described on pages 110–15 affect communication.
5. Give examples illustrating which communication styles described on pages 116–18 operate in mainstream Canadian culture.

After studying the material in this chapter . . .

You should understand:

- the most common misconceptions about listening;
- the five components of the listening process;
- the most common types of ineffective listening;
- the challenges that make effective listening difficult; and
- the skills necessary to listen effectively in informational, critical, and empathic settings.

You should be able to:

- identify situations in which you listen ineffectively and explain the reasons for your lack of effectiveness;
- identify the consequences of your ineffective listening;
- follow the guidelines for informational listening;
- analyze an argument or claim by evaluating the credibility of its proponent, the soundness of its reasoning, and the quality of the evidence offered; and
- apply appropriate response styles in an empathic listening context.

Listening

Chapter Highlights

Most people need to think about listening in a new way.

- There's a difference between hearing and listening.
- Listening isn't a natural ability, and it takes effort and practice to listen well.
- It's probable that people will hear the same message in different ways.

Two approaches can help you become a better listener:

- Minimize faulty listening behaviours.
- Understand some of the reasons why you listen poorly.

Most people use one of four personal listening styles:

- content-oriented,
- people-oriented,
- action-oriented, or
- time-oriented.

There are three ways to listen and respond:

- for information;
- to critically evaluate a speaker's ideas; and
- to help others with their problems.

They call me the Speaker, but . . . they really ought to call me the Listener.

Dennis Hastert

In a world where almost everyone acknowledges the importance of better communication, the need for good listening is obvious. On the most basic level, listening is just as important as speaking. After all, it's impossible for communication to occur without someone receiving a message. (Imagine how ridiculous it would be to speak to an empty room or talk into a cellphone with no signal.)

If rate of occurrence is a measure of importance, then listening easily qualifies as the most important kind of communication. We spend more time listening to others than in any other type of communication. One study revealed that of their total communicating time, university students spent an average of 14 per cent writing, 16 per cent speaking, 17 per cent reading, and a whopping 53 per cent listening.[1] On the job, listening is by far the most common form of communication. On average, employees of major corporations in North America spend about 60 per cent of each working day listening to others.[2]

No matter how importance is measured, listening is arguably just as essential as speaking. When the Conference Board of Canada profiled the most important on-the-job communication skills in 2000, listening and understanding ranked at the top of the list; they are also implicit in the teamwork emphasized elsewhere in the report.[3] A study examining the link between listening and career success revealed that better listeners rose to higher levels in their organizations,[4] and a survey of personnel managers identified listening as the most critical skill for working effectively in teams.[5] In small groups, people who listen well tend to be seen by other members as leaders.[6]

Listening is just as important in personal relationships. In one survey, marriage counsellors identified 'failing to take the other's perspective when listening' as one of the most common communication problems among the couples with whom they work.[7] When another group of adults was asked which communication skills were most important in family and social settings, listening was ranked first.[8] In committed relationships, listening to personal information in everyday conversations is considered an important factor in overall satisfaction.[9] In short, effective listening is essential to effective relational communication.[10]

Nevertheless, experience shows that much of the listening we do is not at all effective. We frequently misunderstand others and are misunderstood in return. We become bored and feign attention while our minds wander. We engage in a battle of interruptions where each person fights to speak without hearing the other's ideas.

Some of this poor listening is inevitable, perhaps even justified. But in other cases we can become better receivers by learning a few basic listening skills. This chapter will help you become a better listener by giving you some important information about the subject. We'll talk about some common misconceptions concerning listening and show you what really happens when listening takes place. We'll discuss some poor listening habits, explain why they occur, and suggest better alternatives.

Misconceptions about Listening

In spite of its importance, listening is misunderstood by most people. Because these misunderstandings so greatly affect our communication, we need to debunk four common misconceptions.

Listening and Hearing Are Not the Same Thing

Hearing is the process in which sound waves strike the eardrum and cause vibrations that are transmitted to the brain. **Listening** occurs when the brain reconstructs these

hearing
The process wherein sound waves strike the eardrum and cause vibrations that are transmitted to the brain.

listening
The process wherein the brain reconstructs electrochemical impulses generated by hearing into representations of the original sound and gives them meaning.

electrochemical impulses into a representation of the original sound and then gives them meaning. Barring illness, injury, or earplugs, hearing can't be stopped: your ears will pick up sound waves and transmit them to your brain whether you want them to or not. Listening, however, isn't automatic. Many times we hear but do not listen. Sometimes we deliberately tune out unwanted signals—everything from a neighbour's lawnmower or the roar of nearby traffic to a friend's boring remarks or a colleague's unwanted criticism.

A closer look at listening—at least the successful variety—shows that it consists of several stages. After hearing, the next stage is **attending**—the act of paying attention to a signal. An individual's needs, wants, desires, and interests determine what is attended to, or *selected*, to use the term introduced in Chapter 2.

The next step in listening is **understanding**—the process of making sense of a message. Chapter 3 discussed many of the ingredients that combine to make understanding possible: a grasp of the syntax of the language being spoken, semantic decoding, and knowledge of the pragmatic rules that help us figure out a speaker's meaning from the context. In addition to these steps, understanding often depends on the ability to organize the information we hear into recognizable form. As early as 1948, Ralph Nichols showed how successful understanding is related to a large number of factors, notably verbal ability, intelligence, and motivation.[11]

Responding to a message consists of giving observable feedback to the speaker. Offering feedback serves two important functions: it helps you clarify your understanding of a speaker's message, and it shows that you care about what the speaker is saying.

Listeners don't always respond visibly to a speaker, but research suggests that they should. One study of 195 critical incidents in banking and medical settings showed that a major difference between effective and ineffective listening had to do with the kind of feedback offered.[12] Good listeners showed that they were attentive through non-verbal behaviours such as keeping eye contact and reacting with appropriate facial expressions. Their verbal behaviour—answering questions and exchanging ideas, for example—also demonstrated their attention. It's easy to imagine how other responses would signal less effective listening. A slumped posture, bored expression, and yawning send a clear message that you are not tuned in to the speaker.

Adding responsiveness to our listening model demonstrates the fact, discussed in Chapter 1, that communication is transactional in nature. Listening isn't just a passive activity. As listeners, we are active participants in a communication transaction. At the same time that we receive messages we also send them.

The final step in the listening process is **remembering**.[13] Research has revealed that people remember only about half of what they hear *immediately after hearing it*.[14] This is true even when people work hard at listening. This situation would probably not be too bad if the half remembered right afterwards were retained, but it isn't. Within two months, half of the half is forgotten, bringing what we remember down to about 25 per cent of the original message. This loss doesn't even take the full two months: people start forgetting *immediately* (within just eight hours the 50 per cent remembered drops to about 35 per cent). Given the amount of information we process every day—from instructors, friends,

attending
The process of focusing on certain stimuli from the environment.

remembering
The act of recalling previously introduced information. Recall drops off in two phases: short-term and long-term.

responding
Providing observable feedback to another person's behaviour or speech.

understanding
The act of interpreting a message by following syntactic, semantic, and pragmatic rules.

TABLE 4.1 Comparison of Communication Activities

	Listening	Speaking	Reading	Writing
Learned	First	Second	Third	Fourth
Used	Most	Next to most	Next to least	Least
Taught	Least	Next to least	Next to most	Most

I can't help hearing, but I don't always listen.

George Burns

residual message
The part of a message that a receiver can recall after short- and long-term memory loss.

Not comprehending, they hear like the deaf.

Heraclitus

the Internet, TV, and other sources—the **residual message** (what we remember) is a small fraction of what we hear.

Listening Is Not a Natural Process

Another common myth is that listening is a natural activity, like breathing. The truth is that listening is a skill much like speaking. Everybody does it, but few people do it well. One study in particular illustrates this point: 144 managers were asked to rate their listening skills. Astonishingly, not one described him- or herself as a 'poor' or 'very poor' listener, whereas 94 per cent rated themselves as 'good' or 'very good'.[15] The favourable self-ratings contrasted sharply with the perceptions of those who reported to the managers, many of whom said their boss's listening skills were weak.

As we have already discussed, some poor listening is inevitable. The good news is that listening can be improved through instruction and training.[16] Despite this fact, the amount of time devoted to teaching listening is far less than that devoted to other types of communication. Table 4.1 reflects this upside-down arrangement.

Listening Requires Effort

Most people assume that listening is fundamentally a passive activity in which the receiver absorbs a speaker's ideas, rather like the way a sponge absorbs water. As we will show later in this chapter, every kind of listening requires mental effort by the receiver. And experience shows that passive listening almost guarantees that the respondent will fail to grasp at least some of the speaker's ideas and will misunderstand others.

All Listeners Do Not Receive the Same Message

We also tend to assume that when two or more people are listening to a speaker, they all are hearing and understanding the same message. In fact, this isn't the case at all. In Chapter 2 we pointed out the many factors that cause each of us to perceive an event differently. Physiological factors, personal interests and needs, and our social roles and cultural backgrounds all shape and distort the raw data we hear into uniquely different messages.

Overcoming Challenges to Effective Listening

Despite the importance of good listening, people seem to get worse at the skill as they grow older.[17] In one experiment, teachers at various grade levels were asked to stop their lectures periodically and ask students what they had just been talking about. Ninety per cent of grade one children could repeat what the teacher had been saying, and 80 per cent of grade twos could do so. But when the test was repeated with teenagers, the results were much less impressive: only 44 per cent of junior high-school students and 28 per cent of high-school students could repeat their teachers' remarks.

Research suggests that adult listening skills are even poorer—at least in some important relationships. One experiment found that people listened more attentively and courteously to strangers than to their spouses. When faced with decision-making tasks, couples interrupted one another more frequently and were generally less polite than they were to strangers.[18]

In the following section we'll take a look at the kinds of poor listening habits that plague communication.

Faulty Listening Behaviours

Most people have one or more habits that keep them from understanding important messages.

Pseudolistening

Pseudolistening is an imitation of the real thing. Pseudolisteners give the appearance of being attentive: they look you in the eye, nod and smile at the right times, and may even answer you occasionally. Behind that appearance of interest, however, something entirely different is going on, because pseudolisteners use a polite facade to mask thoughts that have nothing to do with what the speaker is saying.

Selective Listening

Selective listeners respond only to the parts of a speaker's remarks that interest them, rejecting everything else. We are all selective listeners from time to time—for instance, when we screen out TV or radio ads while keeping an ear cocked for the program to resume. In other cases, selective listening occurs in conversations with people who expect a thorough hearing but get their partner's attention only when the conversation turns to the partner's favourite

I'll defend to the death your right to say that, but I never said I'd listen to it!

Tom Galloway

pseudolistening
An imitation of true listening in which the receiver's mind is elsewhere.

selective listening
A listening style in which the receiver responds only to messages that interest him or her.

Cultural Idiom

keeping an ear cocked
listening alertly

pet
favourite

ambushing

A style in which the receiver listens carefully to gather information to use in an attack on the speaker.

defensive listening

A response style in which the receiver perceives a speaker's comments as an attack.

insensitive listening

Failure to recognize the thoughts or feelings that are not directly expressed by a speaker, instead accepting the speaker's words at face value.

insulated listening

A style in which the receiver ignores undesirable information.

stage hogging

A listening style in which the receiver is more concerned with making his or her own point than with understanding the speaker.

Cultural Idiom

at face value
literally

topic—perhaps money, sex, sports, shopping, some particular person. Unless and until you bring up one of these pet topics, you might as well talk to a tree.

Defensive Listening

Defensive listeners take innocent comments as personal attacks. Teenagers who see a parent's questions about friends and activities as distrustful snooping are defensive listeners, as are touchy parents who view any questioning by their children as a threat to their parental authority. Many defensive listeners are insecure people who suffer from shaky public images and avoid admitting this by projecting their insecurities onto others.

Ambushing

Ambushers listen carefully, but only because they are collecting information to attack what you have to say. The criminal lawyer preparing to cross-examine a witness is a good example of an ambusher. People talking to an ambusher will often become justifiably defensive.

Insulated Listening

Insulated listeners are nearly the opposite of selective listeners. Instead of screening the conversation for topics they want to hear about, they screen for topics they want to avoid and then simply tune out. If you specifically draw their attention to a problem—perhaps an unfinished job, poor grades, or the like—they may seem to have heard you, but they'll promptly forget what you've just said.

Insensitive Listening

People often don't express their thoughts or feelings openly but instead communicate them subtly through choice of words or non-verbal clues or both. **Insensitive listeners** don't receive these messages clearly. They aren't able to look beyond the words and behaviour to understand their hidden meanings; instead, they take a speaker's remarks at face value.

Stage Hogging

Stage hogs differ somewhat from the other types of faulty listeners we've described. It's not just that they don't receive the other person's messages clearly. Instead, stage hogs (sometimes called 'conversational narcissists') try to turn the topic of conversation to themselves rather than showing interest in the speaker.[19] Interruptions are a hallmark of stage hogging, and they are a common feature of Western speech: a study comparing Thai and Anglo-Canadian negotiators found that the Canadians were more likely than Thais to interrupt another person in conversation.[20] Besides preventing the listener from learning potentially valuable information, stage hogging can damage the relationship between the interrupter and the speaker. For example, applicants who interrupt the questions of a potential employer during a job interview are likely to be rated less favourably than job seekers who wait until the interviewer has finished speaking before they respond.[21]

When confronted with stage hogs, people respond in one of two ways. Sometimes the strategy is passive: talking less, tuning out the stage hog, showing boredom non-verbally, or leaving the conversation. Other strategies are more active: trying to recapture the floor, hinting about the stage hog's dominance, or confronting the speaker about his or her narcissism. Reactions like these give stage hogs a taste of their own medicine, turning the conversation into a verbal tug-of-war.

> **Cultural Idiom**
> **a taste of their own medicine**
> retaliating by responding in a similar manner

Reasons for Poor Listening

What causes people to listen poorly? There are several reasons, some of which can be avoided and others that are sad but inescapable facts of life.

Effort

Listening effectively is hard work. The physical changes that occur during careful listening show the effort it takes: heart rate quickens, respiration increases, and body temperature rises.[22] Notice that these changes are similar to the body's reaction to physical effort. This is no coincidence, because listening carefully to a speaker can be just as taxing as more obvious efforts. You can manage the effort that's required to listen well if you prepare yourself for the task. If you know that passive listening won't be enough, you can invest the energy to understand others.

Message Overload

The amount of speech most of us encounter every day makes careful listening to everything we hear impossible. As we've already seen, many of us spend as much as one-third of the time we're awake listening to verbal messages—from instructors, co-workers, friends, family, salespeople, and total strangers. This means we often spend five hours or more a day listening to people talk. If you add this to the amount of time we spend listening to messages on the TV, radio, and Internet, you can see that it's impossible for us to keep our attention totally focused for that amount of time. Therefore, we have to let our attention wander at times. If you can consciously decide which messages are worth your attention, you can devote the time it takes to understand them.

Rapid Thought

Listening carefully is also difficult for a physiological reason. Although we are capable of understanding speech at rates up to 600 words per minute, the average person speaks between 100 and 140 words per minute.[23] Thus, we have a great deal of mental 'spare time' to spend while someone is talking. And the temptation is to use this time in ways that don't relate to the speaker's ideas, such as thinking about personal interests, daydreaming, planning a rebuttal, and so on. The trick is to use this spare time to understand the speaker's ideas better rather than to let your attention wander. Try to rephrase the speaker's ideas in your own words. Ask yourself how the ideas might be useful to you. Consider other angles that the speaker might not have mentioned.

There are people who, instead of listening to what is being said to them, are already listening to what they are going to say themselves.

Albert Guinon

Psychological Noise

Another reason we don't always listen carefully is that we're often wrapped up in personal concerns that are of more immediate importance to us than the messages others are sending.

It's hard to pay attention to someone else when you're anticipating an upcoming test or thinking about the wonderful time you had last night with good friends. Yet, we still feel we have to 'listen' politely to others, and so we continue with our charade. It usually takes a conscious effort to set aside your personal concerns if you expect to give others' messages the attention they deserve.

Figure 4.1 illustrates four ways in which preoccupied listeners lose focus when distracted by psychological noise. Everyone's mind wanders at one time or another, but excessive preoccupation is both a reason for and a sign of poor listening.

Physical Noise

The world in which we live often presents distractions that make it hard to pay attention to others. The sound of traffic, music, other people's talking, and so on interfere with our ability to hear well. Also, fatigue or other forms of discomfort can distract us from paying attention to a speaker's remarks. Consider, for example, how the efficiency of your listening decreases

Easy listening is a style of music, not communication.

Harvey Mackay

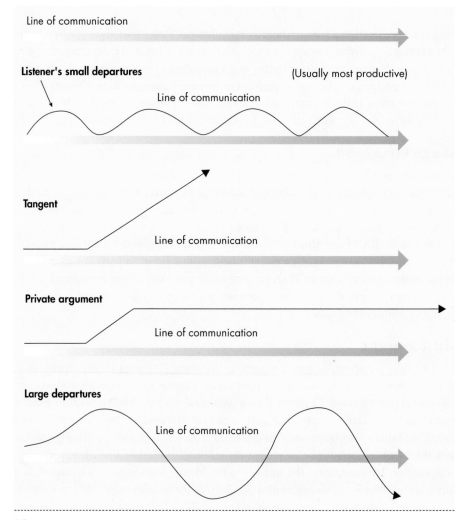

Figure 4.1

Four Thought Patterns

Source: A.D. Wolvin and C.G. Coakley, *Perspectives on Listening* (Norwood, NJ: Ablex, 1993), 115.

when you are seated in a crowded, hot, stuffy room that is surrounded by traffic and other noises. In such circumstances even the best intentions aren't enough to ensure clear understanding. You can often listen better by insulating yourself from outside distractions. This may involve removing the sources of noise: turning off the television, shutting the book you were reading, closing the window, and so on. In some cases, you and the speaker may need to find a more hospitable place to speak in order to make listening work.

Hearing Problems

Sometimes a person's listening ability suffers because of a medical condition, specifically a hearing problem—the most obvious sort of physiological noise, as defined in Chapter 1. After a hearing problem has been diagnosed, it's often possible to treat. The real tragedy occurs when a hearing loss goes undetected. In such cases, both the person with the impairment and others can become frustrated and annoyed at the ineffective communication that results. If you suspect that you or someone you know suffers from hearing loss, it's wise to have a physician or audiologist perform an examination.

Faulty Assumptions

We often give others a mental brush-off because we assume their remarks don't have much value. When one business consultant asked some of her clients why they interrupted colleagues, she received the following responses:

> My idea is better than theirs.
> If I don't interrupt them, I'll never get to say my idea.
> I know what they are about to say.
> They don't need to finish their thoughts since mine are better.
> Nothing about their idea will improve with further development.
> It is more important for me to get recognized than it is to hear their idea.
> I'm more important than they are.[24]

The egotism behind these comments is stunning. Dismissing others' ideas before considering them may be justified sometimes, but it's obviously a mistake to rule out so much of what others say—especially when you consider how you would feel if other people dismissed your comments without hearing you out.

Talking Has More Apparent Advantages

It often appears that we have more to gain by speaking than by listening. Whatever the goal—to win over a prospective employer, to convince others to support your candidate, or to describe the way you want your hair cut—the key to success seems to be the ability to speak well. Another apparent advantage of speaking is the chance it provides to gain the admiration, respect, or liking of others—or so you may think.

Cultural Idiom

give . . . brush-off
to dismiss or not pay attention to

rule out
exclude from consideration

A good listener is a good talker with a sore throat.

Katharine Whitehorn

While the right to talk may be the beginning of freedom, the necessity of listening is what makes that right important.

Walter Lippmann

Tell jokes, and everyone may think you're a real wit. Offer advice, and they might be grateful for your help. Tell them all you know, and they could be impressed by your wisdom.

Although speaking at the right time can lead people to appreciate you, talking too much can result in the kind of stage hogging we alluded to earlier. Not all interruptions are attempts at stage hogging. One study revealed a difference between male and female interrupters.[25] Men typically interrupted conversations far more than women. Their goal was usually to control the discussion. Women interrupted for very different reasons: to communicate agreement, to elaborate on the speaker's idea, or to participate in the topic of conversation. These sorts of responses are more likely to be welcomed as a contribution to the conversation and not as attempts to grab the stage.

If you find yourself hogging the conversation, try a simple experiment: limit the frequency and length of your responses to a fraction of their usual amount. If you were speaking 50 per cent of the time, cut back to 25 per cent—or even less. If you interrupt the speaker every 15 seconds, try to let him or her talk for closer to a minute. You are likely to discover that you're learning more—and probably gaining the appreciation of the other person.

Cultural Differences

The way members of different cultures communicate can affect listening.[26] For instance, one study of young adults from various countries showed marked differences in listening preferences. Young Germans favoured an action-oriented approach: they engaged speakers directly and were highly inquisitive. This style contrasts with the indirect approach of high-context Japanese listeners. Young Israelis were also less vocal than Germans and focused on careful analysis of others' statements. By contrast, young Americans emphasized the social dimension of a conversation and were more focused on how much time a conversation was taking.

Media Influences

A final challenge to serious listening is the influence of contemporary mass media, especially television, radio, and the Internet. A growing amount of programming consists of short segments: news items, commercials, videos, and so on. (Think of YouTube, your Facebook feed, blogs, and MuchMusic.) In the same vein, news consists mainly of brief stories with a declining portion of text and a growing amount of graphical information. This is especially true with news aggregator sites such as Digg or reddit.com/r/canada, which feature catchy headlines on a bulletin board with links to the full story. Sites like these also place personal blogs, tabloid news, and articles from serious newspapers, such as *The Globe and Mail* or the Halifax *Chronicle-Herald* on an equal platform. And 24-hour news networks run headlines across the bottom of the screen (known as a 'news ticker' or 'crawler'), and sometimes weather forecasts across the top, while an announcer simultaneously reads news items. These trends discourage the kind of focused attention that is necessary for careful listening, especially to complicated ideas and feelings.

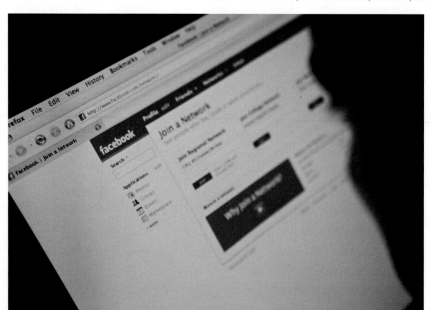

Understanding Diversity

● ● ● ● ● **SIGN OF THE TIMES**

When Joanna Cripps discusses Deaf Culture, she uses capital letters. The lower-case treatment smacks of a negative stereotype created by hearing people, she says, rather than celebrating the lives and experiences of the 450,000 Canadians who are deaf or hearing-impaired.

Deaf people, Ms Cripps included, have a visual language and culture, she explains in an e-mail interview. As the policies, management, and public relations manager of a new Deaf Culture Centre, opening in May in Toronto's Distillery District, she is eager to celebrate that culture with other deaf people—and share it with hearing visitors as well.

The 4,000-square-foot facility, billed as the first of its kind in the world, will showcase deaf culture with displays of historical artifacts, special events and workshops for deaf people, and exhibitions of art created by deaf and hearing-impaired artists.

Rotating exhibits of art will offer visitors a colourful experience of the unique culture that Ms Cripps alludes to: they'll draw extensively on a genre known as De'VIA (short for Deaf View/Image Art), which is visual art created to express the experience of being deaf.

A group of artists who came together in 1989 to explore the nature of 'deaf art' defined De'VIA as having a 'possible tendency' to use intense and contrasting colours and textures, and exaggerated features—for example, hands, mouths, eyes, and ears. (Deaf people often key in on those features when communicating.)

'There's a tendency to vibrant colour, and a visually rich life,' says Anita Small, the centre's director of education, research, and development, who notes that shows already are programmed for the next three years.

Historical exhibits that will be featured on site include artifacts ranging from puppets used by Forrest C. Nickerson, a puppeteer who founded the Canadian Cultural Society of the Deaf, to a display honouring William Hoy, a deaf baseball fan who, in 1901, devised the system of hand signals still used by umpires today.

The centre also pays tribute to American sign language by featuring 3-D signature motifs, created by Bruce Mau Design, that capture the motion of keywords as they're being signed. These images, translated as swirls of motion, have become the inspiration for the centre's logo and visual identity.

Designing such a centre called for flashing lights, instead of bells, in the alarm systems, along with places to set items in order to facilitate discussions using sign language.

'We discovered [members of] the deaf community are very expressive and use a lot of humour,' says Sheldon Levitt, principal at Quadrangle Architects, which designed the space.

Even the door handles of the new facility have a link to the deaf community: they were cast in bronze by 92-year-old sculptor and Order of Canada recipient Dora de Pedery-Hunt, who is, herself, hearing impaired.

The creation of the centre was partially financed by a $175,000 grant from the Department of Canadian Heritage, Cultural Spaces Canada Program.

The balance of the $1.5-million required to cover the budget for the first two years was raised privately by the Canadian Cultural Society of the Deaf and its supporters.

'It is a chance to show the world what deaf culture is all about,' Ms Cripps says. Deaf culture is the result of 'a centuries-long struggle for the freedom to express itself through its own culture, language, and community.

'For us to be able to demonstrate without "preaching" is a plus.'

—*Ian Harvey*, The Globe and Mail, *11 March 2006, M3.*

Question: The author describes the richness of Deaf Culture and communication. How might studying Deaf Culture enrich the lives of hearing people?

Personal Listening Styles

Not everyone listens the same way. Communication researchers have identified four styles, each of which has both strengths and weaknesses.[27]

Content-Oriented Listening

As the label that characterizes them suggests, **content-oriented listeners** are most interested in the quality of messages they hear. They look for details and are good at analyzing an issue from several perspectives. They give weight to the messages of experts and other credible sources of information. Content-oriented listeners often enjoy ideas for their own sake and are willing to spend time exploring them in thorough exchanges of ideas.

A content-oriented approach is valuable when the goal is to evaluate the quality of ideas and when there is value in looking at issues from a wide range of perspectives. It is especially useful when the topic is a complicated one. On the other hand, a content-oriented approach risks annoying people who don't have the same sort of analytical orientation. A content-oriented approach can take more time than others may be willing to give, and the content-oriented listener may challenge ideas in a way that can be perceived as overly critical or even hostile.

People-Oriented Listening

People-oriented listeners are especially concerned with creating and maintaining positive relationships. They tune into others' moods, and they respond to speakers' feelings as well as their ideas. People-oriented listeners are typically less judgmental about what others have to say than are content-oriented types. They are more interested in understanding and supporting people than in evaluating them.[28]

A people orientation comes with a strong concern for relationships that has obvious strengths but also some less obvious drawbacks. It is easy to become overly involved with others' feelings. People-oriented listeners, in an effort to be congenial and supportive, may lose their detachment and ability to assess the quality of information others are giving. Less personally oriented communicators can view these listeners as overly expressive and even intrusive.

Action-Oriented Listening

Unlike people-oriented listeners, who focus on relationships, and content-oriented listeners, who are fascinated with ideas for their own sake, **action-oriented listeners** are most concerned with the task at hand. Their main concern is to figure out what sort of response is required by a message. They want to get to the heart of the matter quickly, and so they appreciate clear, concise messages and often translate others' remarks into well-organized mental outlines.

Action-oriented listening is most appropriate when the goal is taking care of business. These listeners keep a focus on the job at hand and encourage others to be organized and concise. But their no-nonsense approach isn't always appreciated by speakers who lack the skill or inclination to be clear

---

action-oriented listening
A listening style that is primarily concerned with accomplishing the task at hand.

content-oriented listening
A listening style that focuses on the content of a message.

people-oriented listening
A listening style that is primarily concerned with creating and maintaining positive relationships.

Cultural Idiom

give weight to
give priority to

COMMUNICATION ON-SCREEN

The Queen (2006)
Directed by Stephen Frears.

When news of the sudden death of Princess Diana sends a shockwave through Britain and around the world, Her Majesty Queen Elizabeth II (Helen Mirren), retreats behind the walls of Balmoral Castle, unable to comprehend the public response to the tragedy. Over the course of the movie, the Queen is forced to adopt a more people-oriented response, and in so doing transforms the monarchy's centuries-old relationship with the British public.

and direct. Action-oriented listeners seem to minimize emotional issues and concerns, which may be an important part of business and personal transactions.

Time-Oriented Listening

Time-oriented listeners are most concerned with efficiency. They view time as a scarce and valuable commodity, and they grow impatient when they view others as wasting it. A time orientation can be an asset when deadlines and other pressures demand fast action. On the other hand, a time orientation can put off others when it seems to disregard their feelings. Also, an excessive focus on time can hamper the kind of thoughtful deliberation that some jobs require.

As you read the preceding descriptions, you may have found that you use more than one of these listening styles. If so, you aren't alone: 40 per cent of the people who used 'The Listening Styles Profile' reported at least two strong listening preferences.[29] Whichever styles you use, it is important to recognize that you can control the way you listen and to use the styles that best suit the situation at hand. When your relationship with the speaker needs attention, adopt a people-oriented approach. When clarity is the issue, be an action-oriented listener. If analysis is called for, put on your content-oriented persona. And when the clock is what matters most, become a model of time orientation. You can also boost your effectiveness by assessing the listening preferences of your conversational partners and adapting your style to them.

Informational Listening

Informational listening is the approach to take when you want to understand another person. When you are an informational listener, your goal is to make sure you are receiving the same thoughts the other person is trying to convey—not always an easy feat when you consider the forces that interfere with understanding (see pages 99–105).

The situations that call for informational listening are endless and varied: following an instructor's comments in class, listening to a friend's account of a night out, absorbing the sales pitch for a new printer you're thinking of buying, learning about your family history from a relative's tales, swapping ideas in a discussion about politics or sports—the list goes on and on. You can become more effective as an informational listener by approaching others with a constructive attitude and by using some simple but effective skills.

Don't Argue or Judge Prematurely

Since the time of the ancient Greeks and Romans, Western civilization has admired the ability to persuade others.[30] This tradition has led us to measure the success of much communication in terms of whether it changes the way others think and act. Recall, for example, what often happens when people

Learn to listen. Opportunity could be knocking at your door very softly.

Frank Tyger

Cultural Idiom

put off
displease

informational listening
Listening in which the goal is to receive accurately the same thoughts the speaker is trying to convey.

time-oriented listening
A listening style that is primarily concerned with minimizing the time necessary to accomplish the task at hand.

The Chinese characters that make up the verb 'to listen' tell us something significant about this skill.

Ear

Eyes

Undivided Attention

Heart

encounter someone with differing opinions. Rather than try to understand one another, their conversation often turns into an argument or debate (sometimes friendly, and sometimes not) in which the participants try to change one another's minds.

Persuasion is certainly one important goal of communication, but it isn't the only one. Most people would agree with the principle that it's essential to understand a speaker's ideas before judging them. Despite this commonsense fact, all of us are guilty of forming snap judgments, evaluating others before hearing them out. This tendency is greatest when the speaker's ideas conflict with our own.

It's especially tempting to counterattack when others criticize you, even when those criticisms might contain valuable truths and when understanding them might lead to a change for the better. But even when there is no criticism or disagreement, we tend to evaluate others based on sketchy first impressions, forming snap judgments that aren't at all valid. And not all premature judgments are negative. It's also possible to jump to overly favourable conclusions about the quality of a speaker's remarks when we like that person or agree with the ideas being expressed. The lesson is clear: listen first, make sure you understand, and then evaluate or argue, if you choose.

Separate the Message from the Speaker

The first recorded cases of blaming the messenger for an unpleasant message occurred in ancient Greece. When messengers would arrive reporting losses in battles, their generals were known to respond to the bad news by having the messengers put to death. Irrational reaction is still common (though fortunately less violent) today. Consider a few situations in which there is a tendency to get angry with a communicator bearing unpleasant news: an instructor who tries to explain why you did poorly on a major paper; a friend who explains what you did to make a fool of yourself at the party last night; the boss who points out how you could do your job better. At times like this, becoming irritated with the bearer of unpleasant information can not only cause you to miss important information but also harm your relationships.

There's a second way that confusing the message and the messenger can prevent you from understanding important ideas. At times you may mistakenly discount the value of a message because of the person who is presenting it. Even the most boring instructors, the most irritatingly responsible friends, and the most demanding bosses occasionally make good points. If you write off everything a person says before you consider it, you may be cheating yourself out of some valuable information.

Be Opportunistic

Even if you listen with an open mind, sooner or later you will find yourself hearing information that is either so unimportant or so badly delivered that you're tempted to tune out. Although making a quick escape from such

We can communicate an idea around the world in seventy seconds but it sometimes takes years for an idea to get through ¼ inch of human skull.

Charles Kettering

Cultural Idiom

write off
dismiss as worthless or unimportant

Bore: one who has the power of speech but not the capacity for conversation.

Benjamin Disraeli

Letter to the Editor: How to Save Democracy

The following letter is a response to Allan Gregg's 'How To Save Democracy', which appeared in the September 2004 issue of The Walrus (walrusmagazine.com/articles/politics-allan-gregg-how-to-save-democracy/).

The ancient Greek definition of democracy is 'sway' or 'influence' (kratos) of 'the people' (demos). Allan Gregg's piece . . . is less about democratic renewal and more about making Parliament relevant and boosting voter turnout. The interests of Parliament and democracy would be much better served by renewing engagement from the bottom up.

Much of the debate about democracy has a single dimension, as if Parliament and democracy are one and the same. And yet there are plenty of good ideas for a broad-based approach to revitalizing democracy. Gregg himself points out some of the ways forward. These include helping citizens feel connected to the places they live and work. But making elected representatives the gatekeepers of these processes may breed more distrust and cynicism of politicians, not less.

A bold democratic project starts with the interests of citizens, not politicians. It offers widespread opportunities to meaningfully experience social and environmental issues. And maybe after these experiences, these citizens won't vote. Instead they will volunteer, shop consciously, or engage in debate with their friends. Surely this is democracy as well.

John Dewey, the American political philosopher, once commented, 'Democracy begins in conversation.' True democratic renewal requires investment in quality conversation such as more informed citizens and parliamentarians with listening skills. If we achieve authentic conversations, the votes will follow.

—Sanjiv Lingayah

Questions: How does Lingayah's comment illustrate the value of listening for effective communication? What type of listening is he promoting among parliamentarians?

tedious situations is often the best thing to do, there are times when you can profit from paying close attention to apparently worthless communication. This is especially true when you're trapped in a situation where the only alternatives to attentiveness are pseudolistening or downright rudeness.

An opportunistic listener who is willing to invest the effort can find some value in even the worst situations. Consider how you might listen opportunistically when you find yourself locked in a boring conversation with someone whose ideas are worthless. Rather than torture yourself until escape is possible, you could keep yourself amused—and perhaps learn something useful—by listening carefully until you can answer the following (unspoken) questions:

- Is there anything useful in what this person is saying?
- What led the speaker to come up with ideas like these?
- What lessons can I learn from this person that will keep me from sounding the same way in other situations?

Listening with a constructive attitude is important, but even the best intentions won't always help you understand others. The following skills can help you figure out messages that otherwise might be confusing, as well as help you see how those messages can make a difference in your life.

Look for Key Ideas

It's easy to lose patience with long-winded speakers who never seem to get to the point—or have a point, for that matter. Nevertheless, most people do have a central idea, what we call a 'thesis' in Chapter 12. By using your ability to think more quickly than the speaker can talk, you may be able to extract the thesis from the surrounding mass of words you're hearing. If you can't figure out what the speaker is driving at, you can always ask in a tactful way by using the skills of questioning and paraphrasing, which we'll examine next.

Ask Questions

Questioning is about asking for additional information to clarify your idea of the sender's message. If you ask directions to a friend's house, typical questions might be 'Is your place an apartment?' or 'How long does it take to get there from here?'. In more serious situations, questions could include 'What's bothering you?' or 'Why are you so angry?' or 'Why is that so important?'. Notice that a key element of these questions is that they ask the speaker to elaborate on information already given.

Despite the many benefits, not all questions are equally helpful. Whereas **sincere questions** are aimed at understanding others, **counterfeit questions** are really disguised attempts to send a message, not receive one. Counterfeit questions come in several varieties:

- *Questions that make statements.* 'Are you serious?' 'You did what?' Comments like these are certainly not genuine requests for information. Emphasizing certain words can also turn a question into a statement: 'You lent money to *Tony*?' We also use questions to offer advice. The person who responds with, 'Are you going to stand up to him and give him what he deserves?' clearly has stated an opinion about what should be done.
- *Questions that carry hidden agendas.* 'Are you busy Friday night?' is a dangerous question to answer. If you say, 'No,' thinking the person has something fun in mind, you won't like hearing, 'Good, because I need some help moving my piano.'
- *Questions that seek 'correct' answers.* Most of us have been victims of question-askers who want to hear only a particular response. 'Which shoes do you think I should wear?' can be a sincere question—unless the asker has a preference you're being asked to confirm. When this happens, the asker isn't interested in listening to contrary opinions, and 'incorrect' responses get shot down. Some of these questions may venture into delicate territory. 'Honey, do you think I look ugly?' can be a request for a 'correct' answer.
- *Questions that are based on unchecked assumptions.* 'Why aren't you listening to me?' assumes the other person isn't paying attention. 'What's the matter?' assumes that something is wrong. As we explained in Chapter 2, perception-checking is a much better way of checking out assumptions: 'When you kept looking over at the TV, I thought you weren't listening to me, but maybe I was wrong. Were you paying attention?'

There is no such thing as an uninteresting subject. There are only uninterested people.

G.K. Chesterton

----

counterfeit question
A question that disguises the speaker's true motive, which does not include a genuine desire to understand the other person.

sincere question
A question posed with the genuine desire to learn from another person.

Cultural Idiom

long-winded
speaking for a long time

shot down
rejected or defeated

to stand up to
to confront courageously

Unlike counterfeit questions, sincere questions are genuine requests for new information that clarifies a speaker's thoughts or feelings. Although the value of sincere questioning might seem obvious, people don't use this information-seeking approach enough. Communicators are often reluctant to show their ignorance by asking for an explanation of what seems like an obvious point. At times like this, it's a good idea to recall a quote attributed to Confucius: 'He who asks a question is a fool for five minutes. He who does not ask is a fool for life.'

Paraphrase

Questioning is often a valuable tool for increasing understanding. Sometimes, however, questions won't help you understand a speaker's ideas any better. In fact, as the humorous series of drawings in Figure 4.2 suggests, questions can even lead to greater misunderstandings. Now consider another type of feedback—one that would tell you whether you understood what was said before you begin asking additional questions. This sort of feedback, termed **paraphrasing**, involves restating in your own words the message you thought the speaker had just sent, without adding anything new.

> [To a direction-giver] 'So I go through the lights, just past the high school, and I'll see the arena, is that right?'

> [To the boss] 'So you need me both this Saturday and next Saturday—right?'

> [To an instructor] 'When you said, "Don't worry about the low grade on the quiz," did you mean it won't count against my grade?'

In other cases, a paraphrase will reflect your understanding of the speaker's feelings:

> 'You said you understand, but you look confused. Are you?'
> 'You seem to be in a hurry. I get the idea you don't want to talk now. Is that right?'
> 'You said "Forget it," but it sounds like you're mad. Are you?'

Whether your paraphrasing reflects a speaker's thoughts or feelings, and whether it focuses on a specific comment or a general theme, the key to success is to restate the other person's comments in your own words as a way of cross-checking the information. If you simply repeat the speaker's comments verbatim, you will sound foolish—and you still might be misunderstanding what has been said. Notice the difference between simply parroting a statement and really paraphrasing:

Speaker:	I'd like to go, but I can't afford it.
Parroting:	You'd like to go, but you can't afford it.
Paraphrasing:	So if we could find a way to pay for you, you'd be willing to come. Is that right?

Figure 4.2

Asking Questions Doesn't Guarantee Understanding

Speaker:	Wow, you look terrific!
Parroting:	You think I look terrific.
Paraphrasing:	You think I've lost weight?

As these examples suggest, effective paraphrasing is a skill that takes time to develop. You can make your paraphrasing sound more natural by taking any of three approaches, depending on the situation:

1. Change the speaker's wording.

| Speaker: | The gun control registry is just another failed idea of bleeding-heart liberals. |
| Paraphrase: | Let me see if I've got this right: You're mad because you think having a gun control registry sounds good but it's costly and doesn't actually help to keep guns out of the hands of criminals. [Reflects both the speaker's feeling and the reason for it.] |

2. Offer an example of what you think the speaker is talking about.

When the speaker makes an abstract statement, you may suggest a specific example or two to see if your understanding is accurate.

| Speaker: | Craig is such an idiot. I mean, what was he thinking? |
| Paraphrase: | You think that joke about Daria's boyfriend was pretty offensive, huh? [Reflects the listener's guess about speaker's reason for objecting to the behaviour.] |

3. Reflect the underlying theme of the speaker's remarks.

When you want to summarize the theme that seems to have run through another person's conversation, a complete or partial perception check is appropriate:

| Paraphrase: | You keep reminding me to be careful. Sounds like you're worried that something might happen to me. Am I right? [Reflects both the speaker's thoughts and feelings and explicitly seeks clarification.] |

Calvin and Hobbes
by Bill Watterson

Learning to paraphrase isn't easy, but it can be worth the effort, because it offers two very real advantages. First, it boosts the odds that you'll accurately and fully understand what others are saying. We've already seen that using one-way listening or even asking questions may lead you to think that you've understood a speaker when, in fact, you haven't. Paraphrasing, on the other hand, serves as a way of double-checking your interpretation for accuracy. Second, paraphrasing guides you toward sincerely trying to understand another person instead of using non-listening styles such as stage hogging, selective listening, and so on. If you force yourself to reflect the other person's ideas in your own words, you'll spend your mental energy trying to understand that speaker instead of using less constructive listening styles. For this reason, some communication experts suggest that the ratio of questioning and paraphrasing to confronting should be at least 5:1, if not more.[31]

Take Notes

Understanding others is crucial, of course, but comprehending their ideas doesn't guarantee that you will remember them. As you read earlier in this chapter, listeners usually forget almost two-thirds of what they hear.

Sometimes recall isn't especially important. You don't need to retain many details of the vacation adventures recounted by a neighbour or the childhood stories told by a relative. At other times, though, remembering a message—even minute details—is very important. The lectures you hear in class are an obvious example. Likewise, it can be important to remember the details of plans that involve you: the time of a future appointment, directions to a spot where you're meeting friends, or instructions given to you by a manager at work.

At times like these it's smart to take notes instead of relying on your memory. Sometimes these notes may be simple and brief: a phone number jotted on a scrap of paper or a list of things to pick up at the market. In other cases—a lecture, for example—your notes need to be much longer. When detailed notes are necessary, a few simple points will help make them effective:

1. *Don't wait too long before beginning to jot down ideas.* If you don't realize that you need to take notes until five minutes into a conversation, you're likely to forget much of what has been said and miss out on other information as you scramble to catch up.

2. *Record only key ideas.* Don't try to capture every word of a long message. If

---

COMMUNICATION ON-SCREEN

'Who's on First?' (1937)
Performed by Bud Abbott and Lou Costello.

This classic comedy routine made popular in the late 1930s by Abbott and Costello illustrates the importance—and the difficulty—of informational listening. In the sketch, Costello asks Abbott to identify some of the players on his baseball team. With names like Who (the first baseman), What (the second baseman), and I Don't Know (the third baseman), it's easy for Costello to believe that Abbott is being evasive. Much of the humour depends on the two characters' mistaking questioning for paraphrase, exemplified in the following exchange:

Costello:	Now if I pick up the ball and throw to first base, somebody's gotta get it. Now who has it?
Abbott:	Naturally.
Costello:	So I pick up the ball and throw it to Naturally?
Abbott:	No you don't, you throw the ball to Who.

> **Cultural Idiom**
>
> **scramble to catch up**
> to begin in a hurried fashion that which should have been started sooner

Understanding Communication Technology

Young Adults Damaging Hearing with Poor MP3 Player Listening Habits

Some young adults are damaging their ears by listening to digital music players too loud and for extended periods of time, a Hearing Foundation of Canada survey has found.

By the time they hit age 40, teens who listen to music too loud will have significant hearing loss, said foundation advocate Gael Hannan.

Part of the problem is due to what a McMaster University associate professor calls an audio level creep.

People start out their day listening to music at a low level, but to drown out background noise, they continue to turn up the music, said Alex Sévigny.

By the end of the day, they have already gotten used to music at a higher decibel, Sévigny explained.

'It's going to be a strange society where some people have hearing problems in their late 20s and early 30s,' he said.

The Hearing Foundation released the survey of more than 145 young people ahead of their Youth Listening Summit, which begins Monday in the Toronto Area.

The survey found that 30 per cent of the teens were listening to music on their MP3s at 90 decibels or higher and for an average of 2.9 hours a day.

The level deemed safe for listening is 85 decibels or less. Every decibel higher than that profoundly affects hearing, Hannan said.

—**Based on original reporting by The Canadian Press, *The Hamilton Spectator*, 27 November 2008.**

Questions: Do you find that you practice audio level creep? How has having an MP3 player affected your lifestyle and daily routine? Has it made you a better listener or less attentive to the people and things around you? Do you think that MP3 players are bringing on forms of politeness, since the wearer often is oblivious to others speaking to him or her?

Cultural Idiom

pin down
identify specifically

put you off
cause one displeasure

---

you can pin down the most important points, your notes will be easier to follow and much more useful.

3. *Develop a note-taking format.* The exact form you choose isn't important. Some people use a formal outlining scheme with headings designated by Roman numerals, letters, and numbers; others use simple lists. You might come up with useful symbols: boxes around key names and numbers or asterisks next to especially important information. Once you have developed a consistent format, your notes will help you not just to remember information but also to mould others' ideas into a shape that's useful to you.

Critical Listening

critical listening
Listening in which the goal is to judge the quality or accuracy of the speaker's remarks.

Whereas the goal of informational listening is to understand a speaker, the goal of **critical listening** (also called 'evaluative listening') is to judge the quality of a message in order to decide whether to accept or reject it. At first the words *critical* and *evaluative* may put you off, because both words carry the negative connotations of carping and fault-finding. But critical listeners don't have to be hostile. Critical listening—at least in the sense we're discussing here—involves evaluating an idea to test its merit. In this sense, we could say that non-critical listeners are unquestioning, or even naive and gullible. Critical listening is appropriate whenever someone is trying to persuade you to buy a product, to act in a certain way, or to accept a belief—to cite just a few examples. You will be most effective as a critical listener if you follow the guidelines below.

Listen for Information Before Evaluating

The importance of listening for information before evaluating it seems almost too obvious to mention, yet all of us are guilty of judging a speaker's ideas before we completely understand them. The tendency to make premature judgments is especially strong when the idea conflicts with our own beliefs.

You can avoid the tendency to judge before understanding by following the simple rule of paraphrasing a speaker's ideas before responding to them. The effort required to translate the other person's ideas into your own words will keep you from arguing, and if your interpretation is mistaken, you'll know immediately.

Evaluate the Speaker's Credibility

The acceptability of an idea often depends on its source. If a long-time family friend and self-made millionaire invited you to invest your life savings in jojoba fruit futures, you might be grateful for the tip. If your deadbeat brother-in-law made the same offer, you would probably laugh off the suggestion.

Chapter 11 examines credibility in detail, but two questions provide a quick guideline for deciding whether or not to accept a speaker as an authority:

1. *Is the speaker competent?* Does the speaker have the experience or the expertise to qualify as an authority on the subject? Note that someone who is knowledgeable in one area may not be as well qualified to comment in another. For instance, the friend who can answer any question about computer programming might be a terrible adviser when the subject turns to romance.
2. *Is the speaker impartial?* Knowledge alone isn't enough to certify a speaker's ideas as acceptable. People who have a personal stake in a topic are more likely to be biased. The unqualified praise lavished on a product by a sales representative working on commission may be more suspect than the mixed review you get from a user of the same product. This doesn't mean you should disregard any comments you hear from an involved party—only that you should consider the possibility of intentional or unintentional bias.

Examine the Speaker's Evidence and Reasoning

Speakers usually offer some kind of support to back up their statements. A dealer who argues that domestic cars are just as reliable as imports might cite frequency-of-repair statistics from consumer reports or refer you to satisfied customers. A professor arguing that students don't work as hard as they used to might offer test papers or essays from now and 20 years ago to back up the thesis.

Chapter 12 describes several types of supporting material that can be used to prove a point: definitions, descriptions, analogies, statistics, and so on. Whatever form the support

Cultural Idiom

deadbeat
one who does not regularly pay bills

laugh off
dismiss with a laugh

The three things you can't fake are erections, competence and creativity.

Douglas Coupland

takes, you can ask several questions to determine the quality of a speaker's evidence and reasoning:[32]

1. *Is the evidence recent enough?* In many cases, old evidence is worthless. If the honours were earned several years ago, the cuisine from an 'award-winning' restaurant may be barely edible today. The claim 'Tony's a terrible goalie' may have been true in the past, but people do change. Before you accept even the most credible evidence, be sure it isn't obsolete.

2. *Is enough evidence presented?* One or two pieces of support may be exceptions and not conclusive evidence. You might have heard this example of generalizing from limited evidence: 'I never wear seat belts. I knew somebody who wasn't wearing his seatbelt in an accident, and his life was saved because he was thrown clear from the car.' Although not wearing seat belts might have been safer in this instance, experts agree that when you consider all vehicle accidents, the chances of avoiding serious injury are much greater if you wear a seat belt.

3. *Is the evidence from a reliable source?* Even a large amount of recent evidence may be worthless if the source is weak. Your cousin the health-food fanatic might not have the qualifications to talk about the poisonous effects of commercially farmed vegetables; the opinion of an impartial physician, nutritionist, or toxologist would carry more weight. And if someone recommends a new cure for headaches that they read about on the Web, be sure to ask them for the specific source. There is no doubt that much useful information can be found from reputable sites on the Internet; the trick is distinguishing it from the specious information disseminated on the greater number of sites of dubious credibility.

4. *Can the evidence be interpreted in more than one way?* A piece of evidence that supports one claim might also support others. For example, you might hear someone cite statistics showing women are underrepresented in the management of a company as evidence of a conspiracy to exclude them from positions of power. The same statistics, though, could have other explanations: perhaps fewer women have been with the company long enough to be promoted, or perhaps this is a field that has not attracted large numbers of women. Alternative explanations don't necessarily mean that the one being argued is wrong, but they do raise questions that need to be answered before you accept an argument.

Besides taking a close look at the evidence a speaker presents, a critical listener will look at how that evidence is put together to prove a point. Logicians have identified a number of *logical fallacies*—errors in reasoning that can lead to false conclusions. Logicians have identified over 100 fallacies;[33] some of the common ones are discussed in Chapter 11.

Emily Morrice, Montreal Metro Team, Campus Staff (National Focus: McGill University, Concordia University; International Region: North Africa), Power to Change Ministries

Studying human communication opened my eyes to the various media and styles of communication and how the transmitted message can be interpreted and understood in many diverse ways. My focus on mass communication and cultural studies enabled me to learn how a message communicated in one culture can be interpreted radically differently when communicated to someone from another culture. The same is true of mass communication versus communicating to a handful of people. This is monumentally beneficial in my career with an international faith-based NGO.

On a daily basis I engage with university students from all over the world from very diverse cultural and religious backgrounds, and my training in human communication has helped me adapt to and understand the different elements of their perspectives. Whether it be cultural location, language, the power of a family or diaspora's influence, university students travel through many gatekeeping layers to experience and discover a personal faith. At the root of my job is being a good critical and empathic listener. Those are both skills that you can learn using, as long as you take communication seriously! My job educating and guiding these students depends on me being a great communicator and listening to really understand students with strong heritage ties to their roots in Quebec, North Africa, the Caribbean, Southeast Asia, and beyond.

Examine Emotional Appeals

Sometimes emotion alone may be enough to persuade you. You might 'lend' your friend $20 just for old time's sake, even though you don't expect to see the money again soon. In other cases, it's a mistake to let yourself be swayed by emotion when the logic of a point isn't sound. The excitement or fun in an ad or the lure of low monthly payments probably aren't good enough reasons to buy a product you can't afford. Again, the fallacies described in Chapter 11 will help you recognize flaws in emotional appeals.

UNDERSTANDING AND EVALUATING

Think of three recent incidents when trying to understand the other person would have been the most appropriate listening style. Then think of three *different* situations in which an evaluative approach would have been the most appropriate way to listen.

Based on your conclusions (and perhaps those of your classmates), develop a set of guidelines describing when it's best to listen purely for information, suspending judgment and attempting to uncritically understand another person's point of view. Next, describe the circumstances when it is more appropriate to listen evaluatively.

Empathic Listening

advising

A helping response in which the receiver offers suggestions about how the speaker should deal with a problem.

empathic listening

Listening in which the goal is to help the speaker solve a problem.

We listen both informationally and critically out of self-interest. In **empathic listening**, however, the goal is to build a relationship or help the speaker solve a problem.[34] Empathic listening is the approach to use when others seek help for personal dilemmas. Sometimes the problem is a big one: 'I want to end the relationship, but I don't know the best way to do it.' At other times the problem is more modest: 'I can't decide whether to get her the earrings or a new iPod.' Empathic listening is also a good approach to take when you simply want to become better acquainted with others and show them that their opinions and feelings matter to you.

The two goals of helping others and building a relationship aren't mutually exclusive. Empathic listening can accomplish both of them, because when listening helps another person, the relationship between that person and the listener improves.[35] For example, couples who communicate in ways that show they understand one another's feelings and ideas are more satisfied with their marriages than couples who express less understanding. The opposite is also true: in marriages where husbands do not give emotional responses to their wives, the stress level grows.

Whatever the relationship and topic, there are several styles by which you can respond empathically to another person's remarks.[36] Each of these styles has its advantages and disadvantages. As you read them, you can aim toward choosing the best style for the situation at hand.

Advising

Many receive advice, few profit by it.

Publilius Syrus

When approached with another's problem, the most common tendency is to try to help by offering a solution—in other words, by **advising**.[37] Although such a response is sometimes valuable, often it isn't as helpful as you might think.[38] In fact, researchers have discovered that advice is actually unhelpful at least as often as it is helpful.[39]

There are several reasons why advice doesn't work especially well. First, it can be hard to tell when the person with the problem wants to hear the listener's idea of a solution.[40] Sometimes the request is clear: 'What do you think I should do?' At other times, though, it isn't clear whether certain statements are requests for direct advice. Ambiguous statements include requests for opinions ('What do you think of Paolo?'), attempts to solicit information ('Would that be an invasion of privacy?'), and announcements of a problem ('I'm really confused . . .').

Even when someone with a problem asks for advice, offering it may not be helpful. Your suggestion may not offer the best course to follow, in which case it can even be harmful. There's often a temptation to tell others how we would behave in their place, but it's important to

realize that what's right for one person may not be right for another. A related consequence of advising is that it often allows others to avoid responsibility for their decisions. Someone who follows a suggestion of yours that doesn't work out can always pin the blame on you. Finally, in many cases people simply don't want advice: they may not be ready to accept it, and what they might really need is to talk out their thoughts and feelings.

Advice is most welcome under two conditions: when it has been requested and when the adviser seems concerned with respecting the face needs of the recipient.[41]

Before offering advice, you need to be sure that four conditions are present:

1. *Be confident that the advice is correct.* You may be certain about some matters of fact, such as the guidelines for completing a course assignment or the cost of a product you recently had to buy, but resist the temptation to act like an authority on matters you know little about. It is both unfair and unwise to make a suggestion when you aren't positive that it's the best choice. Realize that just because a course of action worked for you doesn't guarantee that it will work for everybody.

2. *Ask yourself whether the person seeking your advice seems willing to accept it.* In this way you can avoid the frustration of making good suggestions only to find that the person with the problem had another solution in mind all the time.

3. *Be certain that the receiver won't blame you if the advice doesn't work out.* You may be offering the suggestions, but the choice and responsibility for accepting them are up to the recipient of your advice.

4. *Deliver your advice supportively, in a face-saving manner.* Advice that is perceived as being offered constructively, in the context of a solid relationship, is much better than critical comments offered in a way that signals a lack of respect for the receiver.[42]

Judging

A **judging** response evaluates the sender's thoughts or behaviours in some way. The judgment may be favourable—'That's a good idea' or 'You're on the right track now'—or unfavourable—'That kind of attitude won't get you anywhere.' But in either case it implies that the person doing the judging is in some way qualified to pass judgment on the speaker's thoughts or behaviours.

Sometimes negative judgments are purely critical. How many times have you heard a response like 'Well, you asked for it!' or 'I told you so!' or 'You're just feeling sorry for yourself'? Although comments like these can sometimes serve as verbal slaps that bring problem-holders to their senses, they usually make matters worse.

Cultural Idiom

pin the blame on
claim the fault lies with

Cultural Idiom

bring someone to his or her senses
cause someone to think more rationally

judging
A reaction in which the receiver evaluates the sender's message either favourably or unfavourably.

At other times negative judgments are less critical. These involve what we usually call *constructive criticism*, which is intended to help the problem-holder improve in the future. This is the sort of response given by friends about everything from the choice of clothing to the choice of friends. Another common setting for constructive criticism occurs in school, where instructors evaluate students' work to help them master concepts and skills. But whether it's justified or not, even constructive criticism runs the risk of arousing defensiveness because it may threaten the self-concept of the person at whom it is directed.

Judgments have the best chance of being received well when two conditions exist:

Criticism, like rain, should be gentle enough to nourish a man's growth without destroying his roots.

Frank A. Clark

1. *The person with the problem should have requested an evaluation from you.* An unsolicited judgment is often likely to trigger a defensive response. But if the person is an employee receiving feedback from a superior or an athlete taking tips from a coach or trainer, the judgment is a natural part of improving one's performance and should be expected, even if it hasn't been asked for.
2. *Your judgment is genuinely constructive and not designed as a put-down.* If you are tempted to use judgments as a weapon, don't fool yourself into thinking that you are being helpful. Often the statement 'I'm telling you this for your own good' simply isn't true.

If you can remember to follow these two guidelines, your judgments will probably be less frequent and better received.

Analyzing

In an **analyzing** statement, the listener offers an interpretation of a speaker's message. Analyses like these are probably familiar to you:

- 'I think what's really bothering you is . . .'
- 'She's only doing it because . . .'
- 'I don't think you really meant . . .'
- 'Maybe the problem started when he . . .'

Interpretations are effective when they help people with problems consider alternative meanings—meanings they would never have thought of without your help. Sometimes a clear analysis will make a confusing problem suddenly clear, either suggesting a solution or at least providing an understanding of what is occurring.

At other times, analysis can create more problems than it solves. There are two problems with analyzing. First, your interpretation may not be correct, in which case it will not help and may create new problems. Second, even if your interpretation is correct, expressing it may not be useful. There's a chance that it will arouse defensiveness (because an accurate

Cultural Idiom

a put-down
an insult, a degrading remark

turned you down
rejected your request or offer

analyzing
A helping style in which the listener offers an interpretation of a speaker's message.

assessment implies superiority and judgment); and even if it doesn't, the person may not be able to understand your view of the problem without working it out personally.

How can you know when it's helpful to offer an analysis? There are several guidelines to follow:

1. *Offer your interpretation in a tentative way, not as absolute fact.* There's a big difference between saying, 'Maybe the reason is . . .' or 'It seems to me that . . .' and insisting: 'Here's where your problem is.'
2. *Your analysis ought to have a reasonable chance of being correct.* An inaccurate interpretation—especially one that sounds plausible—can leave a person more confused than before.
3. *Be sure that the other person will be receptive to your analysis.* Even if you're completely accurate, your thoughts won't help if the problem-holder isn't ready to consider them.
4. *Be sure that your real motive for offering an analysis is to help the other person.* It can be tempting to offer an analysis to show how brilliant you are or even to make the other person feel bad for not having thought of the right answer in the first place. Needless to say, an analysis offered under such conditions isn't helpful.

> **questioning**
> Feedback that usually requests the speaker to supply additional information in order to clarify or expand the receiver's understanding. Also, a style of helping in which the receiver seeks additional information from the sender. Some questioning responses are really disguised advice.

Questioning

Earlier on in this chapter we talked about **questioning** as one way to understand others better. A questioning response can also be a way to help others think about their problems and understand them more clearly.[43] For example, questioning can help a problem-holder define vague ideas more precisely. You might respond to a friend with a line of questioning: 'You said Patrice has been acting "differently" toward you lately. What has she been doing?' Here's another example of a question that helps clarify: 'You told your roommates you wanted them to help out more around the apartment. What would you like them to do?'

Questions can also encourage a problem-holder to examine a situation in more detail by talking either about what happened or about personal feelings; for example, 'How did you feel when they turned you down? What did you do then?'. This type of questioning is particularly helpful when you are dealing with someone who is quiet or is unwilling under the circumstances to talk about the problem very much.

Although questions have the potential to be helpful, they also run the risk of confusing or distracting the person with the problem. The best questioning follows these principles:

1. *Don't ask questions just to satisfy your own curiosity.* You might become so interested in the other person's story that you want to hear more. 'And then what did he say?' you might be tempted to ask. 'What happened next?' Responding to questions like these might confuse the person with the problem, or even leave him or her more agitated than before.

Understanding Communication Technology

Digital Distraction

Our students must be paying attention in class because they're busily using their laptops to type every word from our lectures. Or maybe not.

A quick look from the back of university and college lecture theatres shows that many students with wireless laptops are engaged in non-academic activities, including instant messaging, checking e-mails, playing games, and social networking on sites such as Facebook.

Some faculty members have dealt with this situation by imposing outright bans on laptops in classrooms. But Canadian universities and colleges have spent millions of dollars on wireless networks, so a total ban seems counterproductive or at least a waste of resources.

Perhaps surprisingly, the relative advantages and disadvantages of wireless laptops in the classroom are still being debated in the educational research literature. Anecdotally, stories of students misusing the technology are legion. Jean Boivin, an economics professor at Montreal's École des Hautes études Commerciales, for example, was shocked when he read in a newspaper article that one of his students had lost thousands of dollars day-trading from a wireless laptop in his classroom.

Guy Plourde, a chemistry professor at the University of Northern British Columbia, is likely typical of many faculty members who'd like to see a complete ban on laptops. He says he's frustrated when students—heads raised briefly from their computers—want him to repeat what he said because they didn't pay attention the first time.

Concerns are also being voiced by students themselves. Dawn Lomas of the Learning Success Centre at Ryerson University and Michael Howard of the economics department at the University of Waterloo have both received complaints from students who say they couldn't concentrate in class because other students around them were using their laptops to play games or watch DVDs.

Despite this, most students don't appear to support a total laptop ban. Laurie Harrison, the ombudsperson at Simon Fraser University, has fielded several complaints from students after their professor banned laptops in the classroom.

So what are the alternatives? Margaret Wilson, coordinator of university teaching services at the University of Alberta, suggests that it is best to deal with distractive students individually. Request that they refrain from disturbing others during class and if their actions continue then the professor may appropriately ask them to leave.

But the deeper issue, say most experts, is that students need to be actively engaged in their learning. Teresa

2. *Be sure your questions won't confuse or distract the person you're trying to help.* For instance, asking someone, 'When did the problem begin?' might provide some clue about how to solve it—but it could also lead to a long digression that would only confuse matters. As with advice, it's important to be sure you're on the right track before asking questions.

3. *Don't use questions to disguise your suggestions or criticism.* We've all been questioned by parents, teachers, or other figures who seemed to be trying to trap us or indirectly to guide us. In this way, questioning becomes a strategy used by a questioner who already has some idea of what direction the discussion should take but isn't willing to tell you directly.

Supporting

A **supporting** response can take several forms:

---

supporting

A response style in which the receiver reassures, comforts, or distracts the person seeking help.

Agreement	'You're right—the landlord is being unfair.'
	'Yeah, I thought that class was never going to end.'

Dawson, director of the Learning and Teaching Centre at the University of Victoria, suggests faculty employ such active-learning approaches as shared exercises, problem-based learning and the new clicker technologies that allow simultaneous class response to questions. 'Kinesthetic learners, in particular, need to be active in class and so if we make them sit passively it is harder for them to learn,' she says.

And faculty members can integrate laptops into that active learning. Gary Poole, director of the Centre for Teaching and Academic Growth at the University of British Columbia, believes that it is important for faculty members to 'bring activities to class that invite the constructive use of Internet connections and feature measures of accountability for that use'.

For example, students can be asked to work in groups to either solve a problem requiring Internet access or to find a resource on the Web that is relevant to a topic at hand. 'Each group would then be responsible for reporting to the class and perhaps displaying their findings,' he says. Others suggest that it may be appropriate to have laptop-free periods without necessarily having a complete ban.

Which leads to what I believe is the best suggestion, from Tracy Roberts, an instructional designer with the Centre for Teaching and Educational Technologies at Royal Roads University: have the students come up with the policy, and develop an agreement with them. This approach is consistent with the fact that universities and colleges across Canada increasingly encourage students to take responsibility for their own learning. Students are the ones most affected by both digital distractions and laptop bans. It makes sense to include them in the decision-making process.

So, at the beginning of the semester, I brought up the laptop issue in my first-year physical geography class. At first the students didn't see the point of having the discussion. But once we got beyond the idea of students having 'the right' to bring laptops into the classroom, and whether that right was absolute even if it affected the people around them, the discussion became more productive.

We discussed, for example, whether it was better for people with laptops to sit in a special section of the room so that they wouldn't affect other people. Not only was it a useful discussion on laptops, it also helped to frame issues such as the importance of class attendance, respect for other students, and readiness to actively participate in class. Try it, and let me know how it goes.

—Terence Day, universityaffairs.ca, 5 November 2007

Questions: Do you think that banning laptops will improve students' listening in lecture? Or are these students just employing a different technique of listening, more appropriate to their lifestyles and thinking processes? Do you find that having your laptop open during lecture or class is distracting to you? Try shutting it down and just using paper for a week to see if that makes a difference.

Offers to help	'I'm here if you need me.'
	'Let me try to explain it to him.'
Praise	'I don't care what the boss said: I think you did a great job!'
	'You're amazing, and if he doesn't recognize it, that's his problem.'
Reassurance	'The worst part is over. It will probably get easier from here.'
	'I know you'll do a great job.'
Diversion	'Let's catch a movie and get your mind off this.'
	'That reminds me of the time we . . .'
Acknowledgement	'I can see that really hurts.'
	'I know how important that was to you.'
	'It's no fun to feel unappreciated.'

There's no question about the value of receiving support when faced with personal problems. 'Comforting ability' and social support have been shown to be among the most important communication skills a friend—or a teacher or a parent—can have.[44] In other instances, this kind of comment isn't helpful at all; in fact, it can even make things worse.

COMMUNICATION ON-SCREEN

He's Just Not That Into You (2009)

Directed by Ken Kwapis.

In Baltimore, five women and four men attempt to figure out the signals they receive from the opposite sex. The ensemble cast explores questions about male and female relationships, specifically how women and men communicate. Each character misinterprets signals from his or her partner or the individual he or she is pursuing. Inept listening and questioning skills propel the story forward as the characters discover things about each other and themselves.

Telling a person who is obviously upset that everything is all right or joking about a serious matter can trivialize the problem. People might see your comment as a put-down, leaving them feeling worse than before.

As with the other styles we'll discuss, supporting can be helpful, but only in certain circumstances.[45] For the occasions when supporting is an appropriate response, follow these guidelines:

1. *Make sure your expression of support is sincere.* Phony agreement or encouragement is probably worse than no support at all, because it adds the insult of your dishonesty to whatever pain the other person is already feeling.
2. *Be sure the other person can accept your support.* Sometimes we become so upset that we aren't ready or able to hear anything positive.

Even if your advice, judgments, and analysis are correct and your questions are sincere, and even if your support comes from the best motives, these responses often fail to help. One recent survey demonstrates how poorly such traditional responses work.[46] Mourners who had recently suffered the death of a loved one reported that 80 per cent of the statements made to them were unhelpful. Nearly half of the statements were advice: 'You've got to get out more.' 'Don't question God's will.' Despite their frequency, these responses were helpful only 3 per cent of the time. The next most frequent response was reassurance, such as 'She's out of pain now.' Like advice, this kind of support was helpful only 3 per cent of the time. Far more helpful were expressions that acknowledged the mourner's feelings.

One American Red Cross grief counsellor explained to survivors of the September 11 terrorist attacks in New York that simply being present can be more helpful than trying to reassure grief-stricken family members who had lost loved ones in the tragedy:

> Listen. Don't say anything. Saying 'it'll be okay', or 'I know how you feel' can backfire. Right now that's not what a victim wants to hear. They want to know people are there and care about them. Be there, be present, listen. The clergy refer to it as a 'ministry of presence'. You don't need to do anything, just be there or have them know you're available.[47]

Prompting

Advising, judging, analyzing, questioning, and supporting are all active approaches to helping that call for a great deal of input from the respondent. Another approach to problem-solving is more passive. **Prompting** involves using silences and brief statements of encouragement to draw others out as a way to help them solve their own problems. Consider this example:

Marc: Elena's dad is selling his laptop for only $1,200, but if I want it I have to buy it now. He's got another interested buyer. It's a great deal, and he's only had it a year. But buying it would wipe out my savings. At the rate I spend money, it would take me a year to save up this much again.

Sujit: Uh huh.

Marc: I wouldn't be able to take that ski trip over reading week . . . but I sure could save time with a faster machine. That computer I'm using now is so out of date.

It is hard to know what to say to a person who has been struck by tragedy, but it is easier to know what not to say. Anything critical of the mourner ('don't take it so hard,' 'try to hold back your tears, you're upsetting people') is wrong. Anything which tries to minimize the mourner's pain ('it's probably for the best,' 'it could be a lot worse,' 'she's better off now') is likely to be misguided and unappreciated. Anything which asks the mourner to disguise or reject his feelings ('we have no right to question God,' 'God must love you to have selected you for this burden') is wrong as well.

Harold S. Kushner,
When Bad Things Happen to Good People

---

prompting
Using silence and brief statements of encouragement to draw out a speaker.

Sujit:	That's for sure.
Marc:	You think I should buy it?
Sujit:	I don't know. What do you think?
Marc:	I just can't decide.
Sujit:	[silence]
Marc:	I'm going to do it. I'll never get a deal like this again.

Prompting works especially well when you can't help others make a decision. At times like this your presence can act like a catalyst to help others find their own answers. Prompting will work best when it's done sincerely. Your non-verbal behaviours—eye contact, posture, facial expression, tone of voice—have to show that you are concerned with the other person's problem. Mechanical prompting is likely to irritate instead of help.

Paraphrasing

Earlier we discussed the value of paraphrasing to understand others. The same skill can be used as a helping tool. When you use this approach, be sure to reflect both the thoughts and the feelings you hear being expressed. This conversation between two friends shows how reflecting can offer support and help a person find the answer to her own problem:

Jen:	I've had the strangest feeling about my boss lately.
Carlos:	What's that? [A simple question invites Jen to go on.]
Jen:	I'm starting to think maybe he has this thing about women—or maybe it's just about me.
Carlos:	You mean he's coming on to you? [Carlos paraphrases what he thinks Jen has said.]
Jen:	Oh no, not at all! But it seems like he doesn't take women—or at least me—seriously. [Jen corrects Carlos's misunderstanding and explains herself.]
Carlos:	What do you mean? [Carlos asks another simple question to get more information.]
Jen:	Well, whenever we're in a meeting or just talking around the office and he asks for ideas, he always seems to pick men. He gives orders to women—men, too—but he never asks the women to say what they think.
Carlos:	So you think maybe he doesn't take women seriously, is that it? [Carlos paraphrases Jen's last statement.]
Jen:	Yeah. Well, he sure doesn't seem interested in their ideas. But that doesn't mean he's a total woman-hater or a male chauvinist pig. I know he counts on some women in the office. Our accountant Teresa has been there forever, and he's always saying he couldn't live without her. And when Brenda got the new computer system up and running last month, I know he appreciated that. He gave her a day off and told everybody how she saved our lives.
Carlos:	Now you sound confused. [Reflects her apparent feeling.]
Jen:	I am confused. I don't think it's just my imagination. I mean I'm a good producer, but he has never—not once—asked me for my ideas about how to improve sales or anything. And I can't remember a time when he's asked any other women. But maybe I'm overreacting.
Carlos:	You're not positive whether you're right, but I can tell that this has you concerned. [Carlos paraphrases both Jen's central theme and her feeling.]
Jen:	Yes. But I don't know what to do about it.
Carlos:	Maybe you should . . . [Starts to offer advice but catches himself and decides to ask a sincere question instead.] So what are your choices?

> **Cultural Idiom**
>
> **a male chauvinist pig**
> a male who believes that men are superior to women
>
> **coming on to**
> making a sexual advance to
>
> **where I stand with**
> how I am perceived by

Jen: Well, I could just ask him if he's aware that he never asks women's opinions. But that might sound too aggressive and angry.

Carlos: And you're not angry? [Tries to clarify how Jen is feeling.]

Jen: Not really. I don't know whether I should be angry because he's not taking ideas seriously, or whether he just doesn't take my ideas seriously, or whether it's nothing at all.

Carlos: So you're mostly confused. [Reflects Jen's apparent feeling again.]

Jen: Yes! I don't know where I stand with my boss, and not being sure is starting to get to me. I wish I knew what he thinks of me. Maybe I could just tell him I'm confused about what's going on here and ask him to clear it up. But what if it's nothing? Then I'll look insecure.

Carlos: [Carlos thinks Jen should confront her boss, but he isn't positive that this is the best approach, so he paraphrases what Jen seems to be saying.] And that would make you look bad.

Jen: I'm afraid maybe it would. I wonder if I could talk it over with anybody else in the office and get their ideas . . .

Carlos: . . . see what they think . . .

Jen: Yeah. Maybe I could ask Brenda. She's easy to talk to, and I do respect her judgment. Maybe she could give me some ideas about how to handle this.

Carlos: Sounds like you're comfortable with talking to Brenda first.

Jen: (*warming to the idea.*) Yes! Then if it's nothing, I can calm down. But if I do need to talk to the boss, I'll know I'm doing the right thing.

Carlos: Great. Let me know how it goes.

> *The reality of the other person is not in what he reveals to you, but in what he cannot reveal to you.*
>
> *Therefore, if you would understand him, listen not to what he says but rather to what he does not say.*
>
> Kahlil Gibran

Reflecting a speaker's ideas and feelings in this way can be surprisingly helpful.[48] First, paraphrasing helps the problem-holder sort out the problem. In the dialogue you just read, Carlos's paraphrasing helped Jen pin down the real source of her concern: what her boss thinks of her, not whether he doesn't take women seriously. The clarity that comes from this sort of perspective can make it possible to find solutions that weren't apparent before. Paraphrasing is also helpful because it helps the problem-holder unload more of the concerns he or she has been carrying around, often leading to the relief that comes from catharsis. Finally, listeners who reflect the speaker's thoughts and feelings (instead of judging or analyzing, for example) show their involvement and concern.

Paraphrasing can be helpful, but it is no panacea. A study by noted researcher John Gottman revealed that 'active listening' (a term sometimes used to describe paraphrasing) by itself was not a trait that distinguished happily married couples from troubled ones.[49] Because empathy is the ingredient that makes paraphrasing thoughts and feelings helpful, it is a mistake to think of reflective listening as a technique that you can use mechanically. Carl Rogers, the psychologist generally considered the foremost advocate of active listening, made the case against mechanical paraphrasing strongly: 'I am not trying to "reflect feelings". I am trying to determine whether my understanding of the client's inner world is correct—whether I am seeing it as he or she is experiencing it at this moment.'[50] In other words, reflecting is not an end in itself; rather, it is one way to help others by understanding them better.

There are several factors to consider before you decide to paraphrase:

1. *Is the problem complex enough?* Sometimes people are simply looking for information and not trying to work out their feelings. At times like this, paraphrasing would be out of place. If someone asks you for the time of day, you'd do better simply to give her the information than to respond by saying, 'You want to know what time it is.' If you're fixing dinner, and someone wants to know when it will be ready, it would be exasperating to reply 'You're interested in knowing when we'll be eating.'

2. *Do you have the necessary time and concern?* The kind of paraphrasing we've been discussing here takes a good deal of time. If you're in a hurry to do something besides listen, it's wise to avoid starting a conversation you won't be able to finish. Even more important than time is concern. It's not necessarily wrong to be too preoccupied to help or even to be unwilling to exert the considerable effort that active listening requires. You can't help everyone with every problem. It's far better to state honestly that you're unable or unwilling to help than to pretend to care when you really don't.

3. *Are you genuinely interested in helping the other person?* Sometimes as you listen to others, it's easy to relate their thoughts to your own life or to seek more information just to satisfy your own curiosity. Remember that paraphrasing is a way of helping someone else. The general obligation to reciprocate the other person's self-disclosure with information of your own isn't necessary when the goal is to solve a problem. Research shows that speakers who reveal highly intimate personal information don't expect, or even appreciate, the same kind of disclosure from a conversational partner.[51] Rather, the most competent and socially attractive response is one that sticks to the same topic but is lower in intimacy. In other words, when we are opening up to others, we don't appreciate their pulling a conversational take-away such as '*You're* worried? So am I! Let me tell you about how *I* feel . . .'

4. *Can you withhold judgment?* You've already seen that paraphrasing allows other people to find their own answers. You should use this style only if you can comfortably paraphrase without injecting your own judgments. It's sometimes tempting to rephrase others' comments in a way that leads them toward the solution you think is best without ever clearly stating your intentions. As you will read in Chapter 7, this kind of strategy is likely to backfire by causing defensiveness if it's discovered. If you think the situation meets the criteria for advice described earlier in this chapter, you should offer your suggestions openly.

5. *Is your paraphrasing in proportion to other responses?* Although active listening can be a very helpful way of responding to others' problems, it can become artificial and annoying when it's overused. This is especially true if you suddenly begin to use it as a major response. Even if such responses are potentially helpful, this sudden switch in your behaviour will be so out of character that others might find it distracting. A far better way to use paraphrasing is to gradually introduce it into your repertoire of helpfulness, so that you can become comfortable with it without appearing too awkward. Another way to become more comfortable with this style is to start using it on real but relatively minor problems, so that you'll be more adept at knowing how and when to use it when a big crisis does occur.

When and How to Help

Before committing yourself to helping another person—even someone in obvious distress—make sure your help is welcome. There are many cases in which others prefer to keep their concerns to themselves. In these cases your efforts to get involved may not be useful and can even be harmful. In one survey, some people reported occasions when social support wasn't necessary because they felt capable of handling the problem by themselves.[52] Many regarded uninvited help as an intrusion, and some said it left them feeling more nervous than before. The majority of respondents expressed a preference for being in control of whether their distressing situation should be discussed with even the most helpful friend.

When help is welcome, there is no single best way to provide it. Research shows that all styles can help others accept their situation, feel better, and have a sense of control over their problems.[53] But there is enormous variability in which style will work with a given person.[54] This fact explains why communicators who are able to use a wide variety of helping styles are usually more effective than those who rely on just one or two styles.[55]

You can boost the odds of choosing the best helping style in each situation by considering three factors. First, think about the situation and match your response to the nature of the problem. Sometimes people need your advice. At other times they will find your encouragement and support most helpful, and at still other times they will benefit most from your analysis or judgment. And, as you have seen, there are times when others can find their own answer with help from your probes and paraphrasing.

Second, besides considering the situation, you should think about the other person when deciding which style to use. Some people are able to consider advice thoughtfully, whereas others use suggestions to avoid making their own decisions. Many communicators are extremely defensive and aren't capable of receiving analysis or judgments without lashing out. Still others aren't equipped to think through problems clearly enough to profit from paraphrasing and probing. Sophisticated helpers choose a style that fits the person.

Third, think about yourself when deciding how to respond. Most of us instinctively use one or two helping styles. You may be best at listening quietly, offering a prompt from time to time. Or perhaps you are especially insightful and can offer a truly useful analysis of the problem. Of course, it's also possible to rely on a response style that is unhelpful. You may be overly judgmental or too eager to advise, even when your suggestions aren't invited or productive. As you think about how to respond to another's problems, consider both your strengths and weaknesses.

Summary

Even the best message is useless if it goes unreceived or if it is misunderstood. For this reason, listening—the process of understanding the full meaning of an oral message—is a vitally important part of the communication process. We began our look at the subject by identifying and refuting several myths about listening. Our conclusion here was that effective listening is a skill that needs to be developed in order for us to be truly effective in understanding others.

We next took a close look at five steps in the process of listening: hearing, attending, understanding, responding, and remembering. We described some of the challenges that make effective listening so difficult. We described 7 faulty listening behaviours and 10 more reasons why people often listen poorly. You can become a better listener by recognizing which of these tendencies characterize your communication.

This chapter also discussed several personal listening styles: content-oriented, people-oriented, action-oriented, and time-oriented. The chapter pointed out that most people favour one of these styles and that problems arise when different types of listeners interact. All of these styles have advantages and drawbacks, and effective listeners will use each one when it is most appropriate for the circumstances.

The chapter continued by examining three types of listening. Informational listening is the proper approach to take when the goal is to understand another person's ideas. Information can be best gained with an active approach to listening. This active approach can involve either questioning or paraphrasing—restating the speaker's message in your own words.

Critical listening is appropriate when the goal is to judge the quality of an idea. A critical analysis will be most successful when the listener ensures correct understanding of a message before passing judgment, when the speaker's credibility is taken into account, when the quality of supporting evidence is examined, and when the logic of the speaker's arguments is carefully assessed.

The aim of empathic listening is to help the speaker, not the receiver. Various helping responses include advising, judging, analyzing, questioning, supporting, prompting, and paraphrasing the speaker's thoughts and feelings. Listeners can be most helpful when they use a variety of styles, focus on the emotional dimensions of a message, and avoid being too judgmental.

Key Terms

action-oriented
   listeners 140
advising 152
ambushers 134
analyzing 154
attending 131
content-oriented
   listeners 140
counterfeit question 144
critical listening 148
defensive listening 134

empathic listening 152
hearing 130
informational listening 141
insensitive listeners 134
insulated listeners 134
judging 153
listening 130
paraphrasing 145
people-oriented
   listeners 140
prompting 158

pseudolistening 133
questioning 155
remembering 131
residual message 132
responding 131
selective listening 133
sincere question 144
stage hogs 134
supporting 156
time-oriented listeners 141
understanding 131

Activities

A. Your LQ (Listening Quotient)

Explain the poor listening behaviours listed on pages 133–5 to someone who knows you well. Then ask your informant to describe which, if any, of them, you use. Also explore the consequences of your listening behaviour.

B. Your Listening Style Preferences

You can analyze your effectiveness as a listener by answering the following questions:

1. Which of the listening styles described earlier do you use?
2. Does your listening style change in various situations, or do you use the same style most or all of the time?
3. What are the consequences (beneficial and harmful) of the listening styles you use?
4. How could you adapt your listening styles to improve your communication effectiveness?

C. Informational Listening Practice

Effective informational listening isn't easy. It takes hard work and concentration. You can improve your skill in this important area and convince yourself of the difference good informational listening makes by following these steps:

1. Find a partner with whom you have an important relationship. This may be a family member, lover, friend, fellow worker, or even an 'enemy' with whom you interact frequently.
2. Invite your partner to explain his or her side of an issue that the two of you have difficulty discussing. Your job during this conversation is to understand your partner. You should not even attempt to explain your position. (If you find the prospect of trying to understand the other person distressing, consider how this attitude might interfere with your ability to listen carefully.)
3. As your partner explains his or her point of view, use the skills outlined on pages 141–8 to help you understand. You can discover how well you are grasping your partner's position by occasionally paraphrasing what you think he or she is saying. If your partner verifies your paraphrase as correct, go on with the conversation. If not, try to listen again and play back the message until the partner confirms your understanding.
4. After the conversation is over, ask yourself the following questions:
    a. As you listened, how accurate was your first understanding of the speaker's statements?
    b. How did your understanding of the speaker's position change after you used paraphrasing?
    c. Did you find that the gap between your position and that of your partner narrowed as a result of your both using paraphrasing?

d. How did you feel at the end of your conversation? How does this feeling compare to your usual emotional state after discussing controversial issues with others?

e. How might your life change if you used paraphrasing at home? At work? With friends?

f. See how many pieces of information you can elicit from others by giving out the minimal pieces of information. See how many pieces of information you can elicit from a stranger whom you meet on campus.

Write down what you've learned immediately after having each conversation. See what patterns emerge in the types of people you are most capable to empathize with and get to open up to you and which ones seem unreachable to you.

D. Empathic Response Styles

This exercise will help you improve your ability to listen empathically in the most successful manner. For each of the following statements,

1. Write separate responses, using each of the following styles:
   - advising
   - judging
   - analyzing
   - questioning
   - supporting
   - prompting
   - paraphrasing

2. Discuss the pros and cons of using each response style.

3. Identify which response seems most effective, explaining your decision.

   a. At a party, a guest you have just met for the first time says, 'Everybody seems like they've been friends for years. I don't know anybody here. How about you?'

   b. Your best friend has been quiet lately. When you ask if anything is wrong, she snaps 'No!' in an irritated tone of voice.

   c. A co-worker says, 'The boss keeps making sexual jokes around me. I think it's a come-on, and I don't know what to do.'

   d. It's registration time at university. One of your friends asks if you think he should enroll in the communication class you've taken.

   e. Your roommate remarks, 'It seems like this place is always a mess. We get it cleaned up, and then an hour later it's trashed.'

Further Reading

Burleson, Brant R. 'Emotional Support Skills', in John O. Greene and Brant R. Burleson, eds, *Handbook of Communication and Social Interaction Skills*. Mahwah, NJ: Erlbaum, 2002.
This review of research describes what types of communication provide emotional support.

Leeds, Dorothy. *The Seven Powers of Questions: Secrets to Successful Communication in Life and Work*. New York: Penguin, 2001.
This practical book shows the many ways questions can be useful beyond seeking information. They can encourage others to open up, and even enhance our control over a situation.

Steil, Lyman K., and Richard K. Bommelje. *Listening Leaders: The 10 Golden Rules to Listen, Lead & Succeed*. Edina, MN: Beaver's Pond Press, 2004.
A comprehensive look at how leaders can apply the subtle yet important skill of listening to make a difference in their organizations.

Study Questions

1. Describe situations from your own experience that illustrate the misconceptions about listening outlined on pages 130–2.

2. Recall examples of at least three of the faulty listening behaviours described on pages 133–5.

3. Describe how a situation at work or school might look and sound different, depending on which of the personal listening styles described on pages 140–1 was used.

4. Apply the guidelines in the second half of this chapter to three situations that require good listening: one informational, one critical, and one empathic.

After studying the material in this chapter . . .

You should understand:

- the characteristics of non-verbal communication;
- the differences between verbal and non-verbal communication;
- how culture and gender influence non-verbal communication;
- the functions that non-verbal communication can serve; and
- how the types of non-verbal communication described in this chapter function.

You should be able to:

- identify and describe non-verbal behaviour in various contexts;
- identify non-verbal behaviours that repeat, substitute for, complement, accent, regulate, and contradict verbal messages;
- recognize the emotional and relational dimensions of your own non-verbal behaviour; and
- share your interpretation of another person's non-verbal behaviour in a tentative manner when such sharing is appropriate.

Non-Verbal Communication

Chapter Highlights

Non-verbal communication has several important characteristics.

- Unlike verbal communication, it is always present when people encounter one another and in many situations where they aren't physically present.
- It has great value in conveying information about others, and much of that information isn't something others intentionally want to reveal.
- It is especially useful in suggesting how others feel about you and the relationship, although non-verbal messages are much more ambiguous than verbal communication.

While much non-verbal communication is universal, some factors do shape the way we express ourselves and understand others.

- Culture shapes many non-verbal practices.
- Gender plays a role in the way we communicate.

Non-verbal communication serves many functions, when compared to verbal messages.

- It can repeat, complement, and accent spoken words.
- Sometimes it can substitute for speech.
- It can regulate spoken conversation.
- It can contradict spoken words, or even deceive others.

Non-verbal communication can take many forms. Some of these forms may be obvious:

- posture and gesture,
- face and eyes,
- voice,
- touch,
- physical attractiveness; and clothes.

Other forms are more subtle, involving things like

- personal space and distance,
- use of time, and
- physical environment.

There is often a big gap between what people say and what they feel. An acquaintance says, 'I'd like to get together again' in a way that leaves you suspecting the opposite. (But how do you know?) A speaker tries to appear confident but acts in a way that almost screams out, 'I'm nervous!' (What tells you this?) You ask a friend what's wrong, and the 'Nothing' you get in response rings hollow. (Why does it sound untrue?)

Then, of course, there are times when another's message comes through even though there are no words at all. A look of irritation, a smile, a sigh—signs like these can say more than a torrent of words.

All situations like these have one point in common: the message was sent *non-verbally*. The goal of this chapter is to introduce you to this world of non-verbal communication. Although you have certainly recognized non-verbal messages before, the following pages should introduce you to a richness of information you have never noticed. And though your experience won't transform you into a mind reader, it will make you a far more accurate observer of others—and yourself.

We need to begin our study of non-verbal communication by defining this term. At first this might seem like a simple task. If *non* means 'not' and *verbal* means 'words', then *non-verbal communication* appears to mean 'communication without words'. This is a good starting point after we distinguish between vocal communication (by mouth) and verbal communication (with words). After this distinction is made, it becomes clear that some non-verbal messages are vocal, and some are not. Likewise, although many verbal messages are vocal, some aren't. Table 5.1 illustrates these differences.

What about languages that don't involve words? Do Canadian Sign Language and the Langue des signes québécois, for example, qualify as non-verbal communication? Most scholars would say not.[1] Keeping this fact in mind, we arrive at a working definition of **non-verbal communication:** oral and non-oral messages expressed by other than linguistic means. This rules out sign languages and written words, but it includes messages transmitted by vocal means that don't involve language—sighs, laughs, and other utterances we will discuss soon.

Characteristics of Non-Verbal Communication

Our brief definition only hints at the richness of non-verbal messages. You can begin to understand their prevalence by trying a simple experiment. Spend an hour or so around a group of people who are speaking a language you don't understand. You might find such a

Cultural Idiom

rings hollow
sounds insincere

- - - - - - - - - - - - - - - -

non-verbal communication
Messages expressed by other than linguistic means.

- - - - - - - - - - - - - - - -

TABLE 5.1 Types of Communication

	Vocal Communication	Non-Vocal Communication
Verbal Communication	Spoken words	Written words
Non-Verbal Communication	Tone of voice, sighs, screams, vocal qualities (loudness, pitch, and so on)	Gestures, movement, appearance, facial expression, and so on

Source: Adapted from John Stewart and Gary D'Angelo, Together: *Communicating Interpersonally,* 2nd edn (Reading, MA: Addison-Wesley, 1980), 22. Copyright © 1993 by McGraw-Hill. Reprinted/adapted by permission.

group by visiting an area populated by an ethnic group other than your own, by taking public transportation, or by sitting in a café that caters to a cultural group different from yours, such as those in Vancouver's Chinatown or Toronto's Little India. Your goal is to see how much information you can learn about the people you're observing through means other than the verbal messages they transmit. This experiment will reveal several characteristics of non-verbal communication.

Non-Verbal Communication Exists

Your observations in the experiment show clearly that even without understanding speech it is possible to get an idea about how others are feeling. You probably noticed that some people were in a hurry, whereas others seemed happy, confused, withdrawn, or deep in thought. The point is that without any formal experience you were able to recognize, and to some degree interpret, messages that other people sent non-verbally. In this chapter, we want to sharpen the skills you already have and give you a better grasp of the vocabulary of non-verbal language.

No matter how eloquently a dog may bark, he cannot tell you that his parents were poor but honest.

Bertrand Russell

Non-Verbal Behaviour Has Communicative Value

The pervasiveness of non-verbal communication brings us to its second characteristic: it's virtually impossible *not* to communicate non-verbally. Suppose you were instructed to avoid communicating any messages at all. What would you do? Close your eyes? Withdraw into a ball? Leave the room? The meaning of some non-verbal behaviour can be ambiguous, but it always has communicative value. For example, a study of bereaved First Nations family members in Canada revealed that non-verbal communication was an important part of effective palliative care for First Nations people. The study concluded that respect, communication, appropriate environments, and caregiving were necessary to ensure culturally appropriate care.[2]

Of course, we don't always intend to send non-verbal messages. Unintentional non-verbal behaviours differ from intentional ones.[3] For example, we often stammer, blush, frown, and sweat without meaning to do so. Some theorists argue that unintentional behaviour may provide information, but it shouldn't count as communication. Others draw the boundaries of non-verbal communication more broadly, suggesting that even unconscious and unintentional behaviour conveys messages and thus is worth studying as communication.[4] We take the broad view here because, whether or not our non-verbal behaviour is intentional, others recognize it and take it into account when responding to us.

Although non-verbal behaviour reveals information, we aren't always conscious of what we are communicating non-verbally. In one study, less than a quarter of experimental subjects who had been instructed to show increased or decreased approval of a partner could describe the non-verbal behaviours they used. Furthermore, just because communicators are non-verbally expressive doesn't mean that others will tune into the abundance of unspoken messages that are available. One study

comparing the richness of e-mail to in-person communication confirmed the greater amount of information available in face-to-face conversations, but it also showed that some communicators (primarily men) failed to recognize these messages.[5] A study by Richard Schwier and Shelly Balbar of the University of Saskatchewan investigated the effect of face-to-face versus distant communication on learning in a graduate seminar. The study concluded that both face-to-face and non–face-to-face communication strategies worked for different sorts of learning. They found that a combination of the two appears necessary to promote the student engagement and depth required in a seminar.[6]

The fact that you and everyone around you are constantly sending non-verbal clues is important because it means that you have a constant source of information available about yourself and others. If you can tune into these signals, you will be more aware of how those around you are feeling and thinking, and you will be better able to respond to their behaviour.

Non-Verbal Communication Is Primarily Relational

Some non-verbal messages serve utilitarian functions. For example, a police officer uses hand motions to direct the flow of traffic, as do street surveyors to coordinate their work. But non-verbal communication also serves a far more common (and more interesting) series of social functions.[7]

One of these social functions involves identity management. Chapter 2 discussed how we strive to create an image of ourselves as we want others to view us. Non-verbal communication plays an important role in this process—in many cases more important than verbal communication. Consider, for example, what happens when you attend a party where you are likely to meet strangers you would like to get to know better. Instead of projecting your image verbally ('Hi! I'm attractive, friendly, and easygoing'), you behave in ways that will present this identity. You might smile a lot, and perhaps try to strike a relaxed pose. It's also likely that you dress carefully—even if the image involves looking as if you hadn't given a lot of attention to your appearance.

Along with identity management, non-verbal communication allows us to define the kind of relationships we want to have with others. You can appreciate this fact by thinking about the wide range of ways you could behave when greeting another person. You could wave, shake hands, nod, smile, clap the other person on the back, give a hug, or avoid all contact. Each one of these decisions would send a message about the nature of your relationship with the other person.

Non-verbal communication performs a third valuable social function: conveying emotions that we may be unwilling or unable to express verbally—or ones we may not even be aware of. In fact, non-verbal communication is much better suited to expressing attitudes and feelings than ideas.[8] You can prove this for yourself by imagining how you could express each item on the following list non-verbally:

- You are bored.
- You are attracted to another person in the group.
- You are nervous about trying this experiment.
- You are opposed to stem cell research.
- You want to know if you will be tested on this material.

The first three items in this list involve attitudes. By contrast, the last two items involve ideas, and they would be quite difficult to convey without using words. The same principle

Sometimes you can observe a lot by watching.

Yogi Berra

holds in everyday life: non-verbal behaviour offers many cues about the way people feel—often more than we get from their words alone. In fact, some research suggests that one important element of communicative competence is non-verbal expressiveness.[9]

Non-Verbal Communication Is Ambiguous

Before you get the idea that this book will turn you into a mind reader, it is important to realize that non-verbal communication is often difficult to interpret accurately. To appreciate the ambiguous nature of non-verbal communication, study the photo on this page. What emotions do you imagine the man is feeling? Elation? Relief? In fact, neither of these is even close. The basketball coach in this photo is reacting to a referee's call that he doesn't agree with!

Non-verbal communication can be just as vague in everyday life. For example, relying on non-verbal cues in romantic situations can lead to inaccurate guesses about a partner's interest in a sexual relationship.[10] Workers at Safeway, a chain of grocery stores in the United States and western Canada, discovered first-hand the problems with non-verbal ambiguity when they tried to follow the company's new 'superior customer service' policy that required them to smile and make eye contact with customers. Twelve employees filed grievances over the policy, reporting that several customers had propositioned them after misinterpreting their actions as come-ons.[11]

Although all non-verbal behaviour is ambiguous, some emotions are easier to decode accurately than others. In laboratory experiments, subjects were better at identifying positive facial expressions—happiness, love, surprise, interest—than negative ones such as fear, sadness, anger, and disgust.[12] In real life, however, spontaneous non-verbal expressions are so ambiguous that observers are able to identify the emotions they convey no more accurately than by guessing.[13]

Some people are more skilful than others at accurately decoding non-verbal behaviour.[14] Those who are better senders of non-verbal messages also are better receivers. Decoding ability also increases with age and training, although there are still differences in ability owing to personality and occupation. For instance, extroverts are relatively accurate judges of non-verbal behaviour, whereas dogmatists are not. Women seem to be far better than men

'That was unkind, darling. When their mouths turn up at the corners they want to be friends.'

Young Communicator
PROFILE

●●●●●

Miles Jones, Hip Hop Artist
and Music Producer

Toronto producer, songwriter, and MC Miles Jones has musical wanderlust in his blood. His photographer father, Deadly Hedley Jones, is a former CFNY-FM host and pioneering club DJ. Grandfather Hedley Jones Sr was a Jamaican jazz and ska musician who helped design and build the massively influential rocksteady and reggae recording studio Studio One.

'They could never be stuck in one space,' recalls Miles Jones. 'They were always moving towards the future, to wherever a progressive movement would take them.'

As a youngster, Jones favoured the music of Bob Marley and Stevie Wonder, but by age six, his father had introduced him to 1980s hip-hop artists like Kool Moe Dee, Big Daddy Kane, LL Cool J, and the especially influential Eric B. & Rakim.

'When I heard Rakim rap, it didn't sound like the way anybody else rapped,' says a still-appreciative Jones. 'He could command the mic.'

Encouraged by his schoolteacher mother, Jones wrote poetry as a youth and started freestyling at high-school ciphers. In 2002, he headed to Hamilton to study communication studies and multimedia at McMaster University. Here, he started DJing and made beats that he then sang and rapped over. Two years into his studies, Jones was invited by family friend (and famous Canadian singer-songwriter) Dan Hill to participate in a Canadian Idol songwriter's conference.

'My response to Dan was, "I don't write adult-contemporary music," and he said, "Well, you write lyrics don't you? I

at decoding non-verbal messages. Over 95 per cent of the studies examined in one analysis showed that women are more accurate at interpreting non-verbal signals.[15] Despite these differences, even the best non-verbal decoders do not approach perfect accuracy.

When you do try to make sense out of ambiguous non-verbal behaviour, you need to consider several factors: the *context* in which it occurs (smiling at a joke and smiling at bad news reflect different feelings); the *history* of your relationship with the sender (friendly, hostile, etc.); the other's *mood* at the time; and your *feelings* (when you're feeling insecure, almost anything can seem like a threat). The important idea is that when you become aware think you could do it,'" laughs Jones. 'I went there at 21, the youngest guy in the camp. There were 50 writers from all over the world, you'd be sent into a room, four people at a time, and had four hours to write a song. You'd demo it and then do another in the afternoon. It was intense.'

Armed with new-found confidence and skills, Jones wrote, produced, and recorded his 12-song debut album, *One Chance,* as a thesis project and released it on his own Mojo Recordings label in 2006. Surprisingly mature, the album signalled the emergence of a new Canadian hip-hop talent. Jones now follows on its promise with the musically diverse *Runaway Jones*.

'Post–*One Chance,* I really had a phase of writer's block and didn't know how I was going to approach another album,' Jones admits. 'I needed to be able to create something new, something that wouldn't sound like the 10 other artists I just heard on the radio or saw videos for—something that would make me want to get up and dance.'

He chose to collaborate with a number of favourite producers for inspiration and innovation, including Mr Attic, Slakah the BeatChild, and DJ Serious who crafted both the hip-hop heavy 'Rhyme Like This' and the clubby 'Runaway'.

'Serious is always ahead of the pack, way off doing his own thing,' says Jones. 'He'd already done two hip-hop albums and I think in his head there was no real reason for him to come out with more music unless I could tell him why. He came over and let me hear about 20 tracks, saying "Do you want to hear hip-hop shit or do you want to hear everything?" I chose "Everything."'

On the denser hip-hop tip is 'Never Too Late', produced by Detroit's Black Milk. Jones had written him in 2007 as a fan, 'to say how much I loved his music and what he was doing for hip-hop'. Milk's participation in *Runaway Jones* was later requested.

'The fact that he checked me out and gave me music to hear was really inspiring. Right now, Black Milk is the hip-hop beast producer who's pumping out track after track and everything that he does seems to smash what everyone else is doing in that hip-hop bubble. Everything he does has a feel or sound to it—it's so heavy and emotional in some sense.'

Also contributing are MCs and vocalists including Bronx-based Percee P, London's Shad ('This is the kind of rap that I've always wanted to hear come from Canada'), and Ghanaian born singer-songwriter Kae Sun for whose upcoming album Jones is contributing production.

'I'm really interested in stepping outside of the hip-hop box and producing other artists,' says Jones of his future. 'That's part of why I've created Runaway Jones as a character. Runaway Jones is the one up on stage and touring; Miles Jones is the guy in the studio and making business decisions.'

—*Denise Benson, Eye Weekly, 12 August 2009.*

of non-verbal messages, you should think of them not as facts but rather as clues that need to be checked out.

Non-Verbal Communication Is Different from Verbal Communication

As Table 5.2 shows, non-verbal communication differs in several important ways from spoken and written language. These differences suggest some reasons why it is so valuable to

TABLE 5.2 Some Differences between Verbal and Non-Verbal Communication

	Verbal Communication	Non-Verbal Communication
Complexity	One dimension (words only)	Multiple dimensions (voice, posture, gestures, distance, etc.)
Flow	Intermittent (speaking and silence alternate)	Continuous (it's impossible to avoid communicating non-verbally)
Clarity	Less subject to misinterpretation	More ambiguous
Impact	Has less impact when verbal and non-verbal cues are contradictory	Has stronger impact when verbal and non-verbal cues are contradictory
Intentionality	Usually deliberate	Often unintentional

focus on non-verbal behaviour. For example, while verbal messages are almost always intentional, non-verbal cues are often unintended, and sometimes unconscious.

Non-Verbal Skills Are Important

It's hard to overemphasize the importance of effective non-verbal expression and the ability to read and respond to others' non-verbal behaviour. Non-verbal encoding and decoding skills are a strong predictor of popularity, attractiveness, and socio-emotional well-being.[16] Good non-verbal communicators are more persuasive than people who are less skilled, and they have a greater chance of success in settings ranging from careers to poker to romance. Non-verbal sensitivity is a major part of what some social scientists have called 'emotional intelligence', and researchers have come to recognize that it is impossible to study spoken language without paying attention to its non-verbal dimensions.[17]

Influences on Non-Verbal Communication

A lot of non-verbal communication is universal. For example, researchers have found at least six facial expressions that all humans everywhere use and understand: happiness, sadness, fear, anger, disgust, and surprise.[18] Even children who have been blind since birth reveal their feelings using these expressions. Despite these similarities, there are some important differences in the way people use and understand non-verbal behaviour. We'll look at some of these differences now.

Culture

Cultures have different non-verbal languages as well as verbal ones. For example, if you watch films of former prime minister Jean Chrétien's speeches with the sound turned off, you can often tell whether he's speaking English or French by the changes in his non-verbal behaviour.

The meaning of some gestures varies from one culture to another. The 'okay' gesture made by joining thumb and forefinger to form a circle is a cheery affirmation to most Canadians, but it has less positive meanings in other parts of the world.[19] In France and Belgium it means 'You're worth zero.' In Greece and Turkey it is a vulgar sexual invitation, usually meant as an

COMMUNICATION ON-SCREEN

Top 10 Canadian TV Shows of the Decade

10. Clone High (2002–03)

This one-season wonder was created by Bill Lawrence (*Scrubs*) as a Canada–US co-production, but the US partner dropped the show so quickly that only Canadians saw the full series. A parody of sitcoms, high-school shows, and world history, it featured a premise-explaining theme song, characters based on JFK, Cleopatra, and Gandhi, and a robot who talked like Mr Belvedere. Even with an American creator, how could it not make the list?

9. Mantracker (2006–)

Schlocky, cheesoid TV needs to be represented on a list like this. The obvious choice is the story of Terry Grant, a bad-ass horse-riding, hat-wearing, bearded cowboy who spends every episode hunting down a team of city dwellers released into the wild. It's basically the *Most Dangerous Game* on horseback, or *Dog the Bounty Hunter* without all the Christian moralizing. In other words, something you feel guilty for kind of enjoying.

8. Kenny vs. Spenny (2003–)

A combination of reality competition and sitcom, this show about two mismatched buddies (a neat nut and an evil schemer, like a Canadian *Odd Couple*) shows Kenny and Spenny doing various humiliating things every week in a desperate attempt to one-up each other. Many episodes feature the evil Kenny destroying his supposed friend through deceit, trickery, and blatant cheating. When Trey Parker and Matt Stone joined the show as producers, it seemed to suggest what we already knew: these guys are the new Cartman and Butters.

7. Life With Derek (2005–09)

Canada has produced a number of 'tween' comedies (*Naturally Sadie, Radio Free Roscoe, The Latest Buzz*) that were considerably better acted and better written than their counterparts on the Disney Channel or Nickelodeon. This Family Channel show, about a blended family that—unlike the *Brady Bunch*—can't get along, was perhaps the best of the bunch, a throwback to real-world family problems in a TV landscape increasingly dominated by escapism. It was like *Step By Step* with people who aren't disgusting.

6. The Hour (2005–)

Though *The Rick Mercer Report* was the 2000s' most obvious answer to *The Daily Show*, George Stroumboulopoulos comes closer to matching Jon Stewart's appeal: a comedian and 'personality' performer conducting interviews with many serious, earnest people. After years of interviewers who were totally serious and earnest themselves, or talk-show hosts who only interviewed second-rank entertainers, seeing 'Strombo' chat it up with James Cameron or Barbara Walters demonstrated that Canadian talk shows could successfully follow the US template.

5. Corner Gas (2004–09)

With the success of Brent Butt's half-hour comedy about wacky small-town Saskatchewan residents, we saw how Canadians can step into the breach and do things the United States isn't doing—in this case, rural comedy. The show also took techniques that had become common in US single-camera comedy, like sudden cutaways and flashbacks, and brought them into the Canadian mainstream. It was about a place where life moves slowly, but it helped Canadian shows move a lot faster.

4. Durham County (2007–)

A mashup of cop shows and American Beauty-type stories about the hidden evil of suburbs, this drama starred Hugh Dillon as a big-city cop who tries to start a new life in suburbia, only to discover there's lots of murdering and depravity going on. Though the second season was not as strong as the first, it was The Movie Network's most interesting attempt to do a show in the style of its US counterpart, HBO.

3. Trailer Park Boys (2001–08)

One of the most influential and successful comedy shows of the era, this mock-documentary show about a bunch of beer-swilling lowlifes premiered in 2001, leading to a seven-season run and two films. In mining comedy from the adventures of people who are basically horrible, it preceded shows like *It's Always Sunny In Philadelphia,* and it was doing fake documentary comedy before *Arrested Development* and *The Office* made it cool again.

2. Slings & Arrows (2003–06)

A Canadian show so good that international viewers don't know it's Canadian. A comedy–drama about the pressures of putting on a play at an artistically compromised, financially strapped Shakespeare festival, the show was both an inside look at the insanity of show business and a universal story about the things that go wrong in any workplace. It helped that the great cast was full of big names like Paul Gross and co-creator Mark McKinney (*Kids in the Hall*) and big names to be, like Rachel McAdams. The three seasons of the show were so successful they led to the ultimate compliment any show can receive: a foreign remake, the Brazilian *Som e Fúria*.

1. Intelligence (2006–07)

Created by Chris Haddock, the man behind Da Vinci's Inquest (which didn't make the list because it premiered in the 1990s), this story of drug trafficking, moral ambiguity, and politics was one of the most ambitious Canadian dramas of the decade, a successful attempt to do a serious crime drama like The Wire. It was cancelled by the CBC after only two seasons, leading Haddock to speculate that 'somewhere in the CBC someone is saying "do not promote this show."' That's how you know Canadian TV has made the big time at last: we have TV that's too good for TV.

—*Jaime Weinman*, Maclean's, *6 May 2010.*

Once identified and analyzed, non-verbal communication systems can be taught, like a foreign language. Without this training, we respond to non-verbal communications in terms of our own culture; we read everyone's behaviour as if it were our own, and thus we often misunderstand it. . . .

The language of behaviour is extremely complex. Most of us are lucky to have under control one subcultural system—the one that reflects our sex, class, generation, and geographic region.

Edward and Mildred Hall

insult. Given this sort of cross-cultural ambiguity, it's easy to imagine how an innocent tourist might wind up in serious trouble.

Cultural differences also exist in other forms of non-verbal behaviour. Researchers from Queen's University and the University of Toronto in Canada and Kyoto University in Japan examined the gaze direction (where people are looking), of participants from both countries, in social and non-social contexts. There were significant differences. Canadian participants looked up while thinking only when they knew they were being observed. When they knew they couldn't be seen, Canadian participants looked down. Japanese participants looked down while they were thinking even when they were sure that they were being observed. These results confirm the view that thinking-related gaze behaviours are heavily influenced by cultural display rules and social contexts.[20]

Less obvious cross-cultural differences can damage relationships without the parties ever recognizing exactly what has gone wrong. As anthropologist Edward T. Hall points out, people from the Middle East are likely to conduct business at a much shorter distance than most westerners would feel comfortable with.[21] It is easy to visualize the awkward advance-and-retreat dance that might occur when two diplomats or business people from those cultures meet. The Middle Easterner would probably keep moving forward to close the gap, while her Canadian colleague would keep trying to back away. Both would feel uncomfortable, probably without knowing why.

Even within a culture, various groups can have different non-verbal rules. For example, many teachers use 'quasi-questions' that hint at the information they are seeking. An elementary school teacher might encourage the class to speak up by making an incorrect statement that demands refutation: 'So to get six pieces we divide our pie into quarters, right?'[22] Most English-Canadian students would recognize this behaviour as a way of testing their understanding. But this style of questioning would be unfamiliar to many students raised in traditional Aboriginal cultures, who aren't likely to respond until they are directly questioned by the teacher. As a result, some teachers might view Aboriginal children as unresponsive or slow, when in fact they are simply playing by a different set of rules.

Communicators become more tolerant of others after they understand that unfamiliar non-verbal behaviours are the result of cultural differences. In one study, American adults were presented with videotaped scenes of speakers from Anglo-North America, France, and

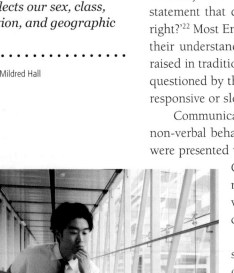

Germany.[23] When the sound was cut off, viewers judged foreigners more negatively than they did their fellow citizens. But when the speakers' voices were added (allowing viewers to recognize that they were from a different country), the critical ratings dropped.

Despite differences like these, many non-verbal behaviours have the same meanings around the world. Smiles and laughter are universal signals of positive emotions, for example, and there is a common set of sour expressions that convey displeasure in every culture.[24] Charles Darwin believed that expressions like these evolved as survival mechanisms that allowed early humans to convey emotional states before the development of language.

Although certain non-verbal expressions may be universal, the way they are used varies widely around the world. In some cultures the overt demonstration of feelings like happiness or anger is discouraged. In others the same feelings are considered perfectly appropriate. Thus a Japanese person might appear much more controlled and placid than someone from Iran, even if their feelings were identical.[25]

Understanding Diversity

● ● ● ● ●   **AN EXPERT SPEAKS MAN TO MANE**

Among the swelling ranks of self-proclaimed male grooming 'experts' (and there are hundreds adding their names to this dubious new form of punditry), criminal investigator Barry Ettinger is an anomaly.

The bald, fiftysomething head of security for a Yellowknife diamond mine has somehow become the unlikely face for the teen-targeted Axe hair brand that has, until now, pitched itself with images of hot women attacking unsuspecting men with lascivious intent.

At a recent Axe media launch in Toronto, Ettinger was the explanatory voice, contextualizing modern male hair peacocking through the prism of his expertise in body language and non-verbal communication. The polygraph examiner and one-time RCMP officer offers insight into male mane rituals—defined as 'hair action . . . [the] surprising acts that happen when a girl can't resist getting into a guy's hair'—and how they achieve their intent.

It seems women really do want to touch before they buy.

And hair is among our most powerful symbols of personal and collective identity.

Our locks, more than even our words, contain the hidden secret to our instant attractiveness, Ettinger claims.

That means those whose flirtation strategies rely heavily on verbal communication are missing the point. All that verbiage accounts for a mere 7 per cent of communication, he says. Intonation makes up another 38 per cent. Unwittingly, the bulk of our communication—55 per cent—is body language, he says.

And hair is a key non-verbal communicator.

'Studies show that hairstyle can outweigh everything else during that first meeting,' Ettinger says. 'It's a sign of health, that you have something to offer. It's psychology. It can be predicted.'

A good hair day provides a psychological image boost that invisibly broadcasts itself as irresistible confidence, he says.

But what good hair giveth, bad hair taketh away.

A bad hair day generates a kind of off-kilter inner turmoil sufficient to send the enchanting waitress at lunch running.

Ettinger recalls a distinct change in the way the world viewed him after he began losing his hair in his thirties. 'Older people who lose their hair are seen as less desirable, less accepted. If I go into a room with guys who are generally the same as me, I know I'll be viewed differently.'

It seems we've instinctively understood the importance of hair-based first impressions for at least 6,000 years, he says.

Hieroglyphs dating back to 4000 BC reveal our ancient selves primping golden locks with animal fat in search of a date on Saturday night. Then, over thousands of years, we devised alternatives from fruit extracts, ashes, clay, and sticks. By AD 100, we'd discovered colour. Then wigs. Today, it's pomades, mousse, gels, putties, pastes, and creams.

And behavioural experts.

The things we do.

—*Robert Cribb,* Toronto Star, *27 March 2010.*

Questions: Hair is perceived by many cultures, Middle Eastern in particular, as a very sexual and alluring feature. That is why it is often covered in a shawl of some sort. Why do you think that hair is so important? What is its communication function in the classroom that you are in right now? Have you made assumptions about people based on the way they wear their hair? If so, what were those assumptions? Were they proven right when you got to know the person better?

The same principle can be seen in action closer to home. For example, we commonly observe that French-Canadian women tend both to be non-verbally more expressive and to interrupt one another more often than is the case with English-Canadian women. This doesn't mean that French-Canadian women always feel more intensely than their English-Canadian counterparts. A more likely explanation is that the two groups follow different cultural rules. Researchers have found that in culturally mixed groups both French- and English-Canadian women moved closer to the other group's style. This non-verbal convergence shows that skilled communicators can adapt their behaviour when interacting with people from different cultural traditions in order to make the exchange more smooth and effective.[26]

Gender

It's easy to identify stereotypical differences in masculine and feminine styles of non-verbal communication. Just think about the exaggerated caricatures of macho men and delicate women that appear from time to time. Many humorous films and plays have been created around the situations that arise when characters try to act like members of the opposite sex. For some examples, see the 'Communication Onscreen' box on page 182.

Although few of us behave like stereotypically masculine or feminine movie characters, there are recognizable differences in the ways men and women look and act. Some of the most obvious differences are physiological: height, depth and volume of the voice, and so on. Other differences are social. For example, females are usually more non-verbally expressive, and they are better at recognizing others' non-verbal behaviour.[27]

Most communication scholars agree that social factors have more influence than biology does in shaping how men and women behave. For example, the ability to read non-verbal cues may have more to do with women's historically less powerful social status: people in subordinate work positions also have better decoding skills.[28] As women continue to gain status in the workplace and home, a paradoxical result may be less sensitivity at reading non-verbal cues.

Cultural norms in the Western world distinguish male from female behaviours.[29] For example, women make more eye contact with conversational partners than men do. They are more vocally expressive than men. Women interact at closer distances, both with men and with other women, than do men in same-sex conversations. Men are more likely to lean forward in conversations than women. They require and are given more personal space. Women are more likely to face conversational partners head-on, whereas men more typically stand at an angle. Women express more emotions via facial expressions than men. Most noticeably, women smile considerably more than men. Women gesture more frequently, whereas men use more expansive gestures.

After looking at differences like these, it might seem as if men and women communicate in radically different ways. In fact, men's and women's non-verbal communication is more similar than different in many respects.[30] Differences like the ones described in the preceding paragraph are noticeable, but they are outweighed by the similarity of our behaviour in areas such as eye contact, posture, and gestures. You can prove this by imagining what it would be like to follow radically different non-verbal rules: standing only an inch away from others, sniffing strangers, or tapping the forehead of someone when you want his or her attention. While biological sex and cultural norms certainly have an influence on

"Beasley, you're a good communicator, look down the table and make eye contact for me!"

Picture a Universal Language

In *The Complete Idiot's Guide to Etiquette,* authors Mary Mitchell and John Corr offer some helpful, if obvious, travel hints: Calculate your finances, pack well, carry proper documentation. 'The pleasant traveller is the well-prepared traveller,' they remark cheerily.

How prepared is well prepared? Gosia Warrink is probing the outer limits. As author of the *Icon Global Picture Dictionary,* Warrink, a designer, offers 98 pages of icons representing every possible item, destination, situation, or person a traveller anywhere on Earth could possibly need.

Handy, maybe, for those excursions to Ulan Bator, say, where English speakers are sparse. Need a haircut in Outer Mongolia? Simply point to your favoured style: buzz, mohawk, mullet.

Waterwings in Vanuatu? Check. An MRI in Uzbekistan? Best of luck getting one, but the icon, tucked next to a drawing of an array of dental instruments, is in the book.

Of course, iconography is a communication medium both primitive and primal, long predating the curious squibs and glyphs we've come to know as our alphabet. Think of cave paintings, the original novellas; or the elaborate narratives painted in the tombs of the Egyptian pharaohs.

Even in the thoroughly modern era, icons are an efficient, language-agnostic means of communication—a simple arrow functions as well in English as in Chinese, Romanian, or Urdu as the international symbol for 'Hey, over here.'

Warrink takes the notion as far as it can logically go, and beyond. Her application ranges from the useful—a vast array of fruits, vegetables, soups, and sushi, and symbols for doctors, dentists, and massage therapists—to the perplexing: a meat grinder, a hand surreptitiously palming a roll of bills (the international symbol for 'bribe'?), and a car that appears to be underwater—useful in Manitoba in springtime,

perhaps, but suspect in most other places out of reach of tsunamis.

Torontonians can take comfort. The CN Tower seems to make an appearance as part of a skyline that appears to be the international symbol for 'downtown'.

Apart from a dizzying breadth of such practicalities, personal aesthetic preferences are helpfully defined here, as well: a living-room suite with a sleek couch and Mies van der Rohe Barcelona chair, alongside a dining room with planar table and Arne Jacobsen ant chair are here, set against a collection of same, tricked out in distinctly ornate Louis XIV. Whatever else Warrink's book might do for you, the Modernists among us will never have to suffer decorative excess.

Useful though the guide may be, it should go without saying that you might want to have a condensed version handy in case of an actual emergency.

Ninety-eight pages of pictures don't exactly make for agile conversation, non-verbal or otherwise. By the time you reach 'poison' (page 11, after deodorant and electric razors but before supermarket and escalator), it could well be too late. . . .

—*Murray Whyte,* Toronto Star, *23 November 2008.*

Questions: As our cities become more multicultural, do you think that using icons to communicate public messages in public places or on public transit will become more common? Given the diversity of languages and cultures, could you ever see a day when we move to icons for more and more of our personal communication, instead of relying so much on the written word? What are some examples that you've noticed from your life or workplace where icons have taken over from words?

non-verbal style, they aren't as dramatic as the 'men are from Mars; women are from Venus' thesis suggests.

Functions of Non-Verbal Communication

Although verbal and non-verbal messages differ in many ways, the two forms of communication operate together on most occasions. The following discussion explains the many functions non-verbal communication can serve and shows how non-verbal messages relate to verbal ones.

●-●-●●-●●

COMMUNICATION ON-SCREEN

Tootsie (1982)
Directed by Sydney Pollack.

The Birdcage (1996)
Directed by Mike Nichols.

Shakespeare in Love (1998)
Directed by John Madden.

One way to recognize differences between masculine and feminine styles of non-verbal communication is to observe the same person playing different gender-related roles. Filmmakers have found this notion intriguing enough to produce several movies in which characters disguise themselves with makeup and costumes—and non-verbal cues—related to masculine and feminine roles.

In *Tootsie*, Michael Dorsey (Dustin Hoffman) is an aspiring New York actor who can't get any roles—at least as a man. In a flash of inspiration, he transforms himself into Dorothy Michaels, a middle-aged woman, and wins a part in a daytime soap opera.

The Birdcage presents another twist on the masculine/feminine theme. In one part of the film, Armand Goldman (Robin Williams) tries to teach his partner, Albert (Nathan Lane), to be more macho. The goal, once again, is disguise: the couple want their son's soon-to-be in-laws to believe they are brothers, not lovers.

The shoe is on the other foot, so to speak, in *Shakespeare in Love*. This time a woman, Viola De Lesseps (Gwyneth Paltrow), disguises herself as a man in order to fulfill her dream of acting in a play written by the young William Shakespeare (Joseph Fiennes). Her gender switching is complicated by her strong romantic feelings for the Bard. Does her non-verbal communication give her away?

emblem
A deliberate non-verbal behaviour with a precise meaning, known to virtually all members of a cultural group.

illustrators
Non-verbal behaviours that accompany and support verbal messages.

Repeating

If someone asked you for directions to the nearest Tim Hortons, you could say, 'Two blocks north', and repeat your answer non-verbally by pointing the way. This sort of repetition isn't just decorative: people remember words reinforced by gestures better than they do words that are merely spoken.[31]

Pointing is an example of what social scientists call an **emblem**: a deliberate non-verbal behaviour with a precise meaning that is known to everyone within a particular cultural group. For example, we all know that a nod of the head means 'yes', a shake of the head means 'no', a wave means 'hello' or 'good-bye', and a hand to the ear means 'I can't hear you.'

Substituting

Emblems can also replace, rather than merely enhance, a verbal message. When a friend asks you what's new, you might shrug your shoulders instead of answering in words. Not all substituting consists of emblems, however. Sometimes substituting responses are more ambiguous and less intentional. A sigh, smile, or frown may substitute for a verbal answer to your question, 'How's it going?' As this example suggests, non-verbal substituting is especially important when people are reluctant to express their feelings in words.

Complementing

Sometimes non-verbal behaviours match the content of a verbal message. Consider, for example, a friend apologizing for being late. Your friend's sincerity would be reinforced if the verbal apology were accompanied by the appropriate non-verbal behaviours: the right tone of voice, facial expression, and so on. We often recognize the significance of complementary non-verbal behaviour when it is missing. If your friend's apology were delivered with a shrug, a smirk, and a light tone of voice, you probably would doubt its sincerity, no matter how profuse the verbal explanation was.

Much complementing behaviour consists of **illustrators**—non-verbal behaviours that accompany and support spoken words. Scratching your head as you search for an idea and snapping your fingers when you get it are both illustrators that complement verbal messages. Research shows that North Americans use illustrators more often when they are emotionally aroused—excited, angry, horrified, agitated, distressed—and trying to explain ideas that are difficult to put into words.[32]

Accenting

Just as we use italics to emphasize an idea in print, we use non-verbal devices to emphasize oral messages. Pointing an accusing finger adds emphasis to criticism (and creates defensiveness in the receiver). Stressing certain words with the voice ('It was *your* idea!') is another way to add non-verbal emphasis.

Regulating

Non-verbal behaviours can control the flow of verbal communication. For example, parties in a conversation often unconsciously send and receive turn-taking cues.[33] When you are ready to yield the floor, the unstated rule is to create a rising vocal intonation pattern; then use a falling intonation pattern or draw out the final syllable of the clause at the end of your statement; finally, stop speaking. If you want to maintain your turn when another speaker seems ready to cut you off, you can suppress the attempt by taking an audible breath, using a sustained intonation pattern (because rising and falling patterns suggest the end of a statement), and avoiding any pauses in your speech. Other non-verbal cues exist for gaining the floor and for signalling that you do not want to speak.

Contradicting

People often simultaneously express different and even contradictory messages in their verbal and non-verbal behaviours. A common example of this sort of mixed message is the experience we've all had of hearing someone with a red face and bulging veins yelling, 'Angry? No, I'm not angry!'

Even though some of the ways in which people contradict themselves are subtle, mixed messages have a strong impact. Research suggests that when a receiver perceives an inconsistency between verbal and non-verbal messages, the non-verbal one carries more weight—more than 12.5 per cent more, according to some studies.[34]

Deliberately sending mixed messages might sound foolish at first, but there are times when we do just that. One deliberate use of mixed messages is to send a message politely but clearly that might be difficult or awkward to convey if it were expressed in words. For instance, think of a time when you became bored with a conversation but your companion kept rambling on. At such a time the most straightforward statement would be, 'I'm tired of listening to you and want to go and do something else.' Although it might feel good to be so direct, this kind of honesty is impolite for anyone over five years of age. Instead of being blunt in situations like this, a face-saving alternative is to express your lack of interest non-verbally. While nodding politely and murmuring, 'Uh-huh' and 'No kidding?' at the appropriate times, you can signal a desire to leave by looking around the room, turning slightly away from the speaker, or even making a point of yawning. In most cases such clues are enough to end the conversation without the awkwardness of expressing outright what's going on.

Deceiving

Deception is perhaps the most interesting type of non-verbal communication, and one that social scientists have studied extensively. As Chapter 6 explains, most of the messages we exchange are not completely truthful. As you will read there, not all deception is self-serving or malicious: much of it is aimed at saving the face of the communicators involved. For example, you might tell a white lie to avoid hurting the feelings of a friend who asks your opinion: 'Mmm, this casserole of yours is delicious. You'll have to give me the recipe.' In a situation like this, it's easy to see how non-verbal factors can make the face-saving deception either succeed or fail.

Take the word butterfly. To use this word it is not necessary to make the voice weigh less than an ounce or equip it with small dusty wings. It is not necessary to invent a sunny day or a field of daffodils. It is not necessary to be in love, or to be in love with butterflies. The word butterfly is not a real butterfly. There is the word and there is the butterfly. If you confuse these two items people have the right to laugh at you.

Leonard Cohen,
'How to Speak Poetry'

Cultural Idiom

the floor
the right or privilege to speak

to cut you off
to interrupt you in order to stop you from proceeding with your remarks

Cultural Idiom

a white lie
harmless untruth

Some people are better at hiding deceit than others. For example, most people—especially women—become more successful liars as they grow older.[35] High self-monitors are usually better at hiding their deception than are people who are less self-aware, and highly expressive liars are judged to be more honest than those who are more subdued.[36] Not surprisingly, people whose jobs may require them to behave in a certain way regardless of how they really feel, such as actors, lawyers, diplomats, and salespeople, are more successful at deception than the general population.[37]

We seem to be worse at catching deceivers when we participate actively in conversations than when we observe from the sidelines.[38] It's easiest to catch liars when they haven't had a chance to rehearse, when they feel strongly about the information being hidden, or when they feel anxious or guilty about their lies.[39] Imagine, for example, that you want to decline an unwanted invitation with a face-saving lie. Your chances of getting away with the deception are best if you have had advance notice of the invitation. If you are caught unprepared, your excuse for not attending is likely to be less persuasive. Trust (or lack of it) also plays a role in determining which deceptive messages will be successful. People who are suspicious that a speaker may be lying pay closer attention to the speaker's non-verbal behaviour (such as talking faster than normal or shifting posture) than do people who are not suspicious.[40] Still, asking questions—even if you are suspicious—isn't especially effective at uncovering deception.[41] As you read earlier, people who focus their attention on catching liars are less effective than those who are busy with other mental tasks.[42] Table 5.3 lists situations in which deceptive messages are most likely to be obvious.

Decades of research have revealed that there are no surefire non-verbal cues that indicate deception. Nonetheless, there are some cues that may reveal less-than-totally-honest

Ulysses: *Fie, fie upon her!*
There's language in her
eyes, her cheek, her
lip,
Nay, her foot speaks; her
wanton spirits look
out
At every joint and motive
in her body.

William Shakespeare,
Troilus and Cressida

Cultural Idiom

surefire
certain to succeed

TABLE 5.3 Leakage of Non-Verbal Clues to Deception

Deception Clues Are Most Likely When the Deceiver	Deception Clues Are Least Likely When the Deceiver
Wants to hide emotions being experienced at the moment.	Wants to hide information unrelated to his or her emotions.
Feels strongly about the information being hidden.	Has no strong feelings about the information being hidden.
Feels apprehensive about the deception.	Feels confident about the deception.
Feels guilty about being deceptive.	Experiences little guilt about the deception.
Gets little enjoyment from being deceptive.	Enjoys the deception.
Needs to construct the message carefully while delivering it.	Knows the deceptive message well and has rehearsed it.

Source: Based on material from Paul Ekman, 'Mistakes When Deceiving', in Thomas A. Sebok and Robert Rosenthal, eds, *The Clever Hans Phenomenon: Communication with Horses, Whales, Apes and People* (New York: New York Academy of Sciences, 1981), 269–78.

communication. For example, deceivers typically make more speech errors—stammers, stutters, hesitations, false starts, and so on—than speakers who are telling the truth. Vocal pitch often rises when people tell lies, and liars hesitate more.[43] Deceivers tend to blink their eyes more often, fidget with their hands, and more rapidly shift their posture. Despite cues like these, it's a mistake to assume that every tongue-tied, fidgeting, eye-blinking person is a liar.

How good are people at detecting lies? The range of effectiveness in uncovering deceptive messages is broad, ranging from 45 to 70 per cent.[44] As we grow older we become better at interpreting contradictory messages. Children between the ages of 6 and 12 use a speaker's words to make sense of a message. But as adults we rely more on non-verbal cues to form many impressions.[45] Adult listeners also use non-verbal behaviours to judge the character of speakers, and differences in non-verbal behaviour influence how much listeners are persuaded by a speaker's message.[46]

Even with an awareness of non-verbal clues, it isn't always easy to detect lies. Training can improve the ability to catch deceivers.[47] Again, the range of effectiveness in uncovering deceptive messages is broad, ranging from 45 to 70 per cent.[48] Sometimes the very suspicion that someone is lying can improve the deceiver's attempts to hide the truth. Research shows that people who probe the messages of deceptive communicators are no better at detecting lies than those who don't investigate the truth of a message. One explanation for this surprising finding is that deceivers who are questioned become more careful about not revealing the truth, and their guardedness results in a better cover-up of deception cues.

Some people are better than others at uncovering deception. Women, for instance, are consistently more accurate than men at detecting lying and what the underlying truth is.[49] The same research showed that as people become more intimate, their accuracy in detecting lies actually declines. This is a surprising fact: intuition suggests that we ought to be better at judging honesty as we become more familiar with others. Perhaps an element of wishful thinking interferes with our accurate decoding of these messages. After all, we would hate to think that a lover would lie to us. When intimate partners do become suspicious, however, their ability to recognize deception increases.[50] Despite their overall accuracy at detecting lies, women are more inclined to fall for the deception of their partners than are men. No matter how skilful or inept we may be at interpreting non-verbal behaviour, training can make us better.[51]

Technology may be gaining ground on deceivers. In 2002, Mayo Clinic researchers reported developing a facial imaging device capable of detecting heat patterns in the skin.[52] Apparently, as with the more familiar polygraph (or lie detector), this device does not actually measure deception but anxiety. Such devices probably have more potential uses in security contexts than in personal situations. Still, the notion of using technology to catch liars is appealing.

Before we finish considering how non-verbal behaviours can deceive, it is important to note that not all deceptive communication is aimed at taking advantage of the recipient. Sometimes deceptive behaviour is a polite way of expressing an idea that would be difficult for the listener to receive if it were expressed in words. In this sense, the ability to deliberately send non-verbal messages that contradict your words can be a kind of communication competence.

Truth . . . Yeah, it's alright.

Michel Foucault,
Madness and Civilization: A History of Insanity in the Age of Reason

Cultural Idiom

cover-up
a plan to escape discovery

Types of Non-Verbal Communication

Now that we've seen how non-verbal messages operate as a form of communication, we can look at the various forms of non-verbal behaviour. In this section we examine how our bodies, artifacts, environments, and the way we use time all send messages.

Posture and Gesture

Stop reading for a moment and notice how you are sitting. What does your position say non-verbally about how you feel? Are there other people near you now? What messages do you get from their postures and movements? Tune your television to any program, turn off the sound, and see what messages are communicated by the movements and body positions of the people on the screen. These simple experiments illustrate the communicative power of **kinesics**, the study of body movement, posture, and gesture.

Posture is a rich channel for conveying non-verbal information. From time to time postural messages are obvious. If you see a person drag through the door or slump over while sitting in a chair, it's apparent that something significant is going on. But most postural cues are more subtle. For instance, the act of mirroring the posture of another person can have positive consequences. One experiment showed that career counsellors who used 'posture echoes' to copy the postures of clients were rated as more empathic than those who did not.[53] Researchers have also found that partners in romantic relationships mirror one another's behaviours.[54]

Posture can communicate vulnerability in situations far more serious than mere social or business settings. One study revealed that rapists sometimes use postural clues to select victims that they believe will be easy to intimidate.[55] Easy targets are more likely to walk slowly and tentatively, stare at the ground, and move their arms and legs in short, jerky motions.

Gestures are a fundamental element of communication—so fundamental, in fact, that people who have been blind from birth use them.[56] One group of ambiguous gestures consists of what we usually call fidgeting—movements in which one part of the body grooms, massages, rubs, holds, pinches, picks, or otherwise manipulates another body part. Social scientists call these behaviours **manipulators**.[57] Social rules may discourage us from performing most manipulators in public, but people still do so without noticing. For example, one study revealed that deceivers bob their heads more often than truth-tellers.[58] Research confirms what common sense suggests—that increased use of manipulators is often a sign of discomfort.[59] But not all fidgeting signals uneasiness. People also are likely to use manipulators when relaxed. When they let their guard down (either alone or with friends), they will be more likely to fiddle with an earlobe, twirl a strand of hair, or clean their fingernails. Whether or not the fidgeter is hiding something, observers are likely to interpret manipulators as a signal of dishonesty; however, because not all fidgeters are liars, it's important not to jump to conclusions about the meaning of manipulators.

Face and Eyes

The face and eyes are probably the most noticed parts of the body, and their impact is powerful. For example, smiling restaurant servers earn larger tips than unsmiling ones, and smiling nuns collect larger donations than ones with glum expressions.[60] The influence of facial

kinesics
The study of body movement, posture, and gesture.

manipulators
Movements in which one part of the body grooms, massages, rubs, holds, pinches, picks, or otherwise manipulates another part.

Cultural Idiom

let their guard down
act or speak naturally without worrying how others will react

I did not know whether I would ever speak to her or not or, if I spoke to her, how I could tell her of my confused adoration. But my body was like a harp and her words and gestures were like fingers running upon the wires.

James Joyce,
'Araby', from *Dubliners*

Understanding Diversity
● ● ● ● ● EXPRESSIVE ITALIANS LET HANDS DO THE TALKING

A recipe for trouble in Italy: make a fist, extend index finger and pinkie, thrust forward and up. A snarl is optional. The gesture—an insult suggesting an unfaithful wife—is part of the array of hand jabs, facial tics, and arm movement that add significance and sentiment to nearly every conversation among Italians.

'There are gestures for everything from making love to making dinner. The hands can often say things better than words,' said Milan design artist Bruno Munari, who compiled a book illustrating some of the most popular Italian gestures. Munari's *Dictionary of Italian Gestures* contains dozens of examples stretching from early-nineteenth-century Naples to modern signals for a cellular telephone call.

Squeezing your chin between thumb and index finger signifies cuteness. Pulling slightly on the skin under the right eye with an index finger shows an agreement has been reached. Consider something foolish? Place hands together as if in prayer and then lower the pinkies.

Technology has added new gestures. The first telephone gesture was a rotating finger, simulating dialing. It was replaced by a push-button movement. Now, with cellular phones widely popular in Italy, the latest phone gesture is a palm pressed to an ear.

With gestures, entire conversations could be conducted in silence.

'What do you want?' (Fingertips pinched together.)

'I'm hungry.' (A curving motion of the hand above the top of the stomach.)

'And something to drink?' (Thumb tipped down toward the mouth.)

'No, everything's fine. It was delicious.' (Shake hand with palm down. Then stick index finger in cheek and rock side to side.)

Some gestures are obvious in their intent. A threat is a thumb slashing across the neck. I'm angry: curl your index finger and bite down.

Others need translation. Rubbing two index fingers together represents an affair or secret meeting. Tapping your forehead with your finger means something is too strange to believe.

'A foreigner can come to Italy and learn the language perfectly, but without knowing the gestures you are not really fluent,' said Munari.

—Brian Murphy, Associated Press, 17 December 1994.

Questions: Do you think that the sort of gestural communication that the article describes Italians using can 'rub off' on other, less-gestural cultures, such as Anglos? Have you noticed that you gesture more when you are around a person who makes heavy use of gestures to communicate?

---

expressions and eye contact doesn't mean that their non-verbal messages are always easy to read. The face is a tremendously complicated channel of expression for several reasons. One is the number of expressions people can produce; another, the speed with which they can change. For example, some videos, shown in slow motion, show expressions fleeting across a subject's face in as short a time as a fifth of a second. Finally, it seems that different emotions show most clearly in different parts of the face: happiness and surprise in the eyes and lower face, anger in the lower face and brows and forehead, fear and sadness in the eyes, and disgust in the lower face.

Ekman and Friesen have identified six basic emotions that facial expressions reflect—surprise, fear, anger, disgust, happiness, and sadness.[61] Expressions reflecting these emotions seem to be recognizable in and between members of all cultures. Of course, **affect blends**—combinations of two or more expressions showing different emotions—are possible. For instance, it's easy to imagine how someone would look if fearful *and* surprised or disgusted *and* angry.

affect blends

Combinations of two or more expressions, each showing a different emotion.

COMMUNICATION ON-SCREEN

Mr Bean (1990–5)

Created by Rowan Atkinson & Robin Driscoll.

Although Mr Bean isn't, strictly speaking, a mime, Rowan Atkinson's most famous persona is perhaps the best-known modern example of a character who communicates almost completely non-verbally. Atkinson first developed the character while a student at Oxford University and refined it throughout his fringe festival career in the 1980s. In 1987, Mr Bean made his most public debut at Montreal's Just for Laughs comedy festival: Atkinson notably insisted his act be scheduled with the francophone acts at the festival rather than on the anglophone side, as he wanted to test the character's physical comedy before a non–English-speaking audience.

Atkinson's non-verbal comedy is arguably at its best in the series of 14 half-hour episodes that ran intermittently on British television in the early 1990s. Once described by Atkinson as 'a child in a grown man's body', Bean bumbles his way through daily life, solving problems presented by everyday tasks and typically leaving a trail of destruction in his wake. Drawing largely on the communicative possibilities offered by his rubbery face, Atkinson manages to tell us exactly what is going on in Mr Bean's curiously structured mind with hardly a word of spoken accompaniment.

disfluencies
Non-linguistic verbalizations, such as 'um', 'er', and 'ah'.

paralanguage
Non-linguistic means of vocal expression: rate, pitch, tone, and so on.

At certain moments, words are nothing; it is the tone in which they are uttered.

Paul Bouget,
Cosmopolis

Research indicates that people are quite accurate at judging facial expressions of these emotions.[62] Accuracy increases when judges know the 'target' or have knowledge of the context in which the expression occurs or when they have seen several samples of the target's expressions.

The eyes themselves can send several kinds of messages. In mainstream Western culture, meeting someone's glance with your eyes is usually a sign of involvement, whereas looking away signals a desire to avoid contact. This is why solicitors on the street—panhandlers, salespeople, petitioners—try to catch our eye. After they've managed to establish contact with a glance, it becomes harder to draw away.

Voice

The voice itself is another form of non-verbal communication. Social scientists use the term **paralanguage** to describe non-verbal, vocal messages. You can begin to understand the power of vocal cues by considering how the meaning of a simple sentence can change just by shifting the emphasis from word to word:

- *This* is a fantastic communication text.
  [Not just any text but this one in particular.]
- This is a *fantastic* communication text.
  [This text is superior, exciting.]
- This is a fantastic *communication* text.
  [The text is good as far as communication goes; it may not be so good as literature or drama.]
- This is a fantastic communication *text*.
  [It's not a play or a CD; it's a text.]

There are many other ways the voice communicates—through tone, speed, pitch, volume, number and length of pauses, and **disfluencies** (such as stammering, use of 'uh', 'um', 'er', and so on). All these factors can do a great deal to reinforce or contradict the message our words convey.

Sarcasm is one instance in which both emphasis and tone of voice help change a statement's meaning to the opposite of its verbal message. Experience this yourself by saying the following three statements. Say them literally first, then sarcastically.

- Thanks for waking me up.
- I really had a wonderful time on my blind date.
- I can't wait to get going on my interpersonal communication paper.

Researchers have identified the communicative value of paralanguage through the use of content-free speech—ordinary speech that has been electronically manipulated so that the words are unintelligible, but the paralanguage remains unaffected. (Hearing a foreign language that you do not understand has the same effect.) Subjects who hear content-free speech can consistently recognize the emotion being expressed, as well as identifying its strength.[63]

The impact of paralinguistic cues is strong. In fact, research shows that listeners pay more attention to the vocal messages than to the words that are spoken when asked to determine a speaker's attitudes.[64] Furthermore, when vocal factors contradict a verbal message, listeners judge the speaker's intention from the paralanguage, not from the words themselves.[65]

Paralanguage can affect behaviour in many ways, some of which are rather surprising. Researchers have discovered that communicators were most likely to comply with requests delivered by speakers whose rate—their talking speed—was similar to their own.[66] Besides *complying* with same-rate speakers, listeners feel more positive in general about people who seem to talk at their own rate. Vocal intensity also can affect how willing people are to respond to another person's requests.[67]

Vocal changes that contradict spoken words are not easy to conceal. If the speaker is trying to conceal fear or anger, the voice will probably sound higher and louder, and the rate of talk may be faster than normal. Sadness produces the opposite vocal pattern: quieter, lower-pitched speech delivered at a slower rate.[68]

Besides reinforcing or contradicting messages, some vocal factors influence the way a speaker is perceived by others. For example, communicators who speak loudly and without hesitations are viewed as more confident than those who pause and speak quietly.[69] People who speak more slowly are judged as having greater conversational control than fast talkers.[70] Research has also demonstrated that people with more attractive voices are rated more highly than those whose voice sounds less attractive.[71] Just what makes a voice attractive can vary. As Figure 5.1 shows, culture can make a difference.

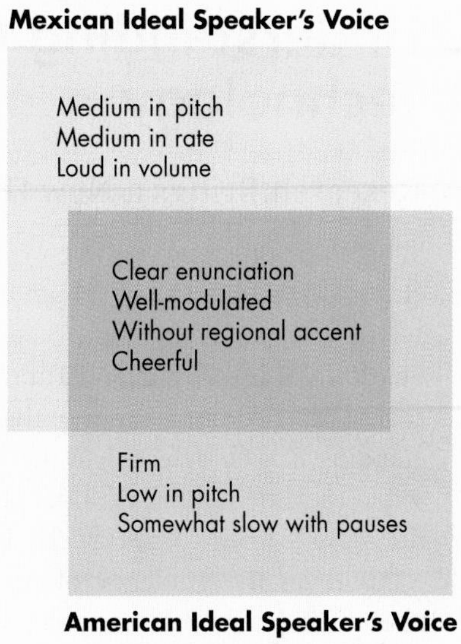

Mexican Ideal Speaker's Voice

Medium in pitch
Medium in rate
Loud in volume

Clear enunciation
Well-modulated
Without regional accent
Cheerful

Firm
Low in pitch
Somewhat slow with pauses

American Ideal Speaker's Voice

Figure 5.1
Ideal Speaker's Voice Types in Mexico and the United States

Touch

Besides being the earliest means we have of making contact with others, touching—or haptics—is essential to our healthy development. During the nineteenth and early twentieth centuries many babies died from a disease then called *marasmus,* which, translated from Greek, means 'wasting away'. In some orphanages the mortality rate was quite high, but even children in 'progressive' homes, hospitals, and other institutions died regularly from the ailment. When researchers finally tracked down the causes of this disease, they found that many infants suffered from lack of physical contact with parents or nurses rather than poor nutrition, medical care, or other factors. They hadn't been touched enough, and as a result they died. From this knowledge came the practice of 'mothering' children in institutions—picking babies up, carrying them around, and handling them several times each day. At one hospital that began this practice, the death rate for infants fell from between 30 and 35 per cent to below 10 per cent.[72]

As a child develops, the need for being touched continues. In his book *Touching: The Human Significance of the Skin,* Ashley Montagu describes research that suggests that allergies, eczema, and other health problems are, in part, caused by a person's lack of contact as an infant with his or her mother.[73] Although Montagu says that these problems develop early in life, he also cites cases where adults suffering from conditions as diverse as asthma and schizophrenia have been successfully treated by psychiatric therapy that uses extensive physical contact.

Touch seems to increase a child's mental functioning as well as physical health. L.J. Yarrow has conducted surveys that show that babies who have been given plenty of physical stimulation by their mothers have significantly higher IQs than those receiving less contact.[74]

Understanding Communication Technology

Research Brings a New Dimension to a Candidate's Choice

What if the difference between winning and losing a close election turned out to be a hum in your voice?

A new study by Kent State University researchers Stanford W. Gregory, Jr, and Timothy J. Gallagher suggests that at least some of the way that people perceive social standing can be detected in the way their voices change when they are talking with people they see as more confident or higher on the social ladder.[1] The researchers focused on the tendency of people in conversation to alter their pitch, volume, pace, and other characteristics of speech to emulate one another. This area of study is known as communication accommodation theory. Dr Gregory's research focuses on accommodation within a little-noticed range of vocal tones which fall below the range of spoken words. The changes are barely detectable, the researchers say, but those who are most inclined to make them typically lose at the ballot box.

The paper analyzes the voices of presidential candidates in their debates since 1960. The researchers found that, in every case, the politician whose voice was most steadfast, as measured by the researchers, won the most votes.

—John Schwartz, *New York Times* online, 17 September 2002.

[1] S.W. Gregory and T.J. Gallagher, 'Spectral Analysis of Candidates' Non-verbal Vocal Communication: Predicting US Presidential Election Outcomes', Social Psychology Quarterly 65 (2002): 298–308.

Touch also plays a large part in how we respond to others and to our environment.[75] For example, touch increases self-disclosure, verbalization of psychiatric patients, and the preference children have for their counsellors. Touch also increases compliance.[76] In one study, subjects were approached by a woman who asked them to return a coin left in the phone booth from which they had just emerged. When the request was accompanied by a light touch on the subject's arm, the probability that the subject would return the coin increased significantly.[77] In a similar experiment, subjects were asked to sign a petition or complete a rating scale. Again, subjects were more likely to co-operate when they were touched lightly on the arm. In the rating-scale variation of the study, the results were especially dramatic: 70 per cent of those who were touched complied, whereas only 40 per cent of the untouched subjects complied (indicating a predisposition not to comply).[78] An additional power of touch is its on-the-job utility. One study showed that fleeting touches on the hand and shoulder resulted in larger tips for restaurant staff.[79]

Touch can communicate many messages. Researchers have catalogued 12 different kinds of touches, including 'positive', 'playful', 'control', and 'ritualistic'.[80] Some kinds of touch indicate varying degrees of aggression. Others signify types of relationships:[81]

- functional/professional (dental examination, haircut);
- social/polite (handshake);
- friendship/warmth (clap on back, Spanish *abrazo*);
- love/intimacy (caresses, hugs); and
- sexual arousal (kisses, strokes).

You might object to the examples following each of these categories, saying that some non-verbal behaviours occur in several types of relationships. A kiss, for example, can mean anything from a polite but superficial greeting to the most intense arousal. What makes a given touch more or less intense? Researchers have suggested a number of factors:

- the part of the body that does the touching;
- the part of the body that is touched;
- the length of time the touch lasts;
- the amount of pressure used;
- whether there is movement after contact is made;
- whether anyone else is present;
- the situation in which the touch occurs; and
- the relationship between the people involved.

In traditional English-Canadian culture, touching is generally more appropriate for women than for men. Men touch their male friends less than they touch their female friends and also less than women touch their female friends. Fear of homosexuality seems to be a strong reason why many men are reluctant to touch one another. Although women are more comfortable about touching than men are, gender isn't the only factor that shapes contact. In general, the degree of touch comfort goes along with openness to expressing intimate feelings, an active interpersonal style, and satisfactory relationships.[82]

Physical Attractiveness

Most people claim that looks aren't the best measure of desirability or character, but then they typically prefer others whom they find attractive.[83] For example, women who are perceived as attractive have more dates, receive higher grades in college, have an easier time persuading men, and receive lighter court sentences. Both men and women whom others view as attractive are rated as being more sensitive, kind, strong, sociable, and interesting than those judged less attractive. Who is most likely to succeed in business? You can safely bet on the attractive job applicant. For example, shorter men have more difficulty finding jobs in the first place, and men over six-foot-two receive starting salaries that average 12.4 per cent higher than comparable applicants under six feet.

The influence of attractiveness begins early in life. Preschoolers were shown photographs of children their own age and asked to choose potential friends and enemies. The researchers found that children as young as three years old agreed as to who was attractive ('cute') and unattractive ('homely'). Furthermore, they valued their attractive counterparts—of both the same and the opposite sex—more highly. Also, preschool girls rated by their peers as pretty were most liked, and those identified as least pretty were least liked. Children who were interviewed rated good-looking children as having positive social characteristics ('He's friendly to other children') and unattractive children as having negative ones ('He hits other children without reason').

Teachers also are affected by students' attractiveness. Physically attractive students are usually judged more favourably—seen as more intelligent, friendly, and popular—than their less attractive counterparts.[84] Fortunately, attractiveness is something we can control without having to call a plastic surgeon. We view others as beautiful or ugly not just on the basis of

In our now more than slightly cockeyed world, there seems to be little provision for someone to get touched without having to go to bed with whomever does the touching. And that's something to think about. We have mixed up simple, healing, warm touching with sexual advances. So much so, that it often seems as if there is no middle way between 'Don't you dare touch me!' and 'Okay, you touched me, so now we should make love!'

A nation which is able to distinguish the fine points between offensive and defensive pass interference, bogies, birdies, and par, a schuss and a slalom, a technical, a personal, and a player-control foul should certainly be able to make some far more obvious distinctions between various sorts of body contact.

Sidney Simon,
Caring, Feeling, Touching

I'm sure you have heard it said that appearance does not matter so much, and that it is what's on the inside that counts. This is, of course, utter nonsense, because if it were true then people who were good on the inside would never have to comb their hair or take a bath, and the whole world would smell even worse than it already does.

Lemony Snicket,
The Miserable Mill

Understanding Communication Technology

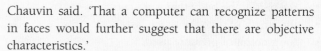

Computer Can Judge Human Attractiveness

Beauty is in the eye of the beholder, the popular saying goes, but new Canadian research suggests this is not really true.

University of Windsor undergraduate student Joshua Chauvin has found that a computer can be trained to rate human facial attractiveness the same way that people rate the looks of others.

For his research, Chauvin trained a computer program called a neural network—which is essentially a pattern recognition program loosely based on the human brain—to mimic how humans assess attractiveness.

He had 100 people rate images of 100 others on attractiveness and then asked the neural network to rate the attractiveness of 33 images.

The findings show that 85 per cent of the time, the neural network's ratings fell within one point of the human subjects' ratings.

'So what [the neural network is] doing is coming up with its own rating for those images based on some sort of understanding of what it thinks the population finds as attractive,' Chauvin told CTV.ca in a telephone interview.

Chauvin was assisted in his research by Dr Marcello Guarini from the Department of Philosophy and Dr Chris Abeare from the Department of Psychology.

He will present his findings this fall at the International Conference for Neural Computation in Madeira, Portugal.

In his research paper, Chauvin points to myriad research that has found that rating facial beauty is consistent across the globe and that specific features, such as facial symmetry, are important for determining facial attractiveness.

'One of the ideas is that there is some sort of objective basis for assessing facial attractiveness. Some sort of biological inclination to like those things and not like others,' Chauvin said. 'That a computer can recognize patterns in faces would further suggest that there are objective characteristics.'

While computers are unlikely to replace humans as beauty-pageant judges, Chauvin said there are some practical implications for his research.

Marketing and advertising companies could use a neural network to assess how their target audience may respond to their casting choices.

'If you want a population's opinion about what attractiveness is, you can take a one-time poll and have them rate any given number of images on attractiveness features,' Chauvin said. 'And then if an advertising campaign has a model, they could input the model into the neural network and find out what the population thinks about that individual without having to poll the population over and over again for each advertisement.'

Chauvin also said the research may one day lead to neural networks identifying telltale facial characteristics of some diseases.

While that research is in its infancy, the next step in Chauvin's study will be to determine if the neural network can also mimic how the subjects assessed the personality characteristics of the faces in the images.

—Andrea Janus, CTV.ca, 18 July 2009.

Questions: Some people might think of what this article is saying as a 'chicken and egg' phenomenon. Do you think that once it is used extensively by professional communicators, the computer program might start influencing people's perception of what is beautiful, rather than simply reflecting popular taste?

the features they're born with but on how they present those features. Posture, gestures, facial expressions, and other behaviours can increase the attractiveness of a person who is otherwise physically unremarkable. Exercise can also improve the way each of us looks. Finally, the way we dress can make a significant difference in the way others perceive us, as we'll see in the next section.

Clothing

Besides protecting us from the elements, clothing is a means of non-verbal communication, providing a relatively straightforward (if sometimes expensive) method of impression management. Clothing can be used to convey economic status, educational level, social status, moral standards, athletic ability and/or interests, belief systems (political, philosophical, religious), and level of sophistication.

Research shows that we do make assumptions about people based on their clothing. Communicators who wear special clothing often gain persuasiveness. For example, experimenters dressed to resemble police officers were more successful than those dressed in civilian clothing in requesting pedestrians to pick up litter and in persuading them to lend a quarter to an over-parked motorist.[85] Likewise, solicitors wearing sheriff's and nurse's uniforms gained greater contributions to law enforcement and health-care campaigns than campaigners in 'plain clothes'.[86]

Uniforms aren't the only kind of clothing that carries influence. In one study, a man and woman were stationed in a hallway so that anyone who wished to go by had to avoid them or pass between them. In one condition, the conversationalists wore 'formal daytime dress'; in the other, they wore 'casual attire'. Passersby behaved differently toward the couple depending on the style of clothing: they responded positively with the well-dressed couple and negatively when the same people were casually dressed.[87] Similar results in other situations show the influence of clothing. We are more likely to obey people dressed in a high-status manner. Pedestrians were more likely to return lost coins to well-dressed people than to those dressed in low-status clothing.[88] We are also more likely to follow the lead of high-status dressers even when it comes to violating social rules. Eighty-three per cent of the pedestrians in one study followed a well-dressed jaywalker who violated a 'wait' crossing signal, whereas only 48 per cent followed a citizen dressed in lower-status clothing.[89] Women who are wearing a suit jacket as part of their outfit are rated as being more powerful than those wearing only a dress or skirt and blouse.[90]

As we get to know others better, the importance of clothing shrinks.[91] This fact suggests that clothing is especially important in the early stages of a relationship, when making a positive first impression is necessary in order to encourage others to get to know us better. This advice is equally important in personal situations and in employment interviews. In both cases, your style of dress (and personal grooming) can make all the difference between the chance to progress further and outright rejection.

Distance

The study of the way people and animals use space has been termed **proxemics**. Preferred spaces are largely a matter of cultural norms. For example, people living in hyperdense Hong Kong manage to live in crowded residential quarters that most North Americans would find intolerable.[92] Edward T. Hall has defined four types used in mainstream Anglo-North American culture.[93] He says that we choose a particular distance depending on how we feel toward the other person at a given time, the context of the conversation, and our personal goals.

Clothes make the man. Naked people have little or no influence on society.

Mark Twain

> **Cultural Idiom**
>
> **jaywalker**
> a person who crosses the street without obeying traffic signals

proxemics
The study of how people and animals use space.

An Exercise in Mutual Evaluation

Since the turn of the century, I have been on one of the least known 'reality shows'.

Five days a week, I am judged and critiqued by almost 100 pop-savvy consumers who rate my dress, speech, moods, manners, and jokes. Unlike the judges from the Idol shows, these judges are not constrained by commercial breaks or the tamed family hour. They have called me stupid and useless, questioned my sexual orientation, hinted that my shirts are too tight—then praised me for being a fine dresser—and hurled invective at me that could crush a weaker soul. They have sometimes made me want to quit my profession, but then I remember Lance Armstrong's mantra that 'Pain is temporary, quitting is forever'—so I go back to them for more judgment. They have great faith in their pronouncements, feeling uniquely qualified to score my critical talents.

The show on which I toil—an obscure little production in Room 233 in an ordinary suburban scene and of little interest to anyone older than 18—might well be called *So You Think You Can Teach*. Every day I stand before 100 teenagers and try to make demand-and-supply curves interesting (I sometimes use my arms to illustrate movements in the curves and end up looking like a man directing jets at Pearson Airport). For many years, I also taught math, which is sometimes a little like being a prison guard, but leavened it by telling anecdotes about my car, my kids, my dog, or my partner. Self-deprecation works, especially if they agree with you.

They keep track of what I wear and have on occasion requested that I wear some shirt that they like. They count the number of pairs of shoes that I own and they know when the grey in my hair has diminished overnight. If I get tongue-tied or trip on an extension cord, they will laugh—sometimes with malice but most often from familiarity with human weakness.

They do most of the things that we all did in school. I remember looking at my teachers with the critical eye of an art appraiser or potential employer, and my friends and I had a ranking system for our teachers based solely on intangibles such as 'fairness' or 'fun'. The good teachers, we concluded, gave little homework, eased off the rules, treated students equally, and allowed lots of parties. Even in Grade 12, we admired the teachers who were relaxed about curriculum and grades, not realizing that we'd pay for this with low grades in first-year English or calculus at university.

The Internet has moved the private domain into the public one. Where opinions might have found an audience of only three or four close friends, or a few more extended family members or work colleagues, they can now find thousands, even millions of people who are interested in the mundane or malicious.

Blogger, MySpace, Facebook, and YouTube have allowed us to expose our private thoughts and acts—and young people translate private thoughts into public ones at the speed of light. For 20 years, I have kept a journal of random thoughts

---

intimate distance

One of Hall's four distance zones, ranging from skin contact to 18 inches (45 centimetres).

personal distance

One of Hall's four distance zones, ranging from 18 inches (45 centimetres) to 4 feet (1.2 metres).

social distance

One of Hall's four distance zones, ranging from 4 to 12 feet (1.2 to 3.6 metres).

Intimate distance begins with skin contact and ranges out to about 18 inches (45 centimetres). The most obvious context for intimate distance involves interaction with people to whom we're emotionally close—and then mostly in private situations. Intimate distance between individuals also occurs in less intimate circumstances: visiting a doctor, dentist, or hairdresser, and during some athletic contests. Allowing someone to move into the intimate zone usually is a sign of trust.

Personal distance ranges from 18 inches (45 centimetres) at its closest point to 4 feet (1.2 metres) at its farthest. Its closer range is the distance at which most relational partners stand in public. We are uncomfortable if someone else 'moves into' this area without invitation. The far range of personal distance runs from about 2.5 to 4 feet (45 to 75 centimetres). This is the zone just beyond the other person's reach—the distance at which we can keep someone 'at arm's length'. This term suggests the type of communication that goes on at this range: interaction is still reasonably personal but less so than communication that occurs a foot (30 centimetres) or so closer.

and no one will ever read it while I am alive. Most of it is silly and innocuous, but part might be considered wildly opinionated, even nasty. I am greedy about my private thoughts, choosing not to share what I think about the eating habits demonstrated at family dinners or the love lives of my friends.

My students are generous to a fault with their private thoughts. They no sooner acquire a thought than they give it away in a fit of dispossession. And there is no shortage of places for them to share. The school cafeteria or hallways are archaic venues for gossiping about teachers compared to RateMyTeachers.ca on the Web. There they can post comments and score teachers in three categories (easiness, clarity, and helpfulness). On a scale of one to five there isn't a lot of wiggle room for interpretation, and kids tend to drift to either end of the spectrum, so I get fives from the adoring students and ones from the kids who just don't like me.

Comments that are only tangentially connected to my ability to teach are made and are often filled with misspellings: 'He spends to much time taking about his dog', 'definetly a really cool guy', 'quit pretending as an university prof'. Many of my raters cannot string together a coherent sentence, but in their defence, they would argue that Simon Cowell can't sing, but he still judges Idol contestants.

In addition to the numerical ratings, students provide a summary judgment of my 'popularity' (in the university equivalent—RateMyProfessors—'hotness' is considered) by selecting an emoticon. So far I have maintained a happy face wearing sunglasses, indicating that I am both popular and cool.

Every three years, I am evaluated by the administration. The process takes most of the school year and involves a fair bit of preparation and introspection and culminates in a public performance for a vice-principal or principal. I receive a written report and sit down face-to-face with my evaluator to discuss how well I've done my job. On RateMyTeachers, I do not know my judges, and what they say about me is written on the Internet version of bathroom walls in indelible ink. Still, I take comfort in the fact that having something written about me is better than nothing at all; I at least make an impression that motivates them to express their opinions in a public forum, much the same way the plebeians did when they wrote about Julius Caesar on the walls of Rome.

Although I do not have the summary powers of an emperor, I still have final judgment about grades and letters of recommendation. I am a benevolent dictator.

—*Kevin Bray,* The Globe and Mail, *7 March 2007, A16. Kevin Bray is a Toronto writer and teacher.*

Question: The writer states that his students judge him on aspects of his appearance, such as his style of dress and his hair. Think of an instructor you've had whose appearance made an impression—favourable or unfavourable—on you. How did this aspect of non-verbal communication colour your perception of the instructor's teaching style?

Social distance ranges from 4 to about 12 feet (1.2 to 3.6 metres). Within it are the kinds of communication that usually occur in business situations. Its closer range, from 4 to 7 feet (1.2 to 2.1 metres), is the distance at which conversations usually occur between salespeople and customers and between people who work together. We use the far range of social distance—7 to 12 feet (2.1 to 3.6 metres)—for more formal and impersonal situations. This is the range at which we generally sit from the boss.

Public distance is Hall's term for the farthest zone, running outward from 12 feet (3.5 metres). The closer range of public distance is the one most instructors use in the classroom. In the farther range of public space—25 feet (7.5 metres) and beyond—two-way communication becomes difficult. In some cases it's necessary for speakers to use public distance owing to the size of their audience, but we can assume that anyone who voluntarily chooses to use it when he or she could be closer is not interested in having a dialogue.

Choosing the optimal distance can have a powerful effect on how we regard others and how we respond to them. For example, students are more satisfied with teachers who reduce

The trouble with being punctual is that nobody's there to appreciate it.

Franklin P. Jones

public distance
One of Hall's four distance zones, extending outward from 12 feet (3.5 metres).

Understanding Diversity

● ● ● ● ● **DRESS FOR DISASTER**

Sharon, an administrative coordinator, was noticeably overt with her flirtation at work.

In a nutshell—she was sexy.

Many of her colleagues assumed her voluptuous curves, enhanced cleavage, and fitted clothes got her the job, but even if that were the case, they failed to protect her from being fired. And she was.

At the end of the day, if you can't back up your beauty with brains and mental power, and follow through—most companies won't keep you.

Women have been capitalizing on their femininity for a long time. According to a survey completed by *Top Sante* magazine, one in five women said they would be prepared to flirt with the boss in order to boost their job prospects. However, research shows that flirting in the workplace will not get you promoted.

Actually, blatant flirting and dressing provocatively can be a liability, not an asset. It often provokes jealousy, creates barriers to being treated sincerely, and makes it easy for others to downgrade successes (albeit maybe unfairly).

Accomplishments are no longer seen as a true reflection of one's inner capabilities but as a reflection of an outer-directed lifestyle.

Let's be honest—miniskirts and stilettos weren't designed for a woman's comfort and aren't practical workplace attire—the only reason for a woman to wear that apparel is to get noticed.

And it does work—you will get noticed, but not always in the way that you anticipated.

Just look at the women on the popular television show *The Apprentice*. When it comes to entrusting the development of your newest multi-million dollar building to a young unknown, who are you most likely to hire to oversee the project—the cutesy girl in the mini or the serious candidate in the pants? We all saw who won.

'That exact portrayal of women on *The Apprentice* is the worst thing for women—it's the demise of the female professional,' says Roz Usheroff, renowned image maker and president of The Usheroff Institute.

'As soon as you promote your beauty instead of your brains, you're not going to be taken seriously. I used to wear short skirts, but found that men would be more interested in checking out my body than checking out my ideas, so now I wear pants,' says Usheroff.

Michelle, a partner in a private investment management firm, gets agitated at the mere mention of the words flirtation and sexuality. 'My image, or the way in which I'm perceived, significantly impacts my career. I read a *Harvard Business Review* study that said people make a first impression within seven seconds of meeting you, and 94 per cent of the time their initial assessment is correct.'

In a male-dominated industry, where it might seem like the ideal environment to want to turn on the feminine charm,

the distance between themselves and their classes. They also are more satisfied with the course itself, and they are more likely to follow the teacher's instructions.[94] Likewise, medical patients are more satisfied with physicians who are not standoffish.[95]

Time

Social scientists use the term **chronemics** for the study of how human beings use and structure time. The way we handle time can express both intentional and unintentional messages.[96] Social psychologist Robert Levine describes several ways that time can communicate.[97] For instance, in a culture like ours that values time highly, waiting can be an indicator of status. 'Important' people (whose time is supposedly more valuable than that of others) may be seen by appointment only, whereas it is acceptable to intrude without

chronemics
The study of how humans use and structure time.

Michelle sees it as being quite the opposite. 'The business I am in is very serious—it's dealing with people's money. And if I want to be taken seriously by my clients and colleagues, then I have to dress seriously.'

'You are constantly creating the perceptions you want, so it's important to ask the question, "How do I want others to see me?"' says David McNally, international entrepreneur, producer of the award-winning film *The Power of Purpose*, and author of the book *Be Your Own Brand*.

Next time you find yourself standing in front of your closet trying to decide what to wear to work, McNally suggests considering this: will what you choose to wear make you distinctive in a way that reflects what you stand for and believe in?

'The advice I gave to my daughters is to dress in a way that addresses your unique style, while at the same time understand that people will make judgments about you by how you dress—that's the reality, because that's the first image we project,' comments McNally, father of five.

My advice is this: dress for success rather than sex-excess—you will be taken more seriously and be much more content with the results.

What Not to Wear
When dressing for work, avoid

- wearing spandex
- showing your midriff
- showing cleavage
- wearing sheer blouses
- sporting really micro minis
- wearing spaghetti-strap tanks
- wearing clothes that are too tight

Wake-Up Call
According to Roz Usheroff, you know you're not being taken seriously when

- your ideas go unnoticed
- your legs get more attention than your voice
- you're overlooked for a sure-win promotion
- an external image consultant is hired to fix you without your consent
- you're asked to serve the coffee and it's not your job
- you're frequently elected to pick up lunch

Is Someone Speaking?
If you answer 'no' to any of these questions you might need an image make-over.

- Do you command respect when you walk into a room?
- Do you grab the attention of the others in the room when you open your mouth to speak?
- Are your ideas/comments heard and acknowledged?
- Are you being taken seriously?
- When you speak with men, do they maintain eye contact, or are their eyes wandering to other parts of your body?

—*Ellen Goldhar*, Toronto Sun, 20 May 2004. *Reprinted by permission of the publisher.*

Question: Choice of clothing can be a powerful form of non-verbal communication. Do you think it is sexist to advise women not to wear provocative clothing at work?

notice on lesser beings. To see how this rule operates, consider how natural it would be for the CEO of a company to arrive, unannounced and uninvited, in a subordinate's office, whereas some employees would never go near the boss's office without an appointment. A related rule is that low-status people must never make more important people wait. It would be a serious mistake to show up late for a job interview, although the interviewer might keep you cooling your heels in the lobby. Important people are often whisked to the head of a restaurant or airport line, whereas the presumably less exalted are forced to wait their turn.

The use of time depends greatly on culture.[98] In some cultures, punctuality is critically important, whereas in others it is barely considered. One psychologist discovered the difference between North and South American attitudes when teaching at a university in Brazil.[99] He found that some students arrived halfway through a two-hour class and that most of them stayed put

> **Cultural Idiom**
>
> **cooling your heels**
> waiting impatiently
>
> **stayed put**
> remained where they were

and kept asking questions when the class was scheduled to end. A half-hour after the official end of the class, the professor finally closed the discussion because there was no indication that the students intended to leave. This flexibility of time is quite different from what is common in most Canadian universities and colleges!

Even within a country, rules of time vary. Sometimes the differences are geographic.[100] In Montreal, the party invitation may say '9 p.m.', but nobody would think of showing up before 9:30. In Calgary, though, guests are expected to show up on time, or perhaps even a bit early. Even within the same geographic area, different groups establish their own rules about the use of time. Consider your own experience. In school, some instructors begin and end class punctually, whereas others are more casual. With some people you feel comfortable talking for hours in person or on the phone, whereas with others time seems to be precious and not meant to be 'wasted'.

territory
Fixed space that an individual assumes some right to occupy.

A team of social scientists studying United Nations deliberations was puzzled by the unexpected and influential role that the ambassador from Ireland was playing in Middle East negotiations. It wasn't until communication patterns were considered that the answer became clear. The Irish ambassador, it turns out, sits alphabetically among delegates from Iran, Israel, Jordan, and Kuwait. This arrangement facilitated communicative ties and, as a result, Ireland discovered itself playing the role of Mideast peace broker.

Aaron Cargile

Territoriality

Whereas personal space is the invisible bubble we carry around as an extension of our physical being, **territory** is fixed space. Any area, such as a room, house, neighbourhood, or country, to which we assume some kind of 'rights' is our territory. Not all territory is permanent. We often stake out space for ourselves in the library, at the beach, and so on by using markers such as books, clothing, or other personal possessions.

The way people use space can communicate a good deal about power and status relationships. Generally, we grant people with higher status more personal territory and greater privacy.[101] We knock before entering the boss's office, whereas an employer can usually walk into a subordinate's work area without hesitating. In traditional colleges and universities, professors have offices, dining rooms, and even washrooms that are private, whereas students, who are presumably less important, have no such sanctuaries.

Environment

The physical environment people create can both reflect and shape interaction. This principle is illustrated right at home. The impressions that household interior designs communicate can be remarkably accurate. Researchers showed 99 students images of the insides or outsides of 12 upper-middle-class homes and then asked them to infer the personality of the owners from their impressions.[102] The students were especially accurate after glancing at interior images. The decorating schemes communicated accurate information about the homeowners' intellectualism, politeness, maturity, optimism, tenseness, willingness to take adventures, family orientations, and reservedness. The home exteriors also gave viewers accurate perceptions of the owners' artistic interests, graciousness, privacy, and quietness.

Besides communicating information about the designer, an environment can shape the kind of interaction that takes place in it. In one experiment, researchers found that the attractiveness of a room influenced the happiness and energy of the people working in it.[103] The experimenters set up three rooms: an 'ugly' one, which resembled a maintenance worker's closet in the basement of a campus building; an 'average' room, which was a professor's office; and a 'beautiful' room, which was furnished with carpeting, drapes, and comfortable furniture. The subjects in the experiment were asked to rate a series of pictures as a way of measuring their energy and feelings of well-being while at work. Results of the experiment showed that, while in the ugly room, the subjects became tired and bored more quickly and took longer to complete their task. When they moved to the beautiful room, however, they rated the faces they were judging higher, showed a greater desire to work, and expressed feelings of importance, comfort, and enjoyment. The results teach a lesson that isn't surprising: workers generally feel better and do a better job when they're in an attractive environment.

In a more therapeutic and less commercial way, physicians have also shaped environments to improve communication. Psychologist Robert Sommer found that redesigning the convalescent ward of a hospital greatly increased the interaction among patients. In the old design, seats were placed shoulder to shoulder around the edges of the ward. When the chairs were grouped around small tables so that patients faced each other at a comfortable distance, the number of conversations doubled.[104]

The design of an entire building can shape communication among its users. Architects have learned that the way housing projects are designed controls to a great extent the contact neighbours have with each other. People who live in apartments near stairways and mailboxes have much more contact with neighbours than do those living in less heavily travelled parts of the building, and tenants generally have more contacts with immediate neighbours than with people even a few doors away.[105] Architects now use this information to design buildings that either encourage communication or increase privacy, and house hunters can use the same knowledge to choose a home that gives them the neighbourhood relationships they want.

So far we have talked about how designing an environment can shape communication, but there is another side to consider. Watching how people use an already existing environment can be a way of telling what kind of relationships they want. For example, Sommer watched students in a college library and found that there's a definite pattern for people who want to study alone. While the library was uncrowded, students almost always chose corner seats at one of the empty rectangular tables.[106] Finally, each table was occupied by one reader. New readers would then choose a seat on the opposite side and far end of an occupied table, thus keeping the maximum distance between themselves and the other readers. One of Sommer's associates tried violating these 'rules' by sitting next to, and across from, other female readers when more distant seats were available. She found that the approached women reacted defensively, either by signalling their discomfort through shifts in posture, by gesturing, or by eventually moving away.

A good house is planned from the inside out. First, you decide what it has to do for its occupants. Then, you let the functions determine the form. The more numerous and various those functions, the more responsive and interesting the house should be. And it may not look at all like you expect.

Dan MacMasters

Summary

Non-verbal communication consists of messages expressed by non-linguistic means. There are non-verbal dimensions to all spoken language, and there are sign languages that are not spoken.

Non-verbal behaviour is an integral part of virtually all communication, and non-verbal skill is a positive predictor of relational success. There are several important characteristics of non-verbal communication. First is the simple fact that it exists—that communication occurs even in the absence of language. This leads to the second characteristic: it is impossible *not* to communicate non-verbally. Humans constantly send messages about themselves that are available for others to receive. The third characteristic is that non-verbal communication is ambiguous; there are many possible interpretations for any behaviour. This ambiguity makes it important for the receiver to verify any interpretation before jumping to conclusions about the meaning of a non-verbal message. Finally, non-verbal communication is different from verbal communication in complexity, flow, clarity, impact, and intentionality.

Some non-verbal communication is influenced by culture and gender. While there are some universal expressions, even the manner in which these expressions are used reflects the communicator's culture and gender. And behaviours that have special meanings in one culture may express different messages in another. We stated that non-verbal communication serves many functions: repeating, substituting, complementing, accenting, regulating, and contradicting verbal behaviour, as well as deceiving.

The remainder of this chapter introduced the many ways in which humans communicate non-verbally: through posture, gesture, use of the face and eyes, voice, touch, clothing, distance, time, territoriality, and physical environment.

Key Terms

affect blends 187

chronemics 196

disfluencies 188

emblem 182

illustrators 182

intimate distance 194

kinesics 186

manipulators 186

non-verbal
   communication 170

paralanguage 188

personal distance 194

proxemics 193

public distance 195

social distance 194

territory 198

Activities

A. Observing and Reporting Non-Verbal Behaviour

This exercise will give you a clear idea of the many non-verbal behaviours that are available to you whenever you encounter another person. It will also help prevent you from jumping to conclusions about the meaning of those behaviours without checking out your

interpretations. You can try the exercise either during or outside of class, and the period of time over which you do it is flexible, from a single class period to several days. In any case, begin by choosing a partner, and then follow these directions:

1. For the first period of time (however long you decide to make it), observe the way your partner behaves. Notice how he or she moves; his or her mannerisms, postures, way of speaking; how he or she dresses; and so on. Jot down your observations. If you're doing this exercise out of class over an extended period of time, there's no need to let your observations interfere with whatever you'd normally be doing: your only job here is to compile a list of your partner's behaviours. In this step, you should be careful not to *interpret* your partner's actions; just record what you see.

2. At the end of the time period, share what you've seen with your partner. He or she will do the same with you.

3. For the next period, your job is not just to observe your partner's behaviour but to interpret it. This time in your conference you should tell your partner what you thought his or her actions revealed. For example, if your partner dressed carelessly, did you think this meant that he or she had overslept, that he or she was losing interest in his or her appearance, or that he or she was trying to be more comfortable? If you noticed your partner yawning frequently, did you think this meant that he or she was bored, tired from a late night, or sleepy after a big meal? Don't feel bad if your guesses weren't all correct. Remember that non-verbal clues tend to be ambiguous. You may be surprised how checking out the non-verbal clues you observe can help build a relationship with another person.

B. Culture and Non-Verbal Communication

1. Identify at least three significant differences between non-verbal practices in two cultures or co-cultures (e.g., ethnic, age, or socioeconomic groups) within your own society.

2. Describe the potential difficulties that could arise out of the differing non-verbal practices when members from the cultural groups interact. Are there any ways of avoiding these difficulties?

3. Now describe the advantages that might come from differing cultural non-verbal practices. How might people from diverse backgrounds profit by encountering one another's customs and norms?

C. Kinesics in Action

You can appreciate the many ways kinesic cues operate by identifying examples from your own experience when body movement served each of the following non-verbal functions:

1. repeating
2. substituting
3. complementing
4. accenting
5. regulating
6. contradicting

D. The Eyes Have It

Prove to yourself the role eye contact plays in social influence by trying a simple experiment.

1.   Choose a situation where you can make simple requests from a series of strangers. You might, for example, ask to cut in line at a store, or you could ask passersby if they have a cell phone you could borrow to make an important phone call.

2.   Make such a request to at least 20 people. Use the same words for each request but alternate your non-verbal behaviour. Half the time make direct eye contact, and the other half of the time avoid looking directly at the other person when you make your request.

3.   Record your results, and see if your eye behaviour played any role in generating compliance to your request.

4.   If eye contact does make a difference, describe how you could apply your findings to real-life situations.

E. Building Vocal Fluency

You can become more adept at both conveying and interpreting vocal messages by following these directions.

1.   Join with a partner and designate one person A and the other B.

2.   Partner A should choose 25 to 50 items from the telephone directory, using his or her voice to convey one of the following attitudes:

   a.   egotism

   b.   friendliness

   c.   insecurity

   d.   irritation

   e.   confidence

3.   Partner B should try to detect the emotion being conveyed.

4.   Switch roles and repeat the process. Continue alternating roles until each of you has both conveyed and tried to interpret at least four emotions.

5.   After completing the preceding steps, discuss the following questions:

   a.   What vocal cues did you use to make your guesses?

   b.   Were some emotions easier to guess than others?

   c.   Given the accuracy of your guesses, how would you assess your ability to interpret vocal cues?

6.   How can you use your increased sensitivity to vocal cues to improve your everyday communication competence?

F. The Rules of Touch

Like most types of non-verbal behaviour, touching is governed by cultural and social rules. Imagine you are writing a guidebook for visitors from another culture. Describe the rules that govern touching in the following relationships. In each case, describe how the gender of the participants affects the rules.

1.   an adult and a 5-year-old

2.   an adult and a 12-year-old

3. two good friends
4. employer and employee

G. Distance Violations

You can test the importance of distance for yourself by violating the cultural rules for use of the proxemic zones outlined on pages 194–5.

1. Join with a partner. Choose which one of you will be the experimenter and which will be the observer.
2. In three situations, the experimenter should deliberately use the 'wrong' amount of space for the context. Make the violations as subtle as possible. You might, for instance, gradually move into another person's intimate zone when personal distance would be more appropriate. (Be careful not to make the violations too offensive!)
3. The observer should record the verbal and non-verbal reactions of others when the distance zones are violated. After each experiment, inform the people involved about your motives and ask whether they were consciously aware of the reason for any discomfort they experienced.

H. The Power of Non-Verbal Insight

Being aware of the communicative power of non-verbal behaviour can often give you an edge in understanding and influencing it. Suppose that your skill at controlling your own non-verbal behaviour became great enough that you were able to present yourself to others in precisely the way you desire (even if the image weren't completely accurate), and your ability to analyze others' non-verbal behaviour gave you a high degree of accuracy in interpreting others' unexpressed feelings.

Go to the park or to some other public place and observe people around you. Ask yourself these questions:

Who is the person I am looking at?

What components of his or her identity can I determine by noting non-verbal behaviour?

What element of non-verbal behaviour is giving me the best clues?

Write down your observations with a brief description of the person you are looking at, including his or her appearance, age, gender, and clothing.

I. Clothing and Impression Management

Using clothing as a method of creating impressions is a fact of life. Discover for yourself how dressing can be a type of deception.

1. Identify three examples from your experience when someone dressed in a manner that disguised or misrepresented his or her true status or personal attributes. What were the consequences of this misrepresentation for you or others?
2. Now identify three occasions in which you successfully used clothing to create a favourable but inaccurate impression. What were the consequences of this deception for others?
3. Based on your conclusions, define any situations when clothing may be used as an unethical means of impression management. List both 'misdemeanours', in which the consequences are not likely to cause serious harm, and 'felonies', in which the deception has the potential to cause serious harm.

Further Reading

Burgoon, Judee K. 'Nonverbal Signals', in Mark L. Knapp and John A Daly, eds, *Handbook of Interpersonal Communication,* 3rd edn. Thousand Oaks, CA: Sage, 2002.
This book investigates non-verbal signals as a big part in interpersonal communication. It demonstrates the importance of this often forgotten component of communication.

Burgoon, Judee K., and Aaron E. Bacue. 'Nonverbal Communication Skills', in John O. Greene and Brant R. Burleson, eds, *Handbook of Communication and Social Interaction Skills.* Mahwah, NJ: Erlbaum, 2003.
This chapter investigates how people can improve their non-verbal communication skills through the use of examples and a systematic method.

Hickson, Mark, Don W. Stacks, and Nina-Jo Moore. *Nonverbal Communication: Studies and Applications.* Los Angeles: Roxbury, 2004.
This book offers a sophisticated introduction to both the theory and the practice of non-verbal communication.

Waldron, Vincent, and Jeffrey Kassing. *Managing Risk in Communication Encounters: Strategies for the Workplace.* Thousand Oaks, CA: Sage, 2010.
This book focuses on the how some daily interactions can be very risky and threaten identities, relationships, and sometimes careers. The authors offer useful guidelines, based on real-life case studies on topics such as voicing dissent, repairing broken relationships, managing privacy, responding to harassment, offering criticism, and communicating emotion.

Study Questions

1. Describe a situation from your own experience in which your non-verbal communication sent a message that your language did not.
2. Recall examples of at least three times that your non-verbal behaviour was ambiguous and misinterpreted by another.
3. Give one example of each form of non-verbal communication functions that you have observed in other people's behaviour. For each example, comment on whether the non-verbal communication function was effective or not.
4. Describe three different situations in which physical attractiveness had an effect on a communication outcome. Describe what the communicator could have changed to make his or her form of attractiveness more appropriate to achieving a different outcome.
5. Give two examples of how choice of clothing affects how someone's communication was perceived by others. How would a different choice of apparel have modified the effect on perception of the person?

Interpersonal Communication

Part II

Professional Profile:

Heather Pullen, MCM, APR

As a starry-eyed journalism school graduate, I was convinced that I was going to change the world. Four years at Carleton University had inspired me to become an investigative journalist—to ask the questions no one else was asking, to expose corruption, and to fight for the rights of the little guy, or gal.

Well, as it turned out, the only fighting I did in the first few years of my career was trying to convince the powers-that-be that a young, female reporter was capable of covering sports. This was in an era when very few women were assigned to sports, and the newspapers I worked for were happy to be perceived as enlightened for sending me into the field (or the dressing room) to get the story. While it wasn't my dream job, it was a start, and it earned me the credibility I needed to move onto other positions.

With this unusual indoctrination to my chosen profession, I learned the importance of versatility, resourcefulness, and curiosity. Throughout my career, those characteristics have helped me respond to challenges and anticipate opportunities. That's because the only *constant* in the world of communication is *change*.

I learned this lesson at the Canadian Broadcasting Corporation, where I worked as a national radio producer for a wide range of programs including children's, news, sports, and current affairs. From there I moved into health care communications where I have led, or helped to lead, public relations teams at several major hospital organizations in Toronto and Hamilton.

In my working life, I have gone from typewriters, carbon paper, and telex machines to computers, e-mails and the Internet. In one short generation, these tools have changed the way we do business, and changed it in an exciting and fulfilling way.

I have also seen a huge evolution in the attitude and capacity of the people we serve. No longer content to simply be on the receiving end of our stories or messages, they are using the same tools we use to inform themselves and, increasingly often, to get engaged in public debates. What was once our *audiences* are now our *stakeholders* and, in the years ahead, communicators will play a vital role in facilitating dialogue and building consensus across communities and amongst constituencies.

Versatility to take on new roles, resourcefulness to find solutions, and curiosity to embrace innovation—these are the characteristics that will help communicators of the future succeed.

Heather Pullen is the manager of public relations and communications at Hamilton Health Sciences, a family of six hospitals and a cancer centre in Hamilton, Ontario. She is an accredited public relations professional and a graduate of McMaster University's Master of Communications Management Program.

After studying the material in this chapter . . .

You should
understand:

- the characteristics that distinguish interpersonal relationships from impersonal ones;
- the content and relational dimensions of every message;
- the role of metacommunication in conveying relational messages;
- the dimensions and influences of intimacy in relationships;
- Knapp's model of relational development and deterioration;
- tension in relationships;
- the reasons for self-disclosure and the Johari Window model of self-disclosure;
- the characteristics of and guidelines for effective and appropriate self-disclosure; and
- the functions served by lies, equivocation, and hints.

You should be
able to:

- identify interpersonal and impersonal communication;
- identify the content and relational dimensions of a message;
- distinguish among types of intimacy and influences on intimacy;
- identify the stages of relationships and the dialectical tensions present in a relationship;
- identify the degree of self-disclosure in your relationships and the functions this serves;
- compose effective and appropriate disclosing messages; and
- identify the types of non-disclosing messages you use, the functions of these messages, and their ethical validity.

Understanding Interpersonal Relationships

Chapter Highlights

Truly interpersonal communication has several characteristics that make it worth studying.

- It is qualitatively different from less personal relationships.
- It has, like all messages, both content and relational dimensions.
- It can address relational matters explicitly through metacommunication.

Intimacy is a special dimension of interpersonal relationships.

- It has several dimensions.
- Men and women sometimes value and express intimacy differently.
- Cultural background influences how we communicate intimacy.

Communication scholars have explored some forces that shape interpersonal relationships.

- Developmental models describe how communication in relationships changes over time.

- Dialectical models describe forces that always operate in relationships.
- No matter which model is used, relationships are constantly changing.

The subject of self-disclosure is an important one in the study of interpersonal relationships.

- People disclose (or withhold) personal information for a variety of reasons.
- Models can help us understand how self-disclosure operates.
- Regardless of the reason, self-disclosure in relationships possesses several characteristics.
- Several guidelines can help you decide whether or not to disclose personal information.

This chapter introduces the vitally important topic of interpersonal relationships. We will begin by exploring what kinds of communication make a relationship interpersonal. Next, we will discuss a number of ways—both subtle and obvious—used to show others how we regard them and what kind of relationship we are seeking with them. We will go on to explore two approaches that characterize how communication operates throughout the lifetime of relationships. Finally, we will look at the role of self-disclosure in interpersonal communication.

Characteristics of Interpersonal Relationships

Our lives begin to end the day we become silent about things that matter.

Martin Luther King, Jr

What is interpersonal communication? How does it differ from other types of interaction? When and how are interpersonal messages communicated? In this section, we will address these important questions as a way of introducing the topic of interpersonal relationships.

What Makes Communication Interpersonal?

The most obvious way to define interpersonal communication is to look at the *context*—the number of people involved. In this sense we could say that all communication between two people, or dyadic communication, is interpersonal. In many ways, dyadic communication is different from the kind that goes on in other contexts, such as the kinds of small groups that will be discussed in chapters 8 and 9. For example, unlike groups involving more than two people, dyads are complete and cannot be subdivided. If one person withdraws from the other, the relationship is finished. This indivisibility means that, unlike the members who make up a group, the partners in a dyad can't form coalitions to get their needs met; instead they must work matters out with one another. Likewise, dyadic communication differs from the kinds of public speeches described in chapters 12 and 13 and from most types of mass communication.

Although looking at communication by context is useful, this approach raises some problems. Consider, for example, a routine transaction between a sales clerk and customer or the rushed exchange when you ask a stranger on the street for directions. While in a purely *contextual* sense communication of this sort meets our definition of 'interpersonal',

'I'm your wife, Arthur. You talk to me. You don't touch base with me.'

it hardly seems personal in any sense of the word. In fact, after transactions like this we commonly remark, 'I might as well have been talking to a machine.'

The impersonal nature of many two-person exchanges has led some scholars to say that quality, not quantity, is what distinguishes interpersonal communication. **Qualitatively interpersonal communication** occurs when people treat one another as unique individuals, regardless of the context in which the interaction occurs or the number of people involved.[1] When quality of interaction is the criterion, the opposite of interpersonal communication is **impersonal communication**, not group, public, or mass communication.

The greater part of our communication, even in dyadic contexts, is relatively impersonal. We chat pleasantly with shopkeepers or fellow commuters on the subway or bus; we discuss the weather or current events with most classmates and neighbours; we deal with co-workers in a polite way. But considering the number of people we communicate with, qualitatively interpersonal interaction is rather scarce. This scarcity isn't necessarily unfortunate. Most of us don't have the time or energy to create personal relationships with everyone we encounter—or even to act in a personal way all the time with the people we know and love best. In fact, the scarcity of qualitatively interpersonal communication contributes to its value. Like precious metals, qualitatively interpersonal relationships are special because of their scarcity. You can get a sense of how interpersonal your relationships are by trying Activity A at the end of the chapter.

Interpersonal Communication and the Internet

There's no question that mediated relationships conducted via e-mail, instant messaging, and telephone pass the test of being contextually interpersonal. But what about their quality? Is online communication a poor substitute for face-to-face contact, or is it a rich medium for developing close personal relationships? In one survey, approximately 25 per cent of the respondents who used the Internet regularly reported spending less time talking in person and on the phone with friends and family members.[2] Another survey revealed that people who relied heavily on the Internet to meet their communication needs grew to rely less and less on their face-to-face networks. More significantly, they tended to feel more lonely and depressed as their online communication increased.[3]

Despite findings like these, a growing body of research disputes the notion that mediated communication lacks quality.[4] Writing (online, of course) in *CMC Magazine,* Brittney G. Chenault summarized research concluding that e-mail, chat rooms, Internet newsgroups, and computer conferences can and do allow electronic correspondents to develop a degree of closeness similar to what can be achieved in person.[5] And a 2005 Statistics Canada survey of Internet use revealed that although users spent substantial time alone, they did not differ significantly in their desire to spend more time with family and friends. In fact, more than one-quarter of the Internet users surveyed singled out spending time with family and friends as their number one priority for the hours when they were not online (see Table 6.1).

Although spending time with family and friends was important to Internet users, Ben Veenhof and colleagues' report on the Statistics Canada survey found that, for every hour of Internet use, people spent one hour less with family members living inside or outside the household (see Figure 6.1).[6] The same report shows that non-users spent more time

Half of all telephone calls do not involve a two-way conversation anymore. The human dimensions of the phenomenon are everywhere, suggested by a bizarre question surfacing in Hollywood where people often conduct business by voice mail, fax, and modem rather than in person. 'Do you need face on that?' people will ask.

Karen Brandon

impersonal communication
Strategies used by communicators to influence the way others view them.

qualitatively interpersonal communication
Interaction in which people treat one another as unique individuals, regardless of the context in which the interaction occurs or the number of people involved.

TABLE 6.1 The Internet and the Way We Spend Our Time

The findings come from the 2005 General Social Survey on time use, which asked respondents to provide a detailed account of all of their activities over a 24-hour period:

Non-users

- Shared their time equally with household members and people from outside the household. Heavy users spent about one hour less with both sets of people.

Moderate users

- Spent about 26 more minutes by themselves than non-users during day. But heavy Internet users were alone nearly two hours (119 minutes) longer than non-users, even when comparing people from similar-sized households.

Heavy users

- Lead a considerably different lifestyle than individuals who do not surf the Web, according to a new study examining its impact on Canadians.
- Devoted less time to socializing with their spouse or partner, as well as their children and friends. And they tended to stay at home, showing less interest in outdoor activities than non-users.
- Devoted significantly less time than non-users to paid work and chores around the home, as well as less time sleeping, relaxing, resting or thinking.
- Spent a considerable amount of their time on the Web using e-mail or chat groups. They were also more likely to spend time conversing with others over the phone.
- Spent an average of 33 minutes less time each day than non-users on domestic work, such as child care and housekeeping.
- Less likely than non-users to say they knew "most" or "many" of the people in their neighbourhood. They were also more likely to describe their sense of belonging to their community as "somewhat" or "very" weak.
- Spent more time reading books than non-users, and moderate users were also likely to spend more time reading newspapers than non-users.
- Although internet users spent less time with others generally, they identified having about the same number of close relationships with people outside the household as non-users.
- Heavy Internet users and non-users spent about the same amount of time, just over two hours, watching television during the day.

All three groups:

- Although Internet users spent substantial time alone, particularly heavy users, they did not differ significantly from non-users in their desire to spend more time with family and friends. In fact, this was the most popular choice for all three groups. More than one-quarter of individuals in each group singled out time with family and friends as their number one priority for spending additional time.

Definitions

Internet use covers personal use of the Internet over a 24-hour period and does not include use of the Internet for other reasons (e.g., work or school).

Non-users are those who did not spend at least five minutes on the Internet at any one time during the day (respondents in the survey were asked not to report activities that were less than five minutes in duration).

Moderate users are those who spent between five minutes and one hour on the Internet during the day.

Heavy users are those who spent more than one hour on the Internet during the day

Source: Statistics Canada, General Social Survey: The Internet and the way we spend our time, 2005.

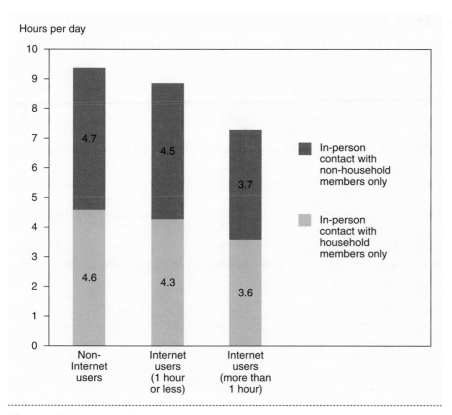

Figure 6.1

Average Time Spent per Day, In-Person Contact with Household Members and Non-Members, Canada, 2005[1]

[1] All figures are adjusted to control for age, sex, number of children aged 14 and under in respondent's household, day of week, education level and time spent at work. Adjusted figures for time spent with households members also control for number of persons living in the household.

Source: Statistics Canada, General Social Survey Cycle 19: Time Use, 2005.

than users in traditional social activities, like socializing with others, having meals with household members, and playing with children (see Table 6.2). Furthermore, people who spent more than one hour on the Internet per day were less likely to know their neighbours (39.9 per cent) than non-users (45.8 per cent)[7]. However, Internet users spent as much time as non-users conversing in-person with other household members and spent more time on the phone than non-users. The study also found that the Internet's heaviest users tend to be young persons, who have lived in their neighbourhoods for shorter periods of time than non-users.

Along with examining the social effects of screen-based media, researchers have also investigated its health effects. A 2009 study compared Canadian and American participants' experiences with physical activity and screen-based media and how these experiences related to various health indicators. They found a generally good relationship between physical activity and positive health indicators (e.g., fitness, weight control, etc.), although they also found a link between physical activity and physical aggression. Screen-based media use was negatively linked to most positive health indicators and positively related to several of the negative health indicators. It is important to note one exception: screen-based media were

TABLE 6.2 Average Time Spent per Day on Traditional Social Activities, Internet Users and Non-Users, Canada, 2005[1] (in minutes per day)

	Non-users		Internet users (1 hour or less)				Internet users (more than 1 hour)			
	Time	Adj. time[1]	Time	Differ-ence	Adj. time[1]	Adj. Differ-ence	Time	Differ-ence	Adj. time[1]	Adj. Differ-ence
Socializing (without meals)	25.6	26.3	20.8	−4.8*	19.5	−6.8**	23.3	−2.3	16.6	−9.7**
Socializing (with meals, excluding restaurant meals)	30.2	30.6	25.1	−5.1*	24.9	−5.7*	22.0	−8.2**	16.6	−14.0**
Socializing at bars, clubs (without meals)	4.1	4.3	3.6	−0.5	2.9	−1.4	4.7	0.6	3.0	−1.3
Playing with children	5.8	5.9	4.6	−1.2	4.5	−1.4*	2.7	−3.1**	2.3	−3.6**
face-to-face, conversation with household members[2]	5.7	5.7	6.5	0.8	7.0	1.3	5.0	−0.7	5.1	−0.6
Talking on the phone	4.4	4.4	6.7	2.3**	6.7	2.3**	7.3	2.9**	7.2	2.8**

* difference from non-users is statistically significant at the 95% confidence level (p < .05)
** difference from non-users is statistically significant at the 99% confidence level (p < .01)
[1] All figures are adjusted to control for age, sex, number of children aged 14 and under in respondent's household, day of week, education level and time spent at work.
[2] Adjusted figures for face-to-face conversation with household members also control for number of persons living in the household.

Source: Statistics Canada, General Social Survey, Cycle 19: Time Use, 2005.

linked to positive peer relationships. These patterns were very similar in both Canada and the United States.

In terms of quantity of Internet use, Figure 6.2 and Table 6.3 demonstrate that Canadians are using electronic communication tools to maintain their personal relationships. Figure 6.2 shows that e-mail use is a large component of Canadians' Internet patterns and grows when Canadians are using the Internet for larger periods of time: those who use the Internet for less than an hour per day spend an average of 22.9 minutes on e-mail, while those who use the Internet for more than one hour spend 50 minutes on e-mail. Table 6.3 illustrates in compelling terms that Canadians of all ages use the Internet in fairly equal amounts to communicate with relatives and friends. The statistics demonstrate a definite upward trend in line with educational achievement, with university-educated people using the Internet to communicate with friends and relatives much more than those who have not had a university education. An interesting finding is that Canadians who are recent immigrants tend to use the Internet to communicate with friends and relatives more than the Canadian-born.

Even more significant than the quantity of online communication is its quality: 55 per cent of Internet users said that e-mail had improved communications with family, and 66 per cent said that their contact with friends had increased because of e-mail. Among women, the rate of satisfaction was even higher: 60 per cent reported better contact with family and 71 per cent with friends. Over three-quarters of the Internet users polled said they never felt ignored by another household member's spending time online.[8] The majority of the Internet users surveyed said that e-mail websites and chat rooms had a 'modestly positive impact' on their ability to communicate more with family members and make new friends. Again,

Understanding Communication Technology

Internet Dangers Exposed

Young Canadians should proceed with caution when putting their personal lives online, Canada's privacy czar warns.

In her annual report to Parliament, Privacy Commissioner Jennifer Stoddart said today's youth are playing out their lives in public in ways their parents and grandparents would find 'unthinkable'. While there are many benefits, surrendering too much personal information can also come with negative long-term consequences.

'Such openness can lead to greater creativity, literacy, networking, and social engagement,' Stoddart said. 'But putting so much of their personal information out into the open can also expose young people to cyber-bullying or leave an enduring trail of embarrassing moments that could haunt them in future.'

With increased texting, blogging, and online posting, unguarded personal information is 'low-hanging fruit' for unscrupulous marketers, illegal data brokers, and identity thieves, Stoddart said. She found that while young people are most likely to embrace new technology, they're least likely to worry about the impact or consider risks associated with posting photos, videos, and personal opinions online.

Pointing to Stoddart's recent high-profile battle with Facebook over retention of personal information, University of Ottawa professor and Internet privacy expert Michael Geist said Canadian privacy law is in a strong position to deal with evolving issues thanks to Stoddart's 'aggressive' defence of privacy rights.

But he conceded most Canadians—especially youth—can use a reminder about long-term repercussions.

'Putting up photos of you and your friends in compromising situations—sometimes there are people who can trace that,' he warned.

Candace Salmon, a 25-year-old Ottawa woman who has grown up in the digital age, isn't worried about using Facebook but uses caution.

'I don't post my phone number or photos which are vulgar or irresponsible,' she said. 'My benchmark is "if I wouldn't want my parents to see it, I won't post it."'

Stoddart's annual report also lists industries that drew the most complaints to her office, including financial institutions (banks, collection agencies, credit bureaus, financial advisers), insurance companies, sales (car dealerships, pharmacies, real estate, stores), and telecommunication and transportation sectors. An Ekos Research poll done for the commissioner's office in March found only 12 per cent of Canadians thought businesses took their obligation to protect consumers' personal information 'very seriously'.

The inquiries branch of the Personal Information Protection and Electronic Documents Act handled 6,344 inquiries, down about 17 per cent from a year earlier.

—Kathleen Harris, National Bureau Chief, *Toronto Sun*, 7 October 2009.

Questions: The author describes how information and communication technologies make us susceptible to surveillance. Do you think that reduced privacy in the digital world is a bad thing for us personally, socially, or culturally? Why or why not?

women had a higher satisfaction rate, with 60 per cent reporting better contact with family and 61 per cent with friends.

For some people, the lack of immediacy in online communication makes it easier to build close relationships. Sociolinguist Deborah Tannen describes a situation where e-mail enhanced a relationship that wouldn't have developed to the same degree in person:

E-mail deepened my friendship with Ralph. Though his office was next to mine, we rarely had extended conversations because he is shy. Face to face he mumbled so I could barely

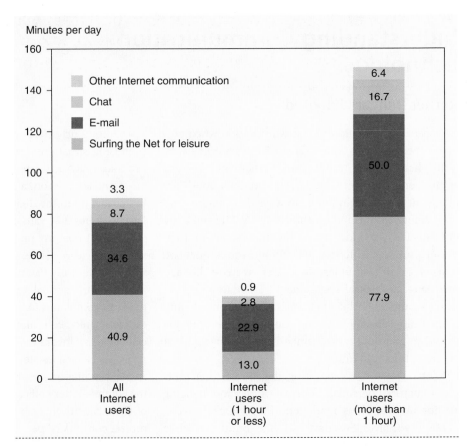

Figure 6.2

Average Time Spent per Day by Internet Users on E-mail, Chatting, and Other Internet Communication, Canada, 2005

Source: Statistics Canada, General Social Survey Cycle 19: Time Use, 2005.

tell he was speaking. But when we both got on e-mail, I started receiving long, self-revealing messages; we poured our hearts out to each other. A friend discovered that e-mail opened up that kind of communication with her father. He would never talk much on the phone (as her mother would), but they have become close since they both got on line.[9]

Stories like these suggest that, rather than weakening opportunities for communication, computer-mediated communication (CMC) provides rich opportunities for establishing and maintaining relationships. An Internet connection makes it possible to send and receive messages to and from people anywhere in the world, at times when it might not be convenient to call.

Content and Relational Messages

content messages
Messages that communicate information about the subject being discussed.

Virtually every verbal statement contains two kinds of messages. **Content messages,** which focus on the subject being discussed, are the most obvious. The content of such statements as 'It's your turn to do the dishes' or 'I'm busy Saturday night' is obvious.

TABLE 6.3 Percentage of Internet/E-mail[1] Users Who Used the Internet in the Previous Month to Communicate with Family and Friends, Canada, 2003

	With relatives	With friends
Total	54.2%	65.4%
Sex		
Male	49.7	63.7
Female	58.8	67.2
Age		
15 to 24	50.1	77.9
25 to 34	58.9	71.2
35 to 44	53.8	61.6
45 to 54	50.5	54.5
55 to 64	56.0	56.7
65 and older	65.0	60.0
Educational attainment		
Less than high school diploma	44.9	60.5
High school diploma	45.7	53.9
Some post-secondary	54.1	69.6
Certificate/diploma from college or trade/technical school	52.6	60.3
University degree	65.1	75.5
Immigration status		
Canadian-born	52.6	64.8
Immigrated before 1985	56.7	63.1
Immigrated 1985 to 1994	57.3	69.1
Immigrated 1995 to 2003	68.0	74.8
Location[2]		
Larger urban centres (CMA/CA)	55.0	67.3
Rural and small town (non CMA/CA)	49.8	56.0

1. This table covers individuals who said they used the Internet or e-mail (or both), for personal use, from any location, in the 12 months preceding the survey.
2. Prince Edward Island is included under 'rural and small town'.

Source: Statistics Canada, General Social Survey Cycle 17: Social Engagement, 2003.

However, content messages aren't the only kind that are exchanged when two people interact. Virtually all communication—both verbal and non-verbal—contains **relational messages**, which make statements about how the parties feel toward one another.[10] These relational messages express communicators' feelings and attitudes involving one or more dimensions.

Affinity

One dimension of relational communication is **affinity**, or the degree to which people like or appreciate one another. As the photo on the next page shows, you can get a good idea of how much each character likes the other, even if you don't know what is being discussed on the content level.

affinity
The degree to which people like or appreciate one another. As with all relational messages, affinity is usually expressed non-verbally.

relational messages
Messages that express the social relationship between two or more individuals.

control
The social need to influence others.

immediacy
The degree of interest and attraction we feel toward and communicate to others. As with all relational messages, immediacy is usually expressed non-verbally.

respect
The degree to which we hold others in esteem.

Respect

Respect is the degree to which we admire others and hold them in esteem. Respect and affinity might seem identical, but they are actually separate dimensions of a relationship.[11] For example, you might like a three-year-old child tremendously without respecting her. Likewise, you could respect a boss's or teacher's talents without liking him. Respect is a tremendously important and often overlooked ingredient in satisfying relationships. It is a better predictor of relational satisfaction than liking, or even loving.[12]

Immediacy

Communication scholars use the term **immediacy** to describe the degree of interest and attraction we feel toward and communicate to others. Immediacy is different from affinity. A situation of high immediacy would be the feeling of connection and excitement that students feel for a very popular professor. The students want to talk to her because they are interested in her subject matter and because they are attracted to her caring and magnetic personality. It's easy to imagine four combinations of these dimensions: high affinity and high immediacy; high affinity and low immediacy; low affinity and low immediacy; and low affinity and high immediacy.

Control

In every conversation and every relationship there is some distribution of **control**: the amount of influence communicators seek. Relational partners can share control equally, or one person can have more and the other(s) less. An uneven distribution of control won't cause problems as long as everyone involved accepts that arrangement. Struggles arise, though, when people disagree on how control should be distributed in their relationship.

You can get a feeling for how relational messages operate in everyday life by recalling the examples at the beginning of this section. Imagine two ways of saying 'It's your turn to do the dishes': one that is demanding and another that is matter-of-fact. Notice how the different non-verbal messages make statements about how the sender views control in this part of the relationship. The demanding tone says, in effect, 'I have a right to tell you what to do around the house,' whereas the matter-of-fact one suggests, 'I'm just reminding you of something you might have overlooked.' Likewise, you can easily visualize two ways to deliver the statement 'I'm busy Saturday night': one with little affection and the other with much liking.

Notice that in each of these examples the relational dimension of the message was never discussed. In fact, most of the time we aren't conscious of the relational messages that bombard us every day. Sometimes we are unaware of relational messages because they match our belief about the amount of affinity, respect, immediacy, and control that is appropriate. For example, you probably won't be offended if your employer tells you to do a certain job because you agree that managers have the right to direct employees. In other cases, however, conflicts arise over relational messages even though content is not disputed. If your manager delivers the order in a condescending, sarcastic, or abusive tone of voice, you probably will be offended. Your complaint wouldn't be with the order itself but rather with the way it was delivered. 'I may work for this company,' you might think, 'but I'm not a slave or an idiot. I deserve to be treated like a human being.'

How are relational messages communicated? As the employer–employee example suggests, they are usually expressed non-verbally. To test this for yourself, imagine how you could act while saying, 'Can you help me for a minute?' in a way that communicates each of the following attitudes:

- superiority
- aloofness
- friendliness
- helplessness
- sexual desire
- irritation

Although non-verbal behaviours are a good source of relational messages, remember that they are ambiguous. The sharp tone you take as a personal insult might stem from fatigue, and the interruption you perceive as an attempt to ignore your ideas might be a sign of pressure that has nothing to do with you. Before you jump to conclusions about relational clues, it's a good idea to practise the skill of perception-checking that you learned in Chapter 2: 'When you use that tone of voice to tell me it's my turn to do the dishes, I get the idea you're mad at me. Is that right?' If your interpretation was indeed correct, you can talk about the problem. On the other hand, if you were overreacting, perception-checking can prevent a needless fight.

Metacommunication

As the preceding example of perception-checking shows, not all relational messages are non-verbal. Social scientists use the term **metacommunication** to describe messages that refer to other messages.[13] In other words, metacommunication is communication about communication. Whenever we discuss a relationship with others, we are metacommunicating: 'It sounds like you're angry at me,' or 'I appreciate how honest you've been.' Metacommunication is an essential ingredient in successful relationships. Sooner or later there are times when it becomes necessary to talk about what is going on between you and the other person. The ability to focus on the kinds of issues described in this chapter and in Chapter 7 can help to keep the relationship on track.

Metacommunication is an important method of solving conflicts in a constructive manner. It provides a way to shift discussions from the content level to relational questions, where the problem often lies. For example, consider a couple bickering because one partner wants to watch television, whereas the other wants to talk. Imagine how much better the chances of a positive outcome would be if they used metacommunication to examine the relational problems that were behind their quarrel: 'Look, it's not the TV watching itself that bothers me. It's that I imagine you watch so much because you're mad at me or bored. Are you feeling bad about us?'

metacommunication
Messages (usually relational) that refer to other messages; communication about communication.

Metacommunication isn't just a tool for handling problems. It is also a way to reinforce the good aspects of a relationship: 'I really appreciate it when you compliment me about my work in front of the boss.' Comments like this serve two functions: they let others know that you value their behaviour, and they boost the odds that the other people will continue the behaviour in the future.

Despite the benefits of metacommunication, bringing relational issues into the open does have risks. Discussing problems can be interpreted in two ways. On the one hand, the other person might see it in a positive light—'Our relationship is working because we can still talk things out.' On the other hand, your desire to focus on the relationship might look like a bad omen—'Our relationship isn't working if we have to keep talking it over.' Furthermore, metacommunication does involve a certain degree of analysis ('It seems like you're angry at me'), and some people resent being analyzed. These cautions don't mean verbal metacommunication is a bad idea. They do suggest, though, that it's a tool that needs to be used carefully.

> **Cultural Idiom**
>
> **on the one hand**
> from one point of view
>
> **on the other hand**
> from the other point of view

> **intimacy**
> A state of closeness between two (or sometimes more) people. Intimacy can be manifested in several ways: physically, intellectually, emotionally, and via shared activities.

Intimacy in Interpersonal Relationships

Even the closest relationships involve a mixture of personal and interpersonal communication. We alternate between a 'we' and a 'me' orientation, sometimes focusing on connecting with others and at other times focusing on our own needs and interests. In the next few pages we will examine how these apparently conflicting drives for intimacy and distance affect our communication.

Dimensions of Intimacy

The dictionary defines *intimacy* as arising from 'close union, contact, association, or acquaintance'. This definition suggests that the key element of intimacy is closeness, one element that 'ordinary people' have reported as characterizing their intimate relationships.[14] However, it doesn't explain what *kinds* of closeness can create a state of intimacy.

In colloquial use, of course, intimacy is almost always used to mean a very particular form of closeness, so much so that the term 'intimate relations' is used as a euphemism for any contact between people with decidedly sexual undertones. If an elementary school teacher refers to her close mentoring relationship with a particular student as 'intimate' when speaking about it with a colleague, it is entirely plausible that the colleague might report the matter to a superior. The association of the word with these connotations extends so far that many department stores call the women's undergarments section 'Intimates'.

In sociological literature, **intimacy** is used somewhat more broadly and can have several qualities. The first is *physical*. Even before birth, the developing fetus experiences a kind of physical closeness with its mother that will never happen again, 'floating in a warm fluid, curling inside a

total embrace, swaying to the undulations of the moving body and hearing the beat of the pulsing heart.'[15] As they grow up, fortunate children are continually nourished by physical intimacy: being rocked, fed, hugged, and held. As we grow older, the opportunities for physical intimacy are less regular but still possible and important. Some, but by no means all, physical intimacy is sexual. In one survey, only one-quarter of the respondents (who were university students) stated that intimacy necessarily contained a romantic or sexual dimension.[16] Other forms of physical intimacy include affectionate hugs, kisses, and even struggles. Companions who have endured physical challenges together—in athletics or emergencies, for example—form a bond that can last a lifetime.

In other cases, intimacy comes from *intellectual* sharing. Not every exchange of ideas counts as intimacy, of course. Talking about next week's mid-term with your instructor or classmates isn't likely to forge strong relational bonds. But when you engage another person in an exchange of important ideas, a kind of closeness develops that can be powerful and exciting.

A third quality of intimacy is *emotion*: exchanging important feelings. This chapter will offer several guidelines for disclosing your thoughts and feelings to others. If you follow those guidelines, you will probably recognize a qualitative change in your relationships.

If we define *intimacy* as being close to another person, then *shared activities* can be some of the ways to achieve this state. Shared activities can include everything from working side by side at a job to meeting regularly at the gym. Although shared activities are no guarantee of intimacy, people who spend time together can develop unique ways of relating that transform the relationship from an impersonal one that could be done with anybody to one with interpersonal qualities. For example, several forms of play often characterize both friendships and romantic relationships. Partners invent private codes, joke around by acting like other people, tease one another, and play games—everything from having punning contests to arm wrestling.[17]

Some intimate relationships exhibit all four qualities: physical intimacy, intellectual exchanges, emotional disclosure, and shared activities. Other intimate relationships exhibit only one or two. Some relationships, of course, aren't intimate in any way. Acquaintances, roommates, and co-workers may never become intimate. In some cases even family members develop smooth but relatively impersonal relationships.

Not even the closest relationships always operate at the highest level of intimacy. At some times you might share all of your thoughts or feelings with a friend, family member, or romantic partner, and at other times you might withdraw. You might freely share your feelings about one topic and stay more aloof in another one. The same principle holds for physical intimacy, which waxes and wanes in most relationships. The dialectical view of relational maintenance described later in this chapter explains how intimacy can wax and wane, even in the closest relationships.

Before I built a wall I'd ask to know
What I was walling in or walling out,
And to whom I was like to give offence.
Something there is that doesn't love a wall,
That wants it down.

Robert Frost,
'Mending Wall'

Male and Female Intimacy Styles

Until recently most social scientists believed that women were better at developing and maintaining intimate relationships than men.[18] This belief grew from the assumption that the disclosure of personal information is the most important ingredient of intimacy. Most research does show that women (taken as a group, of course) are more willing to share their thoughts and feelings than men are.[19] In terms of the amount and depth of information exchanged, female–female relationships are at the top of the disclosure list. Male–female relationships come in second, whereas relationships between men have less disclosure than any other type. At every age, women disclose more than men, and the information they disclose is more personal and more likely to involve feelings. Although both sexes are equally likely to reveal negative information, men are less likely to share positive feelings.[20]

Through the mid-1980s many social scientists interpreted the relative lack of male self-disclosure as a sign that men were unwilling, or even unable, to develop close relationships. Some argued that the female trait of disclosing personal information and feelings makes them more 'emotionally mature' and 'interpersonally competent' than men. Personal growth programs and self-help books urged men to achieve closeness by learning to open up and share their feelings.

Scholarship conducted over the past decade, however, has begun to show that male–female differences aren't as great as they seem,[21] and emotional expression isn't the *only* way to develop close relationships. Unlike women, who value personal talk, men grow close to one another by doing things. In one study more than 75 per cent of the men surveyed said that their most meaningful experiences with friends came from activities other than talking.[22] They reported that through shared activities they 'grew on one another', developed feelings of interdependence, showed appreciation for one another, and demonstrated mutual liking. Likewise, men regarded practical help from other men as a measure of caring. Research like this shows that, for many men, closeness grows from activities that don't depend heavily on disclosure; instead, a friend is a person who does things *for* you and *with* you.

The difference between male and female measures of intimacy helps explain some of the stresses and misunderstandings that can arise between the sexes. For example, a woman who looks for emotional disclosure as a measure of affection may overlook an 'inexpressive' man's efforts to show he cares by doing favours or spending time together. Fixing a leaky faucet or taking a hike may look like ways to avoid getting close, but to the man who proposes them, they may be measures of affection and bids for intimacy. Likewise, differing ideas about the timing and meaning of sex can lead to misunderstandings. Whereas many women think of sex as a way to express intimacy that has already developed, men are more likely to see it as a way to *create* that intimacy.[23] In this sense, the man who encourages sex early in a relationship or after a fight may not just be driven by testosterone—he may view the shared activity as a way to build closeness. By contrast, the woman who views personal talk as the pathway to intimacy may resist the idea of physical closeness before the emotional side of the relationship has been discussed.

Intimacy can also have very negative consequences in cultures other than English-Canadian. Two studies published in 2009 examined how in some cultures that put a high value on female loyalty, honour-related relationship violence is indirectly permitted. Also, in such cultures, women who remain in abusive relationships are rewarded for their sacrifice. The first study compared Latinos and southern US Anglos with northern US Anglos, and the second compared Chileans and Anglo-Canadians. The Latino, Chilean, and southern US Anglo cultures have strong honour traditions, whereas the northern US Anglo and Anglo-Canadian cultures do not. Both studies presented examples of abuse to the participants. Compared to non–honour-culture participants, those from honour cultures were relatively more favourable to the woman if she stayed in the relationship, despite being abused. If the conflict between male and female partners was jealousy-related, honour-culture participants excused the man's abusive language, whereas the man was not excused for his abusive language when the disagreement related to rational choices, such as spending too much money.[24] A woman in an honour-based culture is expected to bear a heavier burden when she enters a relationship with a man than a woman in a non–honour-based culture.

Cultural Influences on Intimacy

The notion of how much intimacy is desirable and how to express it varies from one culture to another.[25] In one study, researchers asked residents of Britain, Japan, Hong Kong, and Italy to describe their use of 33 rules that governed interaction in a wide range of communication behaviours: everything from the use of humour to hand-shaking to the management of money.[26] The results showed that the greatest differences between Asian and European cultures focused on the rules for dealing with intimacy: showing emotions, expressing affection in public, engaging in sexual activity, respecting privacy, and so on. Culture also plays a role in shaping how much intimacy we seek in different types of relationships. For instance, Japanese respondents seem to expect more intimacy in friendships, whereas Anglo-North Americans look for more intimacy in romantic relationships.[27]

A study conducted by researchers from Canada's Queen's and York universities and China's Xi'an University of Architecture and Technology compared the romantic involvements of Canadian and Chinese adolescents. The study also investigated how young people's romantic involvements related to their friendships and parental relationships. The study showed that the Chinese adolescents were less likely to be romantically involved and had generally lower levels of romantic experience, including fewer close romantic relationships. Of all the participants, Chinese girls reported being the least involved in romantic experiences. The link between romance and friendships was important in both cultures: while friendships were more intimate in Canada and parent relationships were closer in China, friendship relationships were positively related to romantic relationships in both cultures. Interestingly, the Chinese adolescents indicated that parents were negatively connected with romantic experiences.[28]

In some collectivist cultures, such as Taiwan and Japan, there is an especially large difference in the way members communicate with members of their 'in-groups' (such as family and close friends) and with those they view as outsiders.[29] They generally do not reach out to strangers, often waiting until they are properly introduced before entering into a conversation. Once introduced, they address outsiders with a degree of formality. They go to extremes to hide unfavourable information about in-group members from outsiders, adhering to the

Understanding Diversity

●●●● ● **CAN'T HELP BEING A FLIRT**

Men preen and puff up their chests like prairie chickens.

Women stare and then cast their eyes down and look up again.

Flirting is so innate most of us don't even know we're doing it. Or so says Lorraine Weygman, a self-described professional flirt and Toronto-based communications expert.

But everyone can use a few tips, and that's what 250 attentive flirters were hoping to find at Toronto's Royal Ontario Museum recently. They had paid $40 a ticket to meet and mingle amongst the statues of Buddha and the Ming Tomb and they were doing their best to get their money's worth.

It was standing-room-only as the men and women, of all ages and sizes, paraded across the floor. Some were dressed in leather, others in conservative business suits. Some even dared to wear polyester sweaters, once popular in the 1970s and so uncool they obviously had become cool again. Or so they thought.

They drank, mingled, and juggled party sandwiches, Vietnamese spring rolls, and crudités, hoping to meet Mr or Ms Right. A cover of the old Buddy Holly song 'That'll Be the Day' played in the background.

'Are you having fun? Did you meet anyone?' a fortysomething woman asks a thirtysomething guy sitting beside her. 'There were two women that I wanted to meet,' he confesses.

But he was too slow, he thinks. Too clumsy. He didn't— what is it they say—'Seize the day, Carpe diem.'

'They were together and then I lost the moment,' he says.

She nods empathetically. She, too, lost the moment. 'I went up to a guy by the bar. He looked lonely. He had his nametag upside down. When I asked him about it, he said: "It made you stop."'

Yeah, she stopped. But that's as far as it got.

Clearly bruised but not battered, these two hardy souls were ready to soldier on in the fine art of flirtation. So both listened attentively as Weygman continued what amounted to a Flirting 101 lecture.

Her aim: to help men and women better understand the message they give out.

'Women usually make the first move,' she told the enthusiastic crowd.

But there were some doubters. 'I wish,' called out one guy.

No, it's true, she says. And she's not the first to say so either. Weygman notes that US social scientists Tim Perper and David Givens studied men and women in cocktail lounges around the world and came to the same conclusion.

Women, she says, usually glance over, smile, lift their eyebrows and then lower their eyelids and look away. The men stand around, puffing up their chests, lighting cigarettes with a flourish, and mixing their martinis, waiting to be chosen.

In fact, these non-verbal forms of flirting are universal, says Weygman, whether you're in downtown Toronto or the

Cultural Idiom
wash dirty laundry in public disclose personal and private problems and concerns to those beyond one's family or group

principle that one doesn't wash dirty laundry in public. By contrast, members of more individualistic cultures, like those in Canada, Australia, and New Zealand, make less of a distinction between personal relationships and casual ones. They are more familiar with strangers and disclose a greater amount of personal information, making them excellent 'cocktail party conversationalists'. Social psychologist Kurt Lewin captured the difference nicely when he noted that Anglo-North Americans are easy to meet but difficult to get to know, whereas Germans are difficult to meet but then easy to know well.[30]

Relational Development and Maintenance

Qualitatively interpersonal relationships aren't stable: they are constantly changing. Communication scholars have explored the way relationships develop and shift from two perspectives: developmental and dialectical.

Brazilian rain forest. And they have evolved this way for one simple reason: it's nature's way of helping us get together to propagate the species.

'Anthropologists have discovered that when you bat your eyes or use certain body language that it is indeed cross-cultural and cross-generational. Flirting is supposed to go towards mating which is supposed to help the survival of the species.'

It is born in us, she says, and even anthropologists—such as Dr Helen Fisher of Rutgers University in New Jersey—say so.

Weygman recounts how, as a teacher, she used to marvel at the fact little girls were already flirting with their male counterparts.

'Girls in fact as young as eight know how to flirt with little boys,' she says. And they get lots of practice at home, routinely flirting with their fathers.

So what do you have to do if you want to give off the right message to that certain someone? What are the non-verbal cues to pay attention to?

Posture is important, says Weygman. Are you standing in an open way? Gaze is also a big factor.

Is a person looking above your head, below your head, off in the distance, or to the left of you? This judges interest.

'When a man looks directly into a woman's eyes, he's penetrating her soul. The longer the stare the more the intimacy.'

Be aware of breathing, timing, and appropriateness, she tells the crowd. Preparation is also important.

If you're going out and you expect to be doing some flirting, remember to prepare and preen.

'Men are very visual; if you dress provocatively, men will come over.'

And if a woman is interested in a man, says Weygman, she'll cross her leg towards him. If she isn't, she'll cross it away from him.

Ultimately, there's one sure cue to determine interest.

'Men and women, if they are interested in each other, their breathing and body language will imitate each other.'

And with that advice, Weygman sent her troops off to wage battle once more and practise their meeting and mingling skills over dessert and martinis.

Buoyed by the lecture, many in the crowd once more began the dance of possibilities: Is he or isn't he? Will she or won't she?

Others left by the nearest exit. In the main lobby of the ROM, two little girls, maybe 4 or 5, waltzed to the beat of swing music as a crowd watched, amused by their antics.

Parents and kids, fresh from the dinosaur show, quickly bundled themselves up against the winter's winds.

'Maybe we'll have better luck out here,' joked one woman, concluding she couldn't have learned much since she was leaving alone.

For her, it was another typical Friday night on her own.

Well, maybe that wasn't quite right, she added. After all, the food had been pretty spectacular.

—*Debra Black,* Toronto Star, *1 April 2002, E1. Reprinted with permission—Torstar Syndication Services.*

Question: The author describes how people who attend singles events are thrown into a situation of forced intimacy. How do you think reading this chapter could help singles negotiate these events with greater success?

A Developmental Perspective

One of the best-known explanations of how communication operates in relationships was created by Mark Knapp, whose **developmental model** broke down the rise and fall of relationships into 10 stages, contained in the two broad phases of 'coming together' and 'coming apart'.[31] Other researchers have suggested that any model of relational communication ought to contain a third part of relational maintenance—communication aimed at keeping relationships operating smoothly and satisfactorily.[32] Figure 6.3 shows how Knapp's 10 stages fit into this 3-part view of relational communication.

The following stages are especially descriptive of intimate, romantic relationships and close friendships. The pattern for other intimate relationships, such as families, would follow different paths. Some valuable relationships don't require a high level of intimacy. They are based on other, equally important foundations: career activities, shared political interests, and religion, to mention just a few.[33]

developmental model

A model claiming that the nature of communication is different in various stages of interpersonal relationships.

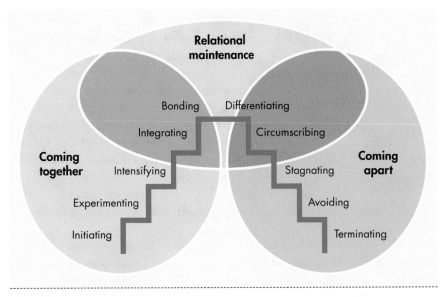

Figure 6.3
Stages of Relational Development

*One word frees us of all the
weight and pain of life; That
word is love.*

Sophocles

Initiating

The stage of initiation involves the initial contact made with another person. Knapp restricts this stage to conversation openers, both in initial contacts and in contacts with acquaintances: 'Nice to meet you,' 'How's it going?' and so on.

Although an initial encounter is necessary to the succeeding interaction, its importance is overemphasized in books offering advice on how to pick someone up at a bar or a party. These books suggest fail-proof openers ranging from 'Excuse me, I'm from out of town, and I was wondering what people do around here at night,' to 'How long do you cook a leg of lamb?' Whatever your preference for opening remarks, this stage is important because you are formulating your first impressions and presenting yourself as interested in the other person.

Initiating relationships can be particularly hard for people who are shy. Making contact with others through the Internet can be helpful for people who have a hard time conversing in person. One study of an online dating service found that participants who identified themselves as shy expressed a greater appreciation for the system's anonymous, non-threatening environment than did non-shy users.[34] The researchers found that many shy users employed the online service specifically to help overcome their inhibitions about initiating relationships in face-to-face settings.

Experimenting

In the stage of experimenting, the conversation develops as people use 'small talk' to get acquainted. We ask: 'Where are you from?' or 'What do you do?' or 'Do you know Jean-Louis Balthazar? He lives in Trois Rivières, too.'

Though small talk might seem meaningless, Knapp points out that it serves four purposes:

1. It is a useful process for uncovering integrating topics and openings for more penetrating conversation.
2. It can be an audition for a future friendship or a way of increasing the scope of a current relationship.
3. It provides a safe procedure for indicating who we are and how another can come to know us better (reduction of uncertainty).
4. It allows us to maintain a sense of community with our fellow human beings.

The relationship during this stage is generally pleasant and uncritical, and the commitments are minimal. Experimenting may last 10 minutes or 10 years.

The willingness to pursue relationships with strangers is partly a matter of personal style. Some people are outgoing and others shy. But culture also plays a role in orientations to newcomers, especially ones from a different ethnic or cultural background. Research suggests that members of some cultures—Chinese and Japanese, for example—are more cautious in their first encounters with strangers and make more assumptions about them based on their backgrounds than do Anglo-North Americans and most Europeans.[35] This fact might explain why people from certain backgrounds appear unfriendly, when in fact they are simply operating by a different set of rules.

Intensifying

It is during the intensifying stage that the kind of truly interpersonal relationship defined earlier in this chapter begins to develop. Several changes in communication patterns occur. Expressions of feelings toward the other become more frequent. Dating couples, for example, use a wide range of communication strategies to describe their feelings of attraction.[36] About a quarter of the time they express their feelings directly, using metacommunication to discuss the state of the relationship. More often they use less-direct methods of communication, such as spending greater amounts of time together, asking for support from one another, doing favours for the partner, giving tokens of affection, hinting and flirting, expressing feelings non-verbally, getting to know the partner's friends and family, and trying to look more physically attractive. Touching is more common during this stage than in either earlier or later ones.[37] Several other changes mark the intensifying stage. Forms of address become more familiar. The parties begin to see themselves as 'we' instead of as separate individuals. It is during the intensifying stage that people begin to express feelings of commitment directly to one another: 'I'm really glad we met.' 'You're the best thing that's happened to me in a long time.'

Integrating

As the relationship strengthens, the parties begin to take on an identity as a social unit. Invitations begin to be addressed to the couple. Social circles merge. The partners begin to take on each other's commitments: 'Sure, we'll spend Thanksgiving with your family.' Common property may begin to be designated—*our* apartment, *our* car, *our* song.[38] Partners develop their own rituals for everything from expressing intimacy to handling daily routines.[39] They even begin to speak alike, using common words and sentence patterns.[40] In this sense, the integration stage is a time when we give up some characteristics of our old selves and become different people.

As we become more integrated with others, our sense of obligation to them grows.[41] We feel obliged to provide a variety of resources such as class notes and money, whether or not the other person asks for them. When intimates do make requests of one another, they are relatively straightforward. Gone are the elaborate explanations, inducements, and apologies. In short, partners in an integrated relationship expect more from one another than they do in less-intimate associations.

Bonding

During the bonding stage, the parties make symbolic public gestures to show the world that their relationship exists. The most common form of bonding in romantic relationships is a

COMMUNICATION ON-SCREEN

Lost in Translation (2003)
Directed by Sofia Coppola.

Actor Bob Harris (Bill Murray) and a young bride, Charlotte (Scarlett Johansson), are both lonely and confused in a luxury Tokyo hotel. They strike up a close friendship, built largely on the respect and trust they develop through self-disclosure. Bob looks at Charlotte wistfully and wonders how he might have built a closer relationship with his own wife. Charlotte looks to Bob for advice about how to remedy her tepid marriage.

The film shows how Charlotte and Bob move through the 'coming together' stages of their platonic relationship, offering each other much-needed support. The audience is left wondering whether their relationship will become romantic. In any case, they clearly learn a great deal about themselves and each other as a result of being 'strangers in a strange land' together.

We are cups, constantly and quietly being filled. The trick is, knowing how to tip ourselves over and let the beautiful stuff out.

Ray Bradbury

wedding ceremony and the legal ties that come with it. Bonding generates social support for the relationship. Both custom and law impose certain obligations on partners who have officially bonded.

Bonding marks a turning point in a relationship. Up until this point, the relationship may have developed at a steady pace: experimenting has gradually moved into intensifying and then into integrating. Now, however, there is a spurt of commitment. The public display and declaration of exclusivity make this a critical period in the relationship.

Relationships don't have to be romantic to have a bonding stage. Business contracts form a bond between associates; initiation into a sorority or fraternity also creates a bond. These acts 'officialize' a relationship and involve a measure of public commitment.

Differentiating

Once two people have formed a commonalty, they need to re-establish individual identities. This is the point where the 'hold me tight' orientation that has existed shifts, and 'put me down' messages begin to occur (see page 229). Partners use a variety of strategies to gain privacy from one another.[42] Sometimes they confront the other party directly, explaining that they don't want to continue a discussion. At other times they are less direct, offering nonverbal cues, changing the topic, or leaving the room.

Differentiation is likely to occur when a relationship begins to experience the first, inevitable stress. This need for autonomy doesn't have to be a negative experience, however. People need to be individuals as well as parts of a relationship, and differentiation is a necessary step toward autonomy. The key to successful differentiation is maintaining a commitment to the relationship while creating the space for being an individual as well.

Circumscribing

So far we have been looking at the growth of relationships. Although some relationships may reach a plateau of development, going on successfully for as long as a lifetime, others pass through several stages of decline and dissolution. In the circumscribing stage, communication between members decreases both in quantity and quality. Restrictions and restraints characterize this stage, and dynamic communication becomes static. Rather than

Understanding Diversity
THE LOVE POLL

What do you think qualifies as cheating? More than 15,000 Canadians coast to coast participated in our online poll.

Percentage who would not be tempted to cheat even if they knew they wouldn't get caught:

Women	74%
Men	47%

Have you ever cheated on a partner?

No	60%
Yes	40%

What do you think qualifies as cheating?

	Yes	No
Flirting	10%	90%
Kissing	69%	31%
Oral sex	77%	23%
Intercourse	85%	15%
Emotional intimacy	51%	49%

Have you ever been cheated on?

No	50%
Yes	50%

Would you try to work it out with a partner if they cheated on you?

Yes	22%
No	32%

If it was a one-time mistake, and they begged for forgiveness

Yes	47%	37%
No	32%	31%

Note: May not add up to 100 due to rounding

Percentage of respondents who would not tell if they witnessed a good friend's partner cheating on them because they feel it is none of their business:

Alberta	26%
British Columbia	30%
Ontario	29%
Quebec	35%

—*Trish McAlaster,* The Globe and Mail, *3 July 2009.*

Questions: What does this poll tell you about relationships in Canada? Do you think the results of this poll are realistic? Where does cheating fit in the relationship stages discussed in this chapter?

discuss a disagreement (which requires some degree of energy on both parts), members opt for withdrawal: either mental (silence or daydreaming and fantasizing) or physical (where people spend less time together). Circumscribing doesn't involve total avoidance; that comes later. Rather, it entails a certain shrinking of interest and commitment.

Stagnating

If circumscribing continues, the relationship begins to stagnate. Members behave toward each other in old, familiar ways without much feeling. No growth occurs. The relationship is a shadow of its former self. We see stagnation in many workers who have lost enthusiasm for their job yet continue to go through the motions for years. The same occurs for some couples who unenthusiastically have the same conversations, see the same people, and follow the same routines without any sense of joy or novelty.

"Gloria, am I supposed to be mailing it in or just going through the motions today?"

Cultural Idiom

bitter jabs
unkind comments

handwriting . . . is clearly on the wall
an indication or foretelling of an unfortunate message

dialectical model
A model claiming that, throughout their lifetime, people in virtually all interpersonal relationships must deal with equally important, simultaneous, and opposing forces such as connection and autonomy, predictability and novelty, and openness versus privacy.

dialectical tensions
Inherent conflicts that arise when two opposing or incompatible forces exist simultaneously.

Avoiding

When stagnation becomes too unpleasant, parties in a relationship begin to create distance between each other. Sometimes this is done under the guise of excuses ('I've been sick lately and can't see you'), and sometimes it is done directly ('Please don't call me; I don't want to see you now'). In either case, by this point the handwriting about the relationship's future is clearly on the wall.

Terminating

Characteristics of this final stage include summary dialogues about where the relationship has gone and the desire to dissociate. The relationship may end with a cordial dinner, a note left on the kitchen table, a phone call, or a legal document stating the dissolution. Depending on each person's feelings, this stage can be quite short, or it may be drawn out over time, with bitter jabs at one another.

The deterioration of a relationship from bonding to circumscribing, stagnating, and avoiding isn't inevitable. One of the key differences between marriages that end in separation and those that are restored to their former intimacy is the communication that occurs when the partners are unsatisfied.[43] Unsuccessful couples deal with their problems by avoidance, indirectness, and less involvement with one another. By contrast, couples who 'repair' their relationship communicate much more directly. They confront one another with their concerns and spend time and effort negotiating solutions to their problems.

Relationships don't always move toward termination in a straight line. Rather, they often move along a back-and-forth pattern, where the trend is toward dissolution.[44] Regardless of how long it takes, termination doesn't have to be totally negative. Understanding each other's investment in the relationship and need for personal growth may dilute the hard feelings. In fact, many relationships aren't so much terminated as redefined. A divorced couple, for example, may find new, less intimate ways to relate to each other.

A Dialectical Perspective

Developmental models, like the one just described, suggest that communication differs in important ways at various points in the life of a relationship. According to these stage-related models, the kinds of interaction that happen during initiating, experimenting, or intensifying are different from the kinds that occur during differentiating, circumscribing, or avoiding.

Not all theorists agree that a stage-related model is the best way to explain interaction in relationships. Some suggest that communicators wrestle with the same kinds of challenges whether a relationship is brand new or decades old. They argue that communicators seek important but inherently incompatible goals throughout virtually all of their relationships. This **dialectical model** suggests that struggling to achieve these goals creates **dialectical tensions**: conflicts that arise when two opposing or incompatible forces exist simultaneously. In recent years, communication scholars have identified the dialectical tensions that make successful communication challenging.[45] They suggest that the struggle to manage these dialectical tensions creates the most powerful dynamics in relational communication. Three of the most powerful dialectical tensions are connection versus autonomy, predictability versus novelty, and openness versus privacy.

Connection versus Autonomy

No one is an island. Recognizing this fact, we seek out involvement with others. But, at the same time, we are unwilling to sacrifice our entire identity to even the most satisfying relationship. The conflicting desires for connection and independence are embodied in the *connection–autonomy dialectic*. Research on relational breakups demonstrates the consequences for relational partners who can't find a way to manage these very different personal needs.[46] Some of the most common reasons for relational breakups involve failure of partners to satisfy one another's needs for connection: 'We barely spent any time together'; 'He wasn't committed to the relationship'; 'We had different needs.' But other relational complaints involve a partner's excessive demands for connection: 'I was feeling trapped'; 'I needed freedom.'

The levels of connection and autonomy that we seek can change over time. In his book *Intimate Behavior,* Desmond Morris suggests that each of us repeatedly goes through three stages: 'Hold me tight,' 'Put me down,' and 'Leave me alone.'[47] This cycle becomes apparent in the first years of life, when children move from the 'hold me tight' stage that characterizes infancy into a new 'put me down' stage of exploring the world by crawling, walking, touching, and tasting. This move for independence isn't all in one direction. The same three-year-old who insists 'I can do it myself' in August may cling to parents on the first day of junior kindergarten in September. As children grow into adolescents, the 'leave me alone' orientation becomes apparent. Teenagers who used to happily spend time with their parents now may groan at the thought of a family vacation or even the notion of sitting down at the dinner table each evening. More time is spent with friends or alone. Although this time can be painful for parents, most developmental experts recognize it as a necessary stage in moving from childhood to adulthood.

As the need for independence from family grows, adolescents take care of their 'hold me tight' needs by associating with their peers. Friendships during the teenage years are vital, and the level of closeness with contemporaries can be a barometer of happiness. This is the time when physical intimacy becomes an option, and sexual exploration may provide a new way of achieving closeness.

In adult relationships, the same cycle of intimacy and distance repeats itself. In marriages, for example, the 'hold me tight' bonds of the first year are often followed by a desire for independence. This need for autonomy can manifest itself in a number of ways, such as the desire to make friends or engage in activities that don't include the spouse, or the need to make a career move that might disrupt the relationship. As we note later on in the discussion of relational stages, this movement from closeness to autonomy may lead to the breakup of

STAGES IN NON-ROMANTIC RELATIONSHIPS

Knapp's model of relational development and decline offers a good description of communication stages in traditional romantic relationships. Some critics have argued that it doesn't characterize other sorts of relationships so well. Identify your position in this debate by following these steps:

1. Explain how well (or how poorly) the model describes one other type of relationship: among co-workers, friends (either close or more distant), parent and child, or another relational context of your choosing.
2. Construct a model describing communication stages in the relationship type you just identified. How does this model differ from Knapp's?

CRITICAL THINKING PROBE

relationships, but it can also be part of a cycle that redefines the relationship in a new form that can recapture or even surpass the intimacy that existed in the past.

Predictability versus Novelty

Stability is an important need in relationships, but too much of it can lead to feelings of staleness. The *predictability–novelty dialectic* reflects this tension. Humorist Dave Barry exaggerates only slightly when he talks about the boredom that can come when husbands and wives know each other too well:

> After a decade or so of marriage, you know everything about your spouse, every habit and opinion and twitch and tic and minor skin growth. You could write a seventeen-pound book solely about the way your spouse eats. This kind of intimate knowledge can be very handy in certain situations—such as when you're on a TV quiz show where the object is to identify your spouse from the sound of his or her chewing—but it tends to lower the passion level of a relationship.[48]

Although too much familiarity can lead to the risk of boredom and stagnation, nobody wants a completely unpredictable relational partner. Too many surprises can threaten the foundations upon which the relationship is based ('You're not the person I married!').

The challenge for communicators is to juggle the desire for predictability with the need for novelty that keeps the relationship fresh and interesting. People differ in their need and desire for stability and surprises, so there is no optimal mixture of the two. As you will read shortly, there are a number of strategies people can use to manage these contradictory drives.

Openness versus Privacy

As Chapter 1 explained, disclosure is one characteristic of interpersonal relationships. Yet, along with the need for intimacy, we have an equally important need to maintain some space between ourselves and others. These sometimes-conflicting drives create the *openness–privacy dialectic*.

Even the strongest interpersonal relationships require some distance. On a short-term basis, the desire for closeness waxes and wanes. Lovers may go through periods of much sharing and times of relative withdrawal. Likewise, they experience periods of passion and then periods of little physical contact. Friends have times of high disclosure where they share almost every feeling and idea and then disengage for days, months, or even longer. Figure 6.4

Understanding Diversity

● ● ● ● ● MAPPING HER MUSICAL LANDSCAPE

'I can't write by a fireplace,' says Inuit singer Elisapie Isaac. 'I need a window. I need to feel connected to something, to see the sky or whatever. I think it's because I'm from this small town where you can see far. No matter what building I'm in, my inspiration is the window.'

Isaac spent almost three years sitting by her window, so to speak, and the songs she found there became the substance of her recent solo recording debut, *There Will Be Stars*. After several years as the singing half of the Quebec electro-folk duo Taima, the 32-year-old performer and film-maker (who began a short Canadian tour on Thursday at Toronto's Drake Hotel) has mapped out her own musical landscape.

'I just wanted it to be sweet and warm, I wanted it to breathe,' she says of the album, which was produced by Éloi Painchaud. She's talking mainly about the shape-shifting sounds on the record. The songs, by contrast, are often about hard, uncomfortable situations: the ragged end of a love affair; the intensity of a deep winter spent in a small Northern settlement (Salluit, in Nunavik); the dislocation many Inuit feel whether they stay in the North or head south, as Isaac did 10 years ago.

'Tears and emotions, that's what motivates me,' she says.

Isaac moved from Montreal to study journalism, then quit school to take a job researching a circumpolar documentary about Inuit people, and made her own half-hour NFB documentary: *Si le temps le permet* (2003), about Aboriginal men in the North and their conflicted feelings about traditional and urban ways. With guitarist Alain Auger, she also started Taima and made a Juno-winning record that sold 25,000 copies.

A second disc was on their agenda, but the initial sessions felt 'a bit forced', Isaac says. She bought a guitar and started writing, not at all sure she could assume the creative functions that, in Taima, had largely been Auger's.

One of the disc's strongest songs was also one of the first written. 'Why Would I Cry?' is a calm and stately tune about reclaiming personal autonomy at the end of a punishing relationship. 'It's a love song, of course, and also an affirmation,' she says. 'I was at a point when I was tired of crying all the time, and this song was the turning point, when I decided that what I choose to do is really my choice.'

'It was also a turning point musically, because the melody and the way it's written are so simple. I knew that was what I wanted to do.' In a way, it was a return to the powerful simplicity of the English hymns and folk songs she sang as a little girl, often on local Northern radio.

Isaac grew up in an adoptive family, after she and a brother were 'given away' to a distant relative. The hard phrase sounds mild in her softly accented English.

'Up north, it's really common for people to be adopted, not taboo in any way,' she says. 'My mother wasn't married, and my grandmother said, "The next baby you have, you should give it to my second cousin, because she's older and she can't have kids." My grandmother passed away before I was born, but my mother respected her decision. She almost had no choice. But I never heard her crying over it, and I have a great relationship with her.'

Her father is a Newfoundlander. Isaac is still getting to know that side of her family, even as she, now the mother of a four-year-old, thinks of making another film about Inuit women in the North, and about the disappearance of traditional rituals.

'There are so many energies, I sometimes wonder, where do I go?' she says. 'I was named after four different women. I used to think that was such a cool thing. But when you're named after four different women, you sort of become those different women. I thought it was such a cool thing, but it kind of messed me up.'

A fine mess, and a fine album too.

—*Robert Everett-Green*, The Globe and Mail, *6 February 2010*.

Questions: How do you think that Elisapie Isaac's relationships have influenced her art? Do you think her blended cultural identity, half Inuit and half Newfoundlander, was a challenge for her? How does her story relate to your life experience and your identity?

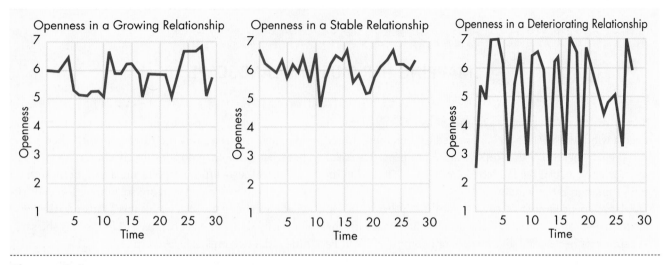

Figure 6.4
Cyclical Phases of Openness and Withdrawal in Relationships

illustrates some patterns of variation in openness uncovered in a study of college students' communication patterns.[49] The students reported the degree of openness in one of their important relationships—a friendship, romantic relationship, or marriage—over a range of 30 conversations. The graphs show a definite pattern of fluctuation between disclosure and privacy in every stage of the relationships.

Strategies for Managing Dialectical Tensions

Managing the dialectical tensions outlined in these pages presents communication challenges. There are a number of strategies by which these challenges can be managed.[50] One of the least functional is *denial* that tensions exist. People in denial insist that 'everything is fine,' that the inevitable tugs of dialectical tensions really aren't a problem. For example, co-workers who claim that they're *always* happy to be members of the team and *never* see conflicts between their personal goals and the organization's are probably operating in a state of denial.

Disorientation is another response to dialectical tensions. In this response, communicators feel so overwhelmed and helpless that they are unable to confront their problems. In the face of dialectical tensions they might fight, freeze, or even leave the relationship. A couple who discover soon after the honeymoon that living a 'happily ever after' conflict-free life is impossible might become so terrified that they would come to view their marriage as a mistake.

In the strategy of *selection,* communicators respond to one end of the dialectical spectrum and ignore the other. For example, a couple caught between the conflicting desires for stability and novelty might find their struggle to change too difficult to manage and choose to stick with predictable, if unexciting, patterns of relating to one another.

Communicators choose the strategy of *alternation* to alternate between one end of the dialectical spectrum at some times and the other end at other times. Friends, for example, might manage the autonomy–connection dialectic by alternating between times when they spend a large amount of time together and other times when they live independent lives.

A fifth strategy is *segmentation,* a tactic in which partners compartmentalize different areas of their relationship. For example, a couple might manage the openness–closedness

Love one another, but make not a bond of love:
Let it rather be a moving sea between the shores of your souls.
Fill each other's cup but drink not from one cup.
Give one another of your bread but eat not of the same loaf.
Sing and dance together and be joyous, but let each one of you be alone,
Even as the strings of a lute are alone though they quiver with the same music.

Kahlil Gibran,
The Prophet

dialectic by sharing almost all their feelings about mutual friends with one another while keeping certain parts of their past romantic histories private.

Moderation is a sixth strategy. This strategy is characterized by compromises, in which communicators choose to back off from expressing either end of the dialectical spectrum. Adult children, for example, might manage the revelation–concealment dialectic with their inquisitive parents by answering some (though not all) unwelcome parental questions.

Communicators can also respond to dialectical challenges by reframing them in terms that redefine the situation so that the apparent contradiction disappears. Consider a couple who wince when their friends characterize them as a 'perfect couple'. On one hand, they want to escape from the 'perfect couple' label that feels confining, but on the other hand, they enjoy the admiration that comes with this identity. By pointing out to their friends that 'ideal couples' aren't always blissfully happy, they can both be themselves and keep the admiration of their friends.

A final strategy for handling dialectical tensions is *reaffirmation*—acknowledging that dialectical tensions will never disappear, accepting or even embracing the challenges they present. The metaphorical view of relational life as a kind of roller coaster reflects this orientation, and communicators who use reaffirmation view dialectical tensions as part of the ride.

Characteristics of Relational Development and Maintenance

Whether you analyze a relationship in terms of stages or dialectical dynamics, two characteristics are true of every interpersonal relationship. As you read about each, consider how it applies to your own experience.

Relationships Are Constantly Changing

Relationships are certainly not doomed to deteriorate, but even the strongest ones are rarely stable for long periods of time. In fairy tales a couple may live 'happily ever after', but in real life this sort of equilibrium is less common. Consider a husband and wife who have been married for some time. Although they have formally bonded, their relationship will probably shift from one dimension of a relational dialectic to another, and forward or backward along the spectrum of stages. Sometimes the partners will feel the need to differentiate from one another, and at other times they will seek intimacy. Sometimes they will feel secure in the predictable patterns they have established, and at other times one or both will be hungry for novelty. The relationship may become more circumscribed, or even stagnant. From this point the marriage may fail, but this fate isn't certain. With effort, the partners may move from the stage of stagnating to experimenting, or from circumscribing to intensifying.

Communication theorist Richard Conville describes the constantly evolving nature of relationships as a cycle in which partners move through a series of stages, returning to ones they previously encountered—although at a new level (see Figure 6.5).[51] In this cycle, partners

COMMUNICATION ON-SCREEN

Bend It like Beckham (2002)
Directed by Gurinder Chadha.

Jesminder 'Jess' Bhamra (Parminder Nagra) is a young teen juggling conflicting goals, relationships, and cultures. Her parents want her to embrace her Indian heritage and traditional Sikh upbringing, but she would rather play soccer in the parks of London. Jess knows her parents would never allow her to participate—so she doesn't tell them. Instead, she makes up stories so she can attend practices and games.

Secrets are a central theme of this movie, as several characters wrestle with the dialectical tension of openness versus privacy. Ultimately, Jess decides to openly pursue her goals and dreams, even if it disappoints the people she loves. In all of her relationships—with family, friends, and lovers—Jess finds that she must balance connection with autonomy, predictability with novelty, and privacy with openness.

One man all by himself is nothing. Two people who belong together make a world.

Hans Margolius

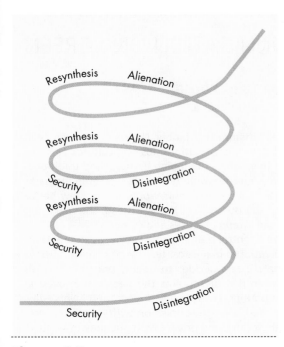

Figure 6.5

A Helical Model of Relational Cycles

self-disclosure

The process of deliberately revealing information about oneself that is significant and that would not normally be known by others.

move from security (integration, in Knapp's terminology) to disintegration (differentiating) to alienation (circumscribing) to resynthesis (intensifying, integrating) to a new level of security. This process repeats itself again and again.

Movement Is Always to a New Place

Even though a relationship may return to a stage it has previously experienced, it will never be the same. For example, most healthy long-term relationships will go through several phases of experimenting, when the partners try out new ways of behaving with one another. Though the same general features characterize each phase, the specifics will feel different each time. As you learned in Chapter 1, communication is irreversible. Partners can never go back to 'the way things were'. Sometimes this fact may lead to regrets: it's impossible to take back a cruel comment or forget a crisis. On the other hand, the irreversibility of communication can make relationships exciting, because it lessens the chance for boredom.

Self-Disclosure in Interpersonal Relationships

'We don't have any secrets,' some people proudly claim. Opening up certainly is important. Earlier in this chapter you learned that one ingredient in qualitatively interpersonal relationships is disclosure. You've also learned that we find others more attractive when they share certain private information with us. Given the obvious importance of self-disclosure, we need to take a closer look at the subject. Just what is it? When is it desirable? How can it best be done?

The best place to begin is with a definition. **Self-disclosure** is the process of deliberately revealing information about oneself that is significant and that others would not normally know. Let's take a closer look at some parts of this definition. Self-disclosure must be *deliberate*. If you accidentally mentioned to a friend that you were thinking about quitting a job or proposing marriage, that information would not fit into the category we are examining here. Self-disclosure must also be *significant*. Revealing relatively trivial information—the fact that you like fudge, for example—does not qualify as self-disclosure. The third requirement is that *others would not know the information being revealed*. There's nothing noteworthy about telling others that you are depressed or elated if they already know how you're feeling.

As Table 6.4 shows, people self-disclose for a variety of reasons. Some involve developing and maintaining relationships, but other reasons often drive revealing personal information. The reasons for disclosing vary from one situation to another, depending on several factors. The first important factor in whether we disclose seems to be how well we know the other person.[52] When the target of disclosure is a friend, the most frequent reason people give for volunteering personal information is relationship maintenance and enhancement. In other words, we disclose to friends in order to strengthen the relationship. The second important reason is self-clarification—to sort out confusion to understand ourselves better.

With strangers, reciprocity becomes the most common reason for disclosing. We offer information about ourselves to strangers in hopes of learning more about them, so we can decide whether and how to continue the relationship. The second most common reason is impression formation. We often reveal information about ourselves to strangers to make

TABLE 6.4 Reasons for Self-Disclosure

Reason	Example/Explanation
Catharsis	'I need to get this off my chest. . . .'
Self-clarification	'I'm really confused about something I did last night. If I tell you, maybe I can figure out why I did it. . . .'
Self-validation	'I think I did the right thing. Let me tell you why I did it. . . .'
Reciprocity	'I really like you . . .' (Hoping for a similar disclosure by the other person.)
Impression management	Salesperson to customer: 'My boss would kill me for giving you this discount . . .' (Hoping disclosure will build on trust.)
Relationship maintenance and enhancement	'I'm worried about the way things are going between us. Let's talk.' Or 'I sure am glad we're together!'
Control	Employee to boss, hoping to get a raise: 'I got a job offer yesterday from our biggest competitor.'

Source: Adapted from V.J. Deriega and J. Grezlak, 'Appropriateness of Self-Disclosure', in G.J. Chelune, ed., *Self-Disclosure* (San Francisco, CA: Jossey-Bass, 1979).

ourselves look good. This information, of course, is usually positive—at least in the early stages of a friendship.

Models of Self-Disclosure

Over several decades, social scientists have created various models to represent and understand how self-disclosure operates in relationships. In the next few pages we will look at two of the best-known models.

Breadth and Depth: Social Penetration

Social psychologists Irwin Altman and Dalmas Taylor describe two ways in which communication can be more or less disclosing.[53] Their **social penetration model** is pictured in Figure 6.6. The first dimension of self-disclosure in this model involves the **breadth** of information volunteered—the range of subjects being discussed. For example, the breadth of disclosure in your relationship with a fellow worker will expand as you begin revealing information about your life away from the job, as well as on-the-job details. The second dimension of disclosure is the **depth** of the information being volunteered, the shift from relatively non-revealing messages to more personal ones.

Depending on the breadth and depth of information shared, a relationship can be defined as either casual or intimate. In a casual relationship, the breadth may be great, but not the depth. A more intimate relationship is likely to have high depth in at least one area. The most intimate relationships are those in which disclosure is great in both breadth and depth. Altman and Taylor see the development of a relationship as a progression from the periphery of their model to its centre, a process that typically occurs over time. Each of your personal relationships probably has a different combination of breadth of subjects and depth of disclosure. Figure 6.7 illustrates a student's self-disclosure in one relationship.

What makes the disclosure in some messages deeper than others? One way to measure depth is by how far it goes in two of the dimensions that

breadth

The range of topics about which an individual discloses.

depth

The level of personal information a person reveals on a particular topic.

social penetration model

A model describing how intimacy can be achieved via the breadth and depth of self-disclosure.

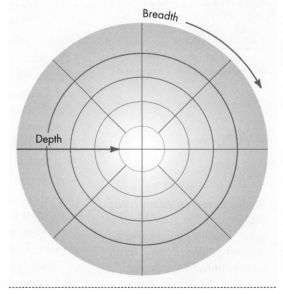

Figure 6.6
Social Penetration Model

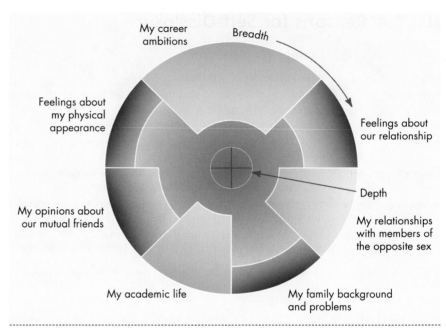

Figure 6.7
Sample Model of Social Penetration

define self-disclosure. Some revelations are certainly more *significant* than others. Consider the difference between saying 'I love my family' and 'I love you.' Other statements qualify as deep disclosure because they are private. Sharing a secret you've told to only a few close friends is certainly an act of self-disclosure, but it's even more revealing to divulge information that you've never told anyone.

Self-Disclosure, Self-Awareness, and Relational Quality: The Johari Window

Another model that helps represent how self-disclosure operates is the **Johari Window.**[54] (The window takes its name from the first names of its creators, Joseph Luft and Harry Ingham.) Imagine a frame inside which is everything there is to know about you: your likes and dislikes, your goals, your secrets, your needs—everything (see Figure 6.8).

Of course, you aren't aware of everything about yourself. Like most people, you're probably discovering new things about yourself all the time. To represent this, we can divide the frame containing everything about you into two parts: the part you know about and the part you don't know about, as in Figure 6.9.

We can also divide this frame containing everything about you in another way. In this division the first part contains the things about you that others know, and the second part contains the things about you that you keep to yourself. Figure 6.10 represents this view.

When we impose these two divided frames one atop the other, we have a Johari Window. By looking at Figure 6.11 you can see the *everything about you* window divided into four parts.

Part 1 represents the information of which both you and the other person are aware. This part is your *open area*. Part 2 represents the *blind area*: information of which you are unaware but the other person knows. You learn about information in the blind area primarily through feedback. Part 3 represents your *hidden area*: information that you know but aren't willing to reveal to

Johari Window
A model that describes the relationship between self-disclosure and self-awareness.

Be more concerned with your character than your reputation, because your character is what you really are, while your reputation is merely what others think you are.

John Wooden

Figure 6.8
The Johari Window: Everything about You

Figure 6.9
The Johari Window: Known to Self; Not Known to Self

Figure 6.10
The Johari Window: Known to Others; Not Known to Others

others. Items in this hidden area become public primarily through self-disclosure, which is the focus of this chapter. Part 4 represents information that is *unknown* to both you and others. At first, the unknown area seems impossible to verify. After all, if neither you nor others know what it contains, how can you be sure it exists? We can deduce its existence because we are constantly discovering new things about ourselves. It is not unusual to discover, for example, that you have an unrecognized talent, strength, or weakness. Items move from the unknown area into the open area either directly when you disclose your insight or through one of the other areas first.

Interpersonal relationships of any depth are virtually impossible if the individuals involved have little open area. Going a step further, you can see that the individual who is less open, that is, who possesses the smaller open area, limits a relationship. Figure 6.12 illustrates this situation with Johari Windows. A's window is set up in reverse so that A's and B's open areas are adjacent. Notice that the amount of communication (represented by the arrows connecting the two open areas) is dictated by the size of the smaller open area of A. The arrows originating from B's open area and being turned aside by A's hidden and blind areas represent unsuccessful attempts to communicate.

You have probably found yourself in situations that resemble Figure 6.12. Perhaps you have felt the frustration of not being able to get to know someone who was too

Ninety percent of all politicians give the other ten percent a bad reputation.

Henry Kissinger

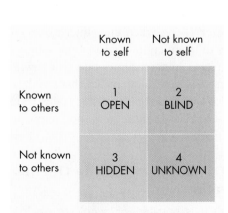

Figure 6.11
The Johari Window: Open; Blind; Hidden; Unknown

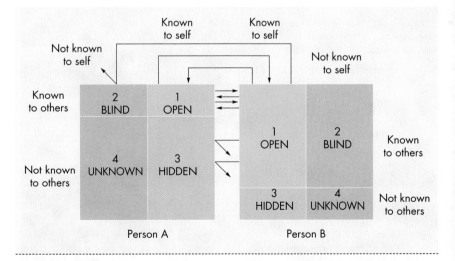

Figure 6.12
The Johari Window: Self-Disclosure Levels in Two-Way Communication

reserved. Perhaps you have blocked another person's attempts to build a relationship with you in the same way. Whether you picture yourself more like Person A or Person B, the fact is that self-disclosure on both sides is necessary for the development of any interpersonal relationship. This chapter will describe just how much self-disclosure is optimal and of what type.

Characteristics of Effective Self-Disclosure

Self-disclosure can certainly be valuable, but using it effectively requires an understanding of how it operates. Here are some findings from researchers that will help you decide when and how disclosure works best.

Self-Disclosure Is Influenced by Culture

The level of self-disclosure that is appropriate in one culture may seem completely inappropriate in another one. Disclosure is especially high in mainstream Anglo-North American society. In fact, people born and bred in English Canada and the United States are more disclosing of themselves—not just to friends but to acquaintances and even strangers—than members of any other culture studied.[55] By contrast, Germans tend to disclose little about themselves except in intimate relationships with a select few, and Japanese people reveal very little about themselves in even their closest relationships.

Cultural differences like this mean that what counts as disclosing communication varies from one culture to another. If you were raised in English Canada, you might view people from certain other cultures as undisclosing or standoffish. But the amount of personal information that people from other traditions disclose might actually be quite revealing by the standards of their culture. The converse is also true: to people from some other cultures, English Canadians probably look like exhibitionists, ready to spew personal information to anyone within earshot.

When communicating with people from different cultures it's important to consider their standards for appropriate disclosure. Don't mistakenly judge them according to your own standards. Likewise, be sensitive about honouring their standards when talking about yourself. In this sense, choosing the proper level of self-disclosure isn't too different from choosing the appropriate way of dressing or eating when encountering members of a different culture: what seems familiar and correct at home may not be suitable with strangers. As you read on, realize that the characteristics and guidelines that suit mainstream English-Canadian culture may not apply in other contexts.

Cultural Idiom

earshot
the distance at which one can hear something or someone

standoffish
unfriendly

Self-Disclosure Usually Occurs in Dyads

Although it is possible for people to disclose a great deal about themselves in groups, such communication usually occurs in one-to-one settings. Revealing significant information about yourself involves a certain amount of risk, and limiting the disclosure to one person at a time minimizes the chance that your disclosure will lead to unhappy consequences.

Effective Self-Disclosure Is Usually Symmetrical

Recall the small amount of successful two-way communication between A and B, as well as B's unsuccessful attempts to communicate in Figure 6.12. In situations such as this one, it's easy to imagine how B would soon limit the amount of disclosure to match that of A. On the other hand, if A were willing to match the degree of disclosure given by B, the relationship would move to a new level of intimacy. In either case, we can expect that the degree of disclosure between partners will often stabilize at a symmetrical level.

Effective Self-Disclosure Occurs Incrementally

Although instances occur in which partners start their relationship by telling everything about themselves to each other, such instances are rare. In most cases, the amount of disclosure increases over time. We begin relationships by revealing relatively little about ourselves; then if our first bits of self-disclosure are well received and bring on similar responses from the other person, we're willing to reveal more. This principle is important to remember. It would usually be a mistake to assume that the way to build a strong relationship would be to reveal the most private details about yourself when first making contact with another person. Unless the circumstances are unique, such baring of your soul would be likely to scare potential partners away rather than bring them closer.

Self-Disclosure Is Relatively Rare

Most conversations—even among friends—focus on everyday mundane topics and disclose little or no personal information.[56] Even partners in intimate relationships rarely talk about personal information.[57] Whether or not we open up to others is based on several criteria, some of which are listed in Table 6.5.

What is the optimal amount of self-disclosure? You might suspect that the correct answer is 'the more, the better', at least in personal relationships. Research has shown that the matter isn't this simple, however.[58] For example, there seems to be a curvilinear relationship between openness and satisfaction in marriage, so that a moderate amount of openness produces better results than either extreme disclosure or withholding. One good measure of happiness is how well the level of disclosure matches the expectations of communicators. If we get what we believe is a reasonable amount of candour from others, we are happy. If they tell us too little—or even too much—we become less satisfied.

Guidelines for Appropriate Self-Disclosure

One fear we've had while writing this chapter is that a few overenthusiastic readers may throw down their books and begin to share every personal detail of their lives with whomever they can find. As you can imagine, this kind of behaviour isn't an example of effective interpersonal communication.

No single style of self-disclosure is appropriate for every situation. Let's take a look at some guidelines that can help you recognize how to express yourself in a way that's rewarding for you and the others involved.[59]

One of the greatest moments in anybody's developing experience is when he no longer tries to hide from himself but determines to get acquainted with himself as he really is.

Norman Vincent Peale

TABLE 6.5 Some Criteria Used to Reveal Family Secrets

Intimate Exchange
Does the other person have a similar problem?
Would knowing the secret help the other person feel better?
Would knowing the secret help the other person manage her problem?

Exposure
Will the other person find out this information, even if I don't tell her?
Is the other person asking me directly to reveal this information?

Urgency
Is it very important that the other person know this information?
Will revealing this information make matters better?

Acceptance
Will the other person still accept me if I reveal this information?

Conversational Appropriateness
Will my disclosure fit into the conversation?
Has the topic of my disclosure come up in this conversation?

Relational Security
Do I trust the other person with this information?
Do I feel close enough to this person to reveal the secret?

Important Reason
Is there a pressing reason to reveal this information?

Permission
Have other people involved in the secret given their permission for me to reveal it?
Would I feel okay telling the people involved that I have revealed the secret?

Membership
Is the person to whom I'm revealing the secret going to join this group (i.e., family)?

Source: Adapted from A.L. Vangelisti, J.P Cauglhin, and L. Timmerman, 'Criteria for Revealing Family Secrets', *Communication Monographs* 68 (2001): 1–27.

Cultural Idiom

opening yourself up
letting yourself become vulnerable

Later that day I got to thinking about relationships. There are those that open you up to something new and exotic, those that are old and familiar, those that bring up lots of questions, those that bring you somewhere unexpected, those that bring you far from where you started, and those that bring you back. But the most exciting, challenging, and significant relationship of all is the one you have with yourself. And if you find someone to love the you you love, well, that's just fabulous.

Carrie Bradshaw,
Sex and the City

Is the Other Person Important to You?

There are several ways in which someone might be important. Perhaps you have an ongoing relationship deep enough so that sharing significant parts of yourself justifies keeping your present level of togetherness intact. Or perhaps the person to whom you're considering disclosing is someone with whom you've previously related on a less personal level. If you now see a chance to grow closer, disclosure may be the path toward developing that personal relationship.

Is the Risk of Disclosing Reasonable?

Take a realistic look at the potential risks of self-disclosure. Even if the probable benefits are great, opening yourself up to almost certain rejection may be asking for trouble. For instance, it might be foolhardy to share your important feelings with someone who you know is likely to either betray or ridicule your confidences. On the other hand, knowing that your partner is trustworthy and supportive makes the prospect of speaking out more reasonable.

Revealing personal thoughts and feelings can be especially risky on the job.[60] The politics of the workplace sometimes require communicators to keep feelings to themselves in order to accomplish both personal and organizational goals. You might, for example, find the opinions of a boss or customer personally offensive but decide to bite your tongue rather than risk your job or lose goodwill for the company.

Are the Amount and Type of Disclosure Appropriate?

A third point to realize is that there are degrees of self-disclosure. Telling others about yourself isn't an all-or-nothing decision. It's possible to share some facts, opinions, or feelings with one person while reserving riskier ones for others. In the same vein, before sharing very important information with someone who does matter to you, you might consider testing reactions by disclosing less personal data.

Is the Disclosure Relevant to the Situation at Hand?

The kind of disclosure that is often characteristic of highly personal relationships usually isn't appropriate in less personal settings. For instance, a study of classroom communication revealed that sharing all feelings—both positive and negative—and being completely honest resulted in less cohesiveness than having a 'relatively' honest climate in which pleasant but superficial relationships were the norm.[61]

Even in personal relationships—with close friends, family members, and so on—constant disclosure isn't a useful goal. The level of sharing in successful relationships rises and falls in cycles. You may go through a period of great disclosure and then spend another period of relative non-disclosure. Even during a phase of high disclosure, sharing everything isn't necessarily constructive. Usually the subject of appropriate self-disclosure involves the relationship rather than personal information. Furthermore, it is usually most constructive to focus your disclosure about the relationship on the 'here and now' as opposed to 'there and then'. 'How am I feeling now?' 'How are we doing now?' These are appropriate topics for sharing personal thoughts and feelings. There are certainly times when it's relevant to bring up the past but only as it relates to what's going on in the present.

Is the Disclosure Reciprocated?

There's nothing quite as disconcerting as talking your heart out to someone only to discover that the other person has yet to say anything to you that is half as revealing as what you've been saying. And you think to yourself, 'What am I doing?' Unequal self-disclosure creates an unbalanced relationship, one doomed to fall apart.

There are few times when one-way disclosure is acceptable. Most of them involve formal, therapeutic relationships in which a client approaches a trained professional with the goal of resolving a problem. For instance, you wouldn't necessarily expect to hear about a physician's personal ailments during a visit to a medical office. Nonetheless, it's interesting to note that one frequently noted characteristic of effective psychotherapists, counsellors, and teachers is a willingness to share their feelings about a relationship with their clients.

Will the Effect Be Constructive?

Self-disclosure can be a vicious tool if it's not used carefully. Psychologist George Bach suggests that every person has a psychological 'belt line'. Below that belt line are areas about which the person is extremely sensitive. Bach says that jabbing at a 'below-the-belt' area is a surefire way to disable another person, although usually at great cost to the relationship. It's important to consider the effects of your candour before opening up to others. Comments

Cultural Idiom

in the same vein
related to this idea

to bite your tongue
to remain silent

Cultural Idiom

talking your heart out
revealing your innermost thoughts and feelings

Hateful to me as are the gates of hell
Is he who, hiding one thing in his heart
Utters another.

Homer,
Iliad

Young Communicator
PROFILE

●●●●●

Joey Coleman, Blogger,
The Globe and Mail

If you don't have an online presence, you're not going to succeed in communications.

I've always used the Internet to communicate my message. From the early UseNets hosted on Hamilton, Ontario-based BBS hosts, to my first Geocities website in 1996, and finally joeycoleman.ca, the experiment has been ongoing.

In 2007, Canada's national news-weekly *Maclean's* hired me as the founding reporter/blogger of their online university news site. Why did *Maclean's* hire me, a student with no professional experience? My blog had a large following; I knew how to communicate; and I knew how to effectively use Web 2.0 tools to collect information. In 2009, I moved my higher-education coverage to Canada's national newspaper *The Globe and Mail's* website.

Today, Twitter is my most-often-used tool. The key to successfully using the social web (blogs, Twitter, Tumblr, Facebook, etc) is authenticity and focus. Find your niche (Hint: communications is not a niche in and of itself), become an expert, write about it, and be human every once in awhile.

Use the tools to connect to people, not to spread propaganda. The Web is not your dumping ground; don't use it as such. You must participate to succeed.

Communicate your niche—mine is higher-education policy—and connect with other people interested in that area. Then, extend your network to related topics. Build relationships. When someone in your network tweets about cheese in Wisconsin—and you're interested in that cheese—respond back. It's off-topic, but that's how you build relationships.

Tweet off-topic yourself. I often tweet about my pinball obsession.

Once you have a relationship, make it mutually beneficial. I've called the Twitter contacts many times for comment and they always take my calls—some of these people don't normally take media calls.

They've used Twitter to reach me, and I've responded when I wouldn't respond to an unknown person. (Hint: Know the functionality of your tools. Twitter direct messages often go to people's cellphones as a text message—it's a great way of getting an immediate message to a reporter in the field.)

As a journalist, I'm always looking for stories and sources. To be effective professional communicators, you must learn my interests as a journalist, then suggest people and stories, and you'll succeed in securing the all-valuable 'earned media', that is, placement of the message you are promoting in the media that I write for.

The Web is not the messiah some people make it out to be. It is a tool that needs to be used properly; misuse is worse than no use, and no use is failure. Most of all, don't spend your entire day talking about social media to other self-proclaimed 'social media experts'!

such as 'I've always thought you were pretty unintelligent' or 'Last year I made love to your best friend' *may* sometimes resolve old business and thus be constructive, but they also can be devastating—to the listener, to the relationship, and to your self-esteem.

Is the Self-Disclosure Clear and Understandable?

When you express yourself to others, it's important that you share yourself in a way that's intelligible. This means describing the *sources* of your message clearly. For instance, it's far better to describe another's behaviour by saying, 'When you don't answer my phone calls or drop by to visit anymore . . .' than to complain vaguely, 'When you avoid me . . .'

It's also vital to express your *thoughts* and *feelings* explicitly. 'I feel worried because I'm afraid you don't care about me' is more understandable than 'I don't like the way things have been going.'

Deception, Hinting, and Equivocation

Although honesty is desirable in principle, it often has risky, potentially unpleasant consequences. This explains why communicators—even those with the best intentions—aren't always completely honest when they find themselves in situations when honesty would be uncomfortable.[62] Three common alternatives to self-disclosure are lies, equivocation, and hinting.

Lies

To most people, lying appears to be a breach of ethics. Although lying to gain unfair advantage over an unknowing victim seems clearly wrong, another kind of untruth isn't so easy to dismiss as completely unethical. White lies, more appropriately called **altruistic lies,** are defined (at least by the people who tell them) as being harmless, or even helpful, to the person to whom they are told.[63] As Table 6.6 shows, at least some of the lies we tell are indeed intended to be helpful, or are at least relatively benign. Whether or not they are innocent, altruistic lies are certainly common. In one study, 130 subjects were asked to keep track of the truthfulness of their everyday conversational statements.[64] Only 38.5 per cent of these statements proved to be totally honest. In another experiment, 147 people between the ages of 18 and 71 kept a log of all the lies they told over a one-week period. Both men and women reported being untruthful in approximately one-fifth of their conversations that lasted over

The injunction against bearing false witness, branded in stone and brought down by Moses from the mountaintop, has always provoked ambivalent, conflicting emotions. On the one hand, nearly everyone condemns lying. On the other, nearly everyone does it every day.

Paul Gray

altruistic lies
Deceptions intended to be unmalicious, or even helpful, to the person to whom they are told.

TABLE 6.6 Some Reasons for Lying

Reason	Example
Acquire resources	'Oh, please let me add this class. If I don't get in, I'll never graduate on time!'
Protect resources	'I'd like to lend you the money, but I'm short myself.'
Initiate and continue interaction	'Excuse me, I'm lost. Do you live around here?'
Avoid conflict	'It's not a big deal. We can do it your way. Really.'
Avoid interaction or take leave	'That sounds like fun, but I'm busy Saturday night.' 'Oh, look what time it is! I've got to run!'
Present a competent image	'Sure, I understand. No problem.'
Increase social desirability	'Yeah, I've done a fair amount of skiing.'

Source: Adapted from categories originally presented in C. Camden, M.T. Motley, and A. Wilson, 'White Lies in Interpersonal Communication: A Taxonomy and Preliminary Investigation of Social Motivations', *Western Journal of Speech Communication* 48 (1984): 315.

COMMUNICATION ON-SCREEN

The Invention of Lying (2009)
Directed by Ricky Gervais & Matthew Robinson.

This comedy is set in a universe very similar to our own but with one glaring difference: no one can tell a lie. To our eyes, the complete honesty that underscores all communication in this world appears both hilarious and deeply discomforting, but something approaching a normal human society nonetheless appears to operate relatively smoothly. That is, until Mark Bellison (Ricky Gervais) suddenly acquires the ability to lie. Gifted with a tremendous advantage over his hapless peers, Bellison inadvertently sparks a religious movement with himself as its leading prophet. As he comes to terms with the interpersonal implications of deception, Bellison is forced to confront what limits, if any, he must place on himself in order to live a happy life.

Cultural Idiom

a put-on
a false show of emotion

---

equivocal language

Language with more than one likely interpretation.

---

10 minutes.[65] Over the course of the week, the subjects reported lying to about 30 per cent of the people with whom they had one-on-one conversations. The rate was much higher in some relationships. For example, dating couples lie to each other in about one-third of their interactions, and college students told at least one lie to their mothers in half of their conversations. In yet another study, subjects recorded their conversations over a two-day period and later counted their own deceptions. The average lie rate: 3 fibs for every 10 minutes of conversation.[66]

What are the consequences of discovering that you've been lied to? In an interpersonal relationship, the discovery can be traumatic. As we grow closer to others, our expectations about their honesty grow stronger. Discovering that you've been deceived requires you to redefine not only the lie you just uncovered but also many of the messages you previously took for granted. Was last week's compliment really sincere? Was your joke really funny, or was the other person's laughter a put-on? Does the other person care about you as much as he or she claimed?

Research has shown that deception does, in fact, threaten relationships;[67] however, not all lies are equally devastating. Feelings of dismay and betrayal are greatest when the relationship is most intense, when the importance of the subject is high, and when there is pre-existing suspicion that the other person isn't being completely honest. Of these three factors, the importance of the information lied about proved to be the key factor in provoking a relational crisis. We may be able to cope with 'misdemeanour' lying, but 'felonies' are a grave threat. In fact, the discovery of major deception can lead to the end of the relationship. More than two-thirds of the subjects in one study reported that their relationship had ended since they discovered a lie. Furthermore, they attributed the breakup directly to the lie. If preserving a relationship is important, honesty—at least about important matters—really does appear to be the best policy.

Equivocation

Lying isn't the only alternative to self-disclosure. When faced with the choice between lying and telling an unpleasant truth, communicators can—and often do—equivocate. As Chapter 3 explained, **equivocal language** has two or more equally plausible meanings. Sometimes people send equivocal messages without meaning to, resulting in confusion. 'I'll meet you at the apartment,' could refer to more than one place. But other times we are deliberately vague. For instance, when a friend asks what you think of an awful outfit, you could say, 'It's really unusual—one of a kind!' Likewise, if you are too angry to accept a friend's apology but don't want to appear petty, you might say, 'Don't mention it.'

The value of equivocation becomes clear when you consider the alternatives. Consider the dilemma of what to say when you receive an unwanted present—an ugly painting, for example—and the giver asks what you think of it. How can you respond? On the one hand, you need to choose between telling the truth and lying. On the other hand, you have a choice of whether to make your response clear or vague. Figure 6.13 displays these choices. After considering the alternatives, it's clear that an equivocal but true response is far preferable to

Is It Ever Right to Lie?

Is it ever right to lie? Suppose the Nazis come to your door asking if you are hiding a Jewish family. You are. Should you say 'No'? Or, on a mundane level, your spouse or lover walks in with a silly new hairdo and asks, 'Do you like it?' Does morality dictate that you ruin the evening? Or can you, in both cases, finesse the answer, not lying but not telling the truth either, perhaps by avoiding an answer to the question?

The demand for honesty is contextual. It depends on what the truth concerns. The Bible tells us not to bear false witness against our neighbor. Perjury, we can agree, is wrong: the consequences can be awful. But it seems to me absolutely crucial to distinguish here between public and private life. Perjury, by its very nature, is public, as is politics. Sex, with a few obvious exceptions, is part of our private life. And just about everyone is less than forthright about sex.

Not all untruths are malicious. Telling the truth can complicate or destroy social relationships. It can undermine precious collective myths. Honesty can be cruel. Sometimes, deception is not a vice but a social virtue, and systematic deception is an essential part of the order of the (social) world.

In many countries—Japan and Western Samoa, for example—social harmony is valued far more than truthfulness as such. To tell another person what he or she wants to hear, rather than what one might actually feel or believe, is not only permitted but expected. Could we not begin to see our own enlightened emphasis on 'seeking the truth at all costs' as one more ethnocentric peculiarity, another curious product of our strong sense of individualism, and a dangerously unsociable conception?

The obvious truth is that our simplest social relationships could not exist without the opaque medium of the lie. The best answer to the question 'What are you thinking?' is often 'Oh, nothing.' Perhaps deception, not truth, is the cement of civilization—cement that does not so much hold us

together as safely separate us and our thoughts. Some things are better left in the dark.

In contrast to Kant, for whom the rule against lying was a moral law, a 'categorical imperative' never to be overridden, utilitarian philosophers insist that lying is wrong only because a lie does, in fact, cause more harm than good. There is no absolute prohibition here, rather perhaps a 'rule of thumb', and there may well be many cases, such as the 'white lies' described above, in which lying causes no harm and may even be commendable. The problem, as Nietzsche so wisely complains, is 'not that you lied to me, but that I no longer believe you'. It is not the breach of the principle against lying that is so troublesome, nor is it the consequences of the lie or the character of the liar. It is that lying compromises and corrupts our relationships.

In other words, the wrongness of lying does not have to do primarily with breaches of principle or miscalculations of harm and good. Lying is wrong because it constitutes a breach of trust, which is not a principle but a very particular and personal relationship between people.

What is wrong with lying, in other words, is not exactly what philosophers have often supposed. Lying undermines relationships by undermining trust. But trust may just as often be supported by mutual myths, by religious faith, by a clear understanding of what is private and personal and what is 'the public's right to know'. Trust is usually violated by lies, but trust can be more deeply damaged by a violation of personal boundaries, which in turn may invite lies and deception to protect what has been violated.

—*Robert C. Solomon*

Questions: Do you feel that lying is ever justified? What are some instances when you have felt obliged to lie? Why did you lie? Can you relate to Robert Solomon's arguments? Do you think he's right that trust makes lying necessary to protect personal boundaries?

the other choices in several respects. First, it spares the receiver from embarrassment. For example, rather than flatly saying 'no' to an unappealing invitation, it may be kinder to say 'I have other plans'—even if those plans are to stay home and watch TV.

Besides saving face for the recipient, honest equivocation can be less stressful for the sender than either telling the truth bluntly or lying. Because equivocation is often easier to accept than the cold, hard truth, it spares the teller from feeling guilty. It's less taxing on the

Cultural Idiom

less taxing on
less demanding of

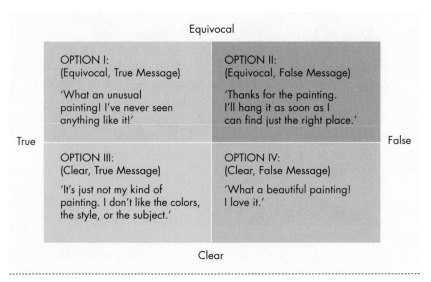

Equivocal

OPTION I: (Equivocal, True Message) 'What an unusual painting! I've never seen anything like it!'	**OPTION II:** (Equivocal, False Message) 'Thanks for the painting. I'll hang it as soon as I can find just the right place.'
OPTION III: (Clear, True Message) 'It's just not my kind of painting. I don't like the colors, the style, or the subject.'	**OPTION IV:** (Clear, False Message) 'What a beautiful painting! I love it.'

True   False

Clear

Figure 6.13
Dimensions of Truthfulness and Equivocation

conscience to say 'I've never tasted anything like this' than to say 'This meal tastes terrible,' even though the latter comment is more precise. Few people want to lie, and equivocation provides an alternative to deceit.[68]

A study by communication researcher Sandra Metts and her colleagues shows how equivocation can save face in difficult situations.[69] Several hundred university students were asked how they would turn down unwanted sexual overtures from a person whose feelings were important to them: either a close friend, a prospective date, or a dating partner. The majority of students chose a diplomatic reaction ('I just don't think I'm ready for this right now') as being more face-saving and comfortable than a direct statement like 'I just don't feel sexually attracted to you.' The diplomatic reaction seemed sufficiently clear to get the message across but not so blunt as to embarrass or even humiliate the other person. (Interestingly, men said they would be able to handle a direct rejection more comfortably than women. The researchers suggest that one reason for the difference is that men stereotypically initiate sexual offers and thus are more likely to expect rejection.)

Besides preventing embarrassment, equivocal language can also save the speaker from being caught lying. If a potential employer asks about your grades during a job interview, you would be safe saying, 'I had a B average last semester,' even though your overall grade average is closer to C. The statement isn't a complete answer, but it is honest as far as it goes. As one team of researchers put it, 'Equivocation is neither a false message nor a clear truth, but rather an alternative used precisely when both of these are to be avoided.'[70]

Given these advantages, it's not surprising that most people will usually choose to equivocate rather than tell a lie. In a series of experiments, subjects chose between telling a face-saving lie, telling the truth, and equivocating. Only 6 per cent chose the lie, and between 3 and 4 per cent chose the hurtful truth. By contrast, over 90 per cent chose the equivocal response.[71] People say they prefer truth-telling to equivocating,[72] but given the choice, they prefer to finesse the truth.

Hinting

Hints are more direct than equivocal statements. Whereas an equivocal message isn't necessarily aimed at changing others' behaviour, a hint seeks to get the desired response from others. Some hints are designed to save the receiver from embarrassment:[73]

Face-Saving Hint	Direct Statement
These desserts are terribly overpriced.	You're too overweight to be ordering dessert.
I know you're busy; I'd better let you go.	I'm bored. I want to get out of this conversation.

Other hints are strategies for saving the sender from embarrassment:

Face-Saving Hint	Direct Statement
I'm pretty sure that smoking isn't permitted here.	Your smoking bothers me.
Gee, it's almost lunchtime. Have you ever eaten at that new Italian restaurant around the corner?	I'd like to invite you out for lunch, but I don't want to risk a 'no' answer to my invitation.

The success of a hint depends on the other person's ability to pick up the unexpressed message. Your subtle remarks might go right over the head of an insensitive receiver—or one who chooses not to respond to them. If this does happen, you still have the choice to be more direct. If the costs of a straightforward message seem too high, you can withdraw without risk.

It's easy to see why people choose hints, equivocations, and white lies instead of complete self-disclosure. These strategies provide an easier way to manage difficult situations than the alternatives for both the speaker and the receiver. In this sense, successful liars, equivocators, and hinters can be said to possess a certain kind of communicative competence. On the other hand, there are certainly times when honesty is the right approach, even if it's painful. At times like these, evaders could be viewed as lacking the competence or the integrity to handle a situation most effectively.

Are hints, benign lies, and equivocations an ethical alternative to self-disclosure? Some of the examples in these pages suggest the answer is a qualified 'yes'. Many social scientists and philosophers agree. Some argue that the morality of a speaker's *motives* for lying ought to be judged, not the deceptive act itself.[74] Others ask whether the *effects* of a lie will be worth the deception. Ethicist Sissela Bok offers some circumstances where deception may be justified: doing good, avoiding harm, and protecting a larger truth.[75] Perhaps the right questions to ask, then, are (1) whether an indirect message is truly in the interests of the receiver, and (2) whether this sort of evasion is the only effective way to behave. Bok suggests another way to check the justifiability of a lie: imagine how others would respond if they knew what you were really thinking or feeling. Would they accept your reasons for not disclosing?

My mother . . . went on worrying and trying to help Noreen without hurting her feelings, by tactful remarks about the advisability of modulating one's voice when singing hymns, and the fact there was plenty of hot water so Noreen didn't need to hesitate about taking a bath. She even bought a razor and a packet of blades and whispered to Noreen that any girl who wore transparent blouses so much would probably like to shave under her arms. None of these suggestions had the slightest effect on Noreen. She did not cease belting out hymns at the top or her voice, she bathed once a fortnight, and the sorrel-coloured hair continued to bloom like a thicket of Indian paintbrush in her armpits.

Margaret Laurence,
A Bird in the House

Cultural Idiom

go right over the head of
be difficult for someone to understand

Ah Mozart! He was happily married—but his wife wasn't.

Victor Borge

Summary

An interpersonal relationship is one in which two or more people meet one another's social needs to a greater or lesser degree. Communication can be considered interpersonal according to either the context or the quality of interaction. Regardless of which definition is used, communication in relationships consists of both content and relational messages. Explicit relational messages are termed *metacommunication*.

Intimacy is a powerful need for most people. Intimacy can be created and expressed in a variety of ways: physically, emotionally, intellectually, and through shared activities. The notion of levels of intimacy has varied according to historical period, culture, and gender. Along with the desire for closeness, a need for distance is equally important. These opposing drives lead to conflicting communication behaviour at different stages in people's lives and their relationships. The challenge is to communicate in a way that strikes a balance between intimacy and distance.

Some communication theorists suggest that intimate relationships pass through a series of stages, each of which is characterized by a unique mode of communication. These stages fall into three broad phases: coming together, relational maintenance, and coming apart. Although the movement within and between these stages does follow recognizable patterns, the amount and direction of movement are not predetermined. Some relationships move steadily toward termination, whereas others shift backward and forward as the partners redefine their desires for intimacy and distance.

Other theorists take a dialectal view, arguing that the same series of opposing desires operates throughout the entire span of relationships. These dialectical drives include autonomy versus connection, predictability versus novelty, and openness versus privacy. Since these opposing forces are inevitable, the challenge is to develop strategies for dealing with them that provide relational satisfaction.

Self-disclosure is the process of deliberately revealing significant information about oneself that would not normally be known. The social penetration model can describe the breadth and depth of self-disclosure. The Johari Window model reveals an individual's open, blind, hidden, and unknown areas. Complete self-disclosure is not common, nor is it always desirable. Several guidelines to help determine when it is and is not appropriate were discussed. The chapter concluded by describing three widely used alternatives to self-disclosure: lies, equivocation, and hints. It discussed the conditions under which these alternatives can be appropriate.

Key Terms

affinity 215

altruistic lies 243

breadth (of
  self-disclosure) 235

content messages 214

control 216

depth (of
  self-disclosure) 235

developmental model 223

dialectical model (of relational maintenance) 228

dialectical tensions 228

equivocal language 244

immediacy 216

impersonal
  communication 209

intimacy 218

Johari Window 236

metacommunication 217

qualitative interpersonal
  communication 209

relational messages 215

respect 216

self-disclosure 234

social penetration
  model 235

Activities

A. Interpersonal Communication: Context and Quality

1. Examine your interpersonal relationships in a contextual sense by making two lists. The first should contain all the two-person relationships in which you have participated during the past week. The second should contain all your relationships that have occurred in small-group and public contexts. Are there any important differences that distinguish dyadic interaction from communication with a larger number of people?

2. Now make a second set of two lists. The first one should describe all of your relationships that are interpersonal in a qualitative sense, and the second should describe all the two-person relationships that are more impersonal. Are you satisfied with the number of qualitatively interpersonal relationships you have identified?

3. Compare the lists you developed in steps 1 and 2. See what useful information each one contains. What do your conclusions tell you about the difference between contextual and qualitative definitions of interpersonal communication?

B. Identifying Relational Messages

To complete this exercise, you will need the help of a partner with whom you communicate on an ongoing basis.

1. Pick three recent exchanges between you and your partner. Although any exchanges will do, the most interesting ones will be those in which you sense that something significant (positive or negative) was going on that wasn't expressed overtly.

2. For each exchange, identify both the content and relational messages that you were expressing. Identify relational messages in terms of dimensions such as affinity, respect, immediacy, and/or control.

3. Explain the concept of relational messages to your partner, and ask him or her to identify the relational messages received from you during the same exchanges. How closely does your partner's perception match your analysis of the relational messages?

4. Now identify the relational messages you interpreted your partner as sending during the three exchanges.

5. Ask your partner to describe the relational messages he or she believed were sent to you on these occasions. How closely did your interpretation match your partner's explanation?

Based on your analysis of these three exchanges, answer the following questions:

1. What significant kinds of relational messages are exchanged in your relationship?

2. How accurate are you in decoding your partner's relational messages? How accurate is your partner in decoding your relational messages?

3. What lessons have you learned from this exercise that can improve the quality of your relationship?

C. Your IQ (Intimacy Quotient)

Answer the following questions as you think about your relationship with a person important in your life.

1. What is the level of physical intimacy in your relationship?
2. What intellectual intimacy do you share?
3. How emotionally intimate are you? Is your emotional intimacy deeper in some ways than in others?
4. Has your intimacy level changed over time? If so, in what ways?

After answering these questions, ask yourself how satisfied you are with the amount of intimacy in this relationship. Identify any changes you would like to occur, and describe the steps you could take to make them happen.

D. Striking a Balance between Intimacy and Distance

Choose an important interpersonal relationship with someone you encounter on a frequent, regular basis. You might choose a friend, family member, or romantic partner.

For at least a week, chart how your communication with this relational partner reflects your desire for either intimacy or distance. Use a seven-point scale, in which behaviour seeking high intimacy receives a seven, whereas behaviour seeking to avoid physical, intellectual, and/or emotional contact receives a one. Use ratings from two through six to reflect intermediate stages. Record at least one rating per day, making more detailed entries if your desire for intimacy or distance changes during that period.

After charting your communication, reflect on what the results tell you about your personal desire for intimacy and distance. Consider the following questions:

1. Which state—intimacy or distance—seemed most desirable for you?
2. To the degree that you seek intimacy, which variety or varieties are most important to you: intellectual, emotional, and/or physical?
3. Was the pattern you charted during this week typical of your communication in this relationship over a longer period of time?
4. Do you seek the same mixture of intimacy and distance in other relationships?
5. Most importantly, are you satisfied with the results you discovered in this exercise? If not, how would you like to change your communication behaviour?

E. Juggling Dialectical Tensions

Identify one situation in which you are trying to manage dialectical tensions in your life. (Describe which of the dialectical forces described in this chapter are in operation.) Then answer the following questions:

1. Which of the strategies for managing dialectical tensions listed on pages 232–3 do you use?
2. How effective is the strategy (or strategies) that you have chosen?
3. Would an alternative strategy be more effective for managing the tensions in this situation?
4. How might things go differently if you choose the alternative strategy?

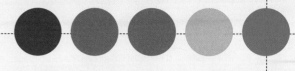

F. Reasons for Disclosing

Recall recent personal examples of times when you have disclosed personal information for each of the reasons listed in Table 6.6. Explain your answer by describing
- the target of your self-disclosure;
- the information you disclosed; and
- your reason(s) for disclosing.

Based on your findings, decide which of the reasons for self-disclosure are most characteristic of your communication. Note: In order to protect privacy, this exercise can be conducted in class by having each member submit anonymous entries.

G. Effective Self-Disclosure

Choose a self-disclosing message that is important enough for you to consider sharing. Use the guidelines on pages 239–43 to craft the message in a way that maximizes the chances of having it received successfully. Share your message strategy with classmates, and get their opinion of whether it needs refinement.

H. The Ethics of Lying and Equivocating

Research shows that virtually everyone lies, equivocates, and hints for a variety of reasons. Explore the ethical legitimacy of your lies and equivocations by following these directions:
1. For a two-day period, keep track of
   a. your lies, equivocations, and hints
   b. your reason for taking one of these approaches in each situation
   c. the positive and negative consequences (for you and the other person) of avoiding self-disclosure.
2. Based on your analysis of the information collected in Step 1, identify the ethical legitimacy of each type of non-disclosing communication. Are any sorts of deception justifiable? Which sorts are not? How would you feel if you discovered the other person had not been straightforward with you under similar circumstances?

Further Reading

Bugeja, Michael. *Interpersonal Divide: The Search for Community in a Technological Age*. New York: Oxford University Press, 2005.
The author argues that media and technology have eroded our sense of community. He analyzes the 'interpersonal divide'—the void that he claims develops when we spend too much time in virtual rather than real communities—and makes the case for face-to-face communication in an increasingly mediated world.

Canary, Daniel J., and Marianne Dainton. *Maintaining Relationships through Communication.* Mahwah, NJ: Erlbaum, 2003.
As its name suggests, this volume explores the ways in which people communicate to maintain various types of relationships. Contexts include interaction among family members, romantic partners, friends, and colleagues. Other chapters address dimensions including culture, long-distance relationships, and computer-medical contexts.

Choril, Nicole. 'Equivocation as an Interactional Event', in William R. Cupach and Brian H. Spitzberg, eds, *The Dark Side of Interpersonal Communication.* Hillsdale, NJ: Erlbaum, 1994.
This chapter describes how equivocation can be a form of strategic ambiguity that greases the wheels of social interaction. It outlines the types of equivocal messages and identifies situations that elicit them.

Conville, Richard, and L. Edna Rogers, eds. *The Meaning of 'Relationship' in Interpersonal Communication.* Westport, CT: Praeger, 1998.
The readings in this volume offer an excellent resource for exploring the nature of interpersonal relationships. Besides offering insights, the references in each chapter will direct serious students to more information on various dimensions of relational communication.

De Kerckhove, Derek. *The Architecture of Intelligence.* Dordecht: Birkhäuser, 2001.
A refreshingly unconventional look at architecture and the Internet. Using Vitruvius's classical text *De Arquitectura* as a starting point, De Kerckhove, Canadian media theorist and director of the McLuhan Centre for Culture and Technology at the University of Toronto, begins a journey into the exciting world of the Internet. On the one hand, he explores the architecture of this revolutionary medium, while on the other hand he considers the wide-ranging opportunities which the Information Technology (IT) world offers for architectonic design, revealing how this new medium for communication is based as much on tradition as on innovation.

Mashek, Debra, J., and Arthur Aron, *Handbook of Closeness and Intimacy.* Mahwah, NJ: Erlbaum, 2004.
This handbook brings together the latest thinking on the scientific study of closeness and intimacy. The chapters address questions including, What are closeness and intimacy? What individual differences and situations play a role in closeness and intimacy? Is there a dark side to closeness and intimacy?

Montgomery, Barbara M., and Leslie A. Baxter, eds. *Dialectical Approaches to Studying Personal Relationships.* New York: Erlbaum, 1998.
This edited collection provides a useful look at how dialectics operate in a variety of interpersonal relationships.

Tannen, Deborah. *I Only Say This Because I Love You: How the Way We Talk Can Make or Break Family Relationships throughout Our Lives.* New York: Random House, 2001.
Tannen explains why talking about even the most innocuous subjects with family members can sometimes be so painful. She looks behind content issues and highlights relational

themes that often trigger criticism, disapproval, and rejection on the one hand and pain on the other. Tannen also explains how some of the dialectical tensions described in this chapter operate, focusing especially on how family communication must balance the need for connection with the desire for control.

Wood, Julia T. *Gendered Lives,* 6th edn. Belmont, CA: Wadsworth, 2005.
Wood shows how gender affects relational communication in a variety of contexts and ways. Chapters examine the influence of gender on various types of relationships: personal (including friendship), romantic, and professional.

Study Questions

1. Think of three relationships that you are currently in, and, for the next two days, list all of the messages you exchange with these three people. Categorize them under the types of relational messages outlined in this chapter: affinity, respect, immediacy, and control.
2. Think of three examples of different types of relationships you are engaged in right now (e.g., school, friendly, workplace, romantic). List examples of metacommunication that you engage in with these different sorts of relationship. Are you more likely to metacommunicate in certain types of relationships?
3. What are your experiences of intimacy in your relationships? Identify three relationships and then discuss how your intimacy functions within them. Do you have different comfort levels in different sorts of relationships (e.g., friendships vs workplace, parental vs romantic)? List how cultural differences play a role in the intimacy you experience in these relationships.
4. Reflect on three of your most important relationships, whether they are in your past or present. They can be friendships, work-relationships, or romantic. Consider how these three relationships map onto the stages of relational development and maintenance. Are all your relationships where you want them to be on the relationship ladder described on pages 223–8?
5. List the three important relationships that you used as examples for the previous question. Now write down whether the dialectical method describes their development better than the stage-based model. Write down how the three most important dialectical tensions (connection versus autonomy, predictability versus novelty, and openness versus privacy) relate to your three important relationships.
6. How does self-disclosure play a role in the three relationships you have been examining? How does your self-disclosure, as well as that of the person you are in a relationship with, correspond to the Johari Window? Map out on a piece of paper the differences in your self-disclosure in all three relationships. Do you disclose more or differently in the three relationships? Why?
7. Using the same three relationships, ask yourself whether you have lied or used equivocation with the people you are in a relationship with. Why did you do it? Did it achieve a positive result for you? Was your lying or equivocation done to protect the relationship or to protect yourself?

After studying the material in this chapter . . .

<table>
<tr>
<td>You should understand:</td>
<td>

- the role of communication climate in interpersonal relationships;
- types of messages that contribute to confirming and disconfirming climates;
- the unavoidable but potentially problematic role of conflict in interpersonal relationships;
- characteristics of non-assertive, directly aggressive, passive-aggressive, indirect, and assertive communications;
- the influence of gender and culture on conflict styles; and
- the differences between win–lose, lose–lose, compromising, and win–win approaches to conflict resolution.

</td>
</tr>
<tr>
<td>You should be able to:</td>
<td>

- identify disconfirming messages and replace them with confirming ones, using the Gibb categories of supportive communication;
- describe the degree to which you use non-assertive, directly aggressive, passive-aggressive, indirect, and assertive messages and choose more satisfying responses as necessary;
- compose and deliver an assertive message, using the behaviour–interpretation–feeling–consequence–intention format; and
- apply the win–win approach to an interpersonal conflict.

</td>
</tr>
</table>

Improving Interpersonal Relationships

Chapter Highlights

Communication climates are intangible but critical ingredients in relational satisfaction. In the first part of this chapter, you will learn

- what makes some messages confirming and other messages disconfirming;
- how communication climates develop; and
- some tips for creating positive communication climates.

The second half of this chapter focuses on conflict in relationships, including

- the nature of conflict;
- how people express conflict;
- the influence of gender and culture on conflict in relationships; and
- methods of conflict resolution, including the win–win approach.

No matter how satisfying your relationships, there are almost certainly ways they could be better. At times even best friends, close families, and productive co-workers become dissatisfied. Sometimes the people involved are unhappy with each other. At other times, one person's problem is unrelated to the relationship. In either case, there's a desire to communicate in a way that makes matters better.

The ideas in this chapter can help you improve the important relationships in your life. We'll begin by talking about the factors that make communication 'climates' either positive or negative before moving on to methods for understanding and resolving interpersonal conflicts.

communication climate

The emotional tone of a relationship as it is expressed in the messages that the partners send and receive.

confirming response

A response that conveys valuing, caring, and/or respecting another person.

Communication Climates in Interpersonal Relationships

Personal relationships are a lot like the weather. Some are fair and warm, others are stormy and cold; some are permanently clouded by smog, others are healthy. Some relationships have stable climates, whereas others change dramatically—calm one moment and turbulent the next. You can't measure interpersonal climate by looking at a thermometer or glancing at the sky, but it's there nonetheless. Every relationship has a feeling, or a pervasive mood, that colours the interactions of the participants. The term **communication climate** refers to the emotional tone of a relationship. A climate doesn't involve specific activities, but instead focuses on the way people feel about each other as they carry out those activities. Consider two communication classes, for example. Both meet for the same length of time and follow the same syllabus. It's easy to imagine how one of these classes might be a friendly, comfortable place to learn, whereas the other might be cold and tense—even hostile. The same principle holds for families, among co-workers, and in other relationships: communication climates are a function more of the way people feel about one another than of the tasks they perform.

Confirming and Disconfirming Messages

What makes some climates positive and others negative? A short but accurate answer is that the *communication climate is determined by the degree to which people see themselves as valued.* When we believe others view us as important, we are likely to feel good about our relationship. On the other hand, the relational climate suffers when we think others don't appreciate or care about us.

Messages that show others that they're valued have been called **confirming responses.**[1] In one form or another, confirming responses say 'you exist,' 'you matter,' 'you're important.' In fact, it's an oversimplification to talk about one type of confirming message: confirming communication really occurs on three increasingly positive levels:[2]

- *Recognition.* The most fundamental act of confirmation is to recognize the other person. Recognition seems easy and obvious, and yet there are many times when we don't respond to others on this basic level. Failure to write or visit a friend is a common example. So is failure to return an e-mail or a phone call. Avoiding eye contact and not approaching someone you know on campus, at a party, or on the street all send negative messages. Of course, this lack of recognition may simply be an oversight. You might not notice your friend, or the pressures of work and school might prevent you from staying in touch. Nonetheless, if the other person *perceives* that you are avoiding contact, the message has the effect of being disconfirming.

- *Acknowledgement.* Acknowledging the ideas and feelings of others is a stronger form of confirmation. Listening is probably the most common form of acknowledgement. Of course, counterfeit listening—ambushing, stage hogging, pseudolistening, and so on—has the opposite effect of acknowledgement. More active acknowledgement includes asking questions, paraphrasing, and reflecting. Not surprisingly, employees rate managers who solicit their suggestions highly—even when the managers don't accept every suggestion.[3] As you read in Chapter 4, reflecting the speaker's thoughts and feelings can be a powerful way to offer support when others have problems.

- *Endorsement.* Whereas acknowledgement signals that you're interested in another's ideas, endorsement means that you agree with them. It's easy to see why endorsement is the strongest type of confirming message, because it communicates the highest form of valuing. The most obvious form of endorsement is agreeing. Fortunately, it isn't necessary to agree completely with another person in order to endorse her or his message. You can probably find something in the message that you endorse. 'I can see why you were so angry,' you might reply to a friend, even if you don't approve of his outburst. Of course, outright praise is a strong form of endorsement and one you can use surprisingly often after you look for opportunities to compliment others. Non-verbal endorsement can also enhance the quality of a relational climate. For example, women rate men who agree with them as more physically attractive than those who fail to do so.[4]

It's hard to overstate the importance of confirming messages. For instance, a positive climate is the best predictor of marital satisfaction.[5] Satisfied couples have a 5:1 ratio of positive to negative statements, whereas the ratio for dissatisfied partners is 1:1.[6] Positive, confirming messages are just as important in families. The satisfaction that siblings feel with one another, for example, drops sharply as aggressive, disconfirming messages increase.[7] Confirmation is just as important in the classroom, where motivation and learning increase when teachers demonstrate a genuine interest and concern for students.[8]

In contrast to confirming communication, messages that deny the value of others have been labelled **disconfirming responses**. These show a lack of regard for the other person either by disputing or by ignoring some important part of that person's message.[9] *Disagreement* can certainly be disconfirming, especially if it goes beyond disputing the other person's ideas and attacks the speaker personally. However, disagreement is not the most damaging kind of

The worst sin towards our fellow creatures is not to hate them, but to be indifferent to them; that's the essence of inhumanity.

George Bernard Shaw

We are here to add what we can to life, not to get what we can from life.

William Osler

disconfirming response
A message that expresses a lack of caring or respect for another person.

TABLE 7.1 Distancing Tactics

Tactic	Description
Avoidance	Evading the other person.
Deception	Lying to or misleading the other person.
Degrading	Treating the other person with disrespect.
Detachment	Acting emotionally disinterested in the other person.
Discounting	Disregarding or minimizing importance of what the other person says.
Humouring	Not taking the other person seriously.
Impersonality	Treating the other person like a stranger; interacting with him or her as a role rather than a unique individual.
Inattention	Not paying attention to the other person.
Non-immediacy	Displaying verbal or non-verbal clues that minimize interest, closeness, or availability.
Reserve	Being unusually quiet and uncommunicative.
Restraint	Curtailing normal social behaviours.
Restrict topics	Limiting conversation to less personal topics.
Shorten interaction	Ending conversations as quickly as possible.

Source: Adapted from J.A. Hess, 'Distance Regulation in Personal Relationships: The Development of a Conceptual Model and a Test of Representational Validity', *Journal of Social and Personal Relationships* 19 (2002): 663–83.

disconfirmation. It may be tough to hear someone say, 'I don't think that's a good idea,' but a personal attack like 'You're crazy' is even tougher to hear. Far worse than disagreements are responses that *ignore* others' ideas—or even their existence.

Not all disconfirming behaviour is unintentional. Table 7.1 lists a number of deliberate tactics that have been used to create distance in an undesired relationship. It's easy to see how each of them is inherently disconfirming.

As you read in Chapter 6, every message has a relational dimension along with its content. This means that, whether we know it or not, we send and receive confirming and disconfirming messages virtually whenever we communicate. Serious conversations about our relationships may not be common, but we convey our attitudes about one another even when we talk about everyday matters. In other words, it isn't *what* we communicate about that shapes a relational climate so much as *how* we speak and act toward one another.

It's important to note that disconfirming messages, like virtually every other kind of communication, are a matter of perception. Communicators are likely to downplay the significance of a potentially hurtful message that they consider to be unintentional.[10] On the other hand, even messages that aren't intended to devalue the other person can be interpreted as disconfirming. Your failure to return an e-mail or phone call might simply be the result of a busy schedule, but if the

other person views the lack of contact as a sign that you don't value the relationship, the effect can be powerful.

How Communication Climates Develop

As soon as two people start to communicate, a relational climate begins to develop. If the messages are confirming, the climate is likely to be a positive one. If they disconfirm one another, the climate is likely to be hostile, cold, or defensive.

Verbal messages certainly contribute to the tone of a relationship, but many climate-shaping messages are nonverbal. The very act of approaching others is confirming, whereas avoiding them can be disconfirming. Smiles or frowns, the presence or absence of eye contact, tone of voice, the use of personal space—all of these and other cues send messages about how the parties feel toward one another.

After a climate is formed, it can take on a life of its own and grow in a self-perpetuating **spiral**—a reciprocating communication pattern in which each person's message reinforces the other's.[11] In positive spirals, one partner's confirming message leads to a similar response from the other person. This positive reaction leads the first person to be even more reinforcing. Negative spirals are just as powerful, though they leave the partners feeling worse about themselves and each other. Research shows how spirals operate in relationships to reinforce the principle 'what goes around comes around'. In one study of married couples, each spouse's response in conflict situations was similar to the other's statement.[12] Conciliatory statements (those that support, accept responsibility, agree, etc.) were likely to be followed by conciliatory responses. Confrontational acts (such as criticism, hostile questions, and fault-finding) were likely to trigger aggressive responses. The same pattern held for other kinds of messages: avoidance triggered avoidance, analysis triggered analysis, and so on.

Escalatory conflict spirals are the most visible way that disconfirming messages reinforce one another.[13] One attack leads to another until a skirmish escalates into a full-blown battle. Although they are less obvious, **de-escalatory conflict spirals** can also be destructive.[14] Rather than fighting, the parties slowly reduce their dependence on one another, withdraw, and become less invested in the relationship.

Spirals rarely go on indefinitely. Most relationships pass through cycles of progression and regression. If the spiral is negative, partners may find the exchange growing so unpleasant that they switch from negative to positive messages without discussing the matter. In other cases they may engage in metacommunication. 'Hold on,' one party might say, 'this is getting us nowhere.' In some cases, however, partners pass the point of no return, leading to the breakup of the relationship. Positive spirals, too, have their limits: even the best relationships go through periods of conflict and withdrawal, although a combination of time and communication skills can eventually bring the partners back into greater harmony.

COMMUNICATION ON-SCREEN

American Beauty (1999)
Directed by Sam Mendes.

To outsiders, Lester and Carolyn Burnham (Kevin Spacey and Annette Bening) look like the perfect couple: attractive, with good jobs and an immaculate suburban home. But we soon learn that life isn't as good as it seems. The Burnhams' relationship with their daughter, Jane (Thora Birch), is superficial. Carolyn is in denial about Lester's crisis, and she ignores his pleas to recapture their lost love. As the film relentlessly moves toward a stunning conclusion, we are presented with a portrait of an American family whose members alternate between avoidance and aggression without demonstrating any apparent skill at managing the serious conflicts that face them.

de-escalatory conflict spiral

A communication spiral in which the parties slowly lessen their dependence on one another, withdraw, and become less invested in the relationship.

escalatory conflict spiral

A reciprocal pattern of communication in which messages, either confirming or disconfirming, between two or more communicators reinforce one another.

spiral

A reciprocal communication pattern in which each person's message reinforces the other's.

Cultural Idiom

hold on
wait

the point of no return
the stage in a process after which there is no possibility of stopping or reversing it

what goes around, comes around
the belief that positive or negative actions done to others will ultimately result in positive or negative things happening to you

evaluative communication

Messages in which the sender judges the receiver in some way, usually resulting in a defensive response. Synonymous with *'you' language.*

Gibb categories

Six sets of contrasting styles of verbal and non-verbal behaviour. Each set describes a communication style that is likely to arouse defensiveness and a contrasting style that is likely to prevent or reduce it. Developed by Jack Gibb.

'you' language

Language that judges another person, increasing the likelihood of a defensive reaction. Synonymous with *evaluative communication.*

TABLE 7.2 The Gibb Categories of Defensive and Supportive Behaviours

Defensive Behaviours	Supportive Behaviours
1. Evaluation	1. Description
2. Control	2. Problem orientation
3. Strategy (Manipulation)	3. Spontaneity (Straightforwardness)
4. Neutrality (Indifference)	4. Empathy
5. Superiority	5. Equality
6. Certainty (Dogmatism)	6. Provisionalism

Creating Positive Communication Climates

It's easy to see how disconfirming messages can pollute a communication climate. But what are some alternative ways of communicating that encourage positive relationships? The work of rhetorical ethicist Jack Gibb provides a picture of what kinds of messages lead to both positive and negative spirals.[15]

After observing groups for several years, Gibb was able to isolate six types of defence-arousing communication and six contrasting behaviours that seemed to reduce the level of threat and defensiveness. The **Gibb categories** are listed in Table 7.2. Using the supportive types of communication and avoiding the defensive ones will increase the odds of creating and maintaining positive communication climates in your relationships.

Evaluation versus Description

The first type of defence-provoking behaviour Gibb noted was **evaluative communication**. Most people become irritated at judgmental statements, which are likely to be interpreted as signalling a lack of respect. Evaluative language has often been described as **'you' language** because most of these statements contain an accusatory use of that word. For example,

- You don't know what you're talking about.
- You're not doing your best.
- You smoke too much.

Unlike evaluative 'you' language, **descriptive communication** focuses on the speaker's thoughts and feelings instead of judging the listener. One form of descriptive communication is **'I' language.**[16] Instead of putting the emphasis on judging another's behaviour, the descriptive speaker explains the effect on him or her of the other's action. For instance, instead of saying, 'You talk too much,' a descriptive communicator would say, 'When you don't give me a chance to say what's on my mind, I get frustrated.' Notice that statements such as this include an account of the other person's behaviour in addition to an explanation of its effect on the speaker and a description of the speaker's feelings.

A Comparison of Dialogue and Debate

People will always have disagreements. The way they handle them both creates and reflects relational climates. The following list contrasts the very different types of communication that characterize dialogue and debate. As you review them, consider how dialogue confirms the other person, even in the face of disagreement, whereas debate is fundamentally disconfirming.

- Dialogue is collaborative: two or more sides work together toward common understanding.
- Debate is oppositional: two sides oppose each other and attempt to prove each other wrong.
- In dialogue, finding common ground is the goal.
- In debate, winning is the goal.
- Dialogue enlarges and possibly changes the participants' points of view.
- Debate affirms the participants' own points of view.
- Dialogue reveals assumptions for re-evaluation.

- Debate defends assumptions as truth.
- Dialogue causes introspection about one's own position.
- Debaters critique the others' positions.
- Dialogue opens the possibility of reaching a better solution than any of the original ones.
- Debate defends one's own positions as the best and excludes other positions.
- Dialogue involves a genuine concern for the other person and seeks not to alienate or offend.
- Debate involves countering the other position without focusing on feelings or relationships and often belittles or deprecates the other position.

—*Adapted from R. Poliner and J. Benson,* Dialogue: Turning Controversy into Community *(Cambridge, MA: Educators for Social Responsibility, 1997).*

Control versus Problem Orientation

A second defence-provoking message involves some attempt to control the other person. A **controlling message** occurs when a sender seems to be imposing a solution on the receiver with little regard for the receiver's needs or interests. The control can range from relatively small matters (where to eat dinner or what show to watch) to large ones (whether to remain in a relationship or how to spend a large tax return).

Whatever the situation, people who act in controlling ways create a defensive climate. Researchers have found that the communication of abusive couples was characterized by opposition to one another's viewpoints.[17] The unspoken message this kind of behaviour communicates is 'I know what's best for you, and if you do as I say, we'll get along.'

By contrast, in **problem orientation**, communicators focus on finding a solution that satisfies both their needs and those of the others involved. The goal here isn't to 'win' at the expense of your partner but rather to work out some arrangement in which everybody feels like a winner. The 'Comparison of Dialogue and Debate' box above shows several important differences between controlling and problem-oriented communication. The last section of this chapter has a great deal to say about 'win–win' problem-solving as a way to find problem-oriented solutions.

Strategy versus Spontaneity

The third communication behaviour that Gibb identified as creating a poor communication climate is **strategy.** A more accurate term to describe this type of behaviour is *manipulation.* Manipulation is the source of irritation in the workplace when a colleague acts friendly to peers while striving to curry favour with the boss.[18] One of the surest ways to make people defensive is to get caught trying to manipulate them. Nobody likes to be a guinea pig or a sucker, and even well-meant manipulation can cause bad feelings.

controlling message
Message in which the sender tries to impose some sort of outcome on the receiver, usually resulting in a defensive reaction.

descriptive communication
Messages that describe the speaker's position without evaluating others. Synonymous with *'I' language.*

'I' language
Language that describes the speaker's position without evaluating others. Synonymous with *descriptive communication.*

problem orientation
A supportive style of communication in which the communicators focus on working together to solve their problems instead of trying to impose their own solutions on one another.

strategy
A defence-arousing style of communication in which the sender tries to manipulate or trick a receiver. Also, the general term for any type of plan, as in the plan for a persuasive speech.

neutrality
A defence-arousing behaviour in which the sender expresses indifference toward a receiver.

spontaneity
Supportive communication behaviour in which the sender expresses a message without any attempt to manipulate the receiver.

superiority
A defence-arousing style of communication in which the sender states or implies that the receiver is inferior.

Cultural Idiom

in the long run
over an extended period of time

Spontaneity is the label Gibb used as a contrast to strategy. A better term might be *straightforwardness*. Despite the misleading label, spontaneous communication doesn't have to be blurted out as soon as an idea comes to you. You might want to plan the wording of your message carefully so that you can express yourself clearly. The important thing is to be honest. A straightforward message may not always get you what you want, but in the long run it's likely to pay dividends in a positive relational climate.

Neutrality versus Empathy

Gibb used the term **neutrality** to describe a fourth behaviour that arouses defensiveness, but a more descriptive term would be *indifference*. A neutral attitude is disconfirming because it communicates a lack of concern for another's welfare. In short, it implies that the other person isn't very important to you.

The damaging effects of neutrality become apparent when you consider the hostility that most people feel towards the large, impersonal organizations they have to deal with: 'They think of me as a number instead of a person'; 'I felt as if I were being handled by computers and not people.' These two common statements reflect reactions to being handled indifferently.

Empathy is an approach that confirms the other person. Having empathy means accepting another's feelings, or putting yourself in another's place. This doesn't mean you need to agree with that person. Gibb noted the importance of non-verbal messages in communicating empathy. He found that facial and bodily expressions of concern are often more important to the receiver than the words used.

Superiority versus Equality

Superiority is a fifth type of communication that creates a defensive climate. When people seem to believe they are better than we are, their attitude is likely to trigger a defensive response.

Flexibility is the key to success in today's job market. With rising tuition fees, a recession, and an evolving industrial landscape, it is important to specialize in a field that can change with the times. At the heart of every major company, communications affords the opportunity to find that niche.

I altered my career path as I gained experience and learned to navigate the work world to suit my interests. Over the past 10 years, I've worked as a floor director at CityTV, research analyst at Queen's Park, and now a transit reporter/communications advisor at the Toronto Transit Commission (TTC). In my current role, I advise commuters of transit delays on CityTV's *Breakfast Television*, CP24, and 680News.

I loved my job at CityTV but was forced to leave when CHUM was sold to CTV and Rogers, as I knew staff would be laid off eventually. And, while politics is inspiring, it is difficult to sustain financial security with an election every four years. When a friend suggested the communications advisor position at the TTC, I was excited. It would provide stable employment with experience and exposure, perfect for my future political ambitions.

When I applied for the position, I didn't think I had a chance. I had a solid background in communications and research, but limited on-air experience. After watching *BT* every day and practising in the mirror, I was able to edge out the competition through two interviews and land my dream job. Remember, to achieve happiness, you must take calculated risks. Trust your education, experience, and ambition—and never sell yourself short.

We often meet people who possess knowledge or talents greater than ours. But your own experiences will tell you that it isn't necessary for these people to project an attitude of superiority. Gibb found ample evidence that many who have superior skills and talents are capable of conveying an attitude of **equality**. These people are able to communicate the view that although they may have greater talent in certain areas, they see others as having just as much worth.

Certainty versus Provisionalism

Dogmatism is another term for the behaviour Gibb calls **certainty**. Messages that suggest the speaker's mind is already made up are likely to generate defensiveness.

In contrast to dogmatic communication is **provisionalism,** in which people may have strong opinions but are willing to acknowledge that they don't have a monopoly on the truth and will change their stand if another position seems more reasonable.

certainty
Messages that dogmatically imply that the speaker's position is correct and that the other person's ideas are not worth considering. Likely to generate a defensive response.

equality
A type of supportive communication suggesting that the sender regards the receiver as worthy of respect.

provisionalism
A supportive style of communication in which the sender expresses a willingness to consider the other person's position.

There is no guarantee that using Gibb's supportive, confirming approach to communication will build a positive climate. But the chances for a constructive relationship will be greatest when communication consists of the kind of constructive approach described here. Besides boosting the odds of getting a positive response from others, supportive communication can leave you feeling better in a variety of ways: more in control of your relationships, more comfortable, and more positive toward others.

Managing Interpersonal Conflict

Even the most supportive communication climate won't guarantee complete harmony. Regardless of what we may wish for or dream about, a conflict-free world just doesn't exist. Even the best communicators, the luckiest people, are bound to wind up in situations where their needs don't match the needs of others. Money, time, power, sex, humour, and aesthetic taste, as well as a thousand other issues, arise and keep us from living in a state of perpetual agreement.

For many people the inevitability of conflict is a depressing fact. They think that the existence of ongoing conflict means that there's little chance for happy relationships with others. Effective communicators know differently, however. They realize that although it's impossible to *eliminate* conflict, there are ways to *manage* it effectively. And those effective communicators know the main theme of this chapter—that managing conflict skilfully can open the door to healthier, stronger, and more satisfying relationships.

A study led by Phillip Sullivan at the University of Windsor examined how hockey players actually benefit from the conflicts that arise naturally among teammates. The traditional view of friction between players is that it is bad for team chemistry. However, if we take a more nuanced view of both conflict and cohesion, certain types of conflict can be seen to foster team unity. After interviewing 62 hockey players, the researchers found that constructive conflict led to greater cohesion among teammates, although negative conflict tended to destroy team morale. This suggests that perfect harmony is not always the best means of maintaining good chemistry.[19]

The Nature of Conflict

Whatever forms they may take, all interpersonal conflicts share certain similarities. Joyce Hocker and William Wilmot provide a thorough definition of conflict. They state that **conflict** is an expressed struggle between at least two interdependent parties who perceive incompatible goals, scarce rewards, and interference from the other parties in achieving their goals.[20] A closer look at the various parts of this definition helps to develop a clearer idea of how conflicts operate.

conflict
An expressed struggle between at least two interdependent parties who perceive incompatible goals, scarce rewards, and interference from the other party in achieving their goals.

Expressed Struggle

A conflict doesn't exist unless both parties know that some disagreement exists. You may be upset for months because a neighbour's barking dog keeps you from getting to sleep at night, but no conflict exists between the two of you until the neighbour learns about your problem. Of course, the expressed struggle doesn't have to be verbal. You can show your displeasure with somebody without saying a word. Giving a dirty look, using the silent treatment, and avoiding the other person are all ways of expressing yourself. But one way or another, both parties must know that a problem exists before they're in conflict.

Perceived Incompatible Goals

Conflicts often look as if one party's gain will be another's loss. For instance, consider the neighbour whose dog keeps you awake at night. Does somebody have to lose? A neighbour who brings a barking dog inside might have to deal with an anxious pet whining or scratching at the back door to go out; however, if he or she lets Fido out to bark at the raccoons, you're still awake and unhappy.

The goals in this situation really aren't completely incompatible—solutions do exist that allow both parties to get what they want. For instance, you could achieve peace and quiet by closing your windows or getting a pair of earplugs. Your neighbour could take the restless dog for a walk around the block instead of letting it out. If any of these solutions proves workable, then the conflict disappears.

Unfortunately, people often fail to see mutually satisfying answers to their problems. And as long as they perceive their goals to be mutually exclusive, they create a self-fulfilling prophecy in which the conflict is very real.

Perceived Scarce Rewards

In a conflict, people believe there isn't enough of a particular resource to go around. The most obvious example of a scarce resource is money—a cause of many conflicts. If an employee asks for a raise and the employer would rather keep the money or use it to expand the business, then the two parties are in conflict.

Time is another scarce commodity. As authors and professionals, we are constantly in the middle of struggles about how to use the limited time we have to spend. Should we work on this book? Spend time with our families? Devote our attention to other research projects? Enjoy the luxury of being alone? With only 24 hours in a day we're bound to end up in conflicts with our families, editors, students, and friends—all of whom want more of our time than we have available to give.

Interdependence

However antagonistic they might feel toward each other, the parties in a conflict are usually dependent on each other. The welfare and satisfaction of one party depend on the actions of the other. If this weren't true, then even in the face of scarce resources and incompatible goals there would be no need for conflict. Interdependence exists between conflicting nations, social groups, organizations, friends, and romantic partners. In each case, if the two parties didn't need each other to solve the problem, both would go their separate ways. In fact, many conflicts go unresolved because the parties fail to understand their interdependence. One of the first steps toward resolving a conflict is to adopt the attitude that 'we're in this together.'

Styles of Expressing Conflict

Communication scholars have identified a wide range of ways communicators handle conflicts.[21] Table 7.3 describes five ways people can act when their needs are not met. Each one has very different characteristics.

Non-Assertion

Non-assertion is the inability or unwillingness to express thoughts or feelings in a conflict. Sometimes non-assertion comes from a lack of confidence. At other times, people lack the awareness or skill to use a more direct means of expression.

The history of man is replete with mechanisms and attempts to control aggression. People have tried to pray it away, wish it away, or play it away. More recently they have tried to psychoanalyze it away. But it does not seem to go away.

George Bach and Herb Goldberg,
Creative Aggression

non-assertion
The inability or unwillingness to express one's thoughts or feelings when necessary.

Understanding Diversity

I AM CANADIAN!

Another deep-thinking tome by another intellectual about the elusive Canadian identity? God help us. Say it isn't so.

Be comforted. This one is different. It's gutsy and exciting. It will start heated and overdue arguments.

And it will have special resonance in Manitoba, where, for historical reasons, it is most likely to be easily understood and embraced. John Ralston Saul, husband of the former governor general Adrienne Clarkson, has been named 'a modern prophet' by *Time* magazine and is no stranger to Canadian readers.

He is the author of five novels but is best known for his non-fiction trilogy, *Voltaire's Bastards, The Doubter's Companion,* and *The Unconscious Civilization.* He is widely considered to be one of the world's most influential thinkers.

In his latest work, he suggests a new and believable understanding of how Canada has come to be what it is: an imperfect refuge from much of the world's established madness of bloodletting and empire, a space lit, against all odds, by a curious faith in the accommodation and inclusiveness of others.

Saul takes on the Really Big Questions of this country's nationhood.

Why do Canadians long for decency rather than supremacy at home and on the international scene? Why do we find conventional patriotism embarrassing? Why haven't we settled into a marriage of convenience with our American neighbours, when many other countries would have seen this as an easy and suitable path to security and power?

Canadians have been arguing for four centuries over which influences have been most important in forging our character: Catholic? Protestant? French? British?

More lately, we have pondered the impact of non-European, Asian, and African values on our way of thinking and being.

For Saul, it's as plain as the nose on our face.

Canada is a Métis nation, deeply indigenized, kept afloat on the currents of Aboriginal beliefs.

Colonists of all origins 'married up' into established Aboriginal families when they arrived, ultimately blending and shaping a new, pragmatic culture of mixed-race farmers, ranchers, and traders.

The result was the internalization of Aboriginal ideas, specifically belief in mutual dependency, the need for partnership, the all-important circle that recognizes and adapts to newcomers, and the pursuit of reconciliation.

These were the hard lessons Aboriginals had learned from the land, forged from the struggle to survive and prosper on it.

According to Saul, these beliefs explain the prevailing Canadian character, and much of the book celebrates Canada's subsequent brand of humanitarian achievement and exercise of 'soft power' in the larger world. These ideas are likely to find favour in Manitoba, which is said to be founded by the Métis prophet Louis Riel and is now home to one of the country's largest and most influential Aboriginal communities.

The problem, Saul explains, is that Canadians are in a state of denial. Not yet understanding and admitting our roots, we have not given ourselves permission to be fully who we are. Nor have we given generations of elite leadership full authority to take us in the direction our hearts want to go.

That makes for a conflicted and cranky population.

Sounding at times like Dr Phil McGraw of TV fame, Saul maintains that once 'we can embrace a language that expresses our story, we will feel a great release. We will discover a remarkable power to act and to do so in such a way that we will feel we are true to ourselves.'

Until then, Saul argues, we can hardly expect Canadian leadership to be anything but passive, hesitant, and downright dysfunctional—not to mention mean-spirited—when compared to the evolved but inarticulate intuition of ordinary citizens.

Ever the cautious optimist, Saul is hopeful that Canadians will escape the bonds of colonial insecurity and recall the unique origins of this country. That, he writes, will unleash a progressive energy the world desperately needs.

A Fair Country has the potential to change the way Canadians see themselves forever.

It offers a romantic and heroic vision, and it's a stirring and unpretentious read.

—*Lesley Hughes, Winnipeg* Free Press, *5 October 2008.*

Questions: Do you like the idea of Canada that John Ralston Saul is promoting? Do you think this is a national myth that could unite Canadians? What are the dangers of adopting Saul's vision of the Canadian identity?

TABLE 7.3 Individual Styles of Conflict

	Non-assertive	Directly Aggressive	Passive-Aggressive	Indirect	Assertive
Approach to Others	I'm not okay; you're okay.	I'm okay; you're not okay.	I'm okay; you're not okay.	I'm okay; you're not okay. (But I'll let you think you are.)	I'm okay; you're okay.
Decision-Making	Lets others choose.	Chooses for others. They know it.	Chooses for others. They don't know it.	Chooses for others. They don't know it.	Chooses for self.
Self-Sufficiency	Low	High or low	Looks high but usually low	High or low	Usually high
Behaviour in Problem Situations	Flees; gives in	Outright attack	Concealed attack	Strategic, oblique	Direct confrontation
Response of Others	Disrespect, guilt, anger, frustration	Hurt, defensiveness, humiliation	Confusion, frustration, feelings of manipulation	Unknowing compliance or resistance	Mutual respect
Success Pattern	Succeeds by luck or charity of others	Beats out others	Wins by manipulation	Gains unwitting compliance of others	Attempts 'win–win' solutions

Source: Adapted with permission from *The Assertive Woman* © 1970, 1987, 1997, and 2000, by Stanlee Phelps and Nancy Austin, San Luis Obispo, CA: *Impact*, 1975, 11; and Gerald Piaget, American Orthopsychiatric Association, 1975. Further reproduction prohibited.

Sometimes people know how to communicate in a straightforward way but choose to behave non-assertively. For example, women on dates are less likely to clearly refuse unwanted sexual advances from people they would like to see again than from people they have no intention of meeting for another date.[22]

Non-assertion is a surprisingly common way of dealing with conflicts. One survey examined the conflict level of husbands and wives in normal 'non-distressed' marriages. Over a five-day period, spouses reported that their partners engaged in an average of 13 behaviours that were 'displeasurable' to them but that they had only *one* confrontation during the same period.[23]

Non-assertion can take a variety of forms. One is *avoidance*—either physical (steering clear of a friend after having an argument) or conversational (changing the topic, joking, or denying that a problem exists). People who avoid conflicts usually believe it's easier to put up with the status quo than to face the problem head-on and try to solve it. *Accommodation* is another type of non-assertive response. Accommodators deal with conflict by giving in and putting the needs of others ahead of their own.

Despite the obvious drawbacks of non-assertion, there are situations when accommodating or avoiding is a sensible approach. Avoidance may be the best course if a conflict is minor and short-lived. For example, you might let a friend's annoying moodiness pass without saying anything, knowing that she's just having one of her rare bad days. Likewise, you might not complain to a neighbour whose sprinkler occasionally hits your front walk. You may also reasonably choose

> **Cultural Idiom**
>
> **steering clear of**
> avoiding
>
> **to face the problem head-on**
> to confront the problem directly

COMMUNICATION ON-SCREEN

'Coach's Corner' (1980–present)

On 'Coach's Corner', a feature on CBC television's *Hockey Night in Canada*, we see two very different styles of handling conflict—and that is the basis of the public's interest in the segment. Former NHL coach Don Cherry is a very successful aggressive communicator. While his on-air behaviour is repellent to many, he manages to bully and dominate his mild-mannered counterpart, Ron MacLean, in a way that makes for engaging viewing. He raises his voice, expresses populist outrage, and uses facial expressions of disgust and disdain to support points, whether he is speaking or not. He reinforces his persona by defending the more brutish and grinding elements of hockey and promoting a nostalgic 'return to basics' approach to issues around safety and violence. The basis of his popularity remains, despite the fact that he breaks Canadian social norms of 'niceness' and is openly aggressive with his counterpart for the duration of his segment.

direct aggression

An expression of the sender's thoughts or feelings or both that attacks the position and dignity of the receiver.

passive aggression

An indirect expression of aggression, delivered in a way that allows the sender to maintain a facade of kindness.

---

to keep quiet if the conflict occurs in an unimportant relationship, as with an acquaintance whose language you find offensive but whom you don't see often. Finally, you might choose to keep quiet if the risk of speaking up is too great: getting fired from a job you can't afford to lose, being humiliated in public, or even risking physical harm.

Direct Aggression

Whereas non-assertors avoid conflicts, communicators who use **direct aggression** embrace them. A directly aggressive message strikes the receiver in a way that attacks his or her position and even dignity. Many directly aggressive responses are easy to spot: 'You don't know what you're talking about.' 'That was a stupid thing to do.' 'What's the matter with you?' Other forms of direct aggression come more from non-verbal messages than from words. It's easy to imagine statements like 'What is it now?' or 'I need some peace and quiet' being expressed in a hostile way.

Verbal aggressiveness may get you what you want in the short run. Yelling 'Shut up' might stop the other person from talking, and saying 'Get it yourself' may save you from some exertion, but the relational damage of this approach probably isn't worth the cost. Direct aggression can be hurtful, and the consequences for the relationship can be long-lasting.[24]

Passive Aggression

Passive aggression, which occurs when a communicator expresses his or her hostility in an indirect way, is far more subtle than its directly aggressive cousin. Psychologist George Bach terms this behaviour **'crazymaking'**[25] and identifies several varieties. For example, 'pseudoaccommodators' pretend to agree with you ('I'll be on time from now on') but don't comply with your request for change. 'Guiltmakers' try to gain control by making you feel responsible for changing to suit them: 'I really should be studying, but I'll give you a ride.' 'Jokers' use humour as a weapon and then hide behind the complaint ('Where's your sense of humour?') when you object. 'Trivial tyrannizers' do small things to drive you crazy instead of confronting you with their complaints: 'forgetting' to give you messages, playing music too loud, and so on. 'Withholders' punish their partners by keeping back something valuable, such as courtesy, affection, or humour.

Indirect Communication

The clearest communication is not necessarily the best approach. **Indirect communication** conveys a message in a roundabout manner, in order to save face for the recipient.[26] Although indirect communication lacks the clarity of an aggressive or assertive message, it involves more initiative than non-assertion. It also has none of the hostility of passive-aggressive cra-zymaking. The goal is to get what you want without arousing the hostility of the other person. Consider the case of the neighbour's annoying dog. One indirect approach would be to strike up a friendly conversation with the owners and ask if anything you are doing is too noisy for them, hoping they would get the hint.

Because it saves face for the other party, indirect communication is often kinder than blunt honesty. If your guests are staying too long, it's probably kinder to yawn and hint about your big day tomorrow than to bluntly ask them to leave. Likewise, if you're not interested in going out with someone who has asked you out to a movie, it may be more compassionate to claim that you're busy than to say 'I'm not interested in seeing you.'

At other times we communicate indirectly in order to protect ourselves. You might, for example, test the waters by hinting instead of directly asking the boss for a raise, or by letting your partner know indirectly that you could use some affection instead of ask-ing outright. At times like these, an oblique approach may get the message across while softening the blow of a negative response.

The advantages of protecting oneself and saving face for others help explain why in-direct communication is the most common way people make requests.[27] The risk of an indirect message, of course, is that the other party will misunderstand you or fail to get the message at all. There are also times when the importance of an idea is so great that hinting lacks the necessary punch. When clarity and directness are your goals, an assertive ap-proach is in order.

Assertion

People who use **assertion** handle conflicts by expressing their needs, thoughts, and feel-ings clearly and directly but without judging others or dictating to them. They have the attitude that most of the time it is possible to resolve problems to everyone's satisfaction. Possessing this attitude and the skills to bring it about doesn't guarantee that assertive communicators will always get what they want, but it does give them the best chance of doing so. An additional benefit of such an approach is that whether or not it satisfies a particular need, it maintains the self-respect of both the assertors and those with whom they interact. As a result, people who manage their conflicts assertively may experience feelings of discomfort while they are working through the problem. They usually feel better about themselves and each other afterward—quite a change from the outcomes of non-assertion or aggression.

Characteristics of an Assertive Message

Knowing *about* assertive messages isn't the same as being able to express them. Communicating assertively works for a variety of messages: those conveying your hopes, your problems, your complaints, and your appreciations. Besides giving you a way to express yourself directly, this format also makes it easier for others to understand you. A complete assertive message has five parts, which we will discuss below.

1. Behavioural Description

As we noted in Chapter 3, a behavioural description is an objective picture of the behaviour in question, without any judging or editorializing. Put in terms of Gibb's categories, it uses

---

assertion
Direct expression of the sender's needs, thoughts, or feelings, deliv-ered in a way that does not attach the receiver's dignity.

crazymaking
Passive-aggressive messages sent in indirect ways that frustrate and confuse the recipient.

indirect communication
Hinting at a message instead of expressing thoughts and feelings directly.

The newest computer can merely compound, at speed, the oldest problem in the relations between human be-ings, and in the end the com-municator will be confronted with the old problem, of what to say and how to say it.

Edward R. Murrow

Cultural Idiom

oblique
evasive, indirect

punch
force or effectiveness

softening the blow of
easing the effect of

test the waters
try

descriptive rather than evaluative language. Notice the difference between a behavioural description and an evaluative judgment:

Behavioural description:	'You asked me to tell you what I really thought about your idea, and then when I gave you my opinion, you told me I was too critical.'
Evaluative judgment:	'Don't be so touchy! It's hypocritical to ask for my opinion and then get mad when I give it to you.'

Judgmental words like 'touchy' and 'hypocritical' invite a defensive reaction. The target of your accusation can reply, 'I'm not touchy *or* hypocritical!' It's harder to argue with the facts stated in an objective, behavioural description. Furthermore, the neutral language reduces the chances of a defensive reaction.

2. Your Interpretation of the Other Person's Behaviour

After describing the behaviour in question, an assertive message expresses the communicator's interpretation. This is where you can use the perception-checking skill outlined in Chapter 2 (pages 54–5). Remember that a complete perception check includes two possible interpretations of the behaviour:

Interpretation A:	'Maybe you reacted defensively because my criticism sounded too detailed—because my standards seemed too high.'
Interpretation B:	'Your reaction made me think that you really didn't want to know my opinion. You were just fishing for a compliment when you asked my opinion.'

> **Cultural Idiom**
>
> **fishing for a compliment**
> trying to get another to say what one wants to hear
>
> **touchy**
> quickly offended with little provocation

Whether you offer two interpretations (as in the previous list) or just one (as in the examples that follow), the key is to label your hunches as such instead of suggesting that you are positive about what the other person's behaviour means.

3. A Description of Your Feelings

Expressing your feelings adds a dimension to a message. For example, consider the difference between these two responses:

- 'When you kiss me on the neck while I'm working [behaviour], I think you probably want to fool around [interpretation], and *I feel aroused* [feeling].'
- 'When you kiss me on the neck while I'm working [behaviour], I think you probably want to fool around [interpretation], and *I feel anxious* [feeling].'

Adding feelings to the situation we presented earlier makes the assertive message clearer as well:

- 'When you said I was too critical after you asked me for my honest opinion [behaviour], it seemed to me that you really didn't want to hear a critical remark [interpretation], and *I felt stupid for being honest* [feeling].'

4. A Description of the Consequences

A consequence statement explains what happens as a result of the behaviour you have described, your interpretation, and the ensuing feeling. There are three kinds of consequences:

- **What happens to you, the speaker:** 'When you forgot to give me the phone message yesterday [behaviour], *I didn't know that my doctor's appointment was delayed, and I wound up sitting in the office for an hour when I could have been studying or working* [consequences]. It seems to me that you don't care enough about how busy I am to even write a simple note [interpretation], and that's why I got so mad [feeling].'

   'I appreciate [feeling] the help you've given me on my term paper [behaviour]. It tells me you think I'm on the right track [interpretation], and *this gives me a boost to keep working on the idea* [consequences].'

- **What happens to the person you're addressing:** 'When you have four or five drinks at a party after I've warned you to slow down [behaviour], you start to act strange: *you make crude jokes that offend everybody, and then I have to drive home* [consequences], and you know I hate driving at night. I don't think you realize how differently you act [interpretation], and I'm worried [feeling] about what will happen if you don't start drinking less.'

- **What happens to others:** 'You probably don't know because you couldn't hear her cry [interpretation], but when you rehearse your lines for the play without closing the doors [behaviour], *the baby can't sleep* [consequence]. I'm especially concerned [feeling] about her because it looks like she's coming down with something.'

   'I thought you'd want to know [interpretation] that when you kid Jamaal about his height [behaviour], he gets embarrassed [feeling] and *usually becomes sulky or leaves* [consequences].'

A consequence statement for our ongoing example might sound like this:

- 'When you said I was too critical after you asked me for my honest opinion [behaviour], it seemed to me that you really didn't want to hear a critical remark [interpretation]. I felt stupid for being honest [feeling]. *Now I'm not sure whether I should tell you what I'm really thinking the next time you ask* [consequence].'

5. A Statement of Your Intentions

Intention statements are the final element in the assertive format. They can communicate three kinds of messages:

- **Where you stand on an issue:** 'When you call us 'girls' after I've told you we want to be called 'women' [behaviour], I get the idea you don't appreciate how important the difference is to us [interpretation] and how demeaning it feels [feeling]. Now I'm in an awkward spot: either I have to keep bringing the subject up, or else drop it and feel bad [consequence]. *I want you to know how much this bothers me* [intention].'

  'I'm really grateful [feeling] to you for speaking up for me in front of the boss yesterday [behaviour]. That must have taken a lot of courage [interpretation]. Knowing that you're behind me gives me a lot of confidence [consequence], and *I want you to know how much I appreciate your support* [intention].'
- **Requests of others:** 'When you didn't call last night [behaviour] I thought you were mad at me [interpretation]. I've been thinking about it ever since [consequence], and I'm still worried [feeling]. *I'd like to know if you are angry* [intention].'

  'I really enjoyed [feeling] your visit [behaviour], and I'm glad you had a good time, too [interpretation]. *I hope you'll come again* [intention].'
- **Descriptions of how you plan to act in the future:** 'I've asked you three times now to repay the $25 I lent you [behaviour]. I'm getting the idea that you've been avoiding me [interpretation], and I'm pretty angry about it [feeling]. I want you to know that unless we clear this up now, *you shouldn't expect me to lend you anything again* [intention].'

Why is it so important to make your intentions clear? Because failing to do so often makes it hard for others to know what you want from them or how to act. Consider how confusing the following statements are because they lack a clear statement of intention.

- 'Thanks for the invitation, but I really should study Saturday night.' [Does the speaker want to be asked out again, or is he indirectly suggesting that he doesn't ever want to go out with you?]
- 'To tell you the truth, I was asleep when you came by, but I should have been up anyway.' [Is the speaker saying that it's okay to come by in the future, or is she hinting that she doesn't appreciate unannounced visitors?]

You can see from these examples that it's often hard to make a clear interpretation of another person's ideas without a direct statement of intention. Notice in the following examples how much more direct the statements become when the speakers make their positions clear:

- 'Thanks for the invitation, but I really should study Saturday night. *I hope you'll ask me again soon.*'

- 'To tell you the truth, I was asleep when you came by, but I should have been up anyway. *Maybe next time you should phone before dropping in so I'll be sure to be awake.*'

In our ongoing example, adding an intention statement would complete the assertive message:

- 'When you said I was too critical after you asked me for my honest opinion [behaviour], it seemed to me that you really didn't want to hear a critical remark [interpretation]. That made me feel stupid for being honest [feeling]. Now I'm not sure whether I should tell you what I'm really thinking the next time you ask [consequence]. *I'd like to get it clear right now: do you really want me to tell you what I think or not [intention]?'*

Before you try to deliver messages using the assertive format outlined here, there are a few points to remember. First, it isn't necessary or even wise to put the elements in the order — order of elements described here in every case. As you can see from reviewing the examples, it's sometimes best to begin by stating your feelings. At other times, you can start by sharing your intentions or interpretations or by describing consequences.

You also should word your message in a way that suits your style of speaking. Instead of saying, 'I interpret your behaviour to mean,' you might choose to say, 'I think . . .' or 'It seems to me . . .' or perhaps 'I get the idea . . .'. In the same way, you can express your intentions by saying, 'I hope you'll understand (or do) . . .' or perhaps 'I wish you would. . . .'. It's important that you get your message across, but you should do it in a way that sounds and feels genuine to you.

Realize that there are some cases in which you can combine two elements in a single phrase. For instance, the statement '. . . and ever since then I've been wanting to talk to you' expresses both a consequence and an intention. In the same way, saying, '. . . and after you said that, I felt confused' expresses a consequence and a feeling. Whether you combine elements or state them separately, the important point is to be sure that each one is present in your statement.

Finally, it is important to realize that it isn't always possible to deliver messages such as the ones here all at one time, wrapped up in neat paragraphs. It will often be necessary to repeat or restate one part many times before your receiver truly understands what you're saying. As you've already read, there are many types of psychological and physical noise that make it difficult for us to understand each other. Just remember: you haven't communicated successfully until the receiver of your message understands everything you've said. In communication, as in many other activities, patience and persistence are essential.

Gender and Conflict Style

While the 'men are from Mars, women are from Venus' theory of gender, which states that men and women actually speak entirely different languages, doesn't hold up under scrutiny, men and women often approach conflicts differently. Even in childhood, males are more likely to be overtly aggressive, demanding, and competitive, whereas females are more co-operative, or at least less directly aggressive. Studies of children from preschool to early adolescence have shown that boys typically try to get their way by ordering one another around:

If you have an apple and I have an apple and we exchange these apples then you and I will still each have one apple. But if you have an idea and I have an idea and we exchange these ideas, then each of us will have two ideas.

George Bernard Shaw

'Lie down.' 'Get off my steps.' 'Gimme your arm.' By contrast, girls are more likely to make proposals for action, beginning with the word 'Let's': 'Let's go find some.' 'Let's ask her if she has any markers.' 'Let's move *these* out *first*.'[28] Whereas boys tell each other what role to take in pretend play ('You be the doctor; I'll be the patient'), girls more commonly ask each other what role they want ('Will you be the patient for a few minutes?') or make a joint proposal ('We can both be doctors'). Furthermore, boys often make demands without offering an explanation ('Look, I want the wire cutters right now'). By contrast, girls often give reasons for their suggestions ('We have to *clean* them first to get rid of the germs'). When girls do have conflicts and disagreements, they are more likely to handle them via indirect aggression such as excluding someone from peer groups and complaining to others.[29] However, gender isn't the only variable that determines how children will handle conflict. For example, girls are more likely to assert themselves with boys when their friends are also present.[30]

Differences like these often persist into adulthood. One survey of university students revealed that men and women viewed conflicts in contrasting ways.[31] Regardless of their cultural background, female students described men as being concerned with power and more interested in content than relational issues. Phrases used to describe male conflict styles included 'The most important thing to males in conflict is their egos'; 'Men don't worry about feelings'; and 'Men are more direct.' By contrast, women were described as being more concerned with maintaining the relationship during a conflict. Phrases used to describe female conflict styles included 'Women are better listeners'; 'Women try to solve problems without controlling the other person'; and 'Females are more concerned with others' feelings.'

Research confirms some of these reports.[32] Limited evidence suggests that women are more likely than men to use indirect strategies instead of confronting conflict head-on. They are also more likely to compromise and give in to maintain relational harmony. Men, by contrast, are more likely to use aggression to get their way.

After a relational conflict begins, men are often more likely than women to withdraw if they become uncomfortable or fail to get their way. The reason why men tend to avoid and women assert may have little to do with gender stereotypes: women may demand more from their partners because historically they have had more to gain by complaining.[33] When men benefit from the status quo, they protect their situation by withdrawing. To understand this 'demand–withdraw' dynamic, consider a stereotypical housekeeping situation in which the woman complains because the man doesn't do his share. Speaking up has the potential to change the woman's situation for the better, whereas avoiding the discussion enables the man to maintain his situation.

Differences like these don't mean that men are incapable of forming good relationships. Instead, the stereotypical male notion of what a good relationship is differs from the stereotypical female notion. For some men, friendship and aggression aren't mutually exclusive. In fact, many strong male relationships are built around competition—at work or in athletics, for example. Women can be competitive, too, but they also are more likely to use logical reasoning and bargaining than aggression.[34] When men communicate with women, they become less aggressive and more co-operative than they are in all-male groups.

Most theorists suggest that the primary reason for differences in conflict style is socialization.[35] Some social scientists have proposed that a 'threshold of assertiveness' may exist for people, especially women, allowing them to behave in an assertive way up to a point, but no further. Because women have typically been perceived as more compliant and co-operative, they may have seen themselves as reaching this threshold sooner than men, at which time they would back off. Because men have been expected to be more assertive—or

Cultural Idiom

back off
stop, quit what they are doing

I accept chaos. I am not sure whether it accepts me. I know some people are terrified of the bomb. But then some people are terrified to be seen carrying a Modern Screen *magazine. Experience teaches us that silence terrifies people the most.*

Bob Dylan

even aggressive—they find it more comfortable to persist in seeking to meet their needs. As sex-role stereotyping becomes less common, it is likely that the differences between male and female conflict styles may become smaller.

Cultural Influences on Conflict

Communication style in situations of conflict varies widely from one culture to another. The English-Canadian preference for a rational, straight-talking, calm yet assertive approach is not the norm in other cultures.[36] In French-Canadian culture, for example, there is typically a greater tolerance for expressions of intense emotion. Similarly, French Canadians are the least likely to keep secrets from their spouses; the most likely are non–French-Canadian residents of Saskatchewan or Manitoba.[37] But ethnicity isn't the only factor that shapes individuals' preferred conflict style: their degree of assimilation also plays an important role. For example, Canadians of Hispanic descent with strong Hispanic cultural identities are more likely to seek accommodation and compromise than Hispanic-Canadians with weaker cultural ties.[38]

Not surprisingly, people from different regions often manage conflict quite differently. In individualistic cultures like that of English Canada, the goals, rights, and needs of each person are considered important, and most people would agree that it is an individual's right to stand up for himself or herself. By contrast, collectivist cultures (more common in Latin America and Asia) consider the concerns of the group to be more important than those of any individual. In these cultures, the kind of assertive behaviour that might seem perfectly appropriate to a North American would seem rude and insensitive.

Another factor that distinguishes the North American and northern European cultures from others is their low-context cultural style.[39] Low-context cultures place a premium on assertiveness, on being direct and literal. By contrast, high-context cultures like that of Japan value self-restraint and avoid confrontation. Preserving and honouring the dignity of the other person are prime goals, and communicators go to great lengths to avoid embarrassing a conversational partner. For this reason, people in these cultures prefer to rely on subtle hints and shared knowledge of social conventions. In Japan, for example, even a simple request like 'Close the door' would be too straightforward.[40] Instead, a remark such as 'It's chilly today' would serve to convey the request in an indirect way. To take a more important example, Japanese people are reluctant to simply say 'no' to a request. A more likely answer would be 'Let me think about it for a while,' which anyone familiar with Japanese culture would recognize as a refusal. When indirect communication is a cultural norm, it is unreasonable to expect more straightforward approaches to succeed.

VALUING DIVERSITY IN CONFLICT STYLES

The preceding section made it clear that conflict styles are shaped by social and cultural influences. Choose a conflict style different from yours—by virtue of gender or culture—and identify the assumptions on which it is based. Next, suggest how people with different styles can adapt their assumptions and behaviours to communicate in a more satisfying manner.

What I have to say is far more important than how long my eyelashes are.

Alanis Morissette

It isn't necessary to look at Eastern cultures to encounter cultural differences in conflict. The style of some other cultures within the Western world differs in important ways from the northern European and North American norm. These cultures see verbal disputes as a form of intimacy and even a game. Canadians visiting Greece, for example, often think they are witnessing an argument when they are overhearing a friendly conversation.[41] A longitudinal study of child development, conducted by Statistics Canada and Human Resources Development Canada, demonstrated that there are many differences between immigrant children and Canadian-born children. For example, immigrant children tend to experience a period of poverty while their families adjust to living in Canada. Many Canadian children grow up in poverty too, but do so mostly because of family dysfunction. As a result, poverty has a smaller effect on immigrant children than their Canadian counterparts. Furthermore, immigrant children tend to experience less conflict in their homes, more family cohesion, and fewer mental health problems than Canadian children. These differences seem to disappear in one generation as immigrants and their children assimilate into English- or French-Canadian culture.[42]

Methods of Conflict Resolution

No matter what the relational style, gender, or culture of the participants, every conflict is a struggle to have one's goals met. Sometimes that struggle succeeds, and at other times it fails. In the remainder of this chapter we'll look at various approaches to resolving conflicts and see which ones are most promising.

Win–Lose

win–lose problem-solving
An approach to conflict resolution in which one party reaches its goal at the expense of the other.

In **win–lose problem-solving**, one party achieves its goal at the expense of the other. People resort to this method of resolving disputes when they perceive a situation as being an 'either–or' one: either I get what I want, or you get your way. The most clear-cut examples of win–lose situations are certain games, such as baseball or poker, in which the rules require a winner and a loser. Some interpersonal issues seem to fit into this win–lose framework: two co-workers seeking a promotion to the same job, for instance, or a couple who disagree on how to spend their limited money.

Power is the distinguishing characteristic in win–lose problem-solving because it is necessary to defeat an opponent to get what you want. The most obvious kind of power is physical. Some parents threaten their children with warnings such as 'Stop misbehaving, or I'll send you to your room.' Adults who use physical power to deal with each other usually aren't so blunt, but the legal system is the implied threat: 'Follow the rules, or we'll lock you up.'

Real or implied force isn't the only kind of power used in conflicts. People who rely on authority of many types engage in win–lose methods without ever threatening physical coercion. In most jobs, supervisors have the potential to use authority in the assignment of working hours, job promotions, desirable or undesirable tasks, and, of course, in the power to fire an unsatisfactory employee. Teachers can use the power of grades to coerce students to act in desired ways.

Even the usually admired democratic principle of majority rule is a win–lose method of resolving conflicts. However fair it may be, this system results in one group's getting its way and another group's being unsatisfied.

There are some circumstances when win–lose problem-solving may be necessary, such as when there are truly scarce resources and where only one party can achieve satisfaction. For instance, if two suitors want to marry the same person, only one can succeed. And to return to an earlier example, it's often true that only one applicant can be hired for a job. But don't be too willing to assume that your conflicts are necessarily win–lose: as you'll soon read, many situations that seem to require a loser can be resolved to everyone's satisfaction.

There is a second kind of situation when win–lose is the best method. Even when co-operation is possible, if the other person insists on trying to defeat you, then the most logical response might be to defend yourself by fighting back. 'It takes two to tango,' the old cliché goes, and it also often takes two to co-operate.

A final and much less frequent situation in which you might be justified in refusing to back down is one in which the other person is clearly harming others. Few people would deny the importance of restraining an aggressor even if that person's freedom is sacrificed in the process.

Lose–Lose

In **lose–lose problem-solving**, neither side is satisfied with the outcome. Although the name of this approach is so discouraging that it's hard to imagine how anyone could willingly use it, in truth lose–lose is a fairly common way to handle conflicts. In many instances the parties will both strive to be winners, but as a result of the struggle, both end up losers. On the international scene many wars illustrate this sad point. A nation that gains military victory at the cost of thousands of lives, large amounts of resources, and a damaged national consciousness hasn't truly won much. On an interpersonal level the same principle holds true. Most of us have seen battles of pride in which both parties strike out and both suffer.

Compromise

Unlike lose–lose outcomes, a **compromise** gives both parties at least some of what they wanted, though both sacrifice part of their goals. People usually settle for compromises when they see partial satisfaction as the best they can hope for. Although a compromise may be better than losing everything, this approach hardly seems to deserve the positive image it has with some people. In his valuable book on conflict resolution, management consultant Albert Filley makes an interesting observation about our attitudes toward this approach.[43] Why is it, he asks, that if someone says, 'I will compromise my values,' we view the action unfavourably, yet we talk admiringly about parties in a conflict who compromise to reach a solution?

The Navajo definition of conflict resolution is to restore harmony. Their experience has convinced them that if one ends a dispute by having a winner and a loser, one dispute may have been ended but another dispute surely will have been started because harmony will not have been restored. Behind this is the Navajo recognition that coercion is not an effective way to bring about genuine change in any individual's long-term behaviour or attitude. Coercion works only as long as one is willing and able to continue the coercion. When the coercion stops, people generally revert to their prior ways, the only real difference being that by then they will have become angry and resentful. Coercion is a short-term, not a long-term answer.

Anne Kaas,
The Better Way: Navajo Peacemaking

compromise
An approach to conflict resolution in which both parties attain at least part of what they seek through self-sacrifice.

lose–lose problem-solving
An approach to conflict resolution in which neither party achieves its goals.

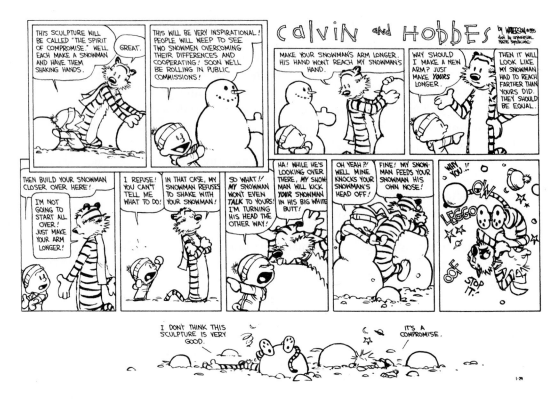

Although compromises may be the best obtainable result in some conflicts, it's important to realize that both people in a dispute can often work together to find much better solutions. In such cases *compromise* is a negative word.

Most of us are surrounded by the results of bad compromises. Consider a common example: the conflict between one person's desire to smoke cigarettes and another's need to breathe clean air. The win–lose outcomes of this conflict are obvious: either the smoker abstains or the non-smoker gets polluted lungs—neither result is very satisfying. But a compromise in which the smoker gets to enjoy only a rare cigarette or must retreat outdoors and in which the non-smoker still must inhale some fumes or feel like an ogre is hardly better. Both sides have lost a considerable amount of both comfort and goodwill. Of course, the costs involved in other compromises are even greater. For example, if a divorced couple compromises on child care by haggling over custody and then finally, grudgingly, agrees to split the time with their children, it's hard to say that anybody has won.

Win–Win

win–win problem-solving
An approach to conflict resolution in which the parties work together to satisfy all their goals.

In **win–win problem-solving,** the goal is to find a solution that satisfies the needs of everyone involved. Not only do the parties avoid trying to win at the other's expense, but they also believe that by working together it is possible to find a solution that allows both to reach their goals.

Some compromises approach this win–win ideal. You and the seller might settle on a price for a used car that is between what the seller was asking and what you wanted to pay. Although neither of you got everything you wanted, the outcome would still leave both of you satisfied. Likewise, you and your companion might agree to see a film that is the second choice for both of you in order to spend an evening together. As long as everyone is satisfied with an outcome, it's accurate to describe it as a win–win solution.

TABLE 7.4 Choosing the Most Appropriate Method of Conflict Resolution

1. Consider deferring to the other person
   - when you discover you are wrong
   - when the issue is more important to the other person than it is to you
   - to let others learn by making their own mistakes
   - when the long-term cost of winning may not be worth the short-term gains

2. Consider compromising
   - when there is not enough time to seek a win–win outcome
   - when the issue is not important enough to negotiate at length
   - when the other person is not willing to seek a win–win outcome

3. Consider competing
   - when the issue is important and the other person will take advantage of your non competitive approach

4. Consider co-operating
   - when the issue is too important for a compromise
   - when a long-term relationship between you and the other person is important
   - when the other person is willing to co-operate.

Although compromises can be a type of win–win outcome, the best solutions are ones in which all the parties get everything they want.

A win–win approach sounds ideal, but it is not always possible, or even appropriate. Table 7.4 suggests some factors to consider when deciding which approach to take when facing a conflict. There will certainly be times when compromising is the most sensible approach. You will even encounter instances when pushing for your own solution is reasonable. Even more surprisingly, you will probably discover that there are times when it makes sense to willingly accept the loser's role.

Steps in Win–Win Problem-Solving

Although win–win problem-solving is often the most desirable approach to managing conflicts, it is also one of the hardest to achieve. In spite of the challenge, it is definitely possible to become better at resolving conflicts. The following discussion outlines a method to increase your chances of being able to handle your conflicts in a win–win manner, so that both you and others have your needs met. As you learn to use this approach you should find that more and more of your conflicts end up with win–win solutions. And even when total satisfaction isn't possible, this approach can preserve a positive relational climate.

As it is presented here, win–win problem-solving is a highly structured activity. After you have practised the approach a number of times, this style of managing conflict will become almost second nature to you. You'll then be able to approach your conflicts without the need to follow the step-by-step approach. But for the time being, try to be patient and trust the value of the following pattern. As you read through the steps, imagine yourself applying them to a problem that's currently bothering you.

> **Cultural Idiom**
> **second nature**
> easy and natural

COMMUNICATION ON-SCREEN

Love Actually (2003)
Directed by Richard Curtis.

This film comprises 10 interwoven romantic stories, with characters who drift in and out of their own storylines to take part in others. As in all love tales, the characters central to the romances face challenges and crises that threaten their relationships. What makes this film unique and especially relevant to this chapter is the variety of approaches to conflict resolution—as well as the variety of outcomes—it presents.

Identify Your Problem and Unmet Needs

Before you speak out, it's important to realize that the problem causing the conflict is yours. Whether you want to return an unsatisfactory piece of merchandise, complain to noisy neighbours because your sleep is being disturbed, or request a change in working conditions from your employer, the problem is yours. Why? Because in each case you are the person who is dissatisfied. You are the one who has paid for the defective article; the merchant who sold it to you has the use of your money. You are the one who is losing sleep as a result of your neighbours' activities; they are content to go on as before. You, not your boss, are the one who is unhappy with your working conditions.

Realizing that the problem is yours will make a big difference when the time comes to approach your partner. Instead of feeling and acting in an evaluative way, you'll be more likely to share your problem in a descriptive way, which will not only be more accurate but also will reduce the chance of a defensive reaction.

After you realize that the problem is yours, the next step is to identify the unmet needs that leave you feeling dissatisfied. Sometimes a relational need underlies the content of the issue at hand. Consider these cases:

- A friend hasn't returned some money you lent long ago. Your apparent need in this situation might be to get the cash back. But a little thought will probably show that this isn't the only, or even the main, thing you want. Even if you were rolling in money, you'd probably want the loan repaid because of your most important need: *to avoid feeling victimized by your friend's taking advantage of you.*
- Someone you care about who lives in a distant city has failed to respond to several e-mails. Your apparent need may be to get answers to the questions contained in the e-mails, but it's likely that there's another, more fundamental need: *the reassurance that you're still important enough to deserve a response.*

As you'll soon see, the ability to identify your real needs plays a key role in solving interpersonal problems. For now, the point to remember is that before you voice your problem to your partner, you ought to be clear about which of your needs aren't being met.

Make a Date

Unconstructive fights often start because the initiator confronts a partner who isn't ready. There are many times when a person isn't in the right frame of mind to face a conflict: perhaps owing to fatigue, being in too much of a hurry to take the necessary time, upset over another problem, or not feeling well. At times like these, it's unfair to 'jump' a person without notice and expect to get his or her full attention for your problem. If you persist, you'll probably have an ugly fight on your hands.

After you have a clear idea of the problem, approach your partner with a request to try to solve it. For example: 'Something's been bothering me. Can we talk about it?' If the answer is 'yes', then you're ready to go further. If it isn't the right time to confront your partner, find a time that's agreeable to both of you.

Describe Your Problem and Needs

Your partner can't possibly meet your needs without knowing why you're upset and what you want. Therefore, it's up to you to describe your problem as specifically as possible. When you do so, it's important to use terms that aren't overly vague or abstract. Recall our discussion of behavioural descriptions in Chapter 3 in order to clarify your problem and specific needs.

Partner Checks Back

After you've shared your problem and described what you need, it's important to make sure that your partner has understood what you've said. As you can remember from the discussion of listening in Chapter 4, there's a good chance—especially in a stressful conflict situation—of your words being misinterpreted.

It's usually unrealistic to insist that your partner paraphrase your problem statement, and fortunately there are more tactful and subtle ways to make sure you've been understood. For instance, you might try saying, 'I'm not sure I expressed myself very well just now—maybe you should tell me what you heard me say so I can be sure I got it right.' In any case, be absolutely sure that your partner understands your whole message before going any further. Legitimate agreements are tough enough, but there's no point in getting upset about a conflict that doesn't even exist.

Solicit Partner's Needs

After you've made your position clear, it's time to find out what your partner needs in order to feel satisfied about this issue. There are two reasons why it's important to discover your partner's needs. First, it's fair. After all, the other person has just as much right as you to feel satisfied, and if you expect help in meeting your needs, then it's reasonable that you behave in the same way. Second, just as an unhappy partner will make it hard for you to become satisfied, a happy partner will be more likely to co-operate in letting you reach your goals. Thus, it is in your own self-interest to discover and meet your partner's needs.

You can learn about your partner's needs simply by asking about them: 'Now I've told you what I want and why. Tell me what you need to feel okay about this.' After your partner begins to talk, your job is to use the listening skills discussed earlier in this book to make sure you understand.

Check Your Understanding of Partner's Needs

Paraphrase or ask questions about your partner's needs until you're certain you understand them. The surest way to accomplish this is to use the paraphrasing skills you learned in Chapter 4.

> *That's the thing about needs. Sometimes when you get them met, you don't need them anymore.*
>
> Carrie Bradshaw,
> *Sex and the City*

COMMUNICATION ON-SCREEN

The New Statesman (1987–92)

Created by Maurice Gran & Laurence Marks.

This British political comedy–drama documents the adventures of Conservative backbench Member of Parliament, Alan B'Stard (Rik Mayall) and his Westminster officemate, backbencher Piers Fletcher-Dervish (Michael Troughton). Both are members of Margaret Thatcher's Conservative revolution, and the show plays on the themes of selfishness and greed that predominated during the Thatcherite era. While the main characters are rather despicable human beings, the program offers multiple examples of all the problem-solving approaches described in this chapter. B'Stard sets up win–win, win–lose, lose–lose, and compromise situations by cheating on his wife, making personal profit from insider knowledge, and generally abusing and mistreating Fletcher-Dervish. The show also illustrates all the different types of aggression.

Negotiate a Solution

Now that you and your partner understand each other's needs, the goal becomes finding a way to meet them. The best way to do this is to develop as many potential solutions as possible and then evaluate them to decide which one best meets the needs of both. The following steps can help communicators develop a mutually satisfying solution.

1. **Identify and define the conflict.** We've discussed this process in the preceding pages. It consists of discovering each person's problem and needs, setting the stage for meeting all of them.
2. **Generate a number of possible solutions.** In this step you and your partner work together to think of as many means as possible to reach their stated ends. The key word here is quantity: it's important to generate as many ideas as you can think of without worrying about which ones are good or bad. Write down every thought that comes up, no matter how unworkable; sometimes a far-fetched idea will lead to a more workable one.
3. **Evaluate the alternative solutions.** This is the time to talk about which solutions will work and which ones won't. It's important for you both to be honest about your willingness to accept an idea. If a solution is going to work, you both have to support it.
4. **Decide on the best solution.** Now that you've looked at all the alternatives, pick the one that looks best to you and your partner. It's important to be sure that you both understand the solution and are willing to try it out. Remember: your decision doesn't have to be final, but it should look potentially successful.

Follow Up on the Solution

Cultural Idiom

to keep on top of
to be in control of

You can't be sure the solution will work until you try it out. After you've tested it for a while, it's a good idea to set aside some time to talk over how things are going. You may find that you need to make some changes or even rethink the whole problem. The idea is to keep on top of the problem and to keep using creativity to solve it.

Win–win solutions aren't always possible. There will be times when even the best-intentioned people simply won't be able to find a way of meeting all their needs. In cases like this, the process of negotiation has to include some compromising. But even then the preceding steps haven't been wasted. The genuine desire to learn what the other person wants and to try to satisfy those desires will build a climate of goodwill that can help you find the best solution to the present problem and also improve your relationship in the future.

One typical comment people have after trying the preceding method of handling conflicts is 'This is a helpful thing sometimes, but it's so rational! Sometimes I'm so uptight I don't care about defensiveness or listening or anything . . . I just want to yell and get it off my chest!'

Cultural Idiom

blowing off steam
releasing excess energy or anger

uptight
anxious

When you feel like this, it's almost impossible to be rational. At times like these, probably the most therapeutic thing to do is to express your feelings in what Bach calls a 'Vesuvius'—an uncontrolled, spontaneous explosion. A Vesuvius can be a terrific way of blowing off steam, and after you do so, it's often much easier to figure out a rational solution to your problem.

So we encourage you to have a Vesuvius with the following qualifications: be sure your partner understands what you're doing and realizes that whatever you say doesn't call for a response. He or she should let you rant and rave for as long as you want without getting defensive or 'tying in'. Then, when your eruption subsides, you can take steps to work through whatever still troubles you.

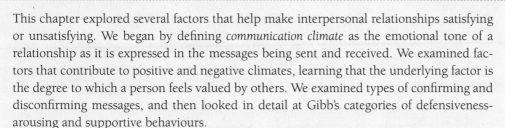

Summary

This chapter explored several factors that help make interpersonal relationships satisfying or unsatisfying. We began by defining *communication climate* as the emotional tone of a relationship as it is expressed in the messages being sent and received. We examined factors that contribute to positive and negative climates, learning that the underlying factor is the degree to which a person feels valued by others. We examined types of confirming and disconfirming messages, and then looked in detail at Gibb's categories of defensiveness-arousing and supportive behaviours.

The second half of the chapter dealt with interpersonal conflict. We saw that conflict is a fact of life in every relationship and that the way conflicts are handled plays a major role in the quality of a relationship. There are five ways people can behave when faced with a conflict: non-assertive, directly aggressive, passive-aggressive, indirect, and assertive. Each of these approaches can be appropriate at times, but the chapter focused on assertive communication skills because of their value and novelty for most communicators. We saw that conflict styles are affected by both gender and culture.

There are four outcomes to conflicts: win–lose, lose–lose, compromise, and win–win. Win–win outcomes are often possible, if the parties possess the proper attitudes and skills. The final section of the chapter outlined the steps in win–win problem-solving.

Key Terms

assertion 269

certainty 263

communication
   climate 256

compromise 277

confirming response 256

conflict 264

controlling message 261

crazymaking 268

de-escalatory conflict
   spiral 259

descriptive
   communication 261

direct aggression 268

disconfirming
   response 257

equality 263

escalatory conflict
   spiral 259

evaluative
   communication 260

Gibb categories 260

'I' language 261

indirect
   communication 269

lose–lose
   problem-solving 277

neutrality 262

non-assertion 265

passive aggression 268

problem orientation 261

provisionalism 263

spiral 259

spontaneity 262

strategy 261

superiority 262

win–lose
   problem-solving 276

win–win
   problem-solving 278

'you' language 260

Activities

A. Your Confirming and Disconfirming Messages

You can gain an understanding of how confirming and disconfirming messages create communication spirals by trying the following exercise.

1. Identify the communication climate of an important personal relationship. Using weather metaphors (sunny, gloomy, calm) may help.
2. Describe several confirming or disconfirming messages that have helped create and maintain the climate. Be sure to identify both verbal and non-verbal messages.
3. Show how the messages you have identified have created either escalatory or de-escalatory conflict spirals. Describe how these spirals reach limits and what events cause them to stabilize or reverse.
4. Describe what you can do to either maintain the existing climate (if positive) or change it (if negative). Again, list both verbal and non-verbal behaviours.

B. Constructing Supportive Messages

This exercise will give you practice in sending confirming messages that reflect Gibb's categories of supportive behaviour. You will find that you can communicate in a constructive way—even in conflict situations.

1. Begin by recalling at least two situations in which you found yourself in an escalatory conflict spiral.
2. Using the Gibb categories, identify your defence-arousing messages, both verbal and non-verbal.
3. Now reconstruct the situations, writing a script in which you replace the defence-arousing behaviours with the supportive alternatives outlined by Gibb.
4. If it seems appropriate, you may choose to approach the other people in each of the situations you have described and attempt to replay the exchange. Otherwise, describe how you could use the supportive approach you developed in Step 3 in future exchanges.

C. Constructing Assertive Messages

Develop your skill at expressing assertive messages by composing responses for each of the following situations:

1. A neighbour's barking dog is keeping you awake at night.
2. A friend hasn't repaid the $20 she borrowed two weeks ago.
3. Your boss made what sounded like a sarcastic remark about the way you put school before work.
4. An out-of-town friend phones at the last minute to cancel the weekend you planned to spend together.

   Now develop two assertive messages you could send to a real person in your life. Discuss how you could express these messages in a way that is appropriate for the situation and that fits your personal style.

D. Problem-Solving in Your Life

1. Recall as many conflicts as possible that you have had in one relationship. Identify which approach best characterizes each one: win–lose, lose–lose, compromise, or win–win.
2. For each conflict, describe the consequences (for both you and the other person) of this approach.
3. Based on your analysis, decide for yourself how successful you and your partner are at managing conflicts. Describe any differences in approach that would result in more satisfying outcomes. Discuss what steps you and your partner could take to make these changes.

E. Choosing an Ethical Conflict Style

At first glance, assertiveness seems like the most ethical communication style to use when you are faced with a conflict. The matter might not be so clear, however. Find out for yourself by following these steps.

1. Decide for yourself whether it is ever justifiable to use each of the other conflict styles: non-assertion, direct aggression, passive aggression, and indirect communication. Support your position on each style with examples from your own experience.
2. Explain your answer to classmates who disagree, and listen to their arguments.
3. After hearing positions that differ from yours, work with your classmates to develop a code of ethics for expressing conflict messages.

Further Reading

Greene, John O., and Brant R. Burleson. *Handbook of Communication and Social Interaction Skills.* Mahwah, NJ: Erlbaum, 2003.
This book focuses specifically on the nature of skills that contribute to effective communication. Chapters address topics such as managing conversations, impression management, arguing, and persuasion. Selected chapters also focus on specific types of interpersonal relationships, including those between romantic partners, spouses, friends, parents and children, people from different cultures, and people in health care.

Hocker, Joyce L., and William W. Wilmot. *Interpersonal Conflict,* 6th edn. New York: McGraw-Hill, 2001.
Interpersonal Conflict is a thorough survey of the nature of interpersonal conflict and how it can be resolved. This is an ideal second step for readers who want to explore the subject in further detail.

Knapp, Mark L., and John A. Daly. *Handbook of Interpersonal Communication,* 3rd edn. Thousand Oaks, CA: Sage, 2002.
Leading scholars have contributed chapters about fundamental issues that involve better relationships including conflict, the role of emotions, culture, personality, and interpersonal influence.

Stone, Douglas, Bruce Patton, and Sheila Heen. *Difficult Conversations: How to Discuss What Matters Most.* New York: Penguin, 2000.
This outstanding book was developed by members of the famous Harvard Negotiation Project. It offers a comprehensive, readable, and (most importantly) effective approach to understanding the potential dangers of unproductive conflicts and how to avoid them. Examples are drawn from a variety of contexts, including work, family, and friendships.

Study Questions

1. What weather-related adjectives would you use to describe the communication climate in your relationship with your best friend? With your employer? With your parents? With your significant other? With an instructor? What kinds of supportive communication described by Gibb (pages 260–4) might improve this climate?

2. How would you describe your friend/employer/parent/significant other/instructor's style of handling concerns about your partnership (pages 265–9)? How would you describe the style you might choose for dealing with your concerns?

3. Describe how you might choose an assertive, win–win approach to addressing your concerns with one of the people you have described in questions 1 or 2. Might your approach be different if your partner had a different cultural or gender identity? What do you think might be different?

Communication in Groups

Part III

Professional Profile:

Andrew Laing

Many of you likely don't realize the enviable position you are in as students of communications in the early twenty-first century. You are both scholars and the main participants in a massive change in the way we communicate with each other brought about by a never-ending transformation of communications technologies. And yet as people embrace Facebook, Twitter, and other new forms of digital communication, there is a feeling of *plus ça change* as one aspect still dominates: the primacy of text and audience. More than any other characteristic, these technologies produce a staggering, mind-bending amount of text, and they also make it increasingly more available to the public. This is the really big trend in communications, so the question is: How do we come to understand this sea of text?

There are a number of approaches, but for me, it is content analysis: the systematic, objective, empirical method of deriving valid inferences about text. I'm a media analyst and arguably one of the country's leading practitioners of and research design experts in content analysis. I fell into my position somewhat by one of life's fortunate accidents—responding to a small postage-stamp advertisement in *The Globe and Mail* for 'Media Analyst'. That was 20 years ago, and the ad still hangs on my office wall. Now I'm president of Canada's foremost news media research firm. Our clients are a *Who's Who* of the country's elite organizations, including RBC Royal Bank, Suncor, Canadian Cancer Society, Sun Life, CN Rail, Rogers Communications, CBC, KPMG, Ontario Ministry of Health, and many more. Cormex is one of more than a dozen firms around the world that conduct news media analysis for private, public, and non-profit sector organizations. These organizations require the systematic, objective assessment of their traditional and social media coverage that content analysis provides in order to benchmark against competitors, manage issues, assess the impact of stakeholder commentary, evaluate key programs and initiatives, and generally to paint a clear 'picture' of what Canadians come to understand about them through the media. To anyone interested in understanding society's issues and how they fit together, my job offers truly great seating.

Ultimately, the key to a career in communications, wherever you see yourself fitting in, is to develop the skills that best suit both you and the marketplace. For me, it was a built-in, hard-wired ability to translate concepts into patterns, one I honed over the years, formalized into research designs, and used to become a leading designer of research that turns communications, through empirical research design, into observable, understandable, actionable patterns.

Andrew Laing is the president of Cormex Research, the country's leading media content analysis firm.

After studying the material in this chapter . . .

You should understand:

- the characteristics of social media and how they differ from those of traditional mass media;
- the history of the development of social media;
- the features of the various types of social media;
- the effects of social media on our sense of self and our mobility, as well as in the realms of marketing and traditional mass media;
- the benefits and dangers of social media; and
- the major theories of mass media, including those of the two Canadian communication pioneers, Harold Innis and Marshall McLuhan.

You should be able to:

- select the right social media outlet for different sorts of messages;
- distinguish between the different varieties of social media and choose the one most appropriate to your task at hand;
- use social media effectively to build a personal digital brand;
- avoid the dangers of social media by policing your image;
- apply Harold Innis's time-binding and space-binding theory to different media; and
- apply Marshall McLuhan's theories of the medium is the message, the tetrad, and hot and cool media.

Social Media and Communication Theory

Chapter Highlights

Social media represent a radical re-thinking of how people and organizations broadcast messages to one another. Social media have several important characteristics:

- They are participatory, dynamic and create community.

Social media can be categorized according to the following types:

- zines, blogs, microblogs,
- social networking websites, wikis,
- social news aggregators,
- social bookmarking websites, and
- social photo and video sharing websites.

Social media are having a major impact on different parts of our lives by

- changing our sense of self;
- affecting how we move, consume, and behave through geotagging;
- changing the way we market goods; and
- transforming traditional mass media.

Social media present both a huge opportunity and pose many risks:

- They provide the opportunity to build a permanent, profitable online brand that promotes your values, goals, and dreams, as long as you police your image.
- They provide a perfect venue for destroying your reputation if used incorrectly.

The communication theories discussed in this chapter are:

- concepts of Harold Innis and Marshall McLuhan;
- flow theories, such as bullet theory, two-step flow theory, and multi-step flow theory;
- social learning theory;
- individual differences theory;
- diffusion of innovation theory;
- cultivation theory;
- agenda-setting theory; and
- cumulative effects theory.

Our lives are all being affected in some way by media. Whether it is popular culture affecting our identities or public relations campaigns facilitating our relationships with one another and with organizations, we are awash in messages. Each of these messages makes us think about the world differently. Even if we reject a message, it still becomes part of our mental landscape. As soon as someone makes you consider something, they have found a way of entering your mindspace. That fact is at the centre of mediated communication.

Mediated communication differs from much of the communication we have studied so far in this text. It consists of messages transmitted through a channel, be it print (newspapers and magazines), broadcast (television, radio, and Internet), entertainment (movies and music), or social media (zines and blogs). As discussed in Chapter 1, we use the term mass communication, or mass media, to refer collectively to these methods of communicating messages to large, widespread audiences. But there is another aspect of mediated communication which does not have to do with mass messages. An e-mail or text message to a friend or phone call to a relative is mediated, in that it depends on a device for its transmission, yet it is intended for one recipient, not for a mass audience. In this sense, mediated communication, though it does not involve face-to-face contact, can possess many of the qualities of interpersonal communication described in this text.

Most of us are inherently interested in the glamour and power of mass communication, and we enjoy learning about it. All of us have been touched by the excitement of feeling the connectivity and instant feeling of celebrity that social media can offer. Some want to explore the possibility of a career in media or public relations. Others just want to be informed users of media. This chapter is designed to help you start analyzing how mediated communication, both traditional and social media, affects your life—for better and for worse. We begin by discussing mediated communication from the perspective of social media. We then take a tour of the different sorts of social media that are popular and powerful at the time of the printing of this book and investigate how they can be effective for communicating messages in various aspects of our lives. We also take a moment to explore how social media may be affecting the mass media, such as newspapers, television, and radio.

In the second half of the chapter, we discuss several mass media theories that have been prevalent in the field of communication studies. Starting with Harold Innis and Marshall McLuhan, the two foundational Canadian communication theorists, we go on a flash tour of the other established communication theories to see how they explain the impact of mediated communication on our social and cultural lives.

Social Media

Social media, which has risen in prominence since 2008, is a form of mediated communication that permits people to develop and categorize networks of friends and acquaintances by various dimensions of affinity, such as likes and dislikes, profession, taste, and ethnic or religious group, among many others. In fact, social media amplify the various forms of interpersonal communication that we have discussed so far in this text. They force us to write more, communicate verbally more, and be much more aware of the impact that the medium we use to communicate has on a receiver's interpretation of our message. For example, someone reading your text message can't understand your emotional state in the same way that someone standing in front of you might. Social media have been at the forefront of a communication revolution. From Facebook to Twitter to LinkedIn to Foursquare, our social lives and economy are being transformed by social media in both subtle and overwhelming ways.

Were Harold Innis with us today, he might say that social media have brought us to the brink of a new form of civilization.

What makes a medium social? While many different answers have been proposed by business gurus, dating coaches, academics, public relations experts, and, of course, the creators of social media services themselves, there is a consensus that the main answer lies in *human interaction*.

A more elaborate definition might say that social media allow for the flow of content, particularly content generated by the users of social media themselves, to other people. Some social media, such as Facebook, permit users to validate membership in their friend lists, facilitating their sharing of posted content with people or organizations with which they have a pre-existing relationship. Other forms, such as blogs, Twitter, or even wikis, permit users to share content with people they may or may not know, thereby supporting the creation of relationships. For example, a person living in Whitehorse can **tweet** messages, images, and links that he or she finds fascinating and accumulate **followers** whom he or she may or may not know, eventually creating a national or perhaps even global community. For the purposes of our discussion in this chapter, we define **social media** as social environments that are meant to be used at little or no cost to publish and share messages and information generated by participants.

Businesses sometimes use the term **user-generated content** when referring to social media, meaning that most of the valuable information available from social media isn't generated by a big organization, such as the CBC or Vidéotron, as is the content of mass media. Instead, social media content is generated by the users themselves. This means that social media is an incarnation of Marshall McLuhan's dictum 'the medium is the message' (see page 319); it is the conversations, stories, photos, links, videos, and works of art that users post to social media sites like Facebook, Twitter, or Digg that make those sites useful. Without the content uploaded and commented on by users, social media would all look exactly the same: empty, meaningless, lifeless shells.

Comparing Social Media and Traditional Mass Media

Social media have two things in common with many other media, including books, letters, or even television shows: they contain messages and they use a channel. The messages can be any form of human or artificial intelligence expression: art, text, videos, music, and so on. The channel can be electronic, through a computer application—or app—available on a server (wikis, Facebook, Twitter), through mobile computing devices (iPad or iPod Touch), or through a smartphone app (Twitter apps for BlackBerry, iPhone, or Android). Surprisingly, social media can also be distributed through physical channels such as zines, graffiti, or slogans that are distributed through viral campaigns or through simple word-of-mouth. For example, a grassroots or telephone-tree campaign can be an efficient way to raise awareness of an upcoming club or group event.

Where social media differ from traditional media is that the former must have a persistent social interface, that is, a software infrastructure that allows users to build and maintain their interpersonal relationships through the social medium. For example, a user's tweets

follower

A twitter user who has subscribed to the tweets of another user.

social media

social environments that are meant to be used at little or no cost to publish and share messages and information generated by participants.

tweet

A message sent through the microblogging service, Twitter.

user-generated content

Social media content that is generated by their users, not by large organizations.

persist on the Twitter website and are available for followers to read and respond to. A history of these conversations is also available, allowing the relationship to build over time. Facebook and other **social networking** systems allow users to create virtual social communities that persist on their respective servers.

Another key difference between social media and traditional mass media is accessibility. In the past, individuals were not empowered to spread their messages globally because they had no access to the gatekeepers of traditional mass media. One of the defining qualities of traditional mass media is that their content is mostly produced at great cost by large corporations. Production also requires high levels of technical expertise and training in communication arts. The only way that most people could communicate through traditional mass media was to write a letter to the editor or to call a phone-in show. If you were very capable, you might find a way to be interviewed by a reporter or talk show host, but that possibility is beyond the reach of the vast majority of citizens.

Social media has given the public easy access to global communication, opening the floodgates to the multitude of messages that users can generate and spread. Social media have suddenly given users the ability to make their voices heard by and their stories known to others all over the world. As a result, social media have shrunk the world.

Social media also differs from traditional mass media in terms of immediacy. It not only takes a long time to create, edit, and produce content for mass media, but there can also be a long time between these stages and broadcast. By comparison, social media is instantaneous; users post information immediately from their smartphones, iPads, or computers. Furthermore, the expected level of production quality and 'finish' is lower for social media content because everyone knows that the content is user-generated.

Finally, social media content is very changeable. When a newspaper is printed, its articles can no longer be edited. The best the newspaper can do is publish a retraction or a correction. Social media content, however, is constantly being edited and re-edited. Think of what happens when a developing story is posted to a newspaper website, such as globeandmail.com. Often the story will start as a stub, basically a headline and a 'lead' (the first line of a news story), and be enhanced throughout the day by staff writers until it becomes a full article. How can traditional newsprint compete with this process? Especially when the electronic version of the paper is being beamed wirelessly to iPads, Kindles, or Kobos?

Although there are significant differences between these two types of media, they are not mutually exclusive. In fact, there exists a form, known as **community media**, that blends some of the qualities of both social and mass media to form a middle ground. Community media are often paid for by cable or large media companies as part of their license application to the Canadian Radio-television and Telecommunications Commission (CRTC). An excellent example of community media is a cable access channel (such as Hamilton's Cable 14 or CPAC, Canada's

community media
A form of media that blends qualities of both social media and traditional mass media.

social networking site
A social medium that allows users to create virtual social communities in which they share content, exchange messages, and build relationships.

national Cable Public Affairs Channel)—a channel that is funded by the cable operators but staffed by a combination of professionally trained technicians and broadcasters and local amateur broadcasters, writers, and interviewers.

Community media are a fascinating compromise between industrial media and social media: they allow a significant amount of user-generated content to appear through talk shows, phone-in shows, and broadcasts of community events, but they also bring professional production quality, access to newswires, and other tools of the industrial media. These latter qualities are possible because of **media convergence,** the tendency of large corporations such as Rogers or Bell Canada Enterprises to own and integrate various types of media outlets (e.g., radio and TV stations, newspapers, book publishing companies, and the Internet) so that content can be shared and rebroadcast. Although critics claim that media convergence reduces consumer choice for information, access to multiple resources allows companies to produce sophisticated community cable programming.

Are Social Media Completely New?

The simple answer to this question is that, while the software programs that drive popular social media services have only been around since the mid-2000s, the technological underpinnings of the Internet which allow social media to connect people the way they do were actually developed in the mid-twentieth century. The Internet's precursor, ARPANET, was developed in 1969, and the World Wide Web was developed by Tim Berners-Lee at CERN (Organisation Européenne pour la Recherche Nucléaire/European Organization for Nuclear Research). Berners-Lee also built the first website, which went live on 6 August 1991. The forerunners of the current forms of social media, which we will discuss in the following sections, were also developed during this time.

Zines: Counter-Cultural, Print-Based Social Media

While a **zine** can appear in various forms, including print or electronic magazine, newsletter, or broadsheet, it is generally defined as a self-published, non-commercial publication that often covers specialized or unconventional subject matter. An active zine culture has existed for many years, with independent artists distributing their publications through special channels which are based on familiarity and community. Because zines often focus on subjects not covered in the mainstream media, there is often a connection made between personal identity and these alternative issues.[1] This means that, through zines, people seek a form of representation that they don't find in mass media content. The connection to alternative communities like punk and Riot Grrrl is a good example. There are also many zines about homosexuality, race issues, and peace activism. The accessibility of the medium has meant that zine-makers are also a very diverse group, including many races, the young and old, and the homosexual and straight. An excellent example of a zine was Jeff Miller's *Ghost Pine* (see page 294). Zine-makers often form communities of readers, authors, and distributors that are almost identical in structure to Facebook and other social networking websites.

GeoCities

Another good example of a precursor to present-day social media is GeoCities, founded by David Bohnett and John Rezner in late 1994. The model was similar to social media inasmuch as users were encouraged to design their own web pages in 'cities' that were

media convergence
The tendency for large corporations to own and integrate various types of media outlets so that content can be shared and rebroadcast. Some critics claim that this reduces consumer choice for information.

zine
A self-published, non-commercial publication, in either print or electronic format, that often covers specialized or unconventional subject matter.

Understanding Diversity

THIS GHOST PINE INTERVIEW IS TRUE

When Jeff Miller launched his *Ghost Pine: All Stories True* punk zine in 1996, he didn't realize he was about to embark on a 13-year journey that would lead him from Ottawa to Montreal, from a punk scene to a vegan kitchen and some odd places in between. Jeff recorded those true-life experiences in *Ghost Pine*, and though the zine folded in 2009 it now lives on in the best-of anthology, *Ghost Pine: All Stories True* (Invisible Publishing, April 2010). . . .

Torontoist: Can you give us an overview of your book, *Ghost Pine: All Stories True*?

Jeff Miller: The book collects the best of my zine, *Ghost Pine*, which came out for 13 years between 1996 and 2009. [It's broken down] into sections that deal with recurring themes time and time again within the zine. This book is [a] collection of stories, and a coming of age. You can see my coming of age when you read through its pages. I thought it would be an interesting document of my progress as a writer and as a human, but also as a document for cultural change. During the time the zine was active there were a lot of changes in the world. I never really wrote a lot about what's happening around me, I often focused on the smaller details of my life. But when I read it now, little details about how the world was a different place back then jumped out at me. I found this interesting and worthwhile exploring in a collection.

. . .

TO: What inspired you to start a zine, way back in 1996?

JM: *Ghost Pine* was inspired by the hardcore punk scene in Ottawa. When I was growing up, there was a vibrant music scene there. A bunch of great bands played every weekend. To me, it was [an] amazing participant-based scene, it didn't feel like there was an audience. Everyone was taking part in some way. I had this idea to keep the scene going, and in order to participate, I needed to do something. Since I was always writing, I thought a zine was the best way to contribute [to] it. The zine evolved from there. It went from being a ranty thing to a selection of autobiographical stories with a beginning, middle, and end, without the same antagonism. The big shift occurred when the fourth issue came out in 1998. I started trying to observe the world, write about my experiences in a way that people could relate to.

TO: Why was the zine called *Ghost Pine*?

JM: Originally it was called *Otaku*, the Japanese word for nerd. At the time thought it as [*sic*] a nice metaphor. The punk scene was about collecting rare records and being on top of that kind of thing. I eventually got tired of that name and wanted to concentrate on the details of everyday life. I wanted a name that would be welcoming, accessible, and reflect what the zine is about. I had this baseball cap since I was a kid, I didn't know where it came from or anything about it, but it featured a picture of a ghost hiding under a pine tree. Under this image, it said 'Ghost Pine'. I really liked this. It was a metaphor for what I wanted to do with the zine, when I explored the small details in life, details or moments that are rather mundane and meaningless, but when you expand upon them, they end up meaning so much in people's lives.

TO: Why did you decide to end the zine in 2009?

JM: I found it more difficult to write about myself. I thought maybe I was less interesting now that I've grown up. I'm a bit shyer now. My life is more stable and change occurs differently when you're older. Some of the things that I was going through didn't really fit in stories in the same way. When I was younger, everything seemed to happen in story form. The timeline was different too. In a period of a month, events would happen that I perceived as life-changing. Now I find the changes happening in my life are more long-term things that can't be summed up so succinctly. . . .

—*Erin Balser, books.torontoist.com, 13 April 2010.*

modelled after existing urban areas, such as Paris or Capitol Hill. This model matched the social media idea of building communities of content by geographic and ethno-cultural affinity.

However, GeoCities never became fully fledged social media and was unavailable in most parts of the world. The most serious problem with the model was that there were very limited opportunities for the audience to contribute feedback. Although 'guestbooks' enabled users to leave comments and notes, this feature allowed only one-way communication between the site owner and the user. All a user could do was leave a message on the site owner's website. Furthermore, GeoCities lacked the ability for users to send exclusive content to friends and family or to form any kind of conversational relationship between users outside of the guestbook. A lack of two-way interactivity made the GeoCities concept fall short of the third element of our definition of social media: relationship- and community-building.

Web 2.0

In 2004, following the initial dot-com boom and bust, communication and multimedia experts coined a new term to name a second wave of Internet development: *Web 2.0*. Web 2.0 emphasized incorporating interactivity and community-building principles into commercial websites, marking a move away from websites as static repositories of information. A good analogy of this change is that websites pre-Web 2.0 were like filing cabinets and Web 2.0 websites were more like libraries. A filing cabinet is a static object that is about the files it contains: you can put a file in it or take a file out of it. A library is a dynamic object that is about you, the user: you can wander the stacks, interact with others, consult the librarian, or use the computer. When *Time* named its 2006 Person of the Year 'You', it was evident that the social media revolution had become truly widespread and was well on its way toward transforming world culture and communication practices.

COMMUNICATION ON-SCREEN

Hackers (1995)
Directed by Iain Softley.

While many may watch *Hackers* because it features a young Angelina Jolie, this film's portrayal of the Internet of the mid-1990s probably carries a bit more academic value. Even in its own time it was seen as far from an honest depiction of the real world of pasty-skinned types tapping away at their 486s in basements across suburban America: the film wildly stylizes and celebrates the computer culture of the time (mostly to the beat of a landmark soundtrack that captured the trance music of the era).

But if you can get over the impossibly beautiful people, this view of the world of Web 0.5 makes for fascinating viewing today. Of particular relevance is its early hinting at the social and egalitarian possibilities raised by a wired community.

Everything old is new again.

Peter Allen

Types of Social Media

Social media are a big part of our lives, but most of us have probably experienced only one or two varieties. In this section we will discuss the different types of social media and a few examples of each.

Blogs

From a contraction of the words 'web' and 'log', a **blog** generally describes a website in which an individual or an organization enters, in reverse-chronological order, regular commentary on events, philosophical musings, and/or personal opinions about an area of expertise. Sometimes bloggers will enrich their commentary with multimedia content, such as images or sound and video clips. The word 'blog' has also entered common English usage as a verb, as in 'I blogged the concert I went to last night.'

blog
A website that features, in reverse-chronological order, an individual's or organization's regular commentary on events, philosophical musings, and/or personal opinions about an area of expertise. Blogs may also include images, sound clips, and video clips.

Blogs started in the mid-1990s. One of the earliest bloggers was Justin Hall, a student at Pennsylvania's Swarthmore College, who started his blog in 1994. Four years later, Bruce Abelson launched OpenDiary. In 1999, Brad Fitzpatrick launched LiveJournal and, with Meg Hourihan, Blogger, which was bought by Google in 2003. In May of that same year, Matt Mullenweg created Wordpress, a set of website-design software tools, mostly used as a basis for blogging.[2] Since then, other blogging engines have been developed, such as Typepad, Tumblr, and Posterous. However, Blogger and Wordpress remain the most popular.

Varieties of Blogs

There are several different sorts of blogs. In this section we describe many of them.

Personal Blogs

Many people maintain their own blogs, sharing information with friends and family or expressing their most intimate thoughts about things they've found on the Internet. Nicolle Brown, a former communications student at McMaster University, keeps a blog (seenbybean. wordpress.com) in which she adds brief snippets of poetic observations and commentary to things on the Internet that she found intriguing or beautiful. Her blog is for herself but is on the Web for all to see, should they stumble across it. Another former McMaster student, Melonie Fullick (who is profiled in Chapter 3 of this book), maintains a beautiful photoblog called Panoptikal (panoptikal.blogspot.com), wherein she posts her photography and adds her thoughts and comments.

Others will maintain a blog to build a personal public brand as an expert in a particular subject area. Joey Coleman, who is profiled in Chapter 6, started a blog (joeycoleman.ca) about higher education when he was a student at the University of Manitoba and was eventually hired by *Maclean's*. Some professors blog to get messages pertaining to their research or political beliefs out to the larger public, beyond the wall of the university or college. Michael Geist, a professor of law at the University of Ottawa, uses his blog (michaelgeist.ca) to promote his perspectives on copyright legislation more widely than if he were to publish them exclusively in scholarly journals. Sidney Eve Matrix, a Queen's National Scholar in the Department of Film and Media at Queen's University, uses her blog (sidneyevematrix. net) to explore ideas 'about trends in the digital production, distribution and consumption of social media including advertising, television, music, movies, gaming, and social networking'.[3]

Cultural Idiom

blogosphere
the collection of all blogs in the world; the universe of blogs

Professional Blogs

Professional blogs, such as Canadian journalist and political commentator David Akin's On the Hill (davidakin.blogware.com) and the Canadian urban music and entertainment news and gossip blog (hiphossip.com), have significantly influenced the distribution of information by breaking stories before the traditional mass media. Political bloggers have made a huge impact by expanding discussions on topics that the traditional mass media have been rather conservative about. From the Israeli–Palestinian conflict to Canada's involvement in the Afghan War to various political scandals, bloggers have blown the conversations wide open, allowing every detail to be published and every opinion, no matter how passionate, to be expressed. Although some traditionalists try to dismiss bloggers as gossips, most members of the public and the traditional mass media recognize the powerful contribution that the blogosphere has made to our global dialogue.

Corporate and Organizational Blogs

As part of their Internet strategy, most corporations and organizations maintain a blog documenting daily corporate life. Corporate blogs, such as that of real estate company Century 21 Canada (century21.ca/Blog) or Thornley Fallis (propr.ca), a Canadian marketing and public relations agency, are used for branding, marketing, and promotional purposes. Not-for-profit organizations, such as the British Columbia Cancer Foundation (bccancerfoundation.wordpress.com); lobbying organizations, such as the Canadian Taxpayers Federation (taxpayer.com/blog); and political offices, such as that of MP Carolyn Bennett (carolynbennett.liberal.ca/blog) also often maintain blogs. For organizations such as these, blogs are an easy, entertaining, and inexpensive means of disseminating key messages.

Vlogs (Video Blogs)

A **vlog** is a blog in which a user produces and publishes video entries as part of the blog's content. The rise of video resources such as YouTube, Google Video, Vimeo, and others has facilitated the rise of Internet television, of which vlogging is a variety. There are not many Canadian vloggers at the time of this writing, with some notable exceptions being FLuffeeTalks, VlogCandy, Kazila, and Nanalew.

The Blogosphere Community

Several blog-specific search engines have been developed over the last several years. Bloglines, Blogscope, and Technorati are three very popular ones. As well, there are blog communities that have grown up in the blogosphere, including Blogster and MyBlogLog. In Canada, several groups have organized their blogosphere, particularly in the world of politics. Each major political party has its own community of bloggers, and Blogging Canadians tries to bring them all together. Another good Canadian resource for blogs is the Canadian Blog Directory (blogscanada.ca).

COMMUNICATION ON-SCREEN

TMZ on TV (2007–)
Created by Harvey Levin.

TMZ on TV (generally shortened to just *TMZ*) is an unusual piece of programming in more ways than one. Unlike countless examples of established 'old-media' property trying to evolve and export themselves to the Web, it came about through precisely the opposite process: first as a successful blog, then adapted into a half-hour daily television newscast. The name stands for the '30-mile zone', an entertainment industry term for the 30-mile radius centred on the intersection of West Beverley Boulevard and North La Cienega Boulevard in Hollywood. In the 1960s, this zone was established to monitor rules for filming in Hollywood; more broadly, however, it serves as shorthand for the bubble-like environment in which Hollywood celebrities carry out their unusual existences.

TimeWarner, a major media conglomerate, developed and launched the original *TMZ* blog in November 2005, with lawyer-turned-journalist Harvey Levin serving as managing editor. *TMZ* broke from traditional American journalistic conventions by importing many of the practices of the notoriously vicious British tabloid press, including paying 'tip fees' to those who provided story material and openly admitting to paying paparazzi for photos. In contrast to the fawning tone usually adopted by traditional entertainment media powerhouses such as *Entertainment Tonight* and *People*, *TMZ* set itself apart with its unapologetic snarkiness. Its aggressive approach to breaking lurid gossip resulted in it routinely scooping the competition and, in so doing, making TimeWarner significant profits.

How much of *TMZ*'s 'edginess' is a natural consequence of its blog format is the subject of some debate. When the time came to adapt itself for television, *TMZ* also innovated: rather than structure itself as a traditional newscast, the program was instead framed as a 'fly-on-the-wall' view of an apparent 'pitch session' of the day's stories from the blog's youngish staff. With his trademark green pen, Levin dutifully writes the ideas on a glass board—to no obvious end—and the audience is brought into the opinionated banter of the newsroom, in some way mirroring the characteristic tone of social media.

vlog
A blog in which the creator produces and publishes video entries as part of the blog's content.

Dangers of Blogging

While blogging is a great way to begin building a personal or organizational brand, it can also expose you to a lot of unwanted attention. Blogging about other people, posting photographs of others without their permission, or making unsubstantiated claims about the motivations, beliefs, activities, or behaviours of others can lead to lawsuits against you or your organization. Posting excessively personal details about yourself, your friends, or your family can be very hurtful. Even if people don't pursue legal action against you, they may no longer trust you.

Finally, revealing too much personal information can lead to **cyberstalking** (the stalking or harrassing of an individual or organization using the Internet or other types of electronic communication), stalking, or even break-ins and assaults. Some dangerous people use the anonymity of the Internet to post terrible comments, filled with threats of violence, sexual assault, or sick personal fantasies, on people's blogs.

Microblogs

Microblogs began in the mid-2000s and were originally known as *tumblelogs,* a term coined by why the lucky stiff (his only known name) in his blog. By 2008, however, the term **microblog** had become predominant. A microblog differs from a traditional blog in the length of its entries. Microblog entries will often consist of only a short, simple sentence, an image, a link, or an embedded video. The content of microblogs tends to be very 'in the moment'; the microblogger will often report on what he or she is doing *on the spot*.

cyberstalking

The stalking or harrassing of an individual or organization using the Internet or other types of electronic communication.

microblog

A blog in which the entries are much shorter than traditional blogs and are 'in the moment'.

Understanding Communication Technology

Cyberstalking

Victims of Violence is a federally registered charity devoted to providing support to Canadian victims of violence. Its website includes an excellent research page on cyberstalking that all young people should read: http://bit.ly/eKimNB.

Microblogs often follow a subscriber or 'follower' model. Twitter has emerged as the most prominent of all the microblogging services because of both clever marketing and an ever-expanding suite of services. Other leading services are Tumblr and some internationally oriented microblogging services such as Emote.In from India, Plurk (which is particularly popular in South-East Asia), Jaiku from Finland, and Identica from Canada. A microblogging site designed specifically for marketers is Six Apart. Many social networking services such as Facebook, Myspace, XING, and LinkedIn offer **status updates,** which may be considered a form of microblogging.

If a user wants to aggregate all of his or her microblogging activities, services such as Lifestream and Profilactic will bring together microblogs from many sites onto one web page. Ping.fm will take your blog post and broadcast it to many social networks through their comments sections.

It is also noteworthy that microblog entries are not exclusively published on the Internet. Rather, they can be pushed straight to a cellphone or a smartphone. It is also possible to receive microblog entries through text messaging, instant messaging, short message service, e-mail, or even digital audio on your smartphone.

Why Has Microblogging Taken Off?

Just as e-mail replaced the written note because it saved communicators time and effort, microblogging services offer a quicker and more efficient means of sending brief messages one-to-one, via direct message, or one-to-many, via broadcast to the microblog's subscribers. Microblogging has simplified the communication process through the brevity of its messages, further reducing the need for niceties and conventions.

Marshall McLuhan might have made the point that social media are returning our culture to an oral, tribal state, drawing it away from the written conventions demanded by handwritten letters toward the conversational style of e-mail and now to the bursts of messaging characterizing the microblog, which are similar to group or town-hall conversations.

An excellent example of this occurrence is how people watching events on television, such as the Stanley Cup finals or the series finale of a popular television show, use Twitter. The event develops, either by suggestion of the organizers or by consensus, what is called a **hashtag,** a short, descriptive label preceded by a pound (#) sign that is included in tweets to make them easily searchable. For instance, the hashtag for this textbook might be #UHC2CanEd, for *Understanding Human Communication,* 2nd Canadian edition. Many people watch the televised proceedings while also participating in the ongoing Twitter conversation, turning what would have been an isolated experience into a communal one. Such was the case during the airing of the *Lost* series finale on 23 May 2010—Twitter traffic was so overwhelming that the service nearly crashed. Hashtags can also be used to bring together followers of conferences or conventions or journalistic coverage of a particular event, such as the student unrest in Iran in 2009.

hashtag
A short, descriptive label preceded by a pound (#) sign that is included in tweets to make them easily searchable.

status update
A short sentence or sentence fragment posted to a social medium that contains a message describing what the communicator is thinking or doing at the time of writing.

"You have to learn to communicate and share your feelings. Open Twitter accounts."

An article published by Bill Heil and Mikolaj Piskorski in the *Harvard Business Review* offers some surprising insights into the world of Twitter. They collected a sample of 300, 542 users in May 2009 and found that 80 per cent were followed by or followed at least one user. They also found that while men and women follow a similar number of Twitter users, men have 15 per cent more followers than women. Even more interesting was the fact that an average man is almost twice as likely to follow another man than a woman. The authors state that this is a stunning result, given that 'on a typical online social network, most of the activity is focused around women—men follow content produced by women they do and do not know, and women follow content produced by women they know.'[4] They also found that the median number of lifetime tweets for a Twitter user is one and that the top 10 per cent of Twitter users in the study contributed 90 per cent of the tweets. Their conclusion was that 'Twitter resembles more of a one-way, one-to-many publishing service more than a two-way, peer-to-peer communication network.'[5]

Social Networking Websites

As we mentioned at the beginning of this chapter, social networking websites enable users, either individuals or organizations, to build networks of 'friends', linked through a variety of potential affinities, with whom they share content, exchange messages, and build relationships. Users build profiles on these sites, sharing pieces of information about themselves, personal photos, notes, and invitations to affinity groups, events, and special interest websites. They then invite others to become their 'friends' and can choose, through privacy settings, how much of their content will be visible to different categories of friends.

There are a massive number of social networking sites that have been developed since 2004; however, we will focus on the four major ones: Facebook, MySpace, LinkedIn, and eHarmony Canada. For a comprehensive list of social networking sites, see the Wikipedia page devoted to cataloguing them, which is updated regularly: en.wikipedia.org/wiki/List_of_social_networking_websites.

Facebook

Facebook was first developed in 2004 as thefacebook.com, a project that provided a very clean interface with a simple blue and white design. It also offered a feeling of exclusivity and prestige, given that it was originally open only to members of the Harvard University community and, later, to other Ivy League colleges. As time passed, thefacebook.com became facebook.com and opened its doors to networks from other universities, then to networks of affinity from workplaces, to high schools, and finally to geographic locations such as countries, cities, and towns.

Canadians have adopted Facebook in droves. In May 2010, the total number of Canadians with Facebook accounts exceeded 16 million, making it the fourth-largest per capita Facebook market, behind Iceland, Norway, and Hong Kong.[6] While Facebook has maintained its clean design, its target market has changed significantly—in 2008 it transformed its status update model to compete with Twitter's microblogging model. In 2010, Facebook introduced the Open Graph model, which allowed it to compete with search engine companies such as Google for the right to organize and structure the World Wide Web through their new 'Facebook Like' button. Website and blog developers may include this button on their sites, enabling users to have a web page mentioned in their Facebook profile and broadcast on the **feeds** of their friends. While this intimately inserted Facebook into the tissue of the Web, it also raised serious privacy issues and caused many people to leave Facebook to join more secure, less profit-oriented social networking services.[7]

feed
The constantly updated, reverse-chronological list of tweets issued by the people that a twitter subscriber is following.

MySpace

MySpace competes with Facebook, although some market researchers say that Facebook (and Twitter) overtook MySpace in popularity in 2009. The often chaotic and garish layouts that adorn many MySpace pages—users can customize the appearance of their pages—and the very late addition of a microblogging 'status update' feature have been blamed by some for the site's decline. However, the fact that its pages are easy to personalize and the addition of special features for musicians have made MySpace an excellent tool for indy bands, models, actresses, and escorts to advertise their wares.

Cultural factors may also influence people choosing either Facebook or MySpace. Social media researcher Danah Boyd made the following observations on the relationship between Facebook and MySpace among teenaged Americans:

> Those who are drawn to Facebook are more likely to represent privileged, educated, stronger socioeconomic backgrounds. They are more likely to be respectful of adult society and more likely to connect with adults who hold power over them. Those drawn to MySpace are more likely to come from immigrant families and from poorer, urban communities. They are more likely to be resistant to normative value and affiliate with subcultures.[8]

LinkedIn

LinkedIn is a social networking site aimed at a professional audience. It permits users to share information about their professional experience, education, training, and achievements. Users can post a photo, their résumé, samples of their work, as well as reference letters. Users also invite other users to be their 'friends' and then share information with them through the link. One distinguishing feature of LinkedIn is that the age of the average user is much higher than that of Facebook or MySpace. The site has also built a profitable revenue model.

eHarmony Canada

eHarmony is a subscription-based social networking website with a twist: it uses proprietary algorithms to match its users together in pairs. Users fill out a detailed questionnaire which covers their likes and dislikes, their psychological profile, and their mental image

of their ideal mate. Then the site matches users based on these reports. Users can then choose whether or not to initiate communication with one or more of their matches (using the site's specific communication process) and, perhaps, eventually to meet in the real world. Although eHarmony promotes itself as a dating website, it is really no different from other social networking sites, except that the process is much more guided and structured by its policies.

Wikis

Wikis are websites that enable collaboration and sharing of information through the creation and simple editing of a number of linked web pages via a web browser such as Firefox, Safari, Opera, or Chrome. Wikis are powered by special software tools installed on **intranets,** or personal servers, which have been sealed off from the general Internet for secure and private use. They are often used for collaborative writing or for tracking the development of a complicated project by allowing individuals to add content and edit the content of others. All edits are catalogued by the wiki software—all previous versions can be viewed at any time.

The most famous and largest example of a wiki is Wikipedia, an open encyclopedia whose contents are created and managed entirely by registered users. It is a crowd-sourced project; the content is not generated by experts but by the collective intelligence and collaborative efforts of people all around the world. Because any user can create or edit a Wikipedia entry, the site features certain social phenomena that don't exist on other sites. 'Editing wars' can be waged, evidenced by the edit history on popular entries. And users sometimes prank an organization by editing its Wikipedia entry with humorous comments and 'facts'.

intranets
Networks that have been sealed off from the general Internet for secure and private use.

social news aggregators
Websites that allow registered users to post news stories to electronic bulletin boards.

wikis
Websites that enable collaboration and sharing of information by creating and editing linked web pages via a web browser.

Social News Aggregators

Social news aggregators are websites that allow registered users to post news stories to electronic bulletin boards. Some of the most popular sites of this kind are Digg, Fark, Reddit, and Slashdot. Of these, the only one to have a Canadian page at the time of printing is Reddit (reddit.com/r/canada). Social news aggregators have spread across the World Wide Web via 'share' buttons on blogs and newspaper and current affairs websites, which enable users to share articles of interest on the social news websites. These websites have been criticized by communication researchers who claim that they are relatively easy to 'game' through the use of artificial intelligence-based 'bots', small software programs who 'like' articles many hundreds if not thousands of times and thus drive up their scores. The prevalence of 'power posters'—the users whose posted articles are read or liked the most—indicates that these users are employing systematic strategies to up the scores of their posts.

Cultural Idiom

drive up
increase

Social Bookmarking Websites

Social bookmarking websites permit registered users to organize, share, and manage their lists of bookmarks of Internet content in a fashion similar to the bookmarks that users save in their web browsers. Users can add descriptions to their bookmarks and tag them with categories. The websites then share the bookmarks in a newsfeed, similar to that of Facebook or Twitter. Delicious, the most popular and pioneering social bookmarking website, has integrated a feature for ranking bookmarks. Users find social bookmarking services useful for consolidating their lists of bookmarks from many computers.

social bookmarking websites

Websites that permit registered users to organize, share, and manage lists of bookmarks of Internet content.

Social Photo and Video Sharing Websites

For Internet users who wish to share content such as photos or videos, social media have sprung up to create communities around these formats. Although there are many examples of this sort of social media, the most popular by far are YouTube and Flickr. YouTube allows users to register and post videos or even to start channels through which they can aggregate videos that they have posted. The site also has a friend function that helps create community among its users and allows them to subscribe and leave comments on each other's blogs. Flickr enables users to post high-quality images to the Internet that may be shared with authorized others.

Social Media, The Self, and Society

Social media are having a big impact on how we interact with one another, but are they changing our personalities and our sense of self? Because the form is still relatively new, there have been no conclusive findings on the subject. A study by Catalina L. Toma of Columbia University indicates that social networking tools have a strong self-affirming value. The participants were asked to spend time on their own or a stranger's Facebook profile and were then given negative feedback on a task. Participants who had spent time on their own Facebook profiles were more accepting of the negative feedback than those who had not, performing identically to those who had performed a self-affirmation exercise before receiving the negative feedback.[9]

Shanyang Zhao, Sherri Grasmuch, and Jason Martin from Temple University investigated how individuals construct their identity on Facebook. They conducted a content analysis of 63 Facebook accounts and found that users predominantly '"show rather than tell" and stress group and consumer identities over personally narrated ones'.[10] These findings suggest a sense of self that is distributed across marketing narratives and narratives attached to specific group identities rather than one that is constructed from users reflecting on and processing their personal experiences and inner identity.

Finally, a team of researchers from Cornell University and the Palo Alto Research Centre explored the impact on impression management of users' status updates on Facebook.[11] They found that, while people are often successful at projecting a positive image through their status updates, it is also often the case that they go too far and are thus perceived as self-important. Adam N. Joinson, a researcher at the University of Bath suggested that people who use Facebook for social connection gratifications use it more frequently, whereas those who use it for content gratifications tend to spend more time on the site.[12] These findings would indicate that there is not a significant loss of a sense of self among Facebook users.

These studies, while limited and preliminary in nature, give us clues that indicate that the 'social media self-concept' will be quite different than the self-concept of the user in 'meatspace'—researchers are just not sure how or why. As sociologist Jean Baudrillard mentions in his seminal book, *Simulation and Simulacra*,[13] we are accelerating the virtual world of digital media so quickly that perhaps one day, the world of simulation may replace the world of physical reality simply because the simulated world is more exciting and we feel better within it than in the real world.

Social Media and Mobility

Parallel to the content revolution occurring in the social media discussed thus far, there is another mobility revolution that is about to wash over our culture and economy. The emergence of smartphones such as the BlackBerry, iPhone, and Android as mass-market consumer technologies has meant that many of us carry in our pockets remarkable portable media devices which include a powerful Internet browser, crystal clear screen, high-quality video and still camera, and sound playback. These devices also have GPS (global positioning system) built in, which permits the device to establish the user's precise location almost anywhere on earth. This has made geotagging a major component of future social media platforms; some of them, such as Twitter, have already integrated it. **Geotagging** enables people to map out their tweets, texts, and photos, generating a giant, interconnected web of messages that are pinned down to earth because the map of messages matches the physical geography so perfectly.

A first such 'location-based social networking service', Foursquare, enables users to 'check in' at locations via the GPS function of their smartphones. It also permits them to leave a comment about the location and form circles of friends, in a similar fashion to other social networking sites. Users then compete to unlock 'badges' which reward them for frequenting different types of locations, such as Tim Hortons or Second Cup coffee shops. Users can even become the 'mayor' of a location if they are the person who has frequented it most regularly. Marketers are quickly realizing the potential of Foursquare for location-based marketing. For example, imagine that you have checked in at your favourite diner—a nearby café can send you a discount for desserts and try to entice you to have dessert at the café instead of at the diner where you are currently seated!

The same concerns that exist with social media's influence on our sense of self apply here. As the real world becomes more and more intertwined with the simulated world of social media, when locations blur with the pure information of our tweets and blogs and

geotagging
The act of tagging a piece of posted content with the GPS coordinates of its author at the moment of posting.

posts, which reality will we choose? This is an important issue and one of the most fascinating things to consider regarding social media. Perhaps one of you will come up with the theory that explains it.

Social Media, Public Relations, and Marketing

Social media are also transforming the world of public relations and marketing. Organizations seek to build lasting relationships and a strong feeling of affinity among their existing clients, potential clients, and stakeholders. In fact, social media allow them to open conversations that the public want to participate in. Through blogs, they attempt to capture the interest of their publics and keep them coming back to the organization's website. Through Facebook, they try to build a feeling of 'belonging to the community' for their brands. And through Twitter, they use clever tweets to keep people thinking about their brand. The emerging key in social media marketing is finding a way of reaching opinion leaders and influencers. What time are they online? Which tweets are they retweeting? Which of the organization's posts are they sharing with their circles of friends on Facebook?

Chris Farias, a successful young entrepreneur who co-founded kitestring creative marketing + design, a marketing and creative design agency which specializes in social media marketing, describes his model of success as

$$\text{Authenticity} + \text{Cool Item/Idea} + \text{Timing}^{14}$$

As a social media marketer, Farias (who is also profiled in this chapter) looks for *social currency,* ideas that will be popular enough that opinion leaders and influencers will want to redistribute it to their networks of Facebook friends and Twitter followers.

However, obtaining such currency requires a lot of sustained effort. Social currency will only be as effective as the amount of time you put into it. You can't just tweet for a couple of days and pick it up a week later. You've lost everyone. You have to do it everyday. You have to be persistent. You have to be topical. You have to be conversational and current. You have to let people in on portions of your private life. You can't set out to make an item go viral, but you can prepare your audience by knowing them, knowing when they're listening and what they're listening to.

> **Cultural Idiom**
>
> **go viral**
> when an item shared on social media is spread by others across their networks and becomes a cultural phenomenon for a short period of time.

Social Media and Traditional Media

Social media are transforming the world of traditional media and media consumption. Dr Andrew Laing, president of Cormex Research (who is profiled in this book), once visited Professor Sévigny's class and asked the 15 students a few simple questions before he gave his lecture:

1. How many of you read the print version of the newspaper at least once a week? (One hand went up.)
2. How many of you have a cable TV subscription? (Seven or eight hands went up.)
3. How many of you read the electronic version of a newspaper at least three times a week? (Every hand shot up.)

Young Communicator
PROFILE

Chris Farias, Imaginitarian
and Partner, kitestring creative
marketing + design

I've known I wanted to work in creative branding since I was little. My favourite part of *Bewitched* was when Darrin and Larry presented their advertising ideas surrounded by leather chairs and afternoon drinks. Samantha would always find some way to ruin it with her mischievousness and magic. In some ways, they're both my hero.

I started kitestring creative marketing + design with my business partner, Jenn Hudder, in 2007. We wanted to work at a studio that was as open to embracing creativity as we were, and it seemed like the best way to find that was to start our own.

I've been a designer and creative marketing strategist for almost a decade now. It's hard to believe how far I've come from St Clair College of Refined Arts in Windsor. I love learning about new design techniques, cultural and technological phenomena, and the latest industry trends. To do what I do, learning never ends, and the practical experience that counts needs to be updated as often as Apple releases a new application.

The funny thing about the newest direction in communicating brands online is that you need to remember some of your earliest teachings to wield it effectively.

Everything I Need to Know About Social Media I Learned in Kindergarten

Using social media is easy, but it's the 'media' part that sends us into a tailspin. Many people fear change, shy away from technology, and hide from the unknown. So, I'm throwing away the media.

What's left? That's right, 'social'.

Being social is easy. We do it everyday. On the phone, in the grocery store, at a party, and at work. The same rules that apply to being social in the real world apply to the online one. And lucky for us, we learned all these rules in kindergarten.

Rule One: Listen

Mrs Miller was my kindergarten teacher. She was about 12 feet tall, if I remember correctly, and she had it out for me. I was basically a mouth with legs. My report card that year came with a note that read 'Chris could talk the leg off a chair.' Being a very visual person, I imagined myself doing just that and found it quite amusing! One thing Mrs Miller did teach me though was to listen. It was ok to talk at the appropriate moments, but when someone was speaking, she urged me to take it all in.

When being social on the interwebs, listen to what others are saying. If you listen more than you talk, you will make friends and have more fuel to add to the conversation later. Being part of the conversation is key and what better way to take part than to actually 'hear' what someone is saying?

Rule Two: Share

Remember wanting to play with something some other kid had? Remember when he didn't give it to you? Remember punching him in the ear? No? Well I do. My playmate was not happy that day.

Sharing information is one way to make friends online. You know things I want to know. Tell me! It will build trust and make you a resource to others.

Rule Three: Be Yourself

While many of the other boys were digging in the indoor sandbox or playing with the blocks, I was over at the 'house' area. This was a section of the classroom that looked just like a tiny house, made just for people my size. Many times I would put on an apron, sit in the rocking chair with two giant pencils, and pretend to knit a scarf. Mrs Miller asked me once why I liked to do this. I told her that I wanted to be just like my Grandma when I grew up. She then grabbed her Polaroid, took a picture, and gave it to me to take home to my Grandma Gilda. That made me happy. It was ok to be me.

It's imperative that your personality shine through online. When you are your true self you come off as transparent and honest. You also attract the people that will like you for who you are. These people will be the ones who will want to work with you and whom you will want to work with. Working with the right people is key to a successful business and a happy you.

Rule Four: Come Prepared

The first day of school was always the best day of the year for me. This was the day I had everything before I started to lose things. My mother would take me to Zellers a few weeks before and we would shop for new pencils and paper, gym shoes, an art smock, and lots of other fun stuff. Because of my wonderful mother I came to school ready to learn, play, and have fun.

It's not the time to start creating your brand the minute you begin communicating on social media. That's the time to showcase it. Before you start your adventures online, you should be prepared. Start a policy. Have a plan of action. Know who you are.

Rule Five: Play Nice

I was at a friend's birthday party. His mother came into the living room and stood before about 12 hungry and excited six-year-old boys. In her very strong Italian accent she stated, 'No pushing. No shoving. No fighting.' All I remember from that day were those words and the cake. I'm a sucker for an ice cream cake.

Picking fights, causing conflict, and making enemies is one way to ruin your brand while using social media. I'm not saying you need to roll over and pee on the floor the minute someone confronts you. You can still stand your ground. But if someone is antagonizing you, it's ok to walk away and not reply. Plus if you do decide to get into that tiff, everyone around you will see that fight happen and you will look like a digital crap disturber to all the on-lookers. Be the nice guy. Don't punch. Don't shove. Don't fight.

When you look at social media in terms of just being social, I think everything becomes clearer. Act the way you should at a regular social event and you'll be just fine. One last thing we all learned in kindergarten that applies to social media: Not everyone needs to know when you have to use the little boys' room.

RECESS!!!

Understanding Communication Technology

Facebook in Canadian Universities

. . . Since its inception, Facebook has grown to become the primary social media tool for written communication amongst large groups, outdoing blogs and sometimes even e-mail.

Post-secondary schools have embraced Facebook for a variety of both professional and personal uses. Professionally, it is now a widely used tool for advertising their programs, athletic teams, and alumni, often creating new Facebook groups for every academic year (in these cases, only the general Facebook group has been included, and not for example, every graduating class group from 1998–2008). Also not included are personal Facebook groups, created by one individual to promote a certain cause and not necessarily related to that school. However, even with these restrictions, there are still almost 1,400 'official' Facebook groups in Canada that relate to universities and colleges. In fact, there are only a handful of schools in Canada that have NOT used Facebook to some degree (mostly smaller private colleges).

Facebook is meant to bind people together by sharing information and communicating updates instantly. Because of this, most Facebook groups are 'open' (i.e., accessible to the general public). This means that even if you are not a college or university student, you can still participate in the lifestyle vicariously. This has some pitfalls, as with other types of social media there is a lack of privacy, which has led to some legal issues. Due to this, some Facebook groups have chosen a 'closed' format (i.e., you can become a member by invitation only), and within post-secondary Facebook groups, just less than 10 per cent of groups choose this route.

Open vs. Closed Facebook Groups

Facebook has become another valuable tool when it comes to prospective students shopping for a post-secondary school. You can now find out if that school's music program is all that great, which society to join, and where the social action is going to be. Knowing this, many schools now have recruitment Facebook groups, where they advertise their school's attributes, mention which cities that

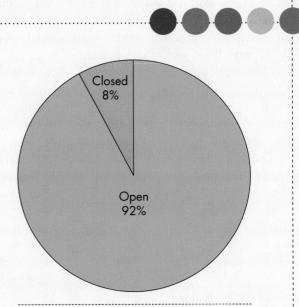

Figure 8.1

Open vs. Closed Facebook Groups

school's representatives will be visiting, or make it easier for you to schedule a personal visit. And Facebook is making the transition from high school to college or university easier. Now if you have to pack up and move to a new city, you will already have several Facebook friends doing the same thing, which makes the first-year experience much more enjoyable.

Prevalence of Facebook Groups in Canadian Post-Secondary Schools

Generally speaking, school size is roughly related to the number of Facebook groups it generates. However, as with blogs, some schools have disproportionately more Facebook groups than the average. The University of Manitoba and the University of Waterloo (both small schools) have 84 and 85 Facebook groups respectively, many more than the average of 5. The University of Ottawa (a medium school) has 63 Facebook groups, and the average for a medium school is 26. And the University of Toronto (a large school) has 99 Facebook groups, compared to the average of 37. Overall it is the universities of Manitoba and Waterloo that have the most number of Facebook groups per capita.

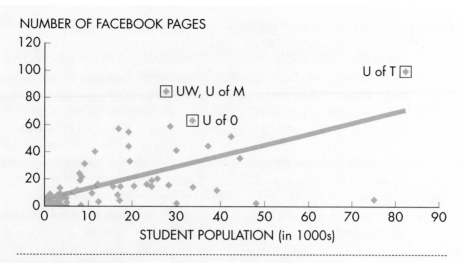

Figure 8.2
Prevalence of Facebook Groups

Type of Facebook Groups in Canadian Post-Secondary Schools

Post-secondary schools employ several types of Facebook groups:

1. **Administrative:** These types of Facebook groups relate to administrative units at a post-secondary school, such as language centres, libraries, staff, and recruitment departments. It can also refer to a general Facebook group that is non-specific. Most post-secondary schools have at least one administrative Facebook group's general all-encompassing one that is used by all members of that school and is not specific. Administrative groups make up about 15 per cent of all Canadian post-secondary Facebook groups.

2. **Alumni:** These are the preferred online tool when it comes to keeping in touch with former students. Almost every post-secondary school will also have one of these types of Facebook groups in addition to the general Facebook group. Alumni groups can be further broken up according to faculty or by graduation year. Despite most post-secondary schools having at

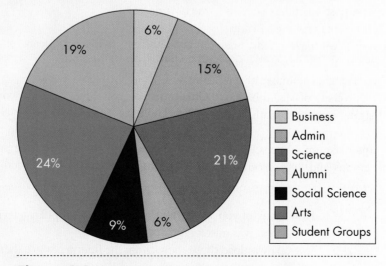

Figure 8.3
Type of Facebook Groups

least one such group, they only make up 6 per cent of post-secondary groups, due to the fact that so many other groups (especially academic ones) are possible for each school.

3. **Student groups:** Societies, non-academic clubs, athletics, student unions, etc. make up this group. About 20 per cent of post-secondary Facebook groups will be of this nature, reflecting the usefulness of Facebook for announcing meetings, sporting events, social activities, etc. The vast majority of this group consists of various cultural clubs (given the great diversity of cultures at most universities and colleges) and appears to be the primary method of communication within these types of Clubs.

Academic Facebook Groups

Academic groups make up the remaining ~60 per cent of post-secondary Facebook groups. Since this group is so large and varied, it's been broken down further into four academic groups: sciences, arts, social sciences, and business. These Facebook groups reflect specific departments or faculties and also academically inclined clubs. This broad grouping has the greatest chance of using closed Facebook groups, due to the course-specific and potentially sensitive nature of some of these groups.

1. **Science Facebook groups** make up 36 per cent of academic Facebook groups and 21 per cent of the overall groups. Most post-secondary schools known for their science programs (e.g., Acadia, Dalhousie, Waterloo, etc.) will have at least one science Facebook group, if not more. In fact Waterloo has the second-highest number of science groups (27 . . . University of Manitoba has 28), reflecting their strong computer, math, and robotics programs.

2. **Arts Facebook groups** make up 39 per cent of academic Facebook groups and 24 per cent of the overall groups, edging out sciences slightly. The University of Toronto, with its varied arts programs and three campuses, has the highest number of Facebook groups (21), just edging out the University of Waterloo with 20.

3. **Social Sciences Facebook groups** make up 15 per cent of academic groups and 9 per cent of the overall groups. The University of Calgary and the University of Windsor, with 8–10 Facebook groups devoted to social sciences, has the highest, mostly relating to their law schools.

4. Finally, **business Facebook groups** make up 11 per cent of academic groups and 6 per cent of the overall groups. The University of Manitoba, with seven groups, has the most, mostly relating to their School of Business. Other prominent universities and colleges with a well-known business school, such as Saint Mary's University or Ryerson University, also have numerous Facebook groups devoted to their business school.

Facebook usage as a social media tool for post-secondary institutions is expected to increase, especially as new features are added. Some schools are already advertising their Facebook groups on their homepage as a primary research tool for prospective students, and making entire web pages devoted to links to their various social media. Static web pages are becoming outdated, and content that is updated daily, or even hourly, is becoming the new norm.

—canadian-universities.net/Facebook/Facebook_in_ Canadian_Universities.html

Questions: Do you think social networking services such as Facebook are going to radically change the way instructors teach? Or will they just be integrated into the other traditional methods? Will the traditional methods be transformed, extended, or replaced?

4. How many of you are current with the most popular television programs? (Almost every hand was raised.)
5. Do you download those shows from the Internet or PVR them? (Every hand shot up.)

While this survey is anecdotal and certainly not scientific, it does signal a massive shift in the way people experience and consume media. Anecdotally again, Professor Sévigny asked many of the same questions of a group of senior citizens at a session on communication literacy. Fascinatingly, the answers were much the same! This suggests that everything that traditional media executives used to think about how to research, develop, and sell media content to the populations of younger and older people must be completely rethought.

Newspapers

When, in 2001, Google News began using computers and artificial intelligence systems to edit a website that brought its reading public the news of the world, many experts began to worry that no one would ever pay for news content again. In fact, Google News has highlighted how inefficient and conformist the international news industry has become, and at the time of this printing, Google has entered into serious discussions with the world's major newsgathering and news publishing organizations about how to construct paywalls to make readers pay for content.

Newspapers are changing as we speak. They are migrating away from print and towards electronic distribution models. They are embracing Twitter and communicating directly with subscribers who want to follow breaking stories in real time. Twitter is pushing users to the newspaper website. In early May 2010, *The Hamilton Spectator* tweeted that a 'crocodilian-type' creature had been spotted in Hamilton Harbour. The newspaper then tweeted updates about the creature throughout the day, finally announcing that the search for the creature had been called off. The experience drove many people, especially young people who appreciated the schlocky humour of the story, to the newspaper's website. The following day's print edition of the paper contained the full story; however, it is very debatable whether these same people picked up a copy.

> **Cultural Idiom**
>
> **paywall**
> a barrier that stops users from accessing the body of a news article if they have not paid for a subscription to the website or, depending on the model, the individual article

Television

Television is undergoing a transformation toward a watch-on-demand model of content delivery. Although broadcasters are caving in to the fact that many people would rather visit their websites to watch TV shows, they are having a lot of trouble finding a revenue model for those sites because no one has quite figured out how to deliver advertising through an online video broadcasting model. Some producers are counting on revenues generated by the stunning quality of Blu-ray discs or the 'extra features' that can be included on them. In September 2010, Steve Jobs, CEO of Apple, Inc., announced a new version of AppleTV that loans out television programs or movies, in the digital equivalent of how we borrow movies from Rogers Video. Time will tell what will end up happening with television in the social media world.

Radio

Radio is a spectacular exception to the trend. Canadians spend an enormous amount of time commuting, which has led to an explosion in the market for satellite radio services like Sirius Canada and XM Canada (even though the two companies have merged, at the time of printing, they were still offering separate subscription services). As well, conventional radio has flourished in the vehicle culture, as well as in busy workplaces where the drone of talk radio or music programming provides a welcome backdrop to a long and sometimes tedious

Understanding Communication Technology

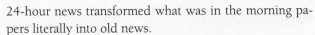

How Google Can Help Newspapers

It's the year 2015. The compact device in my hand delivers me the world, one news story at a time. I flip through my favourite papers and magazines, the images as crisp as in print, without a maddening wait for each page to load.

Even better, the device knows who I am, what I like, and what I have already read. So while I get all the news and comment, I also see stories tailored for my interests. I zip through a health story in *The Wall Street Journal* and a piece about Iraq from Egypt's *Al Gomhuria,* translated automatically from Arabic to English. I tap my finger on the screen, telling the computer brains underneath it got this suggestion right.

Some of these stories are part of a monthly subscription package. Some, where the free preview sucks me in, cost a few pennies billed to my account. Others are available at no charge, paid for by advertising. But these ads are not static pitches for products I'd never use. Like the news I am reading, the ads are tailored just for me. Advertisers are willing to shell out a lot of money for this targeting.

This is a long way from where we are today. The current technology . . . may be relatively old, but it is a model of simplicity and speed compared with the online news experience today. I can flip through pages much faster in the physical edition of *The Journal* than I can on the Web. And every time I return to a site, I am treated as a stranger.

So when I think about the current crisis in the print industry, this is where I begin—a traditional technology struggling to adapt to a new, disruptive world. It is a familiar story: it was the arrival of radio and television that started the decline of newspaper circulation. Afternoon newspapers were the first casualties. Then the advent of 24-hour news transformed what was in the morning papers literally into old news.

Now the Internet has broken down the entire news package with articles read individually, reached from a blog or search engine, and abandoned if there is no good reason to hang around once the story is finished. It's what we have come to call internally the atomic unit of consumption.

Painful as this is to newspapers and magazines, the pressures on their ad revenue from the Internet is causing even greater damage. The choice facing advertisers targeting consumers in San Francisco was once between an ad in the *Chronicle* or *Examiner*. Then came Craigslist, making it possible to get local classifieds for free, followed by Ebay and specialist websites. Now search engines like Google connect advertisers directly with consumers looking for what they sell.

With dwindling revenue and diminished resources, frustrated newspaper executives are looking for someone to blame. Much of their anger is currently directed at Google, whom many executives view as getting all the benefit from the business relationship without giving much in return. The facts, I believe, suggest otherwise.

Google is a great source of promotion. We send online news publishers a billion clicks a month from Google News and more than three billion extra visits from our other services, such as Web Search and iGoogle. That is 100,000 opportunities a minute to win loyal readers and generate revenue—for free. In terms of copyright, another bone of contention, we only show a headline and a couple of lines from each story. If readers want to read on they have to click through to the newspaper's website. (The exception are stories we host through a licensing agreement

workday. Interestingly, alongside the success of conventional and satellite radio, we have seen a surge in the availability of Internet radio stations. Starting such a station doesn't cost a lot of money, and you can broadcast easily to a world audience. Again, workplace listening as well as home listening through computers is driving this growing trend. The interesting problem with Internet radio is that subscribers are not used to paying for online radio content; the business model has yet to be made profitable.

with news services.) And if they wish, publishers can remove their content from our search index, or from Google News.

The claim that we're making big profits on the back of newspapers also misrepresents the reality. In search, we make our money primarily from advertisements for products. Someone types in 'digital camera' and gets ads for digital cameras. A typical news search—for Afghanistan, say—may generate few if any ads. The revenue generated from the ads shown alongside news search queries is a tiny fraction of our search revenue.

It's understandable to look to find someone else to blame. But as Rupert Murdoch has said, it is complacency caused by past monopolies, not technology, that has been the real threat to the news industry.

We recognize, however, that a crisis for newsgathering is not just a crisis for the newspaper industry. The flow of accurate information, diverse views, and proper analysis is critical for a functioning democracy. We also acknowledge that it has been difficult for newspapers to make money from their online content. But just as there is no single cause of the industry's current problems, there is no single solution. We want to work with publishers to help them build bigger audiences, better engage readers, and make more money.

Meeting that challenge will mean using technology to develop new ways to reach readers and keep them engaged for longer, as well as new ways to raise revenue combining free and paid access. I believe it also requires a change of tone in the debate, a recognition that we all have to work together to fulfill the promise of journalism in the digital age.

Google is serious about playing its part. We are already testing, with more than three dozen major partners from the news industry, a service called Google Fast Flip. The theory—which seems to work in practice—is that if we make it easier to read articles, people will read more of them. Our news partners will receive the majority of the revenue generated by the display ads shown beside stories.

Nor is there a choice, as some newspapers seem to think, between charging for access to their online content or keeping links to their articles in Google News and Google Search. They can do both.

This is a start. But together we can go much further toward that fantasy news gadget I outlined at the start. The acceleration in mobile phone sophistication and ownership offers tremendous potential. As more of these phones become connected to the Internet, they are becoming reading devices, delivering stories, business reviews, and ads. These phones know where you are and can provide geographically relevant information. There will be more news, more comment, more opportunities for debate in the future, not less.

The best newspapers have always held up a mirror to their communities. Now they can offer a digital place for their readers to congregate and talk. And just as we have seen different models of payment for TV as choice has increased and new providers have become involved, I believe we will see the same with news. We could easily see free access for mass-market content funded from advertising alongside the equivalent of subscription and pay-for-view for material with a niche readership.

I certainly don't believe that the Internet will mean the death of news. Through innovation and technology, it can endure with newfound profitability and vitality. Video didn't kill the radio star. It created a whole new additional industry.

'How Google Can Help Newspapers', written by Eric Schmidt and published in the Wall Street Journal on Dec. 1, 2009. © Google. Used with permission.

Questions: How do you receive your news? Do you think that Google News will in fact transform the news industry, making it more efficient and responsive to news consumers' needs? Or will it lead to a dehumanization of the news?

Using Social Media Effectively

The main advantage that social media offer is, as we have stressed throughout this chapter, interactivity and community-building. They permit people who may otherwise not have had ready access to a variety of types of content to suddenly have a world of possibilities open to them.

> *As technology advances, it reverses the characteristics of every situation again and again. The age of automation is going to be the age of 'do it yourself'.*
>
> Marshall McLuhan

> *The contemporary artist is always seeking new patterns, new pattern recognition, which is his task, for heaven's sake. The absolute indispensability of the artist is that he alone in the encounter with the present can get the pattern recognition. He alone has the century awareness to tell us what the world is made of. He's more important than the scientist, scientists will be waking up to this shortly and will be resorting en masse to the artist's studio in order to discover the forms of the material they are dealing with . . . the scientist lives in a world of matching, and his idea of proof or verification is just the idea of matching evidence against evidence. When somebody doesn't match but makes a new breakthrough, this is just as disturbing to the scientist as to the educator.*
>
> Marshall McLuhan

A second major advantage that social media confer is that of trust. When your 'friend' on Facebook or someone you follow on Twitter posts something, you can make a judgment call on the person's credibility based on what you know of them. Presumably, you have 'friended' this person or accepted his or her friend request because you felt some affinity toward him or her.

A third major advantage that social media give is the possibility of learning more about your friends by having a privileged glimpse at their lives through the content that they post online: their bookmarks on Delicious, their likes and dislikes as well as photos and notes on Facebook, and their news clippings and videos posted to Reddit or Digg.

All of these advantages allow you to build a profile of your friends in your mind. It is as if you are in a constant (although somewhat one-sided) ongoing conversation with them, and, through the passage of time, you can deepen relationships with people who live far away. Consider that you are in a large interactive community, built on trust through which you share very private photos, notes, news clippings, blog posts, microblog entries, music selections, or likes and dislikes.

In many ways the melding of space-binding technology with a new, emergent time-binding culture signals a massive transformation that our society, culture, and economy is undergoing. We are shifting from a culture of check-boxes, categories, and organized information to one where information flows through a constant, ongoing digital conversation. As Marshall McLuhan famously stated, the greatest skill in the digital age is *pattern recognition*.

When you use social media, you must remember that you are establishing a pattern of online digital behaviour. Every time you post something to Twitter, a photo to Facebook, a status update to MySpace, a video to YouTube, or a bookmark to Delicious, you create a pattern of information that others decode and interpret. You can use this knowledge to build a strong personal brand that lends you credibility and reinforces your professional, moral, or community status. If you are a savvy user of social media, you can craft a permanent personal brand that will be very hard for others to discredit. As a student, you can build a portfolio of your achievements, thoughts, and ideals using social media that others will encounter when they surf the Internet. You can inspire them to respect you and consult you for an opinion. You can move them with beautiful images and thoughts that you post. You can prove to the world that you are an expert and a good communicator of that expertise. In fact, many prospective employers will 'google you' to find out more about you before they interview you. Having a digital footprint that you are proud of will help you get jobs, make friends, and build credibility. However, having negative or unflattering content about you floating in cyberspace can be very dangerous to your reputation, your job, and your relationship prospects. In the next section, we explore some of those dangers.

Dangers of Social Media

Social media are an incredibly powerful way to connect with others and build your reputation and credibility. However, they pose very serious reputational dangers if you are not savvy about how you use them.

The main truth to remember is that everything that you post to social media is *permanent*. As soon as you post an image or a text, or when someone else posts one about you, it is stored on a series of computers at the social media service's headquarters. The moment that another user views the image or reads the text, a copy of it may be stored on the hard drive of his or her computer. This image or text will probably end up being stored on hundreds, thousands, or even tens of thousands of computers worldwide. Furthermore, *you have instantly lost control of that image or text.* Others can interpret it as they choose. They can add comments to it. They can string it together with other pieces of information that they have gathered about you to 'build a story' about you and then disseminate it to millions of other users within minutes. You can probably think of cases where someone sent inappropriate e-mails to a few friends, only to have them forwarded around the world. Another example is how text messages revealed Tiger Woods's marital infidelities.

Some young people do impulsive things. Drunken excess, sexual experimentation, drug-taking, or minor criminal activity such as theft, assault, or vandalism—all of these things can happen. If such activities are done in private and not recorded, it is the word of any witnesses against yours. Any allegations others may make about you are hearsay and are not very credible.

Now, imagine that some of those behaviours had been photographed or videotaped and posted to Facebook or YouTube. These are circumstances that could have nightmarish consequences for your future career and relationships. The thing to remember is that many of the people who have access to your social media profile *are not your friends.* Many of them are quasi-strangers who could easily choose to profit from your momentary misstep. Google CEO Eric Schmidt has recently said that young people may have to change their names and identities to escape from the garish or embarrassing social media profiles they have built.[15]

Protecting Yourself On Social Media

How can you protect yourself in the world of social media? The answer is simple. You must *police your image.* Here are some tips that could help keep you safe:

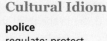

police
regulate; protect

- Always think twice before posting something risqué to social media. Count to a hundred before pressing 'send'.
- Be aware of people taking digital pictures or videos of you. Refuse to sign a release form and tell the photographer/videographer that you do not authorize publication of your image. Be assertive about this.
- Be careful of people who cajole you into compromising situations during Spring Break or at parties, casinos, vacation resorts, or nightclubs. Chances are you may be under the influence of alcohol, drugs, or simply just the pounding music. Your judgment is suspect and you are more prone to impulsive behaviour. Also, locations such as these have a much higher than average number of people whose hidden agenda is to take advantage of you. There is an entire amateur porn industry that proves that 'What happens in Vegas, stays in Vegas' just no longer applies.

In the digital age, there is no privacy and no distance. If you are aware of these facts, you can protect yourself easily and enjoy all of the incredible connectivity and community-building opportunities that social media can offer you.

Understanding Communication Technology

Facing Up to a Question of Privacy

Not so long ago, I found myself in characteristically pugnacious discussion with a senior human rights figure.

The issue was privacy. Her view was that there was an innate and largely unchanging human need for privacy. My view was that privacy was a culturally determined concept. Think of those open multi-seated Roman latrines in Pompeii, and imagine having one installed at work.

The specific point was whether there was a generational difference in attitudes towards privacy, partly as a consequence of Internet social networking. I thought that there was.

As a teenager, I told my parents absolutely nothing and the world little more. Some girls of that era might be photographed bare-breasted at a rock festival, and some guys might be pictured smoking dope but, on the whole, once we left through the front door, we disappeared from sight.

My Generation Y children seem unworried by their mother's capacity to track them and their social lives via Facebook.

In fact, they seem unworried by anybody's capacity to see what they're up to—until, of course, it goes wrong. They seem to want to be in sight, and much effort goes into creating the public identity that they want others to see.

There was an estimate last month that Facebook has something like 130 million unique visits every day. It now acts as a vast marketplace for ideas, preferences, suggestions, and actings-out, extending far beyond the capacity of conventional institutions to influence. And the privacy issues it raises have little to do with the conventional obsessions such as CCTV or government data.

At a conference at the weekend, I heard that some US colleges had taken to looking at the Facebook sites of applicants before they think to alter them in preparation for an interview. This may turn out to be apocryphal, but such a thing could be done.

In this era of supplementing exam grades with personal statements and character assessments, what could be more useful than an unguarded record of a student's true enthusiasms? What else did Tristram do on his horizon-expanding journey to the developing world?

This would have driven me crazy. My daughter's college friends, she says, are 'pretty chilled' about it. There are the odd occasions when a vinous clinch is snapped on a mobile phone and makes the social rounds to the embarrassment of the clinchers, but whatever will be will be.

An EU survey two years ago suggested that this is the pattern more generally. The researchers discovered what seemed to be a paradox: although half of their young respondents were confident in their own ability to protect their online privacy, only a fifth thought it a practical idea to give users in general 'more control over their own identity data'. In other words (and this is my interpretation), they didn't think that their peers could be bothered with extra protection and they felt fairly happy with their own.

Meanwhile, their elders try to get them concerned about issues such as Internet data harvesting by private

Key Theories of Communication

It is interesting that the average person, when asked, will say that society in general is indeed affected by the media, but that he or she personally is not. In fact, most people remain extremely interested in media effects and equally confused about them. Do violent television shows and films cause violence in society? Do print media contribute to society's moral decline? Does spending hours with 'friends' on social media sites actually disconnect people from their families or neighbours?

A quick look at some key theories will help explain the effects that media have both on societies and on the people who inhabit them. Although these theories were all originally companies. A US news report last week concerned the work done to create 'privacy nudges'—software that reminds users at certain moments that the information they are about to divulge has implications for privacy. One privacy campaigner even suggested that people might be rewarded with lottery tickets for not giving out such knowledge.

I have to say, as someone who often elects to receive online mailshots from companies operating in areas in which I'm interested, that this seems to me to miss the main problem. As long as you have the right to say 'no' to a company's blandishments, I don't see a huge problem.

That's why the now notorious Italian bullying video seems much more relevant. At the end of last week, three Google employees were sentenced in absentia for breaching the privacy of a handicapped boy, whose horrid treatment at the hands of his Turin schoolmates had been posted on Google Video. This clip spent several months in circulation.

Almost everyone agrees that the sentence was wrong, perverse, and a kick in the teeth for free speech, with implications that could (but won't) undermine the Internet. And they are quite right. But look at it, for a moment, from the point of view of the boy's parents, or the boy himself. They must have felt powerless and damaged. So how much control or ownership can one have over one's own image and reputation?

The second great question, then, raised with regard to the net is what might be called 'reputation management', or—if you like—public identity management. What is it that you want people to know about you, and can you have control over it?

Last weekend, I was alerted to two new phenomena, both of which caused me to miss a heartbeat. The first was the possibility of using a program, or employing some-

one, to 'suicide' you online. Recently a company in The Netherlands used its Facebook presence to advertise its 'Web 2.0 suicide machine', which would act as 'a digital Dr Kevorkian [and] delete your online presence' from Facebook, MySpace, Twitter, and LinkedIn, not just on your own sites but on everyone else's—leaving just a few 'last words'. Facebook chucked the suicide machine off its premises, so it then suicided itself, ending with the words 'no flowers, no speeches'.

As a journalist, I was horrified by the implications of online suiciding. It means the erasure of documentary history, plus it raises the possibility of doctoring of material on the Internet to render it more palatable to the offended.

The second phenomenon was worse. It was that some people, many perhaps, might seek to undermine any informational authority on the Web by flooding it with false information, thus obliquely protecting their own identities. As an occasional target of such misinformation, sometimes playfully and sometimes maliciously, I know it can play merry hell with everyone's sense of reality.

In other words, it seemed to me that there was a threat much worse than that to privacy, and that was of privacy-induced attempts to bend or erase the truth essential to the value of the Internet. Lack of privacy may be uncomfortable. Lack of truth is fatal.

—David Aaronovitch, *The Australian,* 3 March 2010.

Questions: Do you engage in reputation management? How alert have you been to what identity you are projecting on the Internet? Do you have a different standard for truth online than in real life? Have you told lies or exaggerated about yourself online? If so, why?

---

posed as theories of mass communication, they have been increasingly applied to interpersonal and converging media in recent research.[16]

Harold Innis's Theory of Time-Binding and Space-Binding Media

Harold Innis thought of media in the same way that he thought of the Canadian railway system—a necessary infrastructure that transports goods from one part of the country to another. Railways carry material goods, such as livestock, automobiles, or grain. In the case of newspapers or broadcast media, the goods transported are not of a material nature but are symbolic. Just as we saw in Chapter 1, all communication is symbolic. Broadcast media transport communication symbols to the furthest reaches of Canada, bringing information, education, entertainment, and news to all of its citizens who are capable of interpreting the media's messages. This information is a major factor in empowering those citizens to engage successfully and knowledgably in commerce, politics, education, culture, and society.

For Innis, radical ideas develop in the hinterland and spread inwards toward the centre of power. As the ideas get closer to this centre, they are adopted by an ever-wider cross section of the population, and thus become more conventional themselves. Once a radical message has completed its voyage from the hinterland to the centre of power and has been accepted and adopted by those citizens at the centre, the message has become conventional. Then a new radical message arises to eventually replace the old one, which is now a social convention. Innis claimed that new media create struggles between ideas and systems of power. In his famous article 'Minerva's Owl', he lists how different empires rose and fell because of their reliance on certain types of media, from the clay and stylus at the beginnings of civilization to the parchment and pen during the Dark Ages, to the printing press during the Renaissance, and to the growth of cinema and radio in the twentieth century.[17]

An excellent example of this process is found in the music industry. A new radical band will generally be perceived as 'alternative' when it starts its career. It will be listened to by culturally savvy people, who scorn Top 40 music and commercial bands in favour of novelty and originality. However, this band may eventually become popular beyond the indy fringe and gain currency with the general public. It starts to see its singles being played on commercial radio, rather than campus or alternative Internet stations. Soon, the alternative band is selling millions of albums on iTunes, and its music is being played on Top 40 countdowns all over Canada. The radical alternative new band has become mainstream. Its original fans will now reject the once radical band, calling it a sellout. They will look for a new alternative band to listen to, one that no one in the mainstream knows about.

Harold Innis was also unique as a theorist because he applied the concepts of time and space to media. He made a distinction between two sorts of media: time-binding media and space-binding media.

Time-binding media collapse time by figuratively bringing their audiences back to the *original moment of communication* (see Table 8.1). Thus, the time between, for example, the moment of the first telling of a story and the moment of your hearing or reading it is collapsed. You *re-experience* the same moment in time as the initial telling. For societies that rely on time-binding communication media, time is circular. The stories are written on papyrus, stone, or vellum, for example—all materials that are difficult to work with and not very portable, but very durable. To cap it off, most people in time-binding societies are illiterate. These societies tend to be oral and traditional, and the knowledge they preserve tends to be practical or religious in nature. Why? Because the major medium of storage of information in a time-binding society is the human mind—and we all know how limited its storage capacity can be.

Space-binding media are more portable but less permanent than time-binding media (see Table 8.1). They include modern broadcast media such as radio, television, and mass circulation newspapers. Space-binding media, in opposition to time-binding media, *collapse space*—they convey information that is meant to reach as many citizens as possible over long distances. Another difference is that space-binding media don't last very long. Think of the difference between a DVD and a stone tablet. An average quality DVD will be fortunate to maintain its integrity for 20 years, whereas the stone tablet may still be around a thousand years after it was made. Societies that depend on space-binding media are very different than those dependent on time-binding media. Space-binding societies are prone to rapid change

---

space-binding media
A term coined by Harold Innis to describe types of media, such as television, that collapse space by conveying information that is meant to reach as many citizens as possible over long distances.

time-binding media
A term coined by Harold Innis to describe types of media, such as storytelling, that collapse time by figuratively bringing their audiences back to the original moment of communication.

TABLE 8.1 Characteristics of Time-Binding and Space-Binding Media and Societies

Time-Binding Media	Space-Binding Media
• are very durable • are created by a small class of experts (e.g., scribes or monks) • collapse time and eliminate it as a constraint of the flow of stories and experiences from one generation to the next • include scribe-copied manuscripts on parchment or vellum, oral stories and songs, and traditional dances • carry messages that last for generations, but reach very limited audiences	• are not long-lasting • are easy to work with and transport • collapse space and eliminate it as a constraint on the flow of information • include radio, television, mass circulation newspapers, e-books, CDs, DVDs, Blu-rays, and telephones • carry messages that deteriorate in a short time, but reach vast audiences

Time-Binding Societies	Space-Binding Societies
• are stable and long-lasting • are traditional • favour the preservation of traditional, practical, and religious knowledge • have a circular concept of time; time flows and is not as divisible as in space-binding societies; 'Time is cycling through important rituals.'	• are unstable and prone to rapid change • are materialistic and secular • tend toward imperialism • have a linear concept of time; time is divided into measurable bits and value is attached to the bits; 'Time is money.'

because of the easy flow of information from one end of the society to the other. They are also very materialistic and secular. Space-binding media push standardized information out to millions of receivers, laying the foundation for a common system of education, a powerful national system of news and information, and the storage capacity for all of the records and data generated by a very large and complicated economy. As a result, space-binding societies often tend to become empires.

Marshall McLuhan's Theories

Marshall McLuhan accepted Harold Innis's concept of communication, but he took it in a more psychological direction. We will discuss three of his theories in this section: 'the medium is the message', the tetrad, and hot versus cool media.

McLuhan made the famous observation, quoted earlier in this chapter, that 'the medium is the message.' That is, the medium of communication is actually far more important to the receiver's interpretation of the message than the message's actual content. He said that the media extend our senses—the television extends the eye, clothing extends the skin, radio extends the ear. In essence, McLuhan claimed that media make us cyborgs, biological creatures whose abilities are extended by technology.

For example, imagine that you want to invite a friend to the movies tonight, and you want to increase the probability that he or she will come. How will you do it?

- You could ask your friend face-to-face by saying, 'Would you like to go to the movies tonight? I hear there's a good one playing downtown.' This would feel personal and intimate. The medium of face-to-face oral communication creates a feeling of immediacy and psychological intimacy.
- You could write him or her a note using the same words. This is slightly less personal than speaking face-to-face, but it is still in your handwriting and quite

intimate. Plus, the fact that your friend can look at it again by taking it out of his or her pocket makes it more impactful.

- You could write an e-mail with the same sentences. This may be perceived as less intimate and more of a spur-of-the-moment thought on your part. Your friend may take the invitation more lightly because e-mails are typed in a standardized font—they are not personal. As well, he or she will probably not print it out and carry it in a pocket, like your written note.
- You could telephone your friend and say the same sentences, which is personal but not intimate. There is not only a great physical distance between the two of you, but your voice will also lose a lot of its features because of the quality of the telephone signal. Your 'telephone voice' may sound disinterested, even though you are very eager to go!
- Finally, you could send a text message. Your friend might think that you're being spontaneous and asking him or her to the movies on a whim.

So you see, it is obvious that the same message sent via different media carries a very different value and meaning to your receiver. An effective communicator will take McLuhan's dictum to heart.

Another of McLuhan's ideas that gained enormous currency in the world of communications theory was his **tetrad**, which was composed of his four laws of the media. These laws can be expressed as questions to help us understand the power of a new medium:

1. What does a new medium improve or enhance, make possible or accelerate?
2. When pushed to its limits, the new form will reverse to its original positive characteristics. What is the reversal potential of the new form?
3. What earlier action, form, or service is brought back into play by the new form? What older, previously obsolete form is brought back and becomes an essential part of the new form?
4. What is pushed aside or made obsolete by the new media?

McLuhan insisted that, although it can take years to feel the full effects, all four of these questions are answered simultaneously when a new medium breaks into the culture and begins to change it. Because 'the medium is the message', everything changes as soon as a new medium becomes available, even if people don't know it yet. For example, let's look at the automobile:

- The automobile enhances speed.
- It reverses into gridlock and traffic jams.
- It retrieves the age of knights in shining armour on powerful steeds.
- It throws the horse and buggy into obsolescence.

Let's also look at the cellphone[18]:

- The cellphone enhances the voice.
- It reverses into an 'invisible leash'.
- It retrieves the cries of childhood. 'Mom, Dad—I want attention, NOW!'
- It throws the telephone booth into obsolescence.

McLuhan also understood about where the Internet would take us—he thought that the world was becoming a **global village**, which he considered a place where everyone

global village
A reference to an effect of social media, which makes people more connected with others and involved in their lives, as well as the politics and cultures of other countries.

tetrad
The collective term given to Marshall McLuhan's four laws of media.

is heavily concerned with everyone else's business. He said that, although books were our original teaching machine and are still very important, the nature of their role is changing. We now have many different machines to process information which are all about simultaneity. McLuhan thought that this new connectedness would make us more involved in one another's lives and in the politics and cultures of other countries, that the awareness electronic media would bring us would be accompanied by a sense of responsibility. This term was so prophetic, that it is now used as a sort of shorthand for the social and political life of the World Wide Web.

Finally, McLuhan created the concept of hot and cool media. For McLuhan, **hot media** are high definition, or explicit; they leave very little to the user's imagination. For example, a black-and-white textbook which describes mathematical formulae step by step would be a very hot medium. **Cool media** have the opposite tendency. They are allusive, leaving an awful lot to the imagination of the user, who has to fill in the blanks him- or herself. An excellent example of cool media are comic books which suggest action and use few words. The reader must fill in the rest of the details.

COMMUNICATION ON-SCREEN

McLuhan's Wake (2002)
Directed by Kevin McMahon.

McLuhan's Wake is a visually stunning film, full of poetic insight on McLuhan's life. The film is narrated by performance artist Laurie Anderson and features commentaries from Eric McLuhan (Marshall's son), Neil Postman, Lewis Lapham, and Patrick Watson. By appealing to the five senses and using all forms of media, the film captures how McLuhan viewed the world. McLuhan managed, 30 years before the Internet revolution, to predict with astonishing accuracy how information technology would change our culture and society. While his ideas were dismissed by his contemporaries as outlandish, he is now completely vindicated. This film tells his story.

Flow Theories

Some of the earliest theories of media effects, **flow theories,** deal mainly with how effects travel, or 'flow', from the mass media to their audiences.

Bullet Theory

Early mass media researchers—those who worked between the two world wars—developed an approach based on the idea that the media had direct, powerful effects.[19] According to this theory, later termed **bullet theory,** people who watched, say, violent movies would become violent, and those who read 'immoral' comic books would become immoral. The problem for the researchers was that these powerful, bullet-like effects were very difficult to prove, especially over the long term. Eventually, this theory gave way to a different theoretical model: two-step flow theory.

Two-Step Flow Theory

Research during and after World War II focused on the idea that media effects operate in a two-step process, occurring mostly in interaction with interpersonal communication. Researchers characterized **two-step flow theory** this way: people would hear a message over the radio, perhaps a speech by a political candidate or a commercial message for a new type of laundry soap. Then, rather than immediately pledging their support for the candidate or buying the soap, they would discuss it with opinion leaders—people they knew, such as friends or relatives, whom they viewed as credible sources of information on a particular topic. If the opinion leaders gave positive feedback, the people who had heard the original message might become supporters of the candidate or product.

Multi-Step Flow Theory

Many communication researchers today believe that the theorists who devised two-step flow theory were moving in the correct direction but didn't go far enough. **Multi-step flow theory**

Cultural Idiom

fill in the blanks
supply missing information from one's own knowledge or imagination

bullet theory
A theory that posits that mass media has direct, powerful effects on their audiences.

cool media
According to Marshall McLuhan, media that are allusive require users to use their imaginations to supply missing information.

flow theories
Theories that deal mainly with how effects travel, or 'flow', from the mass media to their audiences.

hot media
According to Marshall McLuhan, media that are explicit and leave very little to users' imaginations.

multi-step flow theory
The theory that mass media effects are part of a complex interaction.

two-step flow theory
The theory that mass media effects operate in a two-step process, mostly in interaction with interpersonal communication.

posits that media effects are part of a complex interaction.[20] In that interaction, opinion leaders have their own opinion leaders, who in turn have opinion leaders. Your friend might be your opinion leader about what sort of computer to buy, but your friend probably formed his or her own opinions on the basis of those developed by other people.

Besides demonstrating how theories become more sophisticated as they are explored over time, flow theories demonstrate the importance of interpersonal communication in the effects of mass communication. They show that mass media don't operate in a vacuum; their effects are filtered on their way to the recipient through the reactions of others. It's worth noting that even though the bullet theory is largely discredited today, we still have daily examples of some types of mediated messages having the direct, powerful effects that early researchers predicted. Many products become overnight successes through advertising, without enough time passing to give interpersonal communication much time to operate. A new blockbuster movie, for example, can earn tens of millions of dollars during its first weekend thanks largely to 'hype'—advertising and positive reviews appearing in the mass media. But for the great majority of mediated messages, effects depend largely on how they interact with interpersonal communication. After a movie's opening weekend, its box office receipts are determined largely by 'word of mouth' communication.

Social Learning Theory

social learning theory
A theory based on the assumption that people learn how to behave by observing others, especially others portrayed in the mass media.

Flow theories aren't the only approach to studying media effects. **Social learning theory** offers a different perspective, beginning with the assumption that people learn how to behave by observing others—especially others portrayed in the mass media. The theory gained prominence from the experiments of Canadian psychologist Albert Bandura in the 1960s.[21] In Bandura's most famous studies, preschool children watched films in which an adult encountered Bobo, a three-foot-tall pop-up clown. One group of preschoolers saw a version in which the adult beat up Bobo and was then rewarded for being a 'strong champion'. Another group saw a version in which the adult assailant was scolded for being a bully and spanked with a rolled-up magazine. After watching the films, the children had their own chance to 'play' with Bobo. Bandura discovered that the children who saw the adult model's aggression being rewarded treated the Bobo doll with greater violence than did those who saw the adult model punished.

The implications of social modelling are obvious. It's easy to imagine how a 13-year-old who has just watched UFC or the movie *Watchmen* might be inspired to lash out at one of his or her friends the first time a disagreement arises. However, the theory also suggests that viewing prosocial models can teach constructive behaviour. The same 13-year-old, if he or she had just watched *Glee*, might be inspired to use one of those characters' non-violent, communicative approaches to problem-solving, rather than using his fists.

Social learning theory makes sense, and the original laboratory studies produced impressive results. But in everyday life the theory doesn't hold up quite so well.[22] After all, behaviour that is modelled from the media might not be successful in the real world. For example, 13-year-olds who try out their martial arts skills on the playground might be punched in the nose by tougher adversaries. The pain of that punch might do more to determine those children's attitudes toward violence than all the television viewing they will ever do. Also, it's worth remembering that all individuals are different, and this fact plays a role in determining how people are influenced by media. For example, boys seem to be influenced more by violent media than girls are, whereas girls seem to be swayed more by the body image of their media models—they often try to be as slim as high fashion models, showing their sensitivity to an influence that seldom has the same effect on boys. Observations such as these led to the development of the individual differences theory.

Individual Differences Theory

As its name suggests, **individual differences theory** looks at how media users with different characteristics are affected by the mass media.[23] Certain users are more susceptible to some types of media messages than are others. For example, a viewer with a high level of education might be more susceptible to a message that includes logical appeals. In addition to level of education, individual differences that help determine how the media affect individuals include age, sex, geographic region, intellectual level, socioeconomic class, level of violence in the home, and so on.

In addition to these demographic factors, there are psychological characteristics that more subtly distinguish media users. **Diffusion of innovations theory** identifies five types of people with different degrees of willingness to accept new ideas from the media.[24] These types also predict who will be first to use and become competent in new media.[25]

1. **Innovators:** These are venturesome people who are eager to try new ideas. They tend to be extroverts and politically liberal. They are the first to try out and become competent in new media, such as the Internet and the iPhone.
2. **Early adopters:** Less venturesome than innovators, these people still make a relatively quick, but informed, choice. Their somewhat more cautious approach makes them important opinion leaders within their social groups.
3. **Early majority:** These people make careful, deliberate choices after frequent interaction with their peers and their opinion leaders. They seldom act as opinion leaders themselves.
4. **Late majority:** More skeptical than the first three groups, these people tend to accept innovations less often. When they do adopt an innovation, they often do so out of economic necessity or increasing peer pressure.
5. **Laggards:** These people tend to be conservative, traditional, and the most resistant to any type of change. Their point of reference tends to be the past, and they tend to be socially isolated. Today, these are the people who are mystified by the Internet and might not even own a computer.

Cultivation Theory

According to **cultivation theory**, the media shape—and sometimes distort—our perceptions of the world.[26] Cultivation theory therefore works hand in hand with the facets of perception discussed in Chapter 2.

Advanced by George Gerbner and his associates at the University of Pennsylvania, cultivation theory predicts that media will teach a common worldview, common roles, and common values. Over time, they suggest, the media 'cultivate' a particular view of the world among users. For example, Gerbner's research found that people who watch a lot of television had a markedly different view of reality than did those who don't. The latter group overestimated their chances of being involved in some type of violence, overestimated the percentage of Americans who have jobs in law enforcement, and found people, in general, to be less trustworthy.

Cultivation theory suggests that the primary effect of television, therefore, is to give habitual viewers a perception that the world is less safe and upright, and more violent, than it

---

cultivation theory
A theory that claims that the media shape—and sometimes distort—our perceptions of the world.

diffusion of innovations theory
A theory that identifies five types of people with different degrees of willingness to accept new ideas from the media: innovators, early adopters, early majority, late majority, and laggards.

early adopters
In diffusion of innovations theory, people who make relatively quick, but informed, choices regarding mass media. Early adopters are important opinion leaders in their respective social groups.

early majority
In diffusion of innovations theory, people who make careful, deliberate choices after frequent interaction with their peers and their opinion leaders. People in this group are seldom opinion leaders.

individual differences theory
A theory that examines how mass media users with different characteristics are affected by media.

innovators
In diffusion of innovations theory, people who are eager to try new ideas. Innovators tend to be extroverts and politically liberal.

laggards
In diffusion of innovations theory, people who tend to be conservative, traditional, and the most resistant to any type of change. Their point of reference tends to be the past, and they tend to be socially isolated.

late majority
In diffusion of innovations theory, people who are more skeptical about accepting innovation and usually do so out of economic necessity or increasing peer pressure.

really is. Gerbner's findings help explain society's increasing tolerance of violence. Researchers suspect that this desensitization has a profound effect on interpersonal communication by making people less caring about the feelings and reactions of other people.

Agenda-Setting Theory

agenda-setting theory
A theory that argues that the media tell people not what to think but what to think about.

cumulative effects theory
A theory that states that media messages are understood through redundancy and have profound effects over time.

Another important approach to media effects was posited by researchers Donald Shaw and Maxwell McCombs in the 1970s. Studying the way political campaigns were covered in the media, they coined the term **agenda-setting theory** to describe the main role of the media. The media, they argued, tell people not what to think but rather what to think about. In other words, the amount of media attention given to an issue affects the level of importance assigned to that issue by consumers of mass media. Shaw and McCombs explained their findings as follows:

> Perhaps more than any other aspect of our environment, the political arena—all those issues and persons about whom we hold opinions and knowledge—is secondhand reality. Especially in national politics, we have little personal or direct contact. Our knowledge comes primarily from the mass media. For the most part, we know only those aspects of national politics considered newsworthy enough for transmission through the mass media.[27]

In other words, the media might not change your point of view about a particular issue, but they will change your perception of what's important.[28]

Although Shaw and McCombs concentrated on political issues and the news media, the idea of agenda setting can easily be applied more broadly to all issues and to all media. For many media users, a social problem, if it is not discussed on the Web, on television, or in newspapers, may not exist at all. Agenda setting has important implications, since the issues that tend to influence government policy are those that have received attention from the public.[29]

Cumulative Effects Theory

Cultural Idiom

driven home
made clear

Not all communication researchers accept the validity of agenda-setting theory. Some point out that while the media do, indeed, tell us what to think about, they do so slowly. **Cumulative effects theory** states that media messages are driven home through redundancy and have profound effects over time. According to this theory, the media latch on to certain themes and messages, which they gradually build up. There is a bandwagon effect as various newspapers, magazines, television and radio networks, websites, and other media take up the themes. Because the media are omnipresent and occupy such a prominent place in most people's lives, the media view becomes the widely accepted one within society.

Cumulative effects theory also describes a 'spiral of silence' that occurs when individuals with divergent views become reluctant to challenge the consensus offered by the media. People unconsciously form perceptions of the distribution of public opinion. If they feel themselves to be in the minority, they are less likely to express their opinions. People who hold majority viewpoints tend to speak out confidently. For example, in times of war, some people might become concerned about civilian casualties inflicted on the other side, but they don't speak out about this issue if they feel that most people disagree.

Summary

Social media has changed the way in which individuals, groups, and organizations communicate. They have broken down boundaries to creativity and broadcasting for individuals that were insurmountable under the regime of the traditional mass media.

There are many different forms of social media, including blogs, microblogs, social networking, wikis, social news aggregators, social bookmarking sites, and social photo and video sharing sites. Each offers a different means of communicating messages, sharing content, and building persistent communities.

Social media are having a major impact on our lives by changing our sense of self; affecting how we travel, consume, and behave through geotagging; changing the way we market goods; and also transforming traditional mass media such as radio, television, and newsprint.

Social media present both a huge opportunity and pose many risks. They provide the opportunity to build a permanent personal online brand that promotes your values, goals, and dreams, but they also provide a perfect venue for destroying your reputation. However, if you police your image online, you can have a very profitable and beneficial experience using social media.

Communication theories provide different models for explaining how messages move from communicators to receivers. They also attempt to explain how media might influence social, cultural, political, and economic effects.

Key Terms

Activities

A. Social Media Autobiography

Construct your social media autobiography by asking yourself the following questions about each type of social media discussed in this chapter.

1. Do I use it?
2. Do my friends use it?
3. Have I posted pictures to it?
4. Has anyone else posted pictures of me to it?
5. Have I posted notes or status updates to it?
6. Have others mentioned me in their notes or their status updates?
7. Have I been tagged in photos or on notes?
8. Have I been tagged on compromising photos? If so, how are they compromising?
9. Do I know everyone who has taken my photo?
10. Have I posted video online?
11. Have others posted video of me online?
12. Is any of this video compromising? If so, in what way?

Summarize your findings in a brief paragraph. You might be surprised at how your social media autobiography reads!

B. Three-Day Digital Media Fast

This activity is deceptively simple. Put away all of your digital media devices for three days. Everytime you get an urge to use one of these devices, log it in a notepad. Write down how you feel when you get the urge. What have you been thinking about? Were you sad? Lonely? Bored? You will be very surprised at how much insight into yourself you can gain by doing this simple exercise. You will learn what place digital technology occupies in your life. This is valuable knowledge in our digital device-saturated world!

C. Social Media Log

Use the following chart to keep a log of all of your uses of social media during the next three days.

Time/Date	Type of Social Media	Activity

Now write a one-paragraph summary of your social media activity and see what it looks like. You'll probably be amazed at how much time you spend on social media websites and what you do while you're on them. This is an excellent exercise for establishing a baseline of self-knowledge concerning social media.

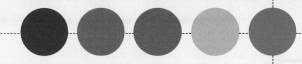

D. Building a Personal Online Brand

This exercise will help you to identify the type of personal brand that you want to create and remind you of the type of material that you should and shouldn't be posting. Answer the following questions as honestly as possible:

1. Do I feel more loved on the Internet than in real life. Why?
2. Why do I want to use social media?
3. What do I want to do professionally?
4. Is my profession of choice one that is based on credibility and trust? How?
5. Am I interested in ever running for political office?
6. Do I envision myself becoming a leader in my industry? An executive? A school principal? A public servant?
7. How do I think having compromising pictures, notes, or videos of myself on social media may impact my future?
8. How do I think having compromising pictures, notes, or videos of myself on social media impacts my credibility as a serious, moral person?
9. Could my social posts ever be misinterpreted negatively?
10. Would I want what I have posted recently to be the basis of my being judged as credible or not credible after I have finished my studies?

This inventory of questions will enable you to get a handle on your perceptions of the effects and potential effects of social media on your life. Now, answer the following questions:

1. How do I want to be perceived by a potential employer?
2. How do I want to be perceived by a potential spouse?
3. How do I want to be perceived by my neighbours?
4. How do I want to be perceived by my friends?
5. How do I want to be perceived by my immediate and extended family?

Now look at the answers to the first set of questions and compare them to your answers to the second set. Do the answers match up? Now answer the following questions:

1. What pictures promote me as I want to be perceived?
2. What videos promote me as I want to be perceived?
3. What notes promote me as I want to be perceived?
4. What status updates promote me as I want to be perceived?
5. What links promote me as I want to be perceived?

Write one-paragraph summaries for your answers to the questions in each section.

E. Posting Content about Your Friends

Imagine that you have videotaped some of your friends doing vulgar, drunken, or lewd things at a party. You think that some of the videos would be very funny to share on social media. Do you decide to share them? What would stop you? What would motivate you to post them anyway?

F. Applying Innis's and McLuhan's Theories to a Medium

Categorize the following list of media according to Innis's theories of space-binding and time-binding media (pages 317–19); McLuhan's tetrad (page 320); and McLuhan's concepts of hot and cool media (page 321).

1. papyrus
2. stone tablet
3. song
4. dance
5. DVD
6. writing paper
7. Moleskine® notebook
8. smartphone
9. Internet
10. HD TV
11. Facebook
12. Twitter
13. a written letter
14. a math textbook with no pictures
15. a newspaper
16. iPad
17. e-mail

G. Making Your Own Zine

This activity involves a little creativity and ingenuity on your part. Take a moment and search for zines on Google. Examine some of the results to get inspiration. Then pick a theme and a catchy title, and make your own zine. It can be as elaborate or as simple as you like. Be creative. Be radical. Be critical of society.

Further Reading

Anderson, Chris. *The Long Tail*, revised and updated edn. New York: Hyperion, 2008.
Anderson makes the point that, once products are marketed and sold online, companies will make money selling small niche products to tiny slices of the public.

Duncombe, Stephen. *Notes from Underground: Zines and the Politics of Alternative Culture*. Bloomington, IN: Microcosm Publishing, 2008.
This book investigates the fascinating world of zines, a countercultural phenomenon that now feels mainstream.

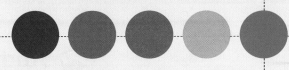

Helprin, Mark. *Digital Barbarism: A Writer's Manifesto.* New York: Harper, 2008.
In this work of protest, Mark Helprin decries how copyright has been eroded and the writer's craft has declined with the digital age.

Innis, Harold. *Empire and Communications.* Oxford: Clarendon Press, 1950.
This book introduces Innis's ideas of time-binding and space-binding media.

Lanier, Jaron. *You are not a Gadget.* New York: Knopf, 2010.
Lanier is considered the father of virtual reality technology. In this book, he argues that the Internet has gone terribly wrong and has led us into a world of conformism and collectivism that will be bad for creativity.

Lessig, Lawrence. *Remix: Making Art and Commerce Thrive in the Hybrid Economy.* New York: Penguin, 2008.
In this fascinating work, Professor Lessig continues his exploration of copyright by examining how both children and adults remix pieces of culture. He draws an interesting distinction between read-only and read-write cultures, explaining how read-write cultures share and creatively adapt the work of others.

McLuhan, Marshall. *Understanding Media: The Extensions of Man.* Cambridge, MA: MIT Press, 1994.
In this, the most read and talked about of McLuhan's books, he elaborates his theory of media, often called 'the medium is the message'. It is in this book that McLuhan describes the difference between hot and cool media.

O'Reilly Radar (radar.oreilly.com)
Tim O'Reilly is a leader in publishing about the digital world. His blog is insightful, intelligent, and sometimes funny. This blog is a great place to keep abreast of the latest developments in digital culture and social media.

Shirky, Clay. *Here Comes Everybody.* New York: Penguin, 2009.
This book describes how the cultural closeness and speed brought about by social media is transforming the way people do business, innovate, invent, and make art. This book is very positive about networked culture.

📓 Study Questions

1. List the social media services that you have used. How do they fit into the categories that are explained on pages 295–303? Do you find that you use them equally? Break the time up from 2008 until now—how have your usage patterns changed or evolved?

2. How do you use your smartphone (e.g., BlackBerry) in your everyday life? Do you use the GPS functions it has? Do you have social media service apps such as Facebook or Twitter or Foursquare installed on it? Do you use it more than your computer to interact with others through social media? Why or why not?

3. Where do you get your news and entertainment? From the television? From the radio? From the newspaper? What percentage comes from social media for each medium now? Do you think that our society is indeed undergoing a permanent shift toward the Internet, or will there always be a place for traditional media?

4. McLuhan is hailed as a prophet by many. As we have seen on pages 319–21, he predicted that technology would change society and turn it into a global village. Do you feel that happening around you? He also said that the 'medium is the message' and that hot and cool media extend or limit our senses. Do you think that McLuhan was exaggerating or just fanciful? How do you see your interactions with your friends, family, and co-workers confirming or contradicting McLuhan's vision of the impact of technology on culture and society?

5. In a media world driven more and more by social media, who do you think are the new agenda setters and the gatekeepers (as defined on pages 323–4)? Are the same elites still in charge or have everyday people achieved more impact?

6. How do you think Innis's theory of innovation (page 317) starting at the periphery and then standardizing as it moves to the centre of power relates to the 'diffusion of innovations' theory (page 323)?

After studying the material in this chapter . . .

You should understand:

- the characteristics that distinguish groups from other collections of people;
- the types of goals that operate in groups;
- the various types of groups;
- the characteristics of groups described in this chapter;
- the advantages and disadvantages of the decision-making methods introduced in this chapter; and
- the cultural influences that shape communication in groups.

You should be able to:

- identify the groups you presently belong to and those you are likely to join in the future;
- list the personal and group goals in groups you observe or belong to;
- identify the rules, norms, roles, and interaction patterns in groups you observe or belong to; and
- choose the most effective decision-making methods for a group task.

The Nature of Groups

Chapter Highlights

Group communication possesses several important characteristics.

- Groups exist for a variety of purposes, and each has its own operating style.
- A true group is distinguished from a collection of individuals by interaction, interdependence, duration over time, and size.
- The stated goals of groups and the personal goals of individual members interact in ways that can affect success.

- Different types of groups exist to fulfill a variety of goals: learning, problem-solving, social, and personal growth.
- A group's rules, norms, roles, patterns of inter-action, and methods of making decisions can shape the way members interact as well as their productivity and satisfaction.
- Powerful but sometimes subtle cultural factors influence the way groups operate.

How important are groups? You can answer this question for yourself by trying a simple experiment. Start by thinking of all the groups you belong to currently and have belonged to in the past: the family you grew up with, the classes you have attended, the companies you have worked for, the teams you have played on, the many social groups you have been a member of—the list is long. Now, one by one, imagine that you had never belonged to each of these groups. Start with the less important ones, and the results aren't too dramatic. Very soon, however, you will begin to see that a great deal of the information you have learned, the benefits you have gained—even your very identity—have all come from group membership.

On the job, groups are the setting in which most work takes place. In one survey, 75 per cent of the professionals surveyed reported that they 'always' or 'often' worked in teams.[1] In the growing multimedia field, the ability to work effectively as part of a team has been identified as the top non-technical job skill.[2] When negotiating is conducted by teams instead of individuals, the results are better for everyone involved.[3]

This doesn't mean that every group experience is a good one. Some are vaguely unrewarding, rather like eating food that has no taste and gives no nourishment. And others are downright miserable. Sometimes it is easy to see why a group succeeds or fails, but in other cases matters aren't so clear.[4]

This chapter will help improve your understanding of the nature of group communication. It will start by explaining just what a group is—because not every collection of people qualifies. It will go on to examine the reasons why people form groups and then look at several types of groups. Finally, it will conclude by looking at some common characteristics that all groups share.

Most of the decisions that affect our lives are not made by individuals, but by small groups of people in executive boardrooms, faculty meetings, town councils, quality circles, dormitory rooms, kitchens, locker rooms, and a host of other meeting places. In a democracy, the small group is the most basic way to get work done.

Arthur Jensen

What Is a Group?

Imagine that you are taking a test on group communication. Which of the following would you identify as groups?

- A crowd of onlookers gawking at a burning building
- Several passengers at an Air Canada ticket counter discussing their hopes of finding space on a crowded flight
- An army battalion

Because all these situations seem to involve groups, your experience as a canny test-taker probably tells you that a commonsense answer will get you in trouble here—and you're right. When social scientists talk about *groups*, they use the word in a special way that excludes each of the preceding examples.

What are we talking about when we use the word *group*? For our purposes a **group** consists of a *small collection of people who interact with each other, usually face to face, over time in order to reach goals*. A closer examination of this definition will show why none of the collections of people described in the preceding quiz qualifies as a group.

group

A small collection of people whose members interact with each other, usually face to face, over time in order to reach goals.

Interaction

Without interaction, a collection of people isn't a group. Consider the first example in our test. Though the onlookers all occupy the same area at the same time, they have virtually nothing to do with each other. Of course, if they should begin interacting—working together to give first aid or to rescue victims, for example—the situation would change. This requirement of interaction highlights the difference between true groups and collections of individuals who merely co-act—simultaneously engaging in a similar activity without communicating with one another. For example, students who passively listen to a lecture don't technically constitute a group until they begin to exchange messages with each other and their instructor. (This explains why some students feel isolated even though they spend so much time on a crowded campus. Despite being surrounded by others, they really don't belong to any group.)

As you read in chapters 3 and 5, there are two types of interaction that go on in any communication setting. The most obvious type is verbal, in which group members exchange words either orally or in writing. But people needn't talk to each other in order to communicate as a group: non-verbal channels can do the job, too. We can see how by thinking again about a hypothetical classroom. Imagine that the course is in its tenth week and that the instructor has been lecturing non-stop for the entire time. During the first few meetings there was very little interaction of any kind: students were too busy scribbling notes and wondering how they would survive the course with grade point averages and sanity intact. But as they became more used to the class, the students began to share their feelings with each other. Now there's a great amount of eye rolling and groaning as the assignments are poured on, and the students exchange resigned sighs as they hear the same tired jokes for the second and third time. Thus, even though there's no verbal exchange of sentiments, the class has become a group—interestingly, one that doesn't include the professor.

The explosion of communication technologies has led to the growth of 'virtual groups'— people who interact with one another without meeting face to face. For a small cost (at least compared with in-person meetings), people, whether within the same office or around the world, can swap ideas via computer networks, speak with one another via telephone conference calls, and even have visual contact thanks to teleconferencing.[5] Despite the lack of personal contact between members, virtual teams actually can be superior to face-to-face teams in at least two ways. First, getting together is fast and easy. A virtual team can meet whenever necessary, even if the members are widely separated. This ease of interaction isn't just useful in the business world. For most groups of students working on class projects, finding a convenient time to meet can be a major headache. Virtual groups don't face the same challenges.

A second advantage of virtual teams is the levelling of status differences. When groups connect via computer networks, rank is much less prominent than when they meet face to face.[6] Because fear of authority figures can squelch creative thinking, virtual teams are a good device for making sure groups find the best solutions to problems.

Interdependence

In groups, members don't just interact: their members are *interdependent*.[7] The behaviour of one person affects all the others in what can be called a 'ripple effect'.[8] Consider your own

People seem to enjoy things more when they know a lot of other people have been left out of the pleasure.

Russell Baker

Pay no attention to what the critics say . . . Remember, a statue has never been set up in honour of a critic.

Jean Sibelius

Understanding Communication Technology

Communicating with Your Own Virtual Group on Facebook

Groups don't have to meet in person. Setting up a telephone conference call is easy and affordable. (Ask your phone company for details.) Also, you can create your own virtual group on the Internet.

As discussed in Chapter 8, Facebook is a popular and powerful resource in social networking and community building. Facebook also allows you to host your own virtual team at no charge, providing a surprising array of services. You and your groupmates can

- send and receive e-mail messages;
- upload and download files;
- create and use your own private chat for real-time conferencing;

- add and edit photos;
- link to other web pages using bookmarks;
- conduct votes and polls online;
- schedule events and reminders on a group calendar;
- create a roster of group members, complete with personal profiles; and
- use Facebook applications to share documents in real time, transmit music, and rate documents.

Sometimes there is no good substitute for face-to-face meetings. But you may be surprised how quick, easy, and effective it can be for a group to work online.

experience in family and work groups: when one member behaves poorly, his or her actions shape the way the entire group functions. The ripple effect can be positive as well as negative: beneficial actions by some members help everyone.

Time

A collection of people who interact for a short while doesn't qualify as a group. As you'll soon read, groups who work together for any length of time begin to take on characteristics that aren't present in temporary aggregations. For example, certain standards of acceptable behaviour begin to evolve, and the way individuals feel about each other begins to affect their behaviour toward the group's task and toward each other. Thus, onlookers at a fire would have trouble qualifying as a group even if they briefly co-operated with one another to help out in the emergency. The time element clearly excludes temporary gatherings such as the passengers gathered around the Air Canada ticket counter. Situations like this one simply don't reflect many of the principles you'll be reading about in the next two chapters.

Size

Our definition of the term *groups* included the word *small*. Most experts in the field set the lower limit of group size at three members. This decision isn't arbitrary—there are some significant differences between two- and three-person communication. For example, the only ways for two people to resolve a conflict are to change one another's minds, give in, or compromise; in a larger group, however, members can form alliances either to put increased pressure on dissenting members or to outvote them.

There is less agreement about when a group stops being small.[9] Though no expert would call a 500-member army battalion a group in our sense of the word (it would be labelled an organization), most experts are reluctant to set an arbitrary upper limit. As long as it is not too large for each member to be able to know and respond to every other member, a group may be considered small. Our focus in these pages will be on collections of people ranging in numbers from 3 to between 7 and 20.

In task-oriented groups, bigger usually isn't better. Research suggests that the optimal size for a group is the smallest number of people capable of performing the task at hand effectively.[10] This definition makes it clear that there is no magic formula for choosing the best group size. The optimal number will change according to the task, as well as contextual factors such as politics, legal requirements, and institutional norms.[11] But generally speaking, as a group becomes larger, it is harder to schedule meetings, the members have less access to important information, and they have fewer chances to participate—three ingredients in a recipe for dissatisfaction.

Goals

Group membership isn't always voluntary, as some family members and most prison inmates will testify. But whether or not people choose to join groups, they usually hope to achieve one or more goals. At first the goal-related nature of group membership seems simple and obvious. In truth, however, there are several types of goals, which we will examine in the following pages.

Goals of Groups and Their Members

We can talk about two types of goals when we examine groups. The first type involves **individual goals**—the motives of individual members—whereas the second involves **group goals**—the outcome the group seeks to accomplish.

Individual Goals

The most obvious reason why individuals join groups is to meet their personal needs. **Task orientation**—getting the job done—is the most obvious type of individual motive for belonging to a group. Some people join study groups, for example, in order to improve their knowledge. Sometimes a member's task-related goals will have little to do with the group's stated purpose. Many merchants, for example, join service clubs such as Kiwanis, Rotary, or Lions primarily because doing so is good for business. The fact that these groups help achieve worthy goals such as helping the blind or disabled is fine, of course, but for many people it is not the prime motive for belonging.[12]

What about groups with no specifically defined purpose? Consider, for instance, gatherings of regulars at the beach on sunny weekends or a group of friends whose members eat

individual goals

The motives of individual members that influence their behaviour in groups.

group goals

Goals that a group collectively seeks to accomplish.

task orientation

Individual goals that involve accomplishing a task.

lunch together several times a week. Collections such as these meet the other criteria for being groups: they interact, meet over time, and have the right number of members. But what are the members' reasons for belonging? In our examples here, the goals can't be sunbathing or eating because these activities could be carried out alone. The answer to our question introduces **social orientation**. In many cases people join together in order to have a sense of belonging, to exercise influence over others, and to gain the liking of others. Notice that none of these factors necessarily has much to do with the task: it's possible to meet social needs without getting the job done. Likewise, a group can be efficient—at least for a short while—without meeting the social needs of its members.

We join many, if not most, groups in order to accomplish both task and social goals. School becomes a place both to learn important information and to meet desirable friends. Our work becomes a means both of putting food on the table and of gaining recognition for our skills. The value of distinguishing between task and social goals becomes clear when we understand that, despite their importance, social goals are often not stated or even recognized by group members. Thus, one way of identifying and overcoming blocks to group effectiveness is to ask yourself whether the group is in fact achieving its members' social goals.

hidden agenda
An individual goal that group members are unwilling to reveal.

social orientation
Individual goals that involve affiliation, influence, and esteem of others.

Group Goals

So far we have discussed the forces that motivate individual group members. In addition to these individual forces, there also exist group goals. For example, athletic teams exist to compete with each other, and academic classes strive to transmit knowledge.

Sometimes there is a close relationship between group and individual goals. In athletic teams the group goal is to win, whereas individual members' goals include helping the group succeed. If you think about it for a moment, however, you'll see that the individual members have other goals as well: improving their physical ability, having a good time, overcoming the personal challenges of competition, and often gaining the social benefits that come from being an athlete. The difference between individual and group goals is even more pronounced when the two are incompatible. Consider, for instance, the case of an athletic team that has one player more interested in being a 'star' (satisfying personal needs for recognition) than in helping the team win. Or recall classes you have known in which the personal goal of some students—to get by with the smallest possible amount of work—was inconsistent with the group goals of gathering and sharing information. Sometimes the gap between individual and group goals is public, but when it is not, an individual's goal becomes a **hidden agenda**. In either case, the discrepancy can be dangerous for the well-being of the group and needs to be dealt with. We'll have more to say about this subject in Chapter 10.

As long as the members' individual goals match those of the group, no conflicts are likely to arise. But when there is a clash between what members seek for themselves and what the group seeks, the collective goal is likely to suffer. The risk that individuals may put their own interests ahead of the group's is especially great when interdependence is low—that is, when members do not have to rely on one another in order to succeed. Jon

Krakauer captures this situation clearly in his account of a team of climbers seeking to reach the peak of Mount Everest:

> There were more than fifty people camped on the Col that night, huddled in shelters pitched side by side, yet an odd feeling of isolation hung in the air. We were a team in name only, I'd sadly come to realize. Although in a few hours we would leave camp as a group, we would ascend as individuals, linked to one another by neither rope nor any deep sense of loyalty. Each client was in it for himself or herself, pretty much. And I was no different: I sincerely hoped Doug got to the top, for instance, yet I would do everything in my power to keep pushing on if he turned around.[13]

COMMUNICATION ON-SCREEN

Spy Game (2001)
Directed by Tony Scott.

Robert Redford plays Nathan Muir, a CIA operative about to retire. When he discovers that his protege, Tom Bishop (Brad Pitt), has been arrested for espionage in China, Muir tries to free him. In the meantime, Muir reminisces about his sometimes tumultuous relationship with the younger agent. Along with his professional skills, Muir uses his knowledge of group dynamics to manipulate the CIA bureaucracy and to rescue his friend. In doing so, he illustrates the clash between individual and group goals.

Types of Groups

So far we have seen that groups fulfill a variety of goals. Another way of examining groups is to look at some of the functions they serve.

Learning Groups

When the term **learning group** comes up, most people think first about school. Although academic classes certainly qualify as learning groups, they aren't the only ones. Members of a scuba-diving class, friends who form a Bible study group, and members of a League of Women Voters chapter all belong to learning groups. Whatever the setting or subject, the purpose of learning groups is to increase the knowledge or skill of each member.

Problem-Solving Groups

Problem-solving groups work to resolve a mutual concern of members. Sometimes the problem involves the group itself, as when a family decides how to handle household chores or when co-workers meet to coordinate vacation schedules. At other times, the problem is external to the group. For instance, neighbours who organize themselves to prevent burglaries or club members who plan a fundraising drive are focusing on external problems.

Problem-solving groups can take part in many activities. One type is gathering information, as when several students compile a report for a class assignment. At other times, a group makes policy—for example, when a club decides whether or not to admit the public to its meetings. In some cases group members may delegate their decision-making power to a smaller group: when hiring, for example, a committee may be formed to interview candidates and decide which one to hire.

Social Groups

We have already mentioned that some groups serve strictly to satisfy the social needs of their participants. Some **social groups** are organized and others are informal. In either case, the inclusion, control, and affection that such groups provide are reasons enough for belonging.

learning group
A group whose goal is to expand its knowledge about some topic other than itself or its individual members.

problem-solving group
A task-related group whose goal is to resolve a mutual concern of its members.

social groups
Groups in which the goal is to satisfy the social needs of its members.

Understanding Communication Technology

Weighing in on Anorexia

YouTube has given everyone with a video camera a place to be seen and heard. And somehow, since its inception two years ago, the website has lured the secretive world of eating disorders onto its world stage.

YouTube broadcaster Carolyn, 29, who asked that her last name not be published, has been locked into a 24/7 battle with her body for 17 years. She's bulimic, sometimes purging several times a day or severely restricting her food. At one point her 5-foot-4-inch frame carried just 83 pounds.

Since last year, Carolyn has broadcast 24 videos about her disease from her home in Montreal, under the user name 'chanceoperations'. The blog has more than 150 subscribers.

'I wanted to try and find a voice,' she says of her public effort to help herself, and others, sort through their eating disorders. 'It's hard when you see somebody who is struggling. You feel the same helplessness somebody would feel toward you.'

A 2001 study published in the *Canadian Medical Association Journal* says 27 per cent of Ontario girls aged 12 to 18 were 'engaged in severely problematic food and weight behaviour'. The site also references a 2000 study, published in the *American Journal of Psychiatry,* that estimates 8 per cent of North American women suffer from either anorexia nervosa or bulimia.

On YouTube, the 'pro-ana' movement, which stands for pro-anorexia, gets a lot of heat. Members maintain their disease is a choice; some call it their lifestyle. Pro-ana communities on myspace.com offer pep talks, diet tips, and forums to discuss the disease.

There are those who believe the virtual network encourages recovery, but Carolyn's blog does not support the pro-ana movement or encourage similar behaviours.

Pro-ana websites popped up a few years ago, but were often shut down over concerns that the content glamorizes eating disorders.

Hand in hand with pro-ana is the 'Thinspiration' movement, videos of stick-thin celebrities or regular girls displaying protruding bones in their backs and hips—inspiration to starve in a flashy package.

'Somebody who would promote a message like that is somebody who is in the stage of their illness where they are still taking a lot of pride in it,' says Jacqueline Carter,

---

growth groups
Groups in which the goal is to help members learn more about themselves.

Groups don't always fall neatly into just one category. For example, learning groups often have other functions. Consider the class for which you are reading this book: besides becoming more knowledgeable about communication, many of the students in your class are probably satisfying social needs by making new friends. Some are probably growing personally by applying the principles they are learning to their own lives. Groups of students—fellow employees or teammates, for instance—may even take the class together in order to focus on solving collective problems. Despite the multiplicity of goals, it's usually possible to characterize a group as primarily focused on learning, problem-solving, social, or growth goals.

Growth Groups

Unlike learning groups, in which the subject matter is external to the members, **growth groups** focus on teaching the members more about themselves. Consciousness-raising groups, marriage encounter workshops, counselling, and group therapy are all types of growth groups. These are unlike most other types of groups in that there is no real collective goal: the entire purpose of the group is to help the members identify and deal with their personal concerns.

staff psychologist with the Eating Disorders Program at Toronto General Hospital.

People with anorexia tend to be ambivalent, seeing the pros and cons of the disease, she says.

Addressing ambivalence in therapy is part of recovery. But as videos promoting extreme thinness only represent one side of the coin, Carter says she can't imagine how they could be helpful.

As well, she notes, there is a huge irony in how individuals associate skeletal bodies with self-esteem. 'It's hard to feel good about yourself when you are starved and obsessed with food and can't work because you are too sick,' she says.

Treating psychological problems, such as eating disorders, with professional help over the Internet, is a new field, says Carter. She believes it could be a great way of helping people who are not close to treatment services. But what's happening on YouTube could push people in either direction.

'The medium itself could potentially be very helpful— but it also has the potential to be quite destructive,' she says.

Sharon Hodgson, a recovered anorexic living in Halifax, Nova Scotia, agrees.

'It's really a grey area because you can make friends with people doing damage to themselves and not realize how their patterns will influence your behaviour,' she says.

Hodgson used to moderate a pro-ana website. In 2006, she created webiteback.com to normalize recovery, and says people who think anorexia is a quick fix to lose weight aren't familiar with the true face of the disease.

That face is Gillian, a YouTube user who has battled anorexia for 13 years, since she was 11. Unable to eat solid food for three years, she's fed through a tube in her nose. Her weight has dropped to as little as 49 pounds.

Carolyn doesn't want to put a rosy face on her illness. She avoids doctors and dentists, partly because of the expense, so she doesn't know the exact toll on her body.

'I do know my teeth are chipped and eroded and discoloured,' she says. 'Every now and then my heart flutters, and my hip bones crack, and I can't digest food properly.'

But, she says, the psychological impact is crystal clear.

Carolyn describes her university degree as a waste since she now struggles to socialize. Focusing her mind on everyday concepts and activities is difficult. YouTube, she acknowledges, is an outlet and a way to connect with people.

—Emily Mathieu, *Toronto Star,* 26 June 2007. Courtesy of Emily Mathieu.

Questions: Do you think that Carolyn has been well served by being able to use the Internet to address the challenges posed by her illness? How might the Internet reverse into a negative for people who suffer from illnesses like anorexia?

Characteristics of Groups

Whatever their function, all groups have certain characteristics in common. Understanding these characteristics is a first step to functioning more effectively in your own groups.

Rules and Norms

Many groups have formal **rules**—explicit, officially stated guidelines that govern what the group is supposed to do and how the members should behave. In a classroom, these rules include how absences will be treated, whether papers must be typed or may be handwritten, and so on. Alongside the official rules, an equally powerful set of standards also operates, often without ever being discussed. Sociologists call these unstated rules norms. **Norms** are shared values, beliefs, behaviours, and procedures that govern a group's operation. For instance, you probably won't find a description of what jokes are and aren't acceptable in the bylaws of any groups you belong to, yet you can almost certainly describe the unstated code if you think about it. Is sexual humour acceptable? How much, and what types? What about

norms
Shared values, beliefs, behaviours, and procedures that govern a group's operation.

rules
Explicit, officially stated guidelines that govern group functions and member behaviour.

religious jokes? How much kidding of other members is proper? Matters such as these vary from one group to another, according to the norms of each one.[14]

There are three categories of group norms: social, procedural, and task. **Social norms** govern relationships between members. How honest and direct will members be with one another? What emotions will and won't be expressed, and in what ways? Matters such as these are handled by the establishment of social norms, which are usually implicit. **Procedural norms** outline how the group should operate. Will the group make decisions by accepting the vote of the majority, or will the members keep talking until consensus is reached? Will one person run meetings, or will discussion be leaderless? **Task norms** focus on how the job itself should be handled. Will the group keep working on a problem until everyone agrees that its solution is the best one possible, or will members settle for an adequate, if imperfect, solution? The answer to this question becomes a task-related norm. All groups have social norms, and all except social groups also have procedural and task norms.

Table 9.1 lists some typical rules and norms. It is important to realize that the actual rules and norms that govern a group may fall short of cultural standards. Consider the matter of punctuality, for example. It is a cultural norm in our society that meetings should begin at the scheduled time, yet some groups operate on the (usually unstated)

---

procedural norms
Norms that describe rules for the group's operation.

social norms
Group norms that govern the way members relate to one another.

task norms
Group norms that govern the way members handle the job at hand.

TABLE 9.1 Typical Rules and Norms in Two Types of Groups

Family

Rules (Explicit)
- If you don't do the chores, you don't get your allowance.
- If you're going to be more than a half-hour late, phone home so the others don't worry about you.
- If the gas gauge reads 'empty', fill up the tank before bringing the car home.
- Don't make plans for Sunday nights. That's time for the family to spend together.
- Daniel gets to watch *Sesame Street* from 5:00 to 6:00 p.m.

Norms (Unstated)
- When Dad is in a bad mood, don't bring up problems.
- Don't talk about Sheila's divorce.
- It's okay to tease Lupe about being short, but don't make comments about Shana's complexion.
- As long as the kids don't get in trouble, the parents won't ask detailed questions about what they do with their friends.
- At family gatherings, try to change the subject when Uncle Max brings up politics.

Business Meetings

Rules (Explicit)
- Regular meetings are held every Monday morning at 9:00 a.m.
- The job of keeping minutes rotates from person to person.
- Meetings last no more than an hour.
- Don't leave the meetings to take phone calls except in emergencies.

Norms (Unstated)
- Use first names.
- It's okay to question the boss's ideas, but if she doesn't concede after the first remark, don't continue to object.
- Tell jokes at the beginning of the meeting, but avoid sexual or ethnic topics.
- It's okay to talk about 'gut feelings', but back them up with hard facts.
- Don't act upset when your ideas aren't accepted, even if you're unhappy.

understanding that the real business won't commence until approximately 10 minutes later. On a more serious level, although it is a cultural norm that other people should be treated politely and with respect, some groups accept rude, uncivil behaviour—failure to listen, sarcasm, even outright hostility—between their members.

It is important to recognize a group's norms. Following them is one way to gain acceptance into the group, and identifying norms that cause problems can sometimes be a way to help the group operate more effectively. For instance, some groups make a habit of responding to new ideas with criticism, sarcasm, or indifference. Pointing this norm out to members might be a way to change the unwritten rules and thereby improve the group's work.

If norms are rarely stated, how is it possible to identify them? There are two sets of clues that can help. First, look for behaviours that occur often.[15] For instance, notice what time meetings begin. Observe the amount of work that members are willing to contribute to the group. See what kinds of humour are and aren't used. Habitual behaviours like these point to the unspoken rules that the group lives by. Second, look for clues that members are being punished for violating norms. Most punishments are subtle, of course: pained expressions from other members when a speaker talks too much, no laughter following an inappropriate joke, and so on.

Roles

Whereas norms may be defined as acceptable group standards, **roles** are the patterns of behaviour expected of members. As with norms, some roles are officially recognized. These **formal roles** are assigned by an organization or group partly to establish order. Formal roles usually come with a title, such as 'assistant coach', 'treasurer', or 'customer

formal roles
Roles assigned to a person by group members or an organization, usually to establish order.

roles
The patterns of behaviour expected of group members.

'Rules Are the Only Thing We've Got'

'What are we? Humans? Or animals? Or savages? What's grownups going to think? Going off—hunting pigs—letting fires out—and now!'

A shadow fronted him tempestuously.

'You shut up, you fat slug!'

There was a moment's struggle and the glimmering conch jigged up and down. Ralph leapt to his feet.

'Jack! Jack! You haven't got the conch! Let him speak.'

Jack's face swam near him.

'And you shut up! Who are you, anyway? Sitting there telling people what to do. You can't hunt, you can't sing—'

'I'm chief. I was chosen.'

'Why should choosing make any difference? Just giving orders that don't make any sense—'

'Piggy's got the conch.'

'That's right—favour Piggy as you always do—'

'Jack!'

Jack's voice sounded in bitter mimicry.

'Jack! Jack!'

'The rules!' shouted Ralph. "You're breaking the rules!'

'Who cares?'

Ralph summoned his wits.

'Because the rules are the only thing we've got!'

—*William Golding*
Lord of the Flies

TABLE 9.2 Informal Roles of Group Members

	Typical Behaviours	Examples
Task Roles		
1. **Initiator/Contributor**	Contributes ideas and suggestions; proposes solutions and decisions; proposes new ideas or states old ones in a novel fashion.	'How about taking a different approach to this chore? Suppose we . . .'
2. **Information Seeker**	Asks for clarification of comments in terms of their factual adequacy; asks for information or facts relevant to the problem; suggests information is needed before making decisions.	'Do you think the others will go for this?' 'How much would the plan cost us?' 'Does anybody know if those dates are available?'
3. **Information Giver**	Offers facts or generalizations that may relate to the group's task.	'I bet Chris would know the answer to that.' '*Newsweek* ran an article on that a couple of months ago. It said . . .'
4. **Opinion Seeker**	Asks for clarification of opinions made by other members of the group and asks how people in the group feel.	'Does anyone else have an idea about this?' 'That's an interesting idea, Ruth. How long would it take to get started?'
5. **Opinion Giver**	States beliefs or opinions having to do with suggestions made; indicates what the group's attitude should be.	'I think we ought to go with the second plan. It fits the conditions we face in the Concord plant best. . . .'
6. **Elaborator/Clarifier**	Elaborates ideas and other contributions; offers rationales for suggestions; tries to deduce how an idea or suggestion would work if adopted by the group.	'If we followed Lee's suggestion, each of us would need to make three calls.' 'Let's see . . . at $0.35 per brochure, the total cost would be $525.00.'
7. **Coordinator**	Clarifies the relationships among information, opinions, and ideas or suggests an integration of the information, opinions, and ideas of subgroups.	'John, you seem most concerned with potential problems. Mary sounds confident that they can all be solved. Why don't you list the problems one at a time, John, and Mary can respond to each one.'
8. **Diagnostician**	Indicates what the problems are.	'But you're missing the main thing, I think. The problem is that we can't afford . . .'
9. **Orienter/Summarizer**	Summarizes what has taken place; points out departures from agreed-on goals; tries to bring the group back to the central issues; raises questions about the direction in which the group is heading.	'Let's take stock of where we are. Helen and John take the position that we should act now. Bill says, 'Wait.' Rusty isn't sure. Can we set that aside for a moment and come back to it after we . . .'
10. **Energizer**	Prods the group to action.	'Come on, guys. We've been wasting time. Let's get down to business.'
11. **Procedure Developer**	Handles routine tasks such as seating arrangements, obtaining equipment, and handing out pertinent papers.	'I'll volunteer to see that the forms are printed and distributed.' 'I'd be happy to check on which of those dates are free.'
12. **Secretary**	Keeps notes on the group's progress.	'Just for the record, I'll put these decisions in the memo and get copies to everyone in the group.'
13. **Evaluator/Critic**	Constructively analyzes group's accomplishments according to some set of standards; checks to see that consensus has been reached.	'Look, we said we only had two weeks, and this proposal will take at least three. Does that mean that it's out of the running, or do we need to change our original guidelines?'
Social/Maintenance Roles		
1. **Supporter/Encourager**	Praises, agrees with, and accepts the contributions of others; offers warmth, solidarity, and recognition.	'I really like that idea, John.' 'Priscilla's suggestion sounds good to me. Could we discuss it further?'
2. **Harmonizer**	Reconciles disagreements; mediates differences; reduces tensions by giving group members a chance to explore their differences.	'I don't think you two are as far apart as you think. Henry, are you saying _____? Benson, you seem to be saying _____. Is that what you mean?'

	Typical Behaviours	Examples
3. Tension Reliever	Jokes or in some other way reduces the formality of the situation; relaxes the group members.	'Let's take a break . . . maybe have a drink.' 'You're a tough cookie, Bob. I'm glad you're on our side!'
4. Conciliator	Offers new options when his or her own ideas are involved in a conflict; willing to admit errors so as to maintain group cohesion.	'Looks like our solution is halfway between you and me, John. Can we look at the middle ground?'
5. Gatekeeper	Keeps communication channels open; encourages and facilitates interaction from those members who are usually silent.	'Susan, you haven't said anything about this yet. I know you've been studying the problem. What do you think about _____?'
6. Feeling Expresser	Makes explicit the feelings, moods, and relationships in the group; shares own feelings with others.	'I'm really glad we cleared things up today.' 'I'm just about worn out. Could we call it a day and start fresh tomorrow?'
7. Follower	Goes along with the movement of the group passively, accepting the ideas of others, sometimes serving as an audience.	'I agree. Yes, I see what you mean. If that's what the group wants to do, I'll go along.'

Source: Adapted from *Groups In Context: Leadership and Participation in Decision-Making Groups* by Gerald Wilson and Michael Hanna, pp. 144–6. © 1986. Reprinted by permission of McGraw-Hill Companies, Inc.

service representative'. By contrast, **informal roles** (sometimes called 'functional roles') are rarely acknowledged with a label.[16] Table 9.2 lists some of the most common informal roles in task-oriented groups. As the list shows, the names given to informal roles describe the functions that the various members perform within the group rather than their formal positions. The easiest functional roles to identify are usually those of leaders and followers, but you can probably think of many other examples in groups you have known.

Informal roles are not formally assigned to members. In fact, they are rarely even recognized as existing. Many informal roles may be filled by more than one member, and some of them may be filled by different people at different times. The important fact is that, at crucial times, every informal role must be filled by someone.

Notice that the informal roles listed in Table 9.2 fall into two categories: task and social. **Task roles** help the group accomplish its goals, while **social roles** (also called 'maintenance roles') help the relationships among the members run smoothly. Not all roles are constructive. Table 9.3 lists several **dysfunctional roles** that prevent a group from working effectively.

informal roles

Roles usually not explicitly recognized by a group that describe functions of group members, rather than their positions. Sometimes called 'functional roles'.

task roles

Roles group members take on in order to help solve a problem.

social roles

Emotional roles concerned with maintaining smooth personal relationships among group members. Also termed 'maintenance functions'.

dysfunctional roles

Individual roles played by group members that inhibit the group's effective operation.

TABLE 9.3 Dysfunctional Roles of Group Members

Dysfunctional Roles	Typical Behaviours	Examples
1. Blocker	Interferes with progress by rejecting ideas or taking a negative stand on any and all issues; refuses to co-operate.	'Wait a minute! That's not right! That idea is absurd.' 'You can talk all day, but my mind is made up.'
2. Aggressor	Struggles for status by deflating the status of others; boasts, criticizes.	'Wow, that's really swell! You turkeys have botched things again.' 'Your constant bickering is responsible for this mess. Let me tell you how you ought to do it.'
3. Deserter	Withdraws in some way; remains indifferent, aloof, sometimes formal; daydreams; wanders from the subject, engages in irrelevant side conversations.	'I suppose that's right . . . I really don't care.'
4. Dominator	Interrupts and embarks on long monologues; is authoritative; tries to monopolize the group's time.	'Bill, you're just off base. What we should do is this. First . . .'
5. Recognition Seeker	Attempts to gain attention in an exaggerated manner; usually boasts about past accomplishments; relates irrelevant personal experiences, usually in an attempt to gain sympathy.	'That reminds me of a guy I used to know . . .' 'Let me tell you how I handled old Marris . . .'
6. Joker	Displays a lack of involvement in the group through inappropriate humour, horseplay, or cynicism.	'Why try to convince these guys? Let's just get the mob to snuff them out.' 'Hey, Carla, wanna be my roommate at the sales conference?'
7. Cynic	Discounts chances for group's success.	'Sure, we could try that idea, but it probably won't solve the problem. Nothing we've tried so far has worked.'

Source: Adapted from *Groups in Context: Leadership and Participation in Decision-Making Groups* by Gerald Wilson and Michael Hanna, pp. 144–6. © 1986. Reprinted by permission of McGraw-Hill Companies, Inc.

Research suggests that the presence of positive social roles and the absence of dysfunctional ones are key ingredients in the effectiveness of groups.[17]

What is the optimal balance between task and social functions? According to Robert Bales, one of the earliest and most influential researchers in the area, the ideal ratio is 2:1, with task-related behaviour dominating.[18] This ratio allows the group to get its work done while at the same time taking care of the personal needs and concerns of the members.

Role Emergence

We said earlier that most group members aren't aware of the existence of informal roles. You will rarely find members saying things like 'You ask most of the questions, I'll give opinions, and she can be the summarizer.' Yet it's fairly obvious that over time certain members do begin to fulfill specific roles. How does this role differentiation come about?

The personal characteristics of the various group members certainly help to determine the role that each will play. But personal skills and traits by themselves aren't enough to earn a member acceptance as possessor of a role, especially in newly formed groups without a formal leader. The process of role emergence has been studied extensively by communication scholar Ernest Bormann, who has identified a predictable series of stages that groups go through in role designation.[19] (Remember that this process is almost never discussed within groups and is rarely performed consciously.)

At first, members will make bids for certain roles. Someone with a particularly analytical mind, for example, might audition for the role of critic by pointing out flaws in a proposal. But in order for this role to 'take', the group members must endorse the bid both verbally and

Studying communications prepared me for my profession in a way that no other post-secondary education could have. Offering dynamic course options, taking a Communication Studies and Multimedia (CSMM) program gave me insight into the world of media, culture, and entertainment, while allowing me the freedom to discover which stream of communications suited me best.

When I decided to start my own business, I knew that the experience I had gained in the CSMM program would be something that would be invaluable to me, especially in the development stages. With a firm grasp on pop culture, media behaviours, and content management, I was well versed in many of the important areas of business development and Internet marketing. In addition to the curriculum, the program provided classmate camaraderie that has been incredibly helpful to me; I continue to stay in touch with many of my fellow CSMM grads, and many have proven to be very helpful contacts in many different business avenues, which is a testament to the diversity of the CSMM degree.

As I move forward in my professional life, I will continue to use and value the knowledge I gained in the CSMM program.

non-verbally—by giving the would-be critic their attention and making positive comments about his or her observations. If the group does not support the first few bids, a sensitive candidate will likely decide to look for a different role.

Role-Related Problems and Solutions

Groups can suffer from at least three role-related problems. The first arises when one or more important informal roles—either task or social—go unfilled. For instance, there may be no information giver to provide vital knowledge or no harmonizer to smooth things over when members disagree.

In other cases the problem isn't an absence of candidates to fill certain roles but rather an overabundance of them. This situation can lead to unstated competition between members, which gets in the way of group effectiveness. You have probably seen groups in which two people both want to be the tension-relieving comedian. In such cases, the problem arises when the members become more concerned with occupying their pet position than with getting the group's job done.

Even when there is no competition over roles, a group's effectiveness can be threatened when one or more members suffer from 'role fixation'—performing a certain role even when the situation doesn't require it.[20] As you learned in Chapter 1, a key ingredient of communication

> **Cultural Idiom**
>
> **occupying their pet position**
> playing their favourite role

●●○●●●

COMMUNICATION ON-SCREEN

Maurice Richard/The Rocket (2005)
Directed by Charles Binamé.

A biopic of the legendary star of the NHL's Montreal Canadiens, this film traces the playing career of Maurice 'The Rocket' Richard, played by Roy Dupuis, from his early days with the team. Of particular interest is the relationship between Richard and his coach, Dick Irvin (Stephen McHattie), whose role is to turn a 17-year-old budding superstar with tremendous raw skill, energy, and boundless love of the game into a team leader who would become a hero of Montreal Canadiens' fans everywhere.

> **Cultural Idiom**
>
> **just the ticket**
> the right thing

competence is flexibility, the ability to choose the right behaviour for a given situation. Members who always take the same role—even a constructive one—lack competence, and they hinder the group. As in other areas of life, too much of a good thing can be a problem. You can avoid role-related trouble by following these guidelines:

- Look for unfilled roles. When a group seems to be experiencing problems, use the list in Table 9.2 as a kind of diagnostic checklist to determine which roles may need filling.
- Make sure unfilled roles are filled. After you have identified unfilled roles, you may be able to help the group by filling them yourself. If key facts are missing, take the role of information seeker and try to dig them out. If nobody is keeping track of the group's work, offer to play secretary and take notes. Even if you are not suited by skill or temperament to a job, you can often encourage others to fill it.
- Avoid role fixation. Don't fall into familiar roles if they aren't needed. You may be a world-class coordinator or critic, but these talents will only annoy others if you use them when they aren't needed. In most cases your natural inclination to be a supporter might be just the ticket to help a group succeed, but if you find yourself in a group where the members don't need or want this sort of support, your encouragement might become a nuisance.

Avoid dysfunctional roles. Some of these roles can be personally gratifying, especially when you are frustrated with a group; however, they do nothing to help the group succeed, and they can damage your reputation as a team player. Nobody needs a blocker or a joker, for instance. Resist the temptation to indulge yourself by taking on any of the dysfunctional roles listed in Table 9.3.

Patterns of Interaction

In Chapter 1 we said that communication involves the exchange of information between and among people. It almost goes without saying that this exchange needs to be complete and efficient for the communicators to reach their goals. In interpersonal and public speaking settings,

CRITICAL THINKING PROBE

FUNCTIONAL AND DYSFUNCTIONAL ROLES

Identify the functional and dysfunctional roles in an established group. You might analyze a group that you belong to (e.g., an athletic team or class group), a group that you can observe in action (e.g., city council, faculty senate), or even a fictional group (e.g., those in the films featured in this chapter's 'Communication On-screen' boxes). How do the roles in the group you are analyzing contribute to the group's success (or lack of it)? How might members take on different roles to make the group more effective?

information exchange is relatively uncomplicated, taking basically two routes: either between the two individuals in an interpersonal dyad or between the speaker and the audience in a public speaking situation. (Actually, this is a slight oversimplification. In public speaking situations, members of an audience also exchange messages with one another through their laughter, restless movements, and so on. Basically, though, it's still fair to say that the exchange of information is two-way.) In groups, however, things aren't so simple. The mathematical formula that identifies the number of possible interactions between individuals is

$$\frac{N \quad (N-1)}{2}$$

where N equals the number of members in a group. Thus, even in a relatively small five-member group, there are 10 possible combinations of two-person conversations and 75 possible multi-person interactions. The complex structure of groups affects both the quantity of information exchanged and the flow of information in other ways, too.

A look at Figure 9.1 (usually called a **sociogram**) will suggest the number and complexity of interactions that can occur in a group. Arrows connecting members indicate remarks shared between them. Two-headed arrows represent two-way conversations, whereas one-headed arrows represent remarks that did not arouse a response. Arrows directed to the centre of the circle indicate remarks made to the group as a whole. A network analysis of this sort can reveal both the amount of participation by each member and the recipients of every member's remarks. Thus, it provides a graphic look at who seems to be making the most significant contributions (at least in terms of quantity), as well as who is not contributing.

In the group pictured in Figure 9.1, person E appears to be connected to the group only through interaction with person A; E never addressed any other members, nor did any of them address E. Also notice that person A is both the most active and the most widely connected member. A addressed remarks to the group as a whole as well as to every other member and was the object of remarks from three individuals as well.

Sociograms don't tell the whole story because they do not indicate the quality of the messages being exchanged. Nonetheless, they are a useful tool in analyzing group communication. Communications theorists have identified several common network layouts, or **topologies**, which tend to have similar-looking sociograms. Each topology has its own strengths and weaknesses when it comes to facilitating effective group communication.

If group members always stayed together and shared every piece of information with one another, their interaction would resemble the topology shown in Figure 9.2—what communication theorists have called an **all-channel network**. In such a group, the physical arrangement influences communication. It's obviously easier to interact with someone you can see well. Lack of visibility isn't a serious problem in dyadic settings, but it can be troublesome in groups. For example, group members seated in a circle are more likely to talk with the people across from them than with those

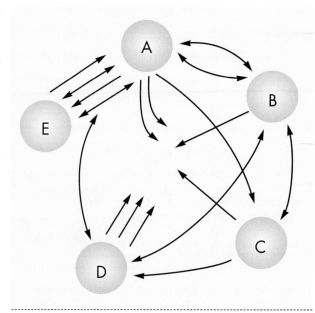

Figure 9.1

Patterns of Interaction in a Five-Person Group

all-channel network

A communication network in which all parties have equal access to one another.

sociogram

Graphic representation of the interaction patterns in a group.

topologies

Common network layouts, such as how the interactions between the participants in a seminar session are laid out, which tend to have similar-looking sociograms.

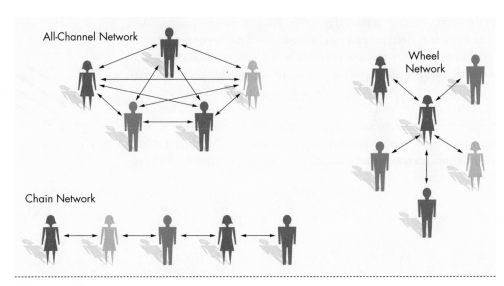

Figure 9.2
Small-Group Communication Networks

on either side.[21] Different things happen when members are seated in rectangular arrangements. Research with 12-person juries showed that those sitting at either end of rectangular tables participated more in discussions and were viewed by other members as having more influence on the decision-making process.[22] Rectangular seating patterns have other consequences as well. Research conducted on six-person groups seated at rectangular tables showed that, as the distance between two persons increased, other members perceived them as being less friendly, less talkative, and less acquainted with each other.[23]

But not all groups meet face to face. The cooks, waiters, and dishwashers at a restaurant rarely sit down together to discuss their work, nor do the nurses, aides, and technicians who staff an 8- or 10-hour hospital shift. When group members aren't in immediate contact with one another, information can flow through a variety of other networks (see Figure 9.2). In a **chain network,** information moves sequentially from one member to another. A chain is an efficient way to deliver simple verbal messages or to circulate written information when it isn't possible for all team members to attend a meeting at one time. You might use this approach to route an important message to members of a team at work, asking each person to initial a memo and pass it along to the next person named on a routing slip. Chain networks are not very reliable for lengthy or complex verbal messages because the content of the message can change as it passes from one person to another.

Another topology is the **wheel network,** in which one person acts as a clearinghouse, receiving and relaying messages to all other members. Like chains, wheel networks are sometimes a practical choice, especially if one member is available to communicate with others all or most of the time. This person can become the informational hub who keeps track of messages and people. Wheel networks can also be useful when relationships are strained between two or more members. In cases like this, the central member can serve as a mediator or facilitator, managing messages as they flow between others.

The success of a wheel network depends heavily on the skill of the **gatekeeper**—the person through whom information flows. If he or she is a skilled communicator, these mediated messages may help the group function effectively. But if the gatekeeper consciously or unconsciously distorts messages to suit personal goals or plays members off against one another, the group is likely to suffer.

Decision-Making Methods

Another way to classify groups is according to the way they make decisions. There are several approaches a group can use to make decisions. We'll look at each of them now, examining their advantages and disadvantages.[24]

Consensus

A decision arrived at by **consensus** is one that all group members support. Consensus decision-making requires that all members of the group have input into the process. The advantages of this approach are obvious: full participation tends to increase the quality of the decision as well as members' commitment to support it. Consensus is especially important in decisions on critical or complex matters. But consensus also has its disadvantages. It takes a great deal of time, which makes it unsuitable for emergencies. In addition, it can often be frustrating: emotions can run high on important matters, and patience in the face of such pressures is difficult. Because of the need to deal with these emotional pressures, consensus calls for more communication skill than do other decision-making approaches. As with many things in life, high rewards come at a proportionately high cost.

Majority Rule

Overzealous high-school civics teachers have encouraged many people to believe that the democratic method of majority decision-making is always superior, but this is not necessarily the case. Majority rule has its advantages in decisions that don't require the support of all group members. When a decision needs the backing of all members in order to be effective, however, majority rule is risky. Remember that even if 51 per cent of the members favour a decision, 49 per cent may still oppose it.

Besides producing unhappy members, decisions made under majority rule are often inferior in quality to decisions hashed out by group members until they reach consensus.[25] Under majority rule, members who recognize that they will be outvoted often participate less than those on the majority side, and the deliberations usually end after a majority opinion has formed—even though minority viewpoints might be worthwhile.

Expert Opinion

Sometimes one group member will be defined as an expert and, as such, will be given the power to make decisions. This method can work well if that person's judgment is truly superior. For example, if a group is backpacking in the wilderness and one member is injured, it would probably be foolish to argue with the advice of a doctor in the group. In most cases,

During a [second-grade] science project . . . one of the 7-year-olds wondered out loud whether the baby squirrel they had in class was a boy or a girl. After pondering the issue for a few minutes, one budding scientist offered the suggestion that they have a class discussion about it and then take a vote.

Cal Downs, Wil Linkugel, and David M. Berg

Cultural Idiom

hashed out
discussed thoroughly

however, matters aren't so simple. Who is the expert? There is often disagreement on this question. Sometimes a member might think he or she is the best qualified to make a decision, but others will disagree. In a case like this, the group probably won't support that person's advice, even if it is sound.

Minority Control

Sometimes a few members of a group will form a committee to decide on a particular matter. This approach works well with non-critical questions, when it would be a waste of time for the whole group to study the issue in detail. When an issue is so important that it needs the support of everyone, it's best at least to have the committee report its findings for the approval of all members.

Authority Rule

Authority rule is the approach most often used by autocratic leaders (see Chapter 10). Though it sounds dictatorial, there are times when such an approach has its advantages. Because it is quick, it may be useful in cases where there simply isn't time for the group to decide what to do. Authority rule is also perfectly acceptable for routine matters that don't require discussion in order to gain approval. When overused, however, this approach causes problems. As Chapter 10 will show, group decisions are usually of higher quality and more likely to gain wide support than those made by an individual. Thus, failure to consult with members can reduce effectiveness even when the leader's decision is a reasonable one.

When the person in authority consults members before making a decision, it is possible to preserve some of the quality and commitment that come with group interaction, but this approach also has its disadvantages. In some cases other group members will be tempted to tell the leader what they think he or she wants to hear; in others they will compete to impress the decision-maker.

Selecting a Decision-Making Method

Which of these decision-making approaches is best? The answer can vary from one culture to another. Consensus is highly valued in Japan. British and Dutch business people also value the 'all members on board' approach. By contrast, people in Germany, France, and Spain tend to prefer strong leaders and view a desire for consensus as somewhat wishy-washy.[26]

Culture notwithstanding, the most effective approach in a given situation depends on the circumstances:

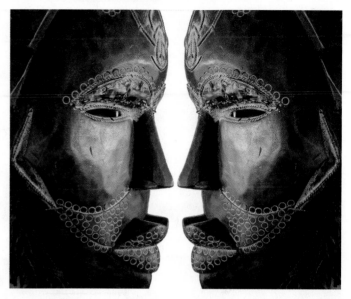

- **The type of decision.** Some decisions are best made by an expert, whereas others will benefit from involving the entire group.
- **The importance of the decision.** If the decision is relatively unimportant, it's probably not worth involving all members of the group. By contrast, critical decisions probably require the participation, and ideally the buy-in, of all members.
- **Time available.** If time is short, it may not be possible to assemble the entire group for deliberations.[27]

When choosing a decision-making approach, weigh the pros and cons of each before you decide which one has the best chance of success in the situation your group is facing.

Cultural Influences on Group Communication

In past generations, most groups in Canada were ethnically and culturally homogeneous. During the twentieth century, however, Canada became home to more then 13.4 million immigrants, and annual rates increased significantly in the 1990s. In 2001, the Canadian census found that 18.4 per cent of the population had been born outside Canada. More than 200 different ethnic origins—defined in the census as the ethnic or cultural group(s) to which an individual's ancestors belonged—were reported.

The proportion of visible minorities in Canada has also increased steadily over the past 20 years. Visible minorities are defined by the Employment Equity Act as 'persons, other than Aboriginal peoples, who are non-Caucasian in race or non-white in colour'. In 1981, visible minorities accounted for 5 per cent of the total population; by 2001, that figure had risen to 13 per cent. The distribution of visible minorities by province ranged from a low of less than 1 per cent in Newfoundland and Labrador to a high of nearly 22 per cent in British Columbia. In Ontario, visible minorities accounted for 19 per cent of the overall population and 37 per cent of the people in Toronto—the highest concentration in the country. In the Atlantic region, only Halifax had a sizable visible minority population (7 per cent). Montreal was the only metropolitan area in Quebec with a large visible minority population (14 per cent). Visible minorities accounted for about 5 per cent of all persons in Regina, almost 6 per cent in Saskatoon, 15 per cent in Edmonton, and about 18 per cent in Calgary. After Toronto, Vancouver had the largest proportion of visible minorities, with 36 per cent.[28]

Fortunately, the growing body of research about communicating across diversity offers encouraging news about what happens when people from different backgrounds get together. While homogeneous groups may be more cohesive,[29] diverse groups often develop better

solutions to problems[30] and enjoy themselves more while working together.[31]

One ingredient in working effectively in diverse groups is understanding the often subtle cultural factors that shape communication. After surveying over 160,000 members of organizations in 60 countries, Geert Hofstede identified five cultural forces that shape the attitudes and behaviours of groups and individuals.[32] We will examine each of them in the following pages.

Individualism versus Collectivism

Some cultures value the individual, whereas others value the group. As Table 9.4 shows, the United States is one of the world's more

TABLE 9.4 Cultural Values in Selected Countries

(Countries ranked lower on each list are closer to the mean)	
Individualistic	**Collectivistic**
United States	Venezuela
Australia	Taiwan
Great Britain	Mexico
Canada	Philippines
Low Power Distance	**High Power Distance**
Israel	Philippines
New Zealand	Mexico
Germany	India
United States	France
Low Uncertainty Avoidance	**High Uncertainty Avoidance**
Singapore	Greece
India	Japan
Philippines	Peru
United States	Mexico
High Task Orientation	**High Social Orientation**
Japan	Sweden
Austria	Norway
Italy	Chile
Mexico	Portugal
Long-Term Focus	**Short-Term Focus**
China (includes Hong Kong and Taiwan)	Pakistan
Japan	Canada
South Korea	Great Britain
Brazil	United States
India	Australia

Source: Based on research summarized in G. Hofstede, *Culture and Organizations: Software of the Mind* (New York: McGraw-Hill, 1997).

Understanding Diversity

⬤ ⬤ ⬤ ⬤ ⬤ BASEBALL IN JAPAN AND THE USA

The concept and practice of group harmony or wa is what most dramatically differentiates Japanese baseball from the American game. It is the connecting thread running through all Japanese life and sports. While 'Let It All Hang Out' and 'Do Your Own Thing' are mottoes of contemporary American society, the Japanese have their own credo in the well-worn proverb 'The Nail That Sticks Up Shall Be Hammered Down'. It is practically a national slogan.

Holdouts, for example, are rare in Japan. A player usually takes what the club deigns to give him and that's that. Demanding more money is evidence that a player is putting his own interests before those of the team.

In the pressure-cooker world of US pro sports, temper outbursts are considered acceptable, and at times even regarded as a salutary show of spirit. In Japan, however, a player's behaviour is often considered as important as his batting average. Batting slumps are usually accompanied by embarrassed smiles. Temper tantrums—along with practical joking, bickering, complaining, and other norms of American clubhouse life—are viewed in Japan as unwelcome incursions into the team's collective peace of mind.

When [Tokyo] Giants top pitcher Takashi Nishimoto ignored the instructions of a coach in practice one summer day in 1985, the coach punched him between the eyes. Nishimoto was also forced to apologize and pay a 100,000 yen fine for insubordination.

Moreover, untoward behaviour is also seen as a sign of character weakness and a 'small heart', as well as being detrimental to the team's image overall. In Japan, a 'real man' is one who keeps his emotions to himself and thinks of others' feelings.

—*Robert Whiting,* You Gotta Have Wa

Questions: Do you think that the different cultural setting in Japan makes for a better sports environment? Do you think that gender norms could lead to workplace clashes between English Canadians and Japanese people? What are the similarities and differences that you see between English Canadians and Japanese people?

individualistic societies, along with Canada, Australia, and Britain. By contrast, Latin American and Asian societies are generally more collectivistic.

In individualistic cultures people tend to feel that their primary responsibility is to themselves, whereas members of collectivistic societies feel loyalties and obligations to the groups of which they are members: the family, the community, the organization they work for, and their working teams. Members of individualistic societies gain most of their identity and self-esteem from their own accomplishments, whereas members of collectivistic societies are identified with the groups to which they belong. Individualistic cultures are also characterized by self-reliance and competition, whereas collectivistic cultures are more attentive to and concerned with the opinions of significant others.[33] Individualistic and collectivistic cultures have very different approaches to communication. For example, individualistic cultures are relatively tolerant of conflicts, state their opinions openly, and use direct, solution-oriented approaches. Members of collectivistic cultures, by contrast, prefer to avoid conflict and often seek less direct ways to express their message.[34]

Cultural Idiom

holdouts
those who refuse to participate until they receive a satisfactory contract offer

speaking out
saying boldly what one thinks

⬤ ⬤ ⬤ ⬤ ⬤ COMMUNICATION ON-SCREEN

The Wizard of Oz (1939)

Directed by Victor Fleming.

This much-loved story illustrates how group members can achieve their personal goals by working together toward a common purpose. The Tin Man wants a heart; the Cowardly Lion wants courage; the Scarecrow wants a brain; and Dorothy wants to go home to Kansas. All the adventurers realize that helping one another is the best way to get what each wants. The characters embody the motto of another famous band of adventurers: 'All for one and one for all'.

collectivistic orientation
A cultural orientation focusing on the welfare of the group as a whole, rather than a concern by individuals for their own success.

individualistic orientation
A cultural orientation focusing on the value and welfare of individual members, as opposed to a concern for the group as a whole.

power distance
The degree to which members are willing to accept a difference in power and status between members of a group.

uncertainty avoidance
The cultural tendency to seek stability and honour tradition instead of welcoming risk, uncertainty, and change.

A fighter pilot soon found he wanted to associate only with other fighter pilots. Who else could understand the nature of the little proposition (right stuff/death) they were all dealing with? And what other subject could compare with it? It was riveting! To talk about it in so many words was forbidden, of course. The very words death, danger, bravery, fear were not to be uttered except in the occasional specific instance or for ironic effect. Nevertheless, the subject could be adumbrated in code or by example . . . They diced that righteous stuff up into little bits, bowed ironically to it, stumbled blindfolded around it, groped, lurched, belched, staggered, bawled, sang, roared, and feinted at it with self-deprecating humor. Nevertheless!—they never mentioned it by name.

Tom Wolfe

It's easy to see how a culture's **individualistic** or **collectivistic orientation** can affect group communication. Members of collectivistic cultures are more likely to be team players, whereas members of individualistic cultures are far more likely to produce and reward stars. As members of highly individualistic cultures, North Americans often need to control their desire to dominate group discussions and to 'win' in problem-solving situations. Consensus may be a desirable outcome, but it doesn't always come easily to individualists. By contrast, members of collectivistic cultures may be reluctant to speak out—especially if it means disagreeing—even when it would be in the best interests of the group.

Power Distance

Some cultures readily accept differences in power and status, whereas others accept them grudgingly, if at all. Most people in Canada and the United States believe in the principle of equality and reject the notion that some people are entitled to greater power or privilege than others. In other cultures, inequality is accepted as a fact of life.[35] **Power distance** refers to the degree to which members are willing to accept a difference in power and status between members of a group. In a culture with a high power distance, group members may willingly subordinate themselves to a leader—especially one whose leadership position is the product of socially accepted factors such as age, experience, training, or status. Members of cultures where low power distance is the norm may be less likely to feel that a particular group needs a leader, or to accept that the person who occupies that role automatically deserves unquestioning obedience. Supervisors, bosses, teachers, and so on certainly have the respect of the groups they lead in cultures where low power distance is the norm—but mostly because they earn it. In low power distance cultures, group members expect leaders to be more considerate of their interests and needs. 'After all,' they assume, 'we're basically equal.'

Uncertainty Avoidance

Some cultures accept—even welcome—risk, uncertainty, and change.[36] Others, characterized by **uncertainty avoidance**, prefer stability and tradition. Geography offers no clue to a culture's tolerance of uncertainty. Among the countries whose people tend to dislike surprises are Greece, Portugal, Turkey, Mexico, and Israel. Among those whose people are more comfortable with change are Denmark, Hong Kong, Ireland, and India.

It should come as no surprise that different attitudes towards uncertainty affect the way members of groups communicate. People who dislike uncertainty are uncomfortable with ambiguous tasks and reluctant to take risks. They tend to worry about the future, be loyal to their employers, and accept seniority as the basis for leadership. They view conflict as undesirable and are often willing to compromise when disagreements arise. By contrast, people from cultures with a higher tolerance for uncertainty are more willing to take risks, more accepting of change, and more willing to break rules for pragmatic reasons. They accept conflict as natural and may be less willing to compromise when disagreements occur.

Task versus Social Orientation

The categories of task and social orientation, discussed earlier in this chapter, were originally labelled 'masculine' and 'feminine', based on the traditional notion that men are assertive and results oriented, whereas women are nurturing. In an era of increasingly flexible gender roles these labels are considered sexist and misleading, so we have substituted different labels. Groups in societies with a strong task orientation (Japan, Austria, Switzerland, and Mexico are examples) focus heavily on getting the job done. By contrast, groups in societies with a high degree of social orientation (including all the Scandinavian countries, as well as Chile, Portugal, and Thailand) are more likely to be concerned about members' feelings and ability to function smoothly as a team. When compared with other countries, Canada is almost exactly in the middle, balanced between task and social concerns.[37]

Task-oriented societies tend to focus on finding ways to improve team performance and ensure individual success through better training and so on. By contrast, groups in socially oriented societies focus more on collective concerns: co-operative problem-solving, maintaining a friendly atmosphere, and good physical working conditions. Problem-solving is still important in these cultures, but group members may be reluctant to take action if the personal costs to members—in stress and hard feelings—are likely to be high.

COMMUNICATION ON-SCREEN

The Right Stuff (1983)
Directed by Philip Kaufman.

This film chronicles the history of the original seven astronauts in the early days of the US space exploration program. In addition to detailing the astronauts' physical accomplishments, the film examines the attitudes that led them to risk death and their reactions to being treated as heroes. It contains many examples of the unspoken norms that these men developed to govern their approach to their jobs, one another, and the world at large.

Short- versus Long-Term Orientation

Some cultures look for quick payoffs, whereas others are willing to defer gratification in pursuit of long-range goals. The willingness to work hard today for a payoff some time in the future is especially common in East Asian cultures, including China, Japan, and South Korea. Western industrialized cultures are much more focused on short-term results.

As long as all group members share the same orientation toward payoffs, the chances for harmony are good. When some people push for a quick fix while others urge patience, conflicts are likely to arise.

It's easy to see how a society's cultural norms—its attitudes toward individuality, power distance, and uncertainty; its task or social orientation; and its emphasis on short- or long-term goals—can affect group behaviour. Whether the group is an athletic team, a military unit, a working group, or a family, the principle is the same. Cultural values shape what groups communicate about and how their members interact. Cultural factors don't account for every difference in group functioning, of course, but common assumptions do exert a subtle yet powerful effect on communication.

Cultural Idiom

payoffs
rewards

Summary

Groups play an important role in many areas of our lives—families, education, employment, and friendships, to name just a few. Groups possess several characteristics that distinguish them from other communication contexts. They involve interaction and interdependence over time among a small number of participants with the purpose of achieving one or more goals. Groups have their own goals, as do individual members. Member goals fall into two categories: task-related and socially related. Sometimes individual and group goals are compatible, and sometimes they are in conflict.

Groups can be classified according to their functions. We have identified four types: learning, problem-solving, social, and growth groups. Whatever the type, every group has certain rules and norms, roles for individual members, patterns of interaction that are shaped by the group's structure, and approaches to decision-making.

Groups don't operate in a vacuum. The culture around them influences the way group members communicate with one another. This chapter has examined five ways in which culture influences interaction: individualism versus collectivism, power distance, uncertainty avoidance, task versus social orientation, and short- versus long-term goals.

Key Terms

all-channel network 349
chain network 350
collectivistic
    orientation 356
consensus 351
dysfunctional roles 345
formal roles 343
gatekeeper 350
group 334
group goals 337
growth groups 340
hidden agenda 338

individual goals 337
individualistic
    orientation 356
informal roles 345
learning group 339
norms 341
power distance 356
problem-solving
    groups 339
procedural norms 342
roles 343
rules 341

social groups 339
social norms 342
social orientation 338
social roles 345
sociogram 349
task norms 342
task orientation 337
task roles 345
topology 349
uncertainty
    avoidance 356
wheel network 350

Activities

A. Your Membership in Groups

To find out what roles groups play in your life, complete the following steps:

1. Use the criteria of interaction, interdependence, time, size, and goals to identify the small groups to which you belong.
2. Describe the importance of each group to you, and evaluate how satisfying the communication is in each one.
3. Based on what you have read in this chapter, describe how communication operates in your groups and how it could be improved.

4. Describe how social media is changing the way you join groups and interact with people. Do you find yourself engaged in more virtual groups than others? Do you derive more or less satisfaction from virtual groups?

5. Discuss whether you think there are specific types of groups that you think are better served as virtual groups.

B. Group and Individual Goals

Think about two groups to which you belong.
1. What are your task-related goals in each?
2. What are your social goals in each?
3. Are your personal goals compatible or incompatible with those of other members?
4. Are they compatible or incompatible with the group goals?
5. What effect does the compatibility or incompatibility of goals have on the effectiveness of the group?

C. Norms and Rules in Action

Describe the explicit rules and desirable norms that you would like to see established in the following new groups, and describe the steps you could take to see that they are established.
1. A group of classmates formed to develop and present a class research project.
2. A group of neighbours meeting for the first time to persuade the city to install a stop sign at a dangerous intersection.
3. A group of eight-year-olds you will be coaching in a team sport.
4. A group of fellow employees who will be sharing new office space.

D. Choosing the Best Decision-Making Approach

Which of the decision-making approaches listed on pages 351–3 would be most appropriate in each of the following situations? Explain why your recommended approach is the best one for each situation.
1. Four apartment mates must decide how to handle household chores.
2. A group of hikers and their experienced guide become lost in a snowstorm and debate whether to try to find their way to safety or to pitch camp and wait for the weather to clear.
3. After trying unsuccessfully to reach consensus, the partners in a new business venture cannot agree on the best name for their enterprise.
4. A 25-member ski club is looking for the cheapest airfare and lodging for its winter trip.
5. A passenger falls overboard during an afternoon sail on your friend's 20-foot sailboat. The wind is carrying the boat away from the passenger.

E. Motives for Group Membership

Members often join a group for reasons unrelated to the group's stated purpose for existing. For example, some people belong to growth groups to fulfill social needs, and others speak out in task-oriented groups to satisfy their egos more than to help solve the stated problem. Develop a set of guidelines that describes when you believe it is and is not ethical to participate in groups without stating any hidden agendas

Further Reading

Keyton, Joann, and Lawrence R. Frey. 'The State of Traits: Predispositions and Group Communication', in Lawrence R. Frey, ed., *New Directions in Group Communication*. Thousand Oaks, CA: Sage, 2002.
This research-based chapter details the influence of individual personality styles on a group's effectiveness.

Rothwell, J. Dan. *In Mixed Company*, 5th edn. Belmont, CA: Wadsworth, 2004.
This book is an easy-to-read, comprehensive look at the process of communication in small groups. Ideal for readers looking for more information on group communication, it does an excellent job of summarizing literally hundreds of research studies in a manner that makes their value in everyday interaction clear.

Zorn, Theodore E., Jr, and George H. Tompson. 'Communication in Top Management Teams', in Lawrence R. Frey, ed., *New Directions in Group Communication*. Thousand Oaks, CA: Sage, 2002.
For career-minded readers, this essay offers insights into the communication skills of high-level managers.

Study Questions

Think back to a group that you participated in recently that was either successful or unsuccessful in meeting its goals. Write a brief description of the group's goals, its setting (physical, virtual) and its members. Then write a line or two about the group's success or failure. Now answer the following questions about your group:

1. What can you speculate are the individual goals of group members? Which of these goals did you find members shared, and which were using hidden agendas? How did those individual goals help or hinder the group in its pursuit of its goal? What could you have done to increase the chances that individual goals didn't interfere with the group's goal?

2. What procedural and task norms would have helped this group be successful? What social norms would have interfered with the group's success?

3. Given the group's task, which of the functional roles described on pages 343–6 do you think were most important to the success of your group? What role-related problems might arise if the roles you listed remain unfilled?

4. Did the group members' cultural backgrounds affect the functioning of the group? How and why? How might you have fixed cultural problems?

5. Would the group have benefited from using social media? How might have a social media approach affected the group's performance?

Persuasion and Public Communication

Part IV

Professional Profile:

Donald Smith

My job is director of operations in the Public Affairs Branch of the Canada Revenue Agency (CRA). That means that I am responsible for national media relations, including the development of media relations policy and strategy. Media monitoring activities are part of the job. I'm also responsible for special event planning and coordination for the minister of National Revenue and the commissioner of the CRA, including speechwriting. In addition, I have liaison responsibilities for CRA's 35 communications specialists located across the country, and I publish the quarterly employee magazine.

The variety of challenges of my job is what makes it so enjoyable. It's a wonderful mix of scheduled deliverables and issues that can and do blow up without warning. So on any given day I have some idea of what I'm going to be doing, but there are frequently surprises, and that's fun.

I got into communications via journalism. I spent the first 10 years of my career as a radio journalist, which led to a job as press secretary to a federal cabinet minister for five years. Next I moved to the federal bureaucracy as a communications account executive, then four years at the Privy Council Office, then to my present job. It wasn't a typical entry into communications, but it wasn't atypical, either, at the time. And I picked up all the skill sets along the way; I didn't actually study public relations until I enrolled in the Master of Communications Management Program at McMaster University at the age of 52. My advice to young communicators is to focus on their formal education in communications and public relations a little earlier in life than I did.

I believe that versatile communicators are the ones who will be the most employable in the next 5 to 10 years. By that I mean communicators will need the traditional skills such as writing, editing, analytical ability, media relations, etc. but will also need the knowledge required to take advantage of social media opportunities. It's not an either/or situation when it comes to traditional media and social media—they will need expertise to work with both.

If I had to name one skill set that a young communicator preparing to enter the field should strive to master, it would be writing. Without question, the development of superior writing skills should be the goal of all aspiring communicators. Senior executives in the public and private sector look to their communications team to provide polished material, be it a news release, speech, letter to the editor, or anything else. Young communicators should look for opportunities to write in order to hone their skills and to start to build a portfolio.

Donald Smith is director of operations in the Public Affairs Branch of the Canada Revenue Agency.

After studying the material in this chapter . . .

You should understand:

- the advantages of solving problems in groups (and the situations where groups are not so effective);
- the characteristics of several common discussion formats;
- the advantages and drawbacks of computer-mediated groups;
- the steps in the rational problem-solving method;
- the developmental stages in a problem-solving group;
- the factors that contribute to group cohesiveness; and
- the various approaches to studying leadership.

You should be able to:

- decide when to use groups to solve problems and whether a face-to-face group meeting or computer-mediated meeting would be more practical;
- use the problem-solving steps outlined in this chapter to help complete a group task;
- suggest ways to build cohesiveness and participation in a group;
- analyze the sources of leadership and power in a group;
- suggest the most effective leadership approach for a specific task; and
- identify the obstacles to effective functioning of a specific group and suggest more effective ways of communicating.

Solving Problems in Groups

Chapter Highlights

In this chapter we will discuss solving problems in groups, including

- when (and when not) to use groups for solving problems;
- what formats are best for different problem-solving situations; and
- the pros and cons of computer-mediated groups.

While groups can solve problems in many different ways, the most successful groups

- tend to follow a structured, six-step approach;
- understand the stages that groups go through while working on a problem; and
- maintain positive relationships and an optimal level of cohesiveness.

You will see that leadership and team-member influence come in many forms:

- Group members can use six types of power.
- The effectiveness of leaders can be defined in different ways.
- There are many different leadership styles, which are effective in different circumstances.

Finally, we'll look at the following pitfalls that can come with group problem-solving and how to avoid them:

- information underload and overload;
- unequal participation; and
- pressure to conform.

In Chapter 9 we described various types of groups—learning, problem-solving, social, and growth groups. Of all these, problem-solving groups have been studied most intensively by social scientists. Once we understand the nature of problem-solving, the reason becomes clear. Solving problems, as we define it here, doesn't refer only to situations where something is wrong. Perhaps *meeting challenges* and *performing tasks* are better terms. After you recognize this fact, you can see that problem-solving occupies a major part of working life. The figures from just one company illustrate the scope of group problem-solving: at 3M Corporation, managers spend a total of 4.4 million hours per year in meetings, at a cost to the company of $78.8 million in salaries.[1] Away from work, groups also meet to solve problems: non-profit organizations plan fundraisers, sports teams work to improve their collective performance, neighbours meet to improve the quality of life where they live, educators and parents work together to improve schools—the list is almost endless.

This chapter will focus on both the task and the relational aspects of problem-solving groups. In addition, it will explore the nature of leadership, defining that important term and suggesting how groups can be led most effectively. Finally, it will list several common problems that task-oriented groups can encounter and describe how to overcome them.

> • • • • • • • • • • • • • • •
>
> *If you can, help others; if you cannot do that, at least do not harm them.*
>
> • • • • • • • • • • • • • • •
>
> Dalai Lama

Problem-Solving in Groups: When and Why

For many people, groups are to problem-solving what Muzak is to music or Twinkies are to food—a joke. The snide remark 'A camel is a horse designed by a committee' reflects this attitude, as does this ditty:

> Search all your parks in all your cities . . .
> You'll find no statues to committees![2]

Cultural Idiom

ditty
a short, simple poem

Muzak
bland instrumental arrangements of popular songs which are often played in elevators, stores, and restaurants

wind up with
have

This unflattering reputation is at least partly justified. Most of us would wind up with a handsome sum if we had a dollar for every hour we've wasted in groups. On the other hand, it's unfair to view all groups as bad, especially when this accusation implies that other types of communication are by nature superior. After all, we've also wasted time listening to boring lectures, reading worthless books, and making trivial conversation.

So what's the truth? Is group problem-solving a waste of effort, or is it the best way to manage a task? As with most matters, the truth falls somewhere between these two extremes. Groups do have their shortcomings, which we will discuss a little later. But problems can be avoided when these shortcomings are recognized. Extensive research has shown that the group approach is the most effective way to handle many tasks.

Advantages of Group Problem-Solving

For more than 50 years, research comparing problem-solving by groups and individuals has shown that, in most cases, groups can produce more solutions to a problem than individuals working alone and that the solutions are of higher quality.[3] Groups have proved superior at a wide range of tasks—everything from assembling jigsaw puzzles to solving complex reasoning problems. There are several reasons why groups are so effective.[4]

Consensus-Building and the Canadian Constitution

For the first 115 years of its life as an independent nation, Canada did not have the right to amend its own Constitution without requesting the formal approval of the British Parliament. The main reason this colonial arrangement had dragged on for so long was that the federal and provincial governments had never been able to agree on a new set of rules for constitutional change. Should all 10 provinces have to agree to a change before it could become law? If not, how many would be enough? What proportion of the population should they represent? Should one province (Quebec in particular) have the power to veto a change that the others were prepared to accept? A means of amending Canada's Constitution in Canada instead of through the British Parliament could not be put in place until questions like these had been answered.

What triggered the final effort to resolve the matter was the May 1980 Quebec referendum on sovereignty-association, for Prime Minister Pierre Trudeau had promised to redefine Quebec's position in Canada if voters rejected the sovereignty option—which they did. Talks with the provinces accordingly resumed in the summer of 1980. By the next fall, however, only two provinces (Ontario and New Brunswick) had agreed to support Trudeau's plan, which centred on the incorporation within the Constitution of a Charter of Rights and Freedoms. The holdouts were hardly united in their objections—each had its own—but together they formed a united front that soon became known as the Gang of Eight.

When the First Ministers' Conference in Ottawa in early November 1981 appeared to be going nowhere on the issue, Trudeau proposed a compromise: agree to removing Constitutional amendment from the hands of the British Parliament now and leave the details of the Charter and amending formula to be worked out later; then, if no agreement was reached within two years, submit the outstanding issues to the public in a national referendum. Seven of the Gang of Eight refused, but—to their shock—Quebec Premier René Lévesque broke ranks and agreed. Accounts

of Lévesque's motivation vary: some say he was reluctant but agreed because a referendum appeared to be the most democratic solution; others that he welcomed the prospect of a showdown with Trudeau that he was sure to win.

In any event, at the end of the meeting Lévesque left to spend the night in Hull, Quebec (across the river from Ottawa), after asking the other premiers to let him know if anything came up before he rejoined them the next morning.

In fact something did come up: late in the night, the other premiers agreed to a compromise negotiated by Justice Minister Jean Chrétien and Saskatchewan Attorney General Roy Romanow. But Lévesque was not informed, let alone consulted. It was only when he arrived for breakfast the next morning that he learned an agreement had been reached during what has come to be known in Quebec as the 'night of the long knives'.

The new compromise was signed by Trudeau and nine premiers, but Lévesque refused to sign. Three weeks later the Quebec government announced that it would invoke its traditional right, as representative of one of Canada's founding peoples, to veto the plan; however, the Supreme Court of Canada ruled that the province had never possessed such a right, either legally or by convention.

Today, more than a quarter of a century after the Constitution Act, 1982, became law—governing both the nine provinces that agreed to it and Quebec—the Quebec provincial government still has not signed it. The decision to throw consensus to the wayside and proceed without Quebec only deepened Quebecers' profound sense of alienation and fanned the flames of separatism.

Questions: A series of communication breakdowns led Quebec Premier René Lévesque to feel that he had been excluded from the constitutional negotiations. Where do you think things went wrong? How could Trudeau, Lévesque, and the other premiers have functioned better as a problem-solving group?

Resources

For many tasks, groups possess a greater collection of resources than do most individuals. Sometimes the resources are physical. Three or four people can put up a tent or dig a ditch much faster than one person can. In other cases, though, pooling resources can actually lead to qualitatively better solutions. Think, for instance, of times when you have studied with other students for a test, and you will remember how much better the group was at

Cultural Idiom

jog your memory
remind yourself

preparing for all the questions that might be asked and at developing answers to them. (Of course, we have to assume that your fellow members cared enough about the exam to have studied for it before the meeting.) Furthermore, interaction among the group's members makes it easier to mobilize their resources. Talking about an upcoming test with others can jog your memory and remind you of things you might not have thought of if you had been working alone.

Accuracy

Another benefit of group work is the increased likelihood of catching errors. At one time or another, we all make stupid mistakes—like the man who built a boat in his basement and then wasn't able to get it out the door. Working in a group increases the chance that foolish errors like this won't slip by. Sometimes, of course, errors aren't so obvious, which makes it even more valuable to have more than one person checking for them. On the other hand, there is always some risk that group members will support each other in a bad idea. We'll discuss this problem later on, when we look at the pressure to conform that can develop in groups.

Commitment

Besides coming up with superior solutions, groups also generate a higher commitment to carrying them out. The idea that people are most likely to accept solutions they have helped create and will work harder to implement them is the principle behind **participative decision-making**, in which the people who will live with a plan help to develop it. This is an especially important principle for those in authority, such as supervisors, teachers, and parents. As professors, we have seen the difference between the sullen compliance of students who have been forced to accept a policy they disagree with and the much more willing co-operation of students who have helped develop it. Though the benefits of participative decision-making are great, we need to insert a qualification here: there are times when an autocratic approach—imposing a decision without discussion—is the most effective. We will discuss this question of when to be democratic and when to be directive in the leadership section of this chapter.

participative decision-making
Development of solutions with input by the people who will be affected.

When to Use Groups for Problem-Solving

Working in a group is not always the best way to solve a problem. Many jobs can be tackled more quickly and easily—even more efficiently—by one or more people working independently. Answering the following questions will help you decide when to solve a problem using a group and when to undertake it alone.[5]

Is the Job Beyond the Capacity of One Person?

Some jobs are simply too big for one person to manage. They may call for more information than a single person possesses or can gather.

For example, a group of friends planning a large New Year's Eve party will probably have a better event if they pool their ideas than if one person tries to think of everything. Some jobs also require more time and energy than one person can spare. Planning the party could involve a variety of tasks: inviting the guests, hiring a band, finding a suitable venue, buying food and drinks, and so on. It's both unrealistic and unfair to expect one or two people to do all this work.

Are Individuals' Tasks Interdependent?

Remember that a group is more than a collection of individuals working side by side. The best tasks for groups are ones where the individuals can help one another in some way. Think of a group of disgruntled tenants considering how to protest unfair rent hikes. In order to get anywhere, they realize that they have to assign areas of responsibility to each member: researching the law, recruiting new members, publicizing their complaints, and so on. It's easy to see that these jobs are all interdependent: recruiting new members, for example, will require publicity; and publicizing complaints will involve showing how the tenants' legal rights are being violated.

One manager let employees know how valuable they were with the following memo:

```
YOU ARX A KXY PXRSON
Xvxn though my typxwritxr is an old modxl, it works vxry
wxll-xxcxpt for onx kxy. You would think that with all thx
othxr kxys functioning propxrly, onx kxy not working would
hardly bx noticxd; but just onx kxy out of whack sxxms to
ruin thx wholx xffort.
     You may say to yoursxlf—Wxll I'm only onx pxrson. No onx
will noticx if I don't do my bxst. But it doxs makx a dif-
fxrxncx bxcausx to bx xffxctivx an organization nxxds activx
participation by xvxry onx to thx bxst of his or hxr ability.
     So thx nxxt timx you think you arx not important, rxmxm-
bxr my old typxwritxr. You arx a kxy pxrson.
```

Even when everyone is working on the same job, there can be interdependence if different members fill the various functional roles described in Chapter 9. Some people might be better at task-related roles like information giving, diagnosing, and summarizing. Others might contribute by filling social roles such as harmonizing, supporting, or relieving tension. People working independently simply don't have the breadth of resources to fill all these functions.

Is There More than One Decision or Solution?

Groups are best suited to tackling problems that have no single, cut-and-dried answer: What's the best way to boost membership in a campus organization? How can funds be raised for a charity? What topic should the group choose for a class project? Gaining the perspectives of every member boosts the odds of finding high-quality answers to questions like these.

By contrast, a problem with only one solution won't take full advantage of a group's talents. For example, phoning merchants to get price quotes or looking up a series of books in the library doesn't require much creative thinking. Jobs like these can be handled by one or two people working alone. Of course, it may take a group meeting to decide how to divide the work to get the job done most efficiently.

> **Cultural Idiom**
>
> **boosts the odds of**
> increases the chances of success
>
> **cut-and-dried**
> unambiguous

Young Communicator
PROFILE

●●●●●

Qianxing Lu, MA Student in Media
Studies, S.I. Newhouse School of
Public Communication

I am currently a graduate student in
the S.I. Newhouse School of Public
Communication at Syracuse University,
one of the world's best schools of communication. I did my undergraduate degree
in communication studies and multimedia
at McMaster University in Canada.

Becoming a leading scholar in mass
communication has been a consistent goal
of mine. Coming from China, one of the nations in which media censorship is the most
practiced, I have been greatly impressed by
the degree of development of media and
leniency for journalism in North America.
However, I am convinced that there will be
media reform in China and I want to be a
part of it, taking what I have learned here in
Canada and the United States back with me.

In the world of academia, communication includes many specific fields ranging from interpersonal communication
to research on government policies in
media that influence almost every media
consumer. Communication is also an area
where interdisciplinary knowledge is most
needed. I have seen numerous fascinating
combinations of communication with psychology, political science, computer science, business, and fine arts.

Although my focus is mainly on communication theory, please keep in mind that
communication is also one of the most practical areas. It teaches you how to read, speak,
and think effectively and always to the point.

●●●●●

COMMUNICATION ON-SCREEN

Apollo 13 (1995)
Directed by Ron Howard.

This film tells the true story of how teamwork and courage
saved the lives of three astronauts who faced death when
their spacecraft malfunctioned on its mission to the moon.
After an onboard explosion, the three astronauts—Jim Lovell
(Tom Hanks), Fred Haise (Bill Paxton), and Jack Swigert (Kevin
Bacon)—were faced with the possibility of becoming marooned
in space, where the options were all grim: running out of oxygen, being poisoned by carbon dioxide, or freezing to death.
The film chronicles how the engineers on the ground worked
with the astronauts to devise a solution to this deadly challenge.
The story shows how a dedicated team can work harmoniously
to triumph over even apparently impossible challenges.

Is There Potential For Disagreement?

Tackling a problem as a group is essential if you need the support of everyone involved. Consider a group of friends planning
a vacation. Letting one or two people choose the destination,
schedule, and budget would be asking for trouble because their
decisions would almost certainly disappoint at least some of the
people who weren't consulted. It would be far smarter to involve
everyone in the most important decisions, even if doing so took
more time. After the key decisions have been settled, it might
be fine to delegate relatively minor issues to one or two people.

Group Problem-Solving Formats

Groups meet to solve problems in a variety of settings and for
a wide range of reasons. The formats they use are also varied.
For example, a group may meet before an audience of people

involved in or affected by the topic under discussion, like the citizens who attend a typical city council meeting or the members of the public who attend the CBC's town hall meetings. Audience members participate in a direct fashion, asking questions, responding to questions, and sometimes voicing their dissent.

Types of Problem-Solving Groups

This list of problem-solving formats and approaches is not exhaustive, but it provides a sense of how a group's structure can shape its ability to come up with high-quality solutions.

Breakout Groups

When a group is too large for all members to take part in discussions, **breakout groups**, also referred to as 'buzz groups', can be used to maximize effective participation. In this approach, a number of subgroups (usually consisting of five to seven members) simultaneously discuss an issue and then report back to the group at large. The best ideas of each breakout group are then assembled to form a high-quality decision.

Problem Census

This approach is useful when groups want to identify important issues or problems. **Problem census** works especially well when some members are more vocal than others because it equalizes participation. Members use a separate card to list each of their ideas. The leader collects all the cards and reads them to the group one by one, posting each on a board visible to everyone. Because the name of the person who contributed each item isn't listed, issues are separated from personalities. As similar items are read, the leader posts and arranges them in clusters. After all items have been read and posted, the leader and members consolidate similar items into a number of ideas that the group needs to address.

Focus Groups

Focus groups are used as a market research tool to enable sponsoring organizations to learn how potential users or the public at large regards a new product or idea. Unlike other groups discussed here, focus groups don't include decision-makers or other members who claim any expertise on a subject. Instead, their comments are used by decision-makers to figure out how people in the wider world might react to ideas.

Parliamentary Procedure

Problem-solving meetings can follow a variety of formats. A session that uses **parliamentary procedure** observes specific rules about how topics may be discussed and decisions made. The standard reference book for parliamentary procedure is the revised edition of *Robert's Rules of Order*. Although the parliamentary rules may seem stilted and cumbersome, when well used they do keep a discussion on track and protect the rights of the minority against domination by the majority.

Panel Discussion

Another common problem-solving format is the **panel discussion**, in which the participants talk over the topic informally, much as they would in an ordinary conversation. A leader (called a 'moderator' in public discussions) may help the discussion along by encouraging some members to comment, cutting off overly talkative ones, and seeking consensus when the time comes for making a decision.

breakout groups
A group discussion strategy used when the number of members is too large for effective discussion. Subgroups simultaneously address an issue and then report back to the group at large.

focus groups
Used in market research by sponsoring organizations to survey potential users or the public at large regarding a new product or idea.

panel discussion
A discussion format in which participants consider a topic more or less conversationally, without formal procedural rules. Panel discussions may be facilitated by a moderator.

parliamentary procedure
A problem-solving method in which specific rules govern the way issues may be discussed and decisions made.

problem census
Used to equalize participation in groups when the goal is to identify important issues or problems. Members first put ideas on cards, which are then compiled by a leader to generate a comprehensive statement of the issue or problem.

symposium
A discussion format in which participants divide the topic in a manner that allows each member to deliver in-depth information without interruption.

COMMUNICATION ON-SCREEN

'The Merchants of Cool: Where Does Cool Come From' (2001)
Directed by Barak Goodman.

In this documentary, which aired on the PBS program *Frontline*, journalist Douglas Rushkoff investigates how young people are targeted by marketing experts. Rushkoff shows how 'cool hunters' spend hours and days conducting surveys, focus groups, and participant research with tweens and teens to find out what young people find attractive, stimulating, terrifying, and beautiful. The merchants of cool want to find out what makes young people get excited about products, how they interact in groups, and why they socialize the way they do. Sombrely serious at times and absolutely hilarious at others, the program is required watching for students who want to understand how young people are targeted by marketing communicators.

Symposium

In a **symposium** the participants divide the topic in a manner that allows each member to deliver in-depth information without interruption. Although this format lends itself to good explanations of each person's decision, the one-person-at-a-time nature of a symposium won't lead to a group decision. The contributions of the members must be followed by the give-and-take of an open discussion.

Forum

A **forum** allows non-members to add their opinions to the group's deliberations before the group makes a decision. This approach is commonly used by public agencies to encourage the participation of citizens in the decisions that affect them.

Computer-Mediated Groups

Face-to-face meetings can be difficult. Just scheduling a session can be maddening: almost every date or time that one person suggests doesn't work for someone else. If the participants come from different locations, the time and cost of a meeting can be significant. Challenges don't end after a meeting time is finally arranged. Some members may be late. Others may have to leave early. And during the meeting interruptions are common: members may be sidetracked by off-the-topic digressions and other distractions. One or more people may dominate the conversation, whereas others rarely speak.

Given the drawbacks of meeting in person, the idea of using technology to create other ways of working together has strong appeal. As we mentioned in Chapter 9, conference calls and teleconferences allow group members to communicate in real time via telephone or computer, as if they were meeting in person. Another approach is an asynchronous discussion, which resembles e-mail: group members don't have to be online at the same time. They can log on to the network at their convenience, check messages others have sent, and contribute their own ideas for other team members to read later.

In the 1990s, communication researchers began to sort out the advantages and disadvantages of computer-mediated meetings as compared to face-to-face interactions.[6] Studies suggest that computer conferencing has several advantages. Most obviously, it is much easier to schedule and 'meet' online because members don't need to leave their desks. Asynchronous meetings are especially convenient because group members can log on at their convenience, independent of other participants. Computer-mediated sessions also encourage more balanced participation: members who might have kept quiet in face-to-face sessions are more comfortable 'speaking out' online. Furthermore, online meetings generate a permanent record of the proceedings, which can be convenient.

Despite their advantages, computer-mediated groups aren't a panacea. The lack of non-verbal cues makes it difficult to convey emotions and attitudes. Meeting in virtual space often means that it takes the group longer to reach a decision than it would if they met face to face. Because typing takes more time and effort than speaking, messages conveyed via computer can lack the detail of spoken ones. In some cases, members may not even bother to type out a message online that they would have shared in person. Finally, the string of separate messages that is generated in a computerized medium can be hard to track, sort out, and synthesize in a meaningful way.

Research comparing the quality of decisions made by face-to-face and online groups is mixed. Some studies have found no significant differences. Others have found that computer-mediated groups generate more ideas than people meeting in person, although they take longer to reach agreement on which ideas are best. The growing body of research suggests that certain types of computer-mediated communication work better than others. For example, asynchronous groups seem to make better decisions than those functioning in a real-time 'chat' mode. Groups using special decision-support software perform better than ones operating without this advantage. Having a moderator also improves the effectiveness of online groups.

What use does this information have for groups who want to decide how to meet? Perhaps the most valuable lesson is that online meetings should not replace face-to-face ones but can be a supplement to in-person sessions. Combining the two forms of interaction can help groups operate both efficiently and effectively. After all, no matter where or how a group meets, the same factors influence its productivity, some of which are listed in Table 10.1.

COMMUNICATION ON-SCREEN

'The Persuaders' (2003)

Directed by Barak Goodman and Rachel Dretzin.

In this *Frontline* documentary, Douglas Rushkoff leads us on a journey to discover how marketers research what consumers want and how they want to be persuaded. This film is full of group communication—from board meetings of advertising executives to focus groups, we are treated to an insider's view of how marketing works. In particular, there is an excellent 10-minute segment featuring Dr Clothaire Rapaille, the famous French market researcher who claims to have uncovered 'culture codes' that unlock the secrets of desire and belief for consumers. Rapaille's research led to the relaunch of the Jeep Wrangler with round headlights and had significant input on the design of the new Boeing Dreamliner mega passenger plane.

Cultural Idiom

tweens
people who are in pre-adolescence, generally between the ages of 10 and 12

TABLE 10.1 Some Communication Factors Associated with Group Productivity

The group contains the smallest number of members necessary to accomplish its goals.

Members care about and agree with the group's goals.

Members are clear about and accept their roles, which match the abilities of each member.

Group norms encourage high performance, quality, success, and innovation.

The group members have sufficient time together to develop a mature working unit and accomplish its goals.

The group is highly cohesive and co-operative.

The group spends time defining and discussing problems it must solve and decisions it must make.

Periods of conflict are frequent but brief, and the group has effective strategies for dealing with conflict.

The group has an open communication structure in which all members may participate.

The group gets, gives, and uses feedback about its effectiveness.

If I'd observed all the rules, I'd never have got anywhere.

Marilyn Monroe

forum

A discussion format in which audience members are invited to add their comments to those of the official discussants.

Source: Adapted from research summarized in S.A. Wheelan, D. Murphy, E. Tsumaura, and S.F. Kline, 'Member Perceptions of Internal Group Dynamics and Productivity', *Small Group Research* 29 (1998): 371–93.

Understanding Communication Technology

Technology for Virtual Meetings

When a group can't or doesn't need to meet in person, an abundance of affordable tools can make virtual meetings easy to set up and conduct. For teleconferences, most phone companies provide a reasonably priced service for connecting three or more people. For the most simple (and free) type of computer conferencing, use one of the common and popular instant messaging (IM) services.

While conference calls and IM services provide the most simple types of virtual conferencing, there are other web-based services that also work very well. For example, Apple iChat (free to Apple users) enables two to four people to teleconference with full video. Skype enables two people to teleconference for free. Both of these services also offer IM and file exchange in parallel to the video conferencing feature.

Another excellent service is offered by Elluminate. Although this is not free software and requires a central installation on a server, the program offers a full suite of web-based meeting productivity tools: file exchange, IM, video and/or audio conferences, and shared screen on which the conversation facilitator can display files that all can see. Elluminate also offers a virtual 'whiteboard' service that enables participants to collaborate in a spontaneous fashion.

A number of fee-based services offer more elaborate tools for conducting computer conferences. One popular service is Webex, which allows users to hold teleconferences that include video, PowerPoint, and other types of multimedia. Participants can also add their own comments. Webex can be combined with a teleconference so participants can speak to one another as well as view a shared computer environment. Another service is Microsoft Live Meeting, formerly called PlaceWare. It presents a 'virtual meeting room' that permits voice and computer sharing and includes a 'whiteboard' where participants can sketch out items for others to see.

Other services allow for file sharing among remote computers. DropBox is an extremely useful service of this type. Users can share large files with other DropBox users who have been authorized to consult the folder. DropBox offers a free service up to 250 megabytes of online storage as well as affordable paid increments up to 5 gigabytes.

Finally, Google Docs, a free service, is leading a revolution in collaborative work. Registered users can use Google's online applications such as word processing, presentation, spreadsheet, form, and drawing software. When someone initiates a document on Google Docs, he or she is the 'owner' of that document and can 'share' it with any other registered Google user they choose. Users may also create folders and share them in their entirety, which makes Google Docs a strong competitor to DropBox.

Approaches and Stages in Problem-Solving

Groups may have the potential to solve problems effectively, but they don't always live up to this potential. What makes some groups succeed and others fail? Researchers spent much of the twentieth century asking this question. Two useful answers emerged from their work.

A Structured Problem-Solving Approach

Although we often pride ourselves on facing problems rationally, social scientists have discovered that logic and reason usually play little part in the way we make decisions.[7] The tendency to use non-rational approaches is unfortunate because research shows that, to a great degree, a group's effectiveness is determined by whether or not it approaches a problem rationally and systematically.[8] Just as a poor blueprint or a shaky foundation can weaken a house, groups can fail by skipping one or more of the necessary steps in solving a problem.

As early as 1910, philosopher and psychologist John Dewey introduced his famous 'reflective thinking' method as a systematic method for solving problems.[9] Since then, other experts have suggested modifications of Dewey's approach. Some emphasize answering key questions, whereas others seek 'ideal solutions' that meet the needs of all members. Research comparing various methods has clearly shown that, although no single approach is best for all situations, a structured procedure produces better results than 'no pattern' discussions.[10]

The following problem-solving model contains the elements common to most structured approaches developed in the last 80 years:

1. Identify the problem.
   a. What are the group's goals?
   b. What are individual members' goals?
2. Analyze the problem.
   a. Word the problem as a probative question.
   b. Gather relevant information.
   c. Identify impelling and restraining forces.
3. Develop creative solutions through brainstorming or the nominal group technique.
   a. Avoid criticism at this stage.
   b. Encourage 'freewheeling' ideas.
   c. Develop a large number of ideas.
   d. Combine two or more individual ideas.
4. Evaluate the solutions.
   a. Which solution will best produce the desired changes?
   b. Which is most achievable?
   c. Which contains the fewest serious disadvantages?
5. Implement the plan.
   a. Identify specific tasks.
   b. Determine necessary resources.
   c. Define individual responsibilities.
   d. Provide for emergencies.
6. Follow up on the solution.
   a. Meet to evaluate progress.
   b. Revise approach as necessary.

Identify the Problem

Sometimes a group's problem is easy to identify. The crew of a sinking ship, for example, doesn't need to conduct a discussion to understand that its goal is to avoid drowning or being eaten by a large fish.

There are many times, however, when the problems facing a group aren't so clear. As an example, think of an athletic team stuck deep in last place well into the season. At first the problem seems obvious: an inability to win any games. But a closer look at the situation might show

COMMUNICATION ON-SCREEN

Thirteen Days (2000)

Directed by Roger Donaldson.

This film chronicles the 1962 nuclear showdown between the United States and the Soviet Union. President John F. Kennedy (Bruce Greenwood) and his team of advisors must come up with a plan that deters the Soviets from completing the installation of missiles in Cuba without triggering a nuclear war. The intense deliberations offer a window into high-stakes decision-making that illustrates the importance of using the input of talented group members to develop an effective solution.

Cultural Idiom

freewheeling
unrestricted thinking

probative question
An open question used to analyze a problem by encouraging exploratory thinking.

Cultural Idiom

boosts the odds
increases the chances of success

damper
something that reduces or restricts

dire straits
extremely difficult situation

that there are unmet goals—and thus other problems. For instance, individual members may have goals that aren't tied directly to winning: making friends and receiving acknowledgment as good athletes, not to mention the simple goal of having fun—of playing in the recreational sense of the word. You can probably see that, if the coach or team members took a simplistic view of the situation by looking only at the team's win–lose record, analyzing player errors, training methods, and so on, some important problems would probably go overlooked. In this situation, the team's performance could probably be best improved by working on the basic problems—the frustration of the players about having their personal needs unmet. What's the moral here? That the way to start understanding a group's problem is to identify the concerns of each member.

What about groups that don't have problems? Several friends planning a surprise birthday party and a family deciding where to go for its vacation don't seem to be in the dire straits of a losing athletic team: they simply want to have fun. In cases like these, it may be helpful to substitute the word *challenge* for the more gloomy word *problem*. However we express it, the same principle applies to all task-oriented groups: the best place to start work is to identify what each member seeks as a result of belonging to the group.

Analyze the Problem

After you have identified the general nature of the problem facing the group, you are ready to look at the problem in more detail. There are several steps you can follow to accomplish this important job.

Word the Problem as a Probative Question

If you have ever seen a formal debate, you know that the issue under discussion is worded as a proposition: 'Canada should increase its spending on higher education', for example. Many problem-solving groups define their task in much the same way: 'We ought to spend our vacation in the mountains,' suggests one family member. The problem with phrasing problems as propositions is that such wording invites people to take sides. Though this approach is fine for formal debates (which are contests rather like football or card games), premature side-taking creates unnecessary conflict in most problem-solving groups.

A far better approach is to state the problem as a question. Note that this should be a **probative question**—an open one that encourages exploratory thinking. Asking, 'Should we vacation in the mountains or at the beach?' still forces members to choose sides. A far better approach involves asking a question to help define the general goals that came out during the problem-identification stage: 'What do we want our vacation to accomplish?' (that is, 'relaxation', 'adventure', 'low cost', and so on).

Notice that this question is truly exploratory. It encourages the family members to work co-operatively instead of forcing them to make a choice and then defend it. The absence of an either–or situation boosts the odds that members will listen openly to one another rather than listening selectively in defence of their own positions. There is even a chance that the co-operative, exploratory climate that comes from wording the question probatively will help the family arrive at consensus about where to vacation, eliminating the need to discuss the matter any further.

Gather Relevant Information

Groups often need to know important facts before they can make decisions or even understand the problem. We remember one group of students who were determined to do well on a class presentation. One of their goals was 'to get an A grade'. They knew that, to do so, they would have to present a topic that interested both the instructor and the students in the audience. Their first job, then, was to do a bit of background research to find out what subjects would be well received. They interviewed the instructor, asking what topics had been successes and failures in previous semesters. They tested some possible subjects on a few classmates and noted their reactions. As a result of this research they were able to modify their original probative question—'How can we choose and develop a topic that will earn us an A grade?'—into a more specific one—'How can we choose and develop a topic that contains humour, action, and lots of information (to demonstrate our research skills to the instructor) and that contains practical information that will improve either the audience's social life, academic standing, or financial condition?'

A problem well stated is a problem half solved.

Charles Kettering

Identify Impelling and Restraining Forces

Once members understand what they are seeking, the next step is to see what forces stand between the group and its goals. One useful tool for this task is **force field analysis**: listing the forces that help and hinder the group.[11] By returning to our earlier example of the troubled athletic team, we can see how the force field operates. Suppose the team defined its problem-question as 'How can we (1) have more fun and (2) grow closer as friends?'

One restraining force in Area (1) was clearly the team's losing record. But, more interestingly, discussion revealed two other dampers on enjoyment: the coach's obsession with winning and his infectiously gloomy behaviour when the team failed. The main restraining force in Area (2) proved to be the lack of socializing among team members in non-game situations. The helping forces in Area 1 included the sense of humour possessed by several members and the confession by most players that winning wasn't nearly as important to them as everyone had suspected. The helping force in Area 2 was the desire of all team members to become better friends. In addition, the fact that members shared many interests was a significant plus.

It's important to realize that most problems have many impelling and restraining forces, all of which need to be identified during this stage. This may call for another round of research. After the force field is laid out, the group is ready to move on to the next step—namely, deciding how to strengthen the impelling forces and weaken the restraining ones.

force field analysis

A method of problem analysis that identifies the forces contributing to resolution of the problem and the forces that inhibit its resolution.

Creativity Killers in Group Discussion

Nothing squelches creativity like criticism. Although evaluating ideas is an important part of problem-solving, judging suggestions too early can discourage members from sharing potentially valuable ideas. Here is a list of creativity-stopping statements that people should avoid making in the development phase of group work.

'That's ridiculous.'
'It'll never work.'
'You're wrong.'

'What a crazy idea!'
'We tried it before, and it didn't work.'
'It's too expensive.'
'There's no point in talking about it.'
'It's never been done like that.'
'We could look like fools.'
'It's too big a job.'
'We could never do that.'
'It's too risky.'
'You don't know what you're talking about.'

Develop Creative Solutions

After the group has set up a list of criteria for success, the next job is to develop a number of ways to reach its goal. Considering more than one solution is important, because the first solution may not be the best one. During this development stage, creativity is essential.[12] The biggest danger is the tendency of members to defend their own idea and criticize others'. This kind of behaviour leads to two problems. First, evaluative criticism almost guarantees a defensive reaction from members whose ideas have been attacked. Second, evaluative criticism stifles creativity. People who have just heard an idea rebuked—however politely—will find it hard even to think of more alternatives, let alone share them openly and risk possible criticism. The following strategies can help groups to be creative and maintain a positive climate.

Brainstorm

Probably the best-known strategy for encouraging creativity and avoiding the dangers just described is **brainstorming**.[13] There are four important rules connected with this strategy:

1. **Criticism is discouraged.** As we have already said, nothing will stop the flow of ideas more quickly than negative evaluation.
2. **'Freewheeling' is encouraged.** Sometimes even the most outlandish ideas prove workable, and even an impractical suggestion might trigger a workable idea.
3. **Quantity is sought.** The more ideas that are generated, the better the chances of coming up with a good one.
4. **Combination and improvement are desirable.** Members are encouraged to 'piggyback' by modifying ideas already suggested and to combine previous suggestions.

brainstorming
A method for creatively generating ideas in groups by minimizing criticism and encouraging a large quantity of ideas without regard to their workability or ownership by individual members.

nominal group technique
Method for including the ideas of all group members in a problem-solving session.

Cultural Idiom

piggyback
adding onto

Although brainstorming is a popular creativity booster, it isn't a guaranteed strategy for developing novel and high-quality ideas. In some experiments, individuals working alone were able to come up with a greater number of high-quality ideas than were small groups.[14]

Use the Nominal Group Technique

Because people in groups often can't resist the tendency to criticize one another's ideas, the **nominal group technique** was developed. It retains the key elements of brainstorming but lets members present their ideas without being attacked. As the following steps show, cycles of individual work alternate with group discussion:

1. Each member works alone to develop a list of possible solutions.
2. In round-robin fashion, each member in turn offers one item from his or her list. The item is listed on a chart visible to everyone. Other members may ask questions to clarify an idea, but no evaluation is allowed during this step.
3. Each member privately ranks his or her choice of the ideas in order, from most preferable (five points) to least preferable (one point). The rankings are collected, and the top ideas are retained as the most promising solutions.
4. A free discussion of the top ideas is held. At this point critical thinking (though not personal criticism) is encouraged. The group continues the discussion until a decision is reached, either by majority vote or by consensus.

> **Cultural Idiom**
>
> **in round-robin fashion**
> go around in a circle, one after another

Evaluate Possible Solutions

After it has listed possible solutions, the group can evaluate the usefulness of each. One good way of identifying the most workable solutions is to ask three questions.

1. **Will this proposal produce the desired changes?** One way to find out is to see whether it successfully overcomes the restraining forces in your force field analysis.
2. **Can the proposal be implemented?** Can the members strengthen impelling forces and weaken restraining ones? Can they influence others to do so? If not, the plan isn't a good one.
3. **Does the proposal contain any serious disadvantages?** Sometimes the cost of achieving a goal is too great. For example, one way to raise money for a group is to rob a bank. Although this plan might be workable, it creates more problems than it solves.

Implement the Plan

Everyone who makes New Year's resolutions knows the difference between making a decision and carrying it out. There are several important steps in developing and implementing a plan of action.

1. **Identify specific tasks to be accomplished.** What needs to be done? Even a relatively simple job usually involves several steps. Now is the time to anticipate all the tasks facing the group. Remember everything now, and you'll avoid a last-minute rush later.
2. **Determine necessary resources.** Identify the equipment, material, and other resources the group will need in order to get the job done.
3. **Define individual responsibilities.** Who will do what? Do all the members know their jobs? The safest plan here is to put everyone's duties in writing, including the due date. This might sound compulsive, but experience shows that it increases the chance of having jobs done on time.
4. **Provide for emergencies.** Murphy's Law states, 'Whatever can go wrong, will.' Anyone experienced in group work knows the truth of this law. People forget or welsh on their obligations, get sick, or quit. Machinery breaks down. (One corollary of Murphy's Law is 'The copying machine will be out of order whenever

> **Cultural Idiom**
>
> **Murphy's Law**
> a folk law of nature claiming that anything that can go wrong will probably go wrong

Cultural Idiom

time cushion
extra time allowance

welsh on
fail to fulfill

it's most needed.') Whenever possible, you ought to develop contingency plans to cover foreseeable problems. Probably the single best suggestion we can give here is to plan on having all work done well ahead of the deadline, knowing that, even with last-minute problems, your time cushion will allow you to finish on time.

Follow Up on the Solution

Even the best plans usually require some modifications after they're put into practice. You can improve the group's effectiveness and minimize disappointment by following two steps:

1. **Meet periodically to evaluate progress.** Follow-up meetings should be part of virtually every good plan. The best time to schedule these meetings is as you put the group's plan to work. At that time, a good leader or member will suggest: 'Let's get together in a week (or a few days or a month, depending on the nature of the task). We can see how things are going and take care of any problems.'

2. **Revise the group's approach as necessary.** These follow-up meetings will often go beyond simply congratulating everyone for coming up with a good solution. Problems are bound to arise, and these periodic meetings, at which the key players are present, are the place to solve them.

Although these steps provide a useful outline for solving problems, they are most valuable as a general set of guidelines and not as a precise formula that every group should follow. As Table 10.2 suggests, certain parts of the model may need emphasis depending on the nature of the specific problem; the general approach will give virtually any group a useful way to consider and solve a problem.

Despite its advantages, the rational, systematic problem-solving approach isn't perfect. The old computer saying 'Garbage in, garbage out' applies here: if the group doesn't possess creative talent, a rational and systematic approach to solving problems won't do much good. Despite its drawbacks, the rational approach does increase the odds that a group can solve problems successfully. Following the guidelines—even imperfectly—will help members

TABLE 10.2 Adapting Problem-Solving Methods to Special Circumstances

Circumstances	Method
Members have strong feelings about the problem.	Consider allowing a period of emotional ventilation before systematic problem- solving.
Task difficulty is high.	Follow the structure of the problem-solving method carefully.
Many possible solutions.	Emphasize brainstorming.
High level of member acceptance required.	Carefully define needs of all members, and seek solutions that satisfy all needs.
High level of technical quality required.	Emphasize evaluation of ideas; consider inviting outside experts.

Source: Adapted from 'Adapting Problem-Solving Methods', *Effective Group Discussion*, 10th ed., John Brilhart and Gloria Galanes, p. 291. Copyright © 2001. Reprinted by permission of McGraw-Hill Companies, Inc.

analyze the problem, come up with solutions, and carry them out better than they could probably do without a plan.

Developmental Stages in Problem-Solving Groups

When it comes to solving problems in groups, research shows that the shortest distance to a solution isn't always a straight line. Communication scholar Aubrey Fisher analyzed tape recordings of problem-solving groups and discovered that many successful groups seem to follow a four-stage process when arriving at a decision.[15] As you read about his findings, visualize how they have applied to problem-solving groups in your experience.

In the **orientation stage,** members approach the problem and one another tentatively. In some groups people may not know one another well, and even in ones where they are well acquainted they may not know one another's positions on the issue at hand. For these reasons, people are reluctant to take a stand during the orientation stage. Rather than state their own positions clearly and unambiguously, they test out possible ideas cautiously and rather politely. There is little disagreement. This cautiousness doesn't mean that members agree with one another; rather, they are sizing up the situation before asserting themselves. The orientation stage can be viewed as a calm before the storm.

After members understand the problem and become acquainted, a successful group enters the **conflict stage.** During this stage, members take strong positions and defend them against those who oppose their viewpoint. Coalitions are likely to form, and the discussion may become polarized. The conflict needn't be personal: it can focus on the issues at hand while preserving the members' respect for one another. Even when the climate does grow contentious, conflict seems to be a necessary stage in group development. The give-and-take of discussion tests the quality of ideas, and weaker ones may suffer a well-deserved death here.[16]

After a period of conflict, effective groups move to an **emergence stage.** One idea might emerge as the best one, or the group might combine the best parts of several plans into a new solution. As they approach consensus, members back off from their dogmatic positions. Statements become more tentative again: 'I guess that's a pretty good idea'; 'I can see why you think that way.'

Finally, an effective group reaches the **reinforcement stage.** At this point not only do members accept the group's decision, but they also endorse it. Whereas members used evidence to back up differing positions in the conflict stage, now they find evidence that will support the decision. Even if members disagree with the outcome, they do not voice their concerns. There is an unspoken drive toward consensus and harmony.

Ongoing groups can expect to move through this four-stage process with each new issue, so that their interaction takes on a cyclic pattern (see Figure 10.1). In fact, a group that deals with several issues at once might find itself in a different stage for each problem. In one series of studies, slightly less than 50 per cent of the problem-solving groups examined followed this pattern.[17] The same research showed that a smaller percentage of groups (about 30 per cent) didn't follow a cyclical pattern. Instead, they skipped the preliminary phases and focused on the solution.

What is the significance of the findings? They tell us that, like children growing toward adulthood, many groups can expect to pass through phases. Knowing that these phases are natural and predictable can be reassuring. It can help curb your impatience when the group is feeling its way through an orientation stage. It can also help you feel less threatened when the inevitable and necessary conflicts take place. Understanding the

conflict stage
A stage in problem-solving groups when members openly defend their positions and question those of others.

emergence stage
A stage in problem-solving when the group moves from conflict toward a single solution.

orientation stage
A stage in problem-solving groups when members become familiar with one another's position and tentatively volunteer their own.

reinforcement stage
A stage in problem-solving groups when members endorse the decision they have made.

Cultural Idiom

sizing up
assessing

Who decides when the applause should die down? It seems like it's a group decision; everyone begins to say to themselves at the same time, 'Well, okay, that's enough of that.'

George Carlin

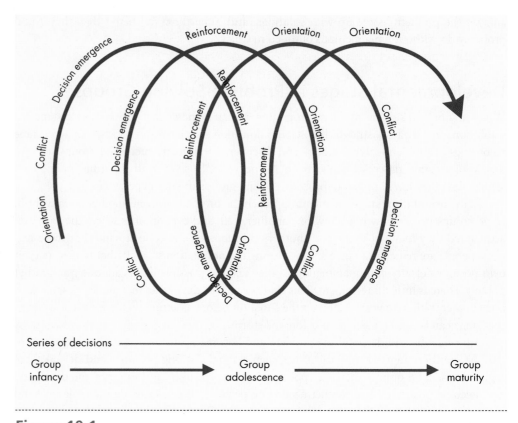

Figure 10.1

Cyclical Stages in an Ongoing Problem-Solving Group

Source: From John K. Brilhart, Gloria J. Galanes, and Katherine Adams, *Effective Group Discussion*, 10th ed. (New York: McGraw-Hill, 2001), p. 335. Reproduced with permission of The McGraw-Hill Companies.

nature of emergence and reinforcement can help you know when it is time to stop arguing and seek consensus.

Maintaining Positive Relationships

The task-related advice in the preceding pages will be little help if the members of a group don't get along. We therefore need to look at some ways to maintain good relationships among members. Many of the principles described earlier in this book apply here. Because these principles are so important, we will review them.

Basic Skills

Groups are most effective when members feel good about one another.[18] Probably the most important ingredient in good personal relationships is mutual respect, and the best way to demonstrate respect for the other person is to listen carefully. A more natural tendency, of course, is to assume you understand the other members' positions and to interrupt or ignore them. Even if you are right, however, this tendency can create a residue of ill feelings. On the other hand, careful listening can at least improve the communication climate—and it may even teach you something.

Never doubt that a small group of thoughtful, committed citizens can change the world; indeed, it's the only thing that ever does.

Margaret Mead

Groups are bound to disagree sooner or later. When they do, the win–win problem-solving methods outlined in Chapter 7 boost the odds of solving the immediate issue in the most constructive way.[19] As you read in Chapter 9, taking votes and letting the majority rule can often leave a sizable minority whose unhappiness may haunt the group's future work. Consensus is harder to reach in the short term but far more beneficial in the long term.

Building Cohesiveness

Cohesiveness can be defined as the totality of forces that causes members to feel themselves part of a group and makes them want to remain in that group. You might think of cohesiveness as the glue that bonds individuals together, giving them a collective sense of identity.

Highly cohesive groups communicate differently than less cohesive ones. Members spend more time interacting, and there are more expressions of positive feelings for one another. They report more satisfaction with the group and its work. In addition, cohesive groups have greater control over the behaviour of their members.[20] With characteristics like these, it's no surprise that highly cohesive groups have the potential to be productive. In fact, one study revealed that cohesiveness proved to be the best predictor of a group's performance, both initially and over time.[21]

Despite its advantages, cohesiveness is no guarantee of success: if the group is united in supporting unproductive norms, members will feel close but won't get the job done. For example, consider a group of employees who have a boss they think is incompetent and unfair. They might grow quite cohesive in their opposition to the perceived tyranny, spending hours after (or during) work swapping complaints. They might even organize protests, work slowdowns, grievances to their union, or mass resignations. All these responses would boost cohesiveness, but they would not necessarily make the company more successful or help the employees.

Research has disclosed a curvilinear relationship between cohesiveness and productivity: up to a certain point, productivity increases as group members become a unified team. Beyond this point, however, the attraction that members feel for one another begins to interfere with the group's efficient functioning. Members may enjoy one another's company, but this enjoyment can keep them from focusing on the job at hand.

The goal, then, is to boost cohesiveness in a way that also gets the job done. There are eight factors that can contribute to both these objectives.

1. Shared or Compatible Goals

People draw closer when they share a similar aim or one solution will satisfy all of them, even if their specific goals are not the same. For example, members of a conservation group might have little in common until a part of the countryside they all value is threatened by development. Some members might value the land because of its beauty; others because it provides a place to hunt or fish; and still others because the nearby scenery increases the value of their property. As long as their goals are compatible, this collection of individuals will find a bond that draws them together.

cohesiveness
The totality of forces that causes members to feel themselves part of a group and makes them want to remain in that group.

All things are subject to interpretation whichever interpretation prevails at a given time is a function of power and not truth.

Friedrich Nietzsche

2. Progress Toward these Goals

While a group is making progress, members feel highly cohesive; when progress stops, cohesiveness decreases. All other things being equal, players on an athletic team feel closest when the team is winning. During extended losing streaks, players are likely to feel less positive about the team and less willing to identify themselves as members of the group.

3. Shared Norms and Values

Although successful groups will tolerate and even thrive on some differences in members' attitudes and behaviour, wide variation in definitions of what actions or beliefs are proper will reduce cohesiveness. If enough members hold different ideas of what behaviour is acceptable, the group is likely to break up. Disagreements over values or norms can arise in many areas, from the kind of humour or degree of candour regarded as acceptable to finances or the proportions of time allotted to work and play.

4. Lack of Perceived Threat between Members

Members of cohesive groups do not see one another as posing any threat to their status, dignity, or well-being (material or emotional). By contrast, the perception that such interpersonal threats do exist can be very destructive. Often competition arises within groups, and as a result members feel threatened. There may be a struggle over who will be the nominal leader. Some members may perceive others as seeking to take over a functional role (problem-solver, information giver, and so on), through either competition or criticism. Sometimes the threat is real, and sometimes it's only imagined, but in either case the group must neutralize it or face the consequences of reduced cohesiveness.

5. Interdependence of Members

Groups become cohesive when individual members' needs can be satisfied only with the help of other members. When a job can be done just as well by one person alone, the need for group membership decreases. Food co-operatives, neighbourhood yard sales, and community political campaigns are all examples of group efforts in which working together allows participants to achieve goals that they could not achieve if they acted alone.

6. Threat from Outside the Group

When members perceive a threat to the group's existence or image (groups have self-concepts, just as individuals do), they grow closer together. Almost everyone knows of a family whose members seem to fight constantly among themselves—until an outsider criticizes one of them. At this point the internal bickering stops, and for the moment the group unites against its common enemy. The same principle also works on a national scale when conflicting groups put aside their differences and join forces in the face of external aggression.

7. Mutual Perceived Attractiveness and Friendship

The factor of mutual attraction and friendship is somewhat circular because friendship and mutual attraction often are a result of the points just listed. Nevertheless, groups often do become close simply because the members like each other. A social group is a good example of a group that stays together because its members enjoy one another's company.

Cultural Idiom

bickering
quarrelling

THE PROS AND CONS OF COHESIVENESS

CRITICAL THINKING PROBE

1. Based on the information on pages 381–3 of this chapter and your own experiences, give examples of groups that meet each of the following descriptions:
   a. a level of cohesiveness so low that it interferes with productivity
   b. an optimal level of cohesiveness
   c. a level of cohesiveness so high that it interferes with productivity.
2. For your answers to (a) and (c), offer advice on how the level of cohesiveness could be adjusted to improve productivity.
3. Are there ever situations where maximizing cohesiveness is more important than maximizing productivity? Explain your answer, supporting it with examples.

8. Shared Group Experiences

When members have been through some unusual or trying experience, they draw together. This explains why soldiers who have been in combat together often feel close and stay in touch for years after; it also accounts for initiation rituals such as the ordeal of fraternity pledging. Many societies have rituals in which all members take part, thus increasing the group's cohesiveness.

It's important to realize that the eight factors just described interact with one another, often in contradictory ways. For instance, group members who have been through thick and thin together may begin to lose their cohesion once that experience is over. Relationships can be strained when friends become less dependent on one another, especially if they begin to feel that the roles they played in the past are no longer appropriate. In cases like this, cohesiveness can be figured as the net sum of all attracting and dividing forces.

> **Cultural Idiom**
>
> **through thick and thin**
> through the good times and the bad

Leadership and Power in Groups

Leadership . . . power . . . influence. For most of us, being in control of events ranks not far below parenthood in the hierarchy of values. 'What are you, a leader or a follower?' we're asked, and we know which position is the better one. Even in groups without designated leaders, some members are more influential than others, and those who aren't out front at least some of the time are likely to feel frustrated.

The following pages will focus on how communication operates to establish influence. We will begin by looking at sources of power in groups, showing that not all influence rests with the person who is nominally in charge. We will then take a look at the communication behaviours that work best when one communicator is designated as the leader—or wants to acquire that role.

Power in Groups

legitimate power
The ability to influence a group owing to one's position within it.

nominal leader
The person who is identified by title as the leader of a group.

power
The ability to influence others' thoughts and/or actions.

We can begin by defining **power** as the ability to influence others. A few examples show that influence can appear in many forms.[22]

- In a tense meeting, apartment dwellers are arguing over crowded parking and late-night noise. One tenant cracks a joke and lightens up the tense atmosphere.
- A project team at work is trying to come up with a new way to attract customers. The youngest member, fresh from a college advertising class, suggests a winning idea.
- Workers are upset after the boss passes over a popular colleague and hires a newcomer for a management position. Despite their anger, they accept the decision after the colleague persuades them that she is not interested in a career move anyhow.
- A teacher motivates students to meet a deadline by awarding bonus points for projects that are turned in early and deducting points for ones turned in late.

These examples suggest that power comes in a variety of forms. We will examine each of them now.

COMMUNICATION ON-SCREEN

Star Trek (2009)
Directed by J.J. Abrams.

In this 're-boot' of the classic 1960s television series, a rewriting of history by villainous Romulans results in a brash and undisciplined James T. Kirk (Chris Pine) growing up fatherless and joining Starfleet Academy late as a jaded 22-year-old. Called away on his first mission as an untested third-year cadet of dubious professionalism, a much more familiar Kirk begins to emerge in a crisis situation. Kirk steps into a leadership vacuum and earns the respect of his crewmates, including his greatest skeptic, Spock (Zachary Quinto).

Kirk's leadership emergence is built around several of his personal attributes: not only does he bring savvy and courage to a brewing galactic confrontation, but he also leverages the talents of his crewmates, who feed off his confidence.

Legitimate Power

Sometimes the ability to influence others comes from **legitimate power** (also known as 'position power'). Legitimate power originates in the holder's title—supervisor, parent, or professor, for example. In many cases we follow the directions of others without knowing much about their qualifications, simply because we respect the role they occupy. In church we honour the request of the minister to stand up or to sit down, and in courts we rise at judges' approach primarily because their positions confer authority on them.

Social scientists use the term **nominal leader** to label the person who is officially designated as being in charge of a group. But nominal leaders are not the only people with legitimate power. Traffic directors at road repair sites are unlikely to be in charge of the project, yet they possess legitimate power in the eyes of motorists, who stop and start at their command.

The easiest way to acquire legitimate power is to have it conferred upon you by an outside authority. But appointment isn't the only path to legitimate power: even in groups that start out with no official leader, members can acquire legitimate power by the acknowledgment of others. Juries elect forepersons, committees elect chairpersons, teams choose captains, and negotiating groups elect spokespeople. The subject of leadership emergence has been studied extensively.[23] Researchers have discovered several communicator characteristics that members who emerge as leaders possess: they speak up in group discussions without dominating others, they demonstrate their competence on the subject being discussed, they observe group norms, and they have the support of other influential members.

Coercive Power

Coercive power may be wielded when influence comes from the threat or actual imposition of some unpleasant consequences. In school, at home, on the job, and in many other settings, we sometimes do what others tell us, not because of any respect for the wisdom of their decisions but rather because the results of not obeying would be unpleasant. Economic hardship, social disapproval, undesirable work, even physical punishment—all are coercive forces that can shape behaviour.

There are three reasons why coercion often isn't the most effective type of power. First, it's likely to create a negative communication climate because nobody likes to be threatened. Second, it can produce a 'boomerang effect', leading some people to defy instructions and do exactly the opposite of what they've been told. Third, coercion may be used to tell others what not to do instead of establishing a clear idea of what you *do* want them to do. Telling an unproductive member, 'If you can't contribute useful information, we'll kick you out of the group' doesn't offer much advice about what would count as 'useful information'.

Social scientists say that coercion has the best chance of success when it involves denial of an expected reward rather than the imposition of a negative consequence.[24] For example, cancelling a promised bonus for members of a working group that doesn't meet its deadline is better than reducing their salaries. Even under circumstances like this, however, coercion alone is not as effective as the next kind of power: rewards.

Reward Power

Reward power involves the grant or promise of desirable consequences. Rewards come in a variety of forms. The most obvious are material reinforcers: money, awards, and so on. Other rewards can be social in nature. The praise of someone you respect can be a powerful motivator. Even spending time with people you like can be reinforcing.

Rewards don't come only from the official leader of a group. The goodwill of other members can sometimes be even more valuable. In a class group, for example, having your fellow students think highly of you might be a more powerful reward than the grade you could receive from the instructor. In fact, subordinates sometimes can reward nominal leaders just as much as the other way around. A boss might work hard to accommodate employees in order to keep them happy, for example.

Expert Power

Expert power exists when we are influenced by people because of what we believe they know or can do. For example, when a medical emergency occurs, most group members would gladly let a doctor, nurse, or paramedic make the decisions because of that person's

coercive power
The power to influence others by the threat or imposition of unpleasant consequences.

expert power
The ability to influence others by virtue of one's perceived expertise on the subject in question.

reward power
The ability to influence others by the granting or promising of desirable consequences.

We only need to look at what we are really doing in the world and at home and we'll know what it is to be Canadian.

Adrienne Clarkson

obvious knowledge. In groups it isn't sufficient to *be* an expert: the other members have to view you as one. This means that it is important to make your qualifications known if you want others to give your opinions extra weight.

Information Power

As its name implies, **information power** comes from a member's knowledge that he or she can help the group reach its goal. Not all useful information comes from experts with special credentials. For instance, a fundraising group seeking donations from local businesses might profit from the knowledge that one member has about which merchants are hospitable to the group's cause. Likewise, a class group working on a term project might benefit from the knowledge of one student who has taken other classes from the instructor who will be grading their work.

Referent Power

Referent power flows from the respect, liking, and trust that others have for a member. If you have high referent power, you may be able to persuade others to follow your lead simply because they believe in you or because they are willing to do you a favour. Members acquire referent power by behaving in ways that others in the group admire and by being genuinely likable. The kinds of confirming communication behaviours described in Chapter 7 can go a long way toward boosting referent power. Listening to others' ideas, honouring their contributions, and taking a win–win approach to meeting their needs all lead to liking and respect.

After our look at various ways group members can influence one another, three important characteristics of power in groups become clearer.[25]

1. **Power is group-centred.** Power isn't something that an individual possesses. Instead, it is conferred by the group. You may be an expert on a particular subject, but if the other members don't think you are qualified to talk, you won't have expert power. You might try to reward other people by praising their contributions, but if they don't value your compliments, then all the praise in the world won't influence them.

2. **Power is distributed among group members.** Power rarely belongs to just one person. Even when a group has an official leader, other members usually have the power to affect what happens. This influence can be positive, coming from information, expertise, or social reinforcement. It can also be negative, coming from punishing behaviours such as criticizing or withholding the contributions that the group needs to succeed. You can appreciate how power is distributed among members by considering the effect that just one member can have by not showing up for meetings or failing to carry out his or her part of the job.

3. **Power isn't an either–or concept.** It's incorrect to assume that power is an either–or concept that members either possess or lack. Rather, it is a matter of degree. Instead of talking about someone as 'powerful' or 'powerless', it's more accurate to talk about how much influence he or she exerts.

By now you can see that power is available to every member of a group. Table 10.3 outlines ways of acquiring the various types of power we have just examined.

---

information power
The ability to influence others by virtue of the otherwise obscure information one possesses.

referent power
The ability to influence others by virtue of the degree to which one is liked or respected.

Me? I'm dishonest, and a dishonest man you can always trust to be dishonest. Honestly. It's the honest ones you want to watch out for, because you can never predict when they're going to do something incredibly . . . stupid.

Jack Sparrow, *Pirates of the Caribbean: The Curse of the Black Pearl*

---

*A leader is best
When people barely know
    that he exists,
Not so good when people
    obey and acclaim him,
Worse when they despise
    him.
'Fail to honour people,
They fail to honour you';
But of a good leader who
    talks little,
When his work is done, his
    aim fulfilled,
They will say, 'We did it
    ourselves.'*

Lao-tzu

TABLE 10.3 Methods for Acquiring Power in Small Groups

Power isn't the only goal to seek in a group. Sometimes being a follower is a comfortable and legitimate role to play. But when you do seek power, the following methods outline specific ways to shape the way others behave and the decisions they make.

Legitimate Authority

1. Become an authority figure. If possible, get yourself appointed or elected to a position of leadership. Do so by following Steps 2–5.
2. Speak up without dominating others. Power comes from visibility, but don't antagonize others by shutting them out.
3. Demonstrate competence on the subject. Enhance legitimate authority by demonstrating information and expertise power.
4. Follow group norms. Show that you respect the group's customs.
5. Gain support of other members. Don't try to carve out authority on your own. Gain the visible support of other influential members.

Information Power

1. Provide useful but scarce or restricted information. Show others that you possess information that isn't available elsewhere.
2. Be certain the information is accurate. One piece of mistaken information can waste the group's time, lead to bad decisions, and destroy your credibility. Check your facts before speaking up.

Expert Power

1. Make sure members are aware of your qualifications. Let others know that you have expertise in the area being discussed.
2. Don't act superior. You will squander your authority if you imply your expertise makes you superior to others. Use your knowledge for the good of the group, not ego building.

Reward and Coercive Power

1. Try to use rewards as a first resort and punishment as a last resort. People respond better to pleasant consequences than unpleasant ones, so take a positive approach first.
2. Make rewards and punishments clear in advance. Let people know your expectations and their consequences. Don't surprise them.
3. Be generous with praise. Let others know that you recognize their desirable behaviour.

Referent Power

1. Enhance your attractiveness to group members. Do whatever you can to gain the liking and respect of other members without compromising your principles.
2. Learn effective presentation skills. Present your ideas clearly and effectively in order to boost your credibility.

Source: Adapted from J. Dan Rothwell, In *Mixed Company: Small Group Communication,* 3rd edn (Fort Worth, TX: Harcourt Brace, 1998), 252–72.

What Makes Leaders Effective?

Even though power is distributed among members of a group, it is still important to explore the special role played by the nominal leader. In the next few pages we will describe the communication-related factors that contribute to leader effectiveness.

Trait Analysis

Over 2,000 years ago, Aristotle proclaimed, 'From the hour of their birth some are marked out for subjugation, and others for command.'[26] This is a radical expression of **trait theories of leadership,** sometimes labelled the 'great man' (or 'great woman') approach. Social scientists began their studies of leader effectiveness by conducting literally hundreds of studies that compared leaders to non-leaders. The results of all this research were mixed. Yet, as Table 10.4 shows, a number of distinguishing characteristics did emerge in several categories.

The majority of these categories involved social skills. For example, leaders talk more often and more fluently and are regarded as more popular, co-operative, and socially skilful.[27] Leaders also possess goal-related skills that help groups perform their tasks. They are somewhat

trait theories of leadership
The belief that it is possible to identify leaders by personal traits, such as intelligence, appearance, or sociability.

TABLE 10.4 Some Traits Associated with Leaders

Factor No.	Factors Appearing in Three or More Studies	Frequency
1	Social and interpersonal skills	16
2	Technical skills	18
3	Administrative skills	12
4	Leadership effectiveness and achievement	15
5	Social nearness, friendliness	18
6	Intellectual skills	11
7	Maintaining a cohesive work group	9
8	Maintaining coordination and teamwork	7
9	Task motivation and application	17
10	General impression	12
11	Group task supportiveness	17
12	Maintaining standards of performance	5
13	Willingness to assume responsibility	10
14	Emotional balance and control	15
15	Informal group control	4
16	Nurturant behaviour	4
17	Ethical conduct, personal integrity	10
18	Communication, verbality	6
19	Ascendance, dominance, decisiveness	11
20	Physical energy	6
21	Experience and activity	4
22	Mature, cultured	3
23	Courage, daring	4
24	Aloof, distant	3
25	Creative, independent	5
26	Conforming	5

more intelligent, possess more task-relevant information, and are more dependable than other members. Just as important, leaders want the role and act in ways that will help them achieve it. Finally, physical appearance seems to play a role in leadership. As a rule, leaders tend to be slightly taller, heavier, and physically more attractive than other members. They also seem to possess greater athletic ability and stamina.

Canadian researchers from the Royal Military College and the University of Western Ontario studied 174 officers in the Canadian Forces to see if they could demonstrate a link between personality traits and leadership success. They found that energy level, internal control, and, especially, dominance were associated with leadership.

On the other hand, trait theories have limited practical value. More recent studies have found that many other factors are important as well, and that not everyone who possesses 'leadership traits' becomes a leader. In the 1980s two organizational researchers, Warren Bennis and Burt Nanus, interviewed 90 American leaders, including Ray Kroc, the founder of McDonald's; John Robinson, a professional football coach; and John H. Johnson, publisher of *Ebony* magazine. Their analysis led to the conclusion that the principle 'leaders must be charismatic' is a myth.

Some are, most aren't. Among the ninety there were a few—but damned few—who probably correspond to our fantasies of some 'divine inspiration', that 'grace under stress' we associated with J.F.K. or the beguiling capacity to spellbind for which we remember Churchill. Our leaders were all 'too human'; they were short and tall, articulate and inarticulate, dressed for success and dressed for failure, and there was virtually nothing in terms of physical appearance, personality, or style that set them apart from their followers. Our guess is that it operates in the other direction; that is, charisma is the result of effective leadership, not the other way around, and that those who are good at it are granted a certain amount of respect and even awe by their followers, which increases the bond of attraction between them.[28]

Leadership Style

As researchers began to realize that personality traits aren't the key to effective leadership, they began to look in other areas. Some scholars theorized that good leadership is a matter of communication style—the way leaders deal with members. Three basic approaches were identified: authoritarian, democratic, and laissez-faire.

The first approach was an **authoritarian leadership style** that relied on legitimate, coercive, and reward power to influence others. The second approach was a **democratic leadership style,** which invited other members to share in decision-making. The third approach was the **laissez-faire leadership style,** in which the leader gave up the power to dictate, transforming the group into a leaderless collection of equals. Early research suggested that the democratic style produced the highest-quality results,[29] but later studies found that matters weren't so simple.[30] For instance, groups with autocratic leaders proved more productive under stressful conditions, but democratically led groups did better when the situation was non-stressful.[31]

Research shows that there is some merit to the styles approach. One extensive study of more than 12,000 managers showed that a democratic approach to leadership correlated highly with success. Effective managers usually sought the advice and opinions of their subordinates, whereas average or unsuccessful ones were more authoritarian and less concerned with the welfare or ideas of the people who reported to them.[32] Despite this fact, a democratic approach isn't always the best one. For example, an autocratic approach gets the job done much more quickly, which can be essential in situations where time is of the essence.

Some researchers have focused on leadership style from a different perspective. Robert R. Blake and Anne A. McCanse developed an approach based on the relationship between the designated leader's concern with the task and with the relationships among members.[33] Their **Leadership Grid** consists of a two-dimensional model, pictured in Figure 10.2. The horizontal axis measures the leader's 'concern for production'. This involves a focus on accomplishing the organizational task, with efficiency being the main concern. The vertical axis measures the leader's concern for people's feelings and ideas. Blake and Mouton suggest that the most effective leader is the one who adopts a 9, 9 style—showing high concern for both task and relationships.

Situational Approaches

Most contemporary scholars are convinced that the best style of leadership varies from one set of circumstances to another.[34] In the 1960s, in an effort to pin down which approach works best in a given type of situation, psychologist Fred Fiedler attempted to find out when a task-oriented approach was most effective and when more relationship-oriented approaches

When one door closes another door opens; but we so often look so long and so regretfully upon the closed door, that we do not see the ones which open for us.

Alexander Graham Bell

authoritarian leadership style

A leadership style in which the designated leader uses legitimate, coercive, and reward power to dictate the group's actions.

democratic leadership style

A style in which the nominal leader invites the group's participation in decision-making.

laissez-faire leadership style

A style in which the designated leader gives up his or her formal role, transforming the group into a loose collection of individuals.

Leadership Grid

A two-dimensional model that identifies leadership styles as a combination of a concern for people and the task at hand.

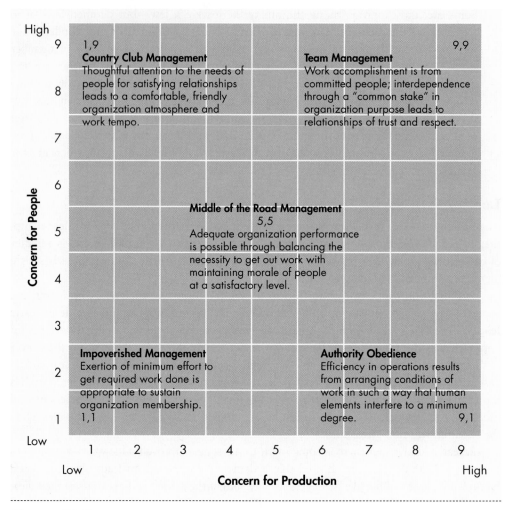

Figure 10.2

The Leadership Grid®

Source: The Leadership Grid® Figure from *Leadership Dilemmas–Grid Solutions,* by Robert R. Blake and Anne Adams McCanse (Houston: Gulf Publishing Co.), 29. Copyright © 1991 by Scientific Methods, Inc. Reproduced by permission of the owners.

were most effective.[35] From his research, Fiedler developed a situational theory of leadership. Although the complete theory is too complex to describe here, the general conclusion of **situational leadership** is that a leader's style should change with the circumstances. A task-oriented approach works best when conditions are either highly favourable (good leader–member relations, strong leader power, and a clear task structure) or highly unfavourable (poor leader–member relations, weak leader power, and an ambiguous task), whereas a more relationship-oriented approach is appropriate in moderately favourable or moderately unfavourable conditions.

More recently, Paul Hersey and Kenneth Blanchard have suggested that a leader's focus on task or relational issues should vary according to the 'readiness' of the group being led (see Figure 10.3).[36] 'Readiness' involves the members' level of motivation, willingness to take responsibility, and the amount of knowledge and experience they have in a given situation. For example, a new, inexperienced group would need more task-related direction, whereas a more experienced group might require more social support and less instruction about how to do the job. A well-seasoned group could probably handle the job well without much supervision at all. Because an employee's readiness changes from one job to another, Hersey and Blanchard suggest that the best way to lead should vary as well.

Overcoming Dangers in Group Discussion

Even groups with the best of intentions often find themselves unable to reach satisfying decisions. At other times, they make decisions that later prove to be wrong. Though there's no foolproof method of guaranteeing high-quality group work, there are several dangers to avoid.

Information Underload and Overload

Information underload occurs when a group lacks information it needs to operate effectively. Sometimes the underload results from overlooking parts of a problem. We know of one group that scheduled a fundraising auction without considering whether there were any other events scheduled for the same time that might attract potential donors. They later found that their event was scheduled opposite an important football game, resulting in a loss of sorely needed funds. In other cases, groups suffer from underload because they simply don't conduct enough research. For example, a group of partners starting a new business has to be aware of all the start-up costs to avoid going bankrupt in the first months of operation. Overlooking one or two important items can make the difference between success and failure.

Sometimes groups can suffer from too much information. **Information overload** occurs when the flow or complexity of material is too great to manage. Having an abundance of information might seem like a blessing, but anyone who has tried to do conscientious library research has become aware of the paralysis that can result from being overwhelmed by an avalanche of books, magazine and newspaper articles, reviews, films, and research studies. When too much information exists, it is hard to sort out the essential from the unessential. Group expert J. Dan Rothwell offers several tips for coping with information overload.[37] First, specialize whenever possible. Try to parcel out areas of responsibility to each member instead of expecting each member to explore every angle of the topic. Second, be selective. Take a quick look

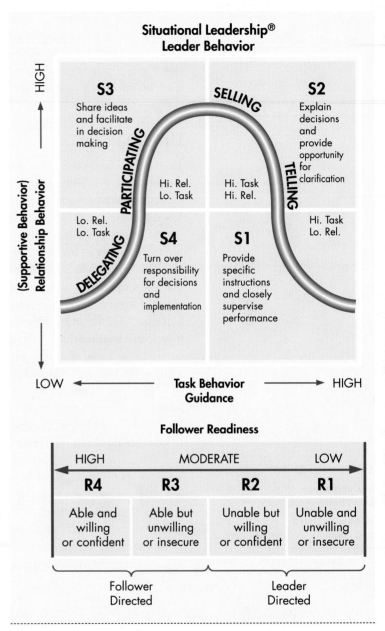

Figure 10.3
Hersey and Blanchard's Leadership Model

Source: 'Situational Leadership Behavior'. From *Management of Organizational Behavior*, 8th edn., © 2001. Adapted/reprinted with permission of Center for Leadership Studies, Escondido, CA 92025. All Rights Reserved.

information overload
Decline in efficiency that occurs when the rate of complexity of material is too great to manage.

at each piece of information to see whether it has real value for your task. If it doesn't, move on to examine more promising material. Third, limit your search. Information specialists have discovered that there is often a curvilinear relationship between the amount of information a group possesses and the quality of its decision. After a certain point, gathering more material can slow you down without contributing to the quality of your group's decisions.

Unequal Participation

The value of involving group members in making decisions—especially decisions that affect them—is great.[38] When people participate, their loyalty to the group increases. (Your own experience will probably show that most group dropouts were quiet and withdrawn.) Broad-based participation has a second advantage: it increases the amount of resources focused on the problem. As a result, the quality of the group's decisions goes up. Finally, participation increases members' loyalty to the decisions that they played a part in making.

The key to effective participation is balance. Domination by a few vocal members can reduce a group's ability to solve a problem effectively. Research shows that the proposal receiving the largest number of favourable comments is usually the one chosen, even if it isn't the best one.[39] Furthermore, ideas of high-status members (who aren't always talkers) are given more consideration than those of lower-status members.[40] The moral to this story? Don't assume that quantity of speech or the status of the speaker automatically defines the quality of an idea. Instead, seek out and seriously consider the ideas of quieter members.

Not all participation is helpful, of course. It's better to remain quiet than to act out the kind of dysfunctional roles described in Chapter 9—cynic, aggressor, dominator, and so on. Likewise, the comments of a member who is uninformed can waste time. Finally, downright ignorant or mistaken input can distract a group.

You can encourage the useful contributions of quiet members in a variety of ways. First, keep the group small. In groups with three or four members, participation is roughly equal, but after size increases to between five and eight, there is a dramatic gap between the contributions of members.[41] Even in a large group you can increase the contributions of quiet members by soliciting their opinions. This approach may seem obvious, but in their enthusiasm to speak out, more verbal communicators can overlook the people who don't speak up. When normally reticent members do offer information, reinforce their contributions. It isn't necessary to go overboard by gushing about a quiet person's brilliant remark, but a word of thanks and an acknowledgment of the value of an idea increase the odds that the contributor will speak up again in the future. A third strategy is to assign specific tasks to normally quiet members. The need to report on these tasks guarantees that they will speak up. A fourth strategy is to use the nominal group technique (p.000), to guarantee that the ideas of all members are heard.

Different strategies can help when the problem is one or more members talking too much—especially when their remarks aren't helpful. If the talkative member is at all sensitive, withholding reinforcement can deliver a diplomatic hint that it may be time to listen more and speak less. A lack of response to an idea or suggestion can work as a hint to cut back on speaking. Don't confuse lack of

LOOK, IF YOU'RE GOING TO HANG OUT WITH US, FIRST THING YOU GOTTA' DO IS LOSE THE BELL. —Hogan.

reinforcement with punishment, however: attacking a member for dominating the group is likely to trigger a defensive reaction and cause more harm than good. If the talkative member doesn't respond to subtle hints, politely expressing a desire to hear from other members can be effective. The next stage in this series of escalating strategies for dealing with dominating members is to question the relevancy of remarks that are apparently off the wall: 'I'm confused about what last Saturday's party has to do with the job we have to do today. Am I missing something?'

Pressure to Conform

There's a strong tendency for group members to go along with the crowd, which often results in bad decisions. A classic study by Solomon Asch illustrated this point. College students were shown three lines of different lengths and asked to identify which of them matched with a fourth line. Although the correct answer was obvious, the experiment was a set-up: Asch had instructed all but one member of the experimental groups to vote for the wrong line. As a result, one-third of the uninformed subjects ignored their own good judgment and voted with the majority. If simple tasks like this one generate such conformity, it is easy to see that following the (sometimes mistaken) crowd is even more likely in the much more complex and ambiguous tasks that most groups face.

Even when there's no overt pressure to follow the majority, more subtle influences motivate members—especially in highly cohesive groups—to keep quiet rather than voice any thoughts that deviate from what appears to be the consensus. 'Why rock the boat if I'm the only dissenter?' members think. 'And if everybody else feels the same way, they're probably right.'

With no dissent, the group begins to take on a feeling of invulnerability: an unquestioning belief that its ideas are correct and even morally right. As its position solidifies, outsiders who disagree can be viewed as the enemy, disloyal to what is obviously the only legitimate viewpoint. Social scientists use the term groupthink to describe the collective striving for unanimity that discourages realistic appraisals of alternatives to a group's chosen decision.[42] Several group practices can discourage this troublesome force.[43] A first step is to recognize the problem of groupthink as it begins to manifest itself. If agreement comes quickly and easily, the group may be avoiding the tough but necessary search for alternatives. Beyond vigilance, a second step to discourage **groupthink** is to minimize status differences. If the group has a nominal leader, he or she must be careful not to use various types of power that come with the position to intimidate members. A third step involves developing a group norm that legitimizes disagreement. After members recognize that questioning one another's positions doesn't signal personal animosity or disloyalty, a constructive exchange of ideas can lead to top-quality solutions. Sometimes it can be helpful to designate a person or subgroup as the 'devil's advocate' who reminds the others about the dangers of groupthink and challenges the trend toward consensus.

Cultural Idiom

go along with the crowd
agree with the majority

off the wall
unconventional, ridiculous

rock the boat
disturb a stable condition

Cultural Idiom

'devil's advocate'
one who argues against a widely held view in order to clarify issues

groupthink
A group's collective striving for unanimity that discourages realistic appraisals of alternatives to its chosen decision.

Summary

Despite the bad reputation of groups in some quarters, research shows that they are often the most effective settings for problem-solving. They command greater resources, both quantitatively and qualitatively, than do either individuals or collections of people working in isolation; their work can result in greater accuracy; and the participative nature of the solutions they produce generates greater commitment from members.

However, groups aren't always the best forum for solving problems. They should be used when the problem is beyond the capacity of one person to solve, when tasks are interdependent, when there is more than one desired solution or decision, and when the agreement of all members is essential.

Groups use a wide variety of discussion formats when solving problems. Some use parliamentary procedure to govern decision-making procedures. Others use moderated panel discussions, symposia, or forums. The best format depends on the nature of the problem and the characteristics of the group.

Since face-to-face meetings can be time-consuming and difficult to arrange, computer-mediated communication can be a good alternative for some group tasks. Some group work can be handled via computer or teleconferencing, where members communicate in real time over digital networks. Other tasks can be handled via asynchronous discussions, in which members exchange messages at their convenience. Mediated meetings provide a record of discussion and may make it easier for normally quiet members to participate, but these meetings can take more time, and they lack the non-verbal richness of face-to-face conversation. Given these pros and cons, smart communicators will give thoughtful consideration to the circumstances before deciding to use the mediated approach.

Groups stand the best chance of developing effective solutions to problems if they begin their work by identifying the problem, avoiding the mistake of failing to recognize the hidden needs of individual members. The next step is analysis of the problem, including identification of forces both favouring and blocking progress. Only at this point should the group begin to develop possible solutions, taking care not to stifle creativity by evaluating any of them prematurely. During the implementation phase of the solution, the group should monitor the situation carefully and make any necessary changes in its plan.

Most groups can expect to move through several stages as they solve a problem. The first of these stages is orientation, during which the members sound each other out. The conflict stage is characterized by partisanship and open debate over the merits of contending ideas. In the emergence stage, the group begins to move toward choosing a single solution. In the reinforcement stage, members endorse the group's decision.

Groups that pay attention only to the task dimension of their interaction risk strains in the relationships among members. Many of these interpersonal problems can be avoided by using the skills described in Chapter 7 as well as by following the guidelines in this chapter for building group cohesiveness and encouraging participation.

Many naive observers of groups confuse the concepts of leader and leadership. We defined leadership as the ability to influence the behaviour of other members through the use of one or more types of power—legitimate, coercive, reward, expert, information, or referent. We saw that many nominal leaders share their power with other members. Leadership has been examined from many perspectives—trait analysis, leadership style, and situational variables.

Smart members will avoid some common dangers that threaten a group's effectiveness. They will make sure to get the information they need, without succumbing to overload.

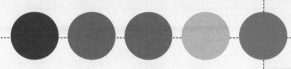

They will make sure that participation is equal by encouraging the contributions of quiet members and keeping more talkative people on track. They will guard against groupthink by minimizing the pressure on members to conform for the sake of harmony or approval.

Key Terms

authoritarian leadership
  style 389
brainstorming 376
breakout groups 369
coercive power 385
cohesiveness 381
conflict stage 379
democratic leadership
  style 389
emergence stage 379
expert power 385
focus groups 369
force field analysis 375
forum 370

groupthink 393
information overload 391
information power 386
information
  underload 390
laissez-faire leadership
  style 389
Leadership Grid 389
legitimate power 384
nominal group
  technique 376
nominal leader 384
orientation stage 379
panel discussion 369

parliamentary
  procedure 369
participative
  decision-making 366
power 384
probative question 374
problem census 369
referent power 386
reinforcement stage 379
reward power 385
situational leadership 390
symposium 369
trait theories of
  leadership 387

Activities

A. When to Use Group Problem-Solving

Explain which of the following tasks would be best managed by a group:
1. collecting and editing a list of films illustrating communication principles
2. deciding what the group will eat for lunch at a one-day meeting
3. choosing the topic for a class project
4. finding which of six companies had the lowest auto insurance rates
5. designing a survey to measure community attitudes toward a subsidy for local artists.

B. Increasing Group Creativity

You can increase your skill at increasing creativity in group discussions by trying the approaches described in this book. Your group should begin by choosing one of the following problems:
1. How can out-of-pocket student expenses (e.g., books, transportation) be decreased?
2. How can the textbook you are using in this (or any other) class be improved?
3. How could your class group (legally) earn the greatest amount of money between now and the end of the term?
4. What strategies can be used effectively when confronted with employer discrimination or harassment? (Assume you want to keep the job.)
5. Imagine that your group has been hired to develop a way of improving the course registration system at your institution. What three recommendations will be most effective?

Choose either brainstorming or the nominal group technique to develop possible solutions to your chosen problem. Explain why you chose the method. Under what conditions would the other method be more appropriate?

C. Stages in Group Development

Identify a problem-solving group, either from your personal experience or from a book or film. Analyze the group's approach to problem-solving. Does it follow the cyclical model pictured in Figure 10.1? Does it follow a more linear approach or no recognizable pattern at all?

D. Power in Groups

Think of examples from groups you have belonged to or observed in which members had and used each type of power discussed on pages 384–7. Describe the types of power you have possessed in groups. Evaluate whether your use of that power has helped or hindered the group's effectiveness.

E. Choosing the Most Effective Leadership Style

Think of two effective leaders you have known. How would you describe the style of each one: autocratic, democratic, or laissez-faire? Task- or relationship-oriented? Imagine that the two leaders were transferred, so that each one was directing the other's group. Would the same style work equally well in each situation? Why or why not?

F. Dealing with Overly Talkative and Quiet Group Members

Balancing participation in group discussions can involve stifling some members and urging others to speak up when they would prefer to be silent. Explore the ethical justification for these actions by answering the following questions.

1. Are there any circumstances when it is legitimate to place quiet group members in the position of speaking up when they would rather remain quiet? When does it become unreasonable to urge quiet members to participate?
2. Does discouraging talkative members ever violate the principles of free speech and tolerance for others' opinions? Describe when it is and is not appropriate to limit a member's contributions.

    After developing your ethical guidelines, consider how you would feel if they were applied to you.

Further Reading

Cochran, Alice. *Roberta's Rules of Order.* San Francisco: Josey-Bass, 2004.
Robert's Rules of Order has served for over 125 years as a guide for using parliamentary procedure to bring order out of meetings that might otherwise be disorganized and even chaotic. Cochran has created a less formal approach that strives for consensus instead of majority rule. For groups that find the traditional approach too confining, this book may be a useful guide.

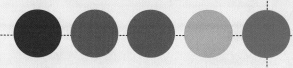

Rothwell, J. Dan. In *Mixed Company: Small Group Communication,* 5th edn. Belmont, CA: Wadsworth, 2004.
This survey of small-group communication combines readability with a comprehensive look at scholarship on the subject. Rothwell pays special attention to how gender and culture affect group work and discusses the features that distinguish effective teams.

Surowiecki, James. *The Wisdom of Crowds.* New York: Doubleday, 2004.
This book explores a deceptively simple idea that has profound implications: groups of people make better decisions than an elite few, no matter how brilliant.

Study Questions

Imagine you are organizing a fundraising plan for a not-for-profit group focused on environmental cleanup of a creek in your area. You announce that you are forming the group on Facebook and Twitter, and a very diverse group of people sign up. At your first meeting, you find that your call out has attracted the following people:

- a gay lawyer who is known as an active community volunteer;
- two teenage girls who are fashionably dressed and currently listening to their iPods;
- two neo-hippies who are sitting quietly, holding their hemp bags;
- two stay-at-home moms, who are primly dressed and constantly texting their children;
- a retired husband and wife who have lived in the neighbourhood for over 30 years and are sad at how soiled it has become;
- two college or university students who want to complete their internship requirements for a communications course;
- a conservative immigrant construction worker from Brazil who has been working in a filthy environment and has had enough; and
- an immigrant from Vietnam who is good at fixing computers but doesn't speak English very well.

Your group has a solid deadline of one month to effectively fundraise for the campaign to have an environmental assessment done of the creek area. You face a town council that doesn't want to spend any money on the environment, and wants to ignore the polluted creek problem.

1. How can you use the structured problem-solving approach outlined on pages 372–8 to develop an effective fundraising plan?
2. What developmental stages in problem-solving groups (described on pages 379–80) can you expect the group to experience as it develops its options? How can awareness of these steps make working together less troublesome and more rewarding?
3. What types of power (described on pages 384–7) can you expect group members to have and use? How could those types of power affect the success of the group, for better or worse?
4. How can you use the advice on pages 381–3 to build cohesiveness as you work on the list of options?
5. Choose either the styles or the situational approach to leadership on pages 389–91 and describe how you would use your chosen style to be an effective leader.

After studying the material in this chapter . . .

You should
understand:

- the characteristics of persuasion and the ethical questions involved;
- the differences between propositions of fact, value, and policy;
- the difference between the goals of convincing and activating;
- the difference between direct and indirect persuasion;
- the importance of setting a clear persuasive purpose;
- the various types of fallacies to avoid;
- the importance of analyzing and adapting to your audience;
- the differences between attitudes, beliefs, and values;
- the components of personal credibility;
- the characteristics of interpersonal persuasion strategies; and
- the components of four types of persuasive writing: news release, opinion editorial (op-ed), blog, and briefing note.

You should be
able to:

- formulate an effective persuasive strategy to convince and to activate an audience;
- formulate a persuasive strategy based on ethical guidelines;
- build persuasive arguments through audience analysis;
- bolster your credibility as a speaker by enhancing your competence, character, and charisma;
- identify and use different interpersonal persuasion strategies; and
- write a persuasive news release, op-ed, blog, and briefing note.

Persuasion, Audiences, and Persuasive Writing

Chapter Highlights

Persuasion has several important characteristics:
- It is not coercive.
- It is usually incremental.
- It is interactive.
- It can be ethical.

Persuasion can be categorized according to the following types:
- type of proposition,
- desired outcome, and
- directness of approach.

Adapting to your audience is an important part of persuasive strategy. To do so, you should
- establish common ground,
- organize your message according to the expected response, and
- neutralize potential hostility.

Understanding the nature of attitudes is essential to being persuasive. Attitudes are
- learned;
- based in our emotions;

- influenced by our thoughts and emotions; and
- related strongly to our beliefs and values.

Three approaches to explaining the structure of attitudes are
- expectancy–value,
- symbolic predispositions, and
- ideology.

Speaker credibility is an essential component of persuasiveness. Characteristics of credibility include
- competence, character, and charisma.

Types of interpersonal persuasion include:
- foot-in-the-door, door-in-the-face,
- social exchange, low-balling,
- that's-not-all, and
- fear-then-relief.

Types of writing covered in this chapter are:
- news release, op-ed, blog, and briefing note.

Jennifer Morrow, a student at Lakehead University in Thunder Bay, Ontario, sums up her understanding of persuasive communication as follows:

> Persuasion is a central part of being human. We must persuade others that we are competent, intelligent, trustworthy and open-minded. Persuasion can also be used to help people who cannot represent themselves—homeless people, abused women, the mentally ill. What could be more important or more fulfilling than that?

Not every student would agree with Jennifer on the joys of persuasive communication, but many college and university students across Canada and around the world are speaking out. They are becoming increasingly engaged in a variety of issues, including global ones such as the growing gap between rich and poor and the need for citizens and their governments to reduce greenhouse gas emissions. Students have staged anti-sweatshop protests at the University of Toronto. University of Ottawa students also recently protested a proposed speech by right-wing commentator Ann Coulter. These students are all engaged in the age-old activity of persuasion. How persuasion works and how to accomplish it successfully are complex topics. Our understanding of persuasion begins with classical wisdom and extends to the latest psychological research. We begin by looking at what we really mean by the term.

Characteristics of Persuasion

persuasion
The process of motivating someone, through communication and relationship-building, to change a particular attitude, belief, value, or behaviour.

Persuasion is the process of motivating someone, through communication and relationship-building, to change a particular attitude, belief, value, or behaviour. Implicit in this definition are several characteristics, which we'll discuss in the sections that follow.

Persuasion Is Not Coercive

Persuasion is not the same thing as coercion. If you held a gun to someone's head and said, 'Do this, or I'll shoot,' you would be acting coercively. Besides being illegal, this approach would be ineffective. As soon as the authorities had led you away in handcuffs, the person would stop following your demands.

This example is a bit far-fetched, but the failure of coercion to achieve lasting results is also apparent in less dramatic circumstances. Children whose parents are coercive often rebel as soon as they can; students who perform out of fear of an instructor's threats rarely appreciate the subject matter; and employees who work for abusive and demanding employers are often unproductive and eager to switch jobs as soon as possible. Persuasion, on the other hand, makes a listener *want* to think or act differently.

Persuasion Is Usually Incremental

Attitudes do not normally change instantly or dramatically. Persuasion is a process. When it is successful, it generally succeeds over time, in increments, and usually small increments at that. The realistic speaker, therefore, establishes goals and expectations that reflect this characteristic of persuasion.

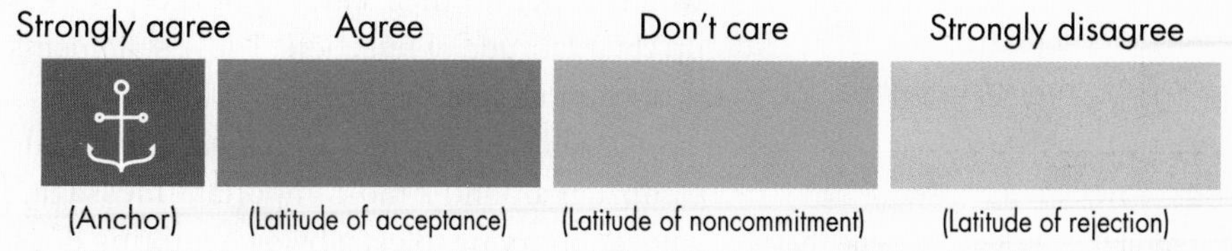

Figure 11.1

Latitudes of Acceptance, Rejection, and Non-Commitment

Communication theorists explain this characteristic of persuasion through **social judgment theory.**[1] This theory tells us that when members of an audience hear a persuasive appeal, they compare it to opinions they already hold. The pre-existing opinion is called an **anchor,** but around this anchor there exist what are called **latitudes of acceptance, latitudes of rejection,** and **latitudes of non-commitment.** A diagram of any opinion, therefore, might look something like Figure 11.1.

People who care very strongly about a particular point of view (they are called 'highly ego-involved' by communication researchers) will have a very narrow latitude of non-commitment. People who care less strongly will have a wider latitude of non-commitment. Research suggests that audience members simply will not respond to appeals that fall within their latitude of rejection. This means that persuasion in the real world occurs in a series of small movements. One persuasive speech may be but a single step in a larger campaign of persuasion. Consider, for instance, the various political communications disseminated in the months and weeks leading up to an election. Candidates watch the opinion polls carefully and adjust their appeals to the latitudes of acceptance and non-commitment of the undecided voters. With such information, a Liberal Party candidate may make pamphlets or information sheets targeted at Green Party voters because she feels that they may be susceptible to vote for her party, given the similarity of many Liberal and Green political positions.

Communicators who heed the principle of social judgment theory tend to seek realistic, if modest, goals in their communications. For example, if you were hoping to change audience views on the issue of abortion, social judgment theory suggests that the first step would be to consider a range of arguments, such as

Abortion is a sin.

Abortion should be absolutely illegal.

Abortion should be allowed only in cases of rape and incest.

A woman should be required to have her husband's permission to have an abortion.

A girl under the age of 18 should be required to have a parent's permission to have an abortion.

Abortion should be allowed during the first three months of pregnancy only.

A girl under the age of 18 should not be required to have a parent's permission before she has an abortion.

A woman should not be required to have her husband's permission to have an abortion.

Abortion should be a woman's personal decision.

Abortion should be discouraged but legal.

Abortion should be available anytime to anyone.

Abortion should be considered simply a form of birth control.

You could then arrange these positions on a continuum and estimate how listeners would react to each one. The statement that best represents the listeners' point of view would be the anchor of your messaging. Other items that might also seem reasonable to them

anchor

The position supported by audience members before a persuasion attempt.

latitudes of acceptance

In social judgment theory, statements that a receiver would not reject.

latitudes of non-commitment

In social judgment theory, statements that a receiver would not care strongly about one way or another.

latitudes of rejection

In social judgment theory, statements that a receiver could not possibly accept.

social judgment theory

Explanation of attitude change that posits that opinions will change only in small increments and only when the target opinions lie within the receiver's latitudes of acceptance and non-commitment.

would make up their latitude of acceptance. Opinions that they would reject would make up their latitude of rejection. Those statements that are left would be the listeners' latitude of non-commitment.

Usually, an organization or an individual will shape a public relations or an advertising campaign around a most important **message.** For example, if you were part of a parents' organization trying to get a bylaw requiring dogs to be leashed when outside passed, your message could be 'Dogs should be leashed so that our children can play outdoors safely.' Once you have a message, you can structure any advertising, informative literature, news releases, op-eds, or other forms of persuasive communication around it. You can also evaluate the success or failure of your 'messaging' by tracking how many citizens' attitudes, beliefs, values, or behaviours you aligned with your campaign's message because of your persuasive communication. If people start signing petitions or leaving comments in online forums supporting your cause, they have adopted your message and you have been successful in persuading them. If they accept parts of your message or start supporting variations of it, then you have been only partially successful in persuading them.

Social judgment theory suggests that you will have the best chance of changing audience attitudes if you begin by presenting an argument based on a position that falls somewhere within the listeners' latitude of non-commitment—even if this isn't the position that you want them to hold ultimately. If you push too hard by arguing a position in your audience's latitude of rejection, your appeals will probably backfire, making your audience more opposed to you than they were to begin with.

> **message**
> A central theme, idea, or value that is transmitted to receivers through persuasive communication.

> **Cultural Idiom**
>
> **backfire**
> produce a result opposite to the one intended
>
> **high-pressure hucksters**
> aggressive and persistent salespeople

Persuasion Is Interactive

The transactional model of communication described in Chapter 1 makes it clear that persuasion is not something you do *to* other people but rather something you do *with* them. The interactive nature of persuasion is best seen in an argument between two people, in which openness to the other person's arguments is essential to settling the dispute. As one observer has pointed out:

> Arguments are not won by shouting down opponents. They are won by changing opponents' minds—something that can happen only if we give opposing arguments a respectful hearing and still persuade their advocates that there is something wrong with those arguments. In the course of this activity, we may well decide that there is something wrong with our own.[2]

In any sort of communication, both the communicator and the audience are active. The communicator can ensure this interactivity by taking an audience survey before communicating, by showing sensitivity to audience reactions during conversation or in writing, or by making him- or herself available for questions and feedback.

Persuasion Can Be Ethical

Even when they understand the difference between persuasion and coercion, some people are still uncomfortable with the idea of persuasive communication. They associate it with high-pressure hucksters: salespeople with their feet stuck in the door, telemarketers who won't take 'no' for an answer, unscrupulous politicians taking advantage of beleaguered taxpayers, and so on. Indeed, many of the principles presented in this chapter have been used by unethical speakers for unethical purposes, but that is not what all—or even most—persuasion is about. Ethical persuasion plays a necessary and worthwhile role in everyone's life.

Through ethical persuasion we influence the lives of others in many worthwhile ways. The person who says, 'I do not want to influence other people' is really saying, 'I don't want to get involved with other people,' and that is an abandonment of one's responsibilities as a human being. Look at the good you can accomplish through ethical persuasion: you can convince a loved one to give up smoking or to exercise more regularly; you can get members of your community to conserve energy or to join together to refurbish a park; you can persuade an employer to hire you for a job where your own talents, interests, and abilities will be put to their best use.

Persuasion is considered ethical if it conforms to accepted standards. But what are the standards today? What if your plan is selfish and not in the best interest of your audience members, but you are honest about your motives—is that ethical? What if your plan is in the best interest of your audience members, but you lie to them to gain their consent? Philosophers and rhetoricians have argued for centuries over questions like these.

There are many ways to define **ethical persuasion**.[3] For our purpose, we will define it as communication in the best interest of the audience that does not depend on false or misleading information to change an audience's attitude or behaviour. The best way to appreciate the value of this simple definition is to consider the many strategies, listed in Table 11.1, that do *not* fit it. For example, plagiarizing material from another source, inventing statistics to support your case, and faking enthusiasm about communicating with someone about something are clearly unethical. Lying may seem an effective alternative to get you out of a bind now and again, but you must remember that every lie you tell must be maintained, which can become very complicated.

ethical persuasion
Persuasion in an audience's best interest that does not depend on false or misleading information to induce change.

TABLE 11.1 Unethical Communication Behaviours

1. Committing Plagiarism
   a. Claiming someone else's ideas as your own
   b. Quoting without citing the source

2. Relaying False Information
   a. Deliberate lying
   b. Ignorant misstatement
   c. Deliberate distortion and suppression of material
   d. Fallacious reasoning to misrepresent truth

3. Withholding Information; Suppression
   a. About self (speaker); not disclosing private motives or special interests
   b. About communication purpose
   c. About sources (not revealing sources; plagiarism)
   d. About evidence; omission of certain evidence (card stacking)
   e. About opposing arguments; presenting only one side

4. Appearing to Be What One Is Not; Insincerity
   a. In words, saying what one does not mean or believe
   b. In delivery (for example, feigning enthusiasm)

5. Using Emotional Appeals to Hinder Truth
   a. Using emotional appeals as a substitute or cover-up for lack of sound reasoning and valid evidence
   b. Failing to use balanced appeals

Adapted from Mary Klaaren Andersen, 'An Analysis of the Treatment of Ethos in Selected Speech Communication Textbooks' (unpublished dissertation, University of Michigan, 1979), 244–7.

Besides being wrong on moral grounds, unethical attempts at persuasion have a major practical disadvantage: if your deception is uncovered, your credibility will suffer. If, for example, prospective buyers uncover your attempt to withhold a structural flaw in the condominium you are trying to sell, they will probably suspect that the property has other hidden problems. Likewise, if your communications professor suspects that you are lifting material from other sources without giving credit, your entire project will be suspect. One unethical act can cast doubt on truthful statements you make in the future. Thus, for pragmatic as well as moral reasons, honesty really is the best policy.

Categorizing Types of Persuasion

There are several ways to categorize the types of persuasive attempts you will make as a speaker. What kinds of subjects will you focus on? What results will you be looking for? How will you go about getting those results? In the following pages we will look at how each of these questions may be used to categorize persuasive attempts.

By Types of Proposition

Persuasive topics may be sorted in terms of the type of thesis statement (referred to as a 'proposition' in persuasion) that you are advancing. There are three categories of proposition: propositions of fact, propositions of value, and propositions of policy.

Propositions of Fact

propositions of fact
Claims bearing on issues in which there are two or more sides of conflicting factual evidence.

propositions of value
Claims bearing on issues involving the worth of some idea, person, or object.

Some persuasive messages focus on **propositions of fact,** issues in which there are two or more sides with conflicting evidence. When presented with a proposition of fact, listeners are required to choose the truth for themselves. The following are some examples:

Caffeine is [*or* is not] addictive.
Canada does [*or* does not] provide more peacekeeping services than other developed countries.
Canada's national health care system is more [*or* is less] efficient than the US system of health care.

As these examples show, many propositions of fact can't be settled with a simple 'yes' or 'no', or with an objective piece of information. Rather, they are open to debate, and answering them requires careful examination and interpretation of evidence, usually collected from a variety of sources. That's why it is possible to debate questions of fact and why these propositions form the basis of persuasive speeches and not informative ones.

Propositions of Value

Propositions of value go beyond issues of truth or falsity and explore the worth of some idea, person, or object. Examples of propositions of value include the following:

An arena full of enthusiastic fans gives [*or* does not give] the home team a decided advantage.
The average Canadian's quality of life is [*or* is not] better than that of the average citizen of the United Kingdom.
Secretly watching pornography is [*or* is not] a form of cheating on your partner.

In order to deal with most propositions of value, you will have to explore certain propositions of fact. For example, you won't be able to debate whether watching pornography behind your partner's back is immoral—a proposition of value—until you have dealt with propositions of fact such as whether your value system considers only physical infidelity to be cheating and whether experts believe that this will create distance in your relationship.

Propositions of Policy

Propositions of policy go one step beyond questions of fact or value; they recommend a specific course of action (a 'policy'). Some questions of policy are the following:

The Supreme Court of Canada is [*or* is not] justified in overturning legislation made by elected officials.

The Canadian government should [*or* should not] financially support NHL teams to keep them in Canadian cities.

Genetic engineering of plants and livestock is [*or* is not] an appropriate way to increase the food supply.

Looking at persuasion according to the type of proposition is a convenient way to generate topics for a persuasive speech because each type of proposition suggests different topics. Selected topics could also be handled differently depending on how they are approached. For example, the central message of a political campaign op-ed could be crafted as a proposition of fact ('Candidate X has done more for this community than Candidate Y'), a proposition of value ('Candidate X is a better person than Candidate Y'), or a proposition of policy ('We should get out and vote for Candidate X'). Remember, however, that a fully developed persuasive op-ed is likely to contain all three types of propositions. If you were preparing an op-ed advocating mandatory drug testing for university athletes (a proposition of policy), you might want to first prove that the use of performance-enhancing drugs among athletes is already widespread (a proposition of fact), that there are considerable health risks associated with this kind of drug use (another proposition of fact), and that the use of performance-enhancing drugs gives some athletes an unfair advantage over others (a proposition of value).

> **convince**
> A speech goal that aims at changing audience members' attitudes, beliefs, or values.
>
> **propositions of policy**
> Claims bearing on issues that involve adopting or rejecting a specific course of action.

By Desired Outcome

We can also categorize persuasion according to two major outcomes: convincing and activating.

Convincing

When you set about to **convince** an audience, you want to change the way its members think. This doesn't mean that you have to swing them from one belief or attitude to a completely different one. Sometimes your audience members will already think the way you want them to, but they will not be firmly enough committed to that way of thinking. When this is the case, your goal is to reinforce, or strengthen, their opinions. For example, let's say your audience already believed that the federal government should be paying down the deficit but did not consider the issue important enough to be made a priority: your job would be to reinforce your audience members' current beliefs. Strengthening an idea or opinion is still a type of change because you are causing an audience to adhere more strongly to a belief or attitude. In other cases, a communication designed to convince will begin to shift attitudes without bringing about a total change of thinking. For example, an effective speech to convince might get a group of skeptics to consider the possibility that social media are a set of tools that all organizations should be integrating into their internal and public communication strategies.

Activating

activate
To move members of an audience toward a specific behaviour.

direct persuasion
Persuasion that does not try to disguise the speaker's persuasive purpose.

When you set about to **activate** an audience, you want to move its members to a specific behaviour. Whereas a speech, conversation, or op-ed designed to convince might spur listeners to action based on the ideas you've convinced them of, it won't be any specific action that you have recommended. In a speech to activate, you do recommend that specific action.

There are two types of action you can ask for—adoption or discontinuance. The former asks an audience to engage in a new behaviour; the latter asks an audience to stop behaving in an established way. If you were communicating for a political candidate and then asked for contributions to that candidate's campaign, you would be asking your audience to adopt a new behaviour. If you communicated against smoking and then asked your audience members to sign a pledge to quit, you would be asking them to discontinue an established behaviour.

By Directness of Approach

We can also categorize persuasion according to the directness of approach used by the speaker.

Direct Persuasion

Direct persuasion does not try to disguise the speaker's persuasive purpose in any way. In direct persuasion the speaker will make his or her purpose clear, usually by stating it outright early in the communication. This is the best strategy to use with a friendly audience, especially when you are asking for a response that the audience is likely to give you. Direct persuasion is the kind we hear in most academic situations. Justine Zaleschuk, a winner of the Canadian Association of Former Parliamentarians essay competition for undergraduate students at Canadian colleges and universities, used direct persuasion in a speech on 'How to Improve Canada's Health Care System'. In her introduction, she announced her intention to persuade in this way:

It seems ironic that the very system created to care for our health and well-being has, itself, been reduced to such a pitiful and sickly state. Medicare has stumbled into the twenty-first century coughing up bills for the increasingly obscene costs of technology and pharmaceuticals. The system is exhausted by the constant headaches of waiting lists and hospital closures. It finds itself hobbling along on its insufficient crutches of underpaid, over-worked staff. With all of this misery the debate has jumped right to the point of whether or not to 'pull the plug' on Medicare in order to pursue the tantalizing alternative of private health care. Yet few have stopped to consider if, possibly, the system merely needs a little bit of work—some modifications in conjunction with some basic upkeep—to survive. Medicare is not due for termination, but rather, consistent maintenance through a commitment to the financial, administrative and human resource aspects of this system of health services.[4]

Indirect Persuasion

Indirect persuasion disguises or de-emphasizes the speaker's persuasive purpose in some way. If you were to open a conversation with the question, 'Is a season ticket to the symphony worth the money?' (when you intended to prove that it was), you would be using indirect persuasion. Any strategy that does not express the speaker's purpose at the outset is based on indirect persuasion.

Although it is meant to operate subtly, indirect persuasion is sometimes easy to spot. A television commercial that shows attractive young people romping on the ski hill on a beautiful day and then flashes the name of a brand of beer, cereal, or soft drink is indisputably using indirect persuasion. Political oratory sometimes relies on methods of indirect persuasion that are more difficult to spot. A political hopeful might be speaking ostensibly on some great social issue when the real persuasive message is 'Please remember my name—and vote for me in the next election.'

COMMUNICATION ON-SCREEN

Yes, Minister (1980–4) and *Yes, Prime Minister* (1986–7)
Created by Antony Jay and Jonathan Lynn.

These two British comedies present the viewer with many examples of the methods of persuasion that this chapter explains. The Right Honourable James Hacker (Paul Eddington), a British politician, constantly comes into conflict with Sir Humphrey Appleby (Sir Nigel Hawthorne), the senior civil servant responsible for implementing his policies. The characters, Sir Humphrey in particular, are constantly using their wiles to persuade other civil servants, members of the press, captains of industry, and other parliamentarians of the value of their plans and objectives. In Sir Humphrey's case, these are usually deviously contrived means of steering Hacker away from any change in government policy that might challenge the civil service. This series contains dozens of classic examples of persuasion—a must watch for students of persuasive and political communication.

---

indirect persuasion
Persuasion that disguises or de-emphasizes the speaker's persuasive goal.

Creating the Persuasive Message

Preparing effective persuasive communication isn't easy, but it can be made easier by observing a few simple rules. These include setting a clear, persuasive purpose and avoiding fallacies.

Set a Clear, Persuasive Purpose

Remember that your objective in persuasive communication is to move the audience to a specific, attainable attitude or behaviour. When communicating to convince, the purpose statement will probably stress an attitude:

> After reading my blog post, my audience will agree that steps should be taken to save whales from extinction.

In communication meant to activate, the purpose statement will stress behaviour:

> After listening to my presentation, my audience members will sign my petition.

Your purpose statement should always be specific, realistic, and worded from the audience's point of view. 'The purpose of this blog post is to save the whales' is not a purpose

Understanding Communication Technology

Radio Is His Medium, Persuasion Is His Message

Terry O'Reilly is poised on a high stool, the kind you can picture Frank Sinatra on, when the singer was crooning into a microphone, recording *All the Way*.

> It's such an ascetic image. A guy. A mic. Headphones.
> Simplicity and sound.
> Not just sound. But the perfection of sound.

This is Mr O'Reilly in his element. He will spend the next three hours 'voicing' Season 3, Show 19, in the CBC radio series *The Age of Persuasion*. His co-writer, Mike Tennant, will sit at the controls suggesting that Mr O'Reilly offer a slightly lighter rendering of 'Bell', when saying 'Alexander Graham Bell', or lauding the beautiful way a particular 'paragraph from hell' has been wrestled to the ground.

'Your voice is resting down nicely,' Mr Tennant will say. Or: 'I'm hearing the pollen of Creemore creeping in a little bit there.' (Mr O'Reilly suffers from allergies and lives in the idyllic rural—and pollen-heavy—Ontario community.)

Today's theme: 'Embracing New Media'. The thesis: that the persuasive power of any new medium takes decades to master.

Regular listeners of Mr O'Reilly's show are invited to conjure the radio host's loamy voice. 'Early nineteenth-century newspaper ads were usually little more than fishmonger's calls, strung in sentences, and committed to print.' (Cue the reading of a particularly droning newspaper ad here.) 'It would take a century and a half for print to graduate from that to classic slogans such as 'Nothing sucks like Electrolux.'

Those who are not regular listeners of the show need to know that four or so years ago, Mr Tennant and Mr O'Reilly and others were having one of their seasonal radio boys lunches when someone was seized by the idea that Mr O'Reilly's annual radio seminars could be broken down into pieces and crafted into a radio show and that the CBC might be the right place to pitch such an idea. This caused Mr O'Reilly to ponder: 'The ad-free CBC is going to air a show about advertising?'

'So we went in and pitched the show to the CBC brass,' says Mr O'Reilly, seated now in his office down the hall from his studio. 'And this is how we pitched it: we said we want to create a show on advertising and we want to aim it at the general public, not at ad guys.'

The show was originally entitled *O'Reilly on Advertising* and launched as a summer replacement series. 'We thought we were only going to do 10 shows,' he says, seeming rather surprised by the popularity of the program, which airs Mondays at 11:30 a.m. on CBC Radio One, repeating Saturdays at 4:30 p.m. And by the fact that the show is being taken into book form: *The Age of Persuasion: How Marketing Ate Our Culture*, will be published by Random House in October.

Mr O'Reilly shouldn't be. Surprised that is. Ever since he landed his first job at a small radio station in 1981, smack in the recession—'I started out in radio because no ad agency would hire me'—he has been smitten by the medium, and it is this passion, and deep historical knowledge, that carries the show.

'Even though it was this detour, I loved it,' he says, describing radio as the toughest 'write' in the business.

statement that has been carefully thought out. Your readers wouldn't be able to jump up and save the whales, even if they were motivated into a frenzy. They might, however, be able to support a specific piece of legislation.

A clear, specific purpose statement will help you stay on track as you go through all the stages of preparation for your persuasive communication. Because the main purpose of your communication is to have an effect on your audience, use this test regularly for every idea, every piece of evidence, and every organizational structure that you think of using. Ask

'There's great radio and there's bad radio and there's not much in the middle. There's a lot of middle ground in TV. You can be wowed by a TV spot that's vapid in the concept department but incredible in the production values department. In radio, that doesn't work. It's either got a motivating idea and great writing or it's completely invisible.'

Mr O'Reilly did head into the agency world: to Campbell-Ewald as his first agency stop after that radio station, followed by Doyle Dane Bernbach, and then Chiat/Day when that agency was just setting up shop in Toronto.

Nissan was Chiat's anchor account. Mr O'Reilly was a copywriter and he had one burning question: 'How come we don't do radio? It seems crazy to me that we're trying to sell cars and we're not talking to people in their cars.' So he did a ton of radio for Nissan.

Still, there were disappointments. 'As a writer, I would hire production companies to direct my work,' he says. 'I would hire people all over the place. . . . But I would end up having to fight the directors to save my work from them.'

In 1990, heading into another recession, he established Pirate Radio in Toronto with partner Rick Shurman. 'I wanted to find a production company that directed audio from a writer's point of view,' Mr O'Reilly recalls. 'I wanted to create a company that respected that idea. So really, I started the company I could not find.'

Today, Pirate splits itself between radio and television work and runs its affairs from a maze of studio and office space in Toronto that has the feel of that fabulous cottage owned by that friend you envy. Writing, casting, voice direction. The company's MO is simple enough: 'We make sound. Great sound. . . . We hope you like how that sounds.'

In conversation, the topic keeps running back to the power of radio. 'At first blush, people think you don't have the tricks, you don't have the locations, you don't have the faces, you don't have all of that at your disposal, when in fact you do,' Mr O'Reilly says. 'The great thing about radio for me is that you can be on the moon, or at the bottom of the ocean, or inside a heart valve, or wherever you want to be with just some great writing and a bag of sound effects.'

It helps enormously that *The Age of Persuasion* is being written in the age of the Internet. Hilarious outtakes of the actor Orson Welles attempting to record a radio spot about Mrs Buckley and her Lincolnshire peas will be plopped into the 'Embracing New Media' show, scheduled to air later this month. ('Idiotic', 'stupid', and 'meaningless' are three of the printable complaints that the actor lobs at the spot's hapless director. Asks the actor, who fights every request to alter his intonation, 'In the depths of your ignorance, what is it you want?')

Sitting on that stool in that studio, Mr O'Reilly laughs again at the replay. Then he clicks into his radio voice to record: 'Radio has the ability, more so than any medium, to paint pictures in your imagination.'

He spends weekends and nights knitting the show together. He spends part of every day responding to e-mails. And this, he reminds, is not his job. 'Most people think most advertising is crap, and they're probably right,' he says. 'But when it's done really well, it's really a wonderful art, and it's so hard to do well.'

—Jennifer Wells, *The Globe and Mail*, 5 June 2009.

Questions: What are your thoughts on advertising? Is it a modern-day art form? How important do you think it is to be critically aware of the effects of advertising on individuals and society?

yourself, 'Will this help me to get my audience and co-communicators to think/feel/behave in the manner I have described in my purpose statement?' If the answer is 'yes', you forge ahead.

Avoid Fallacies

A **fallacy** (from the Latin word meaning 'false') is a mistaken or misleading argument. Although originally the term implied purposeful deception, most logical fallacies are not

fallacy
A mistaken or misleading argument.

recognized as such by those who use them. Scholars have devoted lives and volumes to the description of various types of logical fallacies. In the following sections we take a look at some of the most common ones to keep in mind when building your persuasive argument.[5]

Attack on the Person Instead of the Argument (*Ad Hominem*)

In an **ad hominem** fallacy the speaker attacks the integrity of the person making an argument instead of the argument itself. At its crudest an *ad hominem* argument is easy to detect. Attacking someone's point of view by exclaiming, 'How could anyone believe that fat-headed, ignorant slob?' is hardly persuasive. However, it takes critical thinking to catch more subtle *ad hominem* arguments. Consider this one: 'All this talk about "family values" is hypocritical. Take the Minister for Family Services, who made a speech about the "sanctity of marriage" last year. Now it comes out he was having an affair with his secretary, and his wife is suing him for divorce.' The Minister may well be a hypocrite, but his behaviour doesn't prove anything about the merits of family values.

Reduction to the Absurd (*Reductio ad Absurdum*)

A ***reductio ad absurdum* fallacy** unfairly attacks an argument by extending it to such extreme lengths that it looks ridiculous. For example, 'If we allow developers to build homes on this parcel of land in the Shady Acres ravine, soon we will have no open spaces left. Fresh air and wildlife will be things of the past.' Or 'If we allow the administration to raise tuition this year, soon they will be raising it every year, and before we know it, only the wealthiest students will be able to go to school here.' This extension of reasoning doesn't make any sense: developing one area doesn't necessarily mean that other areas have to be developed, and one tuition increase doesn't mean that others will follow. These policies might be unwise or unfair, but the *ad absurdum* reasoning doesn't prove it.

Either–Or

An **either–or fallacy** sets up false alternatives, suggesting that if the inferior option must be rejected, then the other must be accepted. An angry citizen used either–or thinking to support a proposed city ordinance: 'Either we outlaw alcohol in city parks, or there will be no way to get rid of drunks.' This reasoning overlooks the possibility that there may be other ways to control public drunkenness besides banning all alcoholic beverages. The old saying 'Canada—love it or leave it' is another example of either–or reasoning. Along the same lines is the either–or argument used by Quebec separatists, who claim that Quebec must achieve sovereignty and establish its own government or else lose its culture.

False Cause (*Post Hoc Ergo Propter Hoc*)

A ***post hoc* fallacy** mistakenly assumes that one event causes another because they occur sequentially. An old joke is a useful illustration: Mac approaches Jack and asks, 'Hey, why are you snapping your fingers?' Jack replies, 'To keep the elephants away.' Mac is incredulous: 'What are you talking about? There aren't any elephants within a thousand miles of here.' Jack smiles and keeps on snapping: 'I know. Works pretty well, doesn't it?'

In real life, *post hoc* fallacies aren't always so easy to detect. For example, imagine an education critic pointing out that sexual promiscuity among adolescents began to increase about the same time that prayer in public schools was prohibited by the courts. A causal link may

As far back as I can remember, I've always had a fascination with the media. In my early years, it manifested itself in reading the newspaper every morning—usually the sports section—and watching sports highlights or the news while getting ready for school. I guess I realized from a young age I wasn't going to make it as an NHL superstar or be the one making the news, so the next best thing would be getting paid to talk about it!

After working as the sports editor of my campus newspaper and extensively with campus radio, I took the next step and began interning with two television stations and a magazine upon graduation. I was able to turn those into freelance jobs and put together a rough on-air demo that helped me land a position hosting a morning television show with RogersTV. That lead to sports hosting, producing, and reporting with another local station, which ultimately brought me to my current job as a reporter with CP24.

While my industry is very fluid and 'hands on', studying communications gave me a firm theoretical understanding of underlying issues like gatekeeping, agenda setting, and ownership concentration. In a very transitional industry, this grounding helps me stay a couple steps ahead of the game.

Young Communicator
PROFILE

Gurdeep Ahluwalia, Reporter, CP24

exist in this case: decreased emphasis on spirituality *could* contribute to promiscuity. But you would need evidence to establish a definite connection between the two events.

Appeal to Authority (*Argumentum ad Verecundiam*)

An ***argumentum ad verecundiam* fallacy** involves relying on the testimony of someone who is not an authority in the area under discussion. Relying on an expert is not necessarily a fallacy, of course. A Toronto starlet might be just the right person to offer advice on how to appear more glamorous, and a member of the Vancouver Canucks hockey team could be the best person to comment on what it takes to succeed in organized sports. But an *ad verecundiam* fallacy occurs when the celeb promotes a political candidate or the hockey player tells us why we should buy a certain kind of automobile. When considering endorsements and claims, it's smart to ask yourself whether the source is qualified to make them.

Bandwagon Appeal (*Argumentum ad Populum*)

An ***argumentum ad populum* fallacy** is based on the often dubious notion that because many people favour an idea, you should, too. Sometimes, of course, the mass appeal of an idea can be a sign of its merit. If most of your friends have enjoyed a film or a book, there

argumentum ad populum fallacy

Fallacious reasoning based on the dubious notion that because many people favour an idea, you should, too.

argumentum ad verecundiam fallacy

Fallacious reasoning that tries to support a belief by relying on the testimony of someone who is not an authority on the issue being argued.

'Good God! He's giving the white-collar voters' speech to the blue collars.'

is a good chance that you will as well. But in other cases, widespread acceptance of an idea is no guarantee of its validity. In the face of almost universal belief to the contrary, Galileo reasoned accurately that the earth is not the centre of the universe, and he suffered for his convictions. The lesson here is simple to comprehend but often difficult to follow: when faced with an idea, don't just follow the crowd. Consider the facts carefully, and make up your own mind.

Analyzing the Audience

When you shop for a gift, you consider the person whom you're buying it for; after all, what would be an ideal gift for one person could be a terrible choice for another. In the same way, you need to analyze your audience—examine certain pertinent characteristics of your listeners—when planning persuasive communication. **Audience analysis** is the purest form of receiver orientation. It allows you to adapt to your listeners.

---

audience analysis
A consideration of characteristics including the type, goals, demographics, beliefs, attitudes, and values of listeners.

Cultural Idiom

follow the crowd
do what the majority does

Cultural Idiom

milling around
moving around as a group

student union
a building on college and university campuses where students gather for the purposes of dining, recreation, and other general needs

Cultural Idiom

gimmick
a clever means of drawing attention

Audience Type

There are at least three types of audience you are likely to encounter. We could call these types 'passersby', 'captives', and 'volunteers'. Each type suggests different audience interests. *Passersby*, as the name implies, are people who aren't much interested—at least not in advance—in what you have to say. A crowd milling around the student union or a shopping mall would fit into this category. With passersby, your first concern is to make them aware of you by getting them interested either in the topic you're discussing or in you as a communicator. You might have to pick a really sensational topic or begin developing your topic by using some kind of device or gimmick to get the audience's attention—think of the loud costumes or wild theatrics that street speakers often rely on.

Captives are audience members who have gathered for some reason besides the joy of hearing you speak. Students in a required class often begin as a type of captive audience. With captives you don't have to worry about devices and gimmicks to make them aware of you as a communicator; you do, however, have to use material that will get them interested and keep them interested in your message.

Volunteers are audience members who have gathered together because of a common interest. Students in elective courses, especially those with long waiting lists, would fit into this type. So would gatherings of most clubs, social organizations, and action groups. Even with an audience of volunteers, you still have to maintain their interest; you never lose that responsibility. But when the audience is informed and involved, as volunteers tend to be, you can treat your topic in greater depth without worrying about losing their interest.

Most university and persuasive communication classes are made up of a mixture of captives and volunteers, which means that you don't have to sensationalize your messages or use gimmicks, but you do have to maintain interest and provide depth.

Audience Purpose

Just as you have a purpose for communicating, the people you are communicating with have a purpose for gathering. Sometimes virtually all the members of your audience will have the same ostensible goal. People at a childbirth class are all seeking ways to ensure a relatively painless delivery, and people attending an investment seminar are looking for ways to increase their net worth.

There are other times, however, when audience purpose can't be so easily defined. In some instances, different listeners will have different goals, some of which might not be apparent to the communicator. Consider the listeners gathered for a service at a mosque, church, or synagogue. Whereas most members might listen to a sermon with the hope of applying religious principles to their lives, a few might be interested in being entertained or in merely appearing pious. In the same way, the audience in your communication class probably has a variety of motives for attending. Becoming aware of as many of these motives as possible will help you predict what will interest people. Observing audience demographics helps you make that prediction.

COMMUNICATION ON-SCREEN

Contact (1997)
Directed by Robert Zemeckis.

Based on a novel by the late Carl Sagan, the title has multiple meanings—the main one being astronomer Eleanor Arroway (Jodie Foster)'s contact with extraterrestrial life. Other meanings concern her contact with people, contact with God, and, of interest to us here, contact with a number of audiences, including a pitch session before a foundation board, testimony before Congress, and a lecture to a group of school children. Arroway tailors her messaging to each of these groups—and not always successfully—in an attempt to challenge their pre-existing beliefs.

> **Cultural Idiom**
>
> **stuffy**
> impersonal, not relating to the audience

Demographics

Demographics are characteristics of your audience that can be labelled, such as number of people, gender, age, group membership, and so on. Demographic characteristics, such as the ones discussed here, might affect your message communication planning in a number of ways.[6]

> **demographics**
> Audience characteristics that can be analyzed statistically, such as number of people, gender, age, group membership, and so on.

Number of People

Message appropriateness varies with the size of an audience. With a small audience you can be less formal and more intimate—you can, for example, talk more about your own inner feelings and personal experiences. If you communicated with five people as impersonally as if they were a standing-room-only crowd in a lecture hall, they would probably find you stuffy. On the other hand, if you talked to 300 people about your unhappy childhood, you'd probably make them uncomfortable. Also, the larger your audience, the broader its range of interests and knowledge; with a small audience you can choose a more specific message.

Gender

Traditionally, men and women have tended to be interested in different topics. Although these differences are becoming less pronounced, you might still find that more men than women are interested in hockey or lacrosse and that more women than men are interested in figure skating or modern dance; as a communicator choosing and developing a topic, you must be aware of such prevailing differences in interest. The guideline here might be: *Do not exclude or offend any portion of your audience on the basis of gender.* Every communication trainer has a horror story about a client getting up in front of an audience composed primarily of men and speaking on a subject such as 'Picking up Chicks'. Not only are the women invariably offended, but most men in the audience will feel the same way.

As with any of these demographic characteristics, the point is to analyze, not stereotype, your audience. If you talk down to any of the people you are communicating with, you have probably stereotyped them. The communicator who wants to spread his or her message to a mixed audience on how a man meets a woman, or vice versa, may still do so; the message, however, should be 'meeting people'. That way it can be treated in a manner that would be appropriate for both men and women.

Age

In many areas, younger people and older people have different interests. Your messaging concerning universal health care, child rearing, and school success should therefore reflect the age of your audience. Age-related differences can run deep; Aristotle observed long ago that young people 'have strong passions', that 'their lives are spent not in memory but in expectation', and that they have high ideals because 'they have not been humbled by life or learned its necessary limitations'. Older people, on the other hand, tend to have more practical interests.

Group Membership

The organizations to which the audience members belong provide more clues to their interests. By examining their affiliations, you can surmise audience members' political leanings (Young Conservatives, Young Liberals, University New Democrats, Campus Green Party), religious beliefs (Chinese Christian Fellowship or Campus Hindu Association), or occupation (Canadian Communication Association or Canadian Medical Association). Group membership is often an important consideration in post-secondary classes. Consider the difference between a 'typical' university day class and a 'typical' university night class. At many colleges and universities the evening students are generally older and tend to belong to civic groups, church clubs, and the local chamber of commerce. Daytime students tend to belong to sororities and fraternities, sports clubs, and social action groups.

You have to decide which demographic characteristics are important for a particular message. For example, when Arielle Wittenberg, a student at McMaster University, was working a room at a Liberal Party of Canada function and promoting the message 'A new messaging strategy for the Liberal Party in Hamilton', she knew that religious people were an important demographic. She adapted to her university-aged audience this way:

> Get over the idea that people in the real world are secular, liberal, and morally relativist the way we are in the colleges and universities. Average Canadians who have real lives and real families practise their faiths and traditions. In Hamilton, they often come from diverse communities for whom the Church, Synagogue, Mosque, or Temple is a safe haven and happy place. Places of worship provide cultural continuity. They help to educate children in traditional ways that allow parents to recognize their children. Without their place of worship and their spiritual leader to guide them, many Canadians' existence would be much less orderly and much less lonely.[7]

Cultural Idiom

talk down to
speak to in a condescending way

Of the three elements in speechmaking—speaker, subject and person addressed—it is the last one, the hearer, that determines the speech's end and object.

Aristotle

Understanding Diversity

● ● ● ● ● **THE AGE DEMOGRAPHIC**

When analyzing your audience in terms of age, remember that people of different generations will latch on to different concepts in a speech. These concepts might include memorable events, popular culture 'icons' (i.e., symbols that strongly represent a particular era), or types of music. A small sample of generational differences might play out as in the following chart:

Traditionalists	Baby Boomers	Generation X	Generation Y
• Born: 1922–46 • Population: ~4.5 million • Memorable Events: World War II, Canadian Citizenship Act, Canada–Newfoundland Confederation, television, Medicare, Canadian Bill of Rights • Icons: radio, *Reader's Digest,* Eaton's, Maurice 'the Rocket' Richard • Music: Benny Goodman, Tommy Dorsey, Frank Sinatra, Guy Lombardo, Ella Fitzgerald, Billie Holiday, Charlie Parker, Hank Snow	• Born: 1946–64 • Population: ~10 million • Memorable Events: Expo '67, 'Trudeaumania', Vietnam War, *Apollo 11,* Woodstock, patriation of the Constitution, the Charter of Rights and Freedoms, the '72 Summit Series, Official Languages Act, the October Crisis, the first Quebec Referendum (1980), Multiculturalism Act, John Lennon's murder • Icons: Mickey Mouse, fallout shelters, the peace symbol, *Doonesbury,* Bobby Orr, Pierre Elliott Trudeau, René Levesque, Ken Dryden, Peter Gzowski. • Music: Elvis, The Beatles, The Rolling Stones, Bob Dylan, Jimi Hendrix, Gordon Lightfoot, Ian and Sylvia, Joni Mitchell, The Guess Who, Leonard Cohen	• Born: 1965–78 • Population: ~7 million • Memorable Events: Terry Fox's Marathon of Hope, the *Challenger* disaster, the fall of the Berlin Wall, the Montreal Massacre, Operation Desert Storm • Icons: the personal computer, The *Simpsons, Saturday Night Live,* Brian Mulroney, Wayne Gretzky, Bill Gates, MuchMusic, Don Cherry, Tim Hortons • Music: U2, Madonna, Nirvana, Neil Young, Rush, Bryan Adams, Weird Al Yankovic, Alanis Morissette, Sarah McLachlan, Radiohead, Beck	• Born: 1979–present • Population: ~9.5 million • Memorable Events: the 'Loonie' and 'Toonie', the Quebec Referendum of 1995, the O.J. Simpson trial, the Clinton–Lewinsky scandal, 9/11, the Dot-Com Bubble, same-sex marriage • Icons: the Internet, Nintendo, PlayStation and X-Box, the Apple computer, the iPod, iPhone and iPad the BlackBerry, Beanie Babies, body piercing • Music: The Backstreet Boys, Matchbox 20, Eminem, OutKast, Celine Dion, Metallica, The Tragically Hip, Blur, Shania Twain, Avril Lavigne, Ke$ha, Deadmau5, Sigur Rós, Junior Boys, Michael Bublé, K'Naan, Nora Jones

These four demographic characteristics are important examples, but the list goes on and on. Other important demographic characteristics might be important include ethnic background, educational level, economic status, and hometown.

A final set of factors to consider in audience analysis consists of members' attitudes, beliefs, and values.

Cultural Idiom

Trudeaumania
widespread fascination with Pierre Elliott Trudeau among the Canadian public, especially during the election campaign of 1968

Attitudes, Beliefs, and Values

Audience members' feelings about you, your message, and your intentions for them are central issues in audience analysis. One way to approach these matters is through a consideration of attitudes, beliefs, and values.[8] These characteristics are structured in human consciousness

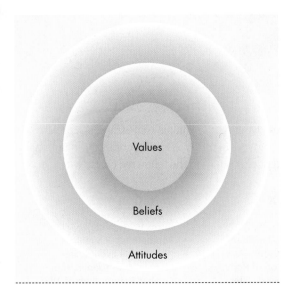

Figure 11.2
Structure of Attitudes, Beliefs, and Values

attitude
A predisposition to respond to an idea, person, or thing favourably or unfavourably.

belief
An underlying conviction about the truth of an idea, often based on cultural training.

value
A deeply rooted belief about a concept's inherent worth.

Fight for your opinions, but do not believe that they contain the whole truth, or the only truth.

Charles A. Dana

like the layers of an onion. They are all closely interrelated, but attitudes lie closer to the surface, whereas beliefs and values underlie them. An **attitude** is a predisposition to respond to something in a favourable or unfavourable way. A **belief** is an underlying conviction about the truth of something, which is often based on cultural training. A **value** is a deeply rooted belief about a concept's inherent worth. An audience might, for example, hold the value that 'freedom is a good thing.' This value might be expressed in a belief such as 'people should be free to choose their political leaders,' which in turn could lead to the attitude that 'voting is an important right and responsibility for all citizens.' Finally, this could lead to a predisposition to vote—in other words, a positive attitude toward voting.

Figure 11.2 shows the relationship among attitudes, beliefs, and values. Experts in audience analysis, such as professional speechwriters or public relations practitioners, often try to concentrate on values. As one team of researchers pointed out, 'Values have the advantage of being comparatively small in number, and owing to their abstract nature, are more likely to be shared by large numbers of people.'[9] Stable Canadian values include good citizenship, a solid work ethic, political freedom, multiculturalism, and justice for all.

You can often make an inference about audience members' attitudes by recognizing the beliefs and values they are likely to hold. For example, a group of Muslim Canadians might hold the value of 'submitting to Allah's will'. This might lead to the belief—based on their religious training—that women are not meant to perform the same functions in society as men. This, in turn, might lead to the attitude that women ought not to pursue careers as firefighters, police officers, or construction workers.

You may also be able to guess how audience members are likely to feel about some issues based on your knowledge of their attitudes on other issues. If your audience is made up of undergraduates who have a positive attitude toward liberation movements, for instance, it's a good bet they will also have positive attitudes toward civil rights and the environment. If they have a negative attitude toward collegiate sports, they probably also have a negative attitude toward fraternities and sororities. This should suggest not only some appropriate topics for each audience but also some ways that those topics could be developed. We will discuss attitudes in more detail because they are always present and most visible, while beliefs and values are more deep-seated.

CRITICAL THINKING PROBE

ATTITUDES, BELIEFS, AND VALUES

Find a persuasive appeal in an advertisement, newspaper editorial, or another source. Identify an attitude, belief, or value that the source of the message is appealing to. Explain why you have identified the appeal the way you have (i.e., why it is an attitude or belief rather than a value, etc.). Explain why, in your opinion, this appeal is or is not effective.

Characteristics of Attitudes

We are surrounded by the attitudes of others. When we open the newspaper, click on a series of blogs about women's fashion, read our Facebook or Twitter feed, listen to CBC radio in the car, or simply spend an afternoon sipping coffee in the student centre, we notice the attitudes of others. Some of them will obviously be deeply held, like those of campus evangelicals preaching; some will be shaky, like the student environmental activist decrying the waste that goes on at your college or university; and others will be complex and subtle, such as how your parents perceive your maintaining or letting go of your ethnic origins. The crucial point to remember is that attitudes are always present.

Attitudes Are Learned

Many researchers, such as cognitive scientist Steven Pinker[10] imply that attitudes can be biologically determined. What's more, in a study published in the *American Journal of Political Science,* researchers analyzed genetic data from twins and their extended families to see if there was a link between genetics and political and social attitudes—the results were undeniable: political and social attitudes seem to have biological roots.[11] However, these findings must not be misinterpreted. We are not born with a set of *pre-programmed attitudes.* While our biological inheritance may increase the probability of us developing certain attitudes, most are formed through our interpretation of our lived experiences. This is not to say that our attitudes are set in stone. They can be changed, either through introspection or through the techniques of persuasion.

Attitudes Are Based in Our Emotions

Our emotional lives play a crucial role in shaping our attitudes. Classical conditioning—repeating a stimulus accompanied by a reward or a punishment—can also play a big role in the formation of attitudes, as can the process of reflecting rationally on our experiences.[12,13] But the largest impact on attitudes comes from our emotional interpretation of a circumstance. We often will not remember what a person said, but we will remember how that person made us feel. For example, a politician who comes to a community event about poverty might not say anything of note, but she may be very charming, warm, and friendly. She might reassure the crowd and make them feel better about their economic situation. As a result, the audience will probably remember how the politician made them feel more than the substance of her speech. Their attitude toward her is shaped by emotion rather than facts and logic.

I've learned that people will forget what you said, people will forget what you did, but people will never forget how you made them feel.

Maya Angelou

Attitudes Influence Our Thoughts and Behaviours

Attitudes organize and structure our ideas about ourselves, others, society, religion, and culture. They enable us to categorize people, places, and things and to attach a value to them. For example, if you are a Liberal or a New Democrat, you probably have a strong intuitive negative reaction to Conservative ideas, and vice versa. Or, if you are Goth or emo, chances are you will have a strong subconscious negative reaction to a preppie or a jock.

Our behaviours can also be shaped by our attitudes.[14] For example, if you have a strong aversion to displays of wealth and hold very modest attitudes toward material things, you may act awkwardly if forced to speak to a person who focuses the conversation on his $10,000 Rolex or his new Porsche Cayman. If you do not engage in the conversation or are unfriendly or dismissive of him, then your attitudes are guiding your behaviours toward him.

Attitudes Are Strongly Related to Our Beliefs and Values

To truly understand the impact of attitudes on our social, cultural, and psychological lives, it is important to reflect on how they relate to our beliefs and our values.

Beliefs are intellectual and cognitive, meaning that they are ideas that people can define easily and cite specifically. They are better defined and more specific than values, which can be large and nebulous. Here are some typical beliefs:

- Canadians are better informed about international current affairs than Americans.
- French Canadians are more passionate lovers than English Canadians, who are more reserved.
- Cats have nine lives.
- Experimenting with drugs just once won't have an impact on your health.
- The moon is made out of green cheese.
- University professors always have above average wisdom.

As you can see from this list, beliefs are thoughts that you hold about the world around you, things that you think are true. However, we often confuse our beliefs with facts (the fact–opinion confusion we discussed in Chapter 3 is based on this idea). Moreover, beliefs can be absolutely false but still held by many people, as the 'cats have nine lives' or 'the moon is made out of green cheese' statements demonstrate. It is interesting to note that the most unverifiable beliefs are often the most strongly held and often justified through a claim to 'faith' in the belief. How often have you heard people whose homes are in the path of a hurricane say that they have faith that their home will not be destroyed, even though the weather service is issuing a strong evacuation recommendation? It often happens—but rarely are they saved from being killed in their home, and if they are, say, through the intervention of a sudden change of wind pattern, they will chalk it up to 'providence' or 'God's will'. Consequently, their belief will be strengthened. All of that, even though what really happened was just a statistical accident. A coincidence, at best.

Values are concepts that we idealize.[15] They tend to be more abstract than our attitudes and more difficult to identify quickly. They are often the 'guiding principles in one's life'[16] or the grand goals that we strive to attain. Shalom H. Schwartz and Wolfgang Bilsky describe values as 'desirable end states or behaviours that transcend specific situations, guide selection or evaluation of behaviour and events and are ordered by relative importance.'[17]

Some values that a person may hold include the following statements:

- It is wrong to lose control of one's behaviour because of drugs or alcohol.
- All human life is sacred.
- Marriage and the family are the central building blocks of society.
- All forms of marriage, gay and straight, are of equal worth and validity.
- We must leave the earth cleaner for coming generations.

It is important to note that people may hold hundreds or even thousands of attitudes but only dozens of values and that those values often help to define their core self-concepts.[18] For example, a female college or university student who holds strong pro-life values may respect her best friend's decision to have an abortion because of an unwanted pregnancy but feel that she has been untrue to herself by not attempting to discourage her friend from this course of action.

Attitudes Are Structured

Following Richard Perloff, the three approaches to describing the structure of attitudes that we will discuss here are

- expectancy–value
- symbolic predispositions
- ideology[19]

Simply put, the **expectancy–value approach** claims that your motivations to change your behaviours are a combination of what you believe about something and how you feel about it. For example, if you are overweight and feeling lonely, you may take on the attitude that losing weight will improve your social life. This is because you believe that losing weight will make you more attractive and sporty, and that others will value your efforts and be more likely to want to be close to you. According to expectancy–value theory, your beliefs and the value you attach to losing weight will determine how likely you are to actually lose the weight.

This theory originates in the definitions of *expectancy* and *value* developed in the seminal works of psychologists Kurt Lewin and Edward Tolman,[20,21] but the theory was first formally defined by John Atkinson, also a psychologist, in 1957.[22] Since then it has been extremely influential in explaining why people are motivated to change certain of their behaviours but not others.[23]

The second type, the **symbolic predispositions approach,** refers to how symbols and the emotional connections we attach to them shape our attitudes. People develop very strong symbolic predispositions to certain attitudes about their country, religion, ethnic loyalty, and racial prejudice. Two French theorists, Algirdas Julien Greimas and Jacques Fontanille, explored the complicated connections between symbols and emotions in human communication, with a particular focus on literature. One of their book's themes is that passions and the symbols used to represent them are organized in systematic and predictable ways that can be applied outside of the novels studied to general human communication.[24] Let us consider a hypothetical example. Suppose that a group of people presumes the guilt of an Aboriginal man for a theft in Dartmouth, Nova Scotia, not because there is a higher statistical probability that an Aboriginal person would commit this crime but because people in Halifax may have a symbolic predisposition to the attitude that Aboriginal people commit such crimes. The symbolic predispositions operating in this example are racial prejudice toward Aboriginal people and ethnic loyalty to one's own group.

Finally, the **ideology approach** is essentially your worldview. You hold a certain set of ideas, beliefs, and metaphors about the world so deeply that they are no longer subject to your cognitive evaluation. Norman Fairclough, a British communication theorist, states that 'ideologies are representations of aspects of the world which can be shown to contribute to establishing, maintaining and changing social relations of power, domination and exploitation. . . . Moreover, if ideologies are primarily representations, they can nevertheless also be "enacted" in ways of acting socially, and "inculcated" in the identities of social agents.'[25] Fairclough claims that these deeply held ideas are excellent means of maintaining power in a society because they become part of people's subconscious reasoning process and guide their attitudes towards an object. In

expectancy–value approach

An approach that claims that a person's motivation to change his or her behaviour is a combination of what the person believes about something and how he or she feels about it.

ideology approach

An approach that claims that our individual worldviews affect our attitudes.

symbolic predispositions approach

An approach that refers to how symbols and the emotional connections we attach to them shape our attitudes.

other words, they make people take things that they might otherwise question for granted.

For example, say that you are in a pub and someone is harassing you. The person stops only when another patron uses physical force on him or her. If you hold a strong ideological commitment to the idea that 'might makes right,' you may have an automatically positive attitude toward the violent behaviour of the person who helped you. If, however, you hold an ideological commitment to the idea that 'non-violence is the only solution,' you may feel relieved that the harasser is gone but form a negative attitude toward the person who helped you. Ideology will have shaped your attitude, and you probably didn't even know it.

Fairclough points out that ideology is most effective when enough people hold the same ideological commitments, for example, that a certain level of poverty is acceptable for a society. However, this can lead to systematic injustice. People won't agitate to eradicate poverty as long as it is below a certain threshold, so certain citizens—usually the most vulnerable, the sick, and the mentally challenged—will remain poor and hopeless.[26]

Attitudes Structure and Persuasion

How would you use these three approaches to understanding the structure of attitudes in your persuasive communication? In this section, we'll look at how they can be used to build a strategy to address a specific problem.

Let's say that you believe strongly in a clean environment and decide to run a campaign persuading students that they should reduce waste in their daily lives by following the three Rs: reduce, reuse, recycle. From an expectancy–value perspective, you want to create a feeling that changing wasteful behaviour will lead to a desirable outcome for the students. This means that you should explore the beliefs that they hold about waste reduction. You could focus on the negative belief that many recycled objects actually end up in landfills and counter it with facts proving that the vast majority of recycled objects, such as tetra paks, are transformed in recycling plants to assume new life as different objects, such as park benches. If you can also convince your audience that people will respect and like them more for visibly recycling their plastics, then it is far more likely that they will change their behaviours.

From a symbolic approach, you would focus on the affective or emotional associations that unbridled waste conjure up. You can sift through the media to find images of landfills brimming with plastic garbage or islands of plastic clogging up hundreds of square kilometres of ocean. Perhaps you could relate terrifying stories of children who have suffered cognitive and physiological defects because of the chemicals that leach out of plastics as they decay near our water supply. These images may create a negative symbolic disposition toward waste and thus may discourage people from behaving wastefully.

From an ideological perspective, you would attack the fundamental principle underlying a particular ideological perspective. That is to say, you would try to shake the students' deeply and subconsciously held beliefs concerning waste. If students have an ideological commitment to the idea that waste reduction and recycling will create costs for business and thus be bad for the economy, your campaign might emphasize the fact that recycling can be a very good thing for the economy. You could find examples of new high-value–added businesses that would implement the infrastructure for recycling and processing waste.

Applying the concepts described in this section will make you better informed about your audience. You will also be more able to adapt to it, which we will discuss next.

Adapting to the Audience

As the previous section shows, it is important to know as much as possible about your audience when practising persuasive communication. For one thing, you should appeal to the values of your audience whenever possible, even if they are not *your* strongest values. This advice does not mean you should pretend to believe in something; according to our definition of *ethical persuasion,* pretense is against the rules. It does mean, however, that you have to stress those values that are felt most forcefully by the members of your audience.[27]

You should also analyze your audience carefully to predict the type of response you will get. Sometimes you have to pick out one part of your audience—a **target audience**, the subgroup you must persuade in order to reach your goal—and aim your communication mostly at those listeners. Some of your audience members might be so opposed to what you are advocating that you have no hope of reaching them. Still others might already agree with you, so they do not need to be persuaded. Between these two segments of your audience are listeners who might be undecided or uncommitted, and they are the ones you should target in your appeals. Of course, you should never ignore those parts of your audience that do not fit your target. To return to our earlier example, if you were communicating about the health risks of smoking, your target might be the smokers in your class and your main purpose to get them to quit. At the same time, you could convince the non-smokers not to start and to use their influence to help their smoking friends quit.

Audience adaptation—changing the way you say something so that it will be more meaningful or effective for a particular group of listeners—is something that we have a tendency to do naturally. Research suggests, for example, that in everyday conversations what we say to children and the elderly is simpler and more redundant than what we say to other adults.[28] Your communication will tend to be successful if you extend this principle of audience adaptation to your listeners by following three important steps.

Establish Common Ground

It helps to stress the similarities between you and your listeners. This approach shows that you understand them; otherwise, why should they listen to you? Emphasizing your common ground demonstrates that you agree on many things; it should then be easy to settle one disagreement—the one related to the attitude or behaviour you would like them to change.

On the surface, former Republican president George W. Bush didn't have much in common with former Liberal prime minister Jean Chrétien. But in welcoming Chrétien on a visit to Detroit, Bush stressed the values that they shared:

> I appreciate so very much the Prime Minister, Jean Chrétien, for joining us here. He has been a steadfast friend. I really enjoy dealing with him on a personal basis. He's a plain-spoken fellow, with a good sense of humour. Probably won't go too good up here in Canada, but he'd be a great Texan. (Laughter and applause.) . . . Mr Prime Minister,

target audience
That part of an audience that must be influenced in order to achieve a persuasive goal.

Speech is power; speech is to persuade, to convert, to compel. It is to bring another out of his bad sense into your good sense.

Ralph Waldo Emerson

this country is doing everything we can to address a common problem, and you need to know, sir, that we're determined and we're patient and we're resolved to win this war against these terrorists, because, like you, we love freedom. We value our freedoms. We want to leave a legacy of freedom behind for our children and our grandchildren.[29]

Organize According to the Expected Response

It is much easier to get an audience to agree with you if its members have already concurred with you on a previous point. Therefore, in persuasive communication you should arrange your points in such a way that you develop a 'yes' response by getting your listeners into the habit of agreeing with you. For example, if you were communicating in favour of organ donation, you might begin by asking your public if they would like to be able to get a kidney if they needed one. Then you might ask them if they would like to have a major role in curbing tragic and needless deaths. The presumed response to both questions is 'yes'. It is only when you have built a pattern of 'yes' responses that you would ask the audience to sign organ donor cards.

If audience members are already in agreement with you, you can organize your material to reinforce their attitudes quickly and then spend most of your time convincing them to take a specific course of action. If, on the other hand, they are hostile to your ideas, you have to spend more time getting the first 'yes' out of them.

Neutralize Potential Hostility

One of the greatest challenges in audience adaptation occurs when you face an audience hostile to you or your ideas. A hostile audience is one that includes a significant number of members who feel adversely about you, your topic, or the communication situation. The disposition of hostile audience members could range from unfriendly to violent. Two guidelines for handling this type of audience are

1. show that you understand their point of view, and
2. if possible, use appropriate humour.

Hear the other side.

Saint Augustine

You must look into people, as well as at them.

Lord Chesterfield

credibility
The believability of a speaker or other source of information.

Whichever approach you use, your success in persuading an audience also depends on your credibility as a communicator.

Building Credibility as a Communicator

Credibility refers to the believability of a communicator. It is the important aspect of a communicator's ability to persuade. Credibility isn't an objective quality; it is a perception in the minds of the audience. In a course like the one you're taking now, students often wonder how they can build their credibility. After all, by the time the communication assignments have been announced, classmates tend to have well-formed impressions of one another. This shows why it's important to earn a good reputation *before* you communicate, through your class comments and the general attitude you've shown.

It is also possible for credibility to change during a speaking event. In fact, researchers speak in terms of *initial credibility* (your credibility when you first prepare to write or speak), *derived credibility* (the credibility you acquire while writing and speaking), and *terminal credibility* (the credibility you still possess once you have finished speaking or have your writing read). It is not uncommon for a student with low initial credibility to increase his or her credibility while communicating and to finish with much higher terminal credibility.

Without credibility, you won't be able to convince your co-communicators that your ideas are worth accepting, even if your material is outstanding. On the other hand, if you can develop a high degree of credibility in the course of your communication, your listeners or readers may well open up to ideas they wouldn't otherwise accept. Members of an audience form judgments about the credibility of a speaker or writer based on their perception of many characteristics, the most important of which might be called the 'Three Cs' of credibility: *competence, character,* and *charisma.*[30]

Competence

Competence refers to your expertise on your topic. Sometimes this competence can come from personal experience that will lead your audience or co-communicators to regard you as an authority on your subject. If everyone in the audience knows you've earned big profits in the stock market, they will probably take your investment advice seriously. If you say that you lost 25 pounds by following a diet-and-exercise program, most audience members will be likely to respect your opinions on weight loss.

The other way to be seen as competent is to be well prepared for speaking. Communication that is well researched, organized, and presented will greatly increase the listeners' or readers' perceptions of the speaker's competence. Your personal credibility will therefore be enhanced by the credibility of your evidence, including the sources you cite, the examples you choose, the way you present statistics, the quality of your visual aids, and the precision of your language.

Character

The second component of credibility, *character,* reflects the importance of gaining the audience's trust in your honesty and impartiality. You should try to find ways to talk about yourself that demonstrate your integrity. You might describe (without boasting, of course) how much time you spent researching the subject, or you might demonstrate your open-mindedness by explaining how you came to change your opinion following your investigation. For example, if you were speaking out against a proposed tax cut in your community, you might begin this way:

●●●●●

COMMUNICATION ON-SCREEN

The West Wing (1999–2006)

Created by Aaron Sorkin.

The seven seasons of this masterpiece of American political drama document the inner workings of the White House senior staff, as well as the President's decision-making processes. The series centres on the administration of charismatic Democrat Jed Bartlet (Martin Sheen), university professor and former governor of New Hampshire, and the various ethical and moral challenges he must face up to as President of the United States.

Sorkin, himself a passionate liberal who had previously written *The American President,* hit his stride in the show's second season, crafting voluminous scripts in which the President and his unusually articulate staff gave voice to many of his own views. Many characters give superbly eloquent speeches throughout the series, most notably President Bartlett himself. A must-see for political junkies and lovers of pomp and circumstance.

You might say I'm an expert on the municipal services of Hamilton. As a lifelong resident, I owe a debt to its schools and recreation programs. I've been protected by its police and firefighters and served by its hospitals, roads, and sanitation crews.

I'm also a taxpayer who's on a tight budget. When I first heard about the tax cut that's been proposed, I liked the idea. But then I did some in-depth investigation into the possible effects—not just to my tax bill, but to the quality of life of our entire community. I looked into our municipal expenses and into the expenses of similar communities where tax cuts have been mandated by law.

Charisma

The term *charisma* as it is used in the popular press often suggests an almost mystical quality. Even the dictionary definitions tend to be vague, evoking special qualities of leadership without specifying what those qualities might be.

Luckily, communication scholars favour a more down-to-earth definition. For them, charisma in the context of public communication refers to the audience's perception of the communicator's enthusiasm and likeability. Whatever the definition, history and research have shown us that audiences are more likely to be persuaded by a charismatic speaker or writer than by a less charismatic one who delivers the same information.

Enthusiasm is sometimes called 'dynamism' by communication scholars. Your audience's or co-communicator's perception of your enthusiasm will depend less on *what* you communicate than on *how* you communicate it. The non-verbal parts of your speech will show far better than your words that you believe in what you are saying. Is your voice animated and sincere? Do your gestures reflect your enthusiasm? Do your facial expressions and eye contact show that you care about your audience? If you are writing persuasively, the anecdotes you relate, the mythology you evoke, and the narrative structure you choose all contribute to being persuasive.

You can boost your likeability by showing that you like and respect your audience. Insincere flattery will probably backfire, but if you can find a way to give your listeners a genuine compliment, they'll be more receptive to your ideas.

Building your credibility by recognizing the roles of competence, character, and charisma is an important part of your persuasive strategy. When combined with a careful consideration of audience adaptation, persuasive structure, and persuasive purpose, it will enable you to formulate the most effective strategy possible.

Understanding Communication Technology

The Power of Authority: The Milgram Experiments

In 1963, Stanley Milgram, an assistant professor of psychology at Yale, published his infamous experiment on obedience to authority. Its conclusion was that most ordinary people were willing to administer what they believed to be painful, even dangerous, electric shocks to innocent people if a man in a white lab coat told them to.

For the first time in four decades, a researcher has repeated the Milgram experiment to find out whether, after all we have learned in the last 45 years, Americans are still as willing to inflict pain out of blind obedience.

The Milgram experiment was carried out in the shadow of the Holocaust. The trial of Adolf Eichmann had the world wondering how the Nazis were able to persuade so many ordinary Germans to participate in the murder of innocents. Professor Milgram devised a clever way of testing, in a laboratory setting, man's (and woman's) willingness to do evil.

The participants—ordinary residents of New Haven—were told they were participating in a study of the effect of punishment on learning. A 'learner' was strapped in a chair in an adjacent room, and electrodes were attached to the learner's arm. The participant was told to read test questions, and to administer a shock when the learner gave the wrong answer.

The shocks were not real. But the participants were told they were—and instructed to increase the voltage with every wrong answer. At 150 volts, the participant could hear the learner cry in protest, complain of heart pain, and ask to be released from the study. After 330 volts, the learner made no noise at all, suggesting he was no longer capable of responding. Through it all, the scientist in the room kept telling the participant to ignore the protests—or the unsettling silence—and administer an increasingly large shock for each wrong answer or non-answer.

The Milgram experiment's startling result—as anyone who has taken a college psychology course knows—was that ordinary people were willing to administer a lot of pain to innocent strangers if an authority figure instructed them to do so. More than 80 per cent of participants continued after administering the 150-volt shock, and 65 per cent went all the way up to 450 volts.

Jerry Burger of Santa Clara University replicated the experiment and has now published his findings in *American Psychologist*. He made one slight change in the protocol, in deference to ethical standards developed since 1963. He stopped when a participant believed he had administered a 150-volt shock. (He also screened out people familiar with the original experiment.)

Professor Burger's results were nearly identical to Professor Milgram's. Seventy per cent of his participants administered the 150-volt shock and had to be stopped. That is less than in the original experiment, but not enough to be significant.

Much has changed since 1963. The civil rights and anti-war movements taught Americans to question authority. Institutions that were once accorded great deference—including the government and the military—are now eyed warily. Yet it appears that ordinary Americans are about as willing to blindly follow orders to inflict pain on an innocent stranger as they were four decades ago.

Professor Burger was not surprised. He believes that the mindset of the individual participant—including cultural influences—is less important than the 'situational features' that Professor Milgram shrewdly built into his experiment. These include having the authority figure take responsibility for the decision to administer the shock, and having the participant increase the voltage gradually. It is hard to say no to administering a 195-volt shock when you have just given a 180-volt shock.

The results of both experiments pose a challenge. If this is how most people behave, how do we prevent more Holocausts, Abu Ghraibs, and other examples of wanton cruelty? Part of the answer, Professor Burger argues, is teaching people about the experiment so they will know to be on guard against these tendencies, in themselves and others.

An instructor at West Point contacted Professor Burger to say that she was teaching her students about his findings. She had the right idea—and the right audience. The findings of these two experiments should be part of the basic training for soldiers, police officers, jailers, and anyone else whose position gives them the power to inflict abuse on others.

—Adam Cohen, *Editorial Observer*, 29 December 2008

Interpersonal Persuasion

cognitive dissonance
The tension caused by holding two conflicting thoughts simultaneously.

door-in-the-face
A persuasion technique in which a persuader makes a large, outrageous first request which is almost certainly to be denied followed by a smaller request which seems more 'reasonable' in the context of the first request.

foot-in-the-door
A persuasion technique based on the idea that if a persuader can overcome initial resistance, he or she can also overcome any other impediments to persuading his or her audience.

interpersonal persuasion
An area of research concerned with how people gain compliance from other people.

low-balling
A persuasion technique in which the persuader makes a first, reasonable request and, once it has been accepted, increases the cost of the transaction.

social exchange
A persuasion technique in which the persuader presents the target person with a material or psychological gift and, in exchange, is granted a request.

Interpersonal persuasion is an area of research concerned with how people gain compliance from other people. That is to say, it is the study of the technique that people use in marketing, sales, or social psychology to persuade others to accept a product or an idea or to change their behaviours. In this section, we will examine several basic compliance-gaining techniques.

Foot-in-the-Door

This is a classic persuasion technique that has been practised since the dawn of time. It is based on the belief that if a persuader can just overcome initial resistance, that is, 'get a **foot-in-the-door**', he or she can also overcome any impediments to the sale or persuasive proposition they are offering. Studies have shown that this approach is effective—if a persuader can convince someone to comply to a small request, then it is much easier to get that person to comply to another, much larger request.[31] This is the reason that some people beg their dates for 'just a little kiss' hoping that it will lead to more. Or a friend will ask to borrow your laptop 'just to check one e-mail' and, once you agree, follow up with a second request to reply to two 'really important' e-mails. Chances are you'll say 'yes' again. Your friend has just used the foot-in-the-door technique to commandeer your computer!

Door-in-the-Face

This technique is the inverse of the foot-in-the-door. In the **door-in-the-face** method, the persuader starts by making a large, outrageous first request which is almost certainly to be denied and then follows it up with a second, smaller request which seems more 'reasonable' in the context of the first one. Robert B. Cialdini and colleagues designed an experiment where participants were asked to counsel juvenile delinquents for two years. All refused. However, 50 per cent of them agreed to a second request to chaperone juvenile delinquents on a trip to the zoo.[32]

Social Exchange

In **social exchange** compliance-gaining the persuader presents the target person with a material or psychological gift. When the persuader later approaches the target person with a request, he or she complies. Social exchange theory explains why lobbyists attempt to gain favour with a politician by giving gifts. This is why politicians, professors, and public servants are very limited in what kinds of contributions they can accept from people who stand to gain something from them.

Low-Balling

In **low-balling**, the persuader makes a first, reasonable request that the target person accepts. The persuader then increases the cost of the transaction. Psychologically, once a person has complied to an earlier request, he or she experiences **cognitive dissonance** (see the box on p. 427) when faced with the possibility of having to walk away from a commitment; therefore, the target person is likely to accept the second, more costly request. The challenge in this compliance-gaining technique is for the persuader to avoid making the second

Cognitive Dissonance

Run by David Straker, ChangingMinds.org is one of the leading international websites for cataloguing and describing the techniques and theories of persuasion. Checking it regularly or signing up to David Straker's Twitter feed (twitter.com/changingminds) is a good idea for students interested in keeping abreast of the latest international developments in persuasion theory and practice.

Description

This is the feeling of uncomfortable tension which comes from holding two conflicting thoughts in the mind at the same time.

Dissonance increases with

- the importance of the subject to us;
- how strongly the dissonant thoughts conflict; and
- our inability to rationalize and explain away the conflict.

Dissonance is often strong when we believe something about ourselves and then do something against that belief. If I believe I am good but do something bad, then the discomfort I feel as a result is cognitive dissonance.

Cognitive dissonance is a very powerful motivator which will often lead us to change one or other of the conflicting belief or action. The discomfort often feels like a tension between the two opposing thoughts. To release the tension we can take one of three actions:

- change our behaviour;
- justify our behaviour by changing the conflicting cognition; or
- justify our behaviour by adding new cognitions.

Dissonance is most powerful when it is about our self-image. Feelings of foolishness, immorality, and so on (including internal projections during decision-making) are dissonance in action.

If an action has been completed and cannot be undone, then the after-the-fact dissonance compels us to change our beliefs. If beliefs are moved, then the dissonance appears during decision-making, forcing us to take actions we would not have taken before.

Cognitive dissonance appears in virtually all evaluations and decisions and is the central mechanism by which we experience new differences in the world. When we see other people behave differently to our images of them, when we hold any conflicting thoughts, we experience dissonance.

Dissonance increases with the importance and impact of the decision, along with the difficulty of reversing it. Discomfort about making the wrong choice of car is bigger than when choosing a lamp.

. . .

Research

[Leon] Festinger first developed this theory in the 1950s to explain how members of a cult who were persuaded by their leader, a certain Mrs Keech, that the earth was going to be destroyed on 21 December and that they alone were going to be rescued by aliens, actually *increased* their commitment to the cult when this did not happen (Festinger himself had infiltrated the cult, and would have been very surprised to meet little green men).[1] The dissonance of the thought of being so stupid was so great that instead they revised their beliefs to meet with obvious facts: that the aliens had, through their concern for the cult, saved the world instead.

In a more mundane experiment, Festinger and [James M.] Carlsmith got students to lie about a boring task. Those who were paid $1 for the task felt uncomfortable lying.[2]

Example

Smokers find all kinds of reasons to explain away their unhealthy habit. The alternative is to feel a great deal of dissonance.

So what?

Using it Cognitive dissonance is central to many forms of persuasion to change beliefs, values, attitudes, and behaviours. The tension can be injected suddenly or allowed to build up over time. People can be moved in many small jumps or one large one.

Defending When you start feeling uncomfortable, stop and see if you can find the inner conflict. Then notice how that came about. If it was somebody else who put that conflict there, you can decide not to play any more with them.

[1] L. Festinger, *A Theory of Cognitive Dissonance* (Stanford, CA: Stanford University Press, 1957).
[2] L. Festinger and J.M. Carlsmith, 'Cognitive Consequences of Forced Compliance', *Journal of Abnormal and Social Psychology* 58 (1959): 203–11.

—From *changingminds.org/explanations/theories/cognitive_dissonance.htm*

fear-then-relief
A persuasion technique in which the persuader causes the target person to feel fear and then, after a short period of time, replaces the fear-causing threat with a gesture of kindness.

that's-not-all
A persuasion technique in which the persuader presents a proposition and a cost, followed by a gift.

request seem outrageous. For example, when a person buys a car, he or she is initially offered a low price. However, when the person goes to sign the deal, he or she is offered additional packages such as extra warranties, undercoating, rust-proofing, etc. Many people, feeling that they have already got a 'great deal' on the car, will make these impulsive purchases, which are highly profitable and significantly raise the dealership's margins on the auto purchase significantly.

That's-Not-All

The **that's-not-all** technique involves the persuader presenting a proposition and a cost without allowing the buyer to respond immediately. After a few seconds of mulling the cost over, the target person is presented with a gift to 'sweeten the deal'. This technique works because of the reciprocity principle—if someone does you a favour, you feel obliged to do one for them. Many of us have experienced this while watching television commercials which offer, for example, a steak knife set for a certain price. After a few minutes, the pitch person will say 'But that's not all—we are also offering you this set of paring knives and this bread cutter at NO ADDITIONAL COST.' The added items convince many people to make the purchase.

Fear-Then-Relief

Fear-then-relief technique occurs when the persuader causes the target person to feel fear and, after a short period of time, replaces the fear-causing threat with a gesture of kindness. In the momentary relief felt at the sudden change in emotions, the target person is more likely to comply. This technique is used by teachers when they tell a student 'You know you are in danger of failing this course.' And, after the fear of failure sinks in, 'But if you stay for study group after school, you will pass.' Chances are the student will agree to stay for the study period. Fear-then-relief is also used in the interrogation of suspects by police or military officers, who put the subject in a state of extreme anxiety and fear in the interrogation room and then relieve that fear. This is the origin of the good cop–bad cop routine that the police often use.

Persuasive Professional Writing: An Introduction Special Section by Philip Savage

There is no getting around it: writing is both essential and, as Gene Fowler knew, 'bloody' hard. However, good writing is key to success as a professional communicator—even in a multimedia era that many say is no longer dependent upon the written word. Many of the third- and fourth-year students I supervise in professional communication internships each year say the same thing in their first weeks of placement. Whether doing web design, writing speeches for politicians, or doing publicity, the basic professional writing skills they learned at university are the most challenging and yet useful parts of their professional training.

Good writing is a cornerstone of being a good communicator. As Heather Pullen, manager of public relations for Hamilton Health Sciences has said, 'The most essential skill for a professional communicator is to be a good, clear, quick writer.' Also, understanding the mechanics of professional writing will enable you to be a more critical participant in our message-saturated culture. By describing practical approaches to getting started in your own writing, this section will give you the basic tools you need to be an effective written communicator in most corporate, not-for-profit, government, or community settings.

The ability to write an effective news release, op-ed, blog, or briefing note can be the difference between success and failure for a campaign or a cause that you are involved with. Whether it is a community pool in your neighbourhood that you want kept open or a campaign for equal pay for woman employees in your workplace, knowing the professional writing skills in this chapter will be an ace in your pocket. Before describing these four forms of professional writing, we discuss two considerations about the practicality of planning writing: purpose and process.

The Purpose of Writing

Writing, whether creative, journalistic, or professional, is a rhetorical act that aims to motivate audiences to change beliefs, attitudes, or behaviour. Rhetoric as commonly understood 'gets bad press'—people associate rhetoric, and professional communication, with manipulation. But we are not talking about improving your 'empty rhetoric' here. Rhetoric in that sense is both unethical and because of that, ineffective over the long term.

I like to quote early broadcast journalist Edward R. Murrow, whose work at CBS exposed the anti-communist fear mongering of Senator Joseph McCarthy in the 1950s. That period and Murrow's integrity are captured in the 2005 George Clooney film *Good Night* and *Good Luck* and especially in Murrow's quote:

> To be persuasive, we must be believable; to be believable we must be credible; to be credible, we must be truthful.

There can be no real change if truth is not at your writing's core. If nothing else this section and indeed this entire book speaks to the need for relationships of trust in your communication.

To be clear about ethical and effective communication you should have two things foremost in your mind as you write: *purpose* and *audience*. Increasingly in an information-overloaded world we require a third dimension, which also is ethically important: *efficiency*. With that in mind, I suggest three questions to ask as you start to write, provided in Table 11.2.[33]

I suggest you 'PAE-up' early. If you don't, you will pay later—with unclear goals you will write many drafts as you try to figure out the answers to what you want to say, to whom and in what form. And if the confusion on any of the three dimensions carries through into the writing, you not only waste the intended audience's time but also add 'noise'

TABLE 11.2 Planning to Write

P	Purpose – What is the purpose of what I write?
A	Audience – Who is the audience for what I write?
E	Efficiency – How can I write it without wasting time?

to the communication. For example, during my professional career (especially at the CBC) I have written applications to the CRTC for new radio station licences.[34] When I wrote these applications I established my PAE goals:

1. Purpose: Our goal is to inform the CRTC about listener service problems and persuade them that the new CBC FM or digital satellite station would best provide the programming the public wanted;

2. Audience: We did not, as you might think, talk primarily to actual radio and TV audiences about our plans. In the report writing we addressed the six to eight individual CRTC commissioners who would sit in judgment at the regulatory hearing and make the decision; and

3. Efficiency: We know that CRTC commissioners have a lot of applications and other hearings. So we made our writing as factual and as concise as possible, giving them the information they needed to justify their decision.

The Process of Writing

Being clear about purpose, audience, and efficiency is great, but you still have to write something. After clarifying goals, it is tempting to go right to the final written piece. However, it is important to both outline and then draft your work before 'polishing the gem' in a final revision or edit. The process includes four steps (see Table 11.3).

Pre-writing includes the PAE sections we discussed with a couple of additions: thinking about the best channel for the writing (perhaps a news release versus a report); and some level of research, that is, collecting new information you need to 'tell the story'.

Outlining is the process of arranging your information, often by using point form or sub-phrases, just before the actual drafting in order to achieve clarity and impact. There are a number of ways to do this. For instance, you might outline the ideas sequentially or chronologically. You might also use a cause-and-effect approach—organizing the various situations and how they led to certain outcomes. Another way is the problem/options/solutions (POS) approach, where you identify a problem facing the group, describe the options for dealing with it (as well as the benefits and costs of each option), and then recommend a preferred solution. Finally, one can always use the journalistic practice of identifying the five Ws (Who, What, When, Where, and Why). This method works well for journalist-type writing, such as news releases. Alternatively, you can mix some of these approaches. For example, when I use the POS approach in my outlines, I tend to make sure that I cover the five Ws as well.[35]

Drafting is when you first begin to write out your sentences. In a way it is 'wrapping sentences around' the outline or framework of your list of ideas and concepts. However, there is a temptation as you start writing full sentences and paragraphs to fine-tune the wording as you go. Don't strive for perfection at this point; keep writing without second-guessing yourself. An extreme form of this practice is known as 'free-writing'. In a quiet and undisturbed setting, write without stopping for 5 to 20 minutes on the subject. Do not worry about grammar, punctuation, fact checking, correct quotes, etc., but try to empty your mind on the subject—almost as a stream of consciousness.[36]

TABLE 11.3 Writing in Four Stages

1. Pre-writing	Doing PAE, plus channel-selection and research.
2. Outlining	Arranging ideas for clarity and impact (e.g., five Ws).
3. Drafting	Writing meaningful words and sentences (e.g., 'free-writing').
4. Editing	Polishing words and sentences (revising then proofreading).

Whether you use free-writing or other drafting approaches, here are a few tips just to keep you writing in the drafting stage (Fowler's bloodletting proper):

1. **Start early.** If you can, start tough writing assignments early in the day (or even days before) the piece is due, avoiding the stress of immediate deadlines.
2. **Turn off the computer (or at least the WiFi connection).** Write about what you know without distractions. Don't stop to check Wikipedia or Google (or worse, friend updates on Facebook!).
3. **Talk it out.** If writing fails you, talk with a friend or colleague ('What do you think about this?' or 'What if I put it like this?'). Or, talk to yourself out loud. Some writers talk into a tape/laptop recorder and then listen back.
4. **Skip around.** If you get a mental block dealing with one section, move to another idea or concept.
5. **Close the door.** Find a time and place to write without distractions.
6. **Take a break.** When it all gets too much, get a breath of fresh air. But be disciplined (e.g., one five-minute break after each hour of writing).

Editing actually has two equally important stages: revising and the final edit. Revising means reviewing your draft to determine if things are missing, repeated, illogical, or lacking in evidence or explanation. Go back to your originally stated goals and audience needs and see if what you drafted actually says what you intended to say to that particular person or group. Often the most productive revising is eliminating unnecessary words and phrases (keeping the goal of efficiency uppermost). A CBC journalist once told me that he always goes over his drafts and removes every adjective and adverb in his first revision. It forces him to look closely at the main construction of his story without 'filler' words and creates a more direct style. He then reads the stripped-down draft and reinserts only the adjectives and adverbs required for comprehension. This trick of the trade also forces you to re-read your work with fresh eyes. Or better yet, have another person read what you have written (new, fresher eyes).[37]

The end stage of the editing is the proofread (or final edit) to ensure that your writing not only conforms to standards of good English—proper spelling, punctuation, and grammar—but also that it is stylistically appropriate.[38]

Four Major Professional Writing Forms

News Releases

The **news release** (historically, press release) is a 'pseudo' news story written in the third-person that provides a reporter or editor with a newsworthy description of a particular person, event, service, or product, often on one single-spaced page of print. News releases are usually time-dependent; they are produced mindful of the various media news cycles (i.e., 'old news is no news').

A common mistake is to think that the audience for the news release is the general public. In fact, the rhetorical purpose is to provide reporters with a professionally and efficiently written package of information with a sharp story angle so that they can write a story in their newspaper or broadcast program or on their website. This means 'getting into the head' of a journalist and realizing that they have a radar for 'puffery, flackery, and hyperbole'.

News releases can be distributed to media outlets via e-mail or social media (usually with a link to the host organization's website) and, depending upon your market, additionally faxed or couriered (the latter if they are part of a full 'press kit' with backgrounders, video, or other physical material, such as product samples).

news release

A document that provides a reporter or editor with a newsworthy description of a particular person, event, service, or product.

TABLE 11.4 News Release Components: A Checklist for Inclusion

- Letterhead, Name, Address, Phone Number, Web Address
- NEWS RELEASE in all caps
- Contact Person's Name (at top or bottom)
- Immediate Release or Release Date
- HEADLINE or TITLE in **boldface** or ALL CAPS
- First paragraph: Date/City, then the five Ws
- Additional Paragraphs: Interesting text and quotes as appropriate
- Final Paragraph: Summary
- Boilerplate
- Information on further contacts, people to talk to
- Basic Font, Page Numbers, and ### or -30- (to indicate end of text)
- Action Plan/Calendar/Photos/Videos/Samples (if necessary)

My colleague, Jane Christmas, manager of public and media relations at McMaster University, refers to the 'humble yet dynamic news release'. She points out that the basic form of the news release has existed for over 100 years—since the days of circus showman and promoter P.T. Barnham in the late nineteenth century and the father of public relations, Edward T. Bernays, in the early twentieth century. But as Jane says, the news release remains the 'workhorse for the PR industry'. At the base of each—regardless of the multimedia complexity now possible—is writing that uses the key components listed in Table 11.4. An example of a real news release is on page 433.

In this example there is a clear headline about a specific event that a reporter or editor could use. In the opening paragraph the five Ws are covered factually in terms of the 'who' (Professors Sammon and Bontis), 'what' (two of six OCUFA awards for teaching), 'when' (announced 3 September 2009), 'where' (in Ontario, with award presentation in Toronto discussed in later paragraphs), and why (for outstanding university teaching, again with more specifics in later paragraphs). Additional paragraphs make good use of quotes from the awarding body and the two professors, which give background and colour on the professors' commitment to teaching. The penultimate paragraph enlarges on the other recipients and gives specifics about the upcoming award presentation, whereas the final paragraph is a 'boilerplate' or generic description of the organization providing the news release, in this case McMaster University.

Op-eds

An **op-ed** is a mini-essay that appears opposite the editorial page in newspapers as a stand-alone feature—historically in print editions but now also on media websites. Originally serving as a kind of extended letter to the editor, op-eds share some characteristics of journalistic columns (e.g., those written by a Jeffrey Simpson in *The Globe and Mail* or by Rex Murphy on CBC's *The National*). An expert or a person engaged directly in specific issues or circumstances usually writes them. If timely and cogent, op-eds can stand out from the rest of the media content in a publication, broadcast, or web page, and may have a significant impact.[39]

Most op-eds run 500 to 750 words long. Like any article, they need to be factual and contain the five Ws. But they do not have to provide an impartial and fully balanced perspective, although they tend to be more persuasive if they acknowledge other points of view. For university students they seem, more than other professional writing formats, quite similar to a traditional short essay. Table 11.5 on page 434 lists the main features of op-eds. Keep

1280 Main Street West, Hamilton, Ontario L8S 4L8, 905-525-9140, mcmaster.ca

NEWS RELEASE

MCMASTER PROFS WIN ONTARIO'S TOP TEACHING AWARD

Hamilton, ON. 3 September 2009 –Two McMaster University professors have been chosen as outstanding university teachers. Sheila Sammon, associate professor of social work, and Nick Bontis, associate professor of business, were two of six professors selected by 15,000 peers across the province in the Ontario Confederation of University Faculty Association (OCUFA) Awards.

'OCUFA's Awards Committee was impressed with Professor Sammon's commitment to student engagement through field practice, class exercise, and by pushing the boundaries of teaching and learning,' said OCUFA President Mark Langer. 'As well, it was extremely impressed by Professor Bontis's innovative thinking and creative teaching. He truly cares about his classes and the success of his students.'

For Sammon, teaching is the best job in the world. 'I have the opportunity to engage with bright minds, to encourage critical thinking, to watch people develop their ideas and life goals, and to collaborate with others,' she says. 'It is particularly important in today's academic environment to focus on the relationships with and between learners. Larger classes, a more diverse student population, increased reliance on technology, shrinking resources for education, and students who are financially stretched require university educators to carefully consider how they teach and why they teach.'

In addition to being a prolific researcher and favourite teacher in the DeGroote School of Business, Bontis is director of the undergraduate program and works tirelessly to ensure the student experience is a positive one. Earlier this year he won the 3M National Teaching Fellow, and the Ontario Undergraduate Student Alliance Top Professor Award.

'I feel blessed to win an award for what I love to do,' says Bontis. 'With each award, my role as a professor at DeGroote becomes emboldened. Students and fellow colleagues significantly increase their expectations of me, and it's my objective to continually over-deliver.'

Sammon and Bontis will each receive a 2008–2009 OCUFA teaching award at a ceremony at the Fairmont-Royal York Hotel in Toronto on 3 October. The four other teaching award recipients are Clare Hasenkampf (University of Toronto), Lorne Sosin (University of Toronto), Gordon Stubley (University of Waterloo), and Cameron Tsujita (University of Western Ontario).

McMaster University, one of four Canadian universities listed among the Top 100 universities in the world, is committed to discovery and learning in teaching, research, and scholarship. It has a student population of 23,000 and more than 135,000 alumni in 128 countries.

For more information, please contact:
Jane Christmas
Manager, Public & Media Relations
McMaster University
905-525-9140 ext. 27988
chrisja@mcmaster.ca

TABLE 11.5 Distinguishing Features of Op-Eds

Timely	Write about a current issue and event.
	No one wants to hear about how Neanderthals could make better decisions in an ice age past. But if you can argue that current government planning follows the same poor neanderthal process and will lead to global warming, do so.
Lively and Strong	New and provocative arguments are good, and even better if strongly and passionately argued.
	You want this kind of reaction from editors and readers: 'Wow! Did you see that unusual perspective on global warming?'
Not Promotional	While you may want to use an op-ed to further your organization (or one of its products or services), this is not the place for it. Build credibility about the range of insights and solutions you have to share.
Right Medium and Right Audience	Choose the media or website that fits the specific policy or decision-making venue you are interested in.
	For an argument against sewage waste flowing into Halifax Harbour, an op-ed in the Halifax *Chronicle Herald* may be most appropriate. However, if you are trying to influence waste-treatment standards set by the federal government, aim for policy-makers and politicians at the federal level by writing in *The Globe and Mail*.
Best Author	As a professional communicator—rather than a subject expert— you probably will not write your own op-eds but would identify the best person in the organization to be the spokesperson for that point of view. However, you may help the appropriate person write the piece.
	If your local environmental organization is against the sewage dumping in Halifax Harbour, but your director has been clearly associated with only one political party, choose a more independent board member who can express similar views.

in mind when reading the 'Best Author' entry that organizations will sometimes submit unsolicited op-eds and sometimes—especially if the organization or its leader is well known by media—they will be invited to comment on a topical issue. In each case the author and those helping to craft the piece need to study the submission criteria of the newspaper, website, or other media outlet.

In July 2005 David Shipley, editor of the op-ed page in *The New York Times*, published some useful tips for authors and explained the process by which he would help edit contributors' articles.[40] A McGill university site published to help its faculty experts gives this advice:

> The style of an op-ed should be lively and provocative, with a clear message and a transparent structure. Reading an op-ed should not be hard work for the general public. Both boilerplate jargon and hyperbolic, righteous indignation should be avoided; strong, colorful language and a memorable phrase or two will catch the editor's attention and lend support to the argument presented. The person in charge of the op-ed page looks for clarity, brevity and newsworthiness, as well as controversy. Intelligent, contrarian views expressed in a unique voice tend to receive a positive response.[41]

Blogs

In a sense, a blog is a series of personal mini-essays (usually about 250 words per entry). Unlike op-eds, blogs are not professionally edited and are not predominantly found in

TABLE 11.6 Blog Characteristics

Personal Commentary	Providing ongoing perspective and views by a single author on a particular topic. Originally some were simply online diaries but were elevated to experts covering politics, economics, or social issues.
Multimedia	A strength of the Web placement is the ability to combine text, images, video, audio, and most important, links to other online media that support or enlarge the insight provided.
Interactive	Most blogs provide a space for readers to leave comments or further the range of discussion with their own links to related content.

traditional media outlets or their websites. However, media outlets will house or link to blogs by their own reporters or outside experts. In addition, a number of companies, public agencies, and not-for profit organizations have their own blogs. In fact, many young professional communicators actually find that writing, managing, or even starting from scratch the organizational blog is a key entry point into professional writing.

The writing of blogs shares some of the basic aspects of writing the op-ed (see Table 11.6), but it is even more concise and is subject to the multimedia audiences' desire for an easy, quicker read. Yet like an op-ed, a good blog is valued for having a unique, passionate, and individual perspective.

Bloggers themselves are often keen to provide tips on how to blog better. The 10 tips in Table 11.7 are adapted from advice that fellow bloggers posted on the Problogger site almost five years ago, still one of the most viewed and valued blogs on blogging.

Briefing Notes

A **briefing note** is typically a 500- to 750-word document written in a strictly formatted structure designed to inform leaders within an organization about issues that require decisions. They developed—particularly in Canada—in the political and public service where Crown ministers at the federal or provincial level were required to make policy decisions or respond to questions on a specific topic. Often a leader is faced with dozens or even hundreds of issues to confront and decide upon daily, thus requiring professional written documents with an emphasis on efficiency and clarity.

briefing note

A document written in a strictly formatted structure designed to inform leaders about issues that require decisions.

TABLE 11.7 Problogger Top 10 Tips

1. Make your opinion known.
2. Link like crazy.
3. Write less – 250 words is enough.
4. Make headlines snappy.
5. Write with passion.
6. Include bullet point lists.
7. Edit your post.
8. Make your posts easy to scan.
9. Be consistent with your style.
10. Litter the post with keywords..

Source: Adapted from problogger.net/archives/2005/12/30/tens-tips-for-writing-a-blog-post/. Accessed 17 May 2010.

TABLE 11.8 Briefing Note Structure

Header	Identify the recipient, author, date, and subject (similar to the header in an inter-office memo).
Issue	One to two sentences with concise statement of the issue or problem. No more than one paragraph.
Background	Two to four paragraphs with relevant information to understand the current situation. Usually includes some history, and in policy environments, the current legislation and policies.
Considerations	Two to four paragraphs showing the keys facts, considerations, and developments that are relevant to the decision to be made.
Options	One to two paragraphs (often bulleted) with observations about the key two to three possible courses of action (often with a summary of cost and benefits included).
Recommendation	One to two paragraphs with a clear recommendation flowing from the background and options (similar to a report's executive summary).

Outside government, briefing notes have spread as a particularly useful professional writing tool to help decision-makers in companies and not-for-profit organizations. These leaders also welcome tightly written communication which distills complex information into short, clear, and well-structured documents and provides recommendations on how to act.

Table 11.8 shows the structure of the briefing note. I use this particular format extensively in the Media Law and Policy course that I teach at McMaster University. My experience is that even students who do not continue in law add it to their portfolio of key writing instruments because of its action-oriented style. A number of public policy courses at Canadian universities, particularly at the graduate level, provide details on the background and value of briefing notes on their websites. I find the University of Victoria's (web.uvic.ca/~sdoyle/E302/Notes/WritingBriefingNotes.html) particularly useful.

The briefing note example on page 437 was prepared by Erin Baxter (who completed my class in 2009 and is currently an MA student in the McMaster University Graduate Program in Communication and New Media).

Skill with briefing notes marks the professional communicator as particularly strategic in their thinking and communication and as analytic 'big thinkers' within an organization. It also allows professional communicators to be integral in the communication of other experts—financial, engineering, policy—who interact with various decision-makers both within and outside the organization. That was my experience writing briefing notes at the CBC through the 1990s and 2000s, in areas as diverse as CRTC licence applications, engineering environmental assessments, network branding, and new programming strategies.

Minister of Canadian Heritage and Official Languages
Ministry of Canadian Heritage

FOR ACTION
Erin Baxter, Student Liason   N06-54317
McMaster University
16 March 2009

Proposal for a two-year pilot internship program for accepted upper-year Canadian
<u>university students studying within accredited Journalism or Communication programs.</u>

ISSUE
The current recession is challenging broadcasters to work within lower budgets, thus, limiting opportunities for Canadian university students to couple theory with practicum through
internships. Potential new CRTC initiatives to increase Canadian Content quotas and the
secure future of broadcasting suggest that Canadian journalistic talent must be cultivated.

BACKGROUND
The Canadian Broadcasting Act sets that the mandate of the Canadian Broadcasting
system is to strengthen the holistic fabric of Canada, promote the ongoing development of Canadian expression, and serve the Canadian public through programming
and employment initiatives. In order to provide this Canadian programming, Canadian
broadcasters must have educated Canadian voices to present viewers with culturally
relevant information. Many of these voices can be found in accredited Canadian universities, learning the theoretical side of broadcast production. These students moving
towards careers in Canadian journalism are of great value to the future of broadcasting
and, therefore, governmental funding is needed to fulfill the Broadcasting Act mandate
to serve these Canadian students with employment initiatives and provide a selection
of eligible students with the practicum experience needed to prepare them for a career
in Canadian journalism.

The CRTC is currently revisiting their decision to exempt new media from Canadian
content regulations outlined in the Broadcasting Act. While a 1999 CRTC Public Notice
stated that the Commission would not regulate new media under the Broadcasting
Act, Canada's cultural sector is concerned about the lack of Canadian material on the
World Wide Web and is calling the CRTC to intervene and establish regulations to ensure Canadian voices are available to Canadians. And as a 2006 report on 'The Future
Environment Facing the Canadian Broadcasting System' discovered, the amount of available Canadian content on the Internet is also a concern for the new 'broadband generation'. Their concern is understandable as 60 per cent of these up-and-coming 12- to
29-year-olds describe the Internet as their medium of choice, and while it is predicted
that upcoming generations will not do away with traditional video content, they will demand this material be available online on a 'time-and-place shifted basis'. Thus, the need
for astute Canadian journalists able to produce such online Canadian content, atop the
60 per cent Canadian content regulations for private and public television broadcasters,
is bound to grow consistently in years to come.

Major broadcasters have recently had to adjust budgets due to a decline in advertising revenues. The CBC, having received $1.1 billion from the Canadian government is struggling to spread their budget for this year and discovering that jobs and programs cannot be sustained with estimated advertising revenue losses of up to $100 million. As a result, the broadcaster is challenged to operate with fewer employees. These budget cuts, which are being felt by other broadcasters including CTVglobemedia and CanWest Global, leave little opportunity for mentorship training as required by productive internships. Consequently, university journalism and communications students seeking to enter into Canadian journalism are left with an uneven balance of theory over practicum and may seek further training outside Canada.

CONSIDERATIONS

In the past, the Ministry of Canadian Heritage and the Canadian Heritage Portfolio have aided Canadian talent and content across the nation through the Canadian Content Development (CCD) as defined in CRTC Public Notice 2006-158, Commercial Radio Policy. The Ministry of Heritage has also been attentive to students seeking employment opportunities through the initiative Young Canada Works (YCW). YCW offers summer employment and internships to students and recent graduates to 'put their skills to the test, build career equity'. Thus, with this precedent of concern for post-secondary graduates, along with the need for Canadian journalists, a government-supplemented internship program will (1) provide opportunities for Canadian students to nurture their journalistic skills, (2) help to facilitate a smooth transition from university to the workplace for Canadian journalism and communication graduates, thereby keeping Canadian talent in Canada, (3) contribute to increasing quality Canadian content available to broadcasters, and, finally, (4) secure a future of informed journalism for future generations.

The federal government already funds an apprenticeship program similar to this internship initiative entitled the Apprenticeship Incentive Grant, which allocates $100 million per year to encourage students aiming for a career in the trades. While the federal government is a large supporter of post-secondary education, providing $9.7 billion in support during the 2008–09 year, a program similar to the Apprenticeship Incentive Grant for university students desiring to contribute to the valuable Canadian journalistic landscape is equally necessary.

RECOMMENDATION

In response to the need for additional Canadian content and the need to cultivate and nurture Canadian
university students the Ministry of Heritage has multiple options:

— Take no action in the development of university students pursuing careers in Canadian journalism and leave the development of this field to post-graduate and college programs that will provide students with the practicum experience this internship initiative is designed to facilitate.
— Reallocate CDD funding to develop journalism students through an alternative bursary program without addressing the need for practicum.
— Implement a two-year pilot program to provide aid to Canadian universities training potential Canadian journalists by funding an enhanced system of internships.

This $1.5 million per year proposal would supplement the cost of 100 Canadian journalism and communication internships. The program would require $15,000 per student for each year of enrolment in the internship, which would be given to the university to cover the administrative costs and provide a minimum $10,000 honorarium to the host broadcaster.

While all of the above suggestions are viable, the third recommendation is most constructive and thus, most strongly suggested as it seeks long-term benefits for a range of parties, including students, universities, as well as current and future broadcasters for a comparably low economic cost. Furthermore, while this proposal is addressed to the Ministry of Heritage, the issue of journalism internships conveniently falls under the jurisdiction of several departments and agencies and, therefore, the weight of the proposed $1.5 million annual budget could be lightened through the co-operative assistance of Human Resources and Skills Development Canada, the CTF, and the CRTC, among others.

Erin E. Baxter

Contacts:
Erin Baxter, 905-525-9140
Department of Communication Studies and Multimedia
Philip Savage, 905-525-9140
Department of Communication Studies and Multimedia

Summary

Persuasion is central to our lives and is something that we practise almost every day. This chapter began by explaining that persuasion is the process of motivating someone, through communication and relationship-building, to change attitudes, beliefs, values, or behaviours. We then discussed the four characteristics of persuasion—non-coercive, usually incremental, interactive, and possibly ethical—and three persuasion categories—type of proposition, desired outcome, and directness of approach.

When creating a persuasive message, it is important to set a clear purpose and to avoid logical fallacies. This chapter describes several fallacies to keep in mind: *ad hominem, reductio ad absurdum,* either–or, post hoc, *argumentum ad verecundiam,* and *argumentum ad populum.*

Analyzing and adapting to your audience is another crucial part of your persuasive strategy. A persuasive communicator considers factors such as audience type; audience purpose; demographics; and attitudes, beliefs, and values to understand his or her audience. Furthermore, he or she uses this information to adapt to the audience by establishing common ground with its members, organizing the message according to the response that he or she expects to receive, and structuring the message to neutralize potential hostility.

Having a solid grasp of attitudes is a central skill for the persuasive communicator. This chapter explained how attitudes are learned, based in our emotions, influence our thoughts and emotions, and bear a strong relationship with our beliefs and values. We also discussed three approaches to structuring attitudes. Expectancy–value combines what we believe about something with how we feel about it. Symbolic predispositions regard mental representations that we hold about facts in the world. Ideology is the set of ideas, beliefs, and metaphors about the world that subconsciously become part of our reasoning processes.

Persuasive communication also requires credibility. The chapter explored the three concepts of credibility: competence, character, and charisma.

One particular form of persuasive communication is found in marketing, sales, and social psychology. Interpersonal persuasion uses a set of techniques to gain compliance from people. This chapter discussed several methods of this type, including foot-in-the-door, door-in-the-face, social exchange, low-balling, that's-not-all, and fear-then-relief.

Finally, we concluded with a section on professional writing, written by Philip Savage. The section explained the fundamentals of writing four basic persuasive products: a news release, an op-ed, a blog, and a briefing note. As the Internet Age makes writing more important to persuasion, knowing how to write these documents will be a valuable skill to people regardless of their professional, community, or faith-based affiliations.

Key Terms

activate 406

ad hominem fallacy 410

anchor 401

argumentum ad populum
   fallacy 411

argumentum ad verecundiam
   fallacy 411

attitude 416

audience analysis 412

belief 416

briefing note 435

cognitive dissonance 426

convince 405

credibility 422

demographics 413

direct persuasion 406

door-in-the-face 426

either–or fallacy 410

ethical persuasion 403

expectancy–value
   approach 419

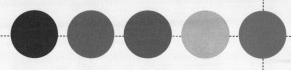

Activities

A. Audience Latitudes of Acceptance

To better understand the concept of latitudes of acceptance, rejection, and non-commitment, formulate a list of perspectives on a topic of your choice. This list should contain 8 to 10 statements that represent a variety of attitudes, as in the list pertaining to the abortion issue on page 401. Arrange this list from your own point of view, from most acceptable to least acceptable. Then circle the single statement that best represents your own point of view: this will be your 'anchor'. Underline those items that also seem reasonable: these make up your latitude of acceptance on this issue. Then cross out the numbers in front of any items that express opinions that you cannot accept: these make up your latitude of rejection. Those statements that are left would be your latitude of non-commitment. Do you agree that someone seeking to persuade you on this issue would do best to advance propositions that fall within this latitude of non-commitment? Why or why not?

B. Personal Persuasion

When was the last time you changed your attitude about something after discussing it with someone? In your opinion, was this persuasion interactive? Not coercive? Incremental? Ethical? Explain your answer.

C. Propositions of Fact, Value, and Policy

Which of the following statements are propositions of fact, propositions of value, and propositions of policy?
1. 'Three Strikes' laws that put criminals away for life after their third conviction are [*or are not*] fair.
2. Elder care should [*or should not*] be the responsibility of government.
3. The mercury in dental fillings is [*or is not*] healthy for the dental patient.
4. Pay raises for MPs should [*or should not*] be delayed until an election has intervened.
5. The democratic process is compromised when an elected member of Parliament crosses the floor to join another party.

6.   Private clinics should [*or* should not] be allowed to perform MRIs and other procedures where hospital wait times are unacceptable.
7.   Elderly people who are wealthy do [*or* do not] receive too many social security benefits.
8.   All forms of tobacco advertising should [*or* should not] be banned.
9.   Gang-related violence is [*or* is not] on the rise.
10. Pit bulls are [*or* are not] dangerous animals.

E. Find the Fallacy

Test your ability to detect shaky reasoning by identifying which fallacy discussed on pages 409–12 is exhibited in each of the following statements.

1.   Some companies claim to be in favour of protecting the environment, but you can't trust them. Businesses exist to make a profit, and the cost of saving the earth is just another expense to be cut.
2.   Take it from me, imported cars are much better than domestics. I used to buy only North American, but the cars made here are all junk.
3.   Hip Hop music ought to be boycotted. After all, the number of assaults on police officers went up right after hip hop became popular.
4.   Carpooling to cut down on the parking problem is a stupid idea. Look around— nobody carpools!
5.   I know that staying in the sun can cause cancer, but if I start worrying about every environmental risk I'll have to stay inside a bomb shelter breathing filtered air, never drive a car or ride my bike, and I won't be able to eat anything.
6.   Theories of Intelligent Design are just a way for Bible-thumping, know-nothing fundamentalists to pass off Creationism as science.

F. Interpersonal Persuasion

Identify several people who have tried to persuade you via interpersonal persuasion. They might be salespeople, politicians, teachers, members of the clergy, coaches, bosses, or anyone else. Identify which interpersonal persuasive technique each used with you. How did the scenarios play out? Did each person follow the technique to the letter? Do you think that he or she had been trained in persuasion?

G. The Credibility of Persuaders

Identify a person who has attempted to persuade you via interpersonal persuasion or mass communication. This person could be a celebrity, an authority figure, an expert, a teacher, a politician, or anyone else. Analyze this person's credibility in terms of the three dimensions discussed in the chapter. Which dimension is most important in terms of this person's effectiveness?

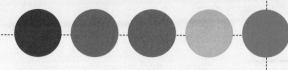

H. Your Attitudes, Beliefs, and Values

Being aware of your own attitudes is a big step toward becoming a good persuader. List 10 attitudes that you think are the most important to you among all the attitudes you hold. Then list the beliefs and values that contribute to and support these attitudes. Do this for different areas of your life, such as politics, morals, cultural prejudices, etc.

I. Analyzing Communication Behaviours

Read Table 11.1 carefully. The behaviours listed there are presented in an order that some communication experts would describe as most serious to least serious. Do you agree or disagree with the order of these ethical faults? State whether you would change the order of any of these behaviours and explain your answer. What other behaviours would you add to this list?

J. Structure of Attitudes

Imagine a situation where you need to persuade three groups of people that tuition rates at your college or university are too high. The three groups are
- parents,
- students, and
- college/university administrators.

Apply the three models of attitude structure described in this chapter (pp. 419–20) to map out a strategy for persuading each group.

K. Persuasive Writing

Imagine that you are working in a community, student, or faith-community group and the group members realize that some persuasive writing is necessary. Think of a scenario first. Perhaps your student group wants to lead an environmental clean-up day on campus. Or maybe you want to alert the world that your faith community is about to start a campaign to raise money for the needy in your area. The members of your group know that you have taken a course in human communication and that you have good writing skills, so you are elected to write the following pieces about your group's cause:
- a news release,
- an op-ed, and
- a blog.

Use the techniques you learned in this chapter to write these pieces.

L. A Briefing Note

Imagine that you are working in a community, student, or faith-community group or for a for-profit corporation. Your boss hears that your school could be a potential grounds for recruiting new members or employees. He or she wants to know all about your college or university and how the students and the administration could be approached.

- Choose an organization, fictional or real, that you are working for.
- Invent a boss and describe him or her in one or two lines.
- Write a briefing note for your boss explaining the situation at the school in terms of how many students there are, how many of them work in part-time jobs already, and give an opinion why they would or would not want to join your organization.

Further Reading

Johannesen, Richard L. *Ethics in Human Communication,* 5th edn. Long Grove, IL: Waveland Press, 2002.
A comprehensive synthesis of key perspectives in communication ethics, this text relates the ethics of public speaking to interpersonal, small-group, and mass communication.

Larson, Charles. *Persuasion: Reception and Responsibility,* 9th edn. Belmont, CA: Wadsworth, 2001.
This book explains theories, research, and ethics of persuasion by looking at popular culture—politics, mass media, advertising, and technology. It focuses on language and critical thinking from a consumer/receiver point of view and contains current verbal and visual examples of persuasion in action.

Perloff, Richard, M. *The Dynamics of Persuasion: Communication and Attitudes in the 21st Century.* New York: Routledge, 2010.
Perloff provides an up-to-date textbook looking at persuasion from social psychological and sociological perspectives. The book puts a special focus on the study of attitudes, beliefs, and values, combining theoretical and applied perspectives.

Pratkais, Anthony R., and Elliot Aronson. *Age of Propaganda: The Everyday Use and Abuse of Persuasion.* New York: W.H. Freeman, 2001.
This work looks at both the history and effectiveness of propaganda. The focus is mass persuasion and manipulation in everything from advertising to political oratory.

Rottenberg, Annette T. *The Structure of Argument,* 4th edn. New York: Bedford/ St Martin's, 2003.
Rottenberg explains how arguments are put together, stressing critical and analytical thinking and offering interesting examples.

Rybacki, Donald, and Karyn Rybacki. *Advocacy and Opposition: An Introduction to Argumentation,* 5th edn. Boston: Allyn and Bacon, 2004.
The authors provide a practical approach to argumentation and critical thinking for the beginning student who needs to construct and present arguments on questions of fact, value, and policy—both in oral and written form. Their work offers a theoretical view of the nature of argument, a discussion of ethical principles of arguing as a form of communication, and a focus on how arguments are created.

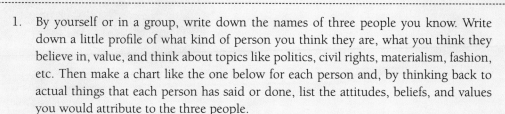

Study Questions

1. By yourself or in a group, write down the names of three people you know. Write down a little profile of what kind of person you think they are, what you think they believe in, value, and think about topics like politics, civil rights, materialism, fashion, etc. Then make a chart like the one below for each person and, by thinking back to actual things that each person has said or done, list the attitudes, beliefs, and values you would attribute to the three people.

Name	Attitudes	Beliefs	Values

Put your chart aside for a day or two and then take it out and compare it to your profiles. Were you right in your initial observations?

2. Keep a log of your encounters with people for three days. In your notebook, take down the types of persuasion techniques (pp. 404–7) they use to try and persuade you to change your attitudes, beliefs, values, or behaviours. Identify whether they are using indirect or direct persuasion. You will be amazed at how many of your everyday interactions are actually based around someone trying to persuade you of something.

3. Tune in to the national news broadcast on one of the major Canadian television channels. Write down the fallacies (pp. 409–12) that you hear in the reasoning of the people being interviewed. How many fallacies can you count in one news broadcast?

4. Pick a topic that is of current interest in your community and try to find examples of the four types of professional writing explained on pages 431–5 (it might be tricky to find a briefing note). Try to see whether there are sentences, concepts, or ideas that are shared between the three items. This will illustrate how much influence these varieties of professional writing can have on media discourse.

After studying the material in this chapter . . .

You should understand:

- the importance of defining a clear speech purpose;
- the differences among a general purpose, a specific purpose, and a thesis;
- the necessity of analyzing a speaking situation;
- the importance of a clear speech organization;
- the basic structure of a speech;
- the steps involved in organizing the body of a speech;
- the importance of effective introductions, conclusions, and transitions;
- the functions and types of supporting material; and
- the elements of a speech that help maintain an audience's attention.

You should be able to:

- choose an effective speaking topic;
- formulate a purpose statement and thesis statement that will help you develop that topic;
- analyze the occasion in any speaking situation;
- construct an effective speech outline using the organizing principles described in this chapter;
- develop an effective introduction, conclusion, and transitions;
- choose supporting material for a speech to make your points clear, interesting, memorable, and convincing;
- emphasize important points in your speech; and
- generate audience involvement.

Speech Writing

Chapter Highlights

Developing your topic begins with defining your purpose. You should understand and be able to state the following simply and clearly:

- your general purpose (to entertain, to inform, or to persuade);
- your specific purpose (expressed in the form of a purpose statement); and
- your central idea (expressed in the form of a thesis statement).

Your next step in developing your topic is to analyze the speaking occasion by considering

- time and space.

There are several tools that are designed to make the important job of structuring your speech easier and more effective. In this chapter we will look at

- working outlines,
- formal outlines, and
- speaking notes.

Following a few simple principles will enable you to build an effective outline. These principles deal with

- standard symbols,
- standard format,

- the rule of division, and
- the rule of parallel wording.

Other principles of speech organization will be examined in depth in this chapter. These include

- organizing your points in a logical order, and
- using transitions.

Beginning and ending your speech effectively will be especially important. With that in mind we will examine rules for effective

- introductions and conclusions.

The effective use of supporting material is one of the most important aspects of speech preparation. In this chapter we will explore

- functions of supporting material,
- types of supporting material, and
- styles of support, including narration and citation.

There are several writing techniques that help make speeches more effective:

- Make it easy to listen.
- Emphasize important points.
- Use clear, simple language.
- Generate audience involvement.

● ● ● ● ●

COMMUNICATION ON-SCREEN

Four Weddings and a Funeral (1994)
Directed by Mike Newell.

Hugh Grant's breakthrough film is a catalogue of social events that also happen to be speaking events. As the film makes clear, however, the effectiveness of speeches can vary considerably depending on circumstance. At the first wedding, Charles (Grant) 'roasts' the groom with great success. At the second wedding, one of his friends tries to imitate his style and fails miserably.

Cultural Idiom

the toast
the speech given before a drink to honour someone

Public speaking can be a horror for the shy person, but it can also be the ultimate act of liberation. . . . I hadn't realized the transformative effect it could have on the speaker herself.

Susan Faludi

A surprising number of people will give speeches that will change their lives. Some of these will be job-related speeches, like the presentation that gets your new company funded or wins you a promotion. Some will be personal, such as the toast at your best friend's wedding or a eulogy for a lost relative. And some will have the potential to change the lives of others, perhaps locally, as you get a civic improvement project started in your hometown, or even globally, as you try to persuade listeners to deal more effectively with global problems like hunger, disease, or environmental threats.

You probably realize that the ability to speak well in public can benefit both your personal and professional life. You may also recognize that successful public speaking can be a liberating, transformative experience that boosts your self-confidence and helps you make a difference in the world. Yet most of us view the prospect of standing before an audience with the same enthusiasm we have for a trip to the dentist or the tax auditor. In fact, giving a speech seems to be one of the most anxiety-producing things we can do.

Countless books, DVDs, and associations offer tips on how to overcome this fear and to become a more comfortable public speaker. Toastmasters International, an organization designed to help people become effective communication leaders, has over 1,000 clubs in Canada, testifying to the popularity of—and need for—this kind of help. While Toastmasters aids those who feel anxious about making the kind of personal speeches we mentioned earlier, it also provides services to organizations—community groups, universities, government agencies, and big businesses—that see the value in having their employees learn to give better sales presentations, to develop and present ideas effectively, to offer and accept constructive criticism, and to hone management skills.[1]

Whether or not you avail yourself of resources such as these, learning to speak comfortably in public is important. Despite the discomfort that speech giving causes, sooner or later you will need to talk to an audience of some kind, as part of a class project, as part of a job, or as part of a community action group. And even in less 'speech-like' situations, you will often need the same skills that are important in speech giving: the ability to talk with confidence, to organize ideas in a clear way, and to make those ideas interesting and persuasive.

Attaining a mastery of public speaking is at least partially a matter of practice. But practice doesn't always make perfect; without a careful analysis of what you are doing, practice has a tendency to make old public speaking habits permanent rather than perfect. This chapter will provide you with tools to analyze and improve your performance as a public speaker.

Choosing a Topic

Often the difference between a successful and an unsuccessful speech is the choice of topic. Your topic should be familiar enough for your audience to understand yet be innovative enough to hold its attention. The following guidelines will help you pick a topic that is right for you, your audience, and your assignment.

Look for a Topic Early

The best student speakers usually choose a topic as soon as possible after a speech is assigned by their instructor, and then they stick with it. One reason to look for a topic early is to have plenty of time to complete the speech and practise it. Adequate practice time is essential to effective speech making, but the reasons for choosing a topic early run even deeper than that. Ideas seem to come automatically to speakers who have a topic in mind; things they read, observe, or discuss that might have otherwise been meaningless suddenly relate to their topic, providing material or inspiration. The earlier you decide on a topic, the more you can take advantage of these happy coincidences.

Choose a Topic That Interests You

Your topic must be interesting to your audience, and the best way to accomplish that is to find a topic that is interesting to you. Your interest in a topic will also improve your ability to create the speech, and it will increase your confidence when it comes time to present it.

Sometimes it's difficult to pinpoint what your interests are—especially when you are being pressed to come up with a speech topic. If that happens to you, you might want to review your favourite media, discuss current events with your family and friends, or just contemplate your interests in solitude. The following checklist could be used as a guide.

> **Cultural Idiom**
>
> **being pressed**
> forced
>
> **stick with**
> continue with

Review	Discuss Current Events	Think About
• newspapers	• international	• activities
• magazines	• national	• hobbies
• books	• local	• special interests
• various multimedia sources	• family	• personal experience
• social media, such as Digg or Reddit Canada	• friends over Facebook and Twitter	• different perspectives on the same idea

Once you have chosen your topic you can begin developing it. Your first step in that task is defining your purpose.

Defining Purpose

No one gives a speech—or expresses *any* kind of message—without having a reason to do so. This is easy to see in those messages that ask for something: 'Please pass the whipped cream,' or 'How about a movie this Friday?' or 'Excuse me, that's my foot you're standing on.' But even in subtler messages, the speaker always has a purpose: to evoke a response from the listener.

> *A speech should not be just a sharing of information, but a sharing of yourself.*
>
> Ralph Archbold

Sometimes purposes are misunderstood or confused by the speaker. This causes wasted time both in the preparation and in the presentation of the speech. It is essential, therefore, that the speaker keep in mind a clear purpose.

The first step in understanding the purpose is to formulate a clear and precise statement of that purpose. This requires an understanding of both *general purpose* and *specific purpose*.

General Purpose

Most students, when asked why they are giving a speech in a college or university class, will quickly cite course requirements. But you have to analyze your motives more deeply than that to develop an effective speech purpose. Even if you are giving your speech only for the grade, you still have to affect your audience in some way to earn that grade. If your motive for speaking is to learn effective speech techniques (as we hope it is), you still have to influence your audience in order to accomplish your goal because influencing an audience is the essence of effective speaking.

When we say you have to influence your audience, we mean you have to change it in some way. If you think about all the possible ways you could change an audience, you'll realize that they all boil down to three options, which happen to be the three **general purposes** for speaking:

1. **To entertain.** To relax your audience by providing it with a pleasant listening experience.
2. **To inform.** To enlighten your audience by teaching it something.
3. **To persuade.** To move your audience toward a new attitude or behaviour.

No speech could ever have just one purpose. A speech designed for one purpose will almost always accomplish a little of the other purposes; even a speech designed purely to entertain might change audience attitudes or teach the audience something new. In fact, these purposes are cumulative in the sense that to inform an audience, you have to make your remarks entertaining enough to hold its interest—at least long enough to convince it that your topic is worth learning about. And you certainly have to inform an audience about your arguments in order to persuade it. That said, two basic characteristics differentiate an informative topic from a persuasive topic.

First, an informative speech generally does not present information that an audience is likely to disagree with. This is a matter of degree. For example, you might want to give a purely informative talk on traditional Chinese medicine, simply describing what its practitioners believe and do. By contrast, a talk in which you either promote or criticize traditional Chinese medicine would clearly be persuasive.

The non-controversial nature of informative speaking does not mean that your speech topic should be uninteresting to your audience but that your approach to it should not engender conflict. You could speak about the animal rights movement, for example, by explaining the points of view of both sides in an interesting but objective manner.

Second, the informative speaker's intent, unlike that of the persuasive speaker, is not to change attitudes or to make the audience members feel differently about the topic. For example, an informative speaker might explain how automobile manufacturers are using GPS navigation technology but will not try to promote a specific brand of car or specific GPS device to the audience. However, the informative speaker does try to make the topic important to the audience and certainly seeks a response—typically attention and interest—from listeners.

---

general purpose
A basic way to affect an audience. There are three options: to entertain, to inform, or to persuade.

Cultural Idiom

boil down to
reduce to the basic elements

Whether your speech is informative or persuasive, deciding your general purpose is like choosing the 'right' answer on a multiple choice question in which all the possible answers are right to a certain degree, but one is more right than the others. Thus, we say that any speech is primarily designed for one of these purposes. A clear understanding of your general purpose gets you on the right track for choosing and developing a topic. Understanding your specific purpose will keep you on that track.

Specific Purpose

Whereas your general purpose is only a one-word label, your **specific purpose** is expressed in the form of a **purpose statement**—a complete sentence that describes exactly what you want your speech to accomplish. The purpose statement usually isn't used word for word in the actual speech; its purpose is to keep you focused as you plan.

If your speech's general purpose is to be informative, you might begin to frame your specific purpose by asking: 'Do I seek to *describe, explain,* or *instruct?*'

Descriptions

A speech of **description** is the most straightforward type of informative speech. With your audience analysis in mind (see Chapter 11), you generally divide this type of speech into the components of the thing you are describing. You might introduce a new product to a group of customers, or you might describe what a career in nursing would be like. Whatever its topic, the speech of description creates a 'word picture' of the essential details that make that thing what it is.

Explanations

Explanations clarify ideas and concepts that are already known but not understood by an audience. For example, your audience members might already know that the stock market can rise and fall rapidly, but they might be baffled by the reasons why this is so. Explanations often deal with the question of why. Why does the stock market rise or fall? Why do we have to wait until the age of 18 to vote? Why are tuition fees increasing *again* this semester?

Instructions

Instructions teach something to the audience in a logical, step-by-step manner. The basis of training programs and orientations, they often deal with the question of how to. Speeches of instruction might deal with *how to* prepare for a test or a job interview. This type of speech often features a demonstration or visual aid. Thus, if you were giving instructions on the perfect golf swing, you might demonstrate with your own club or use a mechanical model to show the physics involved. For instructions on how to perform CPR, you could use a volunteer or a dummy.

> *The secret of success is constancy of purpose.*
>
> Benjamin Disraeli

description
In terms of communication culture, a statement in which the speaker describes his or her position.

explanation
A speech or presentation that clarifies ideas and concepts already known but not understood by an audience.

instruction
A remark that teaches something to an audience in a logical, step-by-step manner.

purpose statement
A complete sentence that describes precisely what a speaker wants to accomplish.

specific purpose
The precise effect that the speaker wants to have on an audience. Expressed in the form of a purpose statement.

Criteria for a Good Purpose Statement

The types of informative speeches described above aren't mutually exclusive. There is considerable overlap, as when you give a speech about objects with the purpose of explaining them. Each style has a particular set of nuances that affect how you would construct your purpose statement. Regardless of your speech's general purpose, however, there are three criteria for a good purpose statement.

1. A Purpose Statement Should Be Receiver-Oriented.

Having a *receiver orientation* means that your purpose is focused on how your speech will affect your audience members. For example, if you were giving an informative talk on how to sue someone in small claims court, this would be an inadequate purpose statement:

> My purpose is to tell my audience about small claims court.

As that statement is worded, your purpose is 'to tell' an audience something, which suggests that the speech could be successful even if no one listens. Your purpose statement should refer to the response you want from your audience: it should tell what the audience members will know or be able to do after listening to your speech. Thus, the preceding purpose statement could be improved in this way:

> After listening to my speech, my audience will know more about small claims court procedures.

That's an improvement, because you have stated what you expect from your audience. But this purpose statement could be improved more through the judicious application of a second criterion.

2. A Purpose Statement Should Be Specific.

To be effective, a purpose statement should be worded specifically, with enough details so that, after your speech, you would be able to measure or test your audience to see if you had achieved your purpose. In the example given earlier, simply 'knowing about small claims court' is too vague; you need something more specific, such as

> After listening to my speech, my audience will know how to win a case in small claims court.

This is an improvement, but it can be made still better by applying a third criterion.

3. A Purpose Statement Should Be Realistic.

You must be able to accomplish your purpose as stated. Some speakers insist on formulating purpose statements such as 'My purpose is to convince my audience to make federal budget deficits illegal.' Unfortunately, unless your audience happens to be the House of Commons, it won't have the power to change Canadian fiscal policy. But any audience can write its members of Parliament or sign a petition. Similarly, an audience will not 'learn how to play championship tennis' or 'understand the danger of business regulation' in one sitting. You must aim for an achievable audience response. In your small claims court speech, it would be impossible for you to be sure that each of your audience members has a winnable case. So a better purpose statement for this speech might sound something like

> After listening to my speech, my audience will be able to list the five steps for preparing a small claims case.

This purpose statement is receiver-oriented, specific, and realistic. It also suggests an organizational pattern for the speech ('the five steps'), which can be a bonus in a carefully worded purpose statement. Consider the following sets of purpose statements:

LESS EFFECTIVE	MORE EFFECTIVE
To talk about professional wrestling (not receiver-oriented).	After listening to my speech, my audience will understand that kids who imitate professional wrestlers can be seriously hurt.
To tell my audience about textbook prices (not specific).	After listening to my speech, the audience will understand the five reasons why textbooks cost more than mass-market books.
After listening to my speech, my audience members will dedicate themselves to fighting cultural imperialism (not realistic).	After listening to my speech, my audience will understand why some Canadians want to restrict the importation of American films and television programs.

The Thesis Statement

So far we have discussed how to select a topic, how to begin focusing that topic through its general purpose, and how to focus it further through its specific purpose. Your next step in the focusing process is to formulate your **thesis statement,** which declares the central idea of your speech. It identifies the one idea that you want your audience to remember after it has forgotten everything else you had to say. The thesis statement for your small claims speech might be worded like this:

> Arguing a case on your own in small claims court is a simple, five-step process that can give you the same results you would achieve with a lawyer.

Unlike your purpose statement, your thesis statement is usually delivered directly to your audience. The thesis statement is usually formulated later in the speech making process, after you have done some research on your topic. The progression from topic to purpose to thesis is, therefore, another focusing process, as you can see in the following examples.

Topic: Grade inflation is good.
General Purpose: To entertain.
Specific Purpose: After listening to my speech, my audience members will be unafraid to march up to their professor and say, 'Give me an "A" or else.'
Thesis Statement: Handing out high grades as if they were Halloween treats makes everybody look good, and it doesn't cause cavities.

Topic: Can the Internet cure the common cold?
General Purpose: To inform.
Specific Purpose: After listening to my speech, my audience members will use the information available on the World Wide Web to be better informed before they see their doctors.

thesis statement
A complete sentence describing the central idea of a speech.

Thesis Statement: Online medical data can save the health care system the cost and spare you the hassle of an unnecessary trip to the doctor.

Topic: Canadians should save more of their incomes.
General Purpose: To persuade.
Specific Purpose: After listening to my speech, audience members will recognize the importance of personal savings and open accounts for this purpose.
Thesis Statement: Because not enough of us are savers, the use of food banks goes up as soon as there are layoffs in the neighbourhood. If you save your money, you can have a buffer against having to go on welfare or using the food bank.

Analyzing the Occasion

In Chapter 11, we discussed the importance of audience analysis in persuasive writing. While this component is also necessary in speech writing, there is another element that must be analyzed: the *occasion*. To be successful, every choice you make in putting together your speech—your choice of purpose, topic, and all the developing material you use—must be appropriate to both of these components.

Analyzing the occasion is a skill that most of us draw upon every day when we engage in all kinds of communication. It is, however, particularly influential in public speaking, where it can strongly affect how our message will be received. The occasion of a speech is determined by the circumstances surrounding it. Three of these circumstances are *time, place,* and *audience expectations*.

Time

Few sinners are saved after the first twenty minutes of a sermon.

Mark Twain

Your speech occupies an interval of time that is surrounded by other events. For example, other speeches might be presented before or after yours, or comments might be made that set a certain tone or mood. External events such as an election, the start of a new semester, or even the weather can colour the occasion in one way or the other. The date on which you give your speech might have some historical significance. If that importance relates in some way to your topic, you can use it to help build audience interest.

The time available for your speech is also an essential consideration. You should choose a topic that is broad enough to say something worthwhile but brief enough to fit your limits. 'Wealth', for example, might be an inherently interesting topic to some students, but it would be difficult to cover such a broad topic in a 10-minute speech and still say anything significant. However, a topic like 'How to Make Extra Money in Your Spare Time' could conceivably be covered in 10 minutes in enough depth to make it worthwhile. All speeches have limits, whether they are explicitly stated or not. If you are invited to say a few words and you present a few volumes, you might not be invited back.

The simplest way to customize a speech is to call members of the audience in advance and ask them what they expect from your session and why they expect it. Then use their quotes throughout your presentation.

Allan Pease

Place

Your speech also occupies a physical space. The beauty or squalor of your surroundings and the noise or stuffiness of the room should all be taken into consideration. These physical surroundings can be referred to in your speech if appropriate. If you were talking about world poverty, for example, you could compare your surroundings to those that might be found in a poorer country.

Young Communicator
PROFILE

Johanna Rienzo, Full-Time Claims Adjuster, Part-Time News Reporter/ Host

Growing up I had a passion for being in the spotlight and was an entertainment junkie! I had an eye for detail and a mind for problem-solving. Throughout my undergraduate years I gained experience in two separate industries: insurance and broadcasting. I dabbled in claims adjusting as an investigative assistant and got a foot in the broadcasting door by interning at many TV and radio stations including Star!, CityTV, Book Television, and 102.1 The Edge. Studying communications taught me how to accept challenges and understand the power of networking, which is what has led me to the positions I currently hold.

Upon graduating I jumped at the opportunity to co-host a weekend show and report for a Rogers TV daily news program. My efforts were remembered by a producer whom I met during one of my internships, and I was offered a position to help produce and report at the Toronto International Film Festival, where I met Edward Norton, Angelina Jolie, and Brad Pitt—a childhood dream come true! These jobs have required proficiency in computer editing, creativity, research, writing, a lot of proofreading, and, above all, tight deadlines!

As a result of my pursuit of a career in claims adjusting, I was hired by an international insurance adjusting company as a claims adjuster. This position involves investigating accidents (vehicle collisions, break and enters, and bodily injuries), content analysis, negotiations, and interpersonal and group communication.

It is a combination of my experiences during my undergraduate years that helps me in each of my current positions. It is important to take what you learn from a textbook and apply it to the real world, which is just what communications teaches you to do. From there, take chances, learn from the past, live in the present, and look towards a bright and abundant future!

Audience Expectations

Finally, your speech is surrounded by audience expectations. A speech presented in a college or university class, for example, is usually expected to reflect a high level of thought and intelligence. This doesn't necessarily mean that it has to be boring or humourless; wit and humour are, after all, indicative of intelligence. But it does mean that you have to put a little more effort into your presentation than if you were discussing the same subject with friends over coffee.

When you are considering the occasion of your speech, it pays to remember that every occasion is unique. Although there are obvious differences between a university seminar, a church sermon, and the roast at a stagette, there are also many subtle differences that will apply only to the circumstances of each unique event.

Knowledge is of two kinds: We know a subject ourselves, or we know where we can find information upon it.

Samuel Johnson

Cultural Idiom

stagette
a celebration in honour of a
woman about to marry

*Words differently arranged
have a different meaning,
and meanings differently
arranged have a different
effect.*

Blaise Pascal

basic speech structure
The division of a speech into introduction, body, and conclusion.

formal outline
A consistent format and set of symbols used to identify the structure
of ideas.

working outline
A constantly changing organizational aid used in planning a
speech.

Introduction
   I. Attention-getter
   II. Preview

Body
   I.
   II.
   III. } Three to five
   IV. main points
   V.

Conclusion
   I. Review
   II. Final remarks

Figure 12.1
Basic Speech Structure

Structuring the Speech

Knowing what you are talking about and *communicating* that knowledge are not the same thing. It's frustrating to realize you aren't expressing your thoughts clearly, and it's equally unpleasant to know that a speaker has something worth saying yet be unable to figure out just what it is because the material is too jumbled to understand.

Being clear to your audience isn't the only benefit of good organization: structuring a message effectively will help you refine your own ideas and construct more persuasive messages.

A good speech is like a good building: both grow from a careful plan. Like any other form of plan, a speech outline is the framework on which your message is built. It contains your main ideas and shows how they relate to one another and your thesis. Virtually every speech outline ought to follow the basic structure outlined in Figure 12.1.

This **basic speech structure** demonstrates the old aphorism for speakers: 'Tell what you're going to say, say it, and then tell what you said.' Although this structure sounds redundant, the research on listening cited in Chapter 4 demonstrates that receivers forget much of what they hear. The clear, repetitive nature of the basic speech structure reduces the potential for memory loss because audiences have a tendency to listen more carefully during the beginning and ending of a speech.[2] Your outline will reflect this basic speech structure.

Outlines come in all shapes and sizes, but the three types that are most important to us here are working outlines, formal outlines, and speaking notes.

Working Outline

A **working outline** is a construction tool used to map out your speech. The working outline will probably follow the basic speech structure but only in rough form. It is for your eyes only. No one else need understand it, so you can use whatever symbols and personal shorthand you find functional. Actually, it is probably a mistake to refer to a 'working outline' in the singular form because you will probably create several drafts as you refine your ideas. As your ideas solidify, your outline will change accordingly, becoming more polished as you go along.

Formal Outline

A **formal outline** such as the one shown on page 459 uses a consistent format and set of symbols to identify the structure of ideas.

A formal outline serves several purposes. In simplified form, it can be used as a visual aid (displayed while you speak or distributed as a handout). It can serve as a record of a speech that was delivered; many organizations send outlines to members who miss meetings at which presentations were given. Finally, in speech classes, instructors often use speech outlines to analyze student speeches. When one is used for that purpose, it is usually a full-sentence outline and includes the purpose, the thesis and topic, and/or title. Most instructors also require a bibliography of sources at the end of the outline. The bibliography should include full research citations, the correct form for which can be found in a style guide, such as *Fit to Print* by Joanne Buckley.[3] There are at least six standard bibliographic styles, and your instructor might assign one of them. Whichever style you use, you should be consistent in form and remember the two primary functions of a bibliographic citation: to demonstrate the credibility of your source and to enable your readers—in this case your professor or fellow students—to find the source if they want to check its accuracy or explore your topic in more detail.

Another person should be able to understand the basic ideas included in your speech by reading the formal outline. In fact, that's one test of the effectiveness of your outline. See if the sample outline on page 459 passes this test for you.

Speaking Notes

Like your working outline, your speaking notes are for your use only, so the format is up to you. Many teachers suggest that speaking notes should be in the form of a brief keyword outline, with just enough information listed to jog your memory but not enough to get lost in.

Many instructors also suggest that you fit your notes on one side of a set of note cards. Some recommend that you also have your introduction and conclusion on note cards, and still others advise that your longer quotations be written out on note cards. For example, the speaking notes for a speech on Quebec separatism might look like the ones in Figure 12.2.

Cultural Idiom

to jog your memory
to remind yourself

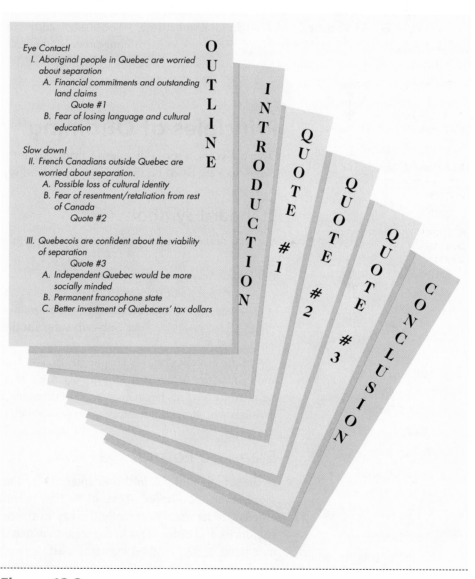

Figure 12.2
Speaking Notes

Understanding Communication Technology

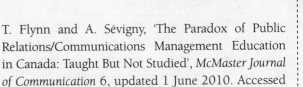

Citing Web Sources

The Internet is becoming an increasingly important source for speech research. When you list a Web source, you should provide the URL (uniform resource locator, or Web address), and the date you found it. You should also include, if possible, the author of the page, the organization that supports it, and the last date it was updated. A complete citation might look something like this:

T. Flynn and A. Sévigny, 'The Paradox of Public Relations/Communications Management Education in Canada: Taught But Not Studied', *McMaster Journal of Communication* 6, updated 1 June 2010. Accessed 3 June 2010 at digitalcommons.mcmaster.ca/mjc.

The first five entries in the bibliography of the sample outline provide other examples of Web citations.

Principles of Outlining

Over the years, a series of rules or principles for the construction of outlines has evolved. These rules are based on the use of the standard symbols and format discussed next.

Standard Symbols

A speech outline generally uses the following symbols:

    I. Main point (Roman numeral)
        A. Subpoint (capital letter)
            1. Sub-subpoint (standard number)
                a. Sub–sub-subpoint (lowercase letter)

In the examples in this chapter, the major divisions of the speech—introduction, body, and conclusion—are not given symbols. They are listed by name, and the Roman numerals for their main points begin anew in each division. An alternative format is to list these major divisions with Roman numerals, main points with capital letters, and so on.

Standard Format

In the sample outlines in this chapter, notice that each symbol is indented a number of spaces from the symbol above it. Besides keeping the outline neat, the indentation of different-order ideas is actually the key to the technique of outlining; it enables you to coordinate and order ideas in the form in which they are most comprehensible to the human mind. If the standard format is used in your working outline, it will help you create a well-organized speech. If it is used in speaking notes, it will help you remember everything you want to say.

Proper outline form is based on a few rules and guidelines, which are discussed in the next sections. The first of these is the rule of division.

Sample Speech Outline

Title: 'Quebec Separatism: Three Different Points of View'

General purpose: To inform

Specific purpose: After listening to my speech, audience members will have a better understanding of what Quebec separatism represents for Aboriginal peoples in Quebec, French Canadians outside Quebec, and the Québécois themselves.

Thesis: Three communities—Aboriginal, French Canadians outside Quebec, and the Québécois—believe they would be affected in very different ways in the event of Quebec's separation from Canada.

INTRODUCTION

I. Attention-getter: In 1995, Canadians came very close to needing a passport to go shopping in Montréal!

II. Thesis statement

III. Preview of main points

BODY

I. Why are Aboriginal people living in Quebec concerned about the idea of separation?
  A. They worry their interests would not be safeguarded in an independent Quebec.
    1. They have outstanding land claims for much of the territory of the current province of Quebec.
    2. They worry that an independent Quebec would not honour the financial commitments made to them by the Government of Canada.
  B. They worry that they might lose their cultures.
    1. They worry that they would not be encouraged to speak their languages and live their cultures.
    2. They worry that an independent Quebec might not provide schooling in Aboriginal languages and culture.

II. Why are French Canadians outside Quebec concerned about the idea of separation?
  A. They worry about preserving their cultural identity.
    1. They currently feel largely ignored by Quebec and fear that they would be abandoned entirely by an independent Quebec.
    2. They worry that the rest of Canada would no longer provide services or education in French.
  B. They worry about prejudice and retaliation.
    1. The rest of Canada might exclude French Canadians from social and economic opportunities.
    2. English-speaking Canadians who resent Quebec's separation might take out their resentment on francophones in the rest of Canada.

III. Why are many Québécois comfortable with the idea of separation?
  A. They believe that an independent Quebec would be fairer and more socially progressive than Canada is now.
    1. Historically, Québécois have had better relations with Aboriginal communities than English Canadians have.
    2. Quebec has done more than other provinces to support Aboriginal education.
  B. They believe that an independent Quebec would ensure a permanent francophone state in North America.
    1. An independent Quebec could be more forceful in arguing for French-language rights outside its borders.
    2. An independent Quebec could negotiate French-language rights for French Canadians outside Quebec as part of the separation agreement.
  C. They believe that an independent Quebec, without responsibilities to the rest of Canada, could provide better governance and make better use of its citizens' tax dollars.

CONCLUSION

I. Review of main points

II. Final remarks: Return to opening example, restate thesis: 'Three communities—Aboriginal peoples, French Canadians outside Quebec, and the Québécois themselves—believe they would be affected in very different ways in the event of Quebec's separation from Canada.'

BIBLIOGRAPHY

Canadian Broadcasting Corporation, 'Quebec Elections 1960–2003', available at archives.cbc.ca/IDD-1-73-651/politics_economy/quebec_elections/. Accessed 1 April 2007.

Canadian Broadcasting Corporation, 'Separation Anxiety: The 1995 Québec Referendum', available at archives.cbc.ca/IDD-1-73-1891/politics_economy/1995_referendum/. Accessed 1 April 2007.

Clarke, George Elliott, 'Building bridges: Cultural pluralism is at the heart of Canadian identity, professor says', News@UofT, 5 May 2003. Accessed 1 April 2007.

Encyclopedia Britannica, 'Canada: Québec Separatism', available at britannica.com/eb/article-43022/Canada. Accessed 1 April 2007.

Global Security. 'Quebec Separatism', available at globalsecurity.org/military/world/war/quebec.htm. Accessed 1 April 2007.

McRoberts, Kenneth. 2004. Beyond Quebec: Taking Stock of Canada. Montreal: McGill-Queen's University Press.

———. 1997. Misconceiving Canada: The Struggle for National Unity. Toronto: Oxford University Press Canada.

Young, Robert A. 1997. Secession of Quebec and the Future of Canada. Montreal: McGill-Queen's University Press.

Understanding Communication Technology

Software for Organization and Outlining

Sometimes the best way to organize ideas is visually. Until recently, the best approach was to write ideas on note cards, spread them out on the table or floor, and rearrange them until a clear plan emerged. Now computers make the task quicker and easier. Any word processor can be used to cut and paste blocks of ideas so you can reorganize the structure of your speech, and more advanced ones include a document map or 'outline view' that shows your organizational structure as you collect your notes.

Now there is even specialized software just for organizing, outlining, and brainstorming as you go. Inspiration® (inspiration.com/Inspiration), a visual tool for developing ideas, is one example. The program's 'diagram view' provides an easy-to-use equivalent to the note card approach. Each idea you type into the computer appears onscreen inside its own box or circle. You can click on these ideas with your mouse and re-arrange them until they fall into patterns that seem clear and effective. Then, with a simple command, the visual map is turned into a traditional outline, suitable for conversion into speaking notes, handouts, or visual aids. Besides serving as an outlining tool, Inspiration makes it easy to create concept maps, process flows, knowledge maps, flow charts, and other visual diagrams.

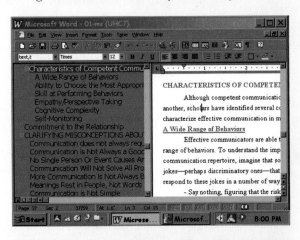

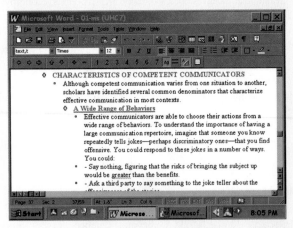

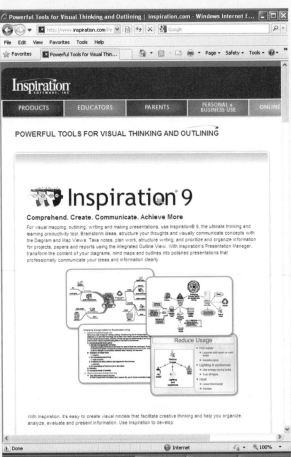

Word-processing programs like Microsoft Word include a document map, shown top, and an outline view, shown bottom, both of which show the organizational structure of the speech you are developing.

The Rule of Division

In formal outlines main points and subpoints always represent a division of a whole. Because it is impossible to divide something into fewer than two parts, you always have at least two main points for every topic. Then, if your main points are divided, you will always have at least two subpoints, and so on. Thus, the rule for formal outlines is 'Never a I *without* a II, never an A *without* a B,' and so on.

Three to five is considered to be the ideal number of main points. It is also considered best to divide those main points into three to five subpoints, when necessary and possible. This practice is followed in the sample outline.

Control yourself when you have two things to say: say first one, then the other, not both at the same time.

George Polya

The Rule of Parallel Wording

Your main points should be worded in a similar or 'parallel' manner. For example, if you were preparing a speech in support of the Canadian Firearms Registry, your main points might look like this:

I. Allowing unregistered guns does not promote public safety: it does not deter crime.
II. Allowing unregistered guns does not promote private security: jurisdictions that permit unregistered guns have more violent crime.
III. Allowing unregistered guns does not promote a civilized society: it increases the danger faced by all members of the community.

Whenever possible, subpoints should also be worded in a parallel manner. For your points to be parallel, they should each contain one, and only one, idea. (After all, they can't really be parallel if one is longer or contains more ideas than the others.) This will enable you to completely develop one idea before moving on to another one in your speech. If you were discussing cures for indigestion, your topic might be divided incorrectly if your main points looked like this:

I. 'Preventive cures' help you before eating.
II. 'Participation cures' help you during and after eating.

You might actually have three ideas there and thus three main points:

I. Prevention cures (before eating).
II. Participation cures (during eating).
III. Post-participation cures (after eating).

Organizing Your Points in a Logical Order

An outline should reflect a logical order for your points. You might arrange them from newest to oldest, largest to smallest, best to worst, or in one of the six ways that follow. The organizing pattern you choose ought to be the one that best develops your thesis.

climax pattern
An organizing plan for a speech that builds ideas to the point of maximum interest or tension.

space pattern
An organizing plan in a speech that arranges points according to their physical location.

time pattern
An organizing plan for a speech based on chronology.

topic pattern
An organizing plan for a speech that arranges points according to logical types or categories.

Time Patterns

Arrangement according to **time patterns**, or chronology, is one of the most common patterns of organization. The period of time could be anything from centuries to seconds. In a speech on airline food on Air Canada, a time pattern might look like this:

I. Early Air Canada food: a gourmet treat
II. The middle period: institutional food at 30,000 feet
III. Today's Air Canada food (unless you're in business class): the passenger with no spare money starves

Arranging points according to the steps that make up a process is another form of time patterning. The topic 'Recording a Hit Song' might use this type of patterning:

I. Find an agent
II. Record the demo tracks
III. Upload to MySpace and Facebook
IV. Promote the song

Time patterns are also the basis of **climax patterns,** which are used to create suspense. For example, if you wanted to create suspense in a speech about Canadian support for American military interventions, you could chronologically trace the steps that eventually led us into Vietnam, Bosnia, or Afghanistan in such a way that you build your audience's curiosity. If you told of these steps through the eyes of a soldier who entered military service right before one of those wars, you would be building suspense as your audience wonders what will become of that soldier.

The climax pattern can also be reversed. When it is, it is called *anticlimactic organization*. If you started your speech by telling the audience that you were going to explain why a specific soldier was killed in a specific war, and then you went on to explain the things that caused that soldier to become involved in that war, you would be using anticlimactic organization. This pattern is helpful when you have an essentially uninterested audience, and you need to build interest early.

Space Patterns

Space patterns are organized according to area. The area could be stated in terms of continents, centimetres, or anything in between. If you were discussing the Canadian North, for example, you could arrange the territories and provinces from west to east:

I. Yukon
II. Northwest Territories
III. Nunavut
IV. Quebec
V. Newfoundland and Labrador

Topic Patterns

A topical arrangement or **topic pattern** is based on types or categories. These categories could be either well known or original; both have their advantages. For example, a division of hockey players according to well-known categories might look like this:

I. Goaltenders
II. Defence

III. Wingers

IV. Centres

Well-known categories are advantageous because audiences quickly understand them. But familiarity also has its disadvantages, such as the 'Oh, this again' syndrome. If the members of an audience feel they have nothing new to learn about the components of your topic, they might not listen to you. To avoid this, you could invent original categories that freshen up your topic by suggesting an original analysis. For example, more original categories for 'hockey players' might look like this:

I. Plumbers—'Grinders' with relatively little talent who work extremely hard and are able to wear skilled opponents down with physical play, aggressive forechecking, and reliable defence.

II. Enforcers—players whose only real purpose is to intimidate their opponents.

III. Passengers—skilled players who seldom play to their full potential and tend to coast, playing well when the team enjoys success but disappearing for long stretches when the team is in a slump.

IV. Franchise players—players with great talent who are also excellent leaders and role models; they make others around them better and promote the team's interests in the media.

Sometimes topics are arranged in the order that will be easiest for your audience to remember. To return to our Canadian North example, the names of the provinces and territories could be arranged so that their first letters spell 'QYNNN'. Acronyms or words used in this way are known as mnemonics. Carol Koehler, a professor of communication and medicine, uses the mnemonic 'CARE' to describe the characteristics of a caring doctor:

C stands for **concentrate.** Physicians should hear with their eyes and ears . . .

A stands for **acknowledge.** Show them that you are listening . . .

R stands for **response.** Clarify issues by asking questions, providing periodic recaps . . .

E stands for **exercise emotional control.** When your 'hot buttons' are pushed . . .[4]

problem–solution pattern
An organizing plan for a speech that describes an unsatisfactory state of affairs and then proposes a plan to remedy the problem.

Problem–Solution Patterns

The **problem–solution pattern,** as you might guess from its no-nonsense name, describes what's wrong and proposes a way to make things better. It is usually (but not always) divisible into two distinct parts, as in this example:

I. The Problem: Homelessness (which could then be broken down into urban homelessness, suburban homelessness, and rural homelessness)

II. The Solution: A national homelessness institute (which would study the root causes of homelessness in the same way that the Canadian Mental Health Association studies the links between lifestyle and mental illness)

Cause–Effect Patterns

cause–effect pattern
An organizing plan for a speech that demonstrates how one or more events result in another event or events.

motivated sequence
A five-step plan used in persuasive speaking; also known as 'Monroe's Motivated Sequence'.

Cause–effect patterns are similar to problem–solution patterns in that they are basically two-part patterns: first you discuss something that happened, then you discuss its effects.

A variation of this pattern reverses the order. Persuasive speeches often have cause–effect or effect–cause as the first two main points. Leo Johnson, a former student at McMaster University, organized the first two points of a speech on 'Poverty in Liberia'[5] like this:

    I. The effects of the problem
        A. A lost generation of children
        B. A large brain drain towards North America
   II. The causes of the problem
        A. Tribal conflict and corrupt government
        B. A lack of support from rich nations like Canada and the United States

The third main point in this type of persuasive speech is often 'solutions', and the fourth 'the desired audience behaviour'. Leo's final points were

   III. Solutions: Convince Canadian politicians and diplomats to help Liberia financially and morally
   IV. Desired Audience Response: Contact local politicians and talk to them about the plight of Liberia

Motivated Sequence

A variation of the problem–solution pattern, developed in the 1930s by Alan H. Monroe, contains five steps and has come to be known as the **motivated sequence:**[6]

    I. **The attention step draws attention to your subject.** ('Cheers for the urban guerillas of Vancouver, the dauntless men and women who let their dogs loose in the parks!'[7])
   II. **The need step establishes the problem.** ('In Canada, we tend to think that freedom for dogs encourages bad behaviour. Nothing could be further from the truth. Freedom actually improves a dog's conduct.')
  III. **The satisfaction step proposes a solution.** ('The time has come for Vancouver and other Canadian cities to unleash their dogs.')
  IV. **The visualization step describes the results of the solution.** ('In the splendid cities of Latin America, well-mannered dogs are accepted almost everywhere as a normal part of life. In Buenos Aires, dogs are welcome in the best hotels, enjoy large play groups in the parks, and are seldom seen on leashes.')
   V. **The action step is a direct appeal for the audience to do something.** ('Demand that parts of Stanley Park become leash-free. Dog lovers of Vancouver, unite!')

COMMUNICATION ON-SCREEN

Memento (2000)

Directed by Christopher Nolan.

The last thing that Leonard Shelby (Guy Pearce) remembers is the murder of his wife. Suffering from a brain injury that does not allow him to create new memories, Leonard relies on a system of tattooed notes and Polaroid photos to try to find his wife's killer. The screenplay by Christopher Nolan, based on his brother Jonathan Nolan's short story 'Memento Mori', is particularly creative precisely because of how it eschews conventional narrative organization. Rather than follow the chronological pattern of organization that we assume as a given for best communicating a story, the movie is instead ordered as a non-linear sequence, beginning at the end and moving backward in time. The result is both an intriguing thriller and a fascinating discourse on the reliability of memory.

Using Transitions

Transitions keep your message moving forward. They perform the following functions:

- They tell how the introduction relates to the body of the speech.
- They tell how one main point relates to the next main point.
- They tell how your subpoints relate to the points they are part of.
- They tell how your supporting points relate to the points they support.

Transitions, to be effective, should refer to the previous point and to the upcoming point, showing how they relate to one another and to the thesis. They usually sound something like this:

'Like [previous point], another important consideration in [topic] is [upcoming point].'

'But [previous point] isn't the only thing we have to worry about. [Upcoming point] is even more potentially dangerous.'

'Yes, the problem is obvious. But what are the solutions? Well, one possible solution is . . .'

Sometimes a transition includes an internal review (a restatement of preceding points), an internal preview (a look ahead to upcoming points), or both:

'So far we've discussed [previous points]. Our next points are [upcoming points].'

You can find several examples of transitions in the sample speech at the end of this chapter.

Beginning and Ending the Speech

The **introduction** and **conclusion** of a speech are vitally important, although they usually occupy less than 20 per cent of your speaking time. Listeners form their impression of a speaker early, and they remember what they hear last; it is, therefore, crucial to make those few moments at the beginning and end of your speech work to your advantage.

The Introduction

There are four functions of the speech introduction. It serves to capture the audience's attention, preview the main points, set the mood and tone of the speech, and demonstrate the importance of the topic.

Capturing Attention

There are several ways to capture an audience's attention. The following discussion shows how some of these ways might be used in a speech entitled 'Communication between Plants and Humans'.

Refer to the Audience
The technique of referring to the audience is especially effective if it is complimentary: 'Julio's speech last week about how animals communicate was so interesting that I decided to explore a related topic: whether people can communicate with plants!'

conclusion
The final structural unit of a speech, in which the main points are reviewed and final remarks are made to motivate the audiences to act or help listeners remember key ideas.

introduction
The first structural unit of a speech, in which the speaker captures the audience's attention and previews the main points to be covered.

transition
A phrase that connects ideas in a speech by showing how one relates to the other.

Refer to the Occasion

A reference to the occasion could allude to the event of your speech, as in 'Even though the focus of this course is human communication, it seems appropriate to talk about whether humans can communicate with plants.'

Refer to the Relationship between the Audience and the Subject

A reference to the relationship that the audience has to the subject will create a feeling of immediacy, as in 'My topic, "Communicating with Plants", ties right in with our study of human communication. We can gain several insights into our communication with one another by examining our interactions with our little green friends.'

Refer to Something Familiar to the Audience

The technique of referring to something familiar to the audience is especially effective if you are discussing a topic that might seem new or strange to that audience. Attention will be attracted to the familiar among the new in much the same way that we are able to pick out a friend's face in a crowd of strangers. For example, 'See that lilac bush outside the window? At this very moment it might be reacting to the joys and anxieties that you are experiencing in this classroom.'

Cite a Startling Fact or Opinion

A statement that surprises audience members is bound to make them sit up and listen. This is true even for a topic that the audience considers old hat; if the audience members think they've heard everything about plant–human communication before, you might mention, 'There is now actual scientific evidence that plants appreciate human company, kind words, and classical music.'

Cultural Idiom

old hat
not new or different

Ask a Question

A rhetorical question causes your audience to think rather than to answer out loud. 'Have you ever wondered why some people seem able to grow beautiful, healthy plants effortlessly, whereas others couldn't make a weed grow in the best soil?' This question is designed to make the audience respond mentally, 'Yeah, why is that?'

Tell an Anecdote

A personal story perks up audience interest because it shows the human side of what might otherwise be dry, boring information. 'The other night, while taking a walk in the country, I happened on a small garden that was rich with lush vegetation. But it wasn't the lushness of the vegetation that caught my eye at first. There, in the middle of the garden, was a man who was talking quite animatedly to a giant sunflower.'

Use a Quotation

Quotable quotes sometimes have a precise, memorable wording that would be difficult for you to equal. Also, they allow you to borrow from the credibility of the quoted source. For example, 'Thorne Bacon, the naturalist, recently said about the possibility of plants and humans communicating, "Personally, I cannot imagine a world so dull, so satiated, that it should reject out of hand arresting new ideas which may be as old as the first amino acid in the chain of life on earth."'

Tell a Joke

If you happen to know (or can find) a joke that suits your subject and occasion, it can help you build audience interest: 'We once worried about people who talked to plants, but that's no longer the case. Now we only worry if the plants talk back.' Be sure, though, that the joke is appropriate to the audience, as well as to the occasion and to you as a speaker.

Previewing Main Points

After you capture the attention of the audience, an effective introduction will almost always state your thesis and give your listeners an idea of the upcoming main points. At a ceremony presenting the Community Award for Graduating Students, Hilary Weston, then lieutenant-governor of Ontario, addressed the students of Toronto's Emory Collegiate Institute this way:

> If I remember my own schooldays correctly, the students attending today's assembly are torn between dreading a series of long-winded, boring speeches and hoping for a good, lengthy break from classes. I'm afraid I can try to address only one of these issues, because my remarks will be short—but I will try very hard not to be too boring!
>
> I always enjoy visiting schools—although, quite often, there is confusion among the students—and even the teachers—as to who is coming to visit. On one occasion, I rolled up to a school, full of beans, only to discover they were rather miffed that I wasn't the other Hillary—Mrs Clinton! They had prepared themselves with lots of questions about Bill and Monica—even from some of the more serious students—with questions about American politics and the role of a modern First Lady.
>
> So, just to set the record straight this time around: I'm not that Hillary, nor am I the Hilary Swank of Oscar fame—although you might think I have a very 'swanky' job! This Hilary was appointed Lieutenant Governor of Ontario by the Prime Minister of Canada just over three years ago.
>
> I'm not here to give you a history lecture, but I would like to tell you a little about my role, so that you can impress your friends and families with your amazing knowledge of the Canadian constitutional process![8]

In this way, Ms Weston previewed her main points:

1. To explain to whom the lieutenant-governor is responsible.
2. To explain what the lieutenant-governor is responsible for.
3. To explain how the lieutenant-governor is appointed.

Sometimes your preview of main points will be even more straightforward:

'I have three points to discuss: They are _____, _____, and _____.'

Sometimes your plan will call for you *not* to refer directly to your main points in your introduction. Perhaps you want to build suspense, create a humorous effect, or stall for time to win over a hostile audience. Whatever the reason, you might preview only your thesis:

'I am going to say a few words about _____.'
'Did you ever wonder about _____?'
'_____ is one of the most important issues facing us today.'

A speech is like a love affair. Any fool can start it, but to end it requires considerable skill.

Lord Mancroft

Setting the Mood and Tone of Your Speech

Notice, in the example just given, how Ms Weston immediately connects with her audience by relating how she felt about guest speakers when she was a student. She also uses an anecdote to keep the tone light and assures the group that she will not be delivering a lecture. This allows her to connect with the students, even though she is considerably older than them and probably also enjoys a higher standard of living than most of them. She shows them that she is going to approach her topic with wit and intelligence. Thus, she sets the mood and tone for her entire speech. Imagine how different that mood and tone would have been if she had said

> Before I start today, I would just like to say that I would never have accepted your invitation to speak here had I known that your school does not offer a French immersion program.

Demonstrating the Importance of Your Topic to Your Audience

Your audience members will listen to you more carefully if your speech relates to them as individuals. Based on your audience analysis, you should state directly *why* your topic is of importance to your audience members. This importance should be related as closely as possible to their specific needs at that specific time. In 1970, when then prime minister Pierre Elliott Trudeau addressed the people of Canada on the subject of the October Crisis, he established the importance of his topic in this way:

> I am speaking to you at a moment of grave crisis, when violent and fanatical men are attempting to destroy the unity and the freedom of Canada. One aspect of that crisis is the threat which has been made on the lives of two innocent men. These are matters of the utmost gravity and I want to tell you what the Government is doing to deal with them.
>
> What has taken place in Montreal in the past two weeks is not unprecedented. It has happened elsewhere in the world on several recent occasions; it could happen elsewhere within Canada. But Canadians have always assumed that it could not happen here and as a result we are doubly shocked that it has.
>
> Our assumption may have been naive, but it was understandable; understandable because democracy flourishes in Canada; understandable because individual liberty is cherished in Canada.
>
> Notwithstanding these conditions—partly because of them—it has now been demonstrated to us by a few misguided persons just how fragile a democratic society can be, if democracy is not prepared to defend itself, and just how vulnerable to blackmail are tolerant, compassionate people.[9]

Demonstrating the Importance of Your Topic to Others

In certain circumstances, a speaker might want to establish the importance of the topic not only to the audience but also to a wider group of people. In 2009, Boyd Neil, senior vice-president of corporate communications at Hill & Knowlton Canada, delivered a speech to the Empire Club of Canada outlining the importance of corporate social responsibility in an age dominated by omnipresent social media. Much of Neil's introduction is devoted to establishing the importance of social media not only to young people but also to organizations.

It's self-evident I think that trust in companies has declined significantly over the past few years although if you want to argue the point I can direct you to quite a number of studies that say so including H&K's own corporate reputation surveys that make the case. It has also become manifest that what can be called social tools—YouTube, Flickr, Facebook, Twitter and blogging among others—have been catalysts for impugning corporate behaviour. Just ask Domino's Pizza or McNeil Consumer Healthcare, TASER International, Continental Airlines or Dalhousie University.

What is less obvious, I think, is how these tools can be used by organizations and companies to build trust. There are a number of hypotheses about social media and trust, which I hope we can test in our short panel discussion. By doing so, I think we will get a better understanding of what those of us who manage reputation both inside and outside organizations have to do differently. I'd like to get things going by posing a few axiomatic beliefs of my own about social media. My point of view comes from four or five years of blogging, engaging in social networks such as Facebook and Twitter, providing counsel to clients on transforming crisis reputation and issue management strategies through the analysis and application of new social tools, teaching new directions in communications for two Canadian universities and discussion online and in person with people much smarter than me, some of whom are here today.[10]

Such an extended preamble might be too long and too general for most speech occasions, but in the context of the fact that social media was probably a relatively new topic to many senior executives in the audience makes it highly appropriate. Only now does Neil introduce the main subject of his talk: social media tools have changed the media and information landscape and organization must adapt. Neil's introduction emphasizes three themes that he will discuss at length in the body of the speech:

1. Large organizations are vulnerable ('It's self-evident I think that trust in companies has declined significantly over the past few years').
2. Social media tools have served to reduce corporate reputation ('It has also become manifest that what can be called social tools—YouTube, Flickr, Facebook, Twitter and blogging among others—have been catalysts for impugning corporate behaviour').
3. Understanding and mastering social media tools will help companies not only avoid reputational crises but improve their reputations ('What is less obvious, I think, is how these tools can be used by organizations and companies to build trust).

The Conclusion

The conclusion, like the introduction, is an especially important part of your speech. Your audience members will tend to be listening carefully, expecting you to provide a convenient summary and a concluding statement that will be easy to remember. The conclusion has three essential functions: to restate your thesis, review your main points, and provide a memorable final remark.

You can restate your thesis by either repeating or paraphrasing it. Either way, your conclusion should include a short summary statement:

> And so, after listening to what I had to say this afternoon, I hope you agree with me that the city cannot afford to lose the services of the Edmonton Humane Society.

You will probably also want to review your main points. This can be done directly: 'I made three main points about the Humane Society today. They are . . .'. But a less direct approach can be even more effective. For an example, first look back at the introduction to Trudeau's October Crisis speech, above, and then read his conclusion to that speech:

> Canada remains one of the most wholesome and humane lands on this earth. If we stand firm, this current situation will soon pass. We will be able to say proudly, as we have for decades, that within Canada there is ample room for opposition and dissent, but none for intimidation and terror.
>
> There are very few times in the history of any country when all persons must take a stand on critical issues. This is one of those times; this is one of those issues. I am confident that those persons who unleashed this tragic sequence of events with the aim of destroying our society and dividing our country will find that the opposite will occur. The result of their acts will be a stronger society in a unified country. Those who would have divided us will have united us.
>
> I sense the unease which grips many Canadians today. Some of you are upset, and this is understandable. I want to reassure you that the authorities have the situation well in hand. Everything that needs to be done is being done; every level of government in this country is well prepared to act in your interests.[11]

Let's take a closer look at how and why this conclusion was effective. In his introduction Trudeau raised three main points and established an atmosphere of uncertainty and alarm, which he highlighted with words like 'crisis', 'violent', 'fanatical', 'fragile', and 'vulnerable'. Now, in his conclusion, he returns to those themes, but this time the atmosphere is one of calm resolve and reassurance. A different emphasis in the language—'wholesome', 'humane', 'ample room', 'stronger society', 'unified country', 'well in hand'—reinforces the message that the situation is under control.

Preview (from conclusion)	Review (from introduction)
1. Canada is facing a moment of grave crisis.	1. If we stand firm, this crisis will pass.
2. Fanatical men are attempting to destroy Canada's unity and freedom.	2. In the end, their actions will have the opposite effect.
3. A democratic society is fragile and must be prepared to defend itself.	3. Government authorities are doing what is necessary to defend our society.

You can ensure that your audience will remember your thesis if you conclude with a striking summary statement. When Natalie St Clair, a student at the University of Ottawa, gave a speech on the dangers of biomedical experimentation in developing countries, she ended it with this concise yet memorable question: 'Testing drugs in Sri Lanka may give impoverished people access to health care, but what good is health care if it comes at the cost of innocent lives?' Finally, your closing remarks will be most effective if you remember these four simple guidelines:

Don't End Abruptly

Make sure that your conclusion accomplishes everything it is supposed to accomplish. Develop it fully. To let your audience know that you're about to conclude, you might want to use signposts such as 'finally . . .', 'in conclusion . . .', or 'to sum up what I've been talking about . . .'.

But Don't Ramble Either

Prepare a definite conclusion, and never, never end by mumbling something like, 'Well, I guess that's about all I wanted to say . . .'.

Don't Introduce New Points

The worst kind of rambling is 'Oh, yes, and something I forgot to mention is . . .'.

Don't Apologize

Don't say, 'I'm sorry I couldn't tell you more about this' or 'I'm sorry I didn't have more time to research this subject' or any of those sad songs. They will only highlight the possible weaknesses of your speech, and there's a good chance those weaknesses were far more apparent to you than to your audience.

Instead, end on a strong note. You can use any of the attention-getters suggested for the introduction to make the conclusion memorable. In fact, one kind of effective closing is to refer to the attention-getter you used in your introduction and remind your audience how it applies to the points you made in your speech.

Supporting Material

It is important to organize ideas clearly and logically. But clarity and logic by themselves won't guarantee that you'll interest, enlighten, or persuade others; these results call for the use of supporting materials. These materials—the facts and information that back up and prove your ideas and opinions—are the flesh that fills out the skeleton of your speech.

Functions of Supporting Material

There are four functions of supporting material.

To Clarify

As we explained in Chapter 3, people of different backgrounds tend to attach different meanings to words. Supporting material can help you avoid confusion by clarifying key terms and ideas. For example, when Ed Rubenstein, the economics analyst at the *National Review*, spoke to a college audience on 'The Economics of Crime', he used supporting material to clarify what he meant by the term *career criminal*:

> The career criminal, according to James Q. Wilson, was long ago identified as: 'typically an impulsive young man who grew up in a discordant family where one or both

parents had a criminal record, discipline was erratic, and human relations were cold and unpredictable. He had a low IQ and poor verbal skills. His behavioural problems appeared early, often by age eight, and included dishonesty and aggressiveness. Even in kindergarten or first grade he was disruptive, defiant, and badly behaved. He had few friends and was not emotionally close to those associates with whom he began stealing and assaulting.'[12]

To Make Interesting

A second function of support is to make an idea interesting or to catch your audience's attention. When Daniel White gave a speech on cloning, he might simply have said, 'There's been a lot of interest in cloning in the media recently.' Instead, he used supporting material to make the same point in a more interesting way:

> 'British Scientists Clone the World's First Adult Mammal.' On February 24 of this year, this headline, or something like it, was plastered on the front page of newspapers all across the nation. Coincidentally, the following weekend the new *Star Trek* episode revealed that Dr Julian Bashir of Deep Space Nine was a product of genetic engineering, the X-Files ran a string of shows dealing with clones, and recently the movie *Multiplicity*, another cloning story, hit the new release section of local video stores.[13]

To Make Memorable

A third function of supporting materials, related to the preceding one, is to make a point memorable. We have already mentioned the value of including 'memorable' statements in a speech conclusion; but it is equally important to make sure that your audience retains important information throughout your speech. Using supporting material is another way to emphasize key points. When Amy Jones wanted to help her audience remember that mosquitoes are a genuine health hazard, she used supporting material in this way:

> We must realize that mosquitoes are more than just a nuisance. In the past nine minutes, 75 more children have died of malaria.[14]

To Prove

Finally, supporting material can be used as evidence, to prove the truth of what you are saying. When Brian Sosnowchik wanted to prove the point that chronic pain is a significant problem in the United States, he used supporting material in this way:

> 'I can't shower because the water feels like molten lava. Every time someone turns on a ceiling fan, it feels like razor blades are cutting through my legs. I'm dying.' Meet David Bogan, financial advisor from Deptford, New Jersey. Porsche, boat, and home owner, and victim of a debilitating car accident that has not only rendered him two years of chronic leg pain, but a fall from the pinnacle of success. Bogan has nothing now. Life to him, life with searing pain, is a worthless tease of agony and distress.
>
> Unfortunately, according to the February 21, 2000 *St. Louis Post-Dispatch,* Bogan is one of 100 million Americans, nearly a third of the population, suffering from chronic pain due to everything from accidents to the simple daily stresses on our bodies. Moreover, in a personal telephone interview on March 30, 2000, Penny Cowan, founder and Executive Director of the American Chronic Pain Association, disclosed, 'Chronic

pain is the most expensive health care problem today, and it certainly doesn't get the appropriate amount of attention from the medical community.'[15]

Types of Supporting Material

As you may have noted, each of the support functions outlined above could be fulfilled by several different types of material. Let's take a look at the main categories of supporting material.

Definitions

It's a good idea to define your key terms, especially if they may be unfamiliar to your audience or if you're using them in an unusual way. A good definition is simple and concise. If you were giving a speech on binge drinking, you might define that term as follows:

> Researchers consider a person who has had five drinks on one occasion during the previous two weeks to be a binge drinker.

Examples

An **example** is a specific case that is used to demonstrate a general idea. Examples can be either factual or hypothetical, personal or borrowed. Rick Hansen, the Canadian wheelchair athlete who travelled around the world to generate awareness of and support for people with disabilities, drew on his own experience for an example of how our lives can be changed for the good. If he had been injured a century earlier, he said, he likely would not have survived:

> But advances in medical technology gave me the opportunity to not only survive but to have hope. I was impacted by a leader in this country who is one of those representations of the thousands of faceless, nameless people who go about their daily lives, in service, asking nothing in return. His name was Stan Strong. Stan wheeled into my life with this incredible grin on his face, with a disability, looking at me and saying: 'Son, what have you got to feel sorry about? Don't you realize that your biggest disability is your attitude at this point? It's time for you to move on. Life can continue.' His inspiration in my life, at a critical moment, was a reflection of all of us in the work that we do—those moments in service when we give for others, when we never know when the penny will drop and when an impact will be so powerfully felt and heard. I was able to move forward in my sport, to represent my country and to be compelled to try to give something back, to wheel around the world.[16]

Hypothetical examples can often be more powerful than factual examples, because hypothetical examples ask audience members to imagine something—thus causing them to become active participants in the thought. Former Alberta premier Ralph Klein used a series of hypothetical examples to convince Albertans to 'Imagine Alberta':

> Now is the perfect time for everyone of us to 'Imagine Alberta' and all it can be: home to the most highly educated and skilled workforce in the world; pioneers in transforming an abundance of resources into new products and opportunities, while protecting our environment; innovators in the development of clean energy; a leader in the war on cancer. Imagine Alberta front and centre on the international stage, creating a quality of life

example
A specific case that is used to demonstrate a general idea.

hypothetical example
An example that asks an audience to imagine an object or event.

second to none, and sharing our good fortune with people across the country, and around the world. . . .

New primary health care networks will soon be up and running, giving Albertans access to care from committed teams of physicians, nurses, dietitians, pharmacists and therapists, all working together.

I imagine a future where these types of innovations take root all across the province . . . where an electronic health record will allow health care providers to instantly access comprehensive, up-to-date information . . . where mental health services are available to everyone who needs them.

I imagine a future where we start to win the fight against cancer . . . where Alberta is known as a worldwide leader in the battle against cancer, renowned for our research, expertise, and leadership.[17]

---

statistics

Numbers arranged or organized to show how a fact or principle is true for a large percentage of cases.

A definition is the enclosing of the wilderness of an idea within a wall of words.

Samuel Butler

Statistics

Statistics are numbers that are arranged or organized to show that a fact or principle is true for a large percentage of cases. Statistics are actually collections of examples, which is why they are often more effective as proof than are isolated examples. A speech claiming that the Canadian Long Gun Registry should not be scrapped might cite the following statistics from a report from the Royal Canadian Mounted Police called 'Canadian Firearms Program Evaluation':

Recently compiled statistics initiated by this evaluation, data from Statistics Canada and all of the Provincial and Territorial Coroners indicate notable decreases of firearm deaths (approximately 12%) in Canada between 2001 and 2004. . . . A survey of Canadian Firearms Registry Online (CFRO) users showed that 81% of trained police officers supported the statement, 'In my experience, CFRO query results have proven beneficial during major operations.' . . . 513 RCMP detachments and federal units, 579 Canadian municipal police agencies and 88 OPP locations query CFRO yearly.[18]

Because statistics can be powerful proof, there are certain rules to follow when using them. You should make sure that they make sense and that they come from a credible source. You should also cite the source of the statistic when you use it. Finally, you should reduce the statistic to a concrete image if possible. For example, $1 billion in $100 bills would be about the same height as a 60-storey building. A concrete image such as this will make the statistics you cite more than 'just numbers'. One observer expressed the idea of Bill Gates's wealth this way:

Examine Bill Gates' wealth compared to yours: consider the average American of reasonable but modest wealth. Perhaps he has a net worth of $100,000. Mr Gates' worth is 400,000 times larger. Which means that if something costs $100,000 to him, to Bill it's as though it costs 25 cents. So for example, you might think a new Lamborghini Diablo would cost $250,000, but in Bill Gates dollars that's 63 cents.[19]

Comparison and Contrast

We use comparisons all the time, often in the form of figures of speech such as similes and metaphors. A simile uses *like* or *as* to equate one thing with another: 'Snow covered the town like a blanket.' A metaphor, by contrast, makes the connection directly, without using *like* or *as:* 'A blanket of snow covered the town'; 'Snow blanketed the town'; 'The town lay under a blanket of snow', and so on. An **analogy** is an extended comparison. Here Jose Kusugak, former president of the Inuit Tapiriit Kanatami (Inuit are United in Canada), uses an analogy to Canadian's sense of fairness overseas to emphasize the importance of fairness when dealing with Aborginal people:

'Tonight, we're going to let the statistics speak for themselves.'

In the more than 30 years that I have been travelling across Canada speaking to all kinds of people on all kinds of subjects, there is one common theme. Canadians are a fair-minded people. I believe as Canadians we believe in fair play. We certainly showed it in times of disaster like the tsunami last December, hurricanes Katrina and Rita and the earthquake this week in Pakistan. We showed it 25 years ago during the Ethiopian famine. In fact the Inuit of Canada on a per-capita basis were the largest donors during that horrible crisis.

It is easy to find fairness and sharing in times of disaster. I regret to say it is harder to find those values in the day-to-day politics in Ottawa in determining our place in Canada and to ensuring a fair quality of life and standard of living for our people.

. . .

Let me paint for you a painful but fair picture of what's happening in some of our communities and what we are trying to do to change the situation.

We have a housing crisis so severe that it will cost more to correct than the cost of settling our land claims. We have a housing emergency due in part by the department's decision 10 years ago to withdraw from providing public housing for Inuit. The other reason is our high birth rate and population boom. The unemployment rate in most of our communities is the highest in Canada. You saw evidence of our cost of living and our average annual wage is far below the national average. We have overcrowding in our communities. We have hidden homelessness and we have a growing population of Inuit youth who have little hope in their lifetime of ever getting their own home because our waiting lists are way too long. When we were going to a restaurant last night we saw some homeless people around the hotel. Here they can actually live outside all year over some heat vent and so on. We can't have that in the Arctic so any homeless person has to go into a house and live with other people so homelessness is hidden.[20]

analogy
An extended comparison that can be used as supporting material in a speech.

Analogies can be used to compare or contrast an unknown concept with a known one. For example, here's the way one doctor explained the importance of regular medical checkups for an audience of men:

> Guys, here's a good analogy to remember: your own preventive checkups are like automobile checkups. While most of us are responsible for, even proud of, how we maintain our vehicles, we don't feel the same sense of accomplishment with our own bodies.
>
> Does getting a tune-up of the car engine guarantee it won't fail? Absolutely not. But it does significantly reduce the risk.
>
> The same thing goes for preventive medical checkups. Do they guarantee nothing bad will happen to you? No, but by understanding the statistical risks people face, and by evaluating and addressing those risks, you improve your odds.
>
> Taking care of your car means regular tune-ups. Taking care of your health means regular checkups.[21]

Anecdotes

An **anecdote** is a brief story with a point, often (but not always) based on personal experience. (The word *anecdote* comes from the Greek, meaning 'unpublished item'.) Politician and Canadian 'father of medicare' Tommy Douglas was famous for his use of anecdotes. In an address to New Democratic supporters, he used the following anecdote to make the point that fighting the good fight for workers' rights is very rewarding:

> About two weeks ago I was very tired and a bit low. We got word that the Canadian Pacific Railway (CPR) had been granted a 17% freight rate increase by the Transport Commission, in spite of appeals to the cabinet. . . . I had the battle of my life with CPR lawyers and officials, and suddenly I felt ten years younger. I've been going on the momentum of that fight with the CPR ever since. I don't know whether it increases the adrenaline in my system, but a fight always makes me feel better.[22]

Quotation/Testimony

A well-chosen quotation allows you to take advantage of someone else's memorable wording. The benefits may be even greater if the quotation and its author are well known. For example, if you were giving a speech on personal integrity, you might quote Mark Twain's famous line: 'Always do right. This will gratify some people, and astonish the rest.' Such a quotation fits Alexander Pope's definition of 'true wit': 'What was often thought, but ne'er so well expressed.'

You can also use quotations as **testimony**, supporting a point by appealing to the authority of someone with particular knowledge of your subject. When former prime minister Jean Chrétien gave a speech in tribute to the recently deceased Pierre Trudeau, he used Trudeau's own words to evoke his feelings for Canada:

> Pierre Elliott Trudeau was a man like no other.
>
> A man of brilliance and learning. A man of action. A man of grace and style. A man of wit and playfulness. A man of extraordinary courage. A complex man, whose love of Canada was pure and simple.
>
> Pierre wrote about 'a man who never learned patriotism in school, but who acquired that virtue when he felt in his bones the vastness of his land and the greatness of its

---

anecdote
A brief personal story used to illustrate or support a point in a speech.

testimony
Supporting material that proves or illustrates a point by citing an authoritative source.

founders'. Pierre, too, came to love this land as he climbed its mountain peaks, con-quered the rapids of its rivers and wandered the streets of its cities.[23]

Sometimes testimony can be paraphrased. A business executive giving a talk on the subject of diversity, for example, referred to a conversation he once had with the prominent civil-rights leader Jesse Jackson as testimony:

At one point in our conversation, Jesse talked about the stages of advancement toward a society where diversity is fully valued. He said the first stage was emancipation—the end of slavery. The second stage was the right to vote and the third stage was the politi-cal power to actively participate in government—to be part of city hall, the Governor's office and Capitol Hill. Jesse was clearly focused, though, on the fourth stage—which he described as the ability to participate fully in the prosperity that this nation enjoys. In other words, economic power.[24]

Styles of Support: Narration and Citation

Most of the forms of support discussed in the preceding section could be presented in either of two ways: through narration or through citation. **Narration** means storytelling: you pres-ent your information in the form of a small drama, with a beginning, middle, and end. In the following example, Canadian Armed Forces General Rick Hillier used narrative in a speech on 'The Men and Women of Canada's Armed Forces':

The Prime Minister as you know went to Afghanistan about a month ago. I had the op-portunity to meet him. We had about 25 or 30 men and women in uniform waiting to greet him and welcome him to Kandahar and to Afghanistan on the tarmac. He was a little bit late so I had a chance to talk to all those folks. A dust storm made the plane 45 minutes late. I was sitting there chatting to them about a variety of things, laughing and talking to about 15 men and eight to 10 female soldiers. Out of those 15 men, nine of them had similar haircuts to Master Corporal Perry and Master Seaman Miller and I am trying to figure out whether my wife would like it if I did that. None of those folks knew who was arriving. We had a tight security blanket on and none of them knew who was arriving. They knew somebody was coming who we wanted them to greet. As the Prime Minister got off the aircraft one of our female master corporals said, 'Sir, I'm really excited to welcome the Prime Minister, to meet the Prime Minister, I thought it was going to be Don Cherry.'[25]

By contrast, **citation** is a simple statement of the facts. Citation is usually more concise than narration, and it is always more precise in that it includes specific details about the source of the information. A citation will always include a phrase such as 'According to the 25 July 2006 edition of *The Walrus* magazine' or 'As Mr Knight made clear in an interview on 24 April of this year'. General Hillier cited some statistics later in his speech:

The last thing I have to tell you is we need recruits. We need Canadians. Now there have been a lot of naysayers out there who don't believe that we can actually recruit the number of men and women that we need. This past year, the fiscal year from April 1 of last year to March 31 just past, we had set a goal of 5,627 new recruits. That allowed

citation
A brief statement of supporting material in a speech.

narration
Presentation of speech supporting material as a story with a begin-ning, middle, and end.

us to meet attrition and to grow by 500 soldiers, which is all the money that we had for increased growth. As of the end of March 31 we were at 106 per cent of target. In fact, we succeeded even with our dinosaur methods of recruiting, even with our slow and ponderous and painful process, because I believe that most young Canadians can see and feel the excitement that I and these men and women who are here with me today feel and believe and see in what we do.[26]

Some types of support, such as anecdotes, naturally lend themselves to narration. Statistics, on the other hand, are nearly always presented in citation form. With the other types of support—examples, quotation/testimony, definitions, analogies—you will often be able to use either narration or citation.

Holding the Audience's Attention

No matter how supporting material is used, a speech will not be successful if it does not hold the audience's attention. We have all been in situations where we attended a speech and, regardless of how passionate we were about the topic or maybe even the speaker, found ourselves nodding off or losing our concentration. That's why speeches have to be written with keeping people captivated as the main goal.

Make It Easy to Listen

Remember the complex nature of listening discussed in Chapter 4. For your speech to be well received, you must make it easy for your audience members to hear, pay attention, understand, and remember. This means that you should speak clearly and with enough volume to be heard by all your listeners. It also means that as you put your speech together, you should be mindful of those techniques, including the three given here, that recognize the way human beings process information.

Limit the Amount of Information You Present

Remember that you have become an expert on this topic and that you won't be able to transmit everything you know to your audience at one sitting. It's better to make careful choices about the three to five main ideas you want to get across and then develop those ideas fully. Too much information leads to overload, anxiety, and a lack of attention on the part of your audience.

Use Familiar Information to Increase Understanding of the Unfamiliar

Move your audience members from information that you can assume they know about, based on your audience analysis, to your newer information. For example, if you are giving a speech about how the stock market works, you could compare the daily activity of a broker with that of a salesperson in a retail store, or you could compare the idea of capital growth (a new concept to some listeners) with interest earned in a savings account (a more familiar concept).

Use Simple Information to Build Understanding of Complex Information

Just as you move your audience members from the familiar to the unfamiliar, you can move them from the simple to the complex. An average college or university audience, for example, can understand the complexities of genetic modification if you begin with the concept of inherited characteristics.

We know more than we can tell.

Michael Polanyi

Emphasize Important Points

Along with making it easy to listen to your speech, you should stress its important points through repetition and the use of signposts.

Repetition

Repetition is one of the age-old rules of learning. People are simply more likely to absorb and understand information that is stated more than once. This is especially true in a speaking situation, where your audience members cannot go back to pick up something they have missed the way they could with a piece of writing. If their minds have wandered the first time you said something, they just might pick it up the second time.

Of course, simply repeating something in the same words might bore the audience members who actually are paying attention, so effective speakers learn to say the same thing in more than one way. CBC executive Sylvain Lafrance used this technique in a speech explaining radio's role in keeping listeners aware of important events taking place both in their own communities and around the world:

> **Cultural Idiom**
>
> **run a point into the ground**
> over-elaborate an idea to the point where the audience is tired of hearing about it

> Citizens waking up in the morning and turning on the radio in Montreal, in Bangkok, or in Shanghai probably want to hear a voice from home telling them about things that will have an impact on their daily lives, but also the things that constitute a threat in today's world, and those that are a source of happiness. These realities are not just local—they are at once local, national, and international. The radio must be a window for citizens onto their streets, their cities, and their countries, and from there to an entire planet that seems to shrink a bit more every day. Our challenge at CBC/Radio-Canada is defining how radio can bring people closer and be open to the world, given today's new realities.[27]

Redundancy can be effective when you use it to emphasize important points.[28] It is ineffective only when (1) you are redundant with obvious, trivial, or boring points, and (2) you run an important point into the ground. There is no sure rule for making certain you have not overemphasized a point. You just have to use your best judgment to make sure that you have stated the point enough that your audience members get it without repeating it so often that they want to give it back.

Signposts

Another way to emphasize important material is by using **signposts,** words or phrases that emphasize the importance of what you are about to say. You can state, simply enough, 'What I'm about to say is important,' or you can substitute some variation of that idea: 'You should understand that . . .', 'The most important thing to remember is . . .', 'The three keys to this situation are . . .', and so on.

Use Clear, Simple Language

Another technique for effective informative speaking is to use clear language—which means using precise, simple wording and avoiding jargon. Dictionaries and thesauruses are handy tools for picking precise vocabulary. The online dictionary and the 'thesaurus' function that can be found under the 'tools/language' tab of most word processing programs can be consulted easily as you plan your speech. You should remember, though, that picking the right word, the most precise word, seldom means using a word that is unfamiliar to your audience. In fact, just the opposite is true. Important ideas do not have to sound complicated.

Along with simple vocabulary, you should strive toward simple syntax by using a direct, short sentence structure. In a speech about the new mandate for the Ontario Women's Health Council, Jane Pepino, the council's chairperson, introduced her main ideas in the following way:

The opportunity for constructive advocacy—to move from talking to doing—needs a place and a forum and often a microphone. The voice of women in this province now has a place to be heard, and a group who are mandated to be their advocates. We have microphones. We have e-mail. We have access to the best and the brightest to advise us on what works and what doesn't. Thanks to women advocating for their own health for many years, the Women's Health Council can begin to advocate for them and with them.[29]

Pepino's vocabulary choices are interesting and clear, and we have a clear sense of where she is going to take this speech as she continues.

Generate Audience Involvement

The final technique for effective speaking is to get your audience involved in your speech. **Audience involvement** is the level of commitment and attention that listeners devote to a speech. Educational psychologists have long known that the best way to teach people something is to have them do it; social psychologists have added to this rule by proving, through many studies, that involving an audience in a message increases the audience members' comprehension of, and agreement with, that message.

There are many ways to encourage audience involvement in your speech. One way is to follow the rules for good delivery by maintaining enthusiasm, energy, eye contact, and so on. Other ways include personalizing your speech, using audience participation, using volunteers, and having a question-and-answer period.

Personalize Your Speech

One way to encourage audience involvement is to give audience members a human being to connect with. In other words, don't be afraid to be yourself and to inject a little of your own personality into the speech. If you happen to be good at storytelling, make a narration part of your speech. If humour is one of your strengths, be funny. If you feel passionate about your topic, show it. Certainly, if you have any personal experience that relates to your topic, use it.

Use Audience Participation

Audience participation—having your listeners actually take part during your speech—is another way to increase their involvement in your message. For example, if you were giving a demonstration of isometric exercises (which don't require too much room for movement), you could have the entire audience stand up and do one or two sample exercises. (Exercise not only involves audience members psychologically, but also keeps them more alert physically.) If you were explaining how to fill out a federal income-tax form, you could give each audience member a sample form to fill out as you explain it. Outlines and checklists can be used in a similar manner for just about any speech.

Here's how one student organization in the United States used audience participation to demonstrate the various restrictions that were once placed on American voting rights:

> Voting is something that a lot of us may take for granted. Today, the only requirements for voting are that you are a US citizen aged 18 or older who has lived in the same place for at least 30 days—and that you have registered. But it hasn't always been that way. Americans have had to struggle for the right to vote. I'd like to illustrate this by asking everyone to please stand.
>
> [Wait, prod class to stand.]
>
> I'm going to ask some questions. If you answer no to any question, please sit down.
>
> Do you have five extra dollars in your pocket right now? If not, sit down. Up until 1964, poll taxes existed in many states.
>
> Have you resided at the same address for at least one year? If not, sit down. Residency requirements of more than 30 days weren't abolished until 1970.
>
> Are you white? If not, sit down. The 15th Amendment gave non-whites the right to vote in 1870 but many states didn't enforce it until the late 1960s.
>
> Are you male? If not, sit down. The 19th Amendment only gave women the right to vote in 1920.
>
> Do you own a home? If not, sit down. Through the mid-1800s only property owners could vote.
>
> Are you Protestant? If not, sit down. That's right. Religious requirements existed in the early days throughout the country.[30]

Use Volunteers

If the action you are demonstrating is too expensive or intricate to allow all audience members to take part, you can select one or two volunteers to help you out. By doing this you will increase the psychological involvement of all the members because they will tend to identify with the volunteers.

Have a Question-and-Answer Period

A way to increase audience involvement that is nearly always appropriate if time allows is to answer questions at the end of your speech. You should encourage your audience to ask questions. Solicit questions, and be patient waiting for the first one. Often no one wants to ask the first question. When the questions do start coming, the following suggestions might help you make your answers more effective:

1. **Listen to the substance of the question.** Don't zero in on irrelevant details; listen for the big picture—the basic, overall question that is being asked. If you are not really sure what the substance of a question is, ask the questioner to paraphrase it. Don't be afraid to let the questioners do their share of the work.

2. **Paraphrase confusing questions.** Use the active listening skills described in Chapter 4. You can paraphrase the question in just a few words: 'If I understand your question, you are asking _____ . Is that right?'

3. **Avoid defensive reactions to questions.** Even if the questioner seems to be calling you a liar or biased or ill-informed, try to listen to the substance of the question and not to the possible attack on your personality.

4. **Answer the question as briefly as possible.** Then check the questioner's comprehension of your answer. Sometimes you can simply check his or her non-verbal response—if he or she seems at all confused, you can ask, 'Does that answer your question?'

Sample Speech

The following speech was presented by former prime minister Jean Chrétien in 1997 to mark the signing of the Ottawa Treaty, an agreement aimed at the elimination of anti-personnel landmines around the world.

This speech uses an impressive array of supporting material: quotations, testimony, examples, definitions, emotional appeals, analogies, personal reflections, and anecdotes. Emphasizing Canada's pre-eminence in the international anti-landmine campaign, Chrétien draws attention to the leading roles played by two members of his government, former foreign minister André Ouellet and in particular his successor, Lloyd Axworthy, in achieving the breakthrough that made this treaty possible. He also includes several references to the personal experiences behind his own commitment to the cause. Allusions to the many Canadian soldiers killed or maimed in war since 1914, including a peacekeeper who was killed by a landmine, and the awarding of the Nobel Peace Prize to Lester Pearson reinforce the message that Canada is well positioned to lead this international effort. At the same time he never lets his audience forget the urgency of taking immediate practical action for real people. This is an exemplary speech, delivered by one of Canada's most experienced and canny politicians.

The outline for this speech might look like this (the numbers in parentheses represent the corresponding paragraphs in the speech):

Introduction
 I. Attention-getter (1)
    The landmine epidemic: death remains after war is finished.

II. Statement of thesis (2)

This conference marks a shift in the movement by highlighting the voices of those most affected by the issue, which are more eloquent than the voices of dignitaries and politicians.

III. Preview of main points (3)

Body

I. Individuals and organizations have worked hard to make the treaty possible. (3–7)

Transition: 'I welcome you to an historic occasion.' (3)

A. Goals and accomplishments of the conference: (3)

1. The majority of the world's nations will agree to the anti-landmine treaty.

2. A global partnership of governments, international institutions, and non-governmental groups will spearhead the movement.

3. Citizens in countries affected by landmines can begin to hope.

B. Several powerful international organizations, celebrities, and dignitaries have lent and will lend support to the cause (5), including

1. The Red Cross and the International Campaign to Ban Landmines

2. Diana, Princess of Wales, who was a supporter of the anti-landmine movement

3. UN Secretary-General Kofi Annan, who has made a pledge to engage the United Nations in the anti-landmine cause

II. Chrétien and Canada have long been committed to the anti-landmine cause. (6–11)

Transition: Preview of main theme, the urgency to act. (6)

A. Canada has a history of commitment to the cause. (6–8)

1. In 1994, Chrétien raised the issue at the G-7 Summit.

2. In 1996, Lloyd Axworthy organized a conference in Ottawa. (6–7)

3. Within 14 months, Canada persuaded 100 countries to ban landmines. (8)

B. Chrétien outlines his personal feelings and pledges to uphold Canada's commitment. (9–11)

1. Chrétien's personal recognition of how many Canadians have been killed or maimed by landmines. (9).

2. His delight at the widespread support for the treaty.(10)

3. His promise of Canada's commitment to continue working to persuade those countries that have not agreed to the treaty. (11)

III. The world and Canada are committed to the cause. (12)

Transition: 'Canada, my country, has never had landmine killing fields.' (12)

A. The consequences of landmines:

1. Many peacekeepers have been killed, among them a Canadian. (12–13)

2. Humans living in the affected regions have suffered devastating losses. (14)

B. A call to the world to make a promise

1. To Admir (15)

2. To the dead (16)

3. To convince other nations. (17)

C. Canada leads the way: (18–21)

1. Canada is the first country to ratify the landmine treaty into law. (18)

2. Canada pledges $100 million. (19)

3. Canada calls on others to follow its lead. (20–1)

Conclusion
  I. Final remarks (22)
 II. Review of main points (22)
III. Restatement of thesis (23)

Speech at the Conference for the Global Ban on Anti-Personnel Landmines, Ottawa, 3 December 1997
Jean Chrétien

Distinguished Guests, Ladies and Gentlemen,

1 We have come together today to bring an end to the landmine epidemic. The sting of death remains long after the guns grow quiet, long after the battles are over.

2 At international conferences, there is always a great deal of talk and debate. But the most powerful voices here in Ottawa will not be the ones inside this conference site. They will be the cries of the victims of landmines—from the ricefields of Cambodia, to the suburbs of Kabul; from the mountainsides of Sarajevo to the plains of Mozambique. A chorus of millions of voices, pleading with the world, demanding the elimination of anti-personnel landmines.

3 I welcome you to an historic occasion. For the first time, the majority of the nations of the world will agree to ban a weapon which has been in military use by almost every country in the world. For the first time, a global partnership of governments, international institutions, and non-governmental groups has come together—with remarkable speed and spirit—to draft the treaty we will sign today. For the first time, those who fear to walk in their fields, those who cannot till their lands, those who cannot return to their own homes—all because of landmines—once again can begin to hope.

4 For all of them, for all of us, this is a day we will never forget.

5 The work of many nations, groups, and individuals has brought us to this moment. The International Committee of the Red Cross, whose surgeons have seen too many bodies shattered by landmines, offered early leadership. The International Campaign to Ban Landmines drove the cause with their enthusiasm and commitment. The late Princess of Wales seized the attention of the world when she exposed the human cost of landmines. And Secretary-General Kofi Annan showed courageous leadership. He recognized that the Ottawa process embodied a solemn commitment made by 156 UN members in 1996. A pledge to 'pursue vigorously an effective, legally binding international agreement to ban the use, stockpiling, production, and transfer of anti-personnel landmines'.

6 At the first G-7 Summit I attended as prime minister, in Naples in 1994, I raised the Canadian concern over the landmine epidemic. In 1995, our foreign minister, André Ouellet, committed Canada to the cause of banning landmines. And in 1996, Lloyd Axworthy brought new energy, commitment, and new urgency to world action. He convened a conference in Ottawa because we were not satisfied with what had been done to end the extermination in slow motion caused by landmines.

7 We knew that it was not good enough to end the landmine epidemic at some distant future date. Not with a hundred million mines planted all over the world. Not with thousands of innocent civilians—men, women, and children—dying every year. We knew we had to act. And we did.

8 At the end of that October conference, on behalf of Canada, Lloyd Axworthy challenged the world to return here just fourteen months later to sign a treaty banning the use, transfer, production, and stockpiling of anti-personnel landmines. His challenge marked a breakthrough. A breakthrough that has led directly to this historic moment. Back then, we believed if only a handful of countries came to sign, it would be an achievement. Today and tomorrow, more than 100 countries will sign this treaty. I want to say to Lloyd—your government is proud of you and your country is proud of you.

9 Like all of you here today, I have so many memories of the landmine campaign. Just last month—as every year—we honoured our war dead at the Cenotaph, just metres from this building. Standing there, I realized that, within weeks, we would be banning a weapon that has killed and maimed Canadian soldiers since the First World War.

10 I will never forget my discussions with prime ministers and presidents as they grappled with the consequences of signing this treaty, and my delight when they said that their governments would be in Ottawa in December. Of course, not all will be here, but even in the case of many who are absent, there is a new commitment to ban exports and end production. A commitment that would not be there if this conference were not taking place.

11 I give you my commitment that Canada will continue to work to persuade those who are not here to sign. We must always recognize that this treaty is open to all but can be hostage to none.

12 Canada, my country, has never had landmine killing fields. But in this century Canadian soldiers and peacekeepers have walked and died in those fields. As Secretary-General Annan knows so well, over 200 UN peacekeepers have died as landmine victims.

13 In June 1994, Master Corporal Mark Ifield, a Canadian peacekeeper in Croatia, was killed by a landmine. We honour those peacekeepers today as we remember all who have fallen victims of this horrible weapon.

14 And we listen to those who still fear like Admir Mujkic, a grade 12 student, in East Tuzla in Bosnia. In an essay, he told us his dream and his fear:

> I want to run through fields with my girlfriend. I want to pick the first violet for her, and to climb the trees in the forest. . . . Should all my life be permanently marked with the word 'mine'?

15 No Admir, it should not. Let us say to all the children of the world that you will walk again through the fields, and climb the trees in the forests, in a world free from mines.

16 And let us swear to those hundreds of thousands who have been murdered by landmines that we will not turn back. To the children whose very futures were stolen from them; to the families that were destroyed; to those who have lost limbs, who have lost lives: this slaughter must end. It will end. And that ending begins here—in Ottawa.

17 We will leave Ottawa proud of what we have done but very conscious of what is left to do. There are still many nations which must join us. There are still hundreds of thousands of victims to help. There are still tens of millions of mines to clear.

18 Certainly the commitment of the Government of Canada does not end with hosting this conference. I am proud to say that, by unanimous consent, both houses of our

Parliament have ratified the treaty, and it has been proclaimed as law, making Canada the first nation in the world to ratify this historic convention.

19　On behalf of our government, I am also proud to announce today the establishment of a $100 million fund to implement this treaty. This means bringing it to life; making it truly global; clearing the mines; helping the victims. Both with immediate medical care and long-term help rebuilding their lives.

20　I know other countries are making similar contributions. I call on all countries to put forward the resources needed to rid the world of these buried killing machines—once and for all.

21　Jody Williams soon will go to Oslo to receive the Nobel Peace Prize. Forty years ago, a Canadian made the same journey. In bestowing the prize on Lester Pearson, the Nobel Academy said: 'No matter how dark the outcome for the world may be, Lester Pearson is no pessimist. His efforts would not have been possible unless he had been supported by a strong faith in the final victory of the good forces of life.'

22　Distinguished guests, ladies and gentlemen, we still have much work to do, but I am no pessimist. And obviously, neither are any of you. Today is a triumph for Jody Williams; for Lloyd Axworthy; for Secretary-General Annan; for all the many others who deserve our thanks. But to borrow those words of forty years ago in Oslo, it is the triumph of something else, something even bigger: it is the triumph of the forces of good in life.

23　Today, in Ottawa, let us celebrate that triumph. And let us commit here and now to even greater triumphs ahead.[31]

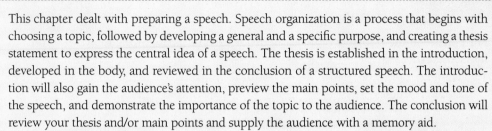

Summary

This chapter dealt with preparing a speech. Speech organization is a process that begins with choosing a topic, followed by developing a general and a specific purpose, and creating a thesis statement to express the central idea of a speech. The thesis is established in the introduction, developed in the body, and reviewed in the conclusion of a structured speech. The introduction will also gain the audience's attention, preview the main points, set the mood and tone of the speech, and demonstrate the importance of the topic to the audience. The conclusion will review your thesis and/or main points and supply the audience with a memory aid.

The process of organizing the body of a speech begins with listing the points you might want to make. These points are then arranged according to the principles of outlining. They are divided, coordinated, and placed in a logical order. Transitions from point to point help make this order apparent to your audience. Organization should follow the pattern that best suits your argument. The most common patterns are based on time (including building to a climax or anticlimax), space, topic, problem–solution, cause–effect, and motivated sequence.

Supporting materials are the facts and information you use to back up what you say. Supporting material has four purposes: to clarify, to make interesting, to make memorable, and to prove. Types of supporting materials include definitions, examples, statistics, analogies, anecdotes, quotations, and testimony. Any piece of support might combine two or more of these types. Support may be narrated (told in story form) or cited (stated briefly).

A key objective in speech writing is to hold the audience's attention. This goal can be achieved by making the speech easy to listen to, emphasizing important points, using clear and simple language, and generating audience involvement.

Key Terms

analogy 475
audience involvement 480
audience participation 481
anecdote 476
basic speech structure 456
cause–effect patterns 464
citation 477
climax pattern 462
conclusion 465
description 451
example 473

explanation 451
formal outline 456
general purpose 450
hypothetical examples 473
instruction 451
introduction 465
motivated sequence 464
narration 477
problem–solution
   pattern 463
purpose statement 451

signpost 480
space pattern 462
specific purpose 451
statistics 474
testimony 476
thesis statement 453
time pattern 462
topic pattern 462
transition 465
working outline 456

Activities

A. Dividing Ideas

For practice in the principle of division, divide each of the following topics into three to five subcategories:

1. clothing
2. academic studies
3. crime
4. health care
5. fun
6. charities

B. Building Outlines

Indicate which items would be main points and which would be subpoints in a speech entitled 'World War II' by fitting them into the following outline form:

Japan desires an eastern empire	I.
Shortage of rubber tires	A.
Events of the war	B.
Nazi policy of expansion	II.
Japan seizes the Philippines	A.
Sugar rationing	B.
Effects of the war on America	C.
Germany attacks France	III.
Causes of the war	A.
Germany attacks Soviet Union	B.

C. Organizational Effectiveness

Take any written statement (of at least three paragraphs) that you consider effective. This statement might be an editorial in your local newspaper, a short magazine article, or even a section of one of your textbooks. Outline this statement according to the rules discussed in this chapter. Was the statement well organized? Did its organization contribute to its effectiveness?

D. The Functions of Support

For practice in recognizing the functions of support, identify three instances of support in Jean Chrétien's speech at the end of this chapter. Explain the function of each instance of support. (Keep in mind that any instance of support could perform more than one function.)

E. The Ethics of Support

Have you ever 'stretched' supporting material to help it conform to a point you were trying to make? (An example might be citing an 'expert' for an idea of your own when discussing a social issue with a friend.) How far can you stretch the facts without stepping onto ethical thin ice?

Further Reading

Leeds, Dorothy. *PowerSpeak: Engage, Inspire, and Stimulate Your Audience.* Franklin Lakes, NJ: Career Press, 2003.
Chapter 5 of this text offers an interesting perspective, presenting clear speech organization as an important leadership trait. In her 'PowerSpeak Outline', Leeds includes suggestions about how much time to spend on each section of a speech.

McCarthy, Edward. *Speechwriting: A Professional Step-by-Step Guide for Executives.* Dayton, OH: The Executive Speaker Co., 1989.
See especially 'Step 3: Do Research for Supporting Material' for another perspective on finding and evaluating evidence.

Morreale, Sherwyn P., and Courtland L. Bovee. *Excellence in Public Speaking.* Fort Worth, TX: Harcourt Brace, 1998.
See especially Chapter 7, 'Supporting Your Speech', Chapter 9, 'Organizing Your Speech', and Chapter 11, 'Outlining Your Speech'.

O'Hair, Dan. *Outlining and Organizing Your Speech,* 2nd edn. New York: Bedford/St Martin's, 2003.
O'Hair offers a workbook that takes students step by step through the process of structuring different types of speeches with various styles of outlines.

The Oxford Dictionary of Quotations, 5th edn. New York: Oxford University Press, 2000.
A valuable reference for quotations and testimony, this volume contains more than 20,000 quotations from over 3,000 people, from Woody Allen to Émile Zola. The quotations are arranged alphabetically by author with comprehensive topical and keyword indexes.

Study Questions

Imagine you are making the case for a new, more advanced 'reuse, reduce, recycle' campaign on campus. Complete the following steps:
1. Create an outline for a speech to kick off your campaign.
2. Describe one piece of supporting material you can use for each main point in the speech. Explain how it will make the speech more interesting, memorable, clear, and persuasive.
3. Make a list of your sources for citations, narratives, and statistics.
4. Write a brief point-form characterization of your audience. How will you connect with them? Will you use audience participation?
5. What are two different techniques you could use to capture attention?

After studying the material in this chapter . . .

You should
understand:

- the differences between facilitative and debilitative stage fright;
- the sources of debilitative stage fright;
- the differences among the various types of delivery;
- the visual and auditory aspects of delivery; and
- the functions and types of visual aids.

You should be
able to:

- overcome debilitative stage fright;
- choose the most effective type of delivery for a particular speech;
- follow the guidelines for effective extemporaneous, impromptu, manuscript, and memorized speeches;
- follow the guidelines for the visual and auditory aspects of delivery;
- choose appropriate visual aids for a presentation; and
- offer constructive criticism of others' presentations.

Public Speaking

Chapter Highlights

Stage fright is one of the most formidable barriers to effective public speaking. In this chapter, we will look at

- the differences between facilitative and debilitative stage fright;
- the sources of debilitative stage fright; and
- ways to overcome debilitative stage fright.

One of the first things to consider when preparing a speech is the style of delivery. In this chapter we will look at four types:

- extemporaneous,
- impromptu,
- manuscript, and
- memorized.

This chapter presents guidelines for effective delivery. These guidelines are of two types:

- those dealing with the visual aspects of delivery, and
- those dealing with the auditory aspects of delivery.

Visual aids are a unique type of supporting material. In this chapter we will examine

- types of visual aids;
- media for the presentation of visual aids; and
- rules for using visual aids.

Finally, this chapter will discuss guidelines for presenting effective criticism of your classmates' speeches.

debilitative stage fright
An intense level of anxiety about speaking before an audience, resulting in poor performance.

facilitative stage fright
A moderate level of anxiety about speaking before an audience that helps improve the speaker's performance.

You've developed a purpose, and you've chosen and researched a topic that suits your own interests, your audience, and the occasion. You feel confident about your ability to organize your ideas in a logical, effective way, and you've built a healthy reserve of supporting material. But all that doesn't solve your primary problem: when you think about the actual act of standing before a group, your self-confidence begins to erode. What if your hands shake or your voice squeaks? What if you forget what you wanted to say? These questions make the prospect of talking to an audience seem threatening.

Because the act of speaking before a group of listeners may be a relatively new one for you, we'll look at the process in this chapter. Our purpose is to make you feel more confident about yourself as a speaker and to give you a clearer idea of how to behave when you're in front of an audience. We will begin with a discussion of stage fright.

Dealing with Stage Fright

Communication scholars call the terror that strikes the hearts of so many novice speakers *communication apprehension* or *speech anxiety,* but those who experience it know it more commonly as *stage fright.*

Facilitative and Debilitative Stage Fright

Although stage fright is a very real problem for many speakers, it is a problem that can be overcome. In fact, research suggests that it can be overcome in basic communication courses such as the one you are taking now.[1] Interestingly, the first step towards feeling less apprehensive about speaking is to realize that a certain amount of nervousness is natural and can be a good thing. This **facilitative stage fright** can help to improve your performance by causing you to think more rapidly and express yourself more energetically than you would if you were totally relaxed. In the same way, a moderate level of tension helps actors and musicians deliver their best performances.

It is only when the level of anxiety is intense that it becomes **debilitative stage fright,** inhibiting effective self-expression. Intense fear causes trouble in two ways. First, the strong emotion keeps you from thinking clearly.[2] This has been shown to be a problem even in the preparation process: students who are highly anxious about giving a speech will find the preliminary steps, including research and organization, to be more difficult.[3] Second, intense fear leads to an urge to do something, anything, to make the problem go away. This urge to escape often causes a speaker to speed up his or her delivery, which results in a rapid, almost machine-gun speaking style. As you can imagine, this boost in speaking rate leads to even more mistakes, which only add to the speaker's anxiety. Thus, a relatively small amount of nervousness can begin to feed on itself until it grows into a serious problem.

Sources of Debilitative Stage Fright

Before we describe how to manage debilitative stage fright, it might be helpful to look at why people are afflicted with the problem.[4]

Previous Negative Experience

People often feel apprehensive about giving a speech because of unpleasant past experiences. Most of us are uncomfortable doing *anything* in public, especially if it is a form of performance in which our talents and abilities are being evaluated. An unpleasant experience in one type of performance can cause you to expect a similar outcome to similar situations in the future.[5] These expectations can be realized through the self-fulfilling prophecies discussed in Chapter 2. A traumatic failure at an earlier speech and low self-esteem from critical parents during childhood are both common examples of experiences that can cause later stage fright.

You might object to the idea that past experiences cause stage fright. After all, not everyone who has bungled a speech or had critical parents is debilitated in the future. To understand why some people are affected more strongly than others by past experiences, we need to consider another cause of speech anxiety.

Irrational Thinking

Cognitive psychologists argue that it is the beliefs people have about events that cause them to feel nervous, not the events themselves. Certain irrational beliefs leave people feeling unnecessarily apprehensive. Psychologist Albert Ellis lists several such beliefs, or examples of **irrational thinking**, which we will call 'fallacies' because of their illogical nature.[6]

Catastrophic Failure
People who succumb to the **fallacy of catastrophic failure** operate on the assumption that if something bad can happen, it probably will. Their thoughts before a speech resemble these:

> 'As soon as I stand up to speak, I'll forget everything I wanted to say.'
> 'Everyone will think my ideas are stupid.'
> 'Somebody will probably laugh at me.'

Although it is naive to imagine that all your speeches will be totally successful, it is equally naive to assume they will all fail miserably. One way to escape the fallacy of catastrophic failure is to take a more realistic look at the situation. Would your audience members really boo you off the stage? Will they really think your ideas are stupid? Even if you did forget your remarks for a moment, would the results be a genuine disaster? It helps to remember that nervousness is more apparent to the speaker than to the audience.[7] Beginning public speakers, when congratulated for their poise during a speech, are apt to make such remarks as 'Are you kidding? I was dying up there.'

COMMUNICATION ON-SCREEN

Akeelah and the Bee (2006)
Directed by Doug Atchison.

An 11-year-old girl from a troubled family reluctantly takes up a challenge from her school principal to enter a spelling bee, where she achieves surprising success. Through succeeding rounds of competition—all the way up to the national final—Akeelah (Keke Palmer)'s insecurity is just one of the obstacles she must overcome. While participating in a spelling bee is not the same as delivering a speech, the similarities—standing on stage before a large and judging public—are clear.

I have a slight inferiority complex still. I go into a room and have to talk myself into going up to people. If I'm the epitome of a woman who is always confident and in control, don't ever believe it of anyone.

Barbara Walters

fallacy of catastrophic failure
The irrational belief that the worst possible outcome will probably occur.

irrational thinking
Beliefs that have no basis in reality or logic; one source of debilitative stage fright.

I don't know the key to success, but the key to failure is trying to please everyone.

Bill Cosby

---

fallacy of approval
The irrational belief that it is vital to win the approval of virtually every person a communicator deals with.

fallacy of overgeneralization
Irrational beliefs in which (1) conclusions (usually negative) are based on limited evidence or (2) communicators exaggerate their shortcomings.

fallacy of perfection
The irrational belief that a worthwhile communicator should be able to handle every situation with complete confidence and skill.

Courage is resistance to fear, mastery of fear—not absence of fear.

Mark Twain

Perfection

Speakers who succumb to the **fallacy of perfection** expect themselves to behave flawlessly. Whereas such a standard of perfection might serve as a target and a source of inspiration (like the desire to make a hole-in-one while golfing), it is totally unrealistic to expect that you will write and deliver a perfect speech—especially as a beginner. It helps to remember that audiences don't expect you to be perfect.

Approval

The mistaken belief called the **fallacy of approval** is based on the idea that it is vital—not just desirable—to gain the approval of everyone in the audience. It is rare that even the best speakers please everyone, especially on topics that are at all controversial. To paraphrase Abraham Lincoln, you can't please all the people all the time—and it is irrational to expect you will.

Overgeneralization

The **fallacy of overgeneralization** might also be labelled the fallacy of exaggeration because it occurs when a person blows one poor experience out of proportion. Consider these examples:

'I'm so stupid! I mispronounced that word.'
'I completely blew it—I forgot one of my supporting points.'
'My hands were shaking. The audience must have thought I was a complete idiot.'

A second type of exaggeration occurs when a speaker treats occasional lapses as if they were the rule instead of the exception. This sort of mistake usually involves extreme labels, such as 'always' or 'never'.

'I *always* forget what I want to say.'
'I can *never* come up with a good topic.'
'I can't do *anything* right.'

Overcoming Debilitative Stage Fright

There are five strategies that can help you manage debilitative stage fright:

1. **Use nervousness to your advantage.** Paralyzing fear is obviously a problem, but a little nervousness can actually help you deliver a successful speech. Most athletes testify that a bit of anxiety before a game boosts their energy. The same thing is true in speaking: being completely calm can take away the passion that is one element of a good speech. Use the strategies below to *control* your anxiety, but don't try to completely eliminate it.

2. **Be rational about your fears.** Some fears about speaking are rational. For example, if you haven't researched or practised your speech then you should be worried. It's also reasonable to be afraid of a hostile audience. But other fears are based on the fallacies you read about on the previous pages. It's not realistic to expect that you'll deliver a perfect speech, or that everyone in the audience will find your remarks totally fascinating. It's not rational to indulge in catastrophic fantasies

about what might go wrong. If you're afraid that you'll freeze up in front of your audience, analyze in advance how likely that is to actually happen. The risk is probably quite small. Then recognize that, even if you did freeze up, it would not be catastrophic.

3. **Maintain a receiver orientation.** Paying too much attention to your own feelings—even when you're feeling good about yourself—will take energy away from communicating with your listeners. Concentrate on your audience members rather than on yourself. Focus your energy on keeping them interested and on making sure they understand you.

4. **Keep a positive attitude.** Build and maintain a positive attitude toward your audience, your speech, and yourself as a speaker. Some communication consultants suggest that public speakers should concentrate on the following three statements immediately before speaking:

I'm glad I have the chance to talk about this topic.
I know what I'm talking about.
I care about my audience.

Repeating these statements (as long as you believe them!) can help you maintain a positive attitude.

Another technique for building a positive attitude is known as **visualization.**[8] It requires you to use your imagination to visualize the successful completion of your speech. This technique has been used successfully with many athletes. Visualization can help make the self-fulfilling prophecy discussed in Chapter 2 work in your favour.

5. **Most important, be prepared!** Preparation is the most important key to controlling speech anxiety. You can feel confident if you know from practice that your remarks are well organized and supported and that your delivery is smooth. Researchers have determined that the highest level of speech anxiety occurs just before speaking, the second-highest level at the time the assignment is announced and explained, and the lowest level during the time you spend preparing your speech.[9] You should take advantage of this relatively low-stress time to think through the problems that might make you nervous during the actual speech. For example, if your anxiety is based on a fear of forgetting what you are going to say, make sure that your speaking aids, whether they are cue cards, outlines, or speaking notes, are complete and effective and that you have practised your speech thoroughly. (We'll go into speech practice in more detail in a moment.) If, on the other hand, your great fear is 'sounding stupid', you can relieve your anxiety by getting started early enough to do lots of research and thinking in advance.

Types of Delivery

There are four basic types of delivery—*extemporaneous, impromptu, manuscript,* and *memorized.* Each type creates a different impression and is appropriate under different conditions. Any speech may incorporate more than one of these types of delivery. For purposes of discussion, however, it is best to consider them separately.

Cultural Idiom

blows . . . out of proportion
exaggerates

freeze up
become immobilized through fear

give . . . the edge
provide an advantage

visualization
A technique for behaviour rehearsal (e.g., for a speech) that involves imagining the successful completion of the task.

Nervousness can give your speech the edge—and the passion—all good speeches need. It has always been so; two thousand years ago Cicero said all public speaking of real merit was characterized by nervousness.

Dorothy Leeds

extemporaneous speech
A speech that is planned in advance but presented in a direct, conversational manner.

impromptu speech
A speech given 'off the top of one's head', without preparation.

Extemporaneous

An **extemporaneous speech** is planned in advance but presented in a direct, spontaneous manner. Extemporaneous speeches are conversational in tone, which means that they give the audience members the impression that you are talking to them, directly and honestly. Extemporaneous speeches *are* carefully prepared, but they are prepared in such a way that they create what actors call 'the illusion of the first time'. In other words, the audience hears your remarks as though they were brand new. This style of speaking is generally accepted to be the most effective, especially for a college or university class. In a classroom, you generally speak before a small audience (5 to 50 people) made up of individuals with diverse backgrounds. Spontaneity is essential with this type of audience, but so is careful message planning. Extemporaneous speaking allows you to benefit from both elements.

Extemporaneous speaking is also the most common type of delivery in the 'outside' world. Most of those involved in communication-oriented careers find that the majority of their public speaking is done before audiences who, in terms of size and diversity of interests represented, resemble those found in a classroom. Professional public speakers recognize the advisability of both careful planning and spontaneity with such an audience.

A speech presented extemporaneously will be researched, organized, and practised in advance, but the exact wording of the entire speech will not be memorized or otherwise predetermined. Because you speak from only brief, unobtrusive notes, you are able to move and maintain eye contact with your audience. In fact, one of the keys to successful extemporaneous speaking is to avoid your notes as much as possible; you should refer to them only to get yourself back on track if you feel a memory lapse coming on or to make sure you've covered all your subpoints before moving on to your next main point. Because extemporaneous speaking creates a casual atmosphere, it can seem normal to stop occasionally and say, 'Let me just make sure I've mentioned everything I wanted to tell you about this.'

The extemporaneous speech does have some disadvantages. It's difficult to stay within exact time limits, to be exact in wording, or to be grammatically perfect. Therefore, if you are speaking as part of a radio or television broadcast, or what you say will be recorded word-for-word, you might want to use a manuscript or memorize your speech. Also, an extemporaneous speech requires time to prepare. On spur-of-the-moment speaking occasions, you will need to deliver an impromptu speech.

Cultural Idiom

off the top of one's head
with little time to plan or think about

spur-of-the-moment
occurring without warning

wrap it up
finish

It usually takes me more than three weeks to prepare a good impromptu speech.

Mark Twain

Impromptu

An **impromptu speech** is a speech you give off the top of your head, without preparation. It is the kind you may have to give in an emergency, such as when a scheduled speaker becomes ill and you are suddenly called upon. Lack of preparation is the main problem with impromptu speeches, but there are some advantages, too. It is, by definition, spontaneous. It is the delivery style necessary for informal talks, group discussions, and comments on others' speeches. It also can be an effective training aid; it can teach you to think on your feet and organize your thoughts quickly. To take full advantage of an impromptu speaking opportunity, remember the following points:

1. **Use the time you have to prepare wisely.** Take advantage of the time between being called on to speak and actually speaking. Even if you have only a minute, you can still scribble a few brief notes to protect against mental blocks.

2. **Don't be afraid to be original.** You don't have to remember what every other expert says about your topic—what do *you* have to say about it? Review your personal experiences and use them. If nothing else, consider questions such as the five Ws and formulate a plan to answer one or more of them.

3. **Observe what is going on around you, and respond to it.** If there are other speakers, you might agree or disagree with what they have said. You can comment on the audience and the occasion as well as on your topic.

4. **Keep a positive attitude.** Remember that audience expectations are low. Audience members know you have not prepared in advance, and they don't expect you to be perfect.

5. **Keep your comments brief.** This might be the most important thing to remember. In particular, be sure not to prolong your conclusion. If you have said everything you want to say or everything you can remember, wrap it up as neatly as possible and sit down. If you have forgotten something, it probably wasn't important anyway. If it was, the audience will ask you about it afterwards.

COMMUNICATION ON-SCREEN

Saving Private Ryan (1998)
Directed by Steven Spielberg.

This film is about American soldiers on a mission to save a fallen paratrooper in Normandy during Word War II. Tom Hanks is Captain John H. Miller, leading his soldiers into dangerous, Nazi-occupied territory. Miller's nerves are shot, but he still manages a speech that rallies his men for a mission that they initially don't believe in. This is an example of an impromptu speech that is delivered effectively and convincingly, given its context.

Manuscript

Manuscript speeches are read word-for-word from a prepared text (see Figure 13.1). They are necessary when you are speaking for the record, such as when you are speaking at legal proceedings or presenting scientific findings. The greatest disadvantage of a manuscript speech is the lack of spontaneity that may result. Manuscript readers have even been known, to their extreme embarrassment, to read their directions by mistake: 'And so, let me say in conclusion, look at the audience with great sincerity . . . Oops!'

Manuscript speeches are difficult and cumbersome, but they are sometimes necessary. Here are some guidelines:

1. While writing, keep in mind that a speech is not the same as a term paper: speeches are usually less formal, more repetitive, and more personal.[10] They use more adverbs, adjectives, and circumlocutions such as 'well' and 'as you can see'. As one expert points out, 'Speeches use more words per square thought than well-written essays or reports.'[11] So, when you're preparing a manuscript speech, write the way you talk, not the way you write a paper.

2. Use short paragraphs. They make it easier to find your place in the script after you've looked up to make eye contact with your audience.

3. Print out the manuscript triple-spaced, in capital letters, in 14-point font or larger. Underline the words you want to emphasize. This makes reading the text while you are at the podium much easier.

4. Use stiff paper so that it won't fold up or fly away during the speech. Print on only one side, and make sure the page numbers are visible.

5. Use the 'numbered lines' feature that most word processors offer. This makes referring to parts of the speech a lot easier both when practising and when giving the speech.

manuscript speech
A speech that is read word-for-word from a prepared text.

Good results are seldom led to
When people feel they're being read to.

Charles Osgood

THE CURRENT BACKLOG OF MORE THAN 800 CLAIMS IS SIMPLY <u>UNACCEPTABLE</u>. THE FACT THAT IT TAKES 13 YEARS ON AVERAGE TO PROCESS A CLAIM IS <u>UNACCEPTABLE</u>. AND THE FACT THAT THE FEDERAL GOVERNMENT ACTS AS BOTH JUDGE AND JURY IS ALSO <u>UNACCEPTABLE</u>. THE TIME IS LONG PAST DUE FOR A NEW APPROACH, AND THAT IS OUR PURPOSE HERE TODAY.

I'M VERY PLEASED TO ANNOUNCE A COMPREHENSIVE PACKAGE OF REFORMS THAT WILL <u>REVOLUTIONIZE</u> THE CLAIMS RESOLUTION PROCESS. THESE REFORMS INCLUDE <u>THREE</u> <u>KEY</u> <u>ELEMENTS</u>: <u>FIRST</u>, WE PROPOSE TO FINALLY CREATE A <u>FULLY</u> <u>INDEPENDENT</u> CLAIMS TRIBUNAL. . . . <u>SECOND</u>, WE PROPOSE TO TRANSFORM THE ISCC INTO A <u>NEUTRAL</u> DISPUTE RESOLUTION BODY. AND <u>FINALLY</u>, WE PROPOSE TO INTRODUCE <u>PRACTICAL</u> <u>MEASURES</u> TO SPEED UP THE RESOLUTION OF SMALL CLAIMS. . . .

NOW, LADIES AND GENTLEMEN, WE BELIEVE THESE MEASURES REPRESENT AN HISTORIC BREAKTHROUGH ON THE INTRACTABLE LOGJAM OF SPECIFIC CLAIMS.

Figure 13.1

Part of a Sample Page from a Manuscript Speech (reduced)

---

memorized speech

A speech learned and delivered by rote without a written text.

Failure to prepare is preparing to fail.

John Wooden

---

6. Rehearse the speech until you can 'read' whole lines without looking at the manuscript.
7. Take your time, vary your speed, and try to concentrate on ideas rather than words.

Memorized

Memorized speeches—those learned by heart and performed without any aids—are the most difficult and often the least effective. They often seem excessively formal. However, like manuscript speeches, they may be necessary on certain occasions. They are used both in oratory contests and as memory-training devices. They are also used in some political situations. For example, in Canadian televised election debates the candidates are allowed to make prepared speeches, but they are not allowed to use notes. Thus, they have to memorize precise, for-the-record wording, and make it sound natural.

The legendary American frontiersman Davy Crockett once gave an object lesson on the benefits and hazards of memorized speeches. When he was running for Congress, Crockett always extemporized, adapting to his audience, but his opponent always gave the same memorized speech. So for one debate Crockett memorized his opponent's entire speech and delivered it first, leaving his adversary with nothing to say.[12]

There is only one guideline for a memorized speech: practise. The speech won't be effective unless you have practised it until you can present it with that 'illusion of the first time' that we mentioned while discussing extemporaneous speeches.

Practising the Speech

In most cases, a delivery that sounds smooth and natural is the result of extensive practice. Once you've chosen the appropriate delivery type for the speech you will be giving, the best way to make sure that you are on your way to an effective delivery is to practise your speech repeatedly and systematically. One way to do that is to go through some or all of the following steps:

1. First, present the speech to yourself. 'Talk through' the entire speech, including your examples and forms of support. (Don't just say, 'This is where I present my statistics' or 'This is where I explain about photosynthesis.')
2. Record your speech and then watch or listen to it. Because we hear our own voices partially through our cranial bone structure, we are sometimes surprised at what we sound like to others. Videotaping is an especially effective tool for rehearsals because it lets you know what the audience will see as well as hear.[13]

Speech Coaches: Being Prepared Is Everything!

When speech coaches are preparing a person to speak in public, they script every element of the speech, from the speaker's rhythm and cadence to his or her gaze direction. Then the speaker practises the speech in realistic surroundings, perhaps even in the arena where it will actually be delivered, until the coach is confident that the speaker has experienced every possible scenario—an interruption from a disruptive audience member, an electrical black out, sound system problems, inattention on the audience's part, or competing factors such as other presentations going on in other corners of the room. Every part of the speech, from the speaker's entry to his or her posture and demeanour, is rehearsed many times. The more the speaker has mastered and over-learned his or her performance, the better the performance will be. Good speech coaches know that thorough preparation for public communication is everything.

3. Present the speech in front of a small group of friends or relatives.
4. Present the speech to at least one listener in the room in which you will present the final speech (or, if that room is not available, a similar room). Have your listener(s) critique your speech according to the guidelines for delivery discussed in the next section.

Guidelines for Delivery

The best way to consider guidelines for delivery is through examination of the non-verbal aspects of presenting a speech. As you read in Chapter 5, non-verbal behaviour can change, or even contradict, the meaning of the words a speaker utters. If audience members want to interpret how you feel about something, they are likely to trust your non-verbal communication more than your words. If you tell them, 'It's great to be here today,' but you stand before them slouched over with your hands in your pockets, looking like you wish you were *anywhere else,* they are likely to discount what you say. This non-verbal behaviour might cause your audience members to react negatively to your speech, and their negative reaction might make you even more nervous. This cycle of speaker and audience reinforcing each other's feelings can work for you, though, if you approach a subject with genuine enthusiasm. Enthusiasm is shown, just as clearly as a lack of it, through both the visual and auditory aspects of your delivery.

Words represent your intellect. The sound, gesture and movement represent your feeling.

Patricia Fripp

Visual Aspects of Delivery

Visual aspects of delivery include appearance, movement, posture, facial expression, and eye contact.

Appearance

Appearance is not a presentation variable as much as a preparation variable. Some communication consultants suggest new clothes, new glasses, and new hairstyles for their clients. In case you consider any of these, be forewarned that you should be attractive to your audience but not flashy. Research suggests that audiences like speakers who are similar to them, but they prefer the similarity to be shown conservatively.[14] Fashionable dressers might not like

Cultural Idiom

flashy
showy, gaudy

someone dressed in dowdy, old-fashioned clothes, but they would also have problems with someone dressed in fashions that are too avant-garde. Speakers are perceived to be more credible when they look businesslike.

Movement

Movement is an important visual aspect of delivery. The way you walk to the front of your audience, for example, will express your confidence and enthusiasm. Nervous energy can cause your body to shake and twitch, which can be distressing both to you and to your audience as you are speaking. One way to control involuntary movement is to move voluntarily when you feel the need to move. Don't feel that you have to stand in one spot or that all your gestures need to be carefully planned in advance. Simply get involved in your message, and let your involvement create the motivation for your movement. That way, when you move, you will emphasize what you are saying in the same way you would emphasize it if you were talking to a group of friends. If you move voluntarily, you will use up the nervous energy that would otherwise cause you to move involuntarily.

Movement can also help you maintain contact with all members of your audience. Those closest to you will feel the greatest contact. This creates what is known as the 'action zone' in the typical classroom, within the area of the front and centre of the room. Movement enables you to extend this action zone in order to include people who would otherwise remain uninvolved. Without overdoing it, you should feel free to move toward, away from, or from side to side of your audience.

Remember: move with the understanding that it will add to the meaning of the words you use. It is difficult to bang your fist on a podium or take a step without conveying emphasis. Make the emphasis natural by allowing your message to create your motivation to move.

Posture

Generally speaking, good posture does not mean standing at military attention. It simply means standing with your spine relatively straight, your shoulders relatively squared off, and your feet set comfortably.

Of course, you shouldn't get too comfortable. There are speakers who are effective even though they sprawl on tabletops and slouch against blackboards, but their effectiveness is usually in spite of their posture rather than because of it. Sometimes speakers are so awesome in stature or reputation that they need an informal posture to encourage their audience to relax. In that case, sloppy posture is more or less justified. But because awesomeness is not usually a problem for beginning speakers, good posture should be the rule.

Good posture can help you control nervousness by allowing your breathing apparatus to work properly; when your brain receives enough oxygen, it becomes easier for you to think clearly. Good posture will also help you get a positive audience reaction because standing up straight makes you more visible. It also increases your audience contact because the audience members will feel that you are interested enough in them to stand formally, yet relaxed enough to be at ease with them.

Once you make good eye contact with a person in the audience, they will feel you are talking to them for the rest of the speech.

Ken Blanchard

Facial Expression

The expression on your face can be more meaningful to your audience than the words you say. Try it yourself with a mirror. Say, 'You're a terrific audience,' for example, with a smirk, with a warm smile, with a deadpan expression, and then with a scowl. It just doesn't mean the same thing. Remember also that it is nearly impossible to control facial expressions from the outside. Like your movement, your facial expressions will reflect your involvement with your message. Don't try to fake it. Just get involved in your message, and your face will take care of itself.

Eye Contact

Eye contact is perhaps the most important non-verbal facet of delivery because it increases your direct contact with your audience. It can also help you control your nervousness. For many people, the most frightening aspect of public speaking is not knowing how audience members will react. Direct eye contact is a form of reality testing that allows you to check audience responses as you speak. Usually, especially when you're addressing your classmates, you will find that your audience is more 'with' you than you think. When you deliberately establish eye contact with people who seem bored, you will often find that they are interested; they just weren't showing their interest because they didn't think anyone was looking.

To maintain eye contact, you could try to meet the eyes of each member of your audience squarely at least once during any given presentation. After you have made definite eye contact, move on to another audience member. You can learn to do this quickly, so you can visually latch on to every member of a good-sized class in a relatively short time.

The characteristics of appearance, movement, posture, facial expression, and eye contact are visual, non-verbal facets of delivery. Now consider the auditory non-verbal messages that you might send during a presentation.

Many a pair of curious ears had been lured by that well-timed pause.

Li Ang

Auditory Aspects of Delivery

As we noted in Chapter 5, your paralanguage—the way you use your voice—says a good deal about you, especially about your sincerity and enthusiasm. In addition, using your voice well can help you control your nervousness. It's another cycle: controlling your vocal characteristics will decrease your nervousness, which in turn will enable you to control your voice even more. But this cycle can also work in the opposite direction. If your voice is out of control, your nerves will probably be in the same state. Controlling your voice is mostly a matter of recognizing and using appropriate *volume, rate, pitch,* and *articulation.*

Volume

The loudness of your voice is determined by the amount of air you push past the vocal folds in your throat. The key to controlling volume, then, is controlling the amount of air you use. The key to determining the *right* volume is audience contact. Your delivery should

> **Cultural Idiom**
>
> **deadpan**
> an expressionless face
>
> **squared off**
> evenly aligned
>
> **squarely**
> directly

'And now a correction: Portions of last night's story on diving mules which were read with an air of ironic detachment should actually have been presented with earnest concern.'

pitch
The highness or lowness of one's voice.

rate
The speed at which a speaker utters words.

be loud enough so that your audience members can hear everything you say but not so loud that they feel you are talking to someone in the next room. Too much volume is seldom the problem for beginning speakers. Usually they either are not loud enough or have a tendency to fade off at the end of a thought. Sometimes, when they lose faith in an idea in mid-sentence, they compromise by mumbling the end of the sentence so that it isn't quite coherent.

One speaker who was criticized for inappropriate volume is Ted Kennedy. One researcher points out that 'Kennedy tended to shout when an audience was small or uninterested or when he sensed he was losing them. Thus, his volume was often inappropriate to the time and place.'[15]

Rate

Your speed in speaking is called your **rate.** There is a range of personal differences in speaking rate. Former prime minister Jean Chrétien is said to speak at around 90 words per minute, whereas one actor who is known for his fast-talking commercials speaks at about 250. Normal speaking speed, however, is between 120 and 150 words per minute. If you talk much more slowly than that, you may lull your audience to sleep. Faster speaking rates are stereotypically associated with speaker competence,[16] but if you speak too rapidly, you will tend to be unintelligible. Once again, your involvement in your message is the key to achieving an effective rate.

Pitch

The highness or lowness of your voice—**pitch**—is controlled by the frequency at which your vocal folds vibrate as you push air through them. Because taut vocal folds vibrate at a greater frequency, pitch is influenced by muscular tension. This explains why nervous speakers have a tendency occasionally to 'squeak', whereas relaxed speakers seem to be more in control. Pitch will tend to follow rate and volume. As you speed up or become louder, your pitch will have a tendency to rise. If your range in pitch is too narrow, your voice will have a singsong quality. If it is too wide, you may sound overly dramatic. You should control your pitch so that your listeners believe you are talking *with* them rather than performing in front of them. Once again, your involvement in your message should take care of this naturally for you.

Keep in mind that any change in the pitch—or the volume or the rate—of your delivery will create emphasis. Whether you slow down or speed up, drop your voice to a whisper or raise it to a scream, the audience will perceive the change as signifying emphasis. One student provided an example of how volume can be used to emphasize an idea. He was speaking of the way possessions like cars communicate things about their owners. 'For example,' he said, with normal volume, 'a Mercedes-Benz says, "I made it," but a Rolls-Royce says, "I'VE GOT MONEY!"' He blared out those last three words with such force that the podium shook.

Articulation

The final non-verbal auditory behaviour, articulation, is perhaps the most important. **Articulation** has a number of meanings, but in this context it means pronouncing all the parts of every word—and nothing else.

It is not our purpose here to condemn regional or ethnic dialects (though a considerable amount of research suggests regional dialects can create negative impressions).[17] What we suggest is not standardized but rather *careful* articulation. Incorrect articulation is usually nothing more than careless articulation. It is caused by (1) leaving off parts of words (deletion), (2) replacing parts of words (substitution), (3) adding parts to words (addition), or (4) overlapping two or more words (slurring).

Deletion

The most common mistake in articulation is **deletion**, or leaving off part of a word. As you are thinking the complete word, it is often difficult to recognize that you are saying only part of it. The most common deletions occur at the ends of words, especially *-ing* words. *Going, doing,* and *stopping* become *goin', doin',* and *stoppin'*. Parts of words can be left off in the middle, too, as in *terr'iss* for *terrorist, Innernet* for *Internet,* and *asst* for *asked*.

Substitution

Substitution takes place when you replace part of a word with an incorrect sound. The ending *-th* is often replaced at the end of a word with a single *t*, as when *with* becomes *wit*. The *th-* sound is also a problem at the beginning of words; *this, that,* and *those* have a tendency to become *dis, dat,* and *dose*.

Addition

Adding extra parts to words causes the articulation problem of **addition**: for example, *incentative* instead of *incentive, athalete* instead of *athlete,* and *orientated* instead of *oriented*. Sometimes this type of addition is caused by incorrect word choice, as when *irregardless* is used for *regardless*.

Another type of addition is the use of 'tag questions', such as *you know?* or *you see?* or *right?* at the end of sentences. To have every other sentence punctuated with one of these barely audible superfluous phrases can be annoying.

Probably the worst type of addition, or at least the most common, is the use of *uh, anda,* and *like* between words. *Anda* is often stuck between two words when *and* isn't even needed. If you find yourself doing that, you might want to pause or swallow instead.[18]

Slurring

Slurring is caused by trying to say two or more words at once—or at least overlapping the end of one word with the beginning of the next. Word pairs ending with *of* are the worst offenders in this category. *Sort of* becomes *sorta, kind of* becomes *kinda,* and *because of* becomes *becausa*. Word combinations ending with *to* are often slurred, as when *want to* becomes *wanna*. Sometimes even more than two words are blended together, as when *that is the way* becomes *thatsaway*. Careful articulation means using your lips, teeth, tongue, and jaw to bite off your words, cleanly and separately, one at a time.

---

addition

The articulation error that involves adding extra parts to words.

articulation

The process of pronouncing all the necessary parts of a word.

deletion

The articulation error that involves leaving off parts of words.

slurring

The articulation error that involves overlapping the end of one word with the beginning of the next.

substitution

The articulation error that involves replacing part of a word with an incorrect sound.

A vessel is known by the sound, whether it be cracked or not.

Demosthenes

Mend your speech a little, lest you may mar your fortune.

William Shakespeare, *King Lear*

Understanding Diversity
● ● ● ● ● A POEM IN PRAISE OF NEWFOUNDLAND ENGLISH

A schoolteacher before her marriage, Rose M. Sullivan (1900–64) wrote many poems about life in her hometown of Trinity, Newfoundland.

The Typical Newfoundlander

The typical Newfoundlander
And I'm proud that I am one
Besides the Queen's good English,
Has a language all his own.
For instance, if you meet one
And inquire about his health,
He's not 'just fine' or 'like the bird'
He's 'first rate b'y, how's yerself?'

Such sayings as 'I bound you will',
'Save up' and 'hard afore',
And 'most to rights' and 'straightened up',
And 'dunch' and 'doubt the fire'
These need no definitions,
We heard them in our cradles,
We know how much a 'yaffle' is
Though it isn't in our tables.

We all know what a 'grapnel' is
A 'haul-off' and a 'killick'
I spent my time around the 'punts',
Although I was a 'twillick'.
There's 'slewed around' and 'went to work'
'Turned to' and 'took a spell',
While of 'clever' looking boys and girls
I'm sure we've all 'heard tell'.

We go around the 'ballycaters',
When there's 'swatches' on the ice,
And only a Newfoundlander
Can 'fall down' and get a 'h'ist'.
You'd never guess a 'bedlamer'
Is an adolescent lad,
While intermittent snow flurries
Are 'dwies' or just a 'scad'.

Now other people say 'down south'.
This I don't understand,
For everybody always says
'Down North' in Newfoundland.
'Bide where you're at' or 'lef'n bide'
You'll hear the old folks say,
We say we're drinkin' 'switchel'
When we drink unsweetened 'tay'.

Some think we live on fish and spuds,
This fairly makes me boil,
Though 'tis a treat when Spring comes 'round,
To get a meal of 'swile',
A local dish is 'fish and brewis',
The youngsters like the 'scrunchions',
And they like the 'lassy sugar'
From the bottom of the puncheons.

Besides the regular meal time,
You'll see 'all hands' 'knock off'
For their 'lev'ner' and their 'fourer',
A 'mug up' or a 'scoff',
We used to have such hearty 'grub'
As 'toutons', 'duffs', and tarts
But the maids have gone romantic
When their cookies are shaped like hearts.
Poor Grandpa, he's 'all crippled up'
With 'rheumatiz' not 'gout',
He 'keels out' on the 'settle'
And says he's 'fair worn out'.
Sometimes he gets his 'dander up'
Because he lost his spring,
He frets and grumbles when he thinks
How his work is all in slings.

Does your clock sometimes be 'random'?
Were you ever on the 'tear'?
Does your house be in a 'ree-raw'?
Do you find things 'shockin' dear'?
Or were you ever real 'put out'?
Did you ever 'notch a beam'?
If you're not a Newfoundlander
You don't know what I mean.
But times bring alterations,
And soon we'll have no more,
Those quaint old local sayings
As in the days of yore.
Still in my heart I'll treasure them,
They'll always seem to be
A precious part of home sweet home,
To simple folk like me.

—*Rose M. Sullivan, Trinity, Trinity Bay*

Question: Rose Sullivan clearly took pleasure and pride in Newfoundland English. Some people, however, feel self-conscious about their regional dialects and make a deliberate effort to change the way they speak. Why do you think this is the case?

Understanding Communication Technology

Historic Canadian Speeches on the Web, in Libraries, and in Books

'Streaming technology' enables you to listen to audio programming and watch video programming over the Internet. This means that you can hear how speeches from history—at least those made since recording technology was invented—actually sounded. You can hear how speakers handled auditory non-verbal characteristics such as volume, rate, pitch, and articulation. When video clips are available, you can even observe how they handled the visual aspects of delivery discussed in this chapter.

Many great Canadians have made speeches before the Empire Club. You can search the full text of all speeches on the organization's website (speeches.empireclub.org/).

The CBC has a very extensive site with many audio and video clips of great recorded speeches. For example, you can find speeches by American presidents, including Truman, Nixon, Reagan, and Obama, visiting Canada at archives.cbc.ca/IDD-1-73-676/politics_economy/presidents/.

The website of the Prime Minister's Office (PMO) of the Government of Canada lists all the most significant speeches given by the Prime Minister (pm.gc.ca/eng/media.asp?category=2). This is often a good source of contemporary speeches. Library and Archives Canada also has an excellent website listing great speeches by Canadian prime ministers (collectionscanada.gc.ca/2/4/index-e.html).

Most Canadian universities and colleges subscribe to a resource called *Canadian Speeches*, which is available in both print and electronic formats. To find this resource, go to your library's catalogue and search for 'Canadian speeches' in the 'Journal Title' field.

Books such as *Great Canadian Speeches* are other useful resources for locating speeches. This particular book has a section called 'Speech Sources'. Such bibliographies can be useful in locating other sources related to the speech you are looking for. To find more books of Canadian speeches, try searching your library's catalogue using keywords like 'Canadian' and 'speeches'.

Up to this point, we have discussed how you can use your physicality and voice to achieve effective speech delivery. In the next sections, we will look at another important aspect of public speaking: visual aids.

Using Visual Aids

Visual aids are graphic devices used in a speech to illustrate or support ideas. They can show how things look (photos of your trek to Nepal or the effects of malnutrition). They can show how things work (a demonstration of a new ski binding, a diagram of how seawater is made drinkable through desalination). Visual aids can also show how things relate to one another (a graph showing the relationships among gender, education, and income). Finally, visual aids can be highly effective as evidence. A photograph of toxic waste in your community, a chart clearly delineating a rise in crime, or a sample of an incorrectly wired electric heater that caused a fire can all be striking evidence for a particular point.

> **visual aids**
> Graphic devices used in a speech to illustrate or support ideas.

Types of Visual Aids

There is a wide variety of types of visual aids. The most common types are discussed in the following sections.

Objects and Models

Sometimes the most effective visual aid is the actual thing you are talking about. This will be the case when that thing is portable and simple enough to use for a demonstration during your speech, such as a new hockey helmet designed to prevent concussion. A **model** is a scaled representation, used when the thing you are discussing is too large (the solar system), too small (a DNA molecule), or simply doesn't exist any more (a Tyrannosaurus rex).

Diagrams

A **diagram** is any kind of line drawing that shows the most important properties of an object. Diagrams do not try to show everything about an item but just those parts that the audience most needs to be aware of and understand. Blueprints and architectural plans are common types of diagrams, as are maps and organizational charts. A diagram is most appropriate when you need to simplify a complex object or event and make it more understandable to the audience. The diagram in Figure 13.2 shows the parts of a grain of wheat.

Word and Number Charts

Word charts and **number charts** are visual depictions of key facts or statistics. Presenting facts and numbers in visual form reinforces what you say about them and makes them easier for your audience to understand and retain. Many speakers will also list the main points of their speech, or some key statistics, as a word chart, often in outline form. Figure 13.3 shows a word chart listing the parts of a grain of wheat. This word chart could be used in conjunction with the diagram in Figure 13.2.

Pie Charts

Pie charts are circle shapes with wedges cut into them. They can be used to show divisions of any whole: where your tax dollars go, the percentage of the population involved in various

---

diagram

A line drawing that shows the most important components of an object.

model

Replica of an object being discussed. Usually used when it would be difficult or impossible to use the actual object.

number chart

A visual aid that lists numbers in tabular form in order to clarify information.

pie chart

A visual aid that divides a circle into wedges, representing percentages of the whole.

word chart

A visual aid that lists words or terms in tabular form in order to clarify information.

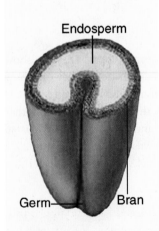

Figure 13.2

Diagram: Wheat Grain

1. BRAN
   Outer layer
   Excellent source of fibre
   Removed in processing

2. GERM
   Excellent source of nutrition
   Removed in processing

3. ENDOSPERM
   Starchy
   Low in nutrients and fibre
   Used in most processed grains and flours

Figure 13.3

Word Chart: Parts of a Wheat Grain

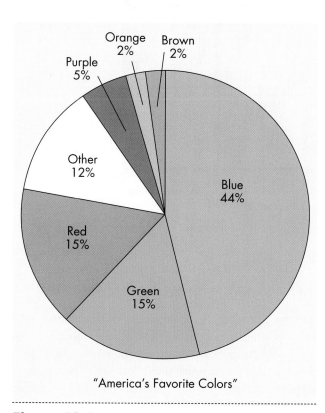

"America's Favorite Colors"

Figure 13.4

Pie Chart: Favourite Colours

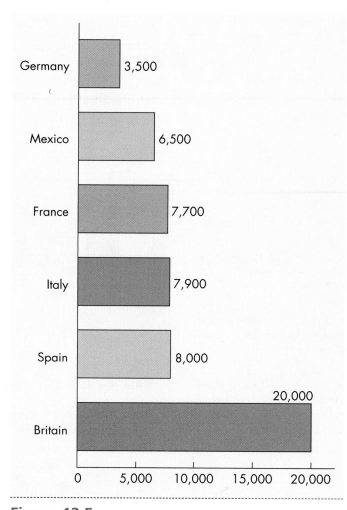

Figure 13.5

Bar Chart: Canadians Travelling Overseas, January–June 2007

occupations, and so on. Pie charts often show percentages adding up to 100 per cent. The wedges of the pie are organized from largest to smallest. The pie chart in Figure 13.4 represents the favourite colours of Americans.[19]

Bar and Column Charts

Bar charts, such as the one shown in Figure 13.5, compare two or more values by stretching them out in the form of horizontal rectangles. **Column charts,** such as the one shown in Figure 13.6 on page 508, perform the same function as bar charts but use vertical rectangles.

Line Charts

A **line chart** maps out the direction of a moving point; it is ideally suited for showing changes over time. The time element is usually placed on the horizontal axis so that the line visually represents the trend over time. The line chart in Figure 13.7 on page 508 is a fictional example, but the same format can be used to chart trends in any number of areas.

bar chart

A visual aid that compares two or more values by showing them as elongated horizontal rectangles.

column chart

A visual aid that compares two or more values by showing them as elongated vertical rectangles.

line chart

A visual aid consisting of a grid that maps out the direction of a trend by plotting a series of points.

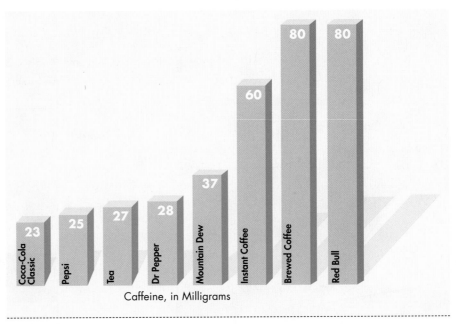

Figure 13.6

Column Chart: Caffeine Content of Popular Drinks

Media for the Presentation of Visual Aids

Visual aids can be presented in several ways. For example, chalkboards or whiteboards can be found in most classrooms. If you will be speaking in a room that doesn't have either, you can buy polymer marking surfaces and their markers in most bookstores and art supply shops.

The main advantage of these write-as-you-go media is that they allow you to be spontaneous and create your visual aids as you speak; for instance, you can use them to show responses from your audience. Their main disadvantage—apart from the odour of whiteboard markers and the squeaking of chalk—is that it may be difficult to prepare visual aids on them in advance, especially if someone else will be using the same room in the same block of time.

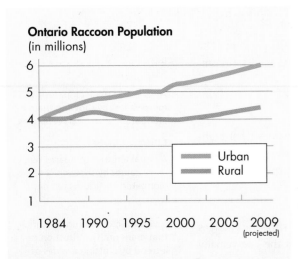

Figure 13.7

Line Chart: Ontario Raccoon Population

Flip Pads and Poster Board

Flip pads are like oversized writing tablets attached to a portable easel. As the name suggests, you reveal visuals on a flip pad one at a time by turning pages. Flip pads combine the spontaneity of the chalkboard (you can write on them as you go) with portability, which means that you can prepare them in advance. If you plan to use the same visuals more than once, you can prepare them in advance on rigid poster board and display them on the same type of easel.

The main disadvantage of flip pads and poster boards, apart from their bulk, is that preparing professional-looking exhibits on them requires a fair amount of artistic ability.

Handouts

The main advantage of handouts is that audience members can keep them for future reference. The main disadvantage is that they can be distracting if you distribute them during your speech: passing them out takes time

Communications is an industry that is always changing and evolving. Your knowledge is always being advanced whether it's learning the newest form of communication or the latest social media outlet. With my lifelong dream of a career in the beauty industry, an education in communications studies was the perfect place to start. This education provided me with a variety of career tools that allowed me to work in a field I am truly passionate about.

After graduating, I was fortunate enough to be given the opportunity to work as an intern at *FASHION Magazine*. While there, I developed a desire to work in public relations and due to the networking opportunities at the magazine, I landed my current position as a communications specialist at Shoppers Drug Mart. Day-to-day my duties include analyzing effective message dissemination, maintaining the company's image through positive messaging, and pitching the right magazines to feature our newest beauty products. Essentially, this opportunity would not have been possible without the solid foundation I received from my education in communication studies. With so many options, I know that the possibilities for my future in the communications industry are endless.

and attention away from your presentation, and audience members will be tempted to focus on them even after you've gone on to talk about something else. It's best, therefore, to pass them out at the end of the speech.

Projectors

Projectors are useful when your audience is too large to view handheld images. They come in several varieties, each of which works well for a specific purpose. *Overhead projectors* have evolved significantly since the days of simple transparencies—large, clear sheets of acetate used to cast an image on a screen. Today most overhead projectors are actually cameras that take a picture of a document and then project that image onto the screen. If you have enough time to take a digital photograph of your visual aid, you can use your laptop with a computer projector for an especially effective presentation. If the room has an ethernet or wireless Internet connection, you could use an online presentation management tool such as Picasa or Flickr. You can also use the Internet to display short films from YouTube or Google Video. An *LCD projector* allows you to use a screen image directly from a computer screen, making it the most direct way to use computer software in presentations.

Other Electronic Media

Many other electronic media are available as presentation aids. Audio aids such as CDs can supply information that could not be presented any other way (comparing musical styles, for example, or demonstrating the differences in the sounds of gas and diesel engines), but in most cases

Understanding Communication Technology

Using PowerPoint

Several specialized programs exist just to produce visual aids. The most popular of these programs is Microsoft's PowerPoint®. In its simplest form, PowerPoint lets you build an effective slide show out of your basic outline. You can choose colour-coordinated backgrounds and consistent formatting that match the tone and purpose of your presentation. The program contains a clip art library that allows you to choose images to accompany your words. It also allows you to import images from outside sources and to build your own charts.

To use PowerPoint, you can enter the program by clicking on the button for 'Blank Presentation' or by activating the 'Wizard' function. Either way, the program will walk you through the stages of creating a slide show. It will, for example, show you a gallery of layout styles and ask you which type you would like.

From this point on it is basically point, click, and follow directions. PowerPoint allows you to choose from several combinations of charts, text, and clip art. These visuals, like any type of computer-generated visual, can

then be run directly from a computer projector, printed onto overhead transparencies, converted to 35mm slides at any photo shop, or simply printed out in handout form. (See pages 508–9 for a discussion of the pros and cons of various presentation media.) Advanced uses of the program produce multimedia presentations with animated slide, sound, and video elements. For more on using PowerPoint, type 'PowerPoint' and 'tutorial' into your favourite search engine.

Before you commit entirely to using PowerPoint, however, make sure you take a moment to check out Keynote, the Macintosh presentation software. Many people prefer Keynote because it is more flexible and allows more beautiful transitions from slide to slide. Another option is to 'open source' which means using non-commercial software programs such as OpenOffice Impress or KPresenter. These programs are designed by groups of software programmers working in a completely open and egalitarian environment. They are a viable alternative to corporate software packages from Microsoft and Apple.

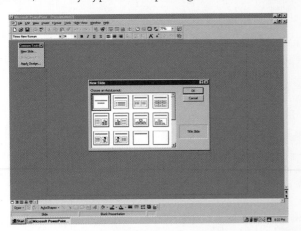

you should use them sparingly. Remember that your presentation already relies heavily on your audience's sense of hearing; it's better to use a visual aid, if possible, than to overwork the audio.

Of course, there are audiovisual aids, including films, videotapes, and sound-on-slides. These should also be used sparingly, however, because they allow audience members to receive information passively, thus relieving them of the responsibility of becoming active participants in the presentation. The general rule when using these media is: *Don't let them get in the way of the direct, person-to-person contact that is the primary advantage of public speaking.*

Understanding Communication Technology

The Pros and Cons of PowerPoint

The Pros

The advantages of PowerPoint are well known. Proponents say that PowerPoint slides can focus the attention of audience members on important information at the appropriate time. They also help listeners appreciate the relationship between different pieces of information. By doing so, they make the logical structure of an argument more transparent.

Some experts think the primary advantage of PowerPoint is that it forces otherwise befuddled speakers to organize their thoughts in advance. Most, however, insist that its primary benefit is in providing two channels of information rather than just one. This gives audiences a visual source of information that is a more efficient way to learn than by listening alone. One psychology professor puts it this way: 'We are visual creatures. Visual things stay put, whereas sounds fade. If you zone out for 30 seconds—and who doesn't?—it is nice to be able to glance up on the screen and see what you missed.'[1]

But for all its popularity, PowerPoint has been receiving some bad press lately, being featured in articles with such downbeat titles as 'PowerPoint Is Evil'[2] and 'Does PowerPoint Make You Stupid?'[3] But the statement that truly put the anti-PowerPoint argument on the map was a 23-page pamphlet with a less dramatic title, *The Cognitive Style of PowerPoint*,[4] because it was authored by Edward R. Tufte, the well-respected author of several influential books on the effective design of visual aids.

The Cons

According to Tufte, the use of low-content PowerPoint slides trivializes important information. It encourages oversimplification by asking the presenter to summarize key concepts in as few words as possible—the ever-present bullet points.

Tufte also insists that PowerPoint makes it easier for a speaker to hide lies and logical fallacies. When dazzling slides are used, the audience stays respectfully still and a speaker can quickly move past gross generalizations, imprecise logic, superficial reasoning, and misleading conclusions.

Perhaps most seriously, opponents of PowerPoint say that it is an enemy of interaction, that it interferes with the spontaneous give-and-take that is so important in effective public speaking. One expert summarized this effect by saying, 'Instead of human contact, we are given human display.'[5]

The Middle Ground?

PowerPoint proponents say that it is just a tool, one that can be used effectively or ineffectively. They are the first to admit that a poorly done PowerPoint presentation can be boring and ineffective, as in the infamous 'triple delivery', in which precisely the same text is seen on the screen, spoken aloud, and printed on the handout in front of you. One proponent insists, 'Tufte is correct in that most talks are horrible and most PowerPoint slides are bad—but that's not PowerPoint's fault. Most writing is awful, too, but I don't go railing against pencils or chalk.'[6]

PowerPoint proponents say that PowerPoint should not be allowed to overpower a presentation—it should be just one element of a speech, not the whole thing. They point out that even before the advent of the personal computer, some people argued that speeches with visual aids stressed format over content. PowerPoint just makes it extremely easy to stress impressive format over less-than-impressive content, but that's a tendency that the effective speaker recognizes and works against. Thus, proponents say, the arguments for and against PowerPoint are really the arguments for and against visual aids. These arguments are merely accentuated now that they apply to one of the most influential media technologies of our day. Opponents shake their heads sadly at this explanation, and insist that every technology changes the humans who use it in some way, and sometimes those changes are subtle and dangerous.

[1.] Steven Pinker . . ., quoted in Laurence Zuckerman, 'Words Go Right to the Brain, but Can They Stir the Heart?' *The New York Times* (17 April 1999): 9.
[2.] Edward Tufte, 'PowerPoint is Evil: Power Corrupts. PowerPoint Corrupts Absolutely', *Wired* (September 2003). Available at wired.com/wired/archive/11.09/ppt2.html.
[3.] Tad Simons, 'Does PowerPoint Make You Stupid?' *Presentations* (March 2004): 25.
[4.] Edward R. Tufte, *The Cognitive Style of PowerPoint* (Cheshire, CT: Graphics Press, 2003).
[5.] Ian Parker, 'Absolute PowerPoint: Can a Software Package Edit Our Thoughts', *The New Yorker* (28 May 2001): 86.
[6.] Don Norman, a design expert cited in Simons, 'Does PowerPoint Make You Stupid?'

Questions: After reviewing the pros and cons of PowerPoint, would you say that PowerPoint is a benefit or a detriment to effective public speaking? What forms of support would you use to back up your argument?

Rules for Using Visual Aids

It's easy to see that each type of visual aid and each medium for its presentation have their own advantages and disadvantages. No matter which type you use, however, there are a few rules to follow.

Simplicity

Keep your visual aids simple. Your goal is to clarify, not confuse. Use only keywords or phrases, not sentences. The 'rule of seven' states that each exhibit you use should contain no more than seven lines of text, each with no more than seven words. Keep all printing horizontal. Omit all non-essential details.

Size

Visual aids should be large enough for your entire audience to see them at one time but portable enough for you to get them out of the way when they no longer pertain to the point you are making.

Attractiveness

Visual aids should be visually interesting and as neat as possible. If you don't have the necessary skills—either artistic or computer—try to get help from a friend or from the audiovisual centre at your college or university.

Appropriateness

Visuals must be appropriate to all the components of the speaking situation—you, your audience, and your topic—and they must emphasize the point you are trying to make. Don't make the mistake of using a visual aid that looks good but has only a weak link to your point—such as showing a map of a city transit system while talking about the condition of the individual cars.

Reliability

You must be in control of your visual aids at all times. Test all electronic media (projectors, computers, and so on) in advance, preferably in the room where you will speak. Just to be safe, have non-electronic backups ready in case of disaster. Be conservative when you choose demonstrations: wild animals, chemical reactions, and gimmicks meant to shock a crowd can often backfire.

Understanding Communication Technology

Stockwell Day's Prop Fail

The federal English-language election debate of 2000 provides an example of how not to use visual aids. When the discussion turned to health care, then prime minister Jean Chrétien insisted that a universal one-tier system was viable. Alexa McDonough, the NDP leader, claimed that recent legislation had opened the door to a two-tiered system. Stockwell Day (then leader of the Alliance Party) held up a sheet of paper with the words 'No 2-Tiered Health Care' written on it. The visual aid was both a violation of the debate rules (Day claimed it was part of his notes) and a matter of ridicule. Conservative leader Joe Clark later mocked Day in the media, saying that he looked more like a game show host than a potential prime minister. The moral of this story is to use props judiciously in public communication.

Finally, when the time comes to use your visual aid, remember to talk to your audience, not to the prop. Some speakers become so wrapped up in their props that they turn their backs on the audience and sacrifice eye contact.

Offering Constructive Criticism

The guidelines presented in this chapter will not only help you to deliver a speech effectively but also allow you to critique the speeches of others. Remember: in your public speaking class you will almost always be asked to evaluate your classmates' speeches. This criticism is extremely important, but it can also be difficult for your classmate to hear. You need to ensure that your criticism is constructive, designed to help the speaker improve. To be constructive, criticism has to be both positive and substantive.

When we say that criticism has to be positive, we mean that you should present it with the positive attitude mentioned earlier. The easiest way to do that is to point out what is *right* about the speech as well as what is *wrong* about it. In fact, negative criticism unaccompanied by positive criticism is often useless because the speaker might become defensive and block out your criticism completely. It is a good idea, therefore, to offer your positive criticism first and then tactfully offer your suggestions for improvement, using the various suggestions for creating a positive communication climate that were discussed in Chapter 7. For example, rather than saying, 'Your ideas about the psychological aspects of diabetes were completely unclear and unsupported,' you might say, 'I found your explanation of the physical aspects of diabetes to be clearly stated and cited with details and examples. However, your explanation of the psychological aspects of the disease left me a little confused. It might be my own fault, but it just did not seem to be as well supported as the rest of your speech.'

When we say that criticism has to be substantive, we mean two things: first, you need to criticize *what* was said as well as *how* it was said. Do not concentrate on delivery traits to the point where you lose track of the speaker's ideas. Second, you need to be specific. Rather than saying, 'I liked this' or 'I didn't like that,' you should provide a detailed explanation of your reasons for liking or disliking parts of the speech.

'It was a little preachy.'

Cultural Idiom

wrapped up in
giving all one's attention to something

COMMUNICATION ON-SCREEN

Battlestar Galactica (2004–09)

Developed by Ronald D. Moore, from the original series created by Glen A. Larson.

This television series, a remake of the short-lived 1978 program of the same title, documents the epic journey home of the last remaining humans after a cataclysm unleashed upon earth by the Cylons, a cyborg race created by humans in their own image. In particular contrast to its flippant predecessor, the series is very much about public relations, politics, and religion—all of which depend on opinion leaders using public speaking to get a message across effectively. Both the Cylons and the humans have to rally support for battles, big decisions, hard choices, and sacrifices. Episodes without any lessons for students of public communication are few and far between.

Summary

One of the most serious problems in public speaking is debilitative (as opposed to facilitative) stage fright. Sources of debilitative stage fright include irrational thinking, which might consist of a belief in one or more of the fallacies mentioned in this chapter. There are several methods of overcoming speech anxiety. The first is to remember that nervousness is natural and should be used to your advantage. The others include being rational, receiver-oriented, positive, and prepared.

There are four types of speech delivery: extemporaneous, impromptu, manuscript, and memorized. In each type, the speaker must be concerned with both visual and auditory aspects of the presentation. Visual aspects include appearance, movement, posture, facial expression, and eye contact. Auditory aspects include volume, rate, pitch, and articulation. The four most common articulation problems are deletion, substitution, addition, and slurring of word sounds.

Visual aids help clarify complicated points and keep an audience informed about where you are in the general scheme of things. This chapter examined several types of visual aids: objects and models, diagrams, word and number charts, pie charts, bar and column charts, and line charts. These visual aids can be presented via flip pads and poster board, handouts, projectors, or other forms of electronic media. Whatever visual aids you use in your public speaking, it is important to ensure that they adhere to the rules regarding simplicity, size, attractiveness, appropriateness, and reliability.

Effective delivery is aided through the constructive criticism of speeches presented in class. Your criticism should include positive as well as negative aspects of the speaker's behaviour. It should also be substantive, which means that it should address what was said as well as how it was said, and it should be specific in terms of what you liked and didn't like about the speech.

Key Terms

addition 503
articulation 503
bar chart 507
column chart 507
debilitative stage fright 492
deletion 503
diagram 506
extemporaneous speech 496
facilitative stage fright 492
fallacy of approval 494

fallacy of catastrophic failure 493
fallacy of overgeneralization 494
fallacy of perfection 494
impromptu speech 496
irrational thinking 493
line chart 507
manuscript speech 497
memorized speech 498

model 506
number chart 506
pie chart 506
pitch 502
rate 502
slurring 503
substitution 503
visual aids 505
visualization 495
word chart 506

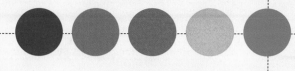

Activities

A. Stage Fright: A Personal Analysis

To analyze your own reaction to stage fright, think back to your last public speech and rate yourself on how rational, receiver-oriented, positive, and prepared you were. How did these attributes affect your anxiety level?

B. Types of Delivery

Find at least one speech for each of the four types of delivery: extemporaneous, impromptu, manuscript, or memorized. In these speeches, decide whether the type of delivery was effective for the topic, speaker, and situation. Explain why or why not. If you think the speeches were not effective, suggest a more appropriate type.

C. Articulation Exercises

Tongue twisters can be used to practise careful articulation out loud. Try these two classics:
- She sells seashells down by the seashore.
- Peter Piper picked a peck of pickled peppers.

Now make up some of your own and try them out. Make twisters for both consonant sounds ('Frank's friendly face flushed furiously') and vowel sounds ('Oliver oiled the old annoying oddity').

D. Inventing Visual Aids

Choose a speech from one of the sources given in the box on page 505. Analyze it for where visual aids might be effective. Describe the visual aids that you think would work best.

Further Reading

Ayers, Joe, and Tim Hopf. *Coping with Speech Anxiety*. Norwood, NJ: Ablex, 1993.
Ayers and Hopf offer a catalogue and explanation of various 'intervention procedures' that help people cope with communication anxiety, including rational-emotive therapy, visualization, systematic desensitization, rhetoritherapy, and anxiety reduction workshops.

Bremmer, Jan, and Herman Roodenburg, eds. *A Cultural History of Gesture*. Ithaca, NY: Cornell University Press, 1992.
This book examines, in a historical–cultural analysis, why certain body movements mean what they do today. For example, Homer promoted the John Wayne walk in ancient Greece by constantly referring to heroes with 'long strides'.

Glenn, Ethel C., Phillip Glenn, and Sandra Forman. *Your Voice and Articulation*, 4th edn. Needham Heights, MA: Allyn and Bacon, 1998.
The authors present a comprehensive discussion of the anatomy and physiology of the human voice. Extensive vocal exercises are included for pitch, volume, rate, and 'vocal colour'. Chapter 2 is devoted to dialects.

Hahner, Jeffrey C., Martin A. Sokoloff, and Sandra L. Salisch. *Speaking Clearly: Improving Voice and Diction*. New York: McGraw-Hill, 2002.
This text comes with a pronunciation guide on CD.

Lee, Charlotte, and Timothy Gura. *Oral Interpretation,* 10th edn. Boston: Houghton Mifflin, 2000.
This book is a collection of prose, drama, and poetry pieces especially designed for oral presentation. See especially Chapter 3, 'Voice Development for Oral Interpretation', and Chapter 4, 'Use of the Body in Oral Interpretation'.

Wells, Lynn K. *The Articulate Voice,* 4th edn. Needham Heights, MA: Allyn and Bacon, 2004.
Wells provides basic information on voice production and techniques for improvement.

Wempen, Faithe. *PowerPoint 2003 Bible*. New York: Wiley, 2003.
Wempen's book is an excellent guide to the use of PowerPoint, but it should be read in conjunction with Edward Tufte's *The Cognitive Style of PowerPoint* (New York: Graphics Press, 2003) to avoid PowerPoint's tendency to trivialize in-depth analysis.

Study Questions

1. For each of the fallacies presented on pages 493–4, think of a time that they have impacted your life. How serious of an impact did they have upon you? Did they hold you back from participating in public communication or from achieving a goal?

2. Imagine that you have been chosen to deliver a speech promoting your school to a group of prospective high-school students. Describe any thoughts you might have that would lead to stage fright and explain how you could use the techniques on pages 494–5 to overcome them.

3. How can you use the visual and vocal aspects of delivery described on pages 499–503 to make your delivery most effective?

4. Think of examples of three PowerPoint presentations that you have seen that fit into the following categories: successful, mediocre, disastrous. Make a small chart to evaluate them, using criteria from the two boxes on PowerPoint on pages 510 and 511. After you have completed your evaluation chart, make suggestions for improvement to each presentation. How would you fix them?

NOTES

Chapter 1

1. For a discussion of the unique character of animal communication, see J. Liska, 'Bee Dances, Bird Songs, Monkey Calls, and Cetacean Sonar: Is Speech Unique?' *Western Journal of Communication* 57 (1993): 1–26.

2. For an in-depth look at this topic, see S.B. Cunningham, 'Intrapersonal Communication: A Review and Critique', in S. Deetz, ed., *Communication Yearbook* 15 (Newbury Park, CA: Sage, 1992).

3. L. Wheeler and J. Nelek, 'Sex Differences in Social Participation', *Journal of Personality and Social Psychology* 35 (1977): 742–54.

4. J. John, 'The Distribution of Free-Forming Small Group Size', *American Sociological Review* 18 (1953): 569–70.

5. D. Smith, 'Are we getting through? Content Analysis of Canada Revenue Agency Media Clippings', MCM Thesis, DeGroote School of Business, McMaster University, 2010.

6. K. Morris, 'Crisis Communications: Challenges faced by Remote and Rural Communities in North Eastern Ontario', *McMaster Journal of Communication* 6 (2009).

7. 'Social Media Reality Check', newswire.ca/socialmediareality-check/.

8. For a summary of the link between social support and health, see S. Duck, 'Staying Healthy . . . with a Little Help from Our Friends?' in *Human Relationships*, 2nd edn (Newbury Park, CA: Sage, 1992).

9. S. Cohen, W.J. Doyle, D.P. Skoner, B.S. Rabin, and J.M. Gwaltney, 'Social Ties and Susceptibility to the Common Cold', *Journal of the American Medical Association* 277 (1997): 1940–4.

10. Three articles in *Journal of the American Medical Association* 267 (22/29 January 1992) focus on the link between psychosocial influences and coronary heart disease: R.B. Case, A.J. Moss, N. Case, M. McDermott, and S. Eberly, 'Living Alone after Myocardial Infarction' (515–19); R.B. Williams, J.C. Barefoot, R.M. Calif, T.L. Haney, W.B. Saunders, D.B. Pryon, M.A. Hlatky, I.C. Siegler, and D.B. Mark, 'Prognostic Importance of Social and Economic Resources among Medically Treated Patients with Angiographically Documented Coronary Artery Disease' (520–4); and R. Ruberman, 'Psychosocial Influences on Mortality of Patients with Coronary Heart Disease' (559–60).

11. S. Cohen and T. Wills, 'Stress, Social Support, and the Buffering Hypothesis', *Psychological Bulletin* 98 (1985): 310–57.

12. J. Caron, R. Tempier, C. Mercier, and P. Leouffre, 'Components of Social Support and Quality of Life in Severely Mentally Ill, Low-Income Individuals in a General Population Group', *Community Mental Health Journal* 34 (1998): 459–76.

13. K.S. Courneya, R.C. Plotnikoff, S.B. Hotz, and N.J. Birkett, 'Social Support and the Theory of Planned Behavior in the Exercise Domain', *American Journal of Health Behavior* 24, 4 (2000): 300–8.

14. J. Ali, 'Mental Health of Canada's Immigrants', *Health Reports* (Ottawa: Statistics Canada, 2002), Catalogue 82-003-XIE: 13 (suppl): 101–11.

15. S. Jafari, S. Baharlou, R. Mathias, 'Knowledge of Determinants of Mental Health Among Iranian Immigrants of BC, Canada: "A Qualitative Study"', *Journal of Immigrant and Minority Health* 12, 1 (February 2010): 100–06.

16. R. Martin, 'Is Laughter the Best Medicine? Humor, Laughter, and Physical Health', *Current Directions in Psychological Science* 11, 6 (2002): 216–20.

17. H.M. Lefcourt and S. Thomas, 'Humor and Stress Revisited' in W. Ruch, ed., *The Sense of Humor: Explorations of a Personality Characteristic* (Berlin: Walter de Gruyter, 1998): 179–202.

18. J. Stewart, *Bridges, Not Walls: A Book about Interpersonal Communication,* 9th edn (New York: McGraw-Hill, 2004): 11.

19. R. Shattuck, *The Forbidden Experiment: The Story of the Wild Boy of Aveyron* (New York: Farrar, Straus & Giroux, 1980): 37.

20. For a fascinating account of Genie's story, see R. Rymer, *Genie: An Abused Child's Flight from Silence* (New York: HarperCollins, 1993). Linguist Susan Curtiss provides a more specialized account of the case in her book *Genie: A Psycholinguistic Study of a Modern-Day 'Wild Child'* (San Diego: Academic Press, 1977).

21. C. Blatchford, 'Custody Granted to Child Abusers', *National Post*, 22 February 2003.

22. A.M. Nicotera, 'Where Have We Been, Where Are We, and Where Do We Go?', in A.M. Nicotera and associates, eds, *Interpersonal Communication in Friend and Mate Relationships* (Albany: SUNY Press, 1993).

23. R.B. Rubin, E.M. Perse, and C.A. Barbato, 'Conceptualization and Measurement of Interpersonal Communication Motives', *Human Communication Research* 14 (1988): 602–28.

24. R.A. Martin, P. Puhlik-Doris, G. Larsen, J. Gray, and K. Weir, 'Individual Divergences in Uses of Humor and Their Relation to Psychological Well-being: Development of the Humor Styles Questionnaire', *Journal of Research in Personality* 37 (2003): 48–75.

25. W. Goldschmidt, *The Human Career: The Self in the Symbolic World* (Cambridge, MA: Basil Blackman, 1990).

26. Job Outlook 2004, *National Association of Colleges and Employers*. Report at jobweb.com/joboutlook/2004outlook/.

27. M.S. Peterson, 'Personnel Interviewers' Perceptions of the Importance and Adequacy of Applicants' Communication Skills', *Communication Education* 46 (1997): 287–91.

28. M.W. Martin and C.M. Anderson, 'Roommate Similarity: Are Roommates Who Are Similar in Their Communication Traits More Satisfied?' *Communication Research Reports* 12 (1995): 46–52.

29. R.B. Rubin and E.E. Graham, 'Communication Correlates of College Success: An Exploratory Investigation', *Communication Education* 37 (1988): 14–27.

30. E. Kirchler, 'Marital Happiness and Interaction in Everyday Surroundings: A Time-Sample Diary Approach for Couples', *Journal of Social and Personal Relationships* 5 (1988): 375–82.

31. R.L. Duran and L. Kelly, 'The Influence of Communicative Competence on Perceived Task, Social and Physical Attraction', *Communication Quarterly* 36 (1988): 41–9.

32. C.E. Shannon and W. Weaver, *The Mathematical Theory of Communication* (Urbana: University of Illinois Press, 1949).

33. M. McLuhan, *Understanding Media: The Extensions of Man*. (Cambridge, MA: MIT Press, 1994).

34. K.R. Colbert, 'The Effects of Debate Participation on Argumentativeness and Verbal Aggression', *Communication Education* 42 (1993): 206–14.

35. See, for example, M. Dunne and S.H. Ng, 'Simultaneous Speech in Small Group Conversation: All-Together-Now and One-at-a-Time?', *Journal of Language and Social Psychology* 13 (1994): 45–71.

36. The issue of intentionality has been a matter of debate by communication theorists. For a sample of the arguments on both sides, see J.O. Greene, ed., *Message Production: Advances in Communication Theory* (New York: Erlbaum, 1997); M.T. Motley, 'On Whether One Can(not) Communicate: An Examination via Traditional Communication Postulates', *Western Journal of Speech Communication* 54 (1990): 1–20; J.B. Bavelas, 'Behaving and Communicating: A Reply to Motley', *Western Journal of Speech Communication* 54 (1990): 593–602; and J. Stewart, 'A Postmodern Look at Traditional Communication Postulates', *Western Journal of Speech Communication* 55 (1991): 354–79.

37. S. Duck, 'Relationships as Unfinished Business: Out of the Frying Pan and into the 1990s', *Journal of Social and Personal Relationships* 7 (1990): 5. For another example of the contextual base of communication, see V. Manusov, 'Reacting to Changes in Nonverbal Behaviors: Relational Satisfaction and Adaptation Patterns in Romantic Dyads', *Human Communication Research* 21 (1995): 456–77.

38. K.J. Gergen, *The Saturated Self: Dilemmas of Identity in Contemporary Life* (New York: Basic Books, 1991): 158.

39. T.P. Mottet and V.P. Richmond, 'Student Nonverbal Communication and Its Influence on Teachers and Teaching: A Review of Literature', in J.L. Chesebro and J.C. McCroskey, eds, *Communication for Teachers* (Needham Heights, MA: Allyn & Bacon, 2001).

40. M. Dainton and L. Stafford, 'The Dark Side of "Normal" Family Interaction', in B.H. Spitzberg and W.R. Cupach, eds, *The Dark Side of Interpersonal Communication* (Hillsdale, NJ: Erlbaum, 1993).

41. For a thorough review of this topic, see B.H. Spitzberg and W.R. Cupach, *Handbook of Interpersonal Competence Research* (New York: Springer-Verlag, 1989).

42. See J.M. Wiemann, J. Takai, H. Ota, and M. Wiemann, 'A Relational Model of Communication Competence', in B. Kovacic, ed., *Emerging Theories of Human Communication* (Albany: SUNY Press, 1997).

43. For a review of the research citing the importance of flexibility, see M.M. Martin and C.M. Anderson, 'The Cognitive Flexibility Scale: Three Validity Studies', *Communication Reports* 11 (1998): 1–9.

44. See G.M. Chen and W.J. Sarosta, 'Intercultural Communication Competence: A Synthesis', in B.R. Burleson and A.W. Kunkel, eds, *Communication Yearbook* 19 (Thousand Oaks, CA: Sage, 1996).

45. See, for example, M.S. Kim, H.C. Shin, and D. Cai, 'Cultural Influences on the Preferred Forms of Requesting and Re-Requesting', *Communication Monographs* 65 (1998): 47–66.

46. M.J. Collier, 'Communication Competence Problematics in Ethnic Relationships', *Communication Monographs* 63 (1996): 314–36.

47. M. Bowman, 'The Diversity of Diversity: Canadian–American Differences and Their Implications for Clinical Training and APA Accreditation', *Canadian Psychology* 41, 4 (2000): 230–43.

48. For an example of the advantages of cultural flexibility, see L. Chen, 'Verbal Adaptive Strategies in U.S. American Dyadic Interactions with U.S. American or East-Asian Partners', *Communication Monographs* 64 (1997): 302–23.

49. For a discussion of the trait versus state assessments of communication, see D.A. Infante, A.S. Rancer, and D.F. Womack, *Building Communication Theory*, 3rd edn (Prospect Heights, IL: Waveland Press, 1996): 159–60. For a specific discussion of trait versus state definitions of communication competence, see W.R. Cupach and B.H. Spitzberg, 'Trait versus State: A Comparison of Dispositional and Situational Measures of Interpersonal Communication Competence', *Western Journal of Speech Communication* 47 (1983): 364–79.

50. B.R. Burleson and W. Samter, 'A Social Skills Approach to Relationship Maintenance', in D. Canary and L. Stafford, eds, *Communication and Relationship Maintenance* (San Diego: Academic Press, 1994), 12.

51. L.K. Guerrero, P.A. Andersen, P.F. Jorgensen, B.H. Spitzberg, and S.V. Eloy, 'Coping with the Green-Eyed Monster: Conceptualizing and Measuring Communicative Responses to Romantic Jealousy', *Western Journal of Communication* 59 (1995): 270–304.

52. See B.J. O'Keefe, 'The Logic of Message Design: Individual Differences in Reasoning about Communication', *Communication Monographs* 55 (1988): 80–103.

53. See, for example, A.D. Heisel, J.C. McCroskey, and V.P. Richmond, 'Testing Theoretical Relationships and Non-relationships of Genetically-Based Predictors: Getting Started with Communibiology', *Communication Research Reports* 16 (1999): 1–9; and J.C. McCroskey and K.J. Beatty, 'The Communibiological Perspective: Implications for Communication in Instruction', *Communication Education* 49 (2000): 1–6.

54. S.L. Kline and B.L. Clinton, 'Developments in Children's Persuasive Message Practices', *Communication Education* 47 (1998): 120–36.

55. M.A. de Turck and G.R. Miller, 'Training Observers to Detect Deception: Effects of Self-Monitoring and Rehearsal', *Human Communication Research* 16 (1990): 603–20.

56. R.B. Rubin, E.E. Graham, and J.T. Mignerey, 'A Longitudinal Study of College Students' Communication Competence', *Communication Education* 39 (1990): 1–14.

57. See, for example, R. Martin, 'Relational Cognition Complexity and Relational Communication in Personal Relationships', *Communication Monographs* 59 (1992): 150–63; D.W. Stacks and M.A. Murphy, 'Conversational Sensitivity: Further Validation and Extension', *Communication Reports* 6 (1993): 18–24; and A.L. Vangelisti and S.M. Draughton, 'The

Nature and Correlates of Conversational Sensitivity', *Human Communication Research* 14 (1987): 167–202.

58. Research summarized in D.E. Hamachek, *Encounters with the Self*, 2nd edn (Fort Worth, TX: Holt, Rinehart and Winston, 1987): 8. See also J.A. Daly, A.L. Vangelisti, and S.M. Daughton, 'The Nature and Correlates of Conversational Sensitivity', in M.V. Redmond, ed., *Interpersonal Communication: Readings in Theory and Research* (Fort Worth, TX: Harcourt Brace, 1995).

59. J. Kruger and D.A. Dunning, 'Unskilled and Unaware of It: How Difficulties in Recognizing One's Own Incompetence Lead to Inflated Self-Assessments', *Journal of Personality and Social Psychology* 77, 6 (December 1999): 1121–34.

60. Adapted from the work of R.P. Hart as reported by M.L. Knapp in *Interpersonal Communication and Human Relationships* (Boston: Allyn & Bacon, 1984), 342–4. See also R.P. Hart and D.M. Burks, 'Rhetorical Sensitivity and Social Interaction', *Speech Monographs* 39 (1972): 75–91; and R.P. Hart, R.E. Carlson, and W.F. Eadie, 'Attitudes toward Communication and the Assessment of Rhetorical Sensitivity', *Communication Monographs* 47 (1980): 1–22.

61. Adapted from J.C. McCroskey and L.R. Wheeless, *Introduction to Human Communication* (Boston: Allyn & Bacon, 1976), 3–10.

62. R.K. Aune, 'A Theory of Attribution of Responsibility for Creating Understanding'. Paper delivered to the Interpersonal Communication Division of the 1998 International Communication Association Conference, Jerusalem, Israel.

63. W.B. Pearce and K.A. Pearce, 'Extending the Theory of the Coordinated Management of Meaning (CMM) through a Community Dialogue Process', *Communication Theory* 10 (2000): 405–23. See also E.M. Griffin, *A First Look at Communication Theory*, 5th edn (New York: McGraw-Hill, 2003), 66–81.

64. J.A.M. Meerloo, *Conversation and Communication* (Madison, CT: International Universities Press, 1952), 91.

65. E. Eisenberg, 'Jamming: Transcendence through Organizing', *Communication Research* 17 (1990): 139–64.

66. Adapted from D.D. Thornburg, 'Jamming, Technology and Learning', *PBS Teacher Source Online*. Available at pbs.org/teachersource/thornburg/thornburg0701.shtm.

67. For a detailed rationale of the position argued in this section, see G.H. Stamp and M.L. Knapp, 'The Construct of Intent in Interpersonal Communication', *Quarterly Journal of Speech* 76 (1990): 282–99. See also J. Stewart, 'A Postmodern Look at Traditional Communication Postulates', *Western Journal of Speech Communication* 55 (1991): 354–79.

68. For a thorough discussion of communication difficulties, see N. Coupland, H. Giles, and J.M. Wiemann, eds, *'Miscommunication' and Problematic Talk* (Newbury Park, CA: Sage, 1991).

69. McCroskey and Wheeless, op. cit., 5.

Chapter 2

1. C.L.M. Shaw, 'Personal Narrative: Revealing Self and Reflecting Other', *Human Communication Research* 24 (1997): 302–19.

2. P.M. Sias, 'Constructing Perceptions of Differential Treatment: An Analysis of Coworkers' Discourse', *Communication Monographs* 63 (1996): 171–87.

3. A. Wilson and B.R. Slugoski, 'Contribution of Conversational Skills to the Production of Judgmental Errors', *European Journal of Social Psychology* 28 (1998): 575–601.

4. J.M. Martz, J. Verette, X.B. Arriaga, L.F. Slovik, C.L. Cox, and C.E. Rusbult, 'Positive Illusion in Close Relationships', *Personal Relationships* 5 (1998): 159–81.

5. J.C. Pearson, 'Positive Distortion: 'The Most Beautiful Woman in the World', in K.M. Galvin and P.J. Cooper, eds, *Making Connections: Readings in Relational Communication*, 2nd edn (Los Angeles: Roxbury, 2000): 186.

6. Summarized in D.E. Hamachek, *Encounters with Others* (New York: Holt, Rinehart and Winston, 1982): 23–30.

7. For a review of these perceptual biases, see D.E. Hamachek, *Encounters with the Self*, 3rd edn (Fort Worth, TX: Harcourt Brace Jovanovich, 1992). See also T.N. Bradbury and F.D. Fincham, 'Attributions in Marriage: Review and Critique', *Psychological Bulletin* 107 (1990): 3–33. For an example of the self-serving bias in action, see R. Buttny, 'Reported Speech in Talking Race on Campus', *Human Communication Research* 23 (1997): 477–506.

8. D. Dunning and A.F. Hayes, 'Evidence for Egocentric Comparison in Social Judgment', *Journal of Personality & Social Psychology* 71 (1996): 213–29.

9. B. Sypher and H.E. Sypher, 'Seeing Ourselves as Others See Us', *Communication Research* 11 (January 1984): 97–115.

10. Reported by D. Myers, 'The Inflated Self', *Psychology Today* 14 (May 1980): 16.

11. C. Symons and B. Johnston, 'Self-reference Affect in Memory: A Meta-Analysis', *Psychological Bulletin* 121 (1997): 371–94.

12. P. Lewicki, 'Self Image Bias in Person Perception', *Journal of Personality and Social Psychology* 45 (1983): 384–93.

13. See, for example, P. Baron, 'Self-Esteem, Ingratiation, and Evaluation of Unknown Others', *Journal of Personality and Social Psychology* 30 (1974): 104–9; and E. Walster, 'The Effect of Self-Esteem on Romantic Liking', *Journal of Experimental and Social Psychology* 1 (1965): 184–97.

14. B. Mullen and G.R. Goethals, 'Social Projection, Actual Consensus and Valence', *British Journal of Social Psychology* 29 (1990): 279–82.

15. P.A. Mongeau and C.M. Carey, 'Who's Wooing Whom II? An Experimental Investigation of Date-Initiation and Expectancy Violation', *Western Journal of Communication* 60 (1996): 195–213.

16. See, for example, D.E. Kanouse and L.R. Hanson, 'Negativity in Evaluations', in E.E. Jones, D.E. Kanouse, H.H. Kelley, R.E. Nisbett, S. Valins, and B. Weiner, eds, *Attribution: Perceiving the Causes of Behavior* (Morristown, NJ: General Learning Press, 1972).

17. V. Manusov, 'It Depends on Your Perspective: Effects of Stance and Beliefs about Intent on Person Perception', *Western Journal of Communication* 57 (1993): 27–41.

18. T. Adler, 'Enter Romance, Exit Objectivity', *APA Monitor* (June 1992): 18.

19. N. Villegas, 'Assessing Reputation Management, Internal Communications and Perceptions in Oakville, Ontario', *McMaster Journal of Communication* 6 (1) (2009).

20. S.B. Algoe, B.N. Buswell, and J.D. DeLamater, 'Gender and Job Status as Contextual Cues for the Interpretation of Facial Expression of Emotion', *Sex Roles* 3 (2000): 183–97.

21. See D.H. Solomon and M.L.M. Williams, 'Perceptions of Social-Sexual Communication at Work: The Effects of Message, Situation, and Observer Characteristics on Judgments of Sexual Harassment', *Journal of Applied Communication Research* 25 (1997): 196–216.

22. J.K. Alberts, U. Kellar-Guenther, and S.R. Corman, 'That's Not Funny: Understanding Recipients' Responses to Teasing', *Western Journal of Communication* 60 (1996): 337–57.

23. M.W. Baldwin and S.D.M. Dandeneau, 'The Inhibition of Socially Rejecting Information Among People with High Versus Low Self Esteem: The Role of Attentional Bias and The Effects of Bias Reduction Training', *Journal of Social and Clinical Psychology* 23(2004): 584–602.

24. M.W. Baldwin, J.R. Baccus, and G.M. Fitzsimons, 'Self-Esteem and The Dual Processing of Interpersonal Contingencies', *Self and Identity* 3 (2004): 81–93.

25. S.J. Unsworth, C.R. Sears, and P.M. Pexman, 'Cultural Influences on Categorization Processes', *Journal of Cross-Cultural Psychology* 36 (2005): 662–88.

26. H. Giles, N. Coupland, and J.M. Wiemann, 'Talk Is Cheap . . . But My Word Is My Bond: Beliefs about Talk', in K. Bolton and H. Kwok, eds, *Sociolinguistics Today: International Perspectives* (London: Routledge & Kegan Paul, 1992).

27. L.A. Samovar and R.E. Porter, *Communication between Cultures*, 2nd edn (Belmont, CA: Wadsworth, 1995), 199.

28. W. Lambert, 'A Social Psychology of Bilingualism', in C. Bratt Paulston and G.R. Tucker, eds, *Sociolinguistics: The Essential Readings* (Oxford: Blackwell, 2003).

29. P. Andersen, M. Lustig, and J. Andersen, 'Changes in Latitude, Changes in Attitude: The Relationship between Climate, Latitude, and Interpersonal Communication Predispositions'. Paper presented at the annual convention of the Speech Communication Association, Boston, 1987; P. Andersen, M. Lustig, and J. Andersen, 'Regional Patterns of Communication in the United States: Empirical Tests'. Paper presented at the annual convention of the Speech Communication Association, New Orleans, 1988.

30. J.B. Stiff, J.P. Dillard, L. Somera, H. Kim, and C. Sleight, 'Empathy, Communication, and Prosocial Behavior', *Communication Monographs* 55 (1988): 198–213.

31. D. Goleman, *Emotional Intelligence: Why It Can Matter More Than I.Q.* (New York: Bantam, 1995).

32. D.T. Regan and J. Totten, 'Empathy and Attribution: Turning Observers Into Actors', *Journal of Personality and Social Psychology* 35 (1975): 850–6.

33. F. Fincham, G. Paleari, and C. Regalia, 'Forgiveness in Marriage: The Role of Relationship Quality, Attributions and Empathy', *Personal Relationships* 9 (2002): 27–37.

34. Hamachek, *Encounters with Others*, 23–4.

35. J. Vorauer, 'The Other Side of the Story: Transparency Estimation in Social Interaction', in G.B. Moskowitz, ed., *Cognitive and Social Psychology: The Princeton Symposium on the Legacy and Future of Social Cognition* (Hillsdale, NJ: Erlbaum, 2001): 261–76.

36. J. Vorauer and M. Ross, 'Self-Awareness and Feeling Transparent: Failure to Express One's Self', *Journal of Experimental Psychology* 35 (1999): 415–40.

37. M. Conway and A. Howell, 'Ego-Involvement Leads to Positive Self-Schema Activation and to a Positivity Bias in Information Processing', *Journal of Motivation and Emotion* 13, 3 (2005): 159–77.

38. M. Das, 'The Identity Development of Mixed Race Individuals in Canada', repository.library.ualberta.ca/dspace/handle/10048/977.

39. Hamachek, *Encounters with the Self*, 5–8. See also J.D. Campbell and L.F. Lavallee, 'Who Am I? The Role of Self-Concept Confusion in Understanding the Behavior of People with Low Self-Esteem', in R. Baumeister, ed., *Self-Esteem: The Puzzle of Low Self-Regard* (New York: Plenum Press, 1993), 3–20.

40. A.W. Combs and D. Snygg, *Individual Behavior*, rev. edn (New York: Harper & Row, 1959), 134.

41. H.S. Sullivan, *The Interpersonal Theory of Psychiatry* (New York: Norton, 1953).

42. C.H. Cooley, *Human Nature and the Social Order* (New York: Scribner's, 1902). Contemporary research supports the power of reflected appraisal. See, for example, R. Edwards, 'Sensitivity to Feedback and the Development of the Self', *Communication Quarterly* 38 (1990): 101–11.

43. J. Bartz and J.E. Lydon, 'Close Relationships and The Working Self Concept: Implicit and Explicit Effects of Priming Attachment on Agency and Communion', *Personality and Social Psychology Bulletin* 30 (2004): 1389–1401.

44. C. McFarland, R. Buehler, and L. MacKay, 'Affective Responses to Social Comparison with Extremely Close Others', *Social Cognition* 19 (2001): 547–86.

45. See also J. Keltikangas, 'The Stability of Self-Concept during Adolescence and Early Childhood: A Six-Year Follow-Up Study', *Journal of General Psychology* 117 (1990): 361–9.

46. P.N. Myers and F.A. Biocca, 'The Elastic Body Image: The Effect of Television Advertising and Programming on Body Image Distortions in Young Women', *Journal of Communication* 42 (1992): 108–34.

47. H. Giles and P. Johnson, 'Ethnolinguistic Identity Theory: A Social Psychological Approach to Language Maintenance', *International Journal of Sociology of Language* 68 (1987): 69–99.

48. S.P. Banks, 'Achieving "Unmarkedness" in Organizational Discourse: A Praxis Perspective on Ethnolinguistic Identity', *Journal of Language and Social Psychology* 6 (1982): 171–90.

49. T.M. Singelis and W.J. Brown, 'Culture, Self, and Collectivist Communication', *Human Communication Research* 21 (1995): 354–89. See also H.R. Markus and S. Kitayama, 'A Collective Fear of the Collective: Implications for Selves and Theories of Selves', *Personality and Social Psychology* 20 (1994): 568–79.

50. J. Servaes, 'Cultural Identity and Modes of Communication', in J.A. Anderson, ed., *Communication Yearbook* 12 (Newbury Park, CA: Sage, 1989): 396.

51. S. Heine, 'Self as a Cultural Product: An Examination of East Asian and North American Selves', *Journal of Personality* 69 (2001): 881–906.

52. A. Bharti, 'The Self in Hindu Thought and Action', in A.J. Marsella, G. DeVos, and F.L.K. Hsu, eds, *Culture and Self: Asian and Western Perspectives* (New York: Tavistock, 1985).

53. W.B. Gudykunst and S. Ting-Toomey, *Culture and Interpersonal Communication* (Newbury Park, CA: Sage, 1988).

54. L.A. Samovar and R.E. Porter, *Communication between Cultures*, 2nd edn (Belmont, CA: Wadsworth, 1995), 91.

55. D. Klopf, 'Cross-Cultural Apprehension Research: A Summary of Pacific Basin Studies', in J. Daly and J. McCroskey, eds, *Avoiding Communication: Shyness, Reticence, and Communication Apprehension* (Beverly Hills, CA: Sage, 1984).

56. T.M. Steinfatt, 'Personality and Communication: Classical Approaches', in J.C. McCroskey and J.A. Daly, eds, *Personality and Interpersonal Communication* (Newbury Park, CA: Sage, 1987), 42.

57. G.W. Allport and H.W. Odbert, 'Trait Names, a Psychological Study', *Psychological Monographs* 47 (1936).

58. J. Kagan, *Unstable Ideas: Temperament, Cognition, and Self* (Cambridge, MA: Harvard University Press, 1989).

59. J.C. McCroskey and V. Richmond, *The Quiet Ones: Communication Apprehension and Shyness* (Dubuque, IA: Gorsuch Scarisbrick, 1980). See also T.J. Bouchard, D.T. Lykken, M. McGue, and N.L. Segal, 'Sources of Human Psychological Differences—The Minnesota Study of Twins Reared Apart', *Science* 250 (12 October 1990): 223–8.

60. K. Schwartz and G. Fouts, 'Music Preferences, Personality Style and Developmental Issues of Adolescents', *Journal of Youth and Adolescence* 32 (3) (2004): 205–13.

61. P.D. MacIntyre and K.A. Thivierge, 'The Effects of Speaker Personality on Anticipated Reactions to Public Speaking', *Communication Research Reports* 12 (1995): 125–33.

62. M. Stein and Y. Kean, 'Disability and Quality of Life in Social Phobia: Epidemiological Findings', *American Journal of Psychiatry* 157 (2000): 1606–13.

63. J. Kolligan, Jr, 'Perceived Fraudulence as a Dimension of Perceived Incompetence', in R.J. Sternberg and J. Kolligen, Jr, eds, *Competence Considered* (New Haven, CT: Yale University Press, 1990).

64. B.J. Zimmerman, A. Bandura, and M. Martinez-Pons, 'Self-Motivation for Academic Attainment: The Role of Self-Efficacy Beliefs and Personal Goal Setting', *American Educational Research Journal* 29 (1992): 663–76.

65. R. Lockwood and Z. Kunda, 'Superstars and Me: Predicting the Impact of Role Models on the Self', *Journal of Personality and Social Psychology* 73, 1 (1997): 91–103.

66. G. Downey and S.I. Feldman, 'Implications of Rejection Sensitivity for Intimate Relationships', *Journal of Personality and Social Psychology* 70 (1996): 1327–43.

67. C.L. Kleinke, T.R. Peterson, and T.R. Rutledge, 'Effects of Self-Generated Facial Expressions on Mood', *Journal of Personality and Social Psychology* 74 (1998): 272–9.

68. R. Rosenthal and L. Jacobson, *Pygmalion in the Classroom* (New York: Holt, Rinehart and Winston, 1968).

69. For a detailed discussion of how self-fulfilling prophecies operate in relationships, see P. Watzlawick, 'Self-Fulfilling Prophecies', in J. O'Brien and P. Kollock, eds, *The Production of Reality*, 3rd edn (Thousand Oaks, CA: Pine Forge Press, 2001), 411–23.

70. C.M. Shaw and R. Edwards, 'Self-Concepts and Self-Presentation of Males and Females: Similarities and Differences', *Communication Reports* 10 (1997): 56–62.

71. E. Goffman, *The Presentation of Self in Everyday Life* (Garden City, NY: Doubleday, 1959), and Relations in Public (New York: Basic Books, 1971).

72. W.R. Cupach and S. Metts, *Facework* (Thousand Oaks, CA: Sage, 1994). See also P. Brown and S.C. Levinson, *Politeness: Some Universals in Language Usage* (Cambridge, England: Cambridge University Press, 1987).

73. W.F. Sharkey, H.S. Park, and R.K. Kim, 'Intentional Self Embarrassment', *Communication Studies* 55 (2004): 379–99.

74. M. Ross, E. Xun, and A. Wilson, 'Language and Bicultural Self', *Personality and Social Psychology Bulletin*, 28 (2002): 1051–62.

75. J. Stewart and C. Logan, *Together: Communicating Interpersonally*, 5th edn (New York: McGraw-Hill, 1998), 120.

76. M.R. Leary and R.M. Kowalski, 'Impression Management: A Literature Review and Two-Component Model', *Psychological Bulletin* 107 (1990): 34–47.

77. V. Brightman, A. Segal, P. Werther, and J. Steiner, 'Ethological Study of Facial Expression in Response to Taste Stimuli', *Journal of Dental Research* 54 (1975): 141.

78. N. Chovil, 'Social Determinants of Facial Displays', *Journal of Nonverbal Behavior* 15 (1991): 141–54.

79. M.R. Leary and R.M. Kowalski, 'Impression Management: A Literature Review and Two-Component Model', *Psychological Bulletin* 107: 34–47.

80. M. Snyder, 'Self-Monitoring Processes', in L. Berkowitz, ed., *Advances in Experimental Social Psychology* (New York: Academic Press, 1979), and 'The Many Me's of the Self-Monitor', *Psychology Today* (March 1983): 341.

81. The following discussion is based on material in Hamachek, *Encounters with the Self*, 24–6.

82. L.M. Coleman and B.M. DePaulo, 'Uncovering the Human Spirit: Moving beyond Disability and "Missed" Communications', in N. Coupland, H. Giles, and J.M. Wiemann, eds, *'Miscommunication' and Problematic Talk* (Newbury Park, CA: Sage, 1991): 61–84.

83. J.W. Vander Zanden, *Social Psychology*, 3rd edn (New York: Random House, 1984), 235–7.

84. J. Brown, C.R. Dykers, J.R. Steele, and A.B. White, 'Teenage Room Culture: Where Media and Identities Intersect', *Communication Research* 21 (1994): 813–27.

85. J.B. Walther, 'Computer-Mediated Communication: Impersonal, Interpersonal, and Hyperpersonal Interaction', *Communication Research* 23 (1996): 3–43.

86. J.T. Hancock and P.J. Durham, 'Impression Formation in Computer-Mediated Communication Revisited: An Analysis of the Breadth and Intensity of Impressions', *Communication Research* 28 (2001): 325–47.

87. *Street Cents*, 2001–2, Episode 7. CBC Television. 26 November 2001. For more on this episode, see cbc.ca/street-cents/guide/2001/07/s04-01.html.

88. A. Lenhart, L. Rainie, and O. Lewis, 'Teenage Life Online' (Washington, DC: Pew Internet and American Life Project, 2001).

89. P.B. O'Sullivan, 'What You Don't Know Won't Hurt Me: Impression Management Functions of Communication Channels in Relationships', *Human Communication Research* 26 (2000): 403–31.

Chapter 3

1. W.S.Y. Wang, 'Language and Derivative Systems', in W.S.Y. Wang, ed., *Human Communication: Language and Its Psychobiological Basis* (San Francisco: Freeman, 1982), 36.

2. O. Sacks, *Seeing Voices: A Journey into the World of the Deaf* (Berkeley: University of California Press, 1989), 17.

3. Adapted from J. O'Brien and P. Kollock, *The Production of Reality*, 3rd edn (Thousand Oaks, CA: Pine Forge Press, 2001), 66.

4. M. Henneberger, 'Misunderstanding of Word Embarrasses Washington's New Mayor', *New York Times* (29 January 1999).

5. C.K. Ogden and I.A. Richards, *The Meaning of Meaning* (New York: Harcourt Brace, 1923), 11.

6. S. Duck, 'Maintenance as a Shared Meaning System', in D.J. Caharg and L. Stafford, eds, *Communication and Relational Maintenance* (San Diego: Academic Press, 1993).

7. D. Crystal, *Language and the Internet* (Cambridge, England: Cambridge University Press, 2001).

8. The Urban Dictionary, urbandictionary.com/define.php?term=leet; urbandictionary.com/define.php?term=geekspeak.

9. S. Tagliamonte and D. Denis, 'OMG, it's so PC! Instant messaging and teen language'. Paper presented at NWAVE 34, New York City, 20–3 October 2005.

10. W.B. Pearce and V. Cronen, *Communication, Action, and Meaning* (New York: Praeger, 1980). See also E.M. Griffin, *A First Look at Communication Theory,* 5th edn (New York: McGraw-Hill, 2003).

11. Genesis 2:19: This biblical reference was noted by D.C. Mader in 'The Politically Correct Textbook: Trends in Publishers' Guidelines for the Representation of Marginalized Groups'. Paper presented at the annual convention of the Eastern Communication Association, Portland, ME, May 1992.

12. G.W. Smith, 'The Political Impact of Name Sounds', *Communication Monographs* 65 (1998): 154–72.

13. Research on the following pages is cited in M.G. Marcus, 'The Power of a Name', *Psychology Today* 9 (October 1976): 75–7, 108.

14. D.H. Naftulin, J.E. Ware, Jr, and F.A. Donnelly, 'The Doctor Fox Lecture: A Paradigm of Educational Seduction', *Journal of Medical Education* 48 (July 1973): 630–5. See also C.T. Cory, ed., 'Bafflegab Pays', *Psychology Today* 13 (May 1980): 12; and H.W. Marsh and J.E. Ware, Jr, 'Effects of Expressiveness, Content Coverage, and Incentive on Multidimensional Student Rating Scales: New Interpretations of the Dr. Fox Effect', *Journal of Educational Psychology* 74 (1982): 126–34.

15. J.S. Armstrong, 'Unintelligible Management Research and Academic Prestige', *Interfaces* 10 (1980): 80–6.

16. S. Pinker, *The Language Instinct* (New York: Harper, 1995), 19.

17. For a summary of research on this subject, see J.J. Bradac, 'Language Attitudes and Impression Formation', in H. Giles and W.P. Robinson, eds, *The Handbook of Language and Social Psychology* (Chichester, England: Wiley, 1990), 387–412.

18. H. Giles and P.F. Poseland, *Speech Style and Social Evaluation* (New York: Academic Press, 1975).

19. A.J. Browne and J. Fisk, 'First Nations Women's Encounters With Mainstream Health Care Services', *Western Journal of Nursing Research* 23, 2 (2001): 126–47.

20. S. Romaine, *Language in Society: An Introduction to Sociolinguistics* (New York: Oxford University Press, 2002), 212.

21. C. Miller and K. Swift, *Words and Women* (New York: HarperCollins, 1991), 27.

22. F. Baider, 'Sexism and Language: What can the Web teach us?' *TEXT Technology* 9 (1999): 2.

23. For a discussion of racist language, see H.A. Bosmajian, *The Language of Oppression* (Lanham, MD: University Press of America, 1983).

24. Ontario Human Rights Commission, *Paying the Price: The Human Cost of Racial Profiling.* Inquiry Report. Available at ohrc.on.ca/en/resources/discussion_consultation/RacialProfileReportEN/pdf.

25. S.L. Kirkland, J. Greenberg, and T. Pyszynski, 'Further Evidence of the Deleterious Effects of Overheard Derogatory Ethnic Labels: Derogation beyond the Target', *Personality and Social Psychology Bulletin* 12 (1987): 216–27.

26. For a review of the relationship between power and language, see J. Liska, 'Dominance-Seeking Language Strategies: Please Eat the Floor, Dogbreath, or I'll Rip Your Lungs Out, O.K.?' in S.A. Deetz, ed., *Communication Yearbook* 15 (Newbury Park, CA: Sage, 1992). See also N.A. Burrell and R.J. Koper, 'The Efficacy of Powerful/Powerless Language on Persuasiveness/Credibility: A Meta-Analytic Review', in R.W. Preiss and M. Allen, eds, *Prospects and Precautions in the Use of Meta-Analysis* (Dubuque, IA: Brown & Benchmark, 1994).

27. D. Tannen, *Talking from 9 to 5* (New York: Morrow, 1994), 101.

28. Geddes, 'Sex Roles in Management: The Impact of Varying Power of Speech Style on Union Members' Perception of Satisfaction and Effectiveness', *Journal of Psychology* 126 (1992): 589–607.

29. L.A. Samovar and R.E. Porter, *Communication between Cultures*, 3rd edn (Belmont, CA: Wadsworth ITP, 1998), 58–9.

30. D. Cyr and A. Sévigny, 'Traduire pour transmettre: le cas des langues amérindiennes', *Linguistica Antverpiensia* N.S. 2 (2004): 167–83.

31. H. Giles, J. Coupland, and N. Coupland, eds, *Contexts of Accommodation: Developments in Applied Sociolinguistics* (Cambridge, England: Cambridge University Press, 1991).

32. See, for example, R.A. Bell and J.G. Healey, 'Idiomatic Communication and Interpersonal Solidarity in Friends' Relational Cultures', *Human Communication Research* 18 (1992): 307–35; and R.A. Bell, N. Buerkel-Rothfuss, and K.E. Gore, 'Did You Bring the Yarmulke for the Cabbage Patch Kid?: The Idiomatic Communication of Young Lovers', *Human Communication Research* 14 (1987): 47–67.

33. Romaine, op. cit., 78.

34. M. Wiener and A. Mehrabian, *A Language within Language* (New York: Appleton-Century-Crofts, 1968).

35. E.S. Kubanyu, D.C. Richard, G.B. Bower, and M.Y. Muraoka, 'Impact of Assertive and Accusatory Communication of Distress and Anger: A Verbal Component Analysis', *Aggressive Behavior* 18 (1992): 337–47.

36. T.L. Scott, 'Teens before Their Time', *Time* (27 November 2000): 22.

37. M.T. Motley and H.M. Reeder, 'Unwanted Escalation of Sexual Intimacy: Male and Female Perceptions of Connotations and Relational Consequences of Resistance Messages', *Communication Monographs* 62 (1995).

38. T. Wallstein, 'Measuring the Vague Meanings of Probability Terms', *Journal of Experimental Psychology* General 115 (1986): 348–65.

39. T. Labov, 'Social and Language Boundaries among Adolescents', *American Speech* 4 (1992): 339–66.

40. K. Barber, *Six Words You Never Knew Had Something to Do With Pigs: And Other Fascinating Facts about the English Language* (Don Mills, ON: Oxford University Press, 2006), 36–8.

41. M. Kakutani, 'Computer Slang Scoffs at Wetware', *Santa Barbara News-Press* (2 July 2000): D1.

42. M. Myer and C. Fleming, 'Silicon Screenings', *Newsweek* (15 August 1994): 63.

43. S.I. Hayakawa, *Language in Thought and Action* (New York: Harcourt Brace, 1964).

44. E.M. Eisenberg, 'Ambiguity as Strategy in Organizational Communication', *Communication Monographs* 51 (1984): 227–42; and E.M. Eisenberg and M.G. Witten, 'Reconsidering Openness in Organizational Communication', *Academy of Management Review* 12 (1987): 418–26.

45. J.K. Alberts, 'An Analysis of Couples' Conversational Complaints', *Communication Monographs* 55 (1988): 184–97.

46. B. Streisand, Crystal Awards Speech, delivered at the Women in Film luncheon, 1992.

47. B. Morrison, 'What You Won't Hear the Pilot Say', *USA Today* (26 September 2000): A1.

48. R.J. Sales and D. Brehm, 'Vest Welcomes Frosh; Prof. Pinker Derides "Euphemism Treadmill"', Massachusetts Institute of Technology News Office (29 August 2001). Available at web. mit.edu/newsoffice/2001/welcome-0829.html.

49. For detailed discussions of the relationship between gender and communication, see D.J. Canary and T.M. Emmers-Sommer, *Sex and Gender Differences in Personal Relationships* (New York: Guilford, 1997); J. Wood, *Gendered Lives: Communication, Gender, and Culture* (Belmont, CA: Wadsworth, 1994); and J.C. Pearson, *Gender and Communication,* 2nd edn (Madison, WI: Brown & Benchmark, 1994).

50. See, for example, A. Haas and M.A. Sherman, 'Reported Topics of Conversation among Same-Sex Adults', *Communication Quarterly* 30 (1982): 332–42.

51. R.A. Clark, 'A Comparison of Topics and Objectives in a Cross Section of Young Men's and Women's Everyday Conversations', in D.J. Canary and K. Dindia, eds, *Sex Differences and Similarities in Communication: Critical Essays and Empirical Investigations of Sex and Gender in Interaction* (Mahwah, NJ: Erlbaum, 1998).

52. J.T. Wood, *Gendered Lives: Communication, Gender, and Culture,* 4th edn (Belmont, CA: Wadsworth, 2001), 141.

53. M.A. Sherman and A. Haas, 'Man to Man, Woman to Woman', *Psychology Today* 17 (June 1984): 72–3.

54. A. Haas and M.A. Sherman, 'Conversational Topic as a Function of Role and Gender', *Psychological Reports* 51 (1982): 453–4.

55. For a summary of research on the difference between male and female conversational behaviour, see H. Giles and R.L. Street, Jr, 'Communication Characteristics and Behavior', in M.L. Knapp and G.R. Miller, eds, *Handbook of Interpersonal Communication* (Beverly Hills, CA: Sage, 1985), 205–61; and A. Kohn, 'Girl Talk, Guy Talk', *Psychology Today* 22 (February 1988): 65–6.

56. A.J. Mulac, J.M. Wiemann, S.J. Widenmann, and T.W. Gibson, 'Male/Female Language Differences and Effects in Same-Sex and Mixed-Sex Dyads: The Gender-Linked Language Effect', *Communication Monographs* 55 (1988): 315–35.

57. L.L. Carli, 'Gender, Language, and Influence', *Journal of Personality and Social Psychology* 59 (1990): 941–51.

58. S. Marinelli, 'Gender Imbalance in Canadian Op-Eds', Honours BA Thesis, Department of Communication Studies & Multimedia, McMaster University.

59. D.J. Canary and K.S. Hause, 'Is There Any Reason to Research Sex Differences in Communication?', *Communication Quarterly* 41 (1993): 129–44.

60. C.J. Zahn, 'The Bases for Differing Evaluations of Male and Female Speech: Evidence from Ratings of Transcribed Conversation', *Communication Monographs* 56 (1989): 59–74. See also L.M. Grob, R.A. Meyers, and R. Schuh, 'Powerful? Powerless Language Use in Group Interactions: Sex Differences or Similarities?', *Communication Quarterly* 45 (1997): 282–303.

61. J.T. Wood and K. Dindia, 'What's the Difference? A Dialogue about Differences and Similarities between Women and Men', in Canary and Dindia, op. cit.

62. D.L. Rubin, K. Greene, and D. Schneider, 'Adopting Gender-Inclusive Language Reforms: Diachronic and Synchronic Variation', *Journal of Language and Social Psychology* 13 (1994): 91–114.

63. D.S. Geddes, 'Sex Roles in Management: The Impact of Varying Power of Speech Style on Union Members' Perception of Satisfaction and Effectiveness', *Journal of Psychology* 126 (1992): 589–607.

64. For a thorough discussion of the challenges involved in translation from one language to another, see L.A. Samovar and R.E. Porter, *Communication between Cultures*, 4th edn (Belmont, CA: Wadsworth, 2001), 149–54.

65. The examples in this paragraph are taken from D. Ricks, *Big Business Blunders: Mistakes in International Marketing* (Homewood, IL: Dow Jones-Irwin, 1983), 41.

66. N. Sugimoto, '"Excuse Me" and "I'm Sorry": Apologetic Behaviors of Americans and Japanese'. Paper presented at the Conference on Communication in Japan and the United States, California State University, Fullerton, CA, March 1991.

67. A summary of how verbal style varies across cultures can be found in Chapter 5 of W.B. Gudykunst and S. Ting-Toomey, *Culture and Interpersonal Communication* (Newbury Park, CA: Sage, 1988).

68. E.T. Hall, *Beyond Culture* (New York: Doubleday, 1959).

69. P. Clancy, 'The Acquisition of Communicative Style in Japanese', in B.B. Schieffelin and E. Ochs, eds, *Language Acquisition and Socialization across Cultures* (Cambridge, England: Cambridge University Press, 1986).

70. Tannen, op. cit., 98–9.

71. Ibid., 99.

72. M.B. Levan, '"Creating a Framework for the Wisdom of the Community": Review of Victim Services in Nunavut, Northwest and Yukon Territories' (September 2003). Available at justice.gc.ca/en/ps/rs/rep/2003/rr03vic-3/rr03vic-3_04_02. html, sec. 4.2.

73. L. Leets and H. Giles, 'Words as Weapons—When Do They Wound?' *Human Communication Research* 24 (1997): 260–301; and L. Leets, 'When Words Wound: Another Look at Racist Speech'. Paper presented at the annual conference of the International Communication Association, San Francisco, May 1999.

74. Almaney and A. Alwan, *Communicating with the Arabs* (Prospect Heights, IL: Waveland, 1982).

75. K. Basso, 'To Give Up on Words: Silence in Western Apache Culture', *Southern Journal of Anthropology* 26 (1970): 213–30.

76. J. Yum, 'The Practice of Uye–ri in Interpersonal Relationships in Korea', in D. Kincaid, ed., *Communication Theory from Eastern and Western Perspectives* (New York: Academic Press, 1987).

77. H. Giles and A. Franklyn-Stokes, 'Communicator Characteristics', in M.K. Asante and W.B. Gudykunst, eds, *Handbook of International and Intercultural Communication* (Newbury Park, CA: Sage, 1989).

78. L. Sinclair, 'A Word in Your Ear', in *Ways of Mankind* (Boston: Beacon Press, 1954).

79. J. Harris, *The Nurture Assumption: Why Children Turn Out the Way They Do* (New York: Free Press, 1999).

80. B. Whorf, 'The Relation of Habitual Thought and Behavior to Language', in J.B. Carrol, ed., *Language, Thought, and Reality* (Cambridge, MA: MIT Press, 1956). See also Harry Hoijer, 'The Sapir–Whorf Hypothesis', in Larry A. Samovar and Richard E. Porter, eds, *Intercultural Communication: A Reader,* 7th edn (Belmont, CA: Wadsworth, 1994), 194–200.

81. R. Ross, *Returning to the Teachings: Exploring Aboriginal Justice* (Toronto: Penguin Books, 1996); and Aboriginal Justice Implementation Commission, *Final Report* (Aboriginal Justice Inquiry of Manitoba, 2001). Available at ajic.mb.ca/reports/ final_ toc.html.

82. H. Hoijer, quoted in T. Seinfatt, 'Linguistic Relativity: Toward a Broader View', in S. Ting-Toomey and F. Korzenny, eds, *Language, Communication, and Culture: Current Directions* (Newbury Park, CA: Sage, 1989).

83. H. Rheingold, *They Have a Word for It* (Los Angeles: J.P. Tarcher, 1988).

84. K.A. Foss and B.A. Edson, 'What's in a Name? Accounts of Married Women's Name Choices', *Western Journal of Speech Communication* 53 (1989): 356–73.

85. See J.N. Martin, R.L. Krizek, T.K. Nakayama, and L. Bradford, 'Exploring Whiteness: A Study of Self-Labels for White Americans', *Communication Quarterly* 44 (1996): 125–44.

86. T. Brown, 'Predictors of Racial Label Preference in Detroit: Examining Trends from 1971 to 1992', *Sociological Spectrum* 19 (1999): 421–42. See also L. Harris, 'On Our Own Terms: AJC Southern Focus Poll', *Atlanta Journal and Constitution* (25 July 1999): 1F.

87. S.J. Boatswain and R.N. Lalond, 'Social Identity and Preferred Ethnic/Racial Labels for Blacks in Canada', *Journal of Black Psychology*, 26 (2000): 216–34.

88. M. Hecht, M.J. Collier, and S.A. Ribeau, *African American Communication: Ethnic Identity and Cultural Interpretation* (Newbury Park, CA: Sage, 1993). See also L.K. Larkey, K.L. Hecht, and J. Martin, 'What's in a Name? African American Ethnic Identity Terms and Self-Determination', *Journal of Language and Social Psychology* 12 (1993): 302–17.

89. D. Niven and J. Zilber, 'Preference for African American or Black', *Howard Journal of Communications* 11 (2000): 267–77.

90. R. King and S. Clarke, 'Contesting Meaning: Newfie and The Politics of Ethnic Labelling', *Journal of Sociolinguistics* 6, 4 (2002): 537–56.

Chapter 4

1. L. Barker, R. Edwards, C. Gaines, K. Gladney, and F. Holley, 'An Investigation of Proportional Time Spent in Various Communication Activities by College Students', *Journal of Applied Communication Research* 8 (1981): 101–9.

2. Research summarized in A.D. Wolvin and C.G. Coakley, 'A Survey of the Status of Listening Training in Some Fortune 500 Corporations', *Communication Education* 40 (1991): 152–64.

3. Conference Board of Canada. 2000. 'Employability Skills 20001'. PDF document accessed on 20 August 2006 at conferenceboard.ca/education/learning-tools/pdfs/esp2000.pdf.

4. B.D. Sypher, R.N. Bostrom, and J.H. Seibert, 'Listening Communication Abilities and Success at Work', *Journal of Business Communication* 26 (1989): 293–303.

5. K.W. Hawkins and B.P. Fullion, 'Perceived Communication Skill Needs for Work Groups', *Communication Research Reports* 16 (1999): 167–74.

6. S.D. Johnson and C. Bechler, 'Examining the Relationship between Listening Effectiveness and Leadership Emergence', *Small Group Research* 29 (1998): 452–71.

7. A.L. Vangelisti, 'Couples' Communication Problems: The Counselor's Perspective', *Journal of Applied Communication Research* 22 (1994): 106–26.

8. A.D. Wolvin, 'Meeting the Communication Needs of the Adult Learner', *Communication Education* 33 (1984): 267–71.

9. K.J. Prage and D. Buhrmester, 'Intimacy and Need Fulfillment in Couple Relationships', *Journal of Social and Personal Relationships* 15 (1998): 435–69.

10. K.K. Hjalone and L.L. Pecchioni, 'Relational Listening: A Grounded Theoretical Model', *Communication Reports* 14 (2001): 59–71.

11. R.G. Nichols, 'Factors in Listening Comprehension', *Speech Monographs* 15 (1948): 154–63.

12. M.H. Lewis and N.L. Reinsch, Jr, 'Listening in Organizational Environments', *Journal of Business Communication* 25 (1988): 49–67.

13. T.L. Thomas and T.R. Levine, 'Disentangling Listening and Verbal Recall: Related but Separate Constructs?', *Human Communication Research* 21 (1994): 103–27.

14. Nichols, op. cit.

15. J. Brownell, 'Perceptions of Effective Listeners: A Management Study', *Journal of Business Communication* 27 (1990): 401–15.

16. N. Spinks and B. Wells, 'Improving Listening Power: The Payoff', *Bulletin of the Association for Business Communication* 54 (1991): 75–7.

17. Reported by R. Nichols and L. Stevens, 'Listening to People', *Harvard Business Review* 35 (September–October 1957): 85–92.

18. W. Winter, A. Ferreira, and N. Bowers, 'Decision-Making in Married and Unrelated Couples', *Family Process* 12 (1973): 83–94.

19. A.L. Vangelisti, M.L. Knapp, and J.A. Daly, 'Conversational Narcissism', *Communication Monographs* 57 (1990): 251–74.

20. G. Barr, 'International Negotiations and Cross-Cultural Communication—A Study in Thailand'. Unpublished MBA project, Royal Roads University, British Columbia, 1998.

21. K.B. McComb and F.M. Jablin, 'Verbal Correlates of Interviewer Empathic Listening and Employment Interview Outcomes', *Communication Monographs* 51 (1984): 367.

22. R.G. Nichols, 'Listening Is a Ten-Part Skill', *Nation's Business* 75 (September 1987): 40.

23. R. Drullman and G.F. Smoorenburg, 'Audio-Visual Perception of Compressed Speech by Profoundly Hearing-Impaired Subjects', *Audiology* 36 (1997): 165–77.

24. N. Kline, *Time to Think: Listening to Ignite the Human Mind* (London: Ward Lock, 1999), 21.

25. A. Mulac, J.M. Wiemann, S.J. Widenmann, and T.W. Gibson, 'Male/Female Language Differences and Effects in Same-Sex and Mixed-Sex Dyads: The Gender-Linked Language Effect', *Communication Monographs* 55 (1988): 315–35.

26. C. Kiewitz, J.B. Weaver III, B. Brosius, and G. Weimann, 'Cultural Differences in Listening Styles Preferences: A Comparison of Young Adults in Germany, Israel, and the United States', *International Journal of Public Opinion Research* 9 (1997): 233–48.

27. L.L. Barker and K.W. Watson, *Listen Up* (New York: St. Martin's Press, 2000).

28. J.L. Chesebro, 'The Relationship between Listening Styles and Conversational Sensitivity', *Communication Research Reports* 16 (1999): 233–8.

29. K.W. Watson, L.L. Barker, and J.B. Weaver, 'The Listening Styles Profile' (New Orleans: SPECTRA, 1995).

30. For a brief summary of ancient rhetoric, see E. Griffin, *A First Look at Communication Theory*, 4th edn (New York: McGraw-Hill, 2000).

31. R. Remer and P. De Mesquita, 'Teaching and Learning the Skills of Interpersonal Confrontation', in D. Cahn, ed., *Intimates in Conflict: A Communication Perspective* (Norwood, NJ: Erlbaum, 1991), 242.

32. Adapted from D.A. Infante, *Arguing Constructively* (Prospect Heights, IL: Waveland, 1988), 71–5.

33. J. Sprague and D. Stuart, *The Speaker's Handbook*, 3rd edn (Fort Worth, TX: Harcourt Brace Jovanovich, 1992), 172.

34. For a detailed look at empathic listening, see S. Spacapan and S. Oskamp, *Helping and Being Helped: Naturalistic Studies* (Newbury Park, CA: Sage, 1992).

35. Research summarized in J. Pearson, *Communication in the Family* (New York: Harper & Row, 1989): 272–5.

36. J.B. Weaver and M.D. Kirtley, 'Listening Styles and Empathy', *Southern Communication Journal* 60 (1995): 131–40.

37. C.E. Currona, J.A. Suhr, and R. MacFarlane, 'Interpersonal Transactions and the Psychological Sense of Support', in S. Duck, ed., *Personal Relationships and Social Support* (London: Sage, 1990).

38. D.J. Goldsmith and K. Fitch, 'The Normative Context of Advice as Social Support', *Human Communication Research* 23 (1997): 454–76.

39. D.J. Goldsmith and K. Fitch, 'The Normative Context of Advice as Social Support', *Human Communication Research* 23 (1997): 454–76. See also D.J. Goldsmith and E.L. MacGeorge, 'The Impact of Politeness and Relationship on Perceived Quality of Advice about a Problem', *Human Communication Research* 26 (2000): 234–63; and B.R. Burleson, 'Social Support', in M.L. Knapp and J.A. Daly, eds, *Handbook of Interpersonal Communication*, 3rd edn (Thousand Oaks, CA: Sage, 2002).

40. D.J. Goldsmith, 'The Sequential Placement of Advice'. Paper presented at the annual convention of the Speech Communication Association (New Orleans, November 1994).

41. D.J. Goldsmith, 'Soliciting Advice: The Role of Sequential Placement in Mitigating Face Threat', *Communication Monographs* 67 (2000): 1–19.

42. D.J. Goldsmith and E.L. MacGeorge, 'The Impact of Politeness and Relationship on Perceived Quality of Advice about a Problem', *Human Communication Research* 26 (2000): 234–63.

43. For a summary of the findings, see B.R. Burleson's review in this issue: 'Psychological Mediators of Sex Differences in Emotional Support: A Reflection on the Mosaic', *Communication Reports* 15 (Winter 2002): 71–9.

44. See research cited in B. Burleson, 'Comforting Messages: Their Significance and Effects', in J.A. Daly and J.M. Wiemann, eds, *Communicating Strategically: Strategies in Interpersonal Communication* (Hillside, NJ: Erlbaum, 1990).

45. D.J. Goldsmith and K. Fitch, 'The Normative Context of Advice as Social Support', *Human Communication Research* 23 (1997): 454–76.

46. M. Davidowitz and R.D. Myricm, 'Responding to the Bereaved: An Analysis of "Helping" Statements', *Death Education* 8 (1984): 1–10.

47. 'Helping Adults, Children Cope with Grief', *Washington Post* (13 September 2001). Available at washingtonpost. com/wp-dyn/articles/A23679-2001Sep13.html.

48. Adapted from B.R. Burleson, 'Comforting Messages: Features, Functions, and Outcomes', in J.A. Daly and J.M. Wiemann, eds, *Strategic Interpersonal Communication* (Hillsdale, NJ: Erlbaum, 1994), 140.

49. J.M. Gottman, J. Coan, S. Carrere, and C. Swanson, 'Predicting Marital Happiness and Stability from Newlywed Interactions', *Journal of Marriage & the Family* 60 (1998): 5–22.

50. C.R. Rogers, 'Reflection of Feelings', *Person-Centered Review* 1 (1986): 375–7.

51. L.A. Hosman, 'The Evaluational Consequences of Topic Reciprocity and Self-Disclosure Reciprocity', *Communication Monographs* 54 (1987): 420–35.

52. R.A. Clark and J.G. Delia, 'Individuals' Preferences for Friends' Approaches to Providing Support in Distressing Situations', *Communication Reports* 10 (1997): 115–21.

53. See, for example, R. Silver and C. Wortman, 'Coping with Undesirable Life Events', in J. Garber and M. Seligman, eds, *Human Helplessness: Theory and Applications* (New York: Academic Press, 1981), 279–340; and C.R. Young, D.E. Giles, and M.C. Plantz, 'Natural Networks: Help-Giving and Help-Seeking in Two Rural Communities', *American Journal of Community Psychology* 10 (1982): 457–69.

54. Clark and Delia, op. cit.

55. Burleson, op. cit.

Chapter 5

1. For a survey of the issues surrounding the definition of non-verbal communication, see M. Knapp and J.A. Hall, *Nonverbal Communication in Human Interaction*, 5th edn (Belmont, CA: Wadsworth, 2002), Chapter 1.

2. L. Kelly, B. Kinkewich, H. Cromarty, N. St Pierre-Hansen, I. Antone, and C. Giles, 'Palliative Care of First Nations People: A Qualitative Study of Bereaved Family Members', *Canadian Family Physician* 55, 4 (April 2009): 394–5.

3. F. Manusov, 'Perceiving Nonverbal Messages: Effects of Immediacy and Encoded Intent on Receiver Judgments', *Western Journal of Speech Communication* 55 (Summer 1991): 235–53.

4. For a discussion of intentionality, see Knapp and Hall, op. cit., 9–12.

5. A.R. Dennis, S.T. Kinney, and Y.T. Hung, 'Gender Differences in the Effects of Media Richness', *Small Group Research* 30 (1999): 405–37.

6. R.A. Schwier and S. Balbar, 'The Interplay of Content and Community in Synchronous and Asynchronous Communication: Virtual Communication in a Graduate Seminar', *Canadian Journal of Learning and Technology/La revue canadienne de l'apprentissage et de la technologie* 28, 2 (Spring 2002).

7. See S.W. Smith, 'Perceptual Processing of Nonverbal Relational Messages', in D.E. Hewes, ed., *The Cognitive Bases of Interpersonal Communication* (Hillsdale, NJ: Erlbaum, 1994).

8. J. Burgeon, D. Buller, J. Hale, and M. de Turck, 'Relational Messages Associated with Nonverbal Behaviors', *Human Communication Research* 10 (Spring 1984): 351–78.

9. J.K. Burgoon, T.B. Birk, and M. Pfau, 'The Association of Socio-Communicative Style and Relational Type of Perceptions of Nonverbal Intimacy', *Communication Research Reports* 14 (1997): 339–49.

10. G.Y. Lim and M.E. Roloff, 'Attributing Sexual Consent', *Journal of Applied Communication Research* 27 (1999): 1–23.

11. 'Safeway Clerks Object to "Service with a Smile"', *San Francisco Chronicle* (2 September 1998).

12. D. Druckmann, R.M. Rozelle, and J.C. Baxter, *Nonverbal Communication: Survey, Theory, and Research* (Newbury Park, CA: Sage, 1982).

13. M.T. Motley and C.T. Camden, 'Facial Expression of Emotion: A Comparison of Posed Expressions versus Spontaneous Expressions in an Interpersonal Communication Setting', *Western Journal of Speech Communication* 52 (Winter 1988): 1–22.

14. See, for example, R. Rosenthal, J.A. Hall, M.R.D. Matteg, P.L. Rogers, and D. Archer, *Sensitivity to Nonverbal Communication: The PONS Test* (Baltimore, MD: Johns Hopkins University Press, 1979).

15. J.A. Hall, 'Gender, Gender Roles, and Nonverbal Communication Skills', in R. Rosenthal, ed., *Skill in Nonverbal Communication: Individual Differences* (Cambridge, MA: Oelgeschlager, Gunn, and Hain, 1979), 32–67.

16. Research supporting these claims is cited in J.K. Burgoon and G.D. Hoobler, 'Nonverbal Signals', in M.L. Knapp and J.A. Daly, eds, *Handbook of Interpersonal Communication*, 3rd edn (Thousand Oaks, CA: Sage, 2002).

17. S.E. Jones and C.D. LeBaron, 'Research on the Relationship between Verbal and Nonverbal Communication: Emerging Interactions', *Journal of Communication* 52 (2002): 499–521.

18. P. Ekman and W.V. Friesen, *Unmasking the Face* (New York: Prentice Hall, 1975).

19. P. Ekman, W.V. Friesen, and J. Baer, 'The International Language of Gestures', *Psychology Today* 18 (May 1984): 64–9.

20. McCarthy, K. Lee, S. Itakura, and D.W. Muir, 'Gaze Display When Thinking Depends on Culture and Context', *Journal of Cross-Cultural Psychology* 39, 6 (2008): 716–29.

21. E. Hall, *The Hidden Dimension* (Garden City, NY: Anchor Books, 1969).

22. D.L. Rubin, '"Nobody Play by the Rule He Know": Ethnic Interference in Classroom Questioning Events', in Y.Y. Kim, ed., *Interethnic Communication: Recent Research* (Newbury Park, CA: Sage, 1986).

23. A.M. Warnecke, R.D. Masters, and G. Kempter, 'The Roots of Nationalism: Nonverbal Behavior and Xenophobia', *Ethnology and Sociobiology* 13 (1992): 267–82.

24. S. Weitz, ed., *Nonverbal Communication: Readings with Commentary* (New York: Oxford University Press, 1974).

25. For a comparison of Japanese and Arab nonverbal communication norms, see D.G. Leathers, *Successful Nonverbal Communication* (New York: Macmillan, 1986), 258–61.

26. M. Booth-Butterfield and F. Jordan, '"Act Like Us": Communication Adaptation among Racially Homogeneous and Heterogeneous Groups'. Paper presented at the Speech Communication Association meeting, New Orleans, 1988.

27. J.A. Hall, 'Male and Female Nonverbal Behavior', in A.W. Siegman and S. Feldstein, eds, *Multichannel Integrations of Nonverbal Behavior* (Hillsdale, NJ: Erlbaum, 1985).

28. J.A. Hall, J.D. Carter, and T.G. Horgan, 'Status Roles and Recall of Nonverbal Cues', *Journal of Nonverbal Behavior* 25 (2001): 79–100.

29. For a comprehensive summary of male–female differences and similarities in nonverbal communication, see P.A. Andersen, *Nonverbal Communication: Forms and Functions* (Mountain View, CA: Mayfield, 1999), 107. For a detailed summary of similarities and differences, see D.J. Canary and T.M. Emmers-Sommer, *Sex and Gender Differences in Personal Relationships* (New York: Guilford, 1997).

30. Andersen, op cit., 107.

31. E.S. Cross and E.A. Franz, 'Talking Hands: Observation of Bimanual Gestures As a Facilitative Working Memory Mechanism'. Paper presented at the Cognitive Neuroscience Society 10th Annual Meeting, New York, 30 March–1 April 2003.

32. Hall, op. cit.

33. C.R. Kleinke, 'Compliance to Requests Made by Gazing and Touching Experimenters in Field Settings', *Journal of Experimental Social Psychology* 13 (1977): 218–33.

34. M.F. Argyle, F. Alkema, and R. Gilmour, 'The Communication of Friendly and Hostile Attitudes: Verbal and Nonverbal Signals', *European Journal of Social Psychology* 1 (1971): 385–402.

35. D.B. Buller and J.K. Burgoon, 'Deception: Strategic and Nonstrategic Communication', in J. Daly and J.M. Wiemann, eds, *Interpersonal Communication* (Hillsdale, NJ: Erlbaum, 1994).

36. J.K. Burgoon, D.B. Buller, L.K. Guerrero, and C.M. Feldman, 'Interpersonal Deception: VI. Effects on Preinteractional and International Factors on Deceiver and Observer Perceptions of Deception Success', *Communication Studies* 45 (1994): 263–80; and J.K. Burgoon, D.B. Buller, and L.K. Guerrero, 'Interpersonal Deception: IX. Effects of Social Skill and Nonverbal Communication on Deception Success and Detection Accuracy', *Journal of Language and Social Psychology* 14 (1995): 289–311.

37. R.G. Riggio and H.S. Freeman, 'Individual Differences and Cues to Deception', *Journal of Personality and Social Psychology* 45 (1983): 899–915.

38. N.E. Dunbar, A. Ramirez Jr, and J.K. Burgoon, 'The Effects of Participation on the Ability to Judge Deceit', *Communication Reports* 16 (2003): 23–33.

39. A. Vrig, L. Akehurst, S. Soukara, and R. Bull, 'Detecting Deceit Via Analyses of Verbal and Nonverbal Behavior in Children and Adults', *Human Communication Research* 30 (2004): 8–41.

40. M.G. Millar and K.U. Millar, 'The Effects of Suspicion on the Recall of Cues to Make Veracity Judgments', *Communication Reports* 11 (1998): 57–64.

41. T.R. Levine and S.A. McCornack, 'Behavior Adaptation, Confidence, and Heuristic-Based Explanations of the Probing Effect', *Human Communication Research* 27 (2001): 471–502. See also D.B. Buller, J. Comstock, R.K. Aune, and K.D. Stryzewski, 'The Effect of Probing on Deceivers and Truth-tellers', *Journal of Nonverbal Behavior* 13 (1989): 155–70; and D.B. Buller, K.D. Stryzewski, and J. Comstock, 'Interpersonal Deception: I. Deceivers' Reactions to Receivers' Suspicions and Probing', *Communication Monographs* 58 (1991): 1–24.

42. T.H. Feely and M.J. Young, 'Self-Reported Cues about Deceptive and Truthful Communication: The Effects of Cognitive Capacity and Communicator Veracity', *Communication Quarterly* 48 (2000): 101–19.

43. P. Rockwell, D.B. Buller, and J.K. Burgoon, 'The Voice of Deceit: Refining and Expanding Vocal Cues to Deception', *Communication Research Reports* 14 (1997): 451–9.

44. P. Kalbfleisch, 'Deceit, Distrust, and Social Milieu: Applications of Deception Research in a Troubled World', *Journal of Applied Communication Research* (1992): 308–34.

45. J. Hale and J.B. Stiff, 'Nonverbal Primacy in Veracity Judgments', *Communication Reports* 3 (1990): 75–83; and J.B. Stiff, J.L. Hale, R. Garlick, and R.G. Rogan, 'Effect of Cue Incongruence and Social Normative Influences on Individual Judgments of Honesty and Deceit', *Southern Speech Communication Journal* 55 (1990): 206–29.

46. J.K. Burgoon, T. Birk, and M. Pfau, 'Nonverbal Behaviors, Persuasion, and Credibility', *Human Communication Research* 17 (1990): 140–69.

47. M.A. deTurck, T.H. Feeley, and L.A. Roman, 'Vocal and Visual Cue Training in Behavior Lie Detection', *Communication Research Reports* 14 (1997): 249–59.

48. Kalbfleisch, op. cit.

49. S.A. McCornack and M.R. Parks, 'What Women Know that Men Don't: Sex Differences in Determining the Truth behind Deceptive Messages', *Journal of Social and Personal Relationships* 7 (1990): 107–18.

50. S.A. McCornack and T.R. Levine, 'When Lovers Become Leery: The Relationship between Suspicion and Accuracy in Detecting Deception', *Communication Monographs* 7 (1990): 219–30.

51. M.A. deTurck, 'Training Observers to Detect Spontaneous Deception: Effects of Gender', *Communication Reports* 4 (1991): 81–9.

52. J. Pavlidis, N.L. Eberhardt, and J.A. Levine, 'Seeing through the Face of Deception', *Nature* 415 (2002).

53. R.E. Maurer and J.H. Tindall, 'Effect of Postural Congruence on Client's Perception of Counselor Empathy', *Journal of Counseling Psychology* 30 (1983): 158–63.

54. V. Manusov, 'Reacting to Changes in Nonverbal Behaviors: Relational Satisfaction and Adaptation Patterns in Romantic Dyads', *Human Communication Research* 21 (1995): 456–77.

55. M.B. Myers, D. Templer, and R. Brown, 'Coping Ability of Women Who Become Victims of Rape', *Journal of*

Consulting and Clinical Psychology 52 (1984): 73–8. See also C. Rubenstein, 'Body Language That Speaks to Muggers', *Psychology Today* 20 (August 1980): 20; and J. Meer, 'Profile of a Victim', *Psychology Today* 24 (May 1984): 76.

56. J.M. Iverson, 'How to Get to the Cafeteria: Gesture and Speech in Blind and Sighted Children's Spatial Descriptions', *Developmental Psychology* 35 (1999): 1132–42.

57. P. Ekman, *Telling Lies: Clues to Deceit in the Marketplace, Politics, and Marriage* (New York: Norton, 1985): 109–110.

58. W. Donaghy and B.F. Dooley, 'Head Movement, Gender, and Deceptive Communication', *Reports* 7 (1994): 67–75.

59. P. Ekman and W.V. Friesen, 'Nonverbal Behavior and Psychopathology', in R.J. Friedman and M.N. Katz, eds, *The Psychology of Depression: Contemporary Theory and Research* (Washington, DC: J. Winston, 1974).

60. R. Sutton and A. Rafaeli, 'Untangling the Relationship between Displayed Emotions and Organizational Sales: The Case of Convenience Stores', *Academy of Management Journal* 31 (1988): 463.

61. P. Ekman and W.V. Friesen, *Unmasking the Face.*

62. P. Ekman, W.V. Friesen, and P. Ellsworth, *Emotion in the Human Face: Guidelines for Research and an Integration of Findings* (Elmsford, NY: Pergamon, 1972).

63. J.A. Starkweather, 'Vocal Communication of Personality and Human Feeling', *Journal of Communication* II (1961): 69; and K.R. Scherer, J. Koiwunaki, and R. Rosenthal, 'Minimal Cues in the Vocal Communication of Affect: Judging Emotions from Content-Masked Speech', *Journal of Psycholinguistic Speech* I (1972): 269–85. See also F.S. Cox and C. Olney, 'Vocalic Communication of Relational Messages'. Paper delivered at annual meeting of the Speech Communication Association, Denver, 1985.

64. K.L. Burns and E.G. Beier, 'Significance of Vocal and Visual Channels for the Decoding of Emotional Meaning', *The Journal of Communication* 23 (1973): 118–30. See also Timothy G. Hegstrom, 'Message Impact: What Percentage Is Nonverbal?' *Western Journal of Speech Communication* 43 (1979): 134–43; and E.M. McMahan, 'Nonverbal Communication as a Function of Attribution in Impression Formation', *Communication Monographs* 43 (1976): 287–94.

65. A. Mehrabian and M. Weiner, 'Decoding of Inconsistent Communications', *Journal of Personality and Social Psychology* 6 (1967): 109–14.

66. D. Buller and K. Aune, 'The Effects of Speech Rate Similarity on Compliance: Application of Communication Accommodation Theory', *Western Journal of Communication* 56 (1992): 37–53. See also D. Buller, B.A. LePoire, K. Aune, and S.V. Eloy, 'Social Perceptions as Mediators of the Effect of Speech Rate Similarity on Compliance', *Human Communication Research* 19 (1992): 286–311; and J. Francis and R. Wales, 'Speech a la Mode: Prosodic Cues, Message Interpretation, and Impression Formation', *Journal of Language and Social Psychology* 13 (1994): 34–44.

67. M.S. Remland and T.S. Jones, 'The Influence of Vocal Intensity and Touch on Compliance Gaining', *Journal of Social Psychology* 134 (1994): 89–97.

68. Ekman, op. cit., 93.

69. C.E. Kimble and S.D. Seidel, 'Vocal Signs of Confidence', *Journal of Nonverbal Behavior* 15 (1991): 99–105.

70. K.J. Tusing and J.P. Dillard, 'The Sounds of Dominance: Vocal Precursors of Perceived Dominance during Interpersonal Influence', *Human Communication Research* 26 (2000): 148–71.

71. M. Zuckerman and R.E. Driver, 'What Sounds Beautiful Is Good: The Vocal Attractiveness Stereotype', *Journal of Nonverbal Behavior* 13 (1989): 67–82.

72. A. Montagu, *Touching: The Human Significance of the Skin* (New York: Harper & Row, 1972), 93.

73. Ibid., 244–9.

74. L.J. Yarrow, 'Research in Dimension of Early Maternal Care', *Merrill-Palmer Quarterly* 9 (1963): 101–22.

75. For a review of research on this subject, see S. Thayer, 'Close Encounters', *Psychology Today* 22 (March 1988): 31–6.

76. See, for example, C. Segrin, 'The Effects of Nonverbal Behavior on Outcomes of Compliance Gaining Attempts', *Communication Studies* 11 (1993): 169–87.

77. C.R. Kleinke, 'Compliance to Requests Made by Gazing and Touching Experimenters in Field Settings', *Journal of Experimental Social Psychology* 13 (1977): 218–23.

78. F.N. Willis and H.K. Hamm, 'The Use of Interpersonal Touch in Securing Compliance', *Journal of Nonverbal Behavior* 5 (1980): 49–55.

79. A.H. Crusco and C.G. Wetzel, 'The Midas Touch: Effects of Interpersonal Touch on Restaurant Tipping', *Personality and Social Psychology Bulletin* 10 (1984): 512–17.

80. S.E. Jones and E. Yarbrough, 'A Naturalistic Study of the Meanings of Touch', *Communication Monographs* 52 (1985): 221–31.

81. R. Heslin and T. Alper, 'Touch: The Bonding Gesture', in J.M. Wiemann and R.P. Harrison, eds, *Nonverbal Interaction* (Beverly Hills, CA: Sage, 1983).

82. D.K. Fromme, W.E. Jaynes, D.K. Taylor, E.G. Hanold, J. Daniell, J.R. Rountree, and M. Fromme, 'Nonverbal Behavior and Attitudes toward Touch', *Journal of Nonverbal Behavior* 13 (1989): 3–14.

83. For a summary, see M.L. Knapp and J.A. Hall, *Nonverbal Communication in Human Interaction*, 3rd edn (New York: Holt, Rinehart and Winston, 1992), 93–132. See also W. Hensley, 'Why Does the Best Looking Person in the Room Always Seem to Be Surrounded by Admirers?' *Psychological Reports* 70 (1992): 457–69.

84. V. Ritts, M.L. Patterson, and M.E. Tubbs, 'Expectations, Impressions, and Judgments of Physically Attractive Students: A Review', *Review of Educational Research* 62 (1992): 413–26.

85. L. Bickman, 'The Social Power of a Uniform', *Journal of Applied Social Psychology* 4 (1974): 47–61.

86. S.G. Lawrence and M. Watson, 'Getting Others to Help: The Effectiveness of Professional Uniforms in Charitable Fund Raising', *Journal of Applied Communication Research* 19 (1991): 170–85.

87. J.H. Fortenberry, J. Maclean, P. Morris, and M. O'Connell, 'Mode of Dress as a Perceptual Cue to Deference', *The Journal of Social Psychology* 104 (1978).

88. L. Bickman, 'Social Roles and Uniforms: Clothes Make the Person', *Psychology Today* 7 (April 1974): 48–51.

89. M. Lefkowitz, R.R. Blake, and J.S. Mouton, 'Status of Actors in Pedestrian Violation of Traffic Signals', *Journal of Abnormal and Social Psychology* 51 (1955): 704–6.

90. L.E. Temple and K.R. Loewen, 'Perceptions of Power: First Impressions of a Woman Wearing a Jacket', *Perceptual and Motor Skills* 76 (1993): 339–48.

91. T.F. Hoult, 'Experimental Measurement of Clothing as a Factor in Some Social Ratings of Selected American Men', *American Sociological Review* 19 (1954): 326–7.

92. Y.K. Chan, 'Density, Crowding, and Factors Intervening in Their Relationship: Evidence from a Hyper-Dense Metropolis', *Social Indicators Research* 48 (1999), 103–24.

93. E.T. Hall, 113–30.

94. M. Hackman and K. Walker, 'Instructional Communication in the Televised Classroom: The Effects of System Design and Teacher Immediacy', *Communication Education* 39 (1990): 196–206. See also J.C. McCroskey and V.P. Richmond, 'Increasing Teacher Influence through Immediacy', in V.P. Richmond and J.C. McCroskey, eds, *Power in the Classroom: Communication, Control, and Concern* (Hillsdale, NJ: Erlbaum, 1992).

95. C. Conlee, J. Olvera, and N. Vagim, 'The Relationships among Physician Nonverbal Immediacy and Measures of Patient Satisfaction with Physician Care', *Communication Reports* 6 (1993): 25–33.

96. D.I. Ballard and D.R. Seibold, 'Time Orientation and Temporal Variation across Work Groups: Implications for Group and Organizational Communication', *Western Journal of Communication* 64 (2000): 218–42.

97. R. Levine, *A Geography of Time: The Temporal Misadventures of a Social Psychologist* (New York: Basic Books, 1997).

98. See, for example, O.W. Hill, R.A. Block, and S.E. Buggie, 'Culture and Beliefs about Time: Comparisons among Black Americans, Black Africans, and White Americans', *Journal of Psychology* 134 (2000): 443–57.

99. R. Levine and E. Wolff, 'Social Time: The Heartbeat of Culture', *Psychology Today* 19 (March 1985): 28–35. See also R. Levine, 'Waiting Is a Power Game', *Psychology Today* 21 (April 1987): 24–33.

100. Burgoon, Buller, and Woodall, op. cit., 148.

101. Mehrabian, op. cit., 69.

102. E. Sadalla, 'Identity and Symbolism in Housing', *Environment and Behavior* 19 (1987): 569–87.

103. A.H. Maslow and N.L. Mintz, 'Effects of Esthetic Surroundings', *Journal of Psychology* 41 (1956): 247–54.

104. L. Festinger, S. Schachter, and K. Back, *Social Pressures in Informal Groups: A Study of Human Factors in Housing* (New York: Harper & Row, 1950).

105. Sommer, op. cit., 78.

106. Ibid., 35.

Chapter 6

1. For further discussion of the characteristics of impersonal and interpersonal communication, see A.P. Bochner, 'The Functions of Human Communication in Interpersonal Bonding', in C.C. Arnold and J.W. Bowers, eds, *Handbook of Rhetorical and Communication Theory* (Boston: Allyn and Bacon, 1984), 550; S. Trenholm and A. Jensen, *Interpersonal Communication* (Belmont, CA: Wadsworth, 1987), 37; and J. Stewart and C. Logan, *Together: Communicating Interpersonally,* 5th edn (New York: McGraw-Hill, 1998).

2. K. O'Toole, 'Study Takes Early Look at Social Consequences of Net Use', *Stanford Online Report*. Accessed 16 February 2000 at stanford.edu/dept/news/report/news/february16/internetsurvey-216.html.

3. R. Kraut, M. Patterson, V. Lundmark, S. Kiesler, T. Mukophadhyay, and W. Scherlis, 'Internet Paradox: A Social Technology That Reduces Social Involvement and Psychological Well-Being?' *American Psychologist* 53 (1998): 1017–31.

4. See J.B. Walther, 'Computer-Mediated Communication: Impersonal, Interpersonal, and Hyperpersonal Interaction', *Communication Research* 23 (1996): 3–43.

5. B.G. Chenault, 'Developing Personal and Emotional Relationships via Computer-Mediated Communication', *CMC Magazine*. Accessed May 1998 at december.com/cmc/mag/1998/may/chenref.html.

6. B. Veenhof, B. Wellman, C. Quell, and B. Hogan, 'How Canadians' Use of the Internet Affects Social Life and Civic Participation', Connectedness Series (December 2008). Statistics Canada Catalogue no. 56F0004M.

7. B. Veenhof, 'The Internet Experience of Younger and Older Canadian', *Innovation Analysis Bulletin* 8, 1 (February 2006). Statistics Canada Catalogue no. 88-003-XTE. Accessed 13 August 2008 at statcan.ca/bsolc/english/bsolc?catno=88-003-X20060019098.

8. UCLA Center for Communication Policy, 'Surveying the Digital Future'. Accessed 25 October 2000 at www.ccp.ucla.edu.

9. D. Tannen, 'Gender Gap in Cyberspace', *Newsweek* (16 May 1994): 41.

10. See J.P. Dillard, D.H. Solomon, and M.T. Palmer, 'Structuring the Concept of Relational Communication', *Communication Monographs* 66 (1999): 46–55.

11. T.S. Lim and J.W. Bowers, 'Facework: Solidarity, Approbation, and Tact', *Human Communication Research* 17 (1991): 415–50.

12. J.R. Frei and P.R. Shaver, 'Respect in Close Relationships: Prototype, Definition, Self-Report Assessment, and Initial Correlates', *Personal Relationships* 9 (2002): 121–39.

13. See C.M. Rossiter, Jr, 'Instruction in Metacommunication', *Central States Speech Journal* 25 (1974): 36–42; and W.W. Wilmot, 'Metacommunication: A Reexamination and Extension', in *Communication Yearbook* 4 (New Brunswick, NJ: Transaction Books, 1980).

14. L.M. Register and T.B. Henley, 'The Phenomenology of Intimacy', *Journal of Social and Personal Relationships* 9 (1992): 467–81.

15. D. Morris, *Intimate Behavior* (New York: Bantam, 1973), 7.

16. K. Floyd, 'Meanings for Closeness and Intimacy in Friendship', *Journal of Social and Personal Relationships* 13 (1996): 85–107.

17. L.A. Baxter, 'A Dialogic Approach to Relationship Maintenance', in D. Canar and L. Stafford, eds, *Communication and Relational Maintenance* (San Diego: Academic Press, 1994).

18. J.T. Wood and C.C. Inman, 'In a Different Mode: Masculine Styles of Communicating Closeness', *Applied Communication Research* 21 (1993): 279–95.

19. See, for example, K. Dindia and M. Allen, 'Sex Differences in Self-Disclosure: A Meta-Analysis', *Psychological Bulletin* 112 (1992): 106–24; I. and P. Backlund, *Exploring GenderSpeak* (New York: McGraw-Hill, 1994), 219; and J.C. Pearson, L.H. Turner and W. Todd-Mancillas, *Gender and Communication,* 2nd edn (Dubuque, IA: W.C. Brown, 1991), 170–1.

20. See, for example, K. Floyd, 'Gender and Closeness among Friends and Siblings', *Journal of Psychology* 129 (1995): 193–202; and K. Floyd, 'Communicating Closeness among Siblings: An Application of the Gendered Closeness Perspective', *Communication Research Reports* 13 (1996): 27–34.

21. E.L. MacGeorge, A.R. Graves, B. Feng, S.J. Gillihan, and B.R. Burleson, 'The Myth of Gender Cultures: Similarities Outweigh Differences in Men's and Women's Provision of and Responses to Supportive Communication', *Sex Roles* 50 (2004): 143–75.

22. C. Inman, 'Friendships among Men: Closeness in the Doing', in J.T. Wood, ed., *Gendered Relationships* (Mountain View, CA: 1996). See also S. Swain, 'Covert Intimacy in Men's Friendships: Closeness in Men's Friendships', in B.J. Risman and P. Schwartz, eds, *Gender in Intimate Relationships: A Microstructural Approach* (Belmont, CA: Wadsworth, 1989).

23. C.K. Reissman, *Divorce Talk: Women and Men Make Sense of Personal Relationships* (New Brunswick: Rutgers University Press, 1990).

24. J.A. Vandello, D. Cohen, R. Grandon, and R. Franiuk, 'Stand by Your Man: Indirect Prescriptions for Honorable Violence and Feminine Loyalty in Canada, Chile, and the United States', *Journal of Cross-Cultural Psychology* 40, 1 (January 2009): 81–104.

25. For a useful survey of cultural differences in interpersonal communication, see W.B. Gudykunst, S. Ting-Toomey, and T. Nishida, eds, *Communication in Personal Relationships across Cultures* (Thousand Oaks, CA: Sage, 1996).

26. M. Argyle and M. Henderson, 'The Rules of Relationships', in S. Duck and D. Perlman, eds, *Understanding Personal Relationships* (Beverly Hills, CA: Sage, 1985).

27. W.B. Gudykunst, 'The Influence of Cultural Variability on Perceptions of Communication Behavior Associated with Relationship Terms', *Human Communication Research* 13 (1986): 147–66.

28. Z. Hong Li, J. Connolly, D. Jiang, D. Pepler, and W. Craig, 'Adolescent Romantic Relationships in China and Canada: A Cross-National Comparison', *International Journal of Behavioral Development* 34, 2 (March 2010): 113–20.

29. H.C. Triandis, *Culture and Social Behavior* (New York: McGraw-Hill, 1994), 230.

30. K. Lewin, *Principles of Topological Psychology* (New York: McGraw-Hill, 1936).

31. M.L. Knapp and A.L. Vangelisti, *Interpersonal Communication and Human Relationships*, 4th edn (Boston: Allyn and Bacon, 2003).

32. D.J. Canary and L. Stafford, eds, *Communication and Relational Maintenance* (San Diego: Academic Press, 1994). See also J. Lee, 'Effective Maintenance Communication in Superior-Subordinate Relationships', *Western Journal of Communication* 62 (1998): 181–208.

33. For a discussion of relational development in non-intimate relationships, see A. Jensen and S. Trenholm, 'Beyond Intimacy: An Alternative Trajectories Model of Relationship Development'. Paper presented at the Speech Communication Association annual meeting, New Orleans, LA, 1988.

34. B.W. Scharlott and W.G. Christ, 'Overcoming Relationship-Initiation Barriers: The Impact of a Computer-Dating System on Sex Role, Shyness, and Appearance Inhibitions', *Computers in Human Behavior* 11 (1995): 191–204.

35. W.B. Gudykunst and S. Ting-Toomey, *Culture and Interpersonal Communication* (Newbury Park, CA: Sage, 1988), 193.

36. J.H. Tolhuizen, 'Communication Strategies for Intensifying Dating Relationships: Identification, Use and Structure', *Journal of Social and Personal Relationships* 6 (1989): 413–34.

37. L.K. Guerrero and P.A. Andersen, 'The Waxing and Waning of Relational Intimacy: Touch As a Function of Relational Stage, Gender and Touch Avoidance', *Journal of Social and Personal Relationships* 8 (1991): 147–65.

38. L.A. Baxter, 'Symbols of Relationship Identity in Relationship Culture', *Journal of Social and Personal Relationships* 4 (1987): 261–80.

39. C.J. Bruess and J.C. Pearson, 'Like Sands through the Hour Glass: These Are the Rituals Functioning in Day-to-Day Married Lives'. Paper delivered at the Speech Communication Association convention, San Antonio, TX, November 1995.

40. H. Giles and P.F. Poseland, *Speech Style and Social Evaluation* (London: Academic Press, 1975).

41. M. Roloff, C.A. Janiszewski, M.A. McGrath, C.S. Burns, and L.A. Manrai, 'Acquiring Resources from Intimates: When Obligation Substitutes for Persuasion', *Human Communication Research* 14 (1988): 364–96.

42. J.K. Burgoon, R. Parrott, B.A. LePoire, D.L. Kelley, J.B. Walther, and D. Perry, 'Maintaining and Restoring Privacy through Different Types of Relationships', *Journal of Social and Personal Relationships* 6 (1989): 131–58.

43. J.A. Courtright, F.E. Millar, L.E. Rogers, and D. Bagarozzi, 'Interaction Dynamics of Relational Negotiation: Reconciliation versus Termination of Distressed Relationships', *Western Journal of Speech Communication* 54 (1990): 429–53.

44. D.M. Battaglia, F.D. Richard, D.L. Datteri, and C.G. Lord, 'Breaking Up Is (Relatively) Easy to Do: A Script for the Dissolution of Close Relationships', *Journal of Social and Personal Relationships* 15 (1998): 829–45.

45. See, for example, L.A. Baxter and B.M. Montgomery, 'A Guide to Dialectical Approaches to Studying Personal Relationships', in B.M. Montgomery and L.A. Baxter, eds, *Dialectical Approaches to Studying Personal Relationships* (New York: Erlbaum, 1998); and L.A. Ebert and S.W. Duck, 'Rethinking

Satisfaction in Personal Relationships from a Dialectical Perspective', in R.J. Sternberg and M. Hojjatr, eds, *Satisfaction in Close Relationships* (New York: Guilford, 1997).

46. Summarized by L.A. Baxter, 'A Dialogic Approach to Relationship Maintenance', in D.J. Canary and L. Stafford, eds, *Communication and Relational Maintenance* (San Diego: Academic Press, 1994).

47. Morris, op. cit., 21–9.

48. D. Barry, *Dave Barry Turns 40* (New York: Fawcett, 1990), 47.

49. C.A. VanLear, 'Testing a Cyclical Model of Communicative Openness in Relationship Development', *Communication Monographs* 58 (1991): 337–61.

50. Adapted from Baxter and Montgomery, op. cit, 185–206.

51. R.L. Conville, *Relational Transitions: The Evolution of Personal Relationships* (New York: Praeger, 1991), 80.

52. L.B. Rosenfeld and W.L. Kendrick, 'Choosing to Be Open: Subjective Reasons for Self-Disclosing', *Western Journal of Speech Communication* 48 (Fall 1984): 326–43.

53. I. Altman and D.A. Taylor, *Social Penetration: The Development of Interpersonal Relationships* (New York: Holt, Rinehart and Winston, 1973).

54. J. Luft, *Of Human Interaction* (Palo Alto, CA: National Press, 1969).

55. W.B. Gudykunst and S. Ting-Toomey, *Culture and Interpersonal Communication* (Newbury Park, CA: Sage, 1988), 197–8; S. Ting-Toomey, 'A Comparative Analysis of the Communicative Dimensions of Love, Self-Disclosure, Maintenance, Ambivalence, and Conflict in Three Cultures: France, Japan, and the United States'. Paper presented at the International Communication Association convention, Montreal, QC, 1987.

56. S. Duck and D.E. Miell, 'Charting the Development of Personal Relationships', in R. Gilmour and S. Duck, eds, *Studying Interpersonal Interaction* (Hillsdale, NJ: Erlbaum, 1991).

57. S. Duck, 'Some Evident Truths about Conversations in Everyday Relationships: All Communications Are Not Created Equal', *Human Communication Research* 18 (1991): 228–67.

58. J.C. Pearson, *Communication in the Family*, 2nd edn (Needham, MA: Allyn & Bacon, 1993), 292–6.

59. Summarized in J. Pearson, *Communication in the Family* (New York: Harper & Row, 1989), 252–7.

60. E.M. Eisenberg and M.G. Witten, 'Reconsidering Openness in Organizational Communication', *Academy of Management Review* 12 (1987): 418–28.

61. L.B. Rosenfeld and J.R. Gilbert, 'The Measurement of Cohesion and Its Relationship to Dimensions of Self-Disclosure in Classroom Settings', *Small Group Behavior* 20 (1989): 291–301.

62. D. O'Hair and M.J. Cody, 'Interpersonal Deception: The Dark Side of Interpersonal Communication?' in B.H. Spitzberg and W.R. Cupach, eds, *The Dark Side of Interpersonal Communication* (Hillsdale, NJ: Erlbaum, 1993).

63. M.E. Kaplar and A.K. Gordon, 'The Enigma of Altruistic Lying: Perspective Differences in What Motivates and Justifies Lie Telling within Romantic Relationships', *Personal Relationships* 11 (2004).

64. R.E. Turner, C. Edgley, and G. Olmstead, 'Information Control in Conversation: Honesty Is Not Always the Best Policy', *Kansas Journal of Sociology* 11 (1975): 69–89.

65. K.L. Bell and B.M. DePaulo, 'Liking and Lying', *Basic and Applied Social Psychology* 18 (1996): 243–66.

66. R.S. Feldman, J.A. Forrest, and B.R. Happ, 'Self-Presentation and Verbal Deception: Do Self-Presenters Lie More?' *Basic and Applied Social Psychology* 24 (2002): 163–70.

67. S.A. McCornack and T.R. Levine, 'When Lies Are Uncovered: Emotional and Relational Outcomes of Discovered Deception', *Communication Monographs* 57 (1990): 119–138.

68. See M.A. Hamilton and P.J. Mineo, 'A Framework for Understanding Equivocation', *Journal of Language and Social Psychology* 17 (1998): 3–35.

69. S. Metts, W.R. Cupach, and T.T. Imahori, 'Perceptions of Sexual Compliance-Resisting Messages in Three Types of Cross-Sex Relationships', *Western Journal of Communication* 56 (1992): 1–17.

70. J.B. Bavelas, A. Black, N. Chovil, and J. Mullett, *Equivocal Communication* (Newbury Park, CA: Sage, 1990), 171.

71. Ibid.

72. See, for example, W.P. Robinson, A. Shepherd, and J. Heywood, 'Truth, Equivocation/Concealment, and Lies in Job Applications and Doctor-Patient Communication', *Journal of Language & Social Psychology* 17 (1998): 149–64.

73. Several of the following examples were offered by M.T. Motley, 'Mindfulness in Solving Communicators' Dilemmas', *Communication Monographs* 59 (1992): 306–14.

74. D.B. Buller and J.K. Burgoon, 'Deception', in *Communicating Strategically: Strategies in Interpersonal Communication* (Hillsdale, NJ: Erlbaum, 1994).

75. S. Bok, *Lying: Moral Choice in Public and Private Life* (New York: Pantheon, 1978).

Chapter 7

1. K.N.L. Cissna and E. Seiburg, 'Patterns of Interactional Confirmation and Disconfirmation', in M.V. Redmond, ed., *Interpersonal Communication: Readings in Theory and Research* (Fort Worth, TX: Harcourt Brace, 1995).

2. Ibid.

3. M.W. Allen, 'Communication Concepts Related to Perceived Organizational Support', *Western Journal of Communication* 59 (1995): 326–46.

4. B. Bower, 'Nice Guys Look Better in Women's Eyes', *Science News* (18 March 1995): 165.

5. See, for example, J. Veroff Douvan, T.L. Orbuch, and L.K. Acitelli, 'Happiness in Stable Marriages: The Early Years', in T.N. Bradbury, ed., *The Development Course of Marital Dysfunction* (New York: Cambridge University Press, 1999), 152–79.

6. D.J. Canary and T.M. Emmers-Sommer, *Sex and Gender Differences in Personal Relationships* (New York: Guildford, 1997).

7. J.J. Teven, M.M. Martin, and N.C. Neupauer, 'Sibling Relationships: Verbally Aggressive Messages and Their Effect

on Relational Satisfaction', *Communication Reports* 11 (1998): 179–86.

8. K. Ellis, 'The Impact of Perceived Teacher Confirmation on Receiver Apprehension, Motivation, and Learning', *Communication Education* 53 (2004): 1–20.

9. For a discussion of reactions to disconfirming responses, see A.L. Vangelisti and L.P. Crumley, 'Reactions to Messages That Hurt: The Influence of Relational Contexts', *Communication Monographs* 64 (1998): 173–96. See also L.M. Cortina, V.J. Magley, J.H. Williams, and R.D. Langhout, 'Incivility in the Workplace: Incidence and Impact', *Journal of Occupational Health Psychology* 6 (2001): 64–80.

10. A.L. Vangelisti, 'Messages That Hurt', in W.R. Cupach and B.H. Spitzberg, eds, *The Dark Side of Interpersonal Communication* (Hillsdale, NJ: Erlbaum, 1994).

11. See W.W. Wilmot, *Dyadic Communication* (New York: Random House, 1987), 149–58, and L.M. Andersson and C.M. Pearson, 'Tit for Tat? The Spiraling Effect of Incivility in the Workplace', *Academy of Management Review* 24 (1999): 452–71. See also L.N. Olson and D.O. Braithwaite, '"If You Hit Me Again, I'll Hit You Back": Conflict Management Strategies of Individuals Experiencing Aggression during Conflicts', *Communication Studies* 55 (2004): 271–86.

12. C. Burggraf and A.L. Sillars, 'A Critical Examination of Sex Differences in Marital Communication', *Communication Monographs* 54 (1987): 276–94. See also D.A. Newton and J.K. Burgoon, 'The Use and Consequences of Verbal Strategies during Interpersonal Disagreements', *Human Communication Research* 16 (1990): 477–518.

13. J.L. Hocker and W.W. Wilmot, *Interpersonal Conflict*, 6th edn (New York: McGraw-Hill, 2001), 33.

14. Ibid., 37.

15. J. Gibb, 'Defensive Communication', *Journal of Communication* 11 (1961): 141–8. See also W.F. Eadie, 'Defensive Communication Revisited: A Critical Examination of Gibb's Theory', *Southern Speech Communication Journal* 47 (1982): 163–77.

16. For a review of research supporting the effectiveness of 'I' language, see R.F. Proctor II and J.R. Wilcox, 'An Exploratory Analysis of Responses to Owned Messages in Interpersonal Communication', *Et Cetera: A Review of General Semantics* 50 (1993): 201–20. See also R.F. Proctor II, 'Responsibility or Egocentrism?: The Paradox of Owned Messages', *Speech Association of Minnesota Journal* 16 (1989): 59–60.

17. T.C. Sabourin and G.H. Stamp, 'Communication and the Experience of Dialectical Tensions in Family Life: An Examination of Abusive and Nonabusive Families', *Communication Monographs* 62 (1995): 213–43.

18. R. Vonk, 'The Slime Effect: Suspicion and Dislike of Likeable Behavior toward Superiors', *Journal of Personality and Social Psychology* 74 (1998): 849–64.

19. P. Sullivan and D. Feltz, 'The Relationship between Intrateam Conflict and Cohesion within Hockey Teams', *Small Group Research* 32, 3 (2001): 342–55.

20. J.L. Hocker and W.W. Wilmot, *Interpersonal Conflict*, 6th edn (New York: McGraw-Hill, 2001), 23.

21. See, for example, L.A. Baxter, W.W. Wilmot, C.A. Simmons, and A. Swartz, 'Ways of Doing Conflict: A Folk Taxonomy of Conflict Events in Personal Relationships', in P.J. Kalbfleisch, ed., *Interpersonal Communication: Evolving Interpersonal Relationships* (Hillsdale, NJ: Erlbaum, 1993).

22. P.J. Lannutti and J.I. Monahan, '"Not Now, Maybe Later": The Influence of Relationship Type, Request Persistence, and Alcohol Consumption on Women's Refusal Strategies', *Communication Studies* 55 (2004): 362–77.

23. G.R. Birchler, R.L. Weiss, and J.P. Vincent, 'Multimethod Analysis of Social Reinforcement Exchange between Maritally Distressed and Nondistressed Spouse and Stranger Dyads', *Journal of Personality and Social Psychology* 31 (1975): 349–60.

24. J.R. Meyer, 'Effect of Verbal Aggressiveness on the Perceived Importance of Secondary Goals in Messages', *Communication Studies* 55 (2004): 168–84.

25. G.R. Bach and H. Goldberg, *Creative Aggression* (Garden City, NY: Doubleday, 1974).

26. See K. Kellermann and B.C. Shea, 'Threats, Suggestions, Hints, and Promises: Gaining Compliance Efficiently and Politely', *Communication Quarterly* 44 (1996): 145–65.

27. J. Jordan and M.E. Roloff, 'Acquiring Assistance from Others: The Effect of Indirect Requests and Relational Intimacy on Verbal Compliance', *Human Communication Research* 16 (1990): 519–55.

28. Research summarized by D. Tannen in *You Just Don't Understand: Women and Men in Conversation* (New York: William Morrow, 1989), 152–7, 162–5.

29. N. Crick, 'Relational and Overt Forms of Peer Victimization: A Multi-informant Approach', *Journal of Consulting and Clinical Psychology* 66 (1998): 337–47.

30. J.F. Benenson, S.A. Ford, and N.H. Apostoleris, 'Girls' Assertiveness in the Presence of Boys', *Small Group Research* 29 (1998): 198–211.

31. M.J. Collier, 'Conflict Competence within African, Mexican, and Anglo American Friendships', in S. Ting-Toomey and F. Korzenny, eds, *Cross-Cultural Interpersonal Communication* (Newbury Park, CA: Sage, 1991).

32. The information in this paragraph is drawn from research summarized by J.T. Wood in *Gendered Lives*, 6th edn (Belmont, CA: Wadsworth, 2005).

33. N.A. Klinetob and D.A. Smith, 'Demand–Withdraw Communication in Marital Interaction: Tests of Interpersonal Contingency and Gender Role Hypotheses', *Journal of Marriage & the Family* 58 (1996): 945–57.

34. See M.J. Papa and E.J. Natalle, 'Gender, Strategy Selection, and Discussion Satisfaction in Interpersonal Conflict', *Western Journal of Speech Communication* 52 (1989): 260–72.

35. See, for example, J.C. Pearson, *Gender and Communication*, 2nd edn (Dubuque, IA: W.C. Brown, 1991), 183–4.

36. For a more detailed discussion of culture, conflict, and context, see W.B. Gudykunst and S. Ting-Toomey, *Culture and Interpersonal Communication* (Newbury Park, CA: Sage, 1988), 153–60.

37. D. Wright and J. Bricker, *What Canadians Think... About Almost Everything* (Toronto: Doubleday, 2005), 287

38. S. Ting-Toomey, K.K. Yee-Jung, R.B. Shapiro, W. Garcia, and T. Wright, 'Ethnic Identity Salience and Conflict Styles in Four Ethnic Groups: African Americans, Asian Americans, European Americans, and Latino Americans'. Paper presented at the annual conference of the Speech Communication Association, New Orleans, November 1994.

39. See, for example, S. Ting-Toomey, 'Rhetorical Sensitivity Style in Three Cultures: France, Japan, and the United States', *Central States Speech Journal* 39 (1988): 28–36.

40. K. Okabe, 'Indirect Speech Acts of the Japanese', in L. Kincaid, ed., *Communication Theory: Eastern and Western Perspectives* (San Diego: Academic Press, 1987): 127–36.

41. The following research is summarized in Tannen, op. cit., 160.

42. Jean-Pierre Voyer, 'A Special Edition on Child Development', *Applied Research Bulletin* (Fall 1999): 20–1.

43. A.C. Filley, *Interpersonal Conflict Resolution* (Glenview, IL: Scott Foresman, 1975), 3.

Chapter 8

1. S. Duncombe, *Zines and the Politics of Alternative Culture* (London: Verso, 2001).

2. E. Ringmar, *A Blogger's Manifesto: Free Speech and Censorship in the Age of the Internet* (London: Anthem Press, 2007).

3. Sidney Eve Matrix Faculty Profile, Queen's University Film and Media. Available at film.queensu.ca/Sidney.html.

4. B. Heil and M. Piskorski, 'New Twitter Research: Men Follow Men and Nobody Tweets', *Harvard Business Review*, 1 June 2009. Available at blogs.hbr.org/cs/2009/06/new_twitter_research_men_follo.html.

5. Ibid.

6. The Canadian Press, '16 Million Canadians on Facebook: Report', published in *The Globe and Mail*, 2 June 2010. Available at theglobeandmail.com/news/technology/personal-tech/16-million-canadians-on-facebook-report/article1589749/.

7. I. Paul, 'It's Quit Facebook Day, Are You Leaving?' *PC World*, 31 May 2010. Available at pcworld.com/article/197621/its_quit_facebook_day_are_you_leaving.html.

8. D. Boyd, 'MySpace Vs. Facebook: A Digital Enactment of Class-Based Social Categories Amongst American Teenagers'. Paper presented at the International Communications Association Conference, Chicago, 23 May 2009. Available at danah.org/papers/talks/ICA2009.html.

9. C.L. Toma, 'Affirming the Self through Online Profiles: Beneficial Effects of Social Networking Sites'. Proceedings of the 28th International Conference on Human Factors in Computing Systems (2010): 1749–52.

10. S. Zhao, S. Grasmuch, and J. Martin, 'Identity Construction on Facebook: Digital Empowerment in Anchored Relationships', *Computers in Human Behavior* 24, 5 (2008): 1816–36.

11. V. Barash, N. Ducheneaut, E. Isaacs, and V. Bellotti, 'Faceplant: Impression (Mis)management in Facebook Status Updates', Proceedings of the Fourth International AAAI Conference on Weblogs and Social Media (2010). Available at aaai.org/ocs/index.php/ICWSM/ICWSM10/paper/viewPDFInterstitial/1465/1858

12. A.N. Joinson, 'Looking At, Looking Up or Keeping Up with People?: Motives and Use of Facebook'. Proceeding of the 26th Annual SIGCHI Conference on Human Factors in Computing Systems (2008): 1027–36. Available at portal.acm.org/citation.cfm?id=1357213.

13. J. Baudrillard, *Simulations and Simulacra*. trans. Sheila Glaser. (Ann Arbor: University of Michigan Press, 1996).

14. Personal communication with Alexandre Sévigny.

15. Z. Kleinman, 'Google Boss Eric Schmidt Warns on Social Use of Media', BBC News, 18 August 2010. Available at bbc.co.uk/news/technology-11009700.

16. P.B. O'Sullivan, 'Bridging the Mass–Interpersonal Divide: Synthesis Scholarship', *Human Communication Research* 25 (1999): 569–88.

17. H. Innis, 'Minerva's Owl'. Available at gutenberg.ca/ebooks/innis-minerva/innis-minerva-00-h.html. Accessed 22 May 2010.

18. *McLuhan's Wake*. Dir. Kevin McMahon, 2002.

19. The name 'bullet theory', also referred to as 'hypodermic needle theory' or 'transmission belt theory', was used not by the early researchers who performed these studies but rather by later theorists. See M.L. DeFleur and S. Ball-Rokeach, *Theories of Mass Communication*, 5th edn (New York: Longman, 1989), 145–66. See also W.J. Severin and J.W. Tankard, Jr, *Communication Theories: Origins, Methods, and Uses in the Mass Media*, 4th edn (New York: Longman, 1997), 322.

20. See, for example, P.M. Sandman, D.M. Rubin, and D.B. Sachsman, *Media: An Introductory Analysis of American Mass Communications*, 3rd edn (Englewood Cliffs, NJ: Prentice Hall, 1982), 4–5.

21. These and other social learning experiments are reported in Bandura's seminal book, *Social Learning Theory* (Englewood Cliffs, NJ: Prentice Hall, 1977). See DeFleur and Ball-Rokeach, op cit., 112–16, for more on this study and social learning and modelling theory.

22. See, for example, S.J. Baran and D.K. Davis, *Mass Communication Theory: Foundations, Ferment, and Future* (Belmont, CA: Wadsworth, 1995), 206.

23. DeFleur and Ball-Rokeach, op cit., 172–86.

24. Diffusion of innovations theory is attributed primarily to E. Rogers, *Diffusion of Innovations*, 3rd edn (New York: Free Press, 1983). See also Severin and Tankard, op cit., 238–9. This research perspective continues to be the foundation for important research. See, for example, T.W. Valents, 'Diffusion of Innovations and Policy Decision-Making', *Journal of Communication* 43, 1 (Winter 1993): 30–45; or M. Meyer, J.D. Johnson, and C. Ethington, 'Contrasting Attributes of Preventive Health Innovations', *Journal of Communication* 47, 2 (Spring 1997): 112–31.

25. See, for example, L. Jeffres and D. Atkin, 'Prediction Use of Technologies for Communication and Consumer Needs', *Journal of Broadcasting and Electronic Media* 40, 3 (Summer

1996): 318–30. See also T. Adams, 'Follow the Yellow Brick Road: Using Diffusion of Innovations Theory to Enrich Virtual Organization in Cyberspace', *Southern Communication Journal* 62, 2 (Winter 1997): 133–48.

26. G. Gerbner, L. Gross, M. Morgan, and N. Signorelli, 'Living with Television: the Cultivation Perspective', in J. Bryant and D. Zillmann, eds, *Media Effects: Advances in Theory and Research* (Hillsdale, NJ: Lawrence Erlbaum, 1994), 17–41. See also Severin and Tankard, op cit., 299–303.

27. D. Shaw and M. McCombs, *The Emergence of American Political Issues: The Agenda-Setting Function of the Press* (St Paul, MN: West Publishing Co., 1977), 7.

28. The way these theories converge can be seen in studies such as H.-B. Brosius and G. Weimann, 'Who Sets the Agenda? Agenda-Setting as a Two-Step Glow', *Communication Research* 23, 5 (October 1996): 561–80. This research examined news items on German television and found that issues tend to flow from the public to the media and within the public.

29. See, for example, J.W. Dearing and E.M. Rogers, *Agenda-Setting* (Thousand Oaks, CA: Sage, 1996), especially Chapter 5.

Chapter 9

1. M.V. Redmond, 'A Plan for the Successful Use of Teams in Design Education', *Journal of Architectural Education* 17 (May 1986): 27–49.

2. 'Professional Occupations in Multimedia', *California Occupational Guide*, Number 2006 (Sacramento, CA: California State Employment Division, 1995), 4. See also 'A Labor Market Analysis of the Interactive Digital Media Industry: Opportunities in Multimedia' (San Francisco: Reagan & Associates, 1997), 15–29.

3. L. Thompson, E. Peterson, and S.E. Brodt, 'Team Negotiation: An Examination of Integrative and Distributive Bargaining', *Journal of Personality and Social Psychology* 70 (1996): 66–78.

4. For a more detailed discussion of the advantages and dis-advantages of working in groups, see S.A. Beebe and J.T. Masterson, *Communicating in Small Groups: Principles and Practices*, 7th edn (Needham Heights: Allyn & Bacon, 2003).

5. See, for example, S. Barnes and L.M. Greller, 'Computer-Mediated Communication in the Organization', *Communication Education* 43 (1994): 129–42.

6. S.L. Herndon, 'Theory and Practice: Implications for the Implementation of Communication Technology in Organizations', *Journal of Business Communication* 34 (January 1997): 121–9.

7. E.A. Marby, 'The Systems Metaphor in Group Communication', in L.R. Frey, ed., *Handbook of Group Communication Theory and Research* (Thousand Oaks, CA: Sage, 1999).

8. J.D. Rothwell, *In Mixed Company: Small Group Communication*, 5th edn (Belmont, CA: Wadsworth, 2004), 29–31.

9. See, for example, J.R. Katzenbach and D.K. Smith, 'The Discipline of Teams', *Harvard Business Review* 86 (March–April 1993): 111–20.

10. J. Hackman, 'The Design of Work Teams', in J. Lorsch, ed., *Handbook of Organizational Behavior* (Englewood Cliffs, NJ: Prentice Hall, 1987), 315–42.

11. Rothwell, op. cit., 42–7.

12. For a discussion of the relationship between individual and group goals, see L. Frey, 'Individuals in Groups', in L.R. Frey and J.K. Barge, eds, *Managing Group Life: Communicating in Decision-Making Groups* (Boston: Houghton Mifflin, 1997).

13. J. Krakauer, *Into Thin Air* (New York: Anchor, 1997), 212–13.

14. See D. Scheerhorn and P. Geist, 'Social Dynamics in Groups', in Frey and Barge, op. cit.

15. S.B. Shimanoff, 'Group Interaction via Communication Rules', in R.S. Cathcart and L.A. Samovar, eds, *Small Group Communication: A Reader*, 5th edn (Dubuque, IA: W.C. Brown, 1988), 50–64.

16. D.S. Gouran, R.Y. Hirokawa, K.M. Julian, and G.B. Leatham, 'The Evolution and Current Status of the Functional Perspective on Communication in Decision-Making and Problem-Solving Groups', in S.A. Deetz, ed., *Communication Yearbook* 16 (Newbury Park, CA: Sage, 1992). See also G.M. Wittenbaum, A.B. Hollingshead, P.B. Paulus, R.Y. Hirokawa, D.G. Ancona, R.S. Peterson, K.A. Jehn, and K. Yoon, 'The Functional Perspective as a Lens for Understanding Groups', *Small Group Research* 35 (2004): 17–43.

17. M.E. Mayer, 'Behaviors Leading to More Effective Decisions in Small Groups Embedded in Organizations', *Communication Reports* 11 (1998): 123–32.

18. R.F. Bales and P.L. Strodbeck, 'Phases in Group Problem Solving', *Journal of Abnormal and Social Psychology* 46 (1951): 485–95.

19. E. Bormann, *Small Group Communication: Theory and Practice* (New York: Harper & Row, 1990).

20. N. Postman, *Crazy Talk, Stupid Talk* (New York: Dell, 1976).

21. B. Steinzor, 'The Spatial Factor in Face-to-Face Discussion Groups', *Journal of Abnormal and Social Psychology* 45 (1950): 522–55.

22. P.L. Strodtbeck and L.H. Hook, 'The Social Dimensions of a Twelve-Man Jury Table', *Sociometry* 24 (1961): 397–415.

23. N.F. Russo, 'Connotations of Seating Arrangements', *Cornell Journal of Social Relations* 2 (1967): 37–44.

24. Adapted from D.W. Johnson and F.P. Johnson, *Joining Together: Group Theory and Group Skills*, 8th edn (Boston: Allyn and Bacon, 2003).

25. R. Hastle, *Inside the Jury* (Cambridge, MA: Harvard University Press, 1983).

26. B. Day, 'The Art of Conducting International Business', *Advertising Age* (6 October 1990): 48.

27. Adapted from R.B. Adler and J.M. Elmhorst, *Communicating at Work: Principles and Practices for Business and the Professions*, 8th edn (New York: McGraw-Hill, 2005), 269.

28. Population Reference Bureau, 'The Changing American Pie, 1999 and 2025'. Accessed 13 October 2004 from prb.org/AmeristatTemplate.cfm?Section=RaceandEthnicity&template=/ContentManagement/ContentDisplay.cfm&ContentID=2743.

29. S.G. Barsade and D.E. Gibson, 'Group Emotion: A View from Top and Bottom', in D.H. Gruenfeld, ed., *Composition*

(Greenwich, CT: JAI Press, 1998). See also K.Y. Williams and C.A. O'Reilly, 'Demography and Diversity in Organizations: A Review of 40 Years of Research', in B. Staw and R. Sutton, eds, *Research in Organizational Behavior* 20 (1998): 77–140.

30. Williams and O'Reilly, op. cit.

31. S.B. Paletz, K. Peng, M. Erez, and C. Maslach, 'Ethnic Composition and Its Differential Impact on Group Processes in Diverse Teams', *Small Group Research* 35 (2004): 128–57.

32. G. Hofstede, *Cultures and Organizations: Software of the Mind* (New York: McGraw-Hill, 1997), 158.

33. See H.C. Triandis, R. Bontempo, M. Villareal, M. Asai, and N. Lucca, 'Individualism and Collectivism: Cross-Cultural Perspectives of Self-Ingroup Relationships', *Journal of Personality and Social Psychology* 54 (1988): 323–38.

34. Research supporting these differences is summarized in S. Ting-Toomey, 'Identity and Interpersonal Bonding', in M.K. Asante and W.B. Gudykunst, eds, *Handbook of International and Intercultural Communication* (Newbury Park, CA: Sage, 1989), 351–73.

35. Hofstede, op. cit., 65–109.

36. Ibid., 110–47.

37. Ibid., 189–210.

Chapter 10

1. L. Tuck, 'Meeting Madness', *Presentations* (May 1995): 20.

2. C. Downs, D.M. Berg, and W.A. Linkugel, *The Organizational Communicator* (New York: Harper & Row, 1977), 127.

3. G.L. Wilson, *Groups in Context: Leadership and Participation in Small Groups* (New York: McGraw-Hill, 2005), 12–13.

4. See, for example, C. Pavitt, 'Do Interacting Groups Perform Better Than Aggregates of Individuals?' *Human Communication Research* 29 (2003): 592–9; G.M. Wittenbaum, 'Putting Communication into the Study of Group Memory', *Human Communication Research* 29 (2004): 616–23; and M.G. Frank, T.H. Feely, N. Paolantonio, and T.J. Servoss, 'Individual and Small Group Accuracy in Judging Truthful and Deceptive Communication', *Group Decision and Negotiation* 13 (2004): 45–54.

5. R.B. Adler and J.M. Elmhorst, *Communicating at Work: Principles and Practices for Business and the Professions*, 8th edn (New York: McGraw-Hill, 2005), 289–90.

6. K.A. Graetz, E.S. Boyle, C.E. Kimble, P. Thompson, and J.L. Garloch, 'Information Sharing in Face-to-Face, Teleconferencing, and Electronic Chat Groups', *Small Group Research* 29 (1998): 714–43.

7. M. Zey, ed., *Decision Making: Alternatives to Rational Choice Models* (Newbury Park, CA: Sage, 1992). For a discussion of how groups 'muddle through' in organizational decision-making, see H. Mintzberg and A. McHugh, 'Strategy Formation in an Adhocracy', *Administrative Science Quarterly* 30 (1985): 160–97.

8. See, for example, A.L. Salazar, R.Y. Hirokawa, K.M. Propp, K.M. Julian, and G.B. Leatham, 'In Search of True Causes: Examination of the Effect of Group Potential and Group

Interaction on Decision Performance', *Human Communication Research* 20 (1994): 529–99.

9. J. Dewey, *How We Think* (New York: Heath, 1910).

10. M.S. Poole, 'Procedures for Managing Meetings: Social and Technological Innovation', in R.A. Swanson and B.O. Knapp, eds, *Innovative Meeting Management* (Austin, TX: 3M Meeting Management Institute, 1991). See also M.S. Poole and M.E. Holmes, 'Decision Development in Computer-Assisted Group Decision Making', *Human Communication Research* 22 (1995): 90–127.

11. K. Lewin, *Field Theory in Social Science* (New York: Harper & Row, 1951), 30–59.

12. See S. Jarboe, 'Group Communication and Creativity Processes', in L.R. Frey, ed., *Handbook of Group Communication Theory and Research* (Thousand Oaks, CA: Sage, 1999).

13. A. Osborn, *Applied Imagination* (New York: Scribner's, 1959).

14. See, for example, M. Diehl and W. Strobe, 'Productivity Loss in Brainstorming Groups: Toward the Solution of a Riddle', *Journal of Personality and Social Psychology* 53 (1987): 497–509; and V. Brown, M. Tumero, T.S. Larey, and P.B. Paulus, 'Modeling Cognitive Interactions during Group Brainstorming', *Small Group Research* 29 (1998): 495–526.

15. B.A. Fisher, 'Decision Emergence: Phases in Group Decision Making', *Speech Monographs* 37 (1970): 53–66.

16. C.R. Frantz and K.G. Jin, 'The Structure of Group Conflict in a Collaborative Work Group during Information Systems Development', *Journal of Applied Communication Research* 23 (1995): 108–27.

17. M. Poole and J. Roth, 'Decision Development in Small Groups IV: A Typology of Group Decision Paths', *Human Communication Research* 15 (1989): 323–56. See also M. Poole and J. Roth, 'Decision Development in Small Groups V: Test of a Contingency Model', *Human Communication Research* 15 (1989): 549–89.

18. S.A. Wheelan, D. Murphy, E. Tsumaura, and S.F. Kline, 'Member Perceptions of Internal Group Dynamics and Productivity', *Small Group Research* 29 (1998): 371–93.

19. S.M. Farmer and J. Roth, 'Conflict-Handling Behavior in Work Groups: Effects of Group Structure, Decision Process, and Time', *Small Group Research* 29 (1998): 669–713.

20. B. Mullen and C. Cooper, 'The Relation between Group Cohesiveness and Performance: An Integration', *Psychological Bulletin* 115 (1994): 210–27.

21. R.T. Keller, 'Predictors of the Performance of Project Groups in R & D Organizations', *Academy of Management Journal* 29 (1986): 715–26. See also B.A. Welch, K.W. Mossholder, R.P. Stell, and N. Bennett, 'Does Work Group Cohesiveness Affect Individuals' Performance and Organizational Commitment?' *Small Group Research* 29 (1998): 472–94.

22. The following types of power are based on the categories developed by J.R. French and B. Raven, 'The Basis of Social Power', in D. Cartright and A. Zander, eds, *Group Dynamics* (New York: Harper & Row, 1968), 565.

23. For a detailed discussion of leadership emergence, see E.G.G. Bormann and N.C. Bormann, *Effective Small Group Communication*, 6th edn (New York: Pearson Custom Publishing, 1997).

24. C. Conrad, *Strategic Organizational Communication: An Integrated Perspective*, 2nd edn (Fort Worth, TX: Holt, Rinehart and Winston, 1990), 139.

25. J.D. Rothwell, *In Mixed Company: Small Group Communication*, 5th edn (Belmont, CA: Wadsworth, 2004), 247–82.

26. Aristotle, *Politics* (New York: Oxford University Press, 1958), Book 7.

27. See B.L. Kelsey, 'The Dynamics of Multicultural Groups', *Small Group Research* 29 (1998): 602–23.

28. W. Bennis and B. Nanus, *Leaders: The Strategies for Taking Charge* (New York: Harper & Row, 1985), 164.

29. K. Lewin, R. Lippitt, and R.K. White, 'Patterns of Aggressive Behavior in Experimentally Created Social Climates', *Journal of Social Psychology* 10 (1939): 271–99.

30. G. Cheney, 'Democracy in the Workplace: Theory and Practice from the Perspective of Communication', *Journal of Applied Communication Research* 23 (1995): 167–200.

31. L.L. Rosenbaum and W.B. Rosenbaum, 'Morale and Productivity Consequences of Group Leadership Style, Stress, and Type of Task', *Journal of Applied Psychology* 55 (1971): 343–58.

32. J. Hall and S. Donnell, 'Managerial Achievement: The Personal Side of Behavioral Theory', *Human Relations* 32 (1979): 77–101.

33. R.R. Blake and A.A. McCanse, *Leadership Dilemmas—Grid Solutions* (Houston: Gulf Publishing Co., 1991).

34. For a discussion of situational theories, see G.L. Wilson, *Groups in Context*, 6th edn (New York: McGraw-Hill, 2002), 190–4.

35. F.E. Fiedler, *A Theory of Leadership Effectiveness* (New York: McGraw-Hill, 1967).

36. P. Hersey and K. Blanchard, *Management of Organizational Behavior: Utilizing Human Resources*, 8th edn (Upper Saddle River, NJ: Prentice Hall, 2001).

37. Rothwell, op. cit., 139–42.

38. M.E. Mayer, 'Behaviors Leading to More Effective Decisions in Small Groups Embedded in Organizations', *Communication Reports* 11 (1998): 123–32.

39. L.R. Hoffman and N.R.F. Maier, 'Valence in the Adoption of Solutions by Problem-Solving Groups: Concept, Method, and Results', *Journal of Abnormal and Social Psychology* 69 (1964): 264–71.

40. E.P. Torrence, 'Some Consequences of Power Differences on Decision Making in Permanent and Temporary Three-Man Groups'. *Research Studies, Washington State College* 22 (1954): 130–40.

41. R.F. Bales, F.L. Strodtbeck, T.M. Mills, and M.E. Roseborough, 'Channels of Communication in Small Groups', *American Sociological Review* 16 (1951): 461–8.

42. I. Janis, *Groupthink: Psychological Studies of Policy Decisions and Fiascoes* (Boston: Houghton Mifflin, 1982).

43. Adapted from Rothwell, op. cit., 223–6.

Chapter 11

1. For an explanation on social judgment theory, see E. Griffin, *A First Look at Communication Theory*, 5th edn (New York: McGraw-Hill, 2003).

2. C. Lasch, 'Journalism, Publicity and the Lost Art of Argument', *Gannett Center Journal* (Spring 1990): 1–11.

3. See, for example, J.A. Jaska and M.S. Pritchard, *Communication Ethics: Methods of Analysis*, 2nd edn (Belmont, CA: Wadsworth, 1994).

4. J. Zaleschuk, 'How to Improve Canada's Health Care System'. Available at hcsc.gc.ca/english/care/romanow/hcc0422.html.

5. There are, of course, other classifications of logical fallacies than those presented here. See, for example, B. Warnick and E. Inch, *Critical Thinking and Communication: The Use of Reason in Argument*, 2nd edn (New York: Macmillan, 1994), 137–61.

6. For an example of how demographics have been taken into consideration in great speeches, see G. Stephens, 'Frederick Douglass' Multiracial Abolitionism: "Antagonistic Cooperation" and "Redeemable Ideals" in the July 5 Speech', *Communication Studies* 48 (Fall 1997): 175–94. On 5 July 1852, Douglass gave a speech entitled 'What to the Slave Is the 4th of July', attacking the hypocrisy of Independence Day in a slaveholding republic. It was one of the greatest anti-slavery speeches ever given, and part of its success stemmed from the way Douglass sought common ground with his multiracial audience.

7. A. Wittenberg, 'A New Messaging Strategy for the Liberal Party in Hamilton', unpublished.

8. For example, see J.E. Kopfman and S. Smith, 'Understanding the Audiences of a Health Communication Campaign: A Discriminant Analysis of Potential Organ Donors Based on Intent to Donate', *Journal of Applied Communication Research* 24 (February 1996): 33–49.

9. R.K. Stutman and S.E. Newell, 'Beliefs versus Values: Silent Beliefs in Designing a Persuasive Message', *Western Journal of Speech Communication* 48, 4 (Fall 1984): 364.

10. S. Pinker, *The Blank Slate* (New York: Viking, 2002).

11. P.K. Hatemi, J.R. Hibbing, S.E. Medland, M.C. Keller, J.R. Alford, K.B. Smith, N.G. Martin, and L.J. Eaves, 'Not by Twins Alone: Using the Extended Family Design to Investigate Genetic Influence on Political Beliefs', *American Journal of Political Science* 54, 3 (June 2010): 798–814.

12. J.P. Dillard, 'Persuasion Past and Present: Attitudes Aren't What They Used to Be', *Communication Monographs* 60 (1993): 90–7.

13. M.P. Zanna and J.K. Rempel, 'Attitudes: A New Look at an Old Concept', in D. Bar-Tal and A. Kruglanski, eds, *The Social Psychology of Knowledge* (New York: Cambridge University Press, 1998), 315–34.

14. R.M. Perloff, *The Dynamics of Persuasion: Communication and Attitudes in the 21st Century*, 4th edn (New York: Routledge, 2010).

15. G.R. Maio and J.M. Olson, 'Values as Truisms: Evidence and Implications', *Journal of Personality and Social Psychology* 74 (1998): 294–311.

16. S.H. Schwartz and W. Bilsky, 'Toward a Universal Psychological Structure of Human Values', *Journal of Personality and Social Psychology* 53, 3 (1987): 550–62.

17. Ibid.

18. M. Rokeach, *The Nature of Human Values* (New York: Free Press, 1973).

19. Perloff, op. cit.

20. E.C. Tolman, *Purposive Behavior in Animals and Men* (New York: Century, 1932).

21. K. Lewin, *A Dynamic Theory of Personality* (New York: McGraw-Hill, 1935).

22. J.W. Atkinson, 'Motivational Determinants of Risk Taking Behavior', *Psychological Review* 64 (1957): 359–72.

23. A. Wigfield, 'Expectancy–Value Theory of Achievement Motivation: A Developmental Perspective', *Educational Psychological Review* 6, 1 (March 1994): 49–78.

24. A.J. Greimas and J. Fontanille, *The Semiotics of Passions: From States of Affairs to States of Feelings*. P. Perron and F. Collins, trans. (Minneapolis and London: University of Minnesota Press, 1993), xxvi, 239.

25. N. Fairclough, *Textual Analysis for Social Research* (New York: Routledge, 2003), 9.

26. Ibid.

27. J. Sprague and D. Stuart, *The Speaker's Handbook*, 3rd edn (Fort Worth, TX: Harcourt Brace Jovanovich, 1992): 172.

28. G. Asburn and A. Gordon, 'Features of Simplified Register in Speech to Elderly Conversationalists', *International Journal of Psycholinguistics* 8,3 (1981): 7–31.

29. G.W. Bush, 'Remarks by the President and Prime Minister Chrétien on US–Canada Smart Borders' (Detroit MI, 9 September 2002). Available at whitehouse.gov/news/releases/2002/09/20020909-4.html.

30. J.A. DeVito, *The Communication Handbook: A Dictionary* (New York: Harper & Row, 1986), 84–6.

31. J.M. Burger, 'The Foot-in-the-Door Compliance Procedure: A Multiple-Process Analysis and Review', *Personality and Social Psychology Review* 3, 4 (November 1999): 303–25.

32. R.B. Cialdini, J.E. Vincent, S.K. Lewis, J. Catalan, D. Wheeler, and B.L. Darby, 'Reciprocal Concessions Procedure for Inducing Compliance: The Door-in-the-Face Technique', *Journal of Personality and Social Psychology* 31, 2 (February 1975): 206–15.

33. There is more detail on a similar process in C. Meyer, *Communicating for Results: A Canadian Student's Guide* (Don Mills, ON: Oxford University Press, 2007), 23–37. Meyer also has specific tools for preparing business communications (e.g., letters, e-mails, memos, and reports) that students would find helpful.

34. In working on major writing projects, both at CBC and elsewhere, I would most often work with other writers in a team. Part of the value of the PAE approach is that you set out the common planning goals among a team of contributors, thus avoiding duplication or even counter-productive writing communication.

35. When I did formal CBC reporting to groups like the CRTC, I often used this outlining method, which is also the basis for the briefing notes in this chapter.

36. Some people use a form of free-writing before they make the outline, or at least partly at that point.

37. Also check for accuracy, completeness, structure, and coherence.

38. Some organizations have their own internal 'house style' for certain types of documents (always follow those first).

Otherwise, you may choose to use an academic publication, such as *The Chicago Manual of Style* (now available online at chicagomanualofstyle.org). I prefer using a journalist's style guide for professional writing; both *The Globe and Mail* and the Canadian Press publish guides suitable for Canadian contexts and spellings.

39. Some believe this is how they get their name: [op]posite the [ed]itorial. Other think of them as opinion-editorials.

40. Accessed 17 May 2010 at nytimes.com/2005/07/31/opinion/31shipley.html?_r=1.

41. McGill University Newsroom, 'Op-ed Writing Tips'. Accessed 17 May 2010 at mcgill.ca/newsroom/facstaffresources/op-ed/.

Chapter 12

1. Toastmasters International, toastmasters.org.

2. See, for example, L. Stern, *The Structures and Strategies of Human Memory* (Homewood, IL: Dorsey Press, 1985). See also C. Turner, 'Organizing Information: Principles and Practices', *Library Journal* (15 June 1987).

3. J. Buckley, *Fit to Print: The Canadian Students' Guide to Essay Writing*, 6th edn (Scarborough, ON: Nelson Education Ltd, 2004).

4. C. Koehler, 'Mending the Body by Lending an Ear: The Healing Power of Listening', *Vital Speeches of the Day* (15 June 1998), 543.

5. L. Johnson, 'Poverty in Liberia'. Student speech presented for 'Celebrate Africa', McMaster University, Dundas, ON, 25 November 2006.

6. A.H. Monroe, *Principles and Types of Speech* (Glenview, IL: Scott, Foresman, 1935).

7. The examples of the steps of the motivated sequence are adapted from Elizabeth Marshal Thomas, 'Canine Liberation', *The New York Times* (1 May 1996): A19.

8. H.M. Weston, 'Announcement of the Lieutenant Governor's Community Volunteer Award for Graduating Students' (Emery Collegiate Institute, Toronto, 11 April 2000). Available at lt.gov.on.ca/sections_english/history/history_middle_frame/hweston_speeches/history_students.html.

9. P.E. Trudeau, 'First Among Equals: Notes for a National Broadcast' (16 October 1970). Available at collectionscanada.ca/2/4/h4-4000-e.html.

10. B. Neil, 'Social Media and Corporate Trust'. Speech presented to the Empire Club of Canada, Toronto, 7 May 2009. Available at speeches.empireclub.org/69578/data?n=18.

11. Trudeau, op. cit.

12. E. Rubenstein, 'The Economics of Crime: The Rational Criminal', *Vital Speeches of the Day* (15 October 1995), 19.

13. D. White, 'Cloning: When Is Enough Enough?' in *Winning Orations, 1997* (Interstate Oratorical Association, 1997), 145. Daniel was coached by Kristine Greenwood.

14. A. Jones, 'The Big Sting', in *Winning Orations, 1998* (Interstate Oratorical Association, 1998), 52. Amy was coached by Judy Woodring.

15. B. Sosnowchik, 'The Cries of American Ailments', in *Winning Orations, 2000* (Interstate Oratorical Association, 2000), 114. Brian was coached by Steve Blivess.

16. R. Hansen, Speech to University of Ottawa, Distinguished Canadian Leadership Awards (2005). Available at canadian-leadership.uottawa.ca/recipients_details-10-e-html.

17. S. Haydu, 'Briefing Note: 2006 Premier's TV Address' (2006). Available at uofaweb.ualberta.ca/govrel//pdfs/Premier's2006TVAddressGRBrief.pdf.

18. RCMP, 'Canadian Firearms Program Evaluation: Final Report' (Regina: RCMP National Program Evaluation Services, 2010), 21 and 28.

19. D. Sherriff, 'Bill Gates—Too Rich', posted on *CRTNET discussion group*, 1 April 1998.

20. J. Kusugak, 'Ongoing Challenges for the Inuit People of Canada'. Speech presented to the Empire Club of Canada, Toronto, 13 October 2005. Available at speeches.empireclub.org/62908/data?n=1.

21. T. Mitchell, 'Hey, Superman, You Won't Be Invincible Forever', *USA Weekend* (8–10 June 2001): 6.

22. T.C. Douglas and L.H. Thomas, *The Making of a Socialist: The Recollections of T.C. Douglas* (Edmonton, University of Alberta Press, 1984), 60.

23. J. Chrétien, 'A Tribute to the Right Honourable Pierre Elliott Trudeau' (Ottawa, 29 September 2000). Available at pco-bcp.gc.ca/default.asp?Language=E&Page=archivechretien&Sub=speeches&Doc=tribute.trudeau.20000929_e.htm.

24. R.C. Notebaert, 'Leveraging Diversity: Adding Value to the Bottom Line', *Vital Speeches of the Day* (1 November 1998), 47.

25. General R. Hillier, 'The Men and Women of the Canadian Armed Forces'. Speech presented to the Empire Club of Canada, Toronto, 11 April 2006. Available at speeches.empireclub.org/62933/data?n=8.

26. Ibid.

27. S. Lafrance, 'The Role of the Media in the Dynamics of Cultural Diversity'. Speech presented to the Radio Development Forum 2004, Beijing, China, 25 October 2004. Available at cbc.radio-canada.ca/speeches/20041025.shtml.

28. J.T. Cacioppo and R.E. Petty, 'Effects of Message Repetition and Position on Cognitive Response, Recall, and Persuasion', *Journal of Personality and Social Psychology* 37 (1979): 97–109.

29. J. Pepino, 'The Mandate of Ontario's Women's Health Council'. Speech presented to the Empire Club of Canada, Toronto, 25 March 1999. Available at empireclub.org/60379/data?n=6.

30. Voter Registration Project, New York Public Interest Research Group, Brooklyn College Chapter, 2004.

31. J. Chrétien, 'Speech at the Treaty-Signing Conference for the Global Ban on Anti-Personnel Landmines', Ottawa, 3 December 1997. Available at collectionscanada.ca/primeministers/h4-4081-e.html.

Chapter 13

1. R.B. Rubin, A.M. Rubin, and F.F. Jordon, 'Effects of Instruction on Communication Apprehension and Communication Competence', *Communication Education* 46 (1997): 104–14. See also P.D. MacIntyre and J.R. MacDonald, 'Public Speaking Anxiety: Perceived Competence and Audience Congeniality', *Communication Education* 47, 4 (October 1998): 359–65. In this study, the group with the highest anxiety showed the largest improvement in perceived competence and perception of audience pleasantness. The speaker's perception of the audience is a key factor in public speaking anxiety.

2. See, for example, J. Borhis and M. Allen, 'Meta-analysis of the Relationship between Communication Apprehension and Cognitive Performance', *Communication Education* 41, 1 (January 1992): 68–76.

3. J.A. Daly, A.L. Vangelisti, and D.J. Weber, 'Speech Anxiety Affects How People Prepare Speeches: A Protocol Analysis of the Preparation Process of Speakers', *Communication Monographs* 62 (December 1995).

4. Researchers generally agree that speech anxiety has three causes: genetics, social learning, and inadequate skills acquisition. See, for example, M.J. Beatty and K.M. Valencic, 'Context-Based Apprehension versus Planning Demands: A Communibiological Analysis of Anticipatory Public Speaking Anxiety', *Communication Education* 49, 1 (January 2000): 58.

5. See, for example, C.R. Sawyer and R.R. Behnke, 'Communication Apprehension and Implicit Memories of Public Speaking State Anxiety', *Communication Quarterly* 45, 3 (Summer 1997): 211–22.

6. Adapted from A. Ellis, *A New Guide to Rational Living* (North Hollywood, CA: Wilshire Books, 1977). G.M. Philips listed a different set of beliefs that he believed contributes to reticence. The beliefs are: (1) an exaggerated sense of self-importance. (Reticent people tend to see themselves as more important to others than others see them.) (2) Effective speakers are born, not made. (3) Skilful speaking is manipulative. (4) Speaking is not that important. (5) I can speak whenever I want to; I just choose not to. (6) It is better to be quiet and let people think you are a fool than prove it by talking (they assume they will be evaluated negatively). (7) What is wrong with me requires a (quick) cure. See J.A. Keaten, L. Kelly, and C. Finch, 'Effectiveness of the Penn State Program in Changing Beliefs Associated with Reticence', *Communication Education* 49, 2 (April 2000): 134.

7. R.R. Behnke, C.R. Sawyer, and P.E. King, 'The Communication of Public Speaking Anxiety', *Communication Education* 36 (April 1987): 138–41.

8. See, for example, J. Ayres and B.L. Heuett, 'The Relationship between Visual Imagery and Public Speaking Apprehension', *Communication Reports* 10, 1 (Winter 1997): 87–94. Besides visualization, treatments for speech anxiety include skills training (such as a public speaking class), systematic desensitization (such as having practice sessions until you feel more comfortable with the real thing), rational-emotive therapy (recognizing irrational beliefs, as discussed earlier in this chapter), interpersonal support (such as coaching), and physical exercise. Students tend to do best when selecting their own treatment. See, for example, K. Kangas Dwyer, 'The Multidimensional Model: Teaching Students to Self-Manage High Communication

Apprehension by Self-Selecting Treatments', *Communication Education* 49, 1 (January 2000): 72.

9. R.R. Behnke and C.R. Sawyer, 'Milestones of Anticipatory Public Speaking Anxiety', *Communication Education* 48, 2 (April 1999): 165.

10. Speeches are also easier to understand than written text. See, for example, D.L. Rubin, T. Hafer, and K. Arata, 'Reading and Listening to Oral-Based versus Literate-Based Discourse', *Communication Education* 49, 2 (April 2000): 121. An interesting study in this area is D.P. Hayes's 'Speaking and Writing: Distinct Patterns of Word Choice', *Journal of Memory and Language* 27 (October 1988): 572–85. This extensive study of written/spoken language differences found these differences so pronounced that 'conversations between college graduates more closely resemble a preschool child's speech to its parents than texts from newspapers'.

11. J. Tarver, 'Can't Nobody Here Use This Language? Function and Quality in Choosing Words', *Vital Speeches of the Day* (1 May 1979): 420–3.

12. M.A. Lofaro and J. Cummings, eds, *Crockett at Two Hundred: New Perspectives on the Man and the Myth* (Knoxville: University of Tennessee Press, 1989).

13. J.S. Hinton and M.W. Kramer, 'The Impact of Self-Directed Videotape Feedback on Students' Self-Reported Levels of Communication Competence and Apprehension', *Communication Education* 47, 2 (April 1998): 151–61. Significant increases in competency and decreases in apprehension were found using this method.

14. See, for example, L.R. Rosenfeld and J.M. Civikly, *With Words Unspoken* (New York: Holt, Rinehart and Winston, 1976), 62.

Also see S. Chaiken, 'Communicator Physical Attractiveness and Persuasion', *Journal of Personality and Social Psychology* 37 (1979): 1387–97.

15. L.P. Devlin, 'An Analysis of Kennedy's Communication in the 1980 Campaign', *Quarterly Journal of Speech* 68 (November 1982): 397–417.

16. A study demonstrating this stereotype is R.L. Street, Jr, and R.M. Brady, 'Speech Rate Acceptance Ranges as a Function of Evaluative Domain, Listener Speech Rate, and Communication Context', *Speech Monographs* 49 (December 1982): 290–308.

17. See, for example, A. Mulac and M.J. Rudd, 'Effects of Selected American Regional Dialects upon Regional Audience Members', *Communication Monographs* 44 (1977): 184–95. Some research, however, suggests that non-standard dialects do not have the detrimental effects on listeners that were once believed. See, for example, F.L. Johnson and R. Buttny, 'White Listener's Responses to 'Sounding Black' and 'Sounding White': The Effect of Message Content on Judgments about Language', *Communication Monographs* 49 (March 1982): 33–9.

18. V. Smith, S.A. Siltanen, and L.A. Hosman, 'The Effects of Powerful and Powerless Speech Styles and Speaker Expertise on Impression Formation and Attitude Change', *Communication Research Reports* 15, 1 (Fall 1998): 27–35. In this study, a powerful speech style was defined as one without hedges and hesitations such as 'uh' and 'anda'.

19. From J. Wypiejewski, ed., *Painting by Numbers: Komar and Melamid's Scientific Guide to Art* (New York: Farrar, Straus & Giroux, 1997).

CREDITS

Photos

page 1: Courtesy of Rikia Saddy; page 2: © iStockphoto.com/ Izabela Habur; page 7: © iStockphoto.com/Alberto Pomares; page 8: CP Images/Darren Calabrese; page 10: Courtesy of Caroline Gdyczynski; page 15 20th Century Fox/Dreamworks/The Kobal Collection; page 16: Norman James/GetStock.com; page 18: ©iStockphoto.com/zhang bo; page 26: ©iStockphoto.com/Sean Locke; page 31: ©iStockphoto.com/Glenda Powers; page 36: Pekka Jaakkola; page 40: Wikipedia; page 42: © iStockphoto.com/ Joshua Hodge Photography; page 43: ©iStockphoto.com/Brad Killer; page 44: CP Images/Pawel Dwulit; page 48: iStock; page 53: Big Soul Productions Inc.; page 55: iStock; page 57: Sangiorzboy/ Dreamstime.com; page 67: © iStockphoto.com/mammamaart; page 68: © iStockphoto.com/Chris Schmidt; page 71: Courtesy of Bianca Freedman; page 82: CP Images/Francis Vachon; page 87: ©iStockphoto.com/Orlando Rosu; page 90: ©iStockphoto. com/Eileen Hart; page 97: ©iStockphoto.com/Nikada; page 98: © iStockphoto.com/michealofiachra; page 99: Photo used courtesy of the Saskatchewan Pork Development Board; page 104: © iStock-photo.com/Skip Odonnell; page 106: © iStockphoto.com/Marcus Clackson; page 110: Courtesy of Melonie Fullick; page 111: © iStockphoto.com page 113: © iStockphoto.com/digitalskillet; page 115: Peter Power/GetStock; page 120: © 2010 Anthony Asael and World of Stock; page 128: © iStockphoto.com/Chris Schmidt; page 131: © iStockphoto.com/Eugene Choi; page 132: © iStockphoto. com/Daniel Laflor; page 134: © iStockphoto.com/Kevin Russ; page 137: © iStockphoto.com/Pali Rao; page 138: © PSL Images / Alamy; page 142: Lite / Dreamstime.com; page 144: Tannis Toohye/ GetStock; page 147: © iStockphoto.com/Chris Schmidt; page 150: © iStockphoto.com/nyul; page 151: Courtesy of Emily Morrice; page 154: © iStockphoto.com/Izabela Habur; page 155: © iStock-photo.com/zhang bo; page 160: © Gabe Palmer / Alamy; page 168: © iStockphoto.com/drbimages; page 171: © imagebroker / Alamy page 173 AP Photo/Kevin Rivoli; page 174 Courtesy of Miles Jones; page 178v © iStockphoto.com/Shelly Perry; page 184: © iStock-photo.com/Joshua Hodge Photography; page 186: AP Photo/Dario Lopez-Mills; page 193: © iStockphoto.com/Chris Schmidt; page 198: © iStockphoto.com/Monika Wisniewska; page 205: Courtesy of Heather Pullen; page 206: © iStockphoto.com/digitalskillet; page 216: © iStockphoto.com/JoseGirarte; page 217: © iStockphoto. com/Loretta Hostettler; page 218: AP Photo/alex Gallardo; page 219: © iStockphoto.com/Nancy Louie; page 220: © iStockphoto. com/Jasmin Awad; page 226: © iStockphoto.com/-ilkeryuksel-; page © iStockphoto.com/ranplett; page 238: © iStockphoto.com/ ranplett; page 242: Courtesy of Joey Coleman; page 246: © iStock-photo.com/Steve Cole; page 254: © iStockphoto.com/RelaxFoto. de; page 256: © iStockphoto.com; page 258: "Mocker/Dreamstime. com; page 260: © David Gee/Alamy; page 262: © iStockphoto. com/Marcus Clackson; page 263: Courtesy of Jessica Martin; page 267: © iStocokphoto.com/Jacob Wackerhausen; page 268: Photo by Dave Sandford/Getty Images; page 280: © iStockphoto.com/ Nigel Carse; page 287: Courtesy of Andrew Laing; page 288: © iStockphoto.com/ Alberto Pomares; page 291: © iStockphoto.com/ pagadesign; page 292: © iStockphoto.com/Andresr; page 296: © iStockphoto.com/Alex Slobodkin; page 299: © iStockphoto.com/ Suprijono Suharjoto; page 300: © iStockphoto.com/Cagri Oner; page 306: Courtesy of Chris Farias; page 302: © iStockphoto.com/ Eyeidea®; page 315: © iStockphoto.com/webphotographeer; page 332: © iStockphoto.com; page 335: © iStockphoto.com/geopaul; page 337: © iStockphoto.com/René Mansi; page 338: CP / Adrien Wyld; page 343: © iStockphoto.com/Jason Lugo; page 345: © iStockphoto.com; page 347: Courtesy of Alex Arnold; page 349: © iStockphoto.com/nicole waring; page 351: © iStockphoto.com/ Kronick; page 353: © iStockphoto.com/Stratesigns, Inc.; page 354: © iStockphoto.com/George Clerk; page 362: © iStockphoto. com/Steve Debenport; page 366: © iStockphoto.com; page 368: Courtesy of Qianxing Lu; page 370: Ron Bull/GetStock; page 373: Beacom Comm/New Line/ The Kobal Collection /Glass.Ben; page 374: © iStockphoto.com/Steve Debenport; page 375: © iStock-photo.com/Dave Bolton; page 381: ©iStockphoto.com; page 383: ©iStockphoto.com/ Kronick; page 384: Paramount/Bad Robot/ The Kobal Collection; page 385: © iStockphoto.com/ Helge Woell; page 361: Courtesy of Donald T. Smith; page 398: CP Images/Tom Hanson; page 400: © iStockphoto.com/Chris Schmidt; page 405: © iStockphoto.com/diego cervo; page 406: © iStockphoto.com/ Suprijono Suharjoto; page 411: Courtesy of Gurdeep Ahluwalia; page 422: © iStockphoto.com/Silvia Boratti; page 413: © iStock-photo.com/Oleg Prikhodko; page 417: © iStockphoto.com/Chris Schmidt; page 420: © iStock.com/Drazen Vukelic; page 423: © iStockphoto.com/Viorika Prikhodko; page 424: © iStockphoto. com/Simon Podgorsek; page 428: © iStockphoto.com/Rtimages; page 445: Courtesy of Johanna Rienzo; page 446: © iStockphoto. comBrian Jackson; page 448: © iStockphoto.com/Joshua Hodge Photography; page 451: © Tony McNicol / Alamy; page 456: © iStockphoto.com/Joshua Hodge Photography; page 463 © iStock-photo.com/Dori Oconnell; page 466: © iStockphoto.com/Gustaf Brundin; page 469: Graham Bezant/GetStock; page 474: © iStockpho-to.com/123render; page 478: © iStockphoto.com; page 481: © iStock-photo.com/Catherine Yeulet; page 490: © iStockphoto.com/Jacom Stephens; page 492: © iStockphoto.com/Sean_Warren; page 501: © iStockphoto.com/René Mansi; page 509: Courtesy of Sarah Hankins.

Cartoons

page 4: David Malki !; page 22: www.octopuspie.com; page 23: Close to Home © 2000 John McPherson. Reprinted with permis-sion of Universal Press Syndicate. All Rights Reserved; page 27: Calvin and Hobbes © 1994 Watterson. Distributed by Universal Press Syndicate. Reprinted with permission. All Rights Reserved; page 28: www.CartoonStock.com; page 39: © The New Yorker Collection 2004 Harry Bliss from cartoonbank.com. All Rights Reserved; page 51: www.CartoonStock.com; page 63: www. CartoonStock.com; page 73: © The New Yorker Collection 1998 Robert Weber from cartoonbank.com. All Rights Reserved; page 84: © The New Yorker Collection 2003 Eric Lewis from cartoonbank. com. All Rights Reserved; page 91 : www.cartoonstock.com; page 101: © Zits Partnership, King Features Syndicate; page 107: David Malki !; page 108: © 2007 Leo Cullum from cartoonbank.com. All Rights Reserved.; page 117: © 2006-2011 Kate Beaton; page 131: David Malki!; page 146: Calvin and Hobbes © 1995 Watterson.